THE CLINICAL MANUAL OF
CHINESE HERBAL
PATENT MEDICINES

A guide to ethical and pure patent medicines

Second Edition

Pangolin Press
Sydney

Pangolin

The Clinical Manual of Chinese Herbal Patent Medicines
A guide to Ethical and Pure Chinese Herbal Patent Medicines

First published 2000
Revised Edition 2003

National Library of Australia Cataloguing-in-Publication data:
Maclean, William
    Clinical Manual of Chinese Herbal Patent Medicines

    Bibliography
    Includes Index
    ISBN 0-646-40800-3
    1. Herbs – Therapeutic use 2. Medicine, Chinese – Handbooks, manuals. 3. Patent medicines – Handbooks, manuals. I. Title II. Title: Chinese Herbal Patent Medicines

Published by Pangolin Press (pangolinpress@bigpond.com)
    PO Box 667
    Glebe, NSW
    Australia 2037

Distributed worldwide by Impulse Books (www.impulsebooks.com)

Cover Design: Yolande Gray Design
Illustrations: Karen Vance

Printed in Hong Kong by Regal Printing Ltd

Disclaimer

The recommendations and information in this book are intended for use by professionals and in no way substitute for advice from a qualified practitioner. Any plant or animal substance intended for medicinal use has the potential to cause allergic reaction in sensitive individuals and unwanted effects may accrue from inaccurate prescription. Neither the author nor the publisher can be held responsible for claims arising from the inappropriate use of any remedy in this book. Do not try self diagnosis or attempt self treatment for any chronic or serious illness without consulting a qualified professional.

Every effort has been made to ensure that the information contained in this volume is as accurate and up to date as possible. However, due to the rapidly changing nature of the industry, formulations, packaging and availability may vary from time to time.

Acknowledgements

Thanks to all those who contributed in some way to this work, and to those who have inspired me to persist with the seemingly endless revisions, checking, double checking, proofing and so on that are the lot of the author and publisher. My special appreciation to my father, Bill Maclean, for hour upon hour of patient and careful proofing, and insightful criticism. Thanks also to those friends and colleagues whose dedication and integrity encouraged me so much – David Legge, Dr Dai Wei Min, Dr Li Dong Sen, Christine Flynn, Jane Lyttleton, Clarence Tsang, Danny Wu, and most of all Kathryn. Dedicated to the fond memory of two gentlemen practitioners and good friends, Peter Townsend and Chris Madden.

Contents

Contents • v

Supplementing Formulae

Shen disorders

Ear, Nose, Throat, Eyes

Pain & Trauma

Men's Health

Pediatric

Skin

Infection & Inflammation

Wind & *Yang*

INTRODUCTION

CHINESE HERBAL PATENT MEDICINES

Patent medicines are medicines manufactured from raw or processed herbal materials into pills, powders or liquid extracts for ingestion, and plasters and liniments for external application. Most are available as 'over the counter' products in herb shops and supermarkets in the Chinatowns of the world. The Chinese have been manufacturing patent medicines for centuries, indeed some of the best known and loved medicines, such as **7.9 Fu Gui Ba Wei Wan, 7.1 Liu Wei Di Huang Wan** and **1.17 Gui Zhi Fu Ling Wan**, were originally produced in patent medicine form. Patent medicines have been a popular and convenient form of health care for centuries, and recent changes to the industry in terms of regulation and quality control, both in and out of China, have led to a resurgence in interest in this ancient system.

Large numbers of patent medicines are produced in China and the range is continually growing. Many are developed from famous proven prescriptions, and are produced (with minor variations) by many different factories. Others may be unique to a single producer, perhaps a secret family recipe handed down through generations.

Dried herb prescriptions vs patent medicines

The practitioner of Chinese herbal medicine has two methods of delivering herbal material to a patient, each with strengths and weaknesses. The first, and still most popular method in China, is the dispensing of dried herbs that are boiled and decocted into a tea. Dried herb prescriptions usually require a consultation and prescription from a qualified physician. The advantage of dried herb prescriptions is flexibility and strength, both of which are advantageous in acute or serious illnesses. The disadvantages of dried herb prescriptions are the inconvenience of daily decoction, poor compliance in prolonged illnesses, difficulties involved in maintenance of a dried herb pharmacy, the degree of expertise required to utilise dried herbs effectively and the cost to the patient. Many practitioners in China and the Western world make use of both systems, starting patients on boiled decoctions until a certain result is attained, then switching to patent medicines for continuation of the treatment.

Advantages of patent medicines

Patent medicines offer some specific advantages to the modern practitioner. They are relatively cheap and easy to take, patient compliance tends to be high, they are easy to store and have a long shelf life. Maintenance of a wide ranging pharmacy is relatively cheap and space efficient. Because patent medicines are generally fairly mild in action, they are less likely to cause problems if incorrectly prescribed. Many of the classic patent medicines have been used for centuries on countless patients and have proved themselves time and again to be both effective and safe. New patent medicines are being produced on the basis of modern research findings, leading to an amalgamation of the best of science and tradition. Technology is being harnessed to improve the extraction ratios and stability of some modern formulae.

There is no question that, in general, patent medicines are not as strong or effective as dried herb decoctions for acute or serious illnesses, although some patent medicines are quite powerful at clearing Toxic and Damp Heat or purging Fire, etc., when taken in the large enough doses. The main advantages of patent medicines, from a clinical point of view, are in the treatment of the chronic problems that make up the bulk of the modern Chinese medicine practice. In my opinion, patent medicines are superior to dried herb prescriptions in several areas. The first is when prolonged and gentle rebuilding of *yin* or Blood is desired. Similarly, dispersal of chronic stagnant *qi* or Blood is best achieved by persistently chipping away at the stagnation over a prolonged period, for which patent medicines are ideal. These patterns require a gradual, persistent and prolonged treatment course. Rebuilding *yin* and Blood, dispersing stagnant Blood and harmonising *qi* distribution are processes that cannot be forced by using large and powerful dried herb prescriptions. They are better dealt with by slow and persistent encouragement of constitutional change, change that for the most part is better carried out by the gentle action of patent medicines.

The other main advantage of patent medicines is in the area of quality control. Dried herbs are not subject to the stringent quality control checks applied to medicines manufactured according to the principles of Good Manufacturing Practice (GMP, *see* p.xii), and may be contaminated with various residues. Occasional batches of dried herbs in the Australian market have been found to be contaminated by industrial pollutants, pesticide residues, heavy metals, moulds and insects. There is no way of being completely sure of the origin, history or quality of any dried herb offered for sale in herb shops. Patent medicines produced in GMP factories however, are guaranteed to be what they claim to be, and to contain only the ingredients listed on the label.

PATENT MEDICINE FORMATS
Pills and Tablets (*wan, pian* 丸, 片)
Pills and tablets come in a number of different sizes and forms. In all cases they are made of finely ground up herbs or concentrated extracts that are bound by pressure, or by the addition of honey, water or some other sticky medium. Upon ingestion, the ingredients are released in the intestine and absorbed slowly and at a constant rate. Depending on the binding medium and the size of the pill, the absorption and metabolism rates can vary. For example, pills bound with a starch paste (usually rice or wheat flour) are absorbed more slowly than those bound with honey, and thus are used when a prolonged action is required. Pills are convenient for fast administration in acute disorders, but are best for chronic problems that require lengthy therapy. They are particularly suited for the long term supplementation required to build *yin* and Blood. They are also the preferred method when a formula requires herbs that are unsuitable for decoction.

There are two common pill types featured in this book, the large traditional honey pill (also known as a bolus) that is usually sealed in a wax coated plastic ball, and the smaller pills coated in licorice powder.

Tablets are produced by squeezing herb powder under pressure to form a uniform disc that can be easily coated with sugar or an enteric coating. This is an advantage if the herbal ingredients are bitter or distasteful, or if the acid environment of the stomach degrades some essential component of the medicine.

Powders (*san* 散)

Powders are finely ground herbs sifted through a uniform mesh. They can be taken directly, chased down with a liquid, or boiled and the resulting liquid taken as a draft. Powders are useful for long term administration in the treatment of chronic disorders. They can be applied externally for skin diseases. They can be blown into the nose or throat for local disorders, or to resuscitate patients from unconsciousness. Powdered herbs are good for local application and are the format of choice for children.

Granules (*chong ji* 冲剂)

Granules are made by decocting herbal ingredients until a thick concentrate is produced. A stabilising excipient is then added, usually a starch of some type (commonly corn starch), in sufficient quantity to form a thick paste. The ground dregs of the decoction, powdered *Dioscorea opposita* root (shan yao) or *Poria cocos* (fu ling) may also be used. The resulting paste is fed through a heated drum sieve that instantly dries it to uniform granules that can be reconstituted to decoction with hot water. The technology required to produced *chong ji* granules has recently improved and the quality of the product is now generally very high. Volatile elements are captured and reintroduced to the final product. Recent developments in low temperature processing (never more than 100°C) ensure that even highly sensitive components are not degraded.

A number of companies are producing individual herbs as *chong ji*. The big advantage is that individual formulae can be constructed from the components.

This format is gradually replacing traditional decoctions in hospitals across China, and more formulae and individual herbs in *chong ji* appear in the over the counter market each year.

Liquid extracts (*kou fu ye* 口服液)

Liquid extracts are a modern format that involves extraction and suspension of herbs in a liquid medium, usually sugar based. They are packaged in sterilised single dose vials. Good for children as the taste of the herbs is disguised. Liquid extracts are absorbed and utilised quickly.

Plasters, syrups, ointments (*gao* 膏)

Plasters are sheets of adhesive material with herbal extracts bound to the sticky surface. They are applied locally for bruising and sprain, pain and arthritic conditions. In general, they warm the local area, invigorate local circulation and promote healing. Syrups are liquid extracts thickened with honey or sugar.

Liniments

Liniments are herbs or herbal oils extracted and suspended in an oil base for long action, or alcohol medium for fast absorption. They are used topically for pain, trauma or skin diseases. Liniments are similar to plasters in action.

QUALITY CONSIDERATIONS

Good Manufacturing Practice

The majority of the patent medicines presented in this volume are produced by Good Manufacturing Practice compliant companies. Good Manufacturing Practice (GMP) is an internationally agreed upon set of principles and procedures which, when followed by manufacturers of medicines and medical devices, helps ensure that the products manufactured will have the required pharmaceutical grade quality. The basic concept of GMP is that quality must be built into each batch of product during all stages of the manufacturing process. It involves quality control and checking at all stages of production, including selection of the herbs and testing for active ingredients and contaminants, extraction and binding methods, and packaging and labelling. GMP has become the standard against which all pharmaceutical practices are judged.

The role of the Therapeutic Goods Administration (TGA)

The Australian Therapeutic Goods Administration (TGA) is responsible for administering the provisions of the Therapeutic Goods Act. The TGA carries out a range of assessment and monitoring activities to ensure therapeutic goods available in Australia conform to GMP standards. Quality control of herbal medicine products is determined in the following ways:

Pre-market assessment

Products assessed as having a higher level of risk (prescription medicines and some nonprescription medicines) are evaluated for quality, safety and efficacy. Once approved for marketing in Australia these products are included in the Australian Register of Therapeutic Goods as 'registered' products and are identified by an AUST R number.

Products assessed as being lower risk (many nonprescription medicines and most patent medicines) are assessed for quality and safety. Once approved for marketing in Australia, these products are included in the Australian Register of Therapeutic Goods as 'listed' products and are identified by an AUST L number.

In assessing the level of risk, factors such as the strength of a product, side effects, potential harm through prolonged use, toxicity and the seriousness of the medical condition for which the product is intended to be used, are all taken into account.

Licensing of manufacturers

Manufacturers of therapeutic goods must be licensed and their manufacturing practices must comply with principles of good manufacturing practice. The aim of licensing and standards is to protect public health by ensuring that medicines and medical devices meet definable standards of quality assurance and are manufactured in conditions that are clean and free of contaminants.

Overseas manufacturers of therapeutic goods supplied to Australia must provide evidence that the goods are manufactured to a standard of GMP equivalent to that expected of Australian manufacturers of similar goods. What this means in practice is that representatives of the TGA inspect and personally approve any factory that applies for GMP status. Inspection and audit of herbal manufacturing facilities can last up to seven days and involve thorough examination of all aspects of the manufacturing process. The rigor of the inspection process ensures that factories that attain Australian GMP status are among the best in the world

Monitoring compliance

Once all government requirements of GMP are met and a factory obtains GMP status, on site inspections are carried out every two years. Any factory that fails to maintain full compliance with GMP standards can lose its certification at any time. In addition, the TGA investigates reports of problems and performs random testing of products on the market to ensure ongoing compliance with the legislation.

Unregistered products

A number of products presented in this manual are not registered by the TGA, although they may be manufactured by a GMP compliant company. This is usually because they are not currently offered for sale in Australia, but are available in Asia, the US or Europe. A relatively large selection of classical formulae, manufactured by the reputable Lanzhou Foci Pharmaceutical Factory, are currently available as practitioner only products in the US and UK. See Selection of Formulae, p.xiv.

We have included a few formulae that are not manufactured by GMP companies. This is generally because they are classified as food products and are therefore not subject to TGA registration.

The issue of contamination

It has long been suspected, and recently shown, that some Chinese patent medicines not produced in GMP compliant factories are contaminated with heavy metals and/ or unlisted pharmaceutical drugs. The problem is further complicated by differing definitions of what constitutes a contaminant.

Heavy metals are sometimes used in patent medicines as an integral part of the prescription, in which case they are listed on the label. Examples of these include the famous sedative cinnabar (mercuric sulphide, *zhu sha*) and the antibiotic realgar (arsenic sulphide, *xiong huang*). When used correctly, these substances are generally considered quite safe. Heavy metal contamination not listed as an ingredient presumably results from industrial pollution on the herbs in the field or as an consequence of the manufacturing process.

Other substances considered contaminating in one country may not be thought so in another. For example, berberine and borneol are listed as contaminants in the US, whereas these substances are therapeutically acceptable to the TGA in Australia and appear in listed products.

When in doubt, only use products that are registered or listed with the TGA, or that are produced in a GMP compliant facility.

ETHICAL CONSIDERATIONS

Endangered species

A number of the medicines described in this volume contain substances derived from animals. In general, items such as the moulted shell of the summer cicadae, earthworms, various beetles or other insects and shells are used. These products are abundant and therapeutically very useful in the correct context.

Unfortunately however, Chinese medicine has a long history of using parts from now rare animals. There are, in the Chinatowns of the world, medicines claiming to contain tiger bone, rhino and saiga antelope horn, as well as seahorse and musk deer gland. In China, these substances have been prized for centuries for their strength (in many cases dubious) and their rarity (and thus high price and the implied status that goes along with being able to afford such items). The practice of listing endangered species on medicine labels continues even though tests have shown that the substance may not be present or that some other product has been substituted (for example cat or dog bone for tiger bone, water buffalo horn for rhino horn). An expensive animal product on the label implies a superior product.

Even though endangered species are probably not being used (both hard to get and wildly expensive), the labelling practice continues to generate an illegal market and encourages poaching of remaining populations. We feel very strongly that no medicine listing an endangered species as an ingredient should be used under any circumstance. None of the medicines in this volume contains parts of endangered species.

SELECTION OF FORMULAE

Medicines are selected primarily on the basis of their availability over the counter in the Australian market, listing with the TGA or because they are produced in factories that comply with the principles of GMP. In addition to the new medicines available in the Australian market, the text includes numerous medicines that are not currently available in Australia, but which can be obtained in North America and Europe. The reason for this is the desire to make this manual a more practical companion to the Clinical Handbook of Internal Medicine series (University of Western Sydney) for those readers outside Australia.

The author of this book practices in Australia and so has an Australian slant, and relies upon the Australian regulatory authority of the TGA. However, the formulae described are essentially the traditional, sometimes ancient, Chinese formulae and are of universal application. Accordingly, the author considers that the information contained in this volume applicable to countries such as the USA and European Union which have a similar approach to Chinese medicine as that practised in Australia.

THE FACTORIES

There are literally hundreds of factories producing patent medicines in China. Of these hundreds of factories, only a dozen or so are deemed to be of sufficient quality to qualify for certification by the Australian TGA as we go to press (2003).

The majority of patent medicines in this book are produced in just five factories. Of these factories, three are famous throughout China and the orient and between them produce hundreds of products for domestic and export consumption. These are the Lanzhou Foci Pharmaceutical Factory, Beijing Tong Ren Tang Pharmaceutical Factory and Tianjin Drug Manufactory. The other two, Guangzhou Qixing Pharmaceutical Factory and the Jing Xian Pharmaceutical Co., also in Guangzhou, are examples of the new and substantial investments in standards of quality and technology that are occurring as China develops and modernises.

Lanzhou Foci Pharmaceutical factory

Lanzhou Foci Pharmaceutical factory in Gansu Province, Western China was founded in 1929. The majority of pills described in the text are produced by this factory. Lanzhou Foci produces more than 100 kinds of products, including pills, tablets, ointments, granules, liquid extracts, syrups and capsules. Their products were exported to Southeastern Asian countries as early as 1930, and now are found in over forty countries including the United States, Japan, Singapore, Thailand, Malaysia, Indonesia, Canada, Australia, the United Kingdom, Hong Kong, Macao and Taiwan.

Lanzhou Foci manufactures a wide range of classical and unique formulae, the pill forms being most commonly available outside China. The trademark for concentrated pills sold outside China is the "Minshan" (Mountain Minshan) brand. The popularity of this factory's products has inspired numerous imitators and fakes.

Beijing Tong Ren Tang Pharmaceutical Factory

Situated in Beijing, this massive company with 11000 employees has been famous for over 300 years. It was established in 1669 by Yue Zunyu who worked in the imperial hospital. Because of its great reputation and effective prescriptions, Tong Ren Tang was able to gain the privilege of providing medicines for the imperial court pharmacy during the years of Emperor Yong Zheng (1723-1735). In 1861, Tong Ren Tang was ordered to prepare medicines for the imperial family directly. Tong Ren Tang specialises in the large honey pill format, although recently it has begun to manufacture increasing numbers of granulated products. Tong Ren Tang produces hundreds of different products in all formats which are revered throughout China for their high quality.

Tianjin Drug Manufactory

Tianjin Drug Manufactory in Shandong province is a large and well respected herb manufacturer specialising in the traditional format of honey pills, as well as tablets.

ARRANGEMENT OF CATEGORIES

I have grouped the medicines according to the most common conditions for which we use them. This arrangement is, however, arbitrary and dependent on clinical experience and personal bias. Many patents could appear in several groups. For example, **1.9 Gui Pi Wan** is a marvellous medicine for *qi* and Blood deficiency type gynecological and postpartum disorders, however it is also widely used for *shen* disturbances, and for fatigue patterns and bleeding syndromes. It is found in the gynecological section, but could just as easily fall into the *shen* calming or supplementing section.

LAYOUT OF THE TEXT

All the information needed to quickly prescribe is described under the relevant headings. In the graphical representation of the pattern identifying features, the bold text indicates an important symptom of the relevant pattern, or the features which differentiate the formula from those with similar action.

Terminology

Translated technical terms with specific meanings in Chinese medicine are capitalised (Liver, Spleen, Gallbladder, Blood, etc.). These terms are defined in the glossary. Difficult to translate terms, selected TCM actions and those that are commonly left untranslated (*qi, yin, yang*, etc.) are defined in the glossary.

Icons

The icons at the edge of the page are a quick summary of certain key features that define a patent medicine, such as whether or not the medicine is listed with the TGA or produced in a GMP compliant factory, available as a practitioner only product, the typical duration of use, pregnancy contraindication, inclusion of animal products and any potential for herb drug interactions. The icon key appears on the inside back cover.

Alternative names

Some patents have traditionally been known by certain common names or by alternative transliterations of Chinese (pin yin or Wade Giles), for example **1.1 Ba Zhen Wan** has long been known as Women's Precious Pills, **1.9 Gui Pi Wan** as Kwei Be Wan, and so on. These alternatives are noted at the top of each page. The main name given is the one common in the Australian market or the standard *pin yin* name, and may vary in other countries.

Factory

The specified factory is important to note as many factories produce medicines of the same name. We recommend only the products of the factories listed in the text.

Indications

The indications are the range of conditions and patterns for which a certain medicine can be used. I have included both TCM and biomedically defined diseases and syndromes, where appropriate. I have tried to be as comprehensive and practical as possible, but be aware that making comparisons between TCM patterns and biomedical diseases is fraught with danger and the potential for misunderstanding. As long as the underlying TCM pattern is diagnosed correctly, the precise biomedical disease the patient has is irrelevant (except from a prognostic point of view). The logic of diagnosis must proceed from the TCM pattern so as to avoid the trap of directly equating a disease with a particular pattern, so often a source of clinical failure. Thus hepatitis is not Damp Heat in the Liver but may in some circumstances appear as that pattern. Always check the pattern identifying features before prescribing.

Pattern identifying features

The pattern identifying features are the symptoms denoting the appropriate pattern for the use of a particular formula. Not all symptoms will, or need be, present to make the diagnosis. Bold text indicates the most important features.

Combinations

Many formulae can be combined to produce a stronger therapeutic effect or to treat a condition for which neither alone is indicated. Suggestions for combinations are drawn from clinical experience and are by no means exhaustive. When combining small pills (from Lanzhou Foci), it is usually convenient to mix them in a generic container, rather than give them separately to the patient. We use opaque plastic jars of various sizes, upon which we fix our clinic label and specific directions for use. This assists in keeping the dosage instructions as simple as possible and avoids any potential confusion. The random selection of pills from the combined jar will ensure the correct mix over the period of treatment.

The proportions in which formulae are mixed depends on the clinical assessment of the individual being treated, the symptom picture and the weighting the practitioner wants to give to the elements in the mix. In general, the higher weighting (and thus higher proportion in a mix) is given to the formula targeting the constitutional elements of a pattern, with formulae for symptomatic relief or secondary patterns in a lower proportion. For many applications, the standard ratio is 2:1, primary constitutional formula to symptomatic or secondary pattern formula. For example, when treating a patient with reflux esophagitis of a Liver *qi* stagnation invading the Stomach type, a good combination is **6.3 Chai Hu Shu Gan Wan** and **2.26 Xiang Lian Wan**. In this case the **6.3 Chai Hu Shu Gan Wan** is the constitutional formula, aimed at correcting the underlying pathology, the Liver *qi* stagnation, while the **2.26 Xiang Lian Wan** is added to provide symptomatic relief of the reflux. Depending on the severity of the reflux, proportionately more **2.26 Xiang Lian Wan** can be added, and as the patient improves the proportion can be reduced. The typical mix of this combination is 2:1 (**6.3 Chai Hu Shu Gan Wan** to **2.26 Xiang Lian Wan**) but 1:1 or even 1:2 may be used in the early stages of treatment to bring quick symptomatic relief. The dose of combined formulae is usually the same as for either formula alone, not doubled.

Dosage

The dosages listed are guides for average sized individuals under common clinical conditions. Dosage must be flexibly applied, and tends to be weight dependent with larger individuals requiring larger doses in general than small individuals. Dose also depends on the severity of the condition being treated. With a few exceptions (noted in the text), the doses of most of the patent medicines in this volume can be experimented with to find the optimum range for the individual being treated. Clinical experience is the ultimate guide.

Children present a special challenge to the delivery of patent medicines. Doses that are too small will be ineffective, while those that are too large may damage the child's delicate *qi*. Often, simply getting the child to ingest the medicine is trouble enough. The following guidelines may be used to determine the correct dose and the frequency of administration. When using medicines not specifically designed for children, one third of the adult dose is given to children 3-7 years old; one half the adult dose for children 7-13 years old. These guidelines should be flexibly applied, and body weight may be a more useful indicator if the child is large or small for his or her age. For children younger than three, special pediatric medicines in powder and granule form are used.

Before attempting to administer any medicine, the importance of the medicine to the child's wellbeing should be clearly communicated to the child. Parents should be advised to remain calm and not force the child against his or her will. Pills should be crushed or cut into small pieces before ingestion. They can also be softened in hot water, and the resulting liquid taken. Medicines for children can be disguised in a palatable medium such as honey or apple sauce. For infants, medicine can be mixed with water or milk and delivered in an eye-dropper or on the nipple. If a child vomits after taking a medicine, reduce the amount given in each dose and give more frequently. Gentle pressure on PC.6 (*nei guan*) or LI.4 (*he gu*) may also assist.

Contraindications

There are certain important contraindications for some of the medicines; these are noted in the text. The main one is pregnancy. Medicines contraindicated during pregnancy are usually Blood invigorating or purgative and can cause uterine contractions, threatening the developing fetus.

Certain herbs and formulae are known to interact with pharmaceutical drugs, either potentiating or negating their activity and thus creating side effects. In addition, new drugs are appearing all the time, so the potential for new interactions is ongoing. Ensure a complete history with all current medications is taken before prescribing. Always exercise appropriate caution when a patient is taking other medications. See Possible Herb Drug Interactions (p.604) for more information.

USING A SPECIFIC MEDIUM TO TAKE THE MEDICINE

Although all medicines can be washed down with water, the therapeutic effect of some patent medicines is enhanced when they are taken with a specific liquid.

Ginger

Ginger can be brewed as a tea and used to wash down patent medicines. Ginger is useful if a medicine causes stomach upsets, nausea, bloating or flatulence. It can be used to protect the stomach when cooling medicines are used, and to enhance the mucolytic action of medicine for Phlegm Damp patterns. To prepare, boil a knob of ginger (about 10-20 grams) for ten minutes in 1-2 cups of water.

In large doses (20-30 grams) ginger is diaphoretic and warming to the internal organs. It is useful to enhance the effects of any medicine used to dispel Wind Cold or treat Cold type pain.

Wine, alcohol

Alcohol is used to enhance the ability of a medicine to promote the circulation of *qi* and Blood, and alleviate pain. Medicines for *bi* syndrome and other chronic pain or stagnation patterns are often taken with wine or steeped and extracted in wine, which is then taken. Alcohol is also used for some supplementing medicines, in particular those used to warm *yang*.

Usually either a neutral spirit such as vodka or a mild wine such as sherry or sake is suitable. The Chinese favor white or yellow wines made from sorghum or millet. The best come from Shaoxing in Jiangsu province. Shaoxing wines are widely available in the Chinatowns and oriental supermarkets found in most major cities. Shaoxing wines are very similar to sherry in alcohol content and flavor. The dose is 25-50 mls (1-2 ounces), at room temperature or slightly warmed.

Rice porridge

Rice porridge (*zhou* or *zook*), a common Chinese breakfast food, is sometimes given with diaphoretic medicines to encourage sweating. Usually some shallots (scallions) or ginger will be added as well. Also good for convalescents recovering from a serious illness or surgery in combination with an appropriate supplementing medicine. When used for convalescents the rice porridge is usually prepared with chicken stock for extra nutrition.

Chicken soup

Chicken soup supplements *qi* and Blood and is an excellent nutritive liquid and immune stimulant. It can be used to enhance the effect of any *qi* and/or Blood supplementing medicine.

Honey

Honey is frequently employed as a binding agent in the large traditional pills (boluses). It is a mild Spleen supplement in its own right and is usually used with supplementing medicines. It can also moisten the lungs to alleviate dry cough, and lubricate the intestines to promote bowel movement. Honey is excellent for making sometimes unpleasant medicines palatable.

Brown sugar

Brown sugar dispels Cold, moves and nourishes Blood. It is especially useful combined with medicines for gynecological conditions associated with Blood deficiency and Cold accumulation.

Cinnamon sticks

Cinnamon sticks warm the channels and dispel Cold. As a tea, they assist medicines aimed at expelling Wind Cold Damp from the channels and joints for the treatment of *bi* syndrome, and can warm the uterus to alleviate dysmenorrhea.

Chrysanthemum flowers

Chrysanthemum flowers cool the Liver and disperse Wind Heat. Good for inflammatory eye conditions and Liver Heat patterns. They can also be used as an eyewash for red sore eyes, in which case they must be boiled for ten minutes, then cooled before application.

Peppermint tea

Peppermint tea dispels Wind Heat and moves Liver *qi*. Used to enhance any medicine for dispeling Wind Heat or alleviating *qi* stagnation.

GENERAL RULES FOR TAKING PATENT MEDICINES

1. Patent medicines are usually best taken on an empty stomach, thirty minutes before eating or one hour after eating, except when they cause gastric irritation or upset, in which case they can be taken on a full stomach.
2. Avoid taking patent medicines with substances that may interact with and bind active ingredients, possibly taking them out of the body through the bowel. These include the tannins found in ordinary tea, bulking agents such as psyllium husks and other fibre containing materials.
3. Use *qi* and *yang* supplementing medicine, those that strengthen the Spleen and Stomach, and those with stimulant herbs, such as ginseng and deer velvet, earlier in the day. Sedatives and *shen* calming medicines should be taken towards the end of the day.
4. It is better to ensure the daily dose is taken rather than be too concerned about timing. If taking patent medicines three time daily proves inconvenient for your patients, it is better for them to take more medicine in fewer doses, rather than less overall.
5. For acute problems, take the appropriate dose of the medicine at frequent intervals, around every 2-3 hours.
6. Persistence pays off. Patent medicines are mostly mild and slow acting, so with the exception of acute disorders, it is usually unrealistic to expect quick results. Many chronic patterns, in particular chronic deficiencies such as *yin* and Blood deficiency, and Blood stagnation, may take some months or longer to correct. If diagnosis is correct, continue therapy for 6 weeks before making a judgement about whether the treatment is working or not. If a medicine does not seem to be working check the diagnosis and make sure the patient is taking the medicine, taking it correctly and in the right dose.

WHEN BUYING PATENT MEDICINES

Make sure the patent medicine you purchase is produced in the factory specified. Read the label and check the trademark if in doubt. Many factories manufacture formulae with the same name, especially the classic formulae and there is always the incentive in retail outlets to try to sell a substitute if the desired product is unavailable. We cannot attest to the quality or efficacy of patent medicines produced by companies other than those we have specified in this book.

Beware of fakes

There is, unfortunately, a flourishing fake medicine industry with formulae made to look like their GMP produced counterparts, so buyer beware. The products of good quality factories are often copied. In particular, the popularity of the products manufactured by the Lanzhou Foci Pharmaceutical Factory has singled it out for mass imitation. The copies may look similar, but are clearly inferior in effect. Look for the Min Shan trademark.

Pill labelling

Many formulae list misleading or narrow indications. This is due to the restricted nature of statements that the Therapeutic Goods Administration allows. The range of allowable statements are designed for over the counter pharmacy products, and are structured so that people with serious illnesses are not tempted to self prescribe. What suppliers are left with are bland and often incorrect statements such as 'Assists in blood circulation', 'For maintenance of peripheral circulation' and 'Helps provide stamina and endurance'.

Availability

Not all the medicines described in this volume are available at all times. Due to the current flux in the industry worldwide, new listed and registered medicines appear and some old stand-bys disappear. Products without TGA registration are not generally available in Australia, but are readily available in North America, the United Kingdom and Europe. We have made every effort to be as comprehensive and up to date as possible. Packaging changes from time to time, and standard formulations may be altered for no apparent reason.

Note 1: Products available outside Australia

The original intent of this book was to record all the commonly available and TGA listed over the counter medicines available in Australia. However, to expand the range of the text and to make it a more useful companion volume to the **Clinical Handbook of Internal Medicine** series (Maclean and Lyttleton, University of Western Sydney Volume 1 [1998], Volume 2 [2002]) I have included a number of products that are not currently available in Australia. These products, derived from classical formulae, are practitioner only products available from companies in America and the United Kingdom. These companies supply patent medicines manufactured in GMP compliant facilities in China, and include Mayway Corporation (Plum Flower Brand), Bio Essence Corporation (Bio Essence Brand) and Nuherbs Co. (Herbal Times and Jade Dragon Brand). Many of these formulae are manufactured under licence by the same Chinese manufacturers represented extensively in this book. For example, the Plum Flower Brand is made by the Lanzhou Foci Pharmaceutical Factory in Gansu, maker of the famous Minshan Brand. Because their products are manufactured by Lanzhou Foci, I have chosen Plum Flower as representative of quality products available outside Australia and thus without official TGA listing.

A number of these formulae are available from several companies. Because of the variation in composition and proportions of herbs of some formulae with the same name supplied by different companies, the herbs listed are those of Plum Flower Brand. These formulae generally follow the classical prescription.

When a formula is available in the US or UK under different names, the suppliers are noted as follows: Plum Flower Brand – (PB), Bio Essence Brand – (BE), Herbal Times Brand – (HT), Jade Dragon Brand – (JD).

WHERE TO BUY PATENT MEDICINES

AUSTRALIA

Champ Firm Pty Ltd
35A Arthur St.,
Cabramatta, NSW 2166
☎ +61 2 9728 3798
🖷 +61 2 9726 2448
champfirm@bigpond.com.au
Wholesale distributor of products
from Lanzhou Foci Pharmaceutical
Factory, Guangzhou Qixing
Pharmaceutical Factory and Tianjin
Drug Manufactory.

Win Duc Herb Co.
60 Dixon St., Haymarket,
Sydney, NSW 2000
☎ +61 2 9281 5554

Everspring Supermarket
421-425 Sussex St.,Haymarket,
Sydney, NSW 2000
☎ +61 2 9211 2980
🖷 +61 2 9281 8048

Acuneeds Australia
622 Camberwell Road,
Camberwell, VIC 3124
(Shop open Monday - Saturday)
☎ +61 3 9889 4100
   or 1800 678 789 (within Australia)
🖷 +61 3 9889 1200
www.acuneeds.com
Full catalogue online with secure
shopping. Australia's leading supplier
of acupuncture and allied equipment,
lasers, stimulators and ear candles,
herbal medicines and textbooks. Shop
online or ask for our extensive colour
catalogue.

China Beijing Tong Ren Tang Australia Pty Ltd
(Head Office)
16-20 Sultram Place,
Adelaide, SA 5000
☎ +61 8 8211 9898
🖷 +61 8 8231 6799
trta@senet.com.au
www.tongrentang.com.au

• **New South Wales Agent**
Dr Ray Wang (Sydney)
☎ +61 2 9565 1940

• **Victorian Agent**
Dr C.J Liu (Melbourne)
☎ +61 3 9887 9738

• **Queensland Agent**
Dr Daniel He (Brisbane)
☎ +61 7 3344 7388

• **Western Australia Agent**
Dr Xu Q Fu (Perth)
  ☎ +61 8 9228 9666

NORTH AMERICA

Mayway Corporation
1338 Mandela Parkway,
Oakland, CA 94607
☎ 1-800-262-9929
☎ (510) 208 3113
🖷 (510) 208 3069
www.mayway.com

Superior Trading Company
837 Washington St,
San Francisco, CA 94108
☎ (415) 495 7988
🖷 (415) 495 7990

Nuherbs Co.

3820 Penniman Ave.,
Oakland, CA 94619
☎ (800) 233 4307
🖷 (800) 550-1928

Bio Essence Corp.

5221 Central Ave.,
Richmond, CA 94804
☎ (510) 558 2000

UNITED KINGDOM & EUROPE

Mayway UK Limited

42 Waterside Trading Centre,
Trumpers Way, Hanwell W7 2QD
☎ 020 8893 6873
🖷 020 8893 6874
www.mayway.demon.co.uk

Patent Medicines for Gynecological Disorders

1.1 BA ZHEN WAN

八珍丸

TRADE MARK

BA ZHEN WAN

AUSTL 55431

200Pills

LANZHOU FOCI PHARMACEUTICAL FACTORY
LANZHOU CHINA

Lanzhou Foci Pharmaceutical Factory (Gansu)
'Eight Precious Pills'
Ba Zhen Wan is packaged in bottles of 200 pills
Also available as: Women's Precious Pills, Women's Precious
Teapills (PF), Nu Ke Ba Zhen Wan

TCM actions

Supplements *qi* and Blood, regulates menstruation and the *chong* and *ren* channels.

Biomedical actions

Energy supplement and stimulant, promotes metabolism, hematinic, regulates menstruation, galactagogue.

INDICATIONS

- *Qi* and Blood deficiency. Especially good for menstrual disorders, and with the appropriate identifying features, **1.1 Ba Zhen Wan** can be used to treat a wide variety of conditions associated with systemic *qi* and Blood deficiency, including scanty menstrual periods or amenorrhea, infertility, habitual miscarriage, mild abnormal uterine bleeding, long menstrual cycle or irregular menstruation, postpartum weakness or insufficient lactation and weakness during pregnancy. Also useful for dull dysmenorrhea and lower abdominal pain that responds favorably to warmth and pressure.
- For non-gynecological conditions associated with *qi* and Blood deficiency, including general fatigue and exhaustion, anemia, postural dizziness, visual weakness, floaters before the eyes, chronic hepatitis, debility, post surgical or post hemorrhage weakness, restless leg syndrome and malnutrition associated with deprivation or anorexia.
- Chronic muscle spasm, neck and shoulder pain that is easily aggravated by physical therapy like massage. There may be dull headaches that are worse when fatigued. The muscles feel firm or tense upon initial palpation but lack tone when palpated deeply.
- Chronic *yin* sores or ulcers that are slow to heal, such as bedsores, tropical ulcers, diabetic ulcers and chronic abscesses.

Composition (each pill contains powdered)

Angelica sinensis (dang gui, chinese angelica) 22mg, *Rehmannia glutinosa* (shu di,

Pattern identifying features

- *Qi* & Blood deficiency
- fatigue
- anemia
- poor appetite

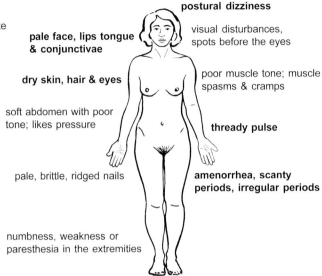

pale face, lips tongue & conjunctivae

dry skin, hair & eyes

soft abdomen with poor tone; likes pressure

pale, brittle, ridged nails

numbness, weakness or paresthesia in the extremities

postural dizziness

visual disturbances, spots before the eyes

poor muscle tone; muscle spasms & cramps

thready pulse

amenorrhea, scanty periods, irregular periods

GYN

processed rehmannia) 22mg, *Paeonia alba* (bai shao, white peony) 15mg, *Atractylodes macrocephala* (bai zhu, atractylodes) 15mg, *Codonopsis pilosula* (dang shen, codonopsis) 15mg, *Poria cocos* (fu ling, hoelen) 15mg, *Ligusticum wallichi* (chuan xiong, cnidium) 11mg, *Glycyrrhiza uralensis* (gan cao, licorice) 7mg

Combinations
- With **7.12 Lu Rong Jiao** for *yang* deficient infertility, characterised by weak progesterone (*yang*) phase of the menstrual cycle (*see* pp.627, 628)
- With **13.14 Ching Wan Hung** topically for chronic bedsores or tropical ulcers.

Dosage and method of administration
8-12 pills three times daily on an empty stomach. The dose may be spread out, or two lots of 12-18 pills may be taken, morning and evening. In severe cases or during the early stages of treatment (the first few weeks), a 50% increase in dose may be used, then reduced as the treatment takes effect.

Cautions and contraindications
Contraindicated during the early phase of acute illness such as colds and flu. Care should be taken in patients with a tendency to abdominal bloating, loose stools or general digestive weakness. Some patients may find **1.1 Ba Zhen Wan** aggravates these symptoms. This can usually be alleviated by taking the pills with a small dose (3-6 pills at the same time) of **2.18 Bao He Wan** or **2.9 Xiang Sha Liu Jun Wan**.

1.2 SI WU WAN

四物丸

Lanzhou Foci Pharmaceutical Factory (Gansu)
'Four Ingredient Pills'
Si Wu Wan is packaged in bottles of 200 pills.
Also available as: Four Substances for Women Teapills (PF)

TCM actions
Supplements Blood, regulates menstruation and the *chong* and *ren* channels.

Biomedical actions
Hematinic, tones the uterus and muscles, galactagogue.

INDICATIONS

- Blood deficiency. The fundamental formula for supplementing Blood and regulating menstruation, and the basic unit from which all Blood supplementing formulae are built. Especially good for menstrual disorders and Heart and Liver Blood deficient patterns. Excellent as an addition to any other formula where increased Blood supplementation is desired.
- Widely used for conditions associated with Blood deficiency, such as anemia, visual weakness, dryness of the skin and eyes, chronic itchy dry skin diseases (such as eczema, dermatitis and psoriasis), and chronic sores or ulcers that are slow to heal, including diabetic ulcers, bedsores and tropical ulcers.
- With the appropriate identifying features, this formula can be used to treat biomedical conditions such as irregular menstruation, scanty periods, amenorrhea, insufficient corpus luteum function, postpartum convalescence, weakness during pregnancy, postpartum weakness and dizziness, postural dizziness, mild dysmenorrhea, infertility and insufficient lactation.

Composition (each pill contains powdered)
Rehmannia glutinosa (shu di, processed rehmannia) 60mg, *Angelica sinensis* (dang gui, chinese angelica) 60mg, *Paeonia alba* (bai shao, white peony) 60mg, *Ligusticum wallichi* (chuan xiong, cnidium) 20mg

Combinations
- With **14.1 Huang Lian Jie Du Wan** for stubborn skin diseases with inflammation, redness and thickening of the dermis (such as psoriasis).
- With **13.14 Ching Wan Hung** topically for chronic bedsores or tropical ulcers.

Pattern identifying features

- **Blood deficiency**
- palpitations
- forgetfulness
- abdominal masses
- dysmenorrhea

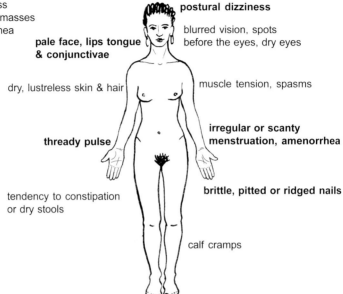

pale face, lips tongue & conjunctivae

dry, lustreless skin & hair

thready pulse

tendency to constipation or dry stools

postural dizziness

blurred vision, spots before the eyes, dry eyes

muscle tension, spasms

irregular or scanty menstruation, amenorrhea

brittle, pitted or ridged nails

calf cramps

GYN

- With **6.1 Xiao Chai Hu Tang Wan** for acute or lingering colds and flu in run down women, or the same associated with the menstrual period.
- With **13.2 Xiao Feng Wan** for skin diseases with itching and dryness.
- With **7.22 Shen Qi Da Bu Wan** with a degree of *qi* deficiency.

Dosage and method of administration

8-12 pills three times daily on an empty stomach. The dose may be spread out, or two lots of 12-18 pills may be taken, morning and evening. In severe cases or during the early stages of treatment (the first few weeks), a 50% increase in dose may be used, then reduced as the treatment takes effect.

Cautions and contraindications

Contraindicated during the early phase of acute illness such as colds and flu. Care should be taken in patients with a tendency to abdominal bloating, loose stools or general digestive weakness. Some patients may find **1.2 Si Wu Wan** aggravates these symptoms. This can usually be alleviated by taking the pills with a small dose (3-6 pills at the same time) of **2.18 Bao He Wan** or **2.9 Xiang Sha Liu Jun Wan**.

1.3 BA ZHEN YI MU WAN

八珍益母丸

Tianjin Darentang Pharmaceutical Factory (Shandong)
'Eight Precious Pills with Motherwort'
Ba Zhen Yi Mu Wan is packaged in bottles of 200 pills.

TCM actions
Supplements *qi* and Blood, quickens Blood, regulates menstruation and the *chong* and *ren* channel.

Biomedical actions
Energy supplement and stimulant, promotes metabolism, hematinic, stimulates Blood circulation, regulates menstruation, emmenagogue.

INDICATIONS

- *Qi* and Blood deficiency with mild Blood stagnation. As a variation of **1.1 Ba Zhen Wan**, this formula has similar action and indications. The difference is the addition of *Leonurus sibirica* (yi mu cao, motherwort) which can gently move stagnant Blood and promote urination. **1.3 Ba Zhen Yi Mu Wan** is better when there is a mild degree of Blood stagnation in addition to *qi* and Blood deficiency. Motherwort also assists in regulating menstruation, and is especially good for postpartum recovery, encouraging complete expulsion of birth products and quick contraction of the uterus back to normal.
- With the appropriate identifying features, this formula can be used to treat conditions such as postpartum Blood stagnation, placental retention, scanty menstrual periods or amenorrhea, mild dysmenorrhea, infertility, habitual miscarriage, premenstrual fluid retention, mild abnormal uterine bleeding with clotting, long menstrual cycle, irregular menstruation, bedsores, tropical ulcers, diabetic ulcers and chronic abscesses.

Composition (each pill contains powdered)
Leonurus sibirica (yi mu cao, motherwort) 46mg, *Angelica sinensis* (dang gui, chinese angelica) 24mg, *Rehmannia glutinosa* (shu di, processed rehmannia) 24mg, *Paeonia alba* (bai shao, white peony) 11mg, *Atractylodes macrocephala* (bai zhu, atractylodes) 11mg, *Poria cocos* (fu ling, hoelen) 11mg, *Ligusticum wallichi* (chuan xiong, cnidium) 11mg, *Glycyrrhiza uralensis* (gan cao, licorice 6mg), *Codonopsis pilosula* (dang shen, codonopsis) 11mg

Pattern identifying features

Blood deficiency with mild Blood stagnation
• fatigue
• poor appetite
• postpartum Blood stagnation
• placental retention
• irregular menstruation

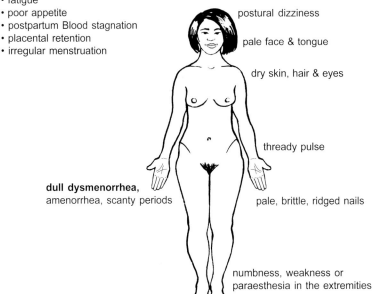

postural dizziness

pale face & tongue

dry skin, hair & eyes

thready pulse

dull dysmenorrhea,
amenorrhea, scanty periods

pale, brittle, ridged nails

numbness, weakness or
paraesthesia in the extremities

GYN

Dosage and method of administration

8-12 pills three times daily on an empty stomach. The dose may be spread out, or two lots of 12-18 pills may be taken, morning and evening. In severe cases, for placental retention, or in the early stages of treatment (the first few weeks), a 50% increase in dose may be used, then reduced as the treatment takes effect.

Cautions and contraindications

Contraindicated during the early phase of acute illness such as colds and flu. Care should be taken in patients with a tendency to abdominal bloating, loose stools or general digestive weakness. Some patients may find **1.3 Ba Zhen Yi Mu Wan** aggravates these symptoms. This can usually be alleviated by taking the pills with a small dose (3-6 pills at the same time) of **2.18 Bao He Wan** or **2.9 Xiang Sha Liu Jun Wan**.

1.4 YI MU TIAO JING TABLET

益母调经片

(Yi Mu Tiao Jing Pian)
Jing Xian Pharmaceutical Co. (Guangzhou)
'Motherwort Pills to Regulate Menstruation'
Yi Mu Tiao Jing Tablets are packaged in bottles of 60 tablets.

**YI MU TIAO
JING TABLET**

AUST L 82981
60 TABLETS

MADE IN CHINA

TCM actions
Supplements *qi* and Blood, regulates *qi* and quickens Blood, regulates menstruation and the *chong* and *ren* channels.

Biomedical actions
Energy supplement and stimulant, promotes metabolism, hematinic, stimulates Blood circulation, regulates menstruation, emmenagogue.

INDICATIONS

• Blood deficiency with mild Blood stagnation causing irregular menstruation, and dysmenorrhea.
• Incomplete expulsion of birth products following labour. Enhances contraction of the uterus back to normal following childbirth.

Composition (each tablet contains extracts equivalent to dry)
Leonurus sibirica (yi mu cao, motherwort) 325mg, *Salvia miltiorrhiza* (dan shen, salvia) 325mg, *Cyperus rotundus* (xiang fu, cyperus) 325mg, *Rehmannia glutinosa* (shu di, processed rehmannia) 225mg, *Atractylodes macrocephala* (bai zhu, atractylodes) 225mg, *Angelica polymorpha* (dang gui, chinese angelica) 175mg, *Ligusticum wallichi* (chuan xiong, cnidium) 175mg, *Paeonia lactiflora* (bai shao, white peony) 200mg

Dosage and method of administration
3-5 tablets, three times daily on an empty stomach.

Cautions and contraindications
Contraindicated during pregnancy and during the early phase of acute illness such as colds and flu. Care should be taken in patients with a tendency to abdominal bloating, loose stools or general digestive weakness. Any discomfort can usually be alleviated by taking the pills with a small dose (3-6 pills at the same time) of **2.18 Bao He Wan** or **2.9 Xiang Sha Liu Jun Wan**.

1.5 BU XUE TIAO JING TABLET

补血调经片

(Bu Xue Tiao Jing Pian)
Jing Xian Pharmaceutical Co. (Guangzhou)
'Supplement Blood and Regulate Menstruation Pills'
Bu Xue Tiao Jing Tablets are packaged in bottles of 60 tablets.

**BU XUE
TIAO JING
TABLET**

AUST L 82422
60 TABLETS

MADE IN CHINA

TCM actions
Supplements *qi* and Blood, warms Kidney *yang*, regulates menstruation and the *chong* and *ren* channels, regulates *qi* and quickens Blood.

Biomedical actions
Energy supplement and stimulant, promotes metabolism, hematinic, stimulates Blood circulation, regulates menstruation, emmenagogue.

INDICATIONS

- Blood deficiency with mild Blood stagnation. Very similar to **1.4 Yi Mu Tiao Jing Tablet**, with more emphasis on Blood supplementing. Useful for patterns with a greater component of Blood deficiency, for example for women following a relatively severe hemorrhage during labour.

GYN

Composition (each tablet contains extracts equivalent to dry)
Rehmannia glutinosa (shu di, processed rehmannia) 450mg, *Angelica polymorpha* (dang gui, chinese angelica) 325mg, *Cyperus rotundus* (xiang fu, cyperus) 325mg, *Spatholobus suberectus* (ji xue teng, spatholobus) 325mg, *Leonurus sibirica* (yi mu cao, motherwort) 125mg, *Salvia miltiorrhiza* (dan shen, salvia) 125mg, *Atractylodes macrocephala* (bai zhu, atractylodes) 125mg, *Ligusticum wallichi* (chuan xiong, cnidium) 125mg, *Dipsacus asper* (xu duan, dipsacus) 125mg, *Zizyphus jujuba* (da zao, chinese dates) 100mg

Dosage and method of administration
3-5 tablets, three times daily on an empty stomach.

Cautions and contraindications
Contraindicated during pregnancy and during the early phase of acute illness such as colds and flu. Care should be taken in patients with a tendency to abdominal bloating, loose stools or general digestive weakness. Any discomfort can usually be alleviated by taking the pills with a small dose (3-6 pills at the same time) of **2.18 Bao He Wan** or **2.9 Xiang Sha Liu Jun Wan**.

1.6 BAI FENG WAN

白凤丸

Tong Ren Tang (Beijing)
'White Phoenix Pills'
Bai Feng Wan is packaged either as
small peppercorn sized honey pills or as a single large honey pill sealed inside a wax ball, ten
balls per box.

TCM actions

Supplements *qi* and Blood, nourishes Kidney *yin*, clears deficient Heat, regulates menstruation and the *chong* and *ren* channels, stops leukorrhea.

Biomedical actions

Hematinic, tones the uterus and muscles, galactagogue.

INDICATIONS

• *Qi* and Blood deficiency patterns with mild Liver *qi* stagnation. This version of **Bai Feng Wan** is very similar to **1.1 Ba Zhen Wan**, with the addition of ginseng and astragalus to supplement *qi* and strengthen the Spleen, and of cyperus and salvia to regulate Liver *qi* and Blood. The black boned chicken makes this a somewhat richer supplement, excellent for relatively severe Blood deficiency. However, its gentle *qi* and Blood moving qualities allow it to powerfully supplement without being cloying.

• Traditionally used in China following menstruation to rebuild Blood and *qi*, and to nourish Blood to keep the skin healthy, soft and elastic.

• With the appropriate identifying features, this formula can be used to treat biomedical conditions such as profuse leukorrhea, irregular menstruation, premenstrual backache, scanty periods, amenorrhea, postpartum convalescence, weakness during pregnancy, postpartum weakness and dizziness, postural dizziness, infertility and insufficient lactation. Excellent for convalescence following severe illness, chemotherapy or surgery.

Composition (each dose [50 small pills] contains)

Black boned chicken 550mg, *Rehmannia glutinosa* (sheng di, rehmannia) 570mg, *Angelica polymorpha* (dang gui, chinese angelica) 210mg, *Panax ginseng* (ren shen, ginseng) 190mg, *Paeonia lactiflora* (bai shao, white peony) 190mg, *Dioscorea opposita* (shan yao, dioscorea) 190mg, *Cyperus rotundus* (xiang fu, cyperus) 190mg, *Salvia miltiorrhiza* (dan shen, salvia) 190mg, *Ostrea gigas* (mu li, oyster shell) 140mg, *Ligusticum wallichi* (chuan xiong, cnidium) 70mg, *Glycyrrhiza uralensis* (gan cao, licorice) 70mg, *Asparagus lucidus* (tian dong,

Pattern identifying features

- *Qi* & **Blood deficiency with deficient Heat**
- **postpartum or illness convalescence**
- **postpartum flushing or heat**
- fatigue, debility
- menstrual disorders
- poor memory, vision

postural dizziness

pale complexion & tongue

insufficient lactation

thready pulse

pale nails

dull abdominal pain

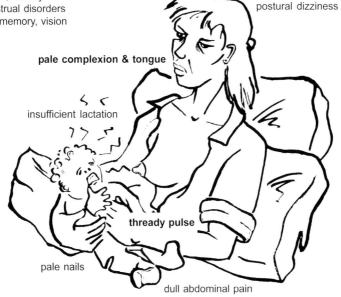

asparagus) 70mg, *Astragalus membranaceous* (huang qi, astragalus) 70mg, *Stellaria dichotoma* (yin chai hu, stellaria root) 55mg, honey 1.9g

Dosage and method of administration

One pill (or a plastic ball of small pills) twice daily on an empty stomach.

Cautions and contraindications

Contraindicated during the early phase of acute illness such as colds and flu. Care should be taken in patients with a tendency to abdominal bloating, loose stools or general digestive weakness. Some patients may find **1.6 Bai Feng Wan** aggravates these symptoms. This can usually be alleviated by taking the appropriate dose with a small quantity (3-6 pills at the same time) of **2.18 Bao He Wan** or **2.9 Xiang Sha Liu Jun Wan**.

1.7 WU JI BAI FENG WAN

乌鸡白凤丸

Tianjin Darentang Pharmaceutical Factory
(Shandong)
'Black Chicken White Phoenix Pills'
Wu Ji Bai Feng Wan is packaged as small peppercorn sized honey pills inside a wax ball, ten balls per box.

TCM actions
Supplements *qi*, Blood and Kidney *yin* and *yang*, regulates menstruation and the *chong* and *ren* channels, quickens Blood.

Biomedical actions
Energy supplement and stimulant, promotes metabolism, hematinic, regulates menstruation, galactagogue, emmenagogue.

INDICATIONS

- Blood deficiency with Liver and Kidney deficiency. The black boned chicken is a special and very nourishing supplement for the Liver and Kidneys, and is especially indicated for postpartum or relatively severe Blood deficiency. Similar to **1.6 Bai Feng Wan**, this version incorporates deer horn resin to powerfully warm and strengthen Kidney *yang* and aid the transformation of *gu qi* into Blood. A well balanced and very popular prescription in China, **1.7 Wu Ji Bai Feng Wan** is able to strongly supplement without causing stagnation. Traditionally used in China following menstruation to rebuild Blood and *qi*, and to nourish Blood to keep the skin healthy, soft and elastic.
- With the appropriate identifying features, this formula can be used to treat biomedical conditions such as infertility, anovulation, scanty periods, amenorrhea, postpartum weakness and postural dizziness, mild dysmenorrhea and insufficient lactation. In addition, it is useful for severe or refractory anemia, to protect bone marrow during chemotherapy or radiotherapy and for chronic sores and ulcers that are slow to heal, such as bedsores, diabetic ulcers and tropical ulcers.

Composition (each dose [50 small pills] contains)
Black boned chicken 1.5g, *Rehmannia glutinosa* (shu di, processed rehmannia) 600mg, *Cervus japonicus* (lu jiao jiao, deer horn resin) 450mg, *Angelica polymorpha* (dang gui, chinese angelica) 335mg, *Paeonia lactiflora* (bai shao, white peony) 300mg, *Panax ginseng* (ren shen, ginseng) 300mg, *Dioscorea opposita* (shan yao, dioscorea) 300mg, *Cyperus rotundus* (xiang fu, cyperus) 300mg, *Salvia miltiorrhiza* (dan shen, salvia) 300mg, *Asparagus lucidius*

Pattern identifying features

- ***Qi* & Blood deficiency, Liver & Kidney deficiency**
- **menstrual disorders**
- cold intolerance
- low libido
- fatigue

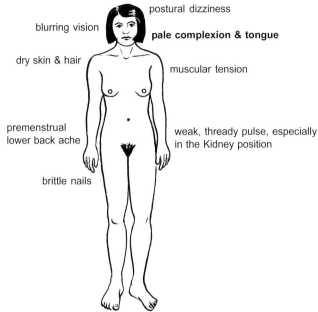

blurring vision

dry skin & hair

premenstrual
lower back ache

brittle nails

postural dizziness

pale complexion & tongue

muscular tension

weak, thready pulse, especially
in the Kidney position

GYN

(tian dong, asparagus) 150mg, *Ligusticum wallichi* (chuan xiong, cnidium) 150mg, *Euryale ferox* (qian shi, euryale seed) 150mg, *Ostrea gigas* (mu li, oyster shell) 110mg, *Scutellaria baicalensis* (huang qin, scute) 85mg, *Glycyrrhiza uralensis* (gan cao, licorice) 75mg, *Stellaria dichotoma* (yin chai hu, stellaria root) 60mg, honey 2.3g

Combinations
- With **13.14 Ching Wan Hung** topically for bedsores or tropical ulcers.

Dosage and method of administration
50 small pills (the contents of one wax ball) twice daily, on an empty stomach.

Cautions and contraindications
Contraindicated during the early phase of acute illness such as colds and flu. Generally well tolerated, however some sensitive patients may find **1.7 Wu Ji Bai Feng Wan** causes abdominal bloating, loose stools or general digestive upset. This can usually be alleviated by taking the dose with a small quantity (3-6 pills at the same time) of **2.18 Bao He Wan** or **2.9 Xiang Sha Liu Jun Wan**.

1.8 TONG REN WU JI BAI FENG WAN

同仁乌鸡白凤丸

Tong Ren Tang (Beijing)
'Black Chicken White Phoenix Pills from
Tong Ren Tang'
Tong Ren Wu Ji Bai Feng Wan is
packaged as large 9 gram honey pills
sealed inside a wax ball, ten balls per box.

TCM actions

Supplements *qi*, Blood and Kidney *yin*, regulates *qi* and menstruation, clears
deficient Heat.

Biomedical actions

Energy supplement and stimulant, hematinic, regulates menstruation.

INDICATIONS

• *Qi* and Blood deficiency (with mild depletion of *yin*), with elements of deficient
Heat and sweating. Similar in general action to **1.6 Bai Feng Wan**, with an
emphasis on cooling heat generated by deficiency.

• An excellent supplementing formula for postpartum Blood deficiency, low grade
afternoon or bone steaming fever and night sweats.

• Irregular menstruation, mild abnormal uterine bleeding, leukorrhea and mild
dysmenorrhea associated with deficiency.

Composition

Black bone chicken, *Panax ginseng* (ren shen, ginseng), *Angelica sinensis* (dang gui,
chinese angelica) *Rehmannia glutinosa* (shu di, processed rehmannia), *Cyperus rotundus*
(xiang fu, cyperus), *Ostrea gigas* (mu li, oyster shell), *Stellaria dichotoma* (yin chai hu,
stellaria root)

Dosage and method of administration

One pill chewed twice daily on an empty stomach.

Pattern identifying features

- **Qi & Blood deficiency with deficient Heat**
- low grade fever, bone steaming fever
- facial flushing, malar flush
- night sweats, easy sweating
- exhaustion, fatigue
- insomnia
- insufficient lactation

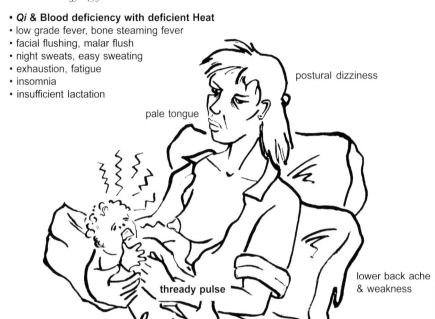

postural dizziness

pale tongue

threadly pulse

lower back ache & weakness

GYN

Cautions and contraindications

Contraindicated during the early phase of acute illness such as colds and flu. Generally well tolerated, however some sensitive patients may find **1.8 Tong Ren Wu Ji Bai Feng Wan** causes abdominal bloating, loose stools or general digestive upset. This can usually be alleviated by taking the dose with a small quantity (3-6 pills at the same time) of **2.18 Bao He Wan** or **2.9 Xiang Sha Liu Jun Wan**.

1.9 GUI PI WAN

归脾丸

Lanzhou Foci Pharmaceutical Factory (Gansu)
'Return the [Health of] Spleen Pills'
Gui Pi Wan is packaged in bottles of 200 pills.
Also available as: Kuei Be Wan, Gui Pi Teapills (PF)

TCM actions
Supplements *qi* and Blood, strengthens the Spleen and Heart, calms the *shen*, strengthens the Spleen's function of keeping Blood in the vessels.

Biomedical actions
Enhances digestive functions, hematinic, hemostatic, sedative for anxiety and mild neurosis, nervine.

INDICATIONS

- Spleen *qi* and Heart Blood deficiency. The focus of this important formula is to nourish *qi* and Blood, strengthen the Spleen's Blood holding capacity, and calm the *shen*.
- Menstrual disorders associated with *qi* and Blood deficiency, such as scanty periods or amenorrhea, irregular menstruation, infertility and premenstrual syndrome with insomnia and anxiety.
- Used for a wide variety of bleeding disorders resulting from the Spleen *qi* failing to hold Blood in the vessels, including uterine bleeding, intermenstrual bleeding, menorrhagia, continuous spotting, easy bruising, rectal bleeding, bleeding hemorrhoids, purpura and clotting disorders.
- Heart and *shen* disorders associated with *qi* and Blood deficiency, and Blood failing to anchor the *shen*, including insomnia, palpitations, poor concentration and memory, anxiety, panic attacks, phobias, mental obsession and obsessive compulsive disorder.
- Postpartum disorders from *qi* and Blood deficiency with weakness, fatigue, anxiety, depression, breathlessness, postural dizziness and anemia.
- With the appropriate identifying features, this formula can be used to treat biomedical conditions such as thrombocytopenic or allergic purpura, Henoch Schönlein purpura, supraventricular tachycardia, cardiac arrhythmia, anemia, neurosis, hypoproteinemia, chronic gastroenteritis, chronic fatigue syndrome and some mild psychiatric disorders.

Pattern identifying features

- **Heart Blood & Spleen** *qi* **deficiency**
- **insomnia**
- **anxiety**, panic attacks
- **bleeding disorders**
- poor memory, forgetfulness
- poor appetite
- fatigue, weakness
- visual disturbances

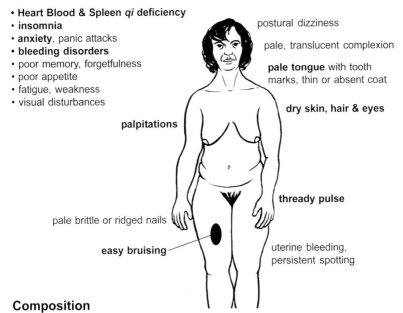

postural dizziness

pale, translucent complexion

pale tongue with tooth marks, thin or absent coat

dry skin, hair & eyes

palpitations

thready pulse

pale brittle or ridged nails

easy bruising

uterine bleeding, persistent spotting

GYN

Composition

Angelica sinensis (dang gui, chinese angelica) 19mg, *Poria cocos* (fu ling, hoelen) 19mg, *Polygala tenuifolia* (yuan zhi, polygala) 19mg, *Atractylodes macrocephala* (bai zhu, atractylodes) 19mg, *Euphoriae longana* (long yan rou, longan) 19mg, *Zizyphus spinoza* (suan zao ren, zizyphus) 10mg, *Saussurea lappa* (mu xiang, saussurea) 5mg, *Astragalus membranaceous* (huang qi, astragalus) 10mg, *Glycyrrhiza uralensis* (gan cao, licorice) 5mg

Combinations

- Taken following menstruation until midcycle (day 4-14, to nourish Blood and *yin*), with **6.4 Xiao Yao Wan** (taken day 15-28 to regulate *qi* and the *yang* phase), for irregular menstruation, infertility and other menstrual disorders.

Dosage and method of administration

8-12 pills three times daily on an empty stomach. The dose may be spread out, or two lots of 12-18 pills may be taken, morning and evening. In severe cases or during the early stages of treatment (the first few weeks), a 50% increase in dose may be used, then reduced as the treatment takes effect.

Cautions and contraindications

Contraindicated during the early phase of acute illness such as colds and flu. Care in patients with a tendency to Dampness or Phlegm, abdominal bloating or loose stools. This can usually be alleviated by taking the pills with a small dose (3-6 pills at the same time) of **2.18 Bao He Wan** or **2.9 Xiang Sha Liu Jun Wan**.

GMP **1.10 DANG GUI JING**

养血当归精

(Yang Xue Dang Gui Jing)
Guangzhou Pangaoshou Pharmaceutical Company (Guangzhou)
'Essence of *Angelica sinensis* to Nourish Blood'
Dang Gui Jing is packaged as liquid in bottles of 150ml.
Also available as: Tang Kwei Gin (PF)

TCM actions
Supplements *qi* and Blood, regulates menstruation and the *chong* and *ren* channels.

Biomedical actions
Energy supplement and stimulant, promotes metabolism, hematinic, regulates menstruation, galactagogue.

INDICATIONS

* *Qi* and Blood deficiency. Very similar in action to **1.1 Ba Zhen Wan**. May be used to treat a wide variety of conditions associated with *qi* and Blood deficiency, including gynecological conditions such as scanty menstrual periods, amenorrhea, infertility, habitual miscarriage, long menstrual cycle or irregular menstruation, postpartum weakness or insufficient lactation and weakness during pregnancy.
* Also used for non-gynecological conditions associated with *qi* and Blood deficiency, including general fatigue and exhaustion, anemia, postural dizziness, visual weakness, floaters before the eyes, generalised weakness, post surgical or post haemorrhage weakness, restless leg syndrome and malnutrition associated with deprivation or anorexia.

Composition
Angelica sinensis (dang gui, chinese angelica), *Codonopsis pilosula* (dang shen, codonopsis), *Rehmannia glutinosa* (shu di, processed rehmannia), *Paeonia alba* (bai shao, white peony), *Poria cocos* (fu ling, hoelen), *Ligusticum wallichi* (chuan xiong, cnidium), *Astragalus membranaceous* (huang qi, astragalus), *Glycyrrhiza uralensis* (zhi gan cao, honey fried licorice root)

Pattern identifying features

- **Blood deficiency**
- anemia
- postpartum or post hemorrhage
  weakness
- fatigue

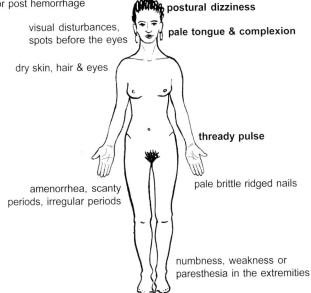

postural dizziness

pale tongue & complexion

visual disturbances,
spots before the eyes

dry skin, hair & eyes

thready pulse

amenorrhea, scanty
periods, irregular periods

pale brittle ridged nails

numbness, weakness or
paresthesia in the extremities

GYN

Dosage and method of administration

10mls, three times daily on an empty stomach.

Cautions and contraindications

Contraindicated during the early phase of acute illness such as colds and flu. Care in patients with a tendency to Dampness or Phlegm, abdominal bloating or loose stools. This can usually be alleviated by taking the formula with a small dose (3-6 pills at the same time) of **2.18 Bao He Wan** or **2.9 Xiang Sha Liu Jun Wan**.

1.11 DANG GUI SU

当归素

Lanzhou Foci Pharmaceutical Factory (Gansu)
'Simply Dang Gui Pills'
Dang Gui Su is packaged in bottles of 200 pills.
Also available as: Dang Gui Extract Wan (HT)

TCM actions
Supplements Blood, regulates menstruation.

Biomedical actions
Hematinic.

INDICATIONS

- Blood deficiency. Especially good for menstrual disorders, such as mild dysmenorrhea, amenorrhea, scanty menstruation, fatigue following menstruation, infertility, postpartum abdominal pain and dizziness, anemia and insufficient lactation.
- For Heart and Liver Blood deficiency patterns causing dizziness, insomnia, poor memory, anxiety, tics and tremors.
- For traumatic injury, superficial suppurative sores, Wind Damp *bi* pain, and postpartum abdominal pain from sluggish Blood circulation or stasis.
- As an adjunct for constipation in the elderly or postpartum women.
- Can be added to other constitutional formulae when enhanced Blood supplementation is desired.

Composition (each pill contains extracts equivalent to)
Angelica sinensis (dang gui, chinese angelica) 284mg

Dosage and method of administration
4-6 pills three times daily on an empty stomach. The dose may be spread out, or two lots of 6-9 pills may be taken, morning and evening.

Cautions and contraindications
Contraindicated during the early phase of acute illness such as colds and flu. Can be used during pregnancy. Very occasionally a sensitive patient may experience mild nausea, diarrhea or loose stools in the early days of treatment. This can be alleviated by reducing the dose or by adding a few pills of **2.9 Xiang Sha Liu Jun Wan** or **2.18 Bao He Wan**.

1.12 SHI XIAO WAN

失 笑 丸

Lanzhou Foci Pharmaceutical Factory (Gansu)
'Break Into a Smile Pills'
Shi Xiao Wan is packaged in bottles of 200 pills.

TCM actions
Quickens Blood, disperses stagnant Blood, stops pain.

Biomedical actions
Analgesic, improves circulation.

INDICATIONS

• Blood stagnation pain. Mostly used for gynecological pain patterns, but can be used for other painful sites such as the stomach, hypochondrium and head. Usually added to a constitutional formula where a degree of Blood stagnation moving action is desired.
• May be used prior to and during menstruation when pain is anticipated, to enhance the analgesic affect of any other treatments.

GYN

Composition (each pill contains powdered)
Salvia miltiorrhiza (dan shen, salvia) 80mg, *Typhae angustifolia* (pu huang, bulrush pollen) 80mg

Combinations
• With **6.4 Xiao Yao Wan** for *qi* and mild Blood stagnation dysmenorrhea.
• With **6.3 Chai Hu Shu Gan Wan** for focal epigastric pain from Liver *qi* invading the Stomach.

Dosage and method of administration
The recommended dose if used alone is 8-12 pills three times daily before meals. However, this formula is usually combined with a constitutional formula, in which case the dose can be reduced by 50-75%.

Cautions and contraindications
Contraindicated during pregnancy. Caution in patients taking warfarin or other blood thinning agents as clotting time may be reduced.

GMP **1.13 WOO GARM YUEN MEDICAL PILLS**

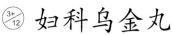

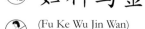

(Fu Ke Wu Jin Wan)
Chan Li Chai Medical Factory (Hong Kong)
'Black and Gold Pills for Gynecological Disorders'
Woo Garm Yuen Medical Pills are packaged as large honey pills in a
yellow wax ball, ten pills per box.

TCM actions
Invigorates *qi* and Blood, disperses stagnant Blood, dispels
Cold, warms the uterus, nourishes Blood.

Biomedical actions
Emmenagogue, regulates menstruation, improves circulation, stops pain, relieves
stagnation in the uterus.

INDICATIONS

• Blood and *qi* stagnation with Cold accumulation and *qi* deficiency affecting the
uterus or other structures of the lower *jiao*. Especially useful for dysmenorrhea
associated with fibroids, endometriosis or cysts. Also for uterine bleeding and
bleeding fibroids. The primary mechanism is the Cold accumulation that causes
poor movement, and subsequent pooling, of Blood in the pelvic basin. A well
balanced formula that equally addresses the Blood stasis and the Cold; best for
excess patterns with little deficiency.

• With the appropriate identifying features, this formula can be used to treat primary
dysmenorrhea, mittlesmertz, gynecological masses, chronic pelvic inflammatory
disease, polycystic ovaries, amenorrhea, intermenstrual bleeding, infertility,
irregular menstrual cycle (especially long cycle) and postpartum placental
retention. It can also be used for prostatic masses and prostatic hypertrophy in
men with Blood stagnation, Cold and *qi* deficiency.

Composition
Artemesia vulgaris (ai ye, mugwort) 13.6%, *Cyperus rotundus* (xiang fu, cyperus) 13.6%,
Atractylodes macrocephala (bai zhu, atractylodes) 12.5%, *Angelica sinensis* (dang gui,
chinese angelica) 8.2%, *Cinnamomum cassia* (rou gui, cinnamon bark) 8.2%, *Curcuma
ezhu* (e zhu, curcuma) 7%, *Typhae angustifolia* (pu huang, bulrush pollen) 6.8%,
Solidago virdaurea (liu ji nu, solidago) 6.8%, *Scutellaria baicalensis* (huang qin, scute)
6.8%, *Citrus reticulata* (qing pi, immature citrus) 5.5%, *Citrus aurantium* (zhi ke,
aurantium) 5.5%, *Zingiber officinalis* (gan jiang, dry ginger) 5.5%

Pattern identifying features

- **Blood stagnation & Cold in the Uterus & lower** *jiao*
- **dark menstrual blood with significant clotting**
- **lower abdominal masses**
- **pale purplish tongue**, or with brown or purple patches on the edges; dark distended sublingual veins
- spider veins around the medial ankle & knee
- cold intolerance, cold extremities
- low abdomen feels cool to the touch

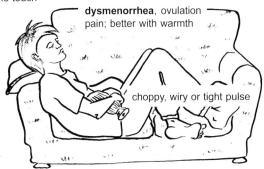

dysmenorrhea, ovulation pain; better with warmth

choppy, wiry or tight pulse

Combinations

- For women with heavy periods with lots of pain and clotting, blood loss may be significant. If so, the focus of the first two weeks of the cycle should be to build blood with a formula like **1.1 Ba Zhen Wan** or **1.16 Tao Hong Si Wu Wan**. Start taking **1.13 Woo Garm Yuen Medical Pills** after midcycle (or just before if there is ovulation pain).
- With **1.33 Hai Zao Jing Wan** or **1.34 Nei Xiao Luo Li Wan** for Phlegm type gynecological cysts and masses.
- With **7.9 Fu Gui Ba Wei Wan** or **7.10 You Gui Wan** for patients with significant *yang* deficiency.
- With **11.1 Qian Lie Xian Capsule** or **11.2 Prostate Gland Pills** for male urinary disturbances from prostate swelling.

Dosage and method of administration

One or two pills per day with warm water, yellow wine (*shao xing jiu*) or ginger tea, on an empty stomach. May be taken through a menstrual period to take advantage of the extra movement of Blood during that time. These pills are often very hard and need to be softened in boiling water for 10 minutes before ingestion.

Cautions and contraindications

Contraindicated during pregnancy and in women with menorrhagia without dark blood or clotting. Some women will experience heavier (and possibly more painful) periods once or twice as the stagnation is moved. Caution in patients on anticoagulant therapy. Watch for bruising or increased tendency to bleeding.

GYN

GMP **1.14 WEN JING TANG WAN**

温经汤丸

Available in the US,
UK and Europe
See Note 1, p.xxi

Lanzhou Foci Pharmaceutical Factory (Gansu)
'Pills to Warm the Menses'
Wen Jing Tang Wan is packaged in bottles of 200 pills.
Available as: Warm Cycle Teapills (PF)

TCM actions
Supplements *qi* and Blood, warms the Uterus, quickens
Blood and gently disperses stagnant Blood.

Biomedical actions
Regulates menstruation, stops pain, relieves stagnation in the
uterus.

INDICATIONS

• Deficient Cold patterns of the Uterus, with Cold congealing the Blood and
Blood stagnation. The focus of the formula is primarily to strengthen *qi* and
Blood while warming and dispelling Cold from the Uterus, and gently dispersing
stagnant Blood. The classical pattern described by Zhang Zhong-jing includes
symptoms of Heat above (typically false Heat)–dry mouth and lips, low grade
fever and warm palms, but these are not especially common and their presence
is not necessary for diagnosis. The key features are the complete unpredictably
of the length and volume of the menstrual period, the coldness of the lower
abdomen which is much relieved with warmth, and the pain which may be
somewhat alleviated with pressure, or at least not made significantly worse when
palpated. Compared to **1.18 Shao Fu Zhu Yu Wan** and **1.13 Woo Garm Yuen
Medical Pills** which are used when the pattern is primarily excess, this formula
is best for patterns of mixed excess and deficiency.
• With the appropriate identifying features, this formula may assist in the treatment
of biomedical conditions such as irregular menstruation, uterine bleeding,
persistent bleeding following termination or miscarriage, infertility, chronic pelvic
inflammatory disease, primary dysmenorrhea and amenorrhea.

Composition
Evodia rutacarpae (wu zhu yu, evodia) 9.5%, *Angelica sinensis* (dang gui, chinese angelica)
9.5%, *Paeonia lactiflora* (chao bai shao, dry fried white peony) 9.5%, *Equus asinus* (e jiao,
donkey skin gelatin) 9.5%, *Codonopsis pilosula* (dang shen, codonopsis) 9.5%, *Pinellia
ternata* (zhi ban xia, processed pinellia) 9.5%, *Ophiopogon japonicus* (mai dong,

Pattern identifying features

- **Cold, deficiency & Blood stagnation affecting the Uterus; Cold below Heat above**
- **irregular menstruation**
- **infertility**
- **dysmenorrhea**
- low grade fever at dusk

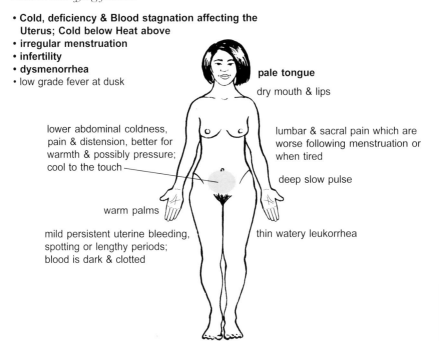

pale tongue

dry mouth & lips

lower abdominal coldness, pain & distension, better for warmth & possibly pressure; cool to the touch

lumbar & sacral pain which are worse following menstruation or when tired

deep slow pulse

warm palms

mild persistent uterine bleeding, spotting or lengthy periods; blood is dark & clotted

thin watery leukorrhea

GYN

ophiopogon) 9.5%, *Cinnamomum cassia* (gui zhi, cinnamon twigs) 6%, *Paeonia suffruticosa* (mu dan pi, moutan) 6%, *Glycyrrhiza uralensis* (gan cao, licorice) 6%, *Ligusticum wallichi* (chuan xiong, cnidium) 6%, *Zingiber officinale* (sheng jiang, ginger) 6%

Combinations
- With **2.13 Li Zhong Wan** for more severe Cold.
- With **10.1 Yunnan Paiyao** for persistent bleeding.
- With **11.4 Tian Tai Wu Yao Wan** for more pronounced *qi* stagnation.

Dosage and method of administration
8-12 pills three times daily on an empty stomach. The dose may be spread out, or two lots of 12-18 pills may be taken, morning and evening. May be taken through the entire period, including during the bleed, to gently encourage the expulsion of stagnant Blood.

Cautions and contraindications
Contraindicated during pregnancy, in women with menorrhagia without dark blood or clotting, and in cases where the excess, i.e. Blood stagnation and Cold is the primary pathogen (*see* **1.18 Shao Fu Zhu Yu Wan** or **1.13 Woo Garm Yuen Medical Pills** for that problem).

1.15 TONG JING WAN

痛经丸

Lanzhou Foci Pharmaceutical Factory (Gansu)
'Dysmenorrhea Pills'
Tong Jing Wan is packaged in bottles of 200 pills.
Also available as: Calm in the Sea of Life Teapills (PF), Period Ease Pills (BE)

TCM actions

Invigorates *qi* and Blood in the lower *jiao*, disperses stagnant Blood, stops pain.

Biomedical actions

Regulates menstruation, improves circulation, stops pain, relieves stagnation in the uterus.

INDICATIONS

• Relatively severe Blood stagnation causing dysmenorrhea or amenorrhea. This is quite a strong Blood moving and analgesic formula, and is suitable for robust patients with little or no deficiency, usually younger women. Can be used during and prior to menstruation for pain associated with gynecological masses and endometriosis.

• Can also be used for Blood stagnation patterns and masses in other structures of the lower *jiao* in women and men, such as in the prostate, testicles (a type of *shan qi*) or urinary bladder causing dysuria or hematuria. Also useful for relatively severe post surgical Blood stagnation or pain.

Composition (each pill contains powdered)

Paeonia lactiflora (bai shao, white peony) 24.5mg, *Prunus persica* (tao ren, peach seed) 24.1mg, *Salvia miltiorrhiza* (dan shen, salvia) 20.4mg, *Lindera strychnifolia* (wu yao, lindera) 20.4mg, *Corydalis turtschaninovii* (yan hu suo, corydalis) 20.4mg, *Cyperus rotundus* (xiang fu, cyperus) 16.4mg, *Angelica polymorpha* (dang gui, chinese angelica) 16.4mg, *Ligusticum wallichi* (chuan xiong, cnidium) 14.4mg, *Carthamus tinctorius* (hong hua, carthamus) 12.4mg, *Panax pseudoginseng* (tian qi, pseudoginseng) 10.2mg

Combinations

• With **1.12 Shi Xiao Wan** or **10.21 Yan Hu Suo Wan** to enhance the analgesic action during episodes of pain.
• With **1.2 Si Wu Wan** for patients with Blood deficiency.

Pattern identifying features

- **Blood stagnation pain**
- lower abdominal pain & distension, worse with pressure
- palpable masses
- dark or clotted menstrual blood
- usually younger women < 35

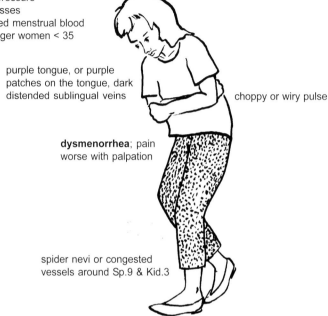

purple tongue, or purple patches on the tongue, dark distended sublingual veins

choppy or wiry pulse

dysmenorrhea; pain worse with palpation

spider nevi or congested vessels around Sp.9 & Kid.3

- With **1.13 Woo Garm Yuen Medical Pills** for relatively severe Blood stagnation and Cold accumulation type dysmenorrhea associated with fibroids or endometriosis.
- With **11.1 Qian Lie Xian Capsules** or **11.2 Prostate Gland Pills** for prostate swelling and perineal pain from Blood stagnation.

Dosage and method of administration

8-12 pills three times daily, on an empty stomach. The dose may be spread out, or two lots of 12-18 pills may be taken, morning and evening. An increased dose can be used in the week prior to an expected painful period. May be taken through a period to promote movement of Blood.

Cautions and contraindications

Contraindicated during pregnancy and in women with menorrhagia without dark blood or clotting. Caution in patients who are very run down or fatigued. Some women will experience heavier, and possibly more painful periods once or twice as the stagnation is moved. Caution in patients taking warfarin or other blood thinning agents as clotting time may be reduced.

1.16 TAO HONG SI WU WAN

桃红四物丸

Lanzhou Foci Pharmaceutical Factory (Gansu)
'Four Ingredient Pills with Safflower and Peach Seed'
Tao Hong Si Wu Wan is packaged in bottles of 200 pills.
Also available as: Tao Hong Si Wu Tang Teapills (PF)

TCM actions

Supplements and quickens Blood, gently disperses stagnant Blood.

Biomedical actions

Emmenagogue, regulates menstruation, improves circulation, stops pain, relieves mild stagnation in the uterus.

INDICATIONS

• Blood deficiency with mild Blood stagnation. Especially good for menstrual disorders and patterns affecting the uterus or other structures of the lower *jiao*. With the appropriate identifying features, this formula can treat mild dysmenorrhea, irregular menstruation, shortened periods with heavy or clotted bleeding, menorrhagia, infertility and masses such as fibroids, endometriosis, Fallopian tube blockage or cysts. Good for gentle expulsion of retained birth products and lochia in the postpartum period. **1.16 Tao Hong Si Wu Wan** is a variation of **1.2 Si Wu Wan** with the addition of peach seed and carthamus to gently invigorate Blood. Many practitioners prefer this formula to **1.2 Si Wu Wan** because of the common complication of stagnant Blood in long term Blood deficiency patterns.

• Used for a wide variety of disorders characterised by Blood deficiency and mild Blood stagnation including circulatory, cardiovascular and hepatic disorders such as varicose veins, spider veins, chronic phlebitis, purplish discoloration of the limbs, numbness or tingling of the extremities, mild angina, liver and spleen swelling and anemia. Also good for post traumatic stress syndrome and chronic depression.

Composition (each pill contains powdered)

Rehmannia glutinosa (shu di, processed rehmannia) 36mg, *Angelica sinensis* (dang gui, chinese angelica) 36mg, *Paeonia lactiflora* (bai shao, white peony) 36mg, *Prunus persica* (tao ren, peach seed) 36mg, *Carthamus tinctorius* (hong hua, carthamus) 18mg, *Ligusticum wallichi* (chuan xiong, cnidium) 18mg

Pattern identifying features

- **Blood deficiency with mild Blood stagnation**
- irregular menstrual cycle (short or long)
- amenorrhea
- infertility
- masses; endometriosis, fibroids

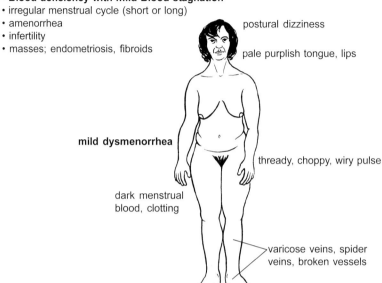

postural dizziness

pale purplish tongue, lips

mild dysmenorrhea

thready, choppy, wiry pulse

dark menstrual blood, clotting

varicose veins, spider veins, broken vessels

Combinations
- With **6.4 Xiao Yao Wan** for depression or post traumatic stress with Liver *qi* stagnation.
- With **13.2 Xiao Feng Wan** for chronic itchy skin diseases with purplish or painful lesions.
- With **5.7 Sunho Multi Ginseng Tablets** for small gynecological masses and circulatory and peripheral vascular disorders.
- With **1.12 Shi Xiao Wan** for severe dysmenorrhea.
- With **2.22 Er Chen Wan** for numbness in the extremities from Blood and Phlegm stagnation following Windstroke.

Dosage and method of administration
8-12 pills three times daily on an empty stomach. The dose may be spread out, or two lots of 12-18 pills may be taken, morning and evening. In severe cases or during the early stages of treatment (the first few weeks), a 50% increase in dose may be used, then reduced as the treatment takes effect. May be taken through a menstrual period to promote movement of Blood.

Cautions and contraindications
Contraindicated during pregnancy and in women with menorrhagia without dark blood or clotting. Some women will experience heavier (and possibly more painful) periods once or twice as the stagnation is moved.

GYN

1.17 GUI ZHI FU LING WAN

桂枝茯苓丸

Lanzhou Foci Pharmaceutical Factory (Gansu)
'Cinnamon Twig and Hoelen Pills'
Gui Zhi Fu Ling Wan is packaged in bottles of 200 pills.
Also available as: Cinnamon and Poria Teapills (PF)

TCM actions
Quickens Blood and gradually disperses stagnant Blood,
warms the uterus, and dissipates abdominal masses.

Biomedical actions
Emmenagogue, regulates menstruation, improves
circulation, stops pain, relieves stagnation in the uterus.

INDICATIONS

- Blood stagnation type masses affecting the reproductive system and lower *jiao*.
  Excellent for small benign gynecological masses such as mild endometriosis,
  fibroids, cysts and chronic inflammatory masses.
- Blood stagnation in the prostate or testicles, with pain that may radiate to the
  groin or lower abdomen, masses and lumps, or Blood stagnation affecting sperm
  quality. Useful following vasectomy reversal.
- With the appropriate identifying features, this formula can be used to treat
  biomedical disorders such as mild primary dysmenorrhea, fibroids, ovarian cysts,
  mittlesmertz, chronic pelvic inflammatory disease, cervical erosion, chronic
  salpingitis, endometriosis and postpartum placental retention, testicular
  varicosities or varicocele, hemaspermia, non liquifation of sperm, antisperm
  antibodies (immunological infertility, especially following vasectomy reversal),
  aspermia, post traumatic, surgical or idiopathic testicular pain and mild
  uncomfortable prostatic swelling.

Composition (each pill contains powdered)
Poria cocos (fu ling, hoelen) 36mg, *Cinnamomum cassia* (gui zhi, cinnamon twigs) 36mg,
Prunus persica (tao ren, peach seed) 36mg, *Paeonia suffruticosa* (mu dan pi, peony root
bark) 36mg, *Paeonia veitchii* (chi shao, red peony) 36mg

Combinations
- With **1.2 Si Wu Wan** to nourish Blood and regulate menstruation. If a stronger
  Blood moving action is desired, combine with **1.16 Tao Hong Si Wu Wan**.

Pattern identifying features

- **small Blood stagnation type masses**
- amenorrhea
- infertility

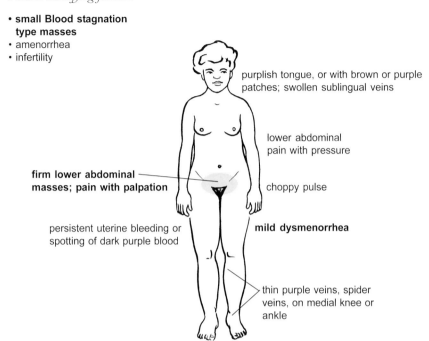

purplish tongue, or with brown or purple patches; swollen sublingual veins

lower abdominal pain with pressure

firm lower abdominal masses; pain with palpation

choppy pulse

persistent uterine bleeding or spotting of dark purple blood

mild dysmenorrhea

thin purple veins, spider veins, on medial knee or ankle

GYN

- Because this is a gentle and relatively neutral formula, it combines well with other formulae to encourage the movement of *qi* and Blood in the lower *jiao*. For example, if the stagnant Blood is due to weak circulation of *yang* and pooling of Blood, combine with **7.9 Fu Gui Ba Wei Wan** or **7.16 Shi Quan Da Bu Wan** to stimulate Kidney *yang* circulation. If due to congealing of Blood from increased viscosity associated with *yin* deficiency, combine with **7.1 Liu Wei Di Huang Wan** or **1.23 Zhi Bai Ba Wei Wan** to nourish *yin* and fluids.

Dosage and method of administration

8-12 pills three times daily on an empty stomach. The dose may be spread out, or two lots of 12-18 pills may be taken, morning and evening. May be taken through the entire period, including during the bleed to encourage the expulsion of stagnant Blood.

Cautions and contraindications

Extreme caution during pregnancy. **1.17 Gui Zhi Fu Ling Wan** was originally designed for bleeding during pregnancy accompanied by abdominal pain, and thus is quite a gentle formula. It is rarely used during pregnancy today, and only by very experienced practitioners.

1.18 SHAO FU ZHU YU WAN

GMP

Available in the US,
UK and Europe
See Note 1, p.xxi

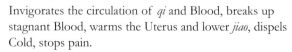

Lanzhou Foci Pharmaceutical Factory (Gansu)
'Remove Stagnant Blood from the Lower Abdomen Pills'
Shao Fu Zhu Yu Wan is packaged in bottles of 200 pills.
Available as: Stasis in the Lower Palace Teapills (PF)

TCM actions
Invigorates the circulation of *qi* and Blood, breaks up
stagnant Blood, warms the Uterus and lower *jiao*, dispels
Cold, stops pain.

Biomedical actions
Vasodilator, analgesic, anti-platelet action, softens and resolves masses.

INDICATIONS

- Blood stagnation and Cold accumulation in the lower *jiao*. The main features are
  lower abdominal pain or palpable masses, which may or may not be painful.
  This is a variation of the classic **5.1 Xue Fu Zhu Yu Wan**, specifically targeted
  at dispelling excess Cold and dispersing stagnant Blood from the lower *jiao*.
- Gynecological disorders with dark clotted bleeding and pain, or palpable masses.
  The main feature is the nature of the pain—fixed, sharp, focal, worse with
  palpation, but alleviated somewhat by Heat.
- Can also be used for Cold and Blood stagnation patterns in men—prostatic or
  testicular swelling and pain.
- With the appropriate identifying features, this formula may assist in the treatment
  of biomedical conditions such as endometriosis, fibroids, ovarian cysts, primary
  and secondary dysmenorrhea, premenstrual backache, mittlesmertz, amenorrhea,
  menorrhagia, uterine bleeding, irregular menstruation, infertility, prostatic
  hypertrophy or early dysplasia, bladder pain, varicocele or other painful testicular
  masses.

Composition
Angelica sinensis (dang gui, chinese angelica) 18.5%, *Typhae angustifolia* (pu huang,
bulrush pollen) 18.5%, *Paeonia veitchii* (chi shao, red peony) 13%, *Trogopterus xanthipes*
(wu ling zhi, flying squirrel feces) 13%, *Corydalis turtschaninovii* (yan hu suo, corydalis)
7%, *Ligusticum wallici* (chuan xiong, cnidium) 7%, *Commiphora myrrha* (mo yao, myrrh)
6.5%, *Cinnamomum cassia* (rou gui, cinnamon bark) 6.5%, *Foeniculum vulgarae* (chao xiao
hui xiang, dry fried fennel seed) 4.5%, *Zingiber officinale* (gan jiang, dry ginger) 3%

Pattern identifying features

- **Blood & Cold stagnation in the lower** *jiao*
- **dysmenorrhea, lower abdominal pain**
- in women, the menses may be irregular, dark or purple & clotty

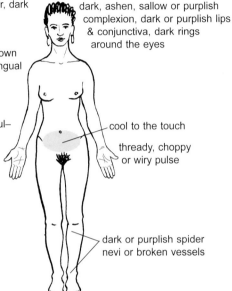

dark, ashen, sallow or purplish complexion, dark or purplish lips & conjunctiva, dark rings around the eyes

purple tongue or with brown or purple patches; sublingual veins dark & distended

lower abdominal pain or palpable masses which may or may not be painful—pain, if present, is relatively sharp or stabbing, fixed in location & worse with pressure, but improves with heat

cool to the touch

thready, choppy or wiry pulse

dark or purplish spider nevi or broken vessels

GYN

Combinations

- With **1.16 Tao Hong Si Wu Wan** for patients with a greater degree of Blood deficiency.

Dosage and method of administration

8-12 pills three times daily on an empty stomach. The dose may be spread out, or two lots of 12-18 pills may be taken, morning and evening. In severe cases or during the early stages of treatment, a 50% increase in dose may be used, then reduced as the treatment takes effect. May be taken through a menstrual period to promote movement of Blood.

Cautions and contraindications

Contraindicated during pregnancy, in women with menorrhagia (other than that associated with Blood stagnation), and with bleeding disorders. Caution in patients on anticoagulant therapy. Watch for bruising or increased tendency to bleeding.

Prolonged use may deplete *qi* and Blood, so a break every 2-3 months, with a change to a simple *qi* and Blood supplement for a few weeks, is recommended.

GMP **1.19 YANG RONG WAN**

养荣丸

Lanzhou Foci Pharmaceutical Factory (Gansu)
'Luxuriantly Nourishing Pills'
Yang Rong Wan is packaged in bottles of 200 pills.

TCM actions

Warms and supplements *qi* and Blood, warms the
Uterus and Kidney *yang*, regulates menstruation and the
chong and *ren* channels.

Biomedical actions

Energy supplement and stimulant, promotes metabolism, hematinic, regulates
menstruation, emmenagogue.

INDICATIONS

* *Qi* and Blood deficiency, Cold accumulation in the Uterus and Spleen and Kidney
  yang deficiency type menstrual disorders and infertility. This is quite a powerful
  formula for regulating and strengthening the function of the *chong* and *ren*
  channels, thus promoting healthy menses and fertility. Typical features include
  irregular periods (usually long cycles), scanty periods, dull dysmenorrhea improved
  with warmth, watery leukorrhea, premenstrual backache and infertility.
* Persistent uterine bleeding, menorrhagia or spotting from Cold in the Uterus
  with underlying Spleen and Kidney deficiency.
* For the post ovulation (progesterone) phase of a cyclical treatment (days 15-28,
  see glossary) to warm and maintain Kidney *yang*.

Composition

Angelica sinensis (dang gui, chinese angelica) 11%, *Rehmannia glutinosa* (shu di,
processed rehmannia) 11%, *Atractylodes macrocephala* (bai zhu, atractylodes) 11%,
Paeonia lactiflora (bai shao, white peony) 8%, *Ligusticum wallichi* (chuan xiong, cnidium)
8%, *Cyperus rotundus* (xiang fu, cyperus) 8%, *Leonurus heterophylla* (yi mu cao,
motherwort) 8%, *Eucommia ulmoides* (du zhong, eucommia) 5%, *Astragalus
membranaceus* (huang qi, astragalus) 5%, *Artemesia argyi* (ai ye, mugwort) 5%, *Poria
cocos* (fu ling, hoelen) 3%, *Equus asinus* (e jiao, donkey skin gelatin) 3%, *Ophiopogon
japonicus* (mai dong, ophiopogon) 3%, *Citrus reticulata* (chen pi, citrus) 3%, *Glycyrrhiza
uralensis* (gan cao, licorice) 3%, *Amomum villosum* (sha ren, cardamon) 2%

Pattern identifying features

- **Qi & Blood deficiency, Cold in the Uterus, Spleen & Kidney *yang* deficiency**
- infertility
- irregular menstruation
- fatigue, weakness, exhaustion
- uterine bleeding, or scanty period with small clots
- cold intolerance

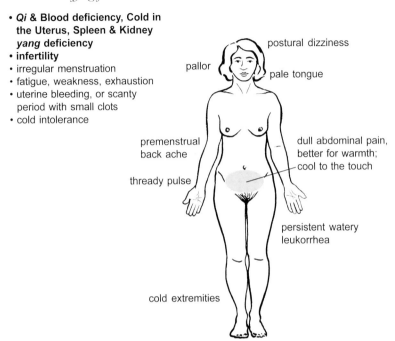

pallor

postural dizziness

pale tongue

premenstrual back ache

thready pulse

dull abdominal pain, better for warmth; cool to the touch

persistent watery leukorrhea

cold extremities

GYN

Combinations

- When used as part of a cyclical treatment, **1.19 Yang Rong Wan** is usually given in the second half of the cycle, days 15-28. In the first half of the cycle, either a Liver and Kidney and Blood supplement (such as a mixture of **7.1 Liu Wei Di Huang Wan** and **1.2 Si Wu Wan**) or *qi* and Blood supplement (such as **1.9 Gui Pi Wan** or **7.16 Shi Quan Da Bu Wan**) is given to strengthen the Kidneys or supplement *qi* and Blood, depending on the patient.

Dosage and method of administration

8-12 pills three times daily on an empty stomach. The dose may be spread out, or two lots of 12-18 pills may be taken, morning and evening. In severe cases or during the early stages of treatment (the first few weeks), a 50% increase in dose may be used, then reduced as the treatment takes effect.

Cautions and contraindications

Contraindicated during the early phase of acute illness such as colds and flu. Care in patients with a tendency to Dampness or Phlegm, abdominal bloating or loose stools, although the cardamon and citrus in this formula generally mean it is well tolerated.

1.20 CU YUN YU TAI CAPSULE

促孕育胎丸 [妇女宝]

(Cu Yun Yu Tai Wan, also listed in Chinese as Fu Nu Bao)

'Promote Pregnancy Pills'

Cu Yun Yu Tai Capsules are packaged in bottles of 36 capsules.

TCM actions
Supplements the Liver and Kidneys, warms the Uterus and Kidney *yang*, regulates the *chong* and *ren* channels, strengthens the Spleen, regulates *qi* and quickens Blood, promotes transformation of *yin* into *yang*.

Biomedical action
Strengthens the progesterone phase of the menstrual cycle, thermogenic, stimulant, promotes ovulation.

INDICATIONS

- Infertility associated with Kidney *yang qi* deficiency, *chong* and *ren* channel dysfunction, and Cold accumulation in the Uterus. This is usually reflected in the basal body temperature chart–the post ovulation progesterone (*yang*) phase fails to rise sufficiently or to maintain an adequate rise long enough. Supports the *yang* phase of the menstrual cycle and promotes transformation of *yin* into *yang* at midcycle to encourage ovulation.
- Used to strengthen *yang* in those women prone to recurrent miscarriage due to *yang* deficiency. Also for low libido and impotence from weak Kidney *yang*.
- With the appropriate identifying features, this formula may be used for primary and secondary infertility, irregular menstruation, long menstrual cycle, low or short progesterone phase of the menstrual cycle, copious thin watery leukorrhea, weakness in the lower back, knees and legs, loss of libido, dizziness and general debility.

Composition (each capsule contains extract equivalent to dry)
Astragalus membranaceous (huang qi, astragalus) 248mg, *Paeonia lactiflora* (bai shao, white peony) 248mg, *Cuscuta hygrophila* (tu su zi, cuscuta) 248mg, *Lycium barbarum* (gou qi zi, lycium fruit) 223mg, *Salvia miltiorrhiza* (dan shen, salvia) 223mg, *Rehmannia glutinosa* (shu di, processed rehmannia) 173mg, *Dioscorea opposita* (shan yao, dioscorea) 173mg, *Epimedium brevicornu* (xian ling pi, epimedium) 124mg, *Curculigo orchioides* (xian mao, curculigo) 124mg, *Dipsacus asper* (xu duan, dipsacus) 124mg, *Panax ginseng* (ren shen, ginseng) 22.5mg

Pattern identifying features

- **Kidney *yang* deficiency, *chong* & *ren* deficiency; Cold in the Uterus**
- **infertility**
- weak *yang* (progesterone) phase of menstrual cycle
- anovulation
- abdominal pain, better for warmth
- poor appetite
- loss of libido

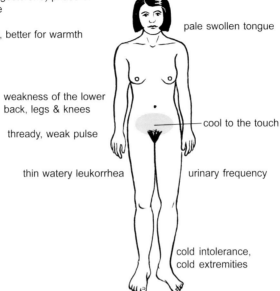

pale swollen tongue

weakness of the lower back, legs & knees

thready, weak pulse

cool to the touch

thin watery leukorrhea

urinary frequency

cold intolerance, cold extremities

GYN

Combinations

- When used as part of a cyclical treatment (*see* glossary), it is usually given in the second half of the cycle, days 15-28. In the first half of the cycle, either a Liver and Kidney and Blood tonic (such as a mixture of **7.1 Liu Wei Di Huang Wan** and **1.2 Si Wu Wan**) or *qi* and Blood supplement (such as **1.9 Gui Pi Wan** or **7.16 Shi Quan Da Bu Wan**) are given to strengthen the Kidneys or supplement *qi* and Blood, depending on the patient.
- With **1.2 Si Wu Wan** for patients with a greater degree of Blood deficiency.

Dosage and method of administration

3-4 capsules, three times daily on an empty stomach.

Cautions and contraindications

Contraindicated during the early phase of acute illness such as colds and flu, and infertility associated with *yin* deficiency or Heat patterns. Caution during pregnancy. Caution for patients on anticoagulant therapy. Watch for bruising or increased tendency to bleeding.

1.21 TIAO JING CU YUN WAN

调经促孕丸

Tong Ren Tang (Beijing)
'Regulate Menses, Promote Pregnancy Pills'
Tiao Jing Cu Yun Wan Pills are packaged in vials
of 50 pills, ten vials per box.

TCM actions
Warms and supplements Kidney and Spleen *yang*, quickens Blood, warms the
Uterus, promotes transformation of *yin* into *yang*.

Biomedical action
Regulates the hypothalamic-ovarian axis, regulates menstruation, strengthens the
progesterone phase of the menstrual cycle, promotes ovulation.

INDICATIONS

• Kidney and Spleen *yang* deficiency, with mild Blood stagnation. A warming and
yang stimulating formula for infertility, long menstrual cycles, scanty periods or
amenorrhea associated with Kidney and Spleen *yang* deficiency. This is quite a
warming formula, specifically designed to promote ovulation and to maintain
the *yang* phase of the menstrual cycle once ovulation has occurred. The astragalus
and salvia assist in promoting ovulation by powerfully mobilising and elevating
yang qi and moving the Blood.
• With the appropriate identifying features, this formula can be used to treat
biomedical conditions such as primary or secondary infertility, amenorrhea,
irregular menstruation, anovulation and corpus luteum failure.

Composition
Cervus japonicus (lu rong, deer velvet), *Epimedium brevicornu* (xian ling pi, epimedium),
Cuscuta hygrophila (tu su zi, cuscuta), *Lycium barbarum* (gou qi zi, lycium fruit),
Dioscorea opposita (shan yao, dioscorea), *Poria cocos* (fu ling, hoelen), *Salvia miltiorrhiza*
(dan shen, salvia), *Astragalus membranaceous* (huang qi, astragalus)

Combinations
• When used as part of a cyclical treatment (*see* glossary), it is given in the second
half of the cycle, days 15-28. In the first half of the cycle, either a Liver and
Kidney and Blood supplement (such as a mixture of **7.1 Liu Wei Di Huang
Wan** and **1.2 Si Wu Wan**) or *qi* and Blood supplement (such as **1.9 Gui Pi Wan**

Pattern identifying features

- **Spleen & Kidney *yang* deficiency**
- **infertility**
- weak *yang* (progesterone) phase of menstrual cycle
- anovulation
- long menstrual cycle, amenorrhea
- cold intolerance
- fatigue, weakness, lassitude
- poor appetite
- loss of libido

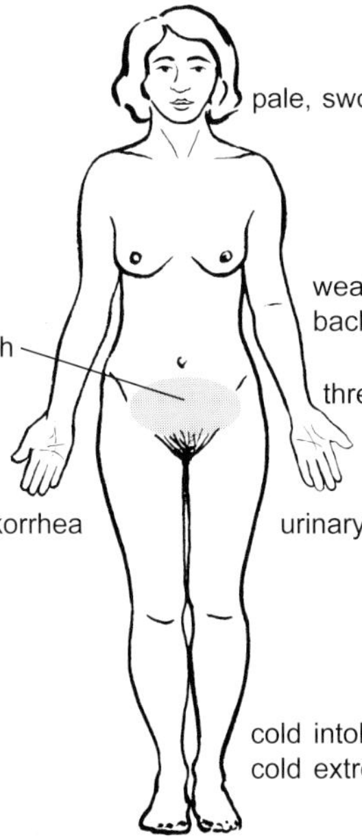

pale, swollen tongue

weakness of the lower back, legs & knees

cool to the touch

thready, weak pulse

thin watery leukorrhea

urinary frequency

cold intolerance, cold extremities

GYN

or **7.16 Shi Quan Da Bu Wan**) is given to strengthen the Kidneys or supplement *qi* and Blood, depending on the patient.

Dosage and method of administration

Fifty pills (one vial) twice daily, on an empty stomach. The dose may be spread out, taking a few pills at frequent intervals throughout the day. When used as part of a cyclical treatment, the appropriate dose is taken from midcycle onwards until menstruation occurs. In the case of amenorrhea, the pills may be taken continually for three months before review.

Cautions and contraindications

Contraindicated during the early phase of acute illness such as colds and flu, and in patients with *yin* deficiency patterns with Heat. This formula is quite warming and may cause some patients to overheat, especially if they are using other warming medications or substances (such as B vitamins).

Caution during pregnancy. Caution for patients on anticoagulant therapy. Watch for bruising or increased tendency to bleeding.

1.22 REHMANNIA GLUTINOSA COMPOUND PILLS

妇科种子丸

Lanzhou Foci Pharmaceutical Factory (Gansu)
'Women's Cultivation (of Fertility) Pills'
Rehmannia Glutinosa Compound Pills are packaged in bottles of 200 pills.
Also available as: Fu Ke Zhong Zi Wan

TCM actions

Nourishes and quickens Blood, supplements and warms Kidney *yang*, warms the Uterus, strengthens the *chong* and *ren* channels.

Biomedical action

Energy supplement and stimulant, promotes metabolism, hematinic, regulates menstruation.

INDICATIONS

- Kidney *qi* or *yang* deficiency, Blood deficiency and Cold accumulation in the Uterus type infertility, dysmenorrhea, amenorrhea, premenstrual backache and other menstrual disorders. Similar in scope and action to **1.19 Yang Rong Wan**.
- Chronic uterine bleeding, spotting or menorrhagia from Cold and *yang* deficiency.
- Can promote transformation of *yin* into *yang* at midcycle and thus encourage ovulation. Warms *yang* and supports the *yang* phase of the menstrual cycle (as measured by the basal body temperature [BBT] chart, *see* glossary).
- Recurrent miscarriage from Kidney *yang* and Blood deficiency (used in between pregnancies).

Composition (each pill contains powdered)

Rehmannia glutinosa (shu di, processed rehmannia) 47.1mg, *Eucommia ulmoides* (du zhong, eucommia) 23.5mg, *Cyperus rotundus* (xiang fu, cyperus) 23.5mg, *Angelica sinensis* (dang gui, chinese angelica) 17.6mg, *Ligusticum wallichi* (chuan xiong, cnidium) 17.6, *Dipsacus asper* (xu duan, dipsacus) 17.6mg, *Artemesia argyi* (ai ye, mugwort) 17.6mg, *Scutellaria baicalensis* (huang qin, scute) 11.8mg, *Commiphora myrrha** (mo yao, myrrh) 11.8mg, *Paeonia lactiflora* (bai shao, white peony) 11.8mg
*Note: The same product in China and the USA uses donkey skin gelatin (e jiao) in place of the myrrh (mo yao).

Pattern identifying features

- **Kidney *yang* deficiency, Blood deficiency, Cold in the Uterus**
- **infertility**
- cold intolerance

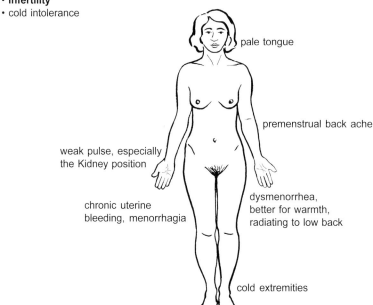

pale tongue

premenstrual back ache

weak pulse, especially
the Kidney position

chronic uterine
bleeding, menorrhagia

dysmenorrhea,
better for warmth,
radiating to low back

cold extremities

GYN

Combinations
- May be used as part of a cyclical treatment (*see* glossary), specifically to support Kidney *yang* in the post-ovulation phase (days 15-28) or to encourage ovulation at midcycle.
- With **7.12 Lu Rong Jiao** or **7.11 Deer Velvet** to increase *yang* transformation.

Dosage and method of administration
8-12 pills three times daily on an empty stomach. The dose may be spread out, or two lots of 12-18 pills may be taken, morning and evening. In severe cases a 50% increase in dose may be used. Usually used in the two weeks prior to menstruation.

Cautions and contraindications
Contraindicated during the early phase of acute illness such as colds and flu. Caution during pregnancy. Care should be taken in patients with a tendency to abdominal bloating, loose stools or general digestive weakness. Some patients may find **1.22 Rehmannia Glutinosa Compound Pills** aggravates these symptoms. This can be alleviated by reducing the dose or by adding a few pills of **2.9 Xiang Sha Liu Jun Wan** or **2.18 Bao He Wan**.

1.23.1 ZHI BAI BA WEI WAN

知柏八味丸

Lanzhou Foci Pharmaceutical Factory (Gansu)
'Eight Flavored Rehmannia Pills with Anemarrhena and
Phellodendron'
Zhi Bai Ba Wei Wan is packaged in bottles of 200 pills
Also available as: Eight Flavor Rehmannia Teapills (PF), Chih Pai
Pa Wei Wan

TCM actions
Supplements Kidney *yin*, moistens dryness and clears
deficient Heat and Fire.

Biomedical actions
Demulcent febrifuge, hematinic, hypoglycemic, antihypertensive, improves kidney
function, regulates adrenal cortex, soothes the urinary tract, reduces excessive
perspiration, depurative, refrigerant.

INDICATIONS

- Kidney *yin* deficiency with deficient Heat or Fire. Especially good for chronic
  gynecological conditions such as menopausal syndrome with heat and/or dryness,
  chronic or recurrent cystitis, interstitial cystitis, vaginal dryness or irritation,
  chronic vaginitis and chronic pelvic inflammatory disease.
- Used for chronic consumptive disorders with low grade fevers and emaciation.
  May be useful as a palliative treatment for the side effects of long term
  corticosteroid use (which damages *yin*).
- Chronic or recurrent sore throat that is worse in the afternoon and evening, or
  when fatigued (in a patient with heat signs).
- With the appropriate identifying features, this formula can be used to treat
  disorders such as those noted above, also chronic tonsillitis, post streptococcal
  glomerulonephritis, chronic nephritis, fever of unknown origin, sperm viscosity
  disorders, diabetes, hyperthyroidism and sore dry or irritated eyes.

Composition (each pill contains powdered)
Rehmannia glutinosa (shu di, processed rehmannia) 35mg, *Cornus officinalis* (shan zhu
yu, cornus) 18mg, *Dioscorea opposita* (shan yao, dioscorea) 18mg, *Poria cocos* (fu ling,
hoelen) 13mg, *Alisma orientalis* (ze xie, alisma) 13mg, *Paeonia suffruticosa* (mu dan pi,
moutan) 13mg, *Anemarrhena aspheloides* (zhi mu, anemarrhena) 9mg, *Phellodendron
amurense* (huang bai, phellodendron) 9mg

Pattern identifying features

- Kidney *yin* deficiency with deficient Heat
- facial or malar flushing
- hot flushes
- night sweats
- heat intolerance, low grade fevers, bone steaming fever, afternoon & tidal fever
- hot hands & feet
- thirst, dry mouth
- irregular or absent periods
- patients are mostly women over 40

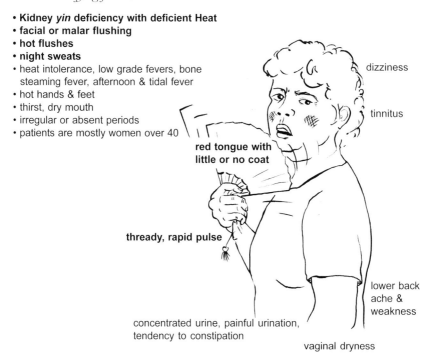

dizziness

tinnitus

red tongue with little or no coat

thready, rapid pulse

lower back ache & weakness

concentrated urine, painful urination, tendency to constipation

vaginal dryness

GYN

Combinations

- With **1.34 Nei Xiao Luo Li Wan** or **11.2 Prostate Gland Pills** for men with a *yin* deficient constitution, prostate swelling and/or elevated prostate specific antigen (PSA).
- With **7.4 Da Bu Yin Wan** or **3.41 Xu Han Ting** for severe sweating.

Dosage and method of administration

8-12 pills three times daily, on an empty stomach. The dose may be spread out, or two lots of 12-18 pills may be taken, morning and evening. In severe cases or during the early stages of treatment (the first few weeks), a 50% increase in dose may be used, then reduced as the treatment takes effect.

Cautions and contraindications

Contraindicated during the early phase of acute illness such as colds and flu. Care should be taken in patients with a tendency to abdominal distension, loose stools or mucus accumulation. This is a cooling formula and overuse can weaken the Spleen.

1.23.2 ZHI BAI DI HUANG WAN

知柏地黄丸

Tong Ren Tang (Beijing)
'Eight Flavored Rehmannia Pills with Anemarrhena and Phellodendron'
Zhi Bai Di Huang Wan is packaged in bottles of 360 little pills.

TCM actions

Supplements Kidney *yin*, moistens dryness and clears deficient Heat and Fire.

Biomedical actions

Demulcent febrifuge, hematinic, hypoglycemic, antihypertensive, improves kidney function, regulates adrenal cortex, soothes the urinary tract, reduces excessive perspiration, depurative, refrigerant.

INDICATIONS

• As for **1.23.1 Zhi Bai Ba Wei Wan**.

Composition (each dose [30 pills] contains powdered)

Rehmannia glutinosa (shu di, processed rehmannia) 1.2g, *Cornus officinalis* (shan zhu yu, cornus) 600mg, *Dioscorea opposita* (shan yao, dioscorea) 600mg, *Poria cocos* (fu ling, hoelen) 400mg, *Alisma orientalis* (ze xie, alisma) 400mg, *Paeonia suffruticosa* (mu dan pi, moutan) 400mg, *Anemarrhena aspheloides* (zhi mu, anemarrhena) 300mg, *Phellodendron amurense* (huang bai, phellodendron) 300mg

Dosage and method of administration

30 pills twice daily. In severe cases or in the early stages of treatment (the first few weeks), a 50% increase in dose may be used, then reduced as the treatment takes effect.

Cautions and contraindications

As for **1.23.1 Zhi Bai Ba Wei Wan**.

1.23.3 ZHI BAI BA WEI PILLS

知柏八味丸

(Zhi Bai Ba Wei Wan)
Jing Xian Pharmaceutical Co. (Guangzhou)
'Eight Flavored Rehmannia Pills with Anemarrhena and Phellodendron'
Zhi Bai Ba Wei Pills are packaged in bottles of 200 pills.

TCM actions
Supplements Kidney *yin*, moistens dryness and clears deficient Heat and Fire.

Biomedical actions
Demulcent febrifuge, hematinic, hypoglycemic, antihypertensive, improves kidney function, regulates adrenal cortex, soothes the urinary tract, reduces excessive perspiration, depurative, refrigerant.

INDICATIONS

• As for **1.23.1 Zhi Bai Ba Wei Wan**.

GYN

Composition (each pill contains extracts equivalent to dry)
Rehmannia glutinosa (shu di, processed rehmannia) 377mg, *Cornus officinalis* (shan zhu yu, cornus) 188mg, *Dioscorea opposita* (shan yao, dioscorea) 188mg, *Poria cocos* (fu ling, hoelen) 141mg, *Alisma orientalis* (ze xie, alisma) 141mg, *Paeonia suffruticosa* (mu dan pi, moutan) 141mg, *Anemarrhena aspheloides* (zhi mu, anemarrhena) 94mg, *Phellodendron amurense* (huang bai, phellodendron) 94mg

Dosage and method of administration
8 pills, three times daily on an empty stomach. In severe cases or in the early stages of treatment (the first few weeks), a 50% increase in dose may be used, then reduced as the treatment takes effect.

Cautions and contraindications
As for **1.23.1 Zhi Bai Ba Wei Wan**.

GMP **1.24 ER XIAN WAN**

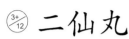

二仙丸

Lanzhou Foci Pharmaceutical Factory (Gansu)
'Two Immortals Pills'
Er Xian Wan is packaged in bottles of 200 pills.
Available as: Two Immortals Teapills (PF)

Available in the US,
UK and Europe
See Note 1, p.xxi

TCM actions

Warms Kidney *yang*, benefits and supplements *yin* and *jing*,
nourishes Blood, clears deficient Heat, regulates the *chong* and
ren channels.

Biomedical actions

Febrifuge, reduces excessive perspiration, regulates and balances the hormones
associated with menopause, antihypertensive.

INDICATIONS

• Kidney *yin* and *yang* deficiency with deficient Heat. The weakness of the Kidneys
fails to support the normal functioning of the *chong* and *ren* channels leading to
reduction or cessation of menstruation. This is an important modern formula
for the treatment of the symptoms of menopause, in particular those associated
with Heat, such as hot flushing, sweats and irritability. However, because *yang* is
also deficient, thermoregulation in general tends to be poor, so patients are often
cold intolerant, and may feel cold, especially in the early hours of the morning.
They tend to easily overheat but can feel quite cold in between flushing episodes.
While primarily designed for women, this formula can be used in men presenting
with Kidney *yin* and *yang* deficiency patterns as well.

• With the appropriate identifying features, this formula can assist in the treatment
of the symptoms of menopausal syndrome, hypertension associated with
menopause, hyperthyroidism and chronic nephritis.

Composition

Curculigo orchioides (xian mao, curculigo) 23%, *Epimedium brevicornu* (xian ling pi,
epimedium) 23%, *Morinda officinalis* (ba ji tian, morinda) 13%, *Anemarrhena aspheloides*
(zhi mu, anemarrhena) 13%, *Phellodendron amurense* (huang bai, phellodendron) 13%,
Angelica sinensis (dang gui, chinese angelica) 12%

Pattern identifying features

- **Kidney *yin* & *yang* deficiency, deficient Heat**
- **amenorrhea, irregular menstrual period**
- **night sweats**, easy sweating
- **hypertension**
- insomnia
- irritability, depression, anxiety
- poor thermoregulation
- fatigue

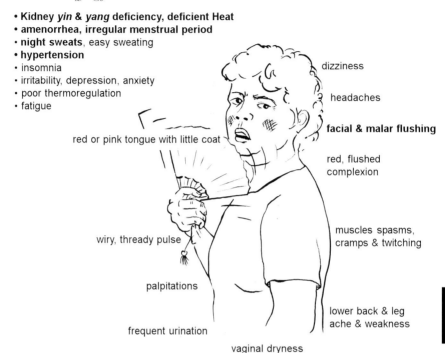

dizziness

headaches

facial & malar flushing

red or pink tongue with little coat

red, flushed complexion

wiry, thready pulse

muscles spasms, cramps & twitching

palpitations

lower back & leg ache & weakness

frequent urination

vaginal dryness

GYN

Combinations
- With **7.1 Liu Wei Di Huang Wan** for relatively severe Kidney *yin* deficiency.
- With **6.5 Jia Wei Xiao Yao Wan** with elements of Liver *qi* stagnation and stagnant Heat.
- With **1.2 Si Wu Wan** for patients with a greater degree of Blood deficiency.

Dosage and method of administration
8-12 pills three times daily, on an empty stomach. The dose may be spread out, or two lots of 12-18 pills may be taken, morning and evening. In severe cases or during the early stages of treatment (the first few weeks), a 50% increase in dose may be used, then reduced as the treatment takes effect.

Cautions and contraindications
Contraindicated during the early phase of acute illness such as colds and flu. Care should be taken in patients with a tendency to abdominal distension, loose stools or mucus accumulation. This is a cooling formula and overuse can weaken the Spleen.

1.25 KUN BAO WAN

坤宝丸

Tong Ren Tang (Beijing)
'Woman's Treasure Pills'
Kun Bao Wan are packaged in bottles of 500 tiny pills, or
in vials of 50 tiny pills, ten vials per box.

WOMEN'S
TREASURE
PILLS
(KUNBAO WAN)
Chinese Herbal Patent Medicines
Manufactured by China Beijing
Tong Ren Tang Holdings Corporation
500 pills
AUST L 78816

TCM actions

Supplements Liver and Kidney *yin*, restrains *yang*,
calms the *shen*, nourishes and cools the Blood, clears deficient Heat, opens the
channels.

Biomedical actions

Regulates the hormones associated with the menstrual cycle, demulcent febrifuge,
sedative.

INDICATIONS

• Liver, Heart and/or Kidney *yin* deficiency with deficient Heat and hyperactive
yang type menopausal syndrome. Considered to be particularly good for
menopausal hypertension, dry scratchy eye disorders, vaginal dryness, headaches
and dizziness or light-headedness associated with *yin* deficiency and *yang* rising.
Also for the emotional aspects and for the generalised aches and pains that
accompany menopause or *yin* deficiency patterns.

Composition (50 pills contains)

Spatholobus suberectus (ji xue teng, spatholobus) 315mg, *Paeonia veitchii* (chi shao, red
peony) 315mg, *Paeonia lactiflora* (bai shao, white peony) 260mg, *Angelica acutiloba*
(dang gui, chinese angelica) 250mg, *Eclipta prostrata* (han lian cao, eclipta) 210mg,
Dendrobium nobile (shi hu, dendrobium) 160mg, *Ligustrum lucidum* (nu zhen zi, privet
fruit) 160mg, *Lycium chinense* (di gu pi, lycium root bark) 160mg, *Rehmannia glutinosa*
(sheng di, rehmannia) 160mg, *Chrysanthemum indicum* (ye ju hua, wild
chrysanthemum) 160mg, *Scutellaria baicalensis* (huang qin, scute) 160mg, *Cynanchum
atratum* (bai wei, swallowwort root) 160mg, *Adenophora tetraphylla* (sha shen,
adenophora) 160mg, *Anemarrhena aspheloides* (zhi mu, anemarrhena) 160mg, *Cuscuta
europea* (tu su zi, cuscuta) 105mg, *Rubus chingii* (fu pen zi, rubus) 105mg, *Polygonum
multiflorum* (he shou wu, polygonum) 105mg, *Lycium barbarum* (gou qi zi, lycium fruit)
105mg, *Ophiopogon japonicus* (mai dong, ophiopogon) 105mg, *Morus alba* (sang ye,
mulberry leaf) 105mg, *Zizyphus jujuba* (da zao, chinese date) 50mg

Pattern identifying features

- **Liver & Kidney *yin* deficiency with *yang* rising & deficient Heat**
- **mood swings, forgetfulness, irrational tears**
- **night sweats, heat at night**
- dry skin, mouth, throat
- insomnia

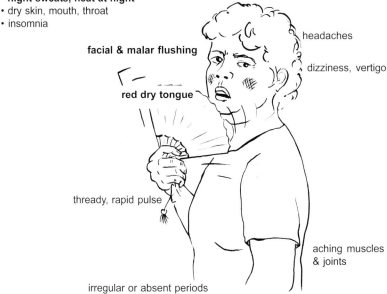

headaches

dizziness, vertigo

facial & malar flushing

red dry tongue

thready, rapid pulse

aching muscles & joints

irregular or absent periods

GYN

Combinations
- With **8.3 An Shen Ding Zhi Wan** or **8.5 Shuian Capsule** for emotional turmoil and mood swings.
- With **7.1 Liu Wei Di Huang Wan** to enhance the Kidney *yin* enriching quality of the treatment.
- With **15.4 Tian Ma Gou Teng Wan** for severe headaches and dizziness associated with menopause.

Dosage and method of administration
25-50 pills twice daily, on an empty stomach. The dose may also be spread out, taking a few pills at frequent intervals throughout the day.

Cautions and contraindications
Contraindicated during the early phase of acute illness such as colds and flu.

1.26 JING AN ORAL LIQUID

静安口服液

(Jing An Kou Fu Ye)
'Peace and Quiet Drink'
Jing Xian Pharmaceutical Co. (Guangzhou)
Jing An Oral Liquid is packaged in vials of 10ml
liquid, 12 vials per box.

TCM actions
Supplements the Liver and Kidney, nourishes and quickens Blood.

Biomedical actions
Nutritive, tonic.

INDICATIONS

- Liver and Kidney *yin* and Blood deficiency type hormonal disorders, including menopausal syndrome, amenorrhea, irregular menstruation, leukorrhea, uterine bleeding, menorrhagia and numbness in the extremities. This formula is mild and gentle, suitable for all *yin* and Blood deficiency patterns. Also suitable for patients with a mild degree of deficient Heat, with symptoms such as flushing, low grade fever, sweating, anxiety, palpitations, dizziness and insomnia or restless sleep with vivid dreams.
- *Yin* and Blood deficiency type visual weakness, dry eyes, excessive lacrimation in Wind or red, sore, irritated eyes.
- Dry, flaky or scaly skin; dry, lustreless hair.

Composition (each vial contains extracts equivalent to dry)
Lycium barbarum (gou qi zi, lycium fruit) 8.4g, *Sesamum indicum* (hei zhi ma, sesame seed) 5.6g, *Morus alba* (sang zi, mulberry fruit) 5.6g, *Carthamus tinctorius* (hong hua, carthamus) 5.6g, *Zizyphus jujuba* (da zao, chinese dates) 4.2g, *Chrysanthemun sinense* (ju hua, chrysanthemum flower) 4.2g, *Citrus reticulata* (chen pi, citrus) 1.4g

Dosage and method of administration
1 vial, two or three times daily.

Cautions and contraindications
Contraindicated during the early phase of acute illness such as colds and flu.

1.27 LADY ORAL LIQUID

女士口服液

(Nu Shi Kou Fu Ye)
'Woman's Drink'
Jing Xian Pharmaceutical Co. (Guangzhou)
Lady Oral Liquid is packaged in vials of 10ml
liquid, 12 vials per box.

TCM actions
Supplements *qi* and Blood, nourishes *yin* and supports *yang*, regulates menstruation,
settles the Heart and calms the *shen*.

Biomedical actions
Nutritive, tonic, regulates menstruation.

INDICATIONS

- *Qi* and Blood deficiency menstrual and *shen* disorders. Typical features include
  fatigue and tiredness, pallor, pale, ridged or brittle nails, insomnia and palpitations,
  vivid dreaming or dream disturbed sleep, irregular menses (especially long cycles,
  scanty periods or missed periods), mild dysmenorrhea, leukorrhea, lower back
  ache, premenstrual back ache and numbness in the extremities.
- Dry, flaky or scaly skin; dry, lustreless hair.

Composition (each vial contains extracts equivalent to dry)
Zizyphus jujuba (da zao, chinese dates) 4g, *Astragalus membranaceous* (huang qi,
astragalus) 3.7g, *Lycium barbarum* (gou qi zi, lycium fruit) 3.7g, *Morus alba* (sang zi,
mulberry fruit) 3g, *Juglans regia* (hu tao ren, walnut) 3g, *Zizyphus spinoza* (suan zao ren,
zizyphus) 2.7g, *Polygonum multiflorum* (he shou wu, ho shou wu) 2.7g, *Coix lachryma-
jobi* (yi ren, coix) 2.7g, *Nelumbus speciosum* (lian zi, lotus seed) 2.2g, *Glycyrrhiza uralensis*
(gan cao, licorice) 540mg, *Ostrea gigas* (mu li, oyster shell) 18mg

Dosage and method of administration
1 vial, two or three times daily.

Cautions and contraindications
Contraindicated during the early phase of acute illness such as colds and flu.

GYN

1.28 GENG NIAN LING

更年灵

Guanghua Pharmaceutical Co. (Guangzhou)
'Miraculous [Pills for] Menopause'
Geng Nian Ling is packaged in bottles of 36 capsules.

TCM actions

Warms Kidney *yang*, nourishes Kidney and Liver *yin*, clears deficiency Heat.

Biomedical actions

Regulates the hormones associated with the menstrual cycle, demulcent febrifuge, sedative, nervine.

INDICATIONS

• Symptoms of menopause. This modern formulation is specifically tailored to be similar in action to **1.24 Er Xian Wan**, combining herbs of opposing natures to facilitate *yin* and *yang* supplementation and clearance of deficiency Heat symptoms. The main features are symptoms such as irregular menstruation, spotting, uterine bleeding, facial flushing, sweats, vaginal dryness, palpitations, insomnia or frequent waking, forgetfulness and irritability.

Composition (each capsule contains)

Ligustrum lucidum (nu zhen zi, privet fruit) 800mg, *Epimedium brevicornu* (xian ling pi, epimedium) 550mg, Thiamine hydrochloride (Vitamin B1) 10mg, Pyridoxine hydrochloride (Vitamin B6) 10mg

Dosage and method of administration

1-2 capsules, two to three times daily on an empty stomach, to a maximum of 5 capsules daily

Cautions and contraindications

None noted.

1.29 BU GAI ZHUANG GU CAPSULE

补钙壮骨丸

(Bu Gai Zhuang Gu Wan)
Jing Xian Pharmaceutical Co. (Guangzhou)
'Pills to Supplement Calcium and Strengthen Bones'
Bu Gai Zhuang Gu Capsule is packaged in bottles of 36 capsules.

KING TIM®

**BU GAI
ZHUANG GU
CAPSULE**

AUST L 82420
36 CAPSULES

MADE IN CHINA

TCM actions
Warms and supplements Kidney *yang*, nourishes Kidney and Liver *yin*, strengthens tendons and bones, supplements *qi* and Blood.

Biomedical actions
Stimulant and tonic, supports thermogenesis and osteogenesis.

INDICATIONS

- Osteoporosis associated with Kidney *yang* deficiency. Used to support and promote osteogenesis in those with, or at risk of, osteoporosis. In combination with weight bearing exercise, assists the Kidneys in maintenance of strong bones. Assists healing of bones following trauma or surgery. Used after Blood moving herbs (such as **10.3 Die Da Zhi Tong Capsule**) have been applied for about two weeks to clear any Blood stagnation.
- Also used for Kidney *yang* deficiency type infertility or impotence, urinary disorders, Wind Cold Damp *bi* syndrome, chronic lower back ache and hypertension.

Composition (each capsule contains extracts equivalent to dry)
Epimedium brevicornu (xian ling pi, epimedium) 450mg, *Dioscorea opposita* (shan yao, dioscorea) 350mg, *Angelica polymorpha* (dang gui, chinese angelica) 320mg, *Rehmannia glutinosa* (shu di, processed rehmannia) 270mg, *Eucommia ulmoides* (du zhong, eucommia) 250mg, *Lycium barbarum* (gou qi zi, lycium fruit) 200mg, *Morinda officinalis* (ba ji tian, morinda) 180mg, *Curculigo orchioides* (xian mao, curculigo) 150mg, *Cornus officinalis* (shan zhu yu, cornus) 135mg, *Ostrea gigas* (mu li, oyster shell powder) 25mg

Dosage and method of administration
2 capsules, three times daily on an empty stomach.

Cautions and contraindications
This formula is quite warming and may overheat some patients. Contraindicated unmodified in patients with *yin* deficiency and internal Heat patterns.

GYN

1.30 TANGKWEI ESSENCE OF CHICKEN

当归鸡精

(Dang Gui Ji Jing)
Cerebos Thailand Ltd (Thailand)
Tangkwei Essence of Chicken is packaged in
68ml jars of liquid extract, six jars to a box.

TCM actions
Supplements *qi* and Blood, promotes
transformation of Blood into mothers milk.

Biomedical action
Supplement to powerfully nourish blood and build energy, tones the uterus and
muscles, galactagogue.

INDICATIONS

• Blood and *qi* deficiency. The formula of choice for postpartum Blood deficiency,
  especially with insufficient lactation. Based on **1.1 Ba Zhen Wan**, the black
  boned chicken makes this formula a rich and fast acting supplement, ideal for all
  mothers. In addition to its main use to strengthen postpartum women, it can be
  used to treat a wide range of *qi* and Blood deficiency problems such as fatigue
  and exhaustion, dizziness, anemia, weight loss and lustreless or falling hair.
• Excellent as support in patients with significant convalescent or nutritional needs,
  for example patients with cancer or other severe illness.

Composition (each jar contains extracts equivalent to dry)
Black bone chicken, *Angelica sinensis* (dang gui, chinese angelica) 13.3g, *Codonopsis
pilosula* (dang shen, codonopsis) 2g, *Ligusticum wallichi* (chuan xiong, cnidium) 1.1g,
Paeonia alba (bai shao, white peony) 880mg, *Atractylodes macrocephala* (bai zhu,
atractylodes) 880mg, *Poria cocos* (fu ling, hoelen) 880mg, *Rehmannia glutinosa* (shu di,
processed rehmannia) 880mg, *Glycyrrhiza uralensis* (gan cao, licorice) 475mg

Dosage and method of administration
In the early days following childbirth, one jar may be taken daily either neat or
diluted with warm water. As energy or milk improves, one jar every second or third

Pattern identifying features

- *Qi* & **Blood deficiency**
- **postpartum fatigue, exhaustion**
- weight loss
- poor appetite
- anemia

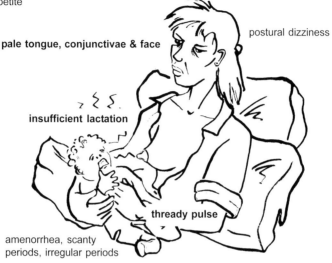

pale tongue, conjunctivae & face

postural dizziness

insufficient lactation

thready pulse

amenorrhea, scanty
periods, irregular periods

day is sufficient. For prolonged breast feeding, or in women with other extensive demands on their energy, one or two jars weekly are useful for maintenance. **1.30 Tangkwei Essence of Chicken** can also be used as a base for Blood enriching soups and stews.

Cautions and contraindications

Contraindicated during the early phase of acute illness such as colds and flu. Caution in women with adequate milk production, as the extra milk stimulated can overwhelm the childs' feeding capacity and predispose to mastitis by congesting the milk ducts. Contraindicated during mastitis.

Care should be taken in patients with a tendency to abdominal distension, loose stools or nausea. Some patients may find **1.30 Tangkwei Essence of Chicken** aggravates these symptoms. This can usually be alleviated by diluting it with a strong ginger root tea or taking it after food.

GMP **1.31 SHIH SAN TAI PAO WAN**

十三太保丸

(Shi San Tai Bao Wan)
Tianjin Drug Manufactory (Shandong)
'Pills to Powerfully Protect [during the
first] Thirteen [weeks of pregnancy]'
Shih San Tai Pao Wan is packaged as
large honey pills sealed in wax balls.

TCM actions

Supplements *qi* and Blood, alleviates food stagnation, dries Dampness, regulates *qi* and Blood, strengthens the Kidneys and corrects the *qi* mechanism.

Biomedical action

Hematinic, energy stimulant.

INDICATIONS

- Gastro-intestinal problems during pregnancy associated with disruption to the *qi* mechanism (*see* glossary). Symptoms include nausea and vomiting, abdominal distension and discomfort, sluggish stools or constipation, belching and loss of appetite. The mode of action of this formula is aimed at re-establishing the correct flow of Spleen and Stomach *qi*, which is easily disrupted by physiological stagnation of the developing fetus and the obstruction to the normal descent of *chong mai qi*. The descending action of the magnolia bark and immature citrus is balanced by the ascending nature of the astragalus and notopterygium, the four acting together to stimulate the normal pivotal dynamo of middle *jiao qi* movement.
- Wind Cold *gan mao* during menstruation or pregnancy. Also for acute or recurrent headaches and lower back and leg pain during pregnancy and menstruation, or in a patient with Blood deficiency.
- Threatened miscarriage. May be useful for incompetent cervix as both immature citrus and astragalus can assist in improving tissue tone and elevating *yang*. Even though this formula is indicated for miscarriage, intervention during the first trimester is usually not appropriate as there may be genetic factors at work. Better to strengthen the Kidneys and Spleen of those prone to miscarriage in between pregnancies.

Pattern identifying features

- **Blood deficiency with disruption to the *qi* mechanism**
- abdominal distension & discomfort
- nausea, morning sickness

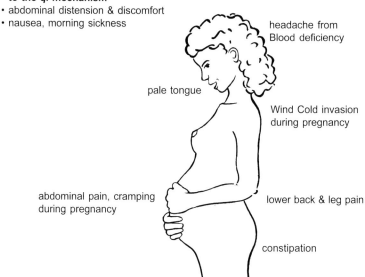

headache from Blood deficiency

pale tongue

Wind Cold invasion during pregnancy

abdominal pain, cramping during pregnancy

lower back & leg pain

constipation

Composition

Angelica sinensis (dang gui, chinese angelica) 18.18%, *Ligusticum wallichi* (chuan xiong, cnidium) 18.18%, *Cuscuta chinensis* (tu su zi, cuscuta) 18.18%, *Paeonia lactiflora* (bai shao, white peony) 13.63%, *Fritillaria cirrhosa* (chuan bei mu, fritillaria) 12.10%, *Astragalus membranaceous* (huang qi, astragalus) 6.10%, *Magnolia officinalis* (hou po, magnolia bark) 5.30%, *Citrus aurantium* (zhi ke, immature citrus) 4.54%, *Notopterygium incisum* (qiang huo, notopterygium) 3.79%

Dosage and method of administration

One pill twice daily on an empty stomach.

Cautions and contraindications

Any medicine used during pregnancy must be used with caution.

1.32 RU JIE XIAO TABLET

乳结消

(Ru Jie Xiao)
Jing Xian Pharmaceutical Co. (Guangzhou)
'Reduce Accumulation in the Breast'
Ru Jie Xiao Tablets are packaged in bottles of 60 sugar coated tablets.

TCM actions
Invigorates and regulates Liver *qi*, quickens Blood, disperses stagnant Blood, transforms Phlegm, dissipates nodules and swellings.

Biomedical actions
Softens and reduces masses and lumps, benefits circulation, assists in regulating menstrual hormones.

INDICATIONS

- Liver *qi*, Phlegm accumulation and/or Blood stasis type breast cysts, lumps and masses. The masses will typically have a cyclical pattern, proliferating towards the end of the menstrual cycle. They are generally well defined and may or may not be tender. In addition, they are generally not inflammatory or suppurative, or associated with fever. This formula is also useful for other benign gynecological masses, such as ovarian cysts, fibroids and endometriosis of the same etiology.
- With the appropriate identifying features, this formula may be used to treat breast cysts, fibrocystic breast disease, hyperplasia of breast tissue, uterine fibroids and ovarian cysts.

Composition (each tablet contains extract equivalent to dry)
Bupleurum falcatum (chai hu, bupleurum) 377mg, *Salvia miltiorrhiza* (dan shen, salvia) 377mg, *Paeonia lactiflora* (bai shao, white peony) 293mg, *Citrus aurantium* (zhi ke, aurantium) 293mg, *Prunella vulgaris* (xia ku cao, prunella) 260mg, *Ranunculus ternatus* (mao zhua cao, ranunculus) 234mg, *Curcuma longa* (yu jin, curcuma) 202mg, *Angelica polymorpha* (dang gui, chinese angelica) 176mg, *Epimedium brevicornu* (xian ling pi, epimedium) 117mg, *Glycyrrhiza uralensis* (gan cao, licorice) 117mg

Pattern identifying features

- **Liver *qi*, Phlegm & Blood stagnation**
- premenstrual symptoms
- irritability

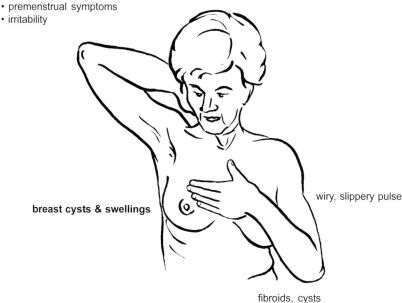

breast cysts & swellings

wiry, slippery pulse

fibroids, cysts

GYN

Combinations
- With **6.4 Xiao Yao Wan** or **6.3 Chai Hu Shu Gan Wan** for fibrocystic breast disease from Liver *qi* stagnation with Phlegm accumulation.
- With **1.33 Hai Zao Jing Wan** to enhance the Phlegm softening and transforming action of the formula.
- With **1.13 Woo Garm Yuen Medical Pills** or **1.14 Wen Jing Tang Wan** for ovarian cysts from Cold and *yang* deficiency.

Dosage and method of administration
3-5 tablets, three times daily on an empty stomach. Patients should expect to see some reduction in the size of the lump within one or two months.

Cautions and contraindications
Caution during pregnancy, in women with menorrhagia, and in patients with bleeding disorders. Caution in patients on anticoagulant therapy (aspirin, warfarin, coumarin). Watch for bruising or increased tendency to bleeding.

1.33 HAI ZAO JING WAN

海藻晶丸

Lanzhou Foci Pharmaceutical Factory (Gansu)
'Brilliant Sargassum Pills'
Hai Zao Jing Wan is packaged in bottles of 200 pills.
Also available as: Sargassum Teapills (PF), Haiodin

TCM actions
Disperses Phlegm, softens hardness, reduces swelling.

Biomedical actions
Softens and reduces masses and lumps.

INDICATIONS

- Phlegm type masses, nodules and lumps, that is, those that are soft or rubbery and well defined. Most commonly used for benign masses in the neck, such as thyroid nodules and goitre.
- Can assist in the treatment of breast cysts, parotid adenomas, lipomas, sebaceous cysts, ovarian cysts and fibroids, glandular and lymphatic congestion, lymphadenopathy, and testicular swellings such as varicocele and hydrocele.

Composition (each pill contains powdered)
Sargassum pallidum (hai zao, sargassum seaweed) 160mg

Combinations
- With **1.32 Ru Jie Xiao Tablets**, **6.4 Xiao Yao Wan** or **6.3 Chai Hu Shu Gan Wan** for thyroid swelling or fibrocystic breast disease arising from Liver *qi* stagnation with Phlegm accumulation.
- With **8.1 Tian Wang Bu Xin Dan** for thyroid swelling or nodules, insomnia and palpitations associated with Heart and Kidney *yin* deficiency and Phlegm accumulation.
- With **6.3 Chai Hu Shu Gan Wan** or **6.2 Si Ni Wan** for swelling in the neck associated with *qi* and Phlegm stagnation.
- With **11.3 Ji Sheng Ju He Wan** or **11.4 Tian Tai Wu Yao Wan** for testicular swellings from Phlegm accumulation
- With **1.13 Woo Garm Yuen Medical Pills** for ovarian cysts.
- With **2.9 Xiang Sha Liu Jun Wan** or **2.23 Ping Wei San** for chronic lymphatic congestion from poor fluid metabolism.

The image on the right shows product packaging with text:
TRADE MARK
HAI ZAO JING WAN
AUSTL 72801
200 PILLS
LANZHOU FOCI PHARMACEUTICAL FACTORY
LANZHOU CHINA

Pattern identifying features

• **Phlegm type nodules & swellings**
• rubbery, smooth well defined swellings

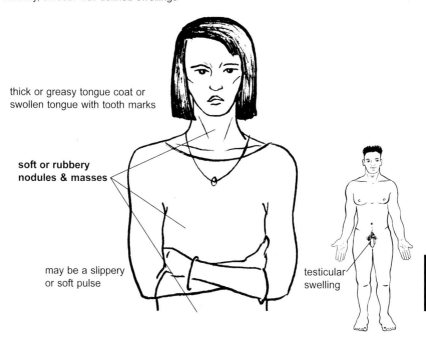

thick or greasy tongue coat or
swollen tongue with tooth marks

**soft or rubbery
nodules & masses**

may be a slippery
or soft pulse

testicular
swelling

GYN

• With **6.4 Xiao Yao Wan** for lymphatic congestion associated with Liver *qi* stagnation.
• With **3.34 Bai He Gu Jin Wan** for chronic swollen lymph glands and other nodules that form in patients with Lung *yin* deficiency.
• With **8.8 Wen Dan Wan** or **14.1 Huang Lian Jie Du Wan** for nodules and masses associated with Phlegm Heat.

Dosage and method of administration

When used alone, the dose is 8-12 pills three times daily on an empty stomach. The dose may be spread out, or two lots of 12-18 pills may be taken, morning and evening. This herb is usually combined with a constitutional formula, however, and so the dose can be reduced by 50-75% depending on the dose of the main formula.

Cautions and contraindications

1.33 Hai Zao Jing Wan (and any preparation containing iodine) should be used cautiously in patients with a hyperthyroid condition, as they may aggravate the condition.

1.34 NEI XIAO LUO LI WAN

内消瘰疬丸

Lanzhou Foci Pharmaceutical Factory (Gansu)
'Internally Reducing Cervical Lymphadenitis Pills'
Nei Xiao Luo Li Wan is packaged in bottles of 200 pills.
Also available as: Nei Xiao Luo Li Teapills (PF)

TCM actions
Softens and disperses Phlegm, softens hardness, reduces masses, clears Heat.

Biomedical actions
Softens and reduces masses and lumps, anti-inflammatory.

INDICATIONS

- Benign masses, nodules and lumps associated with Phlegm, hard Phlegm and/ or mild Blood stagnation. These masses are rubbery and well defined, or firm, tender and irregular. Most commonly used for swollen tender cervical lymph nodes, thyroid nodules, hyperthyroidism, thyroiditis and goitre. Even though this formula is focused on softening and dispersing Phlegm and Phlegm Heat nodules, it can be used for Blood masses as it can soften hardness and assist the breakdown of the mass.
- Useful as an adjunct formula to assist in the softening and dispersal of masses such as endometriosis, ovarian cysts and fibroids, breast masses, inflammatory nodules, glandular and lymphatic congestion, hepatosplenomegaly, adenoma, testicular swellings (including post surgical) and chronic boils. Also used for internal inflammatory masses such as chronic diverticulitis and appendicitis.

Composition (each pill contains powdered)

Prunella vulgaris (xia ku cao, prunella) 40.2mg, *Scrophularia ningpoensis* (xuan shen, scrophularia) 25mg, *Fritillaria thunbergii* (zhe bei mu, fritillaria) 10mg, *Angelica sinensis* (dang gui, chinese angelica) 9.15mg, *Mentha haplocalycis* (bo he, mint) 9.15mg, *Citrus aurantium* (zhi ke, aurantium) 9.15mg, *Rheum palmatum* (da huang, rhubarb) 9.15mg, *Forsythia suspensa* (lian qiao, forsythia) 9.15mg, *Platycodon grandiflorum* (jie geng, platycodon) 9.15mg, *Ampelopsis japonica* (bai lian, ampelopsis) 5mg, *Trichosanthes kirilowii* (tian hua fen, trichosanthes root) 5mg, *Rehmannia glutinosa* (sheng di, raw rehmannia) 5mg, *Glycyrrhiza uralensis* (gan cao, licorice) 5mg

Pattern identifying features

- **Phlegm, hard Phlegm &/or mild Blood stagnation**
- rubbery, painless or tender masses, nodules & lumps; inflammatory masses

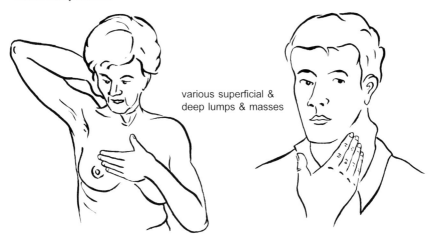

various superficial & deep lumps & masses

GYN

Combinations
- With **6.3 Chai Hu Shu Gan Wan, 6.1 Xiao Chai Hu Tang Wan,** or **6.4 Xiao Yao Wan** for patients with *qi* and Phlegm stagnation masses, such as hypochondriac pain from early liver cirrhosis, or fibrocystic breast disease.
- With **6.1 Xiao Chai Hu Tang Wan** for chronic breast abscess.
- With **7.1 Liu Wei Di Huang Wan** or **1.23 Zhi Bai Ba Wei Wan** for hard Phlegm accumulations or nodules in patients with a *yin* deficient constitution.
- With **1.2 Si Wu Wan** for endometriosis and fibroids with Blood deficiency.
- With **11.1 Qian Lie Xian Capsule** or **11.2 Prostate Gland Pills** for Phlegm type prostate swelling from chronic prostatitis.
- With **6.6 Long Dan Xie Gan Wan** for inflamed and tender lymph nodes in the neck, or acute thyroid swelling.

Dosage and method of administration
8-12 pills three times daily on an empty stomach. The dose may be spread out, or two lots of 12-18 pills may be taken, morning and evening. In severe cases or during the early stages of treatment (the first few weeks), a 50% increase in dose may be used, then reduced as the treatment takes effect.

Cautions and contraindications
Contraindicated during pregnancy.

1.35 FU YAN QING TABLET

妇炎清

(Fu Yan Qing)
Jing Xian Pharmaceutical Co. (Guangzhou)
'Clear Female Inflammation'
Fu Yan Qing Tablets are packaged in bottles of 60 tablets.

TCM actions
Clears Damp Heat and Toxic Heat, and drains Dampness from the lower *jiao*, nourishes Blood, stops pain.

Biomedical actions
Anti-inflammatory, diuretic, disinfectant.

INDICATIONS

- Damp Heat and/or Toxic Heat in the Uterus and lower *jiao*. Used for a variety of presentations of lower *jiao* Damp and Toxic Heat with colored malodorous leukorrhea, heat and pain, including biomedical disorders such as endometritis, inflammation of the cervix, vulvitis, acute pelvic inflammatory disease, salpingitis, adnexitis, pruritus vulvae, genital herpes, *Trichomonas*, *Chlamydia*, thrush and other genital infections, anal fissure and fistula.
- Also good for infection and inflammation of the urinary tract, *Lin* syndrome associated with Heat, Damp Heat and Toxic Heat.

Composition (each tablet contains extracts equivalent to dry)
Lygodium japonicum (hai jin sha, lygodium spore) 325mg, *Plantago asiatica* (che qian zi, plantago) 325mg, *Poria cocos* (fu ling, hoelen) 225mg, *Polyporus umbellatus* (zhu ling, polyporus) 225mg, *Scutellaria baicalensis* (huang qin, scute) 225mg, *Angelica polymorpha* (dang gui, chinese angelica) 225mg, *Paeonia lactiflora* (bai shao, white peony) 225mg, *Phellodendron amurense* (huang bai, phellodendron) 175mg, *Polygonum aviculare* (bian xu, knotweed) 150mg, *Viola yedoensis* (zi hua di ding, viola) 100mg

Combinations
- With **14.5 Chuan Xin Lian Antiphlogistic Tablets** for severe Toxic Heat and infection by *Trichomonas*.
- With **14.1 Huang Lian Jie Du Wan** for severe Damp or Toxic Heat.
- With **13.13 Fu Yin Tai Liniment** for vulvitis and itch.

Pattern identifying features

- **Damp Heat/Toxic Heat in the lower *jiao***
- infection of the genito-urinary system
- urinary tract infection

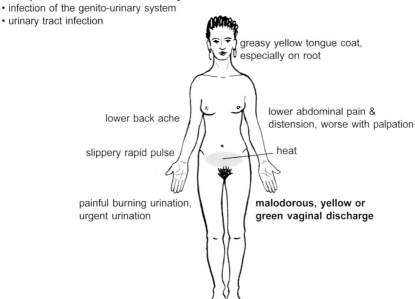

greasy yellow tongue coat, especially on root

lower back ache

lower abdominal pain & distension, worse with palpation

slippery rapid pulse

heat

painful burning urination, urgent urination

malodorous, yellow or green vaginal discharge

GYN

Dosage and method of administration
3-5 tablets, three times daily on an empty stomach.

Cautions and contraindications
Contraindicated in patients with Cold Damp chronic vaginal discharge and with urinary pain and vaginal irritation from *yin* deficiency.

1.36 BI XIE SHENG SHI WAN

萆薢胜湿丸

Lanzhou Foci Pharmaceutical Factory (Gansu)
'*Dioscorea hypoglauca* Pills to Overcome Dampness'
Bi Xie Sheng Shi Wan is packaged in bottles of 200 pills.
Also available as: Subdue the Dampness Teapills (PF)

TCM actions
Clears Damp Heat from the lower *jiao* (Dampness greater than Heat), promotes urination, cools the Blood.

Biomedical actions
Anti-inflammatory, diuretic, disinfectant.

INDICATIONS

• Damp Heat in the Uterus and lower *jiao*. This is a good formula for a variety of presentations of lower *jiao* Damp Heat, with Dampness the dominant feature. These include disorders such as acute pelvic inflammatory disease, pruritus vulvae, vulvitis, genital herpes, genital infection by organisms including *Trichomonas*, *Chlamydia*, and *Candida* (thrush), anal fissure and fistula and thick coloured leukorrhea. This formula is an excellent alternative to **6.6 Long Dan Xie Gan Wan** for recurrent outbreaks of Damp Heat type genital sores and lower *jiao* discharges in women and men. This formula appears to be more effective for these conditions and is more suitable for prolonged use.
• For urinary tract infection (Damp Heat *lin* syndrome) with cloudy or concentrated urine and dysuria.
• Damp Heat in the skin with weeping, red, itchy lesions, such as eczema, dermatitis and vesicular skin diseases. These typically occur in the lower body.

Composition (each pill contains powdered)
Coix lachryma-jobi (yi ren, coix), 24mg, *Poria cocos* (fu ling, hoelen) 19.2mg, *Dioscorea hypoglauca* (bei xie, fish poison yam) 16mg, *Phellodendron amurense* (huang bai, phellodendron) 16mg, *Dictamnus albus* (bai xian pi, dictamnus) 16mg, *Tetrapanax papyriferae* (tong cao, tetrapanax) 16mg, *Alisma orientale* (ze xie, alisma) 14mg, *Atractylodes lancea* (cang zhu, red atractylodes) 12.8mg, *Paeonia suffruticosa* (mu dan pi, moutan) 12.6mg, *Gardenia florida* (shan zhi zi, gardenia fruit) 12.8mg

Pattern identifying features

- **Damp Heat in the lower *jiao***
- Damp > Heat
- pelvic infection
- urinary tract infections
- vesicular skin lesions

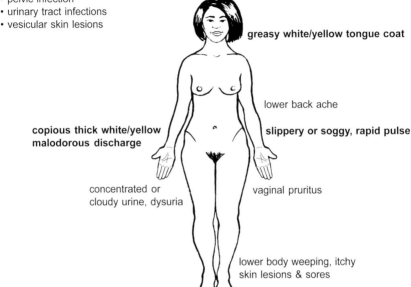

greasy white/yellow tongue coat

lower back ache

copious thick white/yellow malodorous discharge

slippery or soggy, rapid pulse

concentrated or cloudy urine, dysuria

vaginal pruritus

lower body weeping, itchy skin lesions & sores

GYN

Combinations
- With **13.4 Ke Yin Wan** for severe Damp Heat in the skin.
- With **14.1 Huang Lian Jie Du Wan** for severe Damp Heat in the reproductive system.
- With **1.34 Nei Xiao Luo Li Wan** for painful palpable inflammatory masses in the lower abdomen (e.g. salpingitis) from Damp Heat.
- With **14.5 Chuan Xin Lian Antiphlogistic Tablets** for acute prostatitis.

Dosage and method of administration
8-12 pills three or four times daily on an empty stomach, however in most acute cases this can be safely doubled. The dose should be spread out evenly, and in severe cases may be taken every two hours. Generally not recommended for use longer than a few weeks, except in constitutional cases to gradually leach out residual Damp Heat at a lower dose (~18-24 pills per day).

Cautions and contraindications
Generally well tolerated, but can weaken the Spleen and cause digestive upsets when overused.

1.37 YU DAI WAN

愈带丸

Lanzhou Foci Pharmaceutical Factory (Gansu)
'Pills to Resolve Vaginal Discharge'
Yu Dai Wan is packaged in bottles of 200 pills.
Also available as: Stop Discharge Pill (BE)

TCM actions
Clears Damp Heat from the Uterus, stops leukorrhea,
nourishes and supplements Blood.

Biomedical actions
Diuretic, disinfectant, hematinic.

INDICATIONS

- Damp Heat in the Uterus causing thick, yellow or green, malodorous leukorrhea, itch, irritation and discomfort. There may be streaks of blood. The main ingredient, ailanthus, is especially effective in this condition because it not only clears Damp Heat but astringes discharge at the same time. Can be used for both acute and chronic or recurrent cases. Being based on **1.2 Si Wu Wan** it is suitable for vaginal discharge from Damp Heat with underlying Liver Blood deficiency that enables the Damp Heat to linger.
- Dysenteric disorder from Damp Heat.
- With the appropriate identifying features, this formula can assist in the treatment of biomedical conditions such as acute or chronic pelvic inflammatory disease, acute or chronic vaginitis, infection by pathogens such as *Trichomonas* and *Candida*, salpingitis, vaginitis, cervicitis and dysentery.

Composition (each pill contains powdered)
Ailanthus altissima (chun gen pi, ailanthus) 75mg, *Paeonia lactiflora* (bai shao, white peony) 25mg, *Rehmannia glutinosa* (shu di, processed rehmannia) 20mg, *Angelica polymorpha* (dang gui, chinese angelica) 15mg, *Ligusticum wallichi* (chuan xiong, cnidium) 15mg, *Phellodendron amurense* (huang bai, phellodendron) 10mg, *Alpinia officinarum* (gao liang jiang, galangal) 10mg

Combinations
- With severe infection combine with **14.8 Wu Wei Xiao Du Wan, 14.5 Chuan Xin Lian Antiphlogistic Tablets, 14.2 Huang Lian Su Tablets** or **14.6 Fu Fang Nan Ban Lan Gen**.

Pattern identifying features

- **Acute or chronic & lingering Damp Heat in the uterus**
- **leukorrhea**
- Dysenteric disorder
- pain during intercourse

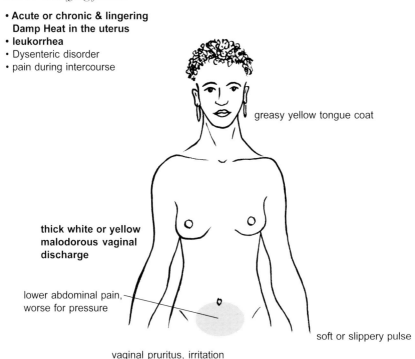

greasy yellow tongue coat

thick white or yellow malodorous vaginal discharge

lower abdominal pain, worse for pressure

soft or slippery pulse

vaginal pruritus, irritation

GYN

• With a component of Liver Fire, combine with **6.6 Long Dan Xie Gan Wan**.

Dosage and method of administration

8-12 pills three times daily on an empty stomach. The dose may be spread out, or two lots of 12-18 pills may be taken, morning and evening. In the early stages of treatment or in severe cases a 50% increase in dose may be used, then reduced as the treatment takes effect.

Cautions and contraindications

Not suitable for Cold Damp type leukorrhea. Care should be taken in patients with a tendency to abdominal bloating, loose stools or general digestive weakness. Some patients may find the rehmannia and Chinese angelica in **1.37 Yu Dai Wan** aggravates these symptoms. This can usually be alleviated by taking the pills with a small dose (3-6 pills at the same time) of **2.22 Er Chen Wan** or **2.18 Bao He Wan**.

GMP 1.38 CHIEN CHIN CHIH TAI WAN

千金止帶丸

(Qian Jin Zhi Dai Wan)
Tianjin Lerentang Pharmaceutical Factory (Shandong)
'Thousand Gold Pieces Pills to Stop Discharge'
Chien Chin Chih Tai Wan is packaged in bottles of 120 pills.

TCM actions
Clears Damp Heat from the lower *jiao*, stops leukorrhea
and pain, strengthens the Spleen.

Biomedical actions
Anti-inflammatory, disinfectant.

INDICATIONS

- Mild acute, subacute or recurrent Damp or Damp Heat in the Uterus and lower *jiao* causing yellow or creamy leukorrhea. Suitable for deficiency, excess or mixed patterns. This formula is interesting in that it contains warming, supplementing, astringent and Damp Heat clearing herbs and is thus best for a variety of complex and chronic conditions, as well as recurrent or latent problems. The focus of the formula is the salty cold indigo, which has Damp and Toxic Heat clearing ability (antibiotic and anti-inflammatory action). Therefore, even though the Damp Heat aspects are the primary focus, the formula recognises the importance of deficiency (here Spleen *qi*, Blood and Kidney *yang*) in enabling Damp Heat to linger and stagnate.
- With the appropriate identifying features, this formula can be used to treat conditions such as leukorrhea, *Candida* (thrush), chronic pelvic inflammatory disease, salpingitis, oophoritis, chronic prostatitis, chronic pyelonephritis, chronic or cloudy urinary problems (such as turbid or milky *lin* syndrome), albuminuria and chyluria.

Composition
Indigo Pulverata Levis (qing dai, indigo) 16%, *Angelica sinensis* (dang gui, chinese angelica) 10%, *Atractylodes macrocephala* (bai zhu, atractylodes) 5%, *Codonopsis pilosula* (dang shen, codonopsis) 12%, *Dipsacus asper* (xu duan, dipsacus) 10%, *Saussurea lappa* (mu xiang, saussurea) 10%, *Ostrea gigas* (mu li, oyster shell) 12%, *Foeniculum vulgarae* (xiao hui xiang, fennel seed) 5%

Pattern identifying features

- **Damp Heat in the lower *jiao* with Spleen & Kidney deficiency**
- pain during intercourse

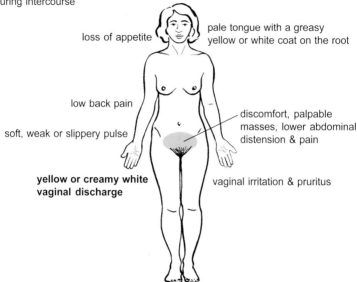

loss of appetite

pale tongue with a greasy yellow or white coat on the root

low back pain

soft, weak or slippery pulse

discomfort, palpable masses, lower abdominal distension & pain

yellow or creamy white vaginal discharge

vaginal irritation & pruritus

GYN

Combinations
- With **7.1 Liu Wei Di Huang Wan** or **1.23 Zhi Bai Ba Wei Wan** for chronic or recurrent urinary discomfort from smouldering Damp Heat and Kidney deficiency.
- With **11.1 Qian Lie Xian Capsules** or **11.2 Prostate Gland Pills** for chronic prostatitis from smouldering Damp Heat.

Dosage and method of administration
5 pills, three times daily on an empty stomach.

Cautions and contraindications
Not recommended for severe or acute Damp Heat or Toxic Heat discharges with no underlying deficiency (*see* **6.6 Long Dan Xie Gan Wan** or **1.35 Fu Yan Qing Tablet**).

1.39 YANG YAN QU BAN TABLET

养颜去斑片

(Yang Yan Qu Ban Pian)

Jing Xian Pharmaceutical Co. (Guangzhou)
'Tablets to Nourish the Face and Eliminate Spots'
Yang Yan Qu Ban Tablets are packaged in bottles of 60 sugar coated tablets.

AUST L 82984
60 TABLETS

MADE IN CHINA

TCM actions

Regulates *qi* and quickens Blood, supplements Blood, strengthens the Spleen.

Biomedical actions

Hematinic, regulates menstruation.

INDICATIONS

- Hyperpigmentation of the skin (melasma, chloasma, melasma gravidarum), especially the face associated with Liver *qi* stagnation, Liver and Spleen disharmony, Blood deficiency and/or Blood stagnation. Features include coffee colored spots or patches on the face, trunk and abdomen, the hyerpigmentation of pregnancy (used postpartum) and pigmentation that complicates hormonal disorders and use of the oral contraceptive pill.

Composition (each tablet contains extracts equivalent to dry)

Codonopsis pilosula (dang shen, codonopsis) 325mg, *Vitex trifolia* (man jing zi, vitex fruit) 325mg, *Salvia miltiorrhiza* (dan shen, salvia) 250mg, *Curcuma longa* (yu jin, curcuma) 250mg, *Cyperus rotundus* (xiang fu, cyperus) 250mg, *Atractylodes macrocephala* (bai zhu, atractylodes) 250mg, *Paeonia lactiflora* (bai shao, white peony) 250mg, *Ligusticum wallichi* (chuan xiong, cnidium) 225mg

Dosage and method of administration

3-5 tablets, three times daily on an empty stomach.

Cautions and contraindications

Contraindicated during pregnancy.

Patent Medicines for the Gastro-intestinal System

2.1 XING JUN SAN

行军散

Five Pagodas Pharmacy Co. (Thailand)
'Marching Powder'
Xing Jun San is a highly aromatic green powder
packaged in small 10 gram or large 25 gram jars.

TCM actions
Fragrantly dispels and dries Dampness (especially
deeply rooted Damp), dispels Summerdamp,
regulates the Stomach and Intestines, stops nausea
and vomiting.

Biomedical actions
Eliminates pathogens from the digestive system, anti-emetic, antidiarrheal.

INDICATIONS

- Summerdamp invasion, Sudden Turmoil Disorder (*see* glossary) and gastro-
  intestinal upsets characterised by acute nausea and vomiting, abdominal cramps
  and diarrhea. This is a strong, fragrant and dispersing formula, and when used
  correctly it generally works quickly. In acute situations, it does not need to be
  used for long, usually no longer than 3-5 days. If the patient does not improve in
  that time he/she should be reassessed.
- Also useful given in small doses when patients with Spleen deficiency diarrhea
  patterns fail to improve or get worse with Spleen supplementing formulae, an
  outcome suggesting hidden or deeply rooted Dampness.
- With the appropriate identifying features, this formula may be used to treat
  biomedical disorders such as acute viral or bacterial gastroenteritis, food
  poisoning, summer flu, stomach flu, acute colitis, travellers diarrhea, 'Bali belly'
  and motion sickness.

Composition (each 100 grams of powder contains)
Magnolia officinalis (hou po, magnolia bark) 11.8g, *Ligusticum wallichi* (chuan xiong,
cnidium) 9.3g, *Atractylodes lancea* (cang zhu, red atractylodes) 9.3g, *Agastache rugosa*
(huo xiang, agastache) 7.1g, *Citrus reticulata* (chen pi, citrus) 7.1g, *Eugenia caryophyllata*
(ding xiang, cloves) 7.1g, *Saussurea lappa* (mu xiang, saussurea) 7.1g, *Aquilaria
agallocha* (chen xiang, aquilaria) 7.1g, *Cinnamomum cassia* (gui zhi, cinnamon) 7.1g,
Glycyrrhiza uralensis (gan cao, licorice) 4.8g, Menthol 4.7g, *Acorus gramineus* (shi chang
pu, acorus) 3.5g, *Angelica dahurica* (bai zhi, angelica) 3.5g, *Mentha haplocalycis* (bo he,

Pattern identifying features

- **Summerdamp invasion**
- acute gastric upset
- lethargy
- heaviness

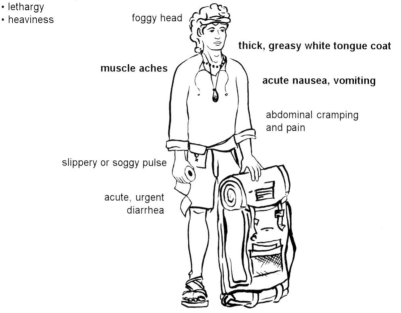

foggy head

thick, greasy white tongue coat

muscle aches

acute nausea, vomiting

abdominal cramping and pain

slippery or soggy pulse

acute, urgent diarrhea

GIT

mint) 3.5g, *Lysimachiae foeni-graeci* (ling ling xiang) 3.3g, *Asarum seiboldi* (xi xin, asarum) 2.3g, *Dryobalanops camphora* (bing pian, borneol) 1.4g

Dosage and method of administration

Summerdamp: Half to one teaspoon of powder in a little water every 2-3 hours in the acute phase. If the patient does not improve (especially nausea) within 30 minutes, the dose can be repeated. It is useful to continue treatment for 1-2 days following resolution of the symptoms (at a smaller dose) to ensure that all Dampness has been cleared.

For leaching hidden Dampness: ¼ teaspoon 2-3 times daily for two or so weeks.

For motion sickness: ¼ teaspoon every hour or as needed.

Cautions and contraindications

Contraindicated during pregnancy. Not suitable for prolonged use. In acute conditions, a good result should be observed within 24-72 hours If improvement is not apparent, review the patient and reconsider the prescription. Not suitable for patients with high fever and thirst.

2.2.1 HUO HSIANG CHENG CHI PIEN

藿香正气片

(Huo Xiang Zheng Qi Pian)
Tianjin Drug Manufactory (Shandong)
'Agastache *Qi* Correcting Tablets'
Huo Hsiang Cheng Chi Pien is packaged
in vials of 8 uncoated pills, 12 vials per box.

TCM actions
Supports *zheng qi* while dispeling Damp pathogens, regulates and harmonises the
Stomach and Intestines, stops vomiting and diarrhea.

Biomedical actions
Anti-emetic, antidiarrheal, stomachic, alleviates acute gastric conditions.

INDICATIONS

- Acute Wind Cold invasion with internal Dampness, the Dampness either pre-
  existing or carried in with the Wind. This pattern is common towards the end of
  Summer and typically appears in clusters, sweeping through an office or school.
  The main symptoms are acute nausea and vomiting, fullness in the chest, upper
  abdominal pain and diarrhea. Also used for Summerdamp attack and Sudden
  Turmoil Disorder (*see* glossary) without the exterior symptoms.
- For patients with a tendency to internal Dampness manifested in digestive
  symptoms such as borborygmus, abdominal distension, nausea, loss of appetite
  and abdominal pain. It can also be prescribed for patients who get worse with
  Spleen *qi* supplementing herbs. May also be useful, in short bursts, for children
  with acute exacerbation of an underlying Damp condition, such as chronic sinus
  or ear congestion, or abdominal pain that is stirred up in windy weather.
- With the appropriate identifying features, this formula can be used to treat
  biomedical conditions such as acute viral or bacterial gastroenteritis, food
  poisoning, summer flu, stomach flu, travellers diarrhea, influenza, acute colitis
  and motion sickness.

Composition
Agastache rugosa (huo xiang, agastache) 13.32%, *Poria cocos* (fu ling, hoelen) 13.25%,
Areca catechu (da fu pi, betel husk) 13.25%, *Angelica dahurica* (bai zhi, angelica)
13.25%, *Perilla frutescens* (zi su ye, perilla) 13.25%, *Magnolia officinalis* (hou po,
magnolia bark) 9.4%, *Atractylodes lancea* (cang zhu, red atractylodes) 9.4%, *Citrus
reticulata* (chen pi, citrus) 9.4%, *Glycyrrhiza uralensis* (gan cao, licorice) 5.5%

Pattern identifying features

- **Summerdamp invasion, Wind Cold with internal Damp**
- **acute gastric upsets**
- chills & fever (chills may be greater than fever)
- lethargy
- heaviness

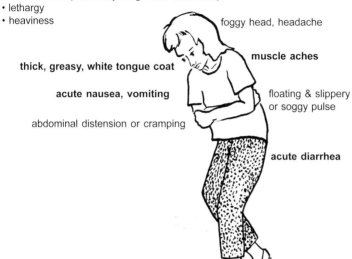

foggy head, headache

muscle aches

thick, greasy, white tongue coat

acute nausea, vomiting

floating & slippery
or soggy pulse

abdominal distension or cramping

acute diarrhea

Dosage and method of administration

For acute cases, 4-8 tablets every 2 hours. For longer use (2-3 weeks maximum) in leaching out hidden or latent Dampness, reduce the dose by 50-75%. Not suitable for small children due to the dimensions of the tablet.

Cautions and contraindications

Not suitable for digestive upsets due to Heat or Damp Heat, (those with thirst, constipation, yellow tongue coat, fever with no chills, etc.).

2.2.2 HUO XIANG ZHENG QI WAN

藿香正气丸

Lanzhou Foci Pharmaceutical Factory (Gansu)
'Agastache *Qi* Correcting Pills'
Huo Xiang Zheng Qi Wan is packaged in bottles of 200 pills.

TCM actions
Supports *zheng qi*, dispels Damp pathogens, regulates and harmonises the Stomach and Intestines, stops vomiting and diarrhea.

Biomedical actions
Anti-emetic, antidiarrheal, stomachic, alleviates acute gastric conditions.

INDICATIONS

- As for **2.2.1 Huo Hsiang Cheng Chi Pien**.

Composition (each pill contains powdered)
Pogostemon cablin (huo xiang, agastache) 23mg, *Magnolia officinalis* (hou po, magnolia bark) 15mg, *Platycodon grandiflorum* (jie geng, platycodon) 15mg, *Citrus reticulata* (chen pi, citrus) 15mg, *Glycyrrhiza uralensis* (gan cao, licorice) 15mg, *Pinellia ternata* (ban xia, pinellia) 15mg, *Atractylodes macrocephala* (bai zhu, atractylodes) 15mg, *Angelica dahurica* (bai zhi, angelica) 8mg, *Perilla frutescens* (zi su ye, perilla) 8mg, *Poria cocos* (fu ling, hoelen) 8mg, *Zingiber officinale* (sheng jiang, ginger) 29mg, *Zizyphus jujuba* (da zao, chinese dates) 47mg

Dosage and method of administration
12-15 pills three times daily on an empty stomach. The dose may be spread out, or two lots of 18-22 pills may be taken, morning and evening. In severe cases, take a dose every two hours or so.

Cautions and contraindications
As for **2.2.1 Huo Hsiang Cheng Chi Pien**.

2.2.3 COLD AND ABDOMINAL DISCOMFORT RELIEVER

藿香正气片

(Huo Xiang Zheng Qi Pian)
Tong Ren Tang (Beijing)
'Agastache *Qi* Correcting Tablets'
Cold and Abdominal Discomfort Reliever is packaged in bottles of 60 sugar coated tablets.

TCM actions
Supports *zheng qi*, dispels Damp pathogens, regulates and harmonises the Stomach and Intestines, stops vomiting and diarrhea.

Biomedical actions
Anti-emetic, antidiarrheal, stomachic, alleviates acute gastric conditions.

INDICATIONS

• As for **2.2.1 Huo Hsiang Cheng Chi Pien**.

Composition (each tablet contains)
Pinellia ternata (ban xia, pinellia) 186mg, *Platycodon grandiflorum* (jie geng, platycodon) 160mg, *Areca catechu* (da fu pi, betel husk) 97mg, *Glycyrrhiza uralensis* (gan cao, licorice) 97mg, *Perilla frutescens* (zi su ye, perilla) 97mg, *Poria cocos* (fu ling, hoelen) 94mg, *Angelica dahurica* (bai zhi, angelica) 94mg, *Pogostemon cablin* (huo xiang, agastache essential oil) 2.8mg, *Citrus reticulata* (chen pi, citrus essential oil) 1.9mg

Dosage and method of administration
4 tablets three times daily. In severe cases a dose can be taken every 2 hours or so.

Cautions and contraindications
As for **2.2.1 Huo Hsiang Cheng Chi Pien**.

GIT

GMP

2.3 SO HUP YUEN MEDICAL PILLS

追风苏合丸

(Zhui Feng Su He Wan)
Chan Li Chai Medical Factory (Hong Kong)
'Chase Away Wind and Make Complete Pills'
So Hup Yuen Medical Pills are packaged as large honey pills in a yellow wax ball, ten pills per box.

TCM actions

Fragrantly dispels and dries Dampness (especially deeply rooted Damp), warms and regulates the Stomach and Intestines, alleviates *gu* syndrome, stops nausea and vomiting.

Biomedical actions

Eliminates pathogens from the digestive system, anti-emetic, antidiarrheal.

INDICATIONS

- Cold Damp in the gastro-intestinal system. Similar in action to **2.1 Xing Jun San**, this formula is quite fragrant, warming and dispersing, and useful for locating and leaching out hard to eliminate Dampness. Useful for odd or resistant gastro-intestinal complaints such as abdominal distension and chronic diarrhea that fails to respond to standard approaches. May be useful in treating *gu* syndrome (*see* glossary). Also suitable for acute Wind Cold invasion with gastro-intestinal upset.
- With the appropriate identifying features, the formula can be used for biomedical conditions such as chronic infections of the gastrointestinal tract, chronic candidiasis, leaky gut syndrome, acute gastroenteritis (either viral or bacterial), summer flu, travellers diarrhea, influenza and acute colitis.

Composition

Agastache rugosa (huo xiang, agastache) 6.72%, *Eugenia caryophyllata* (ding xiang, cloves) 6.72%, *Piper longum* (bi ba, long pepper) 6.72%, *Santalum album* (tan xiang, sandalwood) 6.72%, *Myristica fragrans* (rou dou kou, nutmeg) 6.72%, *Notopterygium incisum* (qiang huo, notopterygium) 6.72%, *Ledebouriella divaricata* (fang feng, siler) 6.72%, *Mentha haplocalycis* (bo he, mint) 6.72%, *Glycyrrhiza uralensis* (gan cao, licorice) 6.72%, *Cyperus rotundus* (xiang fu, cyperus) 6.72%, *Terminalia chebula* (he zi, terminalia) 6.72%, *Atractylodes macrocephala* (bai zhu, atractylodes) 6.72%, *Aquilaria agallocha* (chen xiang, aquilaria) 6.72%, *Saussurea lappa* (mu xiang, saussurea) 6.72%, *Asarum seiboldi* (xi xin, asarum) 4.52%, *Dryobalanops camphora* (bing pian, borneol) 1.4%

Pattern identifying features

- **Cold Dampness in the
  gastrointestinal system**
- physical & mental exhaustion
- gastrointestinal symptoms worse
  with supplementing formulae
- loss of appetite, ravenous hunger
  or odd food cravings

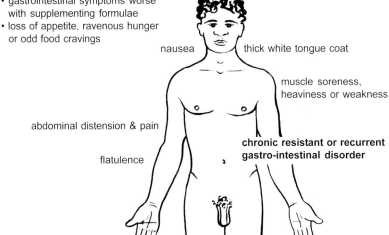

nausea

thick white tongue coat

muscle soreness,
heaviness or weakness

abdominal distension & pain

flatulence

**chronic resistant or recurrent
gastro-intestinal disorder**

chronic diarrhea or
alternating constipation
and diarrhea

GIT

Combinations
- With a small dose of **14.2 Huang Lian Su Tablets** for *gu* syndrome.

Dosage and method of administration
One pill twice daily, on an empty stomach. These pills are often very hard and need
to be softened in boiling water for 10 minutes before ingestion.

Cautions and contraindications
Not suitable for digestive upsets due to Heat or Damp Heat, (those with thirst,
constipation, yellow tongue coat, fever with no chills, etc.).

2.4 FU KE AN

腹可安

Jing Xian Pharmaceutical Co. (Guangzhou)
'Calm the Abdomen'
Fu Ke An is packaged in bottles of 60 sugar coated tablets.

TCM actions
Clears Damp Heat, astringes the Intestines and stops
diarrhea, stops pain.

AUST L 90966
60 TABLETS
MADE IN CHINA

Biomedical actions
Antidiarrheal, alleviates acute gastric conditions.

INDICATIONS

• Acute and chronic diarrhea associated with Damp Heat invasion of the Large
Intestine. The first two herbs in this formula, chinese polygonum and iron holly
bark, have specific activity against the common organisms that cause acute
diarrhea. The main features are indigestion with spasmodic cramping abdominal
or epigastric pain, acid reflux, nausea and vomiting, diarrhea, rectal and anal
pain, fever and malaise. This formula can be used to treat gastroenteritis, dysentery
and colitis.

Composition (each tablet contains extracts equivalent to dry)
Polygonum chinense (huo tan mu, chinese polygonum) 872mg, *Ilex rotunda* (jiu bi ying,
iron holly bark) 722mg, *Plantago asiatica* (che qian zi, plantago) 448mg, *Punica
granatum* (shi liu pi, pomegranate skin) 448mg

Combinations
• With **14.1 Huang Lian Jie Du Wan** for severe Damp Heat.
• With **14.5 Chuan Xin Lian Antiphlogistic Tablets** for dysentery from *Shigella* sp.

Dosage and method of administration
3-4 tablets, three times daily. In severe cases the dose can be increased to 3-4 tablets
every 2 hours.

Cautions and Contraindications
Not suitable for acute diarrhea from Summerdamp or Cold Damp invasion (*see* **2.1
Xing Jun San, 2.2 Huo Hsiang Cheng Chi Pien**, or **2.23 Ping Wei San**).

2.5 BAO JI PILLS

保济丸

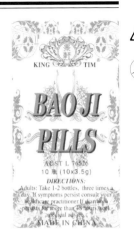

(Bao Ji Wan)
Jing Xian Pharmaceutical Co. (Guangzhou)
'Protect and Relieve Pills'
Bao Ji Pills are packaged in vials of tiny pills, 3.5 grams per vial.

TCM actions
Clears Damp Heat from the Intestines, stops diarrhea.

Biomedical actions
Antidiarrheal, anti-emetic, stomachic, alleviates acute
gastric conditions.

INDICATIONS

- Acute diarrhea and/or nausea and vomiting from Damp Heat invading the Large
  Intestine. Usually occurs during hot and humid weather, especially late Summer
  when heat and humidity are the prevailing climatic features. Similar in action
  and indication to **2.6 Po Chai Pills**, this version has fewer astringent and
  antidiarrheal herbs.
- With the appropriate identifying features (*see* illustration, p.85), this formula may
  be used to treat acute gastroenteritis (either viral or bacterial), summer flu,
  travellers diarrhea, hangover, overindulgence in rich food and food poisoning.

Composition (each bottle [3.5g] contains extracts equivalent to dry)
Uncaria rhyncophylla (gou teng, gambir) 2.9g, *Magnolia officinalis* (hou po, magnolia
bark) 2.9g, *Trichosanthes kirilowi* (tian hua fen, trichosanthes root) 2.9g, *Angelica
dahurica* (bai zhi, angelica) 2.9g, *Pogostemon cablin* (huo xiang, agastache) 2.9g,
Atractylodes lancea (cang zhu, red atractylodes) 2.9g, *Saussurea lappa* (mu xiang,
saussurea) 2.4g, *Citrus reticulata* (chen pi, citrus) 2.4g, *Setaria italica* (gu ya, sprouted
rice) 2.4g, *Mentha haplocalycis* (bo he, mint) 1.4g

Dosage and method of administration
1-2 bottles, three times daily. In severe cases a dose can be taken every 2 hours.

Cautions and contraindications
None noted.

GIT

2.6 PO CHAI PILLS

保济丸

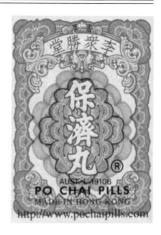

(Bao Ji Wan)
Li Chung Shing Tong Ltd (Hong Kong)
'Protect and Relieve Pills'
Po Chai Pills are packaged in vials of 100 tiny pills, eight vials to a box.

TCM actions

Clears Damp Heat from the Intestines, stops diarrhea.

Biomedical actions

Antidiarrheal, anti-emetic, stomachic, alleviates acute gastric conditions.

INDICATIONS

- Acute diarrhea and/or nausea and vomiting from Damp Heat invasion of the Large Intestine. Usually occurs during hot and humid weather, especially late Summer when heat and humidity are the prevailing climatic features. The main difference between this formula and **2.1 Xing Jun San** and **2.2 Huo Hsiang Cheng Chi Pien**, is that this formula is best for the lower intestinal manifestations and diarrhea. Also used for digestive upsets (diarrhea, abdominal distesion and pain) resulting from overindulgence in rich food and alcohol
- With the appropriate identifying features, this formula may be used to treat acute gastroenteritis (either viral or bacterial), summer flu, travellers diarrhea, hangover, overindulgence and food poisoning.

Composition (w/v)

Poria cocos (fu ling, hoelen) 14%, *Saussurea lappa* (mu xiang, saussurea) 8%, *Atractylodes lancea* (cang zhu, red atractylodes) 8%, *Pogostemon cablin* (huo xiang, agastache) 8%, *Angelica dahurica* (bai zhi, angelica) 8%, *Pueraria lobata* (ge gen, kudzu) 7%, *Magnolia officinalis* (hou po, magnolia bark) 7%, *Coicis lachryma-jobi* (yi ren, coix) 7%, Sun Kook Tea 7%, *Trichosanthes kirilowi* (gua lou, trichosanthes) 5.5%, *Hordeum vulgare* (mai ya, sprouted barley) 5.5%, *Mentha haplocalycis* (bo he, mint) 4.5%, *Halloysitum rubrum* (chi shi zhi, kaolin) 3.5%, *Chrysanthemum morifolium* (ju hua, chrysanthemum) 3.5%, *Citrus reticulata* (chen pi, citrus) 3.5%

Pattern identifying features

- **Acute Damp Heat invasion of the Large Intestine**
- **travellers diarrhea**
- headache, hangover
- fever

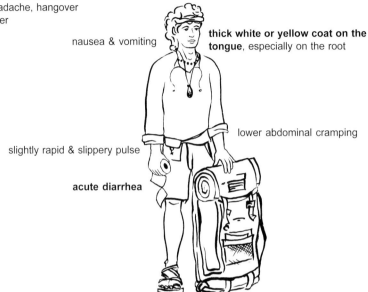

nausea & vomiting

thick white or yellow coat on the tongue, especially on the root

lower abdominal cramping

slightly rapid & slippery pulse

acute diarrhea

GIT

Combinations
- With **14.5 Chuan Xin Lian Antiphlogistic Tablets** or **14.1 Huang Lian Jie Du Wan** for Damp Heat with pus or blood in the stool.

Dosage and method of administration
1-2 vials every two hours. Half dose for children. Continue the formula for a couple of days following the resolution of symptoms to ensure all Damp Heat is leached from the system.

Cautions and contraindications
None noted.

GMP **2.7 SI JUN ZI WAN**

四君子丸

Available in the US,
UK and Europe
See Note 1, p.xxi

Lanzhou Foci Pharmaceutical Factory (Gansu)
'Four Gentlemen Pills'
Available as: Four Gentlemen Teapills (PF)

TCM actions

Strengthens the Spleen and supplements *qi*.

Biomedical actions

Enhances and regulates digestive functions, strengthens immunity and resistance.

INDICATIONS

• Spleen *qi* deficiency. This is the fundamental formula from which all *qi* supplementing and Spleen strengthening formulae are built. Used for all Spleen (and Lung) *qi* deficiency patterns, with symptoms of fatigue, weakness, pallor, loss of appetite, weak digestion, **abdominal distension**, loose stools, a pale tongue and a weak pulse.

• Can be used alone, or more commonly, combined with another formula when a greater *qi* supplementing effect is desired.

Composition

Codonopsis pilosula (dang shen, codonopsis) 29%, *Poria cocos* (fu ling, hoelen) 29%, *Atractylodes macrocephala* (bai zhu, atractylodes) 29%, *Glycyrrhiza uralensis* (gan cao, licorice) 7%

Combinations

• With **6.4 Xiao Yao Wan** for Liver *qi* stagnation with pronounced *qi* deficiency.
• With **4.3 Wu Pi Yin** for mild edema during pregnancy.
• With **7.23 Yu Ping Feng Wan** for Spleen and Lung *qi* deficiency.
• With **1.11 Dang Gui Su** for *qi* and mild Blood deficiency.

Dosage and method of administration

8-12 pills three times daily on an empty stomach. The dose may be spread out, or two lots of 12-18 pills may be taken, morning and evening. In severe cases or the early stages of treatment (the first few weeks), a 50% increase in dose may be used, then reduced as the treatment takes effect. For the same problem in children *see* **12.6 Healthy Child Tea**.

Cautions and contraindications

Contraindicated during the early phase of acute illness such as colds and flu.

2.8 LIU JUN ZI WAN

六君子丸

Available in the US, UK and Europe
See Note 1, p.xxi

Lanzhou Foci Pharmaceutical Factory (Gansu)
'Six Gentlemen Pills'
Available as: Six Gentlemen Teapills (PF)

TCM actions
Strengthens the Spleen and supplements *qi*, transforms Phlegm Damp, stops vomiting.

Biomedical actions
Enhances and regulates digestive functions, strengthens immunity and resistance, mucolytic, anti-emetic.

INDICATIONS

- Spleen *qi* deficiency with Phlegm Damp. A variation of **2.7 Si Jun Zi Wan**, with the addition of pinellia and citrus to transform the Phlegm Damp that commonly complicates Spleen *qi* deficiency. In addition to the basic Spleen *qi* deficient symptom picture, there are signs of Phlegm Damp, such as pronounced abdominal distension, a thick greasy tongue coat, nausea or vomiting and diarrhea.
- Excellent for morning sickness from deficiency, chronic gastro-intestinal weakness and chronic cough from Spleen *qi* deficiency with Phlegm Damp.

Composition
Codonopsis pilosula (dang shen, codonopsis) 19%, *Atractylodes macrocephala* (bai zhu, atractylodes) 15%, *Poria cocos* (fu ling, hoelen) 15%, *Pinellia ternata* (ban xia, pinellia) 15%, *Citrus reticulata* (chen pi, citrus) 15%, *Glycyrrhiza uralensis* (gan cao, licorice) 7%, *Zingiber officinalis* (sheng jiang, ginger) 7%, *Zizyphus jujuba* (da zao, chinese dates) 7%

Dosage and method of administration
8-12 pills three times daily on an empty stomach. The dose may be spread out, or two lots of 12-18 pills may be taken, morning and evening. In severe cases or the early stages of treatment (the first few weeks), a 50% increase in dose may be used, then reduced as the treatment takes effect. For the same problem in children *see* **12.6 Healthy Child Tea**.

Cautions and contraindications
Contraindicated during the early phase of acute illness such as colds and flu.

GIT

2.9 XIANG SHA LIU JUN WAN

香砂六君子丸

Lanzhou Foci Pharmaceutical Factory (Gansu)
'Six Gentlemen Pills with Cardamon and Saussurea'
Xiang Sha Liu Jun Wan is packaged in bottles of 200 pills.
Also available as: Six Gentlemen Plus Teapills (PF), Aplotaxis
Amomum Pills

TCM actions

Strengthens the Spleen, supplements and regulates *qi*,
transforms Phlegm Damp.

Biomedical actions

Enhances and regulates digestive functions, strengthens immunity and resistance,
mucolytic, stomachic, anti-emetic.

INDICATIONS

- Spleen *qi* deficiency with Phlegm Damp and *qi* stagnation. A variation of **2.8 Liu Jun Zi Wan**, this formula adds saussurea and cardamon to regulate *qi* and alleviate food stagnation. The main focus of this formula is on strengthening digestive function, with resolving Phlegm Damp and moving *qi* secondary. Its action is focused in the upper digestive tract–the Stomach and epigastrium. Because the complications of Spleen *qi* deficiency that this formula deals with are so common, it is generally preferred over **2.7 Si Jun Zi Wan** or **2.8 Liu Jun Zi Wan**.
- An excellent formula for patients prone to mucus congestion, and those who suffer from recurrent sinus congestion, allergies, sore throats, ear infections or, in children, glue ear. May be used for both adults and children.
- Chronic respiratory weakness and congestion with cough or wheezing and copious white sputum that collects in the lungs or sinuses.
- With the appropriate identifying features, this formula may be used to treat biomedical conditions such as peptic ulcer disease, chronic gastritis, dyspepsia, chronic colitis, chronic diarrhea, irritable bowel syndrome, morning sickness, hypoglycemia, general debility, narcolepsy, chronic bronchitis, chronic sinus congestion and poor concentration.

Composition (each pill contains powdered)

Atractylodes macrocephala (bai zhu, atractylodes) 32.3mg, *Poria cocos* (fu ling, hoelen) 32.3mg, *Zizyphus jujuba* (da zao, chinese dates) 21.5mg, *Codonopsis pilosula* (dang shen,

Pattern identifying features

• **Spleen *qi* deficiency with Phlegm Damp, *qi* & food stagnation**
• **loss of appetite**
• nausea, vomiting
• sleepiness after eating
• flatulence, belching, borborygmus
• loose stools, chronic diarrhea
• fatigue, heaviness in head & body
• indigestion
• early satiety

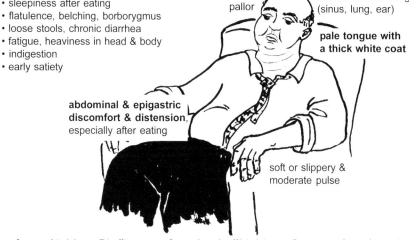

chronic mucus congestion (sinus, lung, ear)

pallor

pale tongue with a thick white coat

abdominal & epigastric discomfort & distension, especially after eating

soft or slippery & moderate pulse

codonopsis) 16mg, *Pinellia ternata* (ban xia, pinellia) 16mg, *Citrus reticulata* (chen pi, citrus) 13mg, *Amomum villosum* (sha ren, cardamon) 13mg, *Saussurea lappa* (mu xiang, saussurea) 11.3mg, *Glycyrrhiza uralensis* (gan cao, licorice) 11.3mg, *Zingiber officinalis* (sheng jiang, ginger) 10.7mg

GIT

Combinations
• With a small dose of **2.18 Bao He Wan** for severe indigestion, bad breath, foul belching or undigested food in the stools from food stagnation.
• With **2.22 Er Chen Wan** for persistent nausea or vomiting.
• With **2.26 Xiang Lian Wan** for reflux and heartburn.
• With **2.23 Ping Wei San** for severe Dampness.
• With **7.23 Yu Ping Feng Wan** for allergies and frequent colds.
• With **9.18 Xin Yi San** for chronic sinus congestion from Phlegm Damp.

Dosage and method of administration
8-12 pills three times daily on an empty stomach. The dose may be spread out, or two lots of 12-18 pills may be taken, morning and evening. In severe cases or during the early stages of treatment (the first few weeks), a 50% increase in dose may be used, then reduced as the treatment takes effect. For the same problem in children *see* **12.6 Healthy Child Tea**.

Cautions and contraindications
Contraindicated during the early phase of acute illness such as colds and flu.

2.10 XIANG SHA YANG WEI WAN

香砂养胃丸

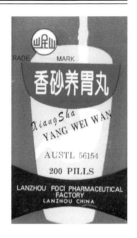

Lanzhou Foci Pharmaceutical Factory (Gansu)
'Cardamon and Saussurea Pills to Nourish the Stomach'
Xiang Sha Yang Wei Wan is packaged in bottles of 200 pills.
Also available as: Appetite and Digestion Pill, Hsiang Sha Yang
Wei Pien

TCM actions

Regulates *qi* in the middle *jiao*, alleviates food stagnation,
fragrantly disperses Dampness, warms and strengthens
the Spleen, harmonises the Stomach and directs Stomach
qi downward.

Biomedical actions

Enhances and regulates digestive functions, eases spasms in the gastro-intestinal
system, alleviates indigestion.

INDICATIONS

• Stagnation of *qi* and Dampness in the Spleen and Stomach with a mild degree
of Spleen deficiency. The main focus of this formula is on moving *qi*, drying the
Damp and redirecting *qi* downwards. Particularly good when Stomach *qi* fails to
descend causing reflux, heartburn, abdominal bloating, nausea or vomiting and
variable bowel habits. An excellent formula for chronic indigestion and dyspepsia
in an otherwise apparently robust individual.

• For mental cloudiness, poor concentration, forgetfulness, foggy headedness,
depression and heaviness of spirit, from a 'mist' of Phlegm Damp enveloping
and obscuring the Heart and mind.

Composition (each pill contains powdered)

Atractylodes macrocephala (bai zhu, atractylodes) 16mg, *Poria cocos* (fu ling, hoelen)
16mg, *Citrus reticulata* (chen pi, citrus) 16mg, *Pinellia ternata* (ban xia, pinellia) 16mg,
Saussurea lappa (mu xiang, saussurea) 11mg, *Pogostemon cablin* (huo xiang, agastache)
11mg, *Cyperus rotundus* (xiang fu, cyperus) 11mg, *Alpinia katsumadai* (cao dou kou,
katsumadai cardamon) 11mg, *Magnolia officinalis* (hou po, magnolia bark) 11mg,
Amomum villosum (sha ren, cardamon) 11mg, *Citrus aurantium* (zhi shi, aurantium)
11mg, *Glycyrrhiza uralensis* (gan cao, licorice) 5mg, *Zizyphus jujuba* (da zao, chinese
dates) 5mg, *Zingiber officinalis* (sheng jiang, ginger) 8mg

Pattern identifying features

- **Spleen Damp & *qi* stagnation;
  Spleen deficiency**
- poor appetite
- reduced sense of taste
- early satiety

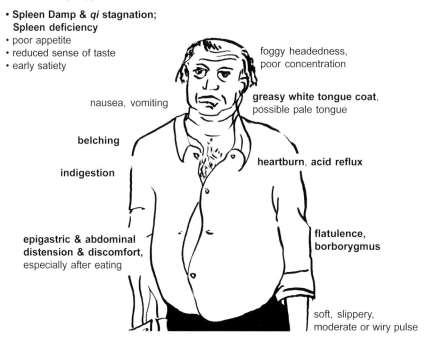

nausea, vomiting

foggy headedness,
poor concentration

greasy white tongue coat,
possible pale tongue

belching

heartburn, **acid reflux**

indigestion

**epigastric & abdominal
distension & discomfort**,
especially after eating

**flatulence,
borborygmus**

soft, slippery,
moderate or wiry pulse

Combinations
- With **2.26 Xiang Lian Wan** for acid reflux from Liver and Stomach *qi* stagnation
  with Spleen deficiency.
- With **2.27 Wei Te Ling** for severe hyperacidity.
- With **6.3 Chai Hu Shu Gan Wan** when there is a significant emotional
  component and obvious Liver *qi* stagnation.
- With **2.23 Ping Wei San** for patients with severe Dampness.
- With **8.11 Jian Nao Yi Zhi Capsule** for mental cloudiness.

Dosage and method of administration
8-12 pills three times daily, on an empty stomach. The dose may be spread out, or
two lots of 12-18 pills may be taken, morning and evening. In severe cases or during
the early stages of treatment (the first few weeks), a 50% increase in dose may be
used, then reduced as the treatment takes effect.

Cautions and contraindications
Not suitable for indigestion from Heat or Phlegm Heat in the Stomach.

GIT

2.11 BU ZHONG YI QI WAN

补中益气丸

Lanzhou Foci Pharmaceutical Factory (Gansu)
'Supplement the Middle and Benefit *qi* Pills'
Bu Zhong Yi Qi Wan is packaged in bottles of 200 pills.
Also available as: Central Chi Teapills (PF), Tonify the Middle
Formula (JD), Tonify the Middle and Qi Pill (BE)

TRADE MARK

BU ZHONG YI QI WAN

AUSTL 60713

200 PILLS

LANZHOU FOCI PHARMACEUTICAL FACTORY
LANZHOU CHINA

TCM actions
Supplements *qi* and strengthens the Spleen, Lung and *wei qi*, elevates the *yang* energy of the body.

Biomedical actions
Tonic, digestive stimulant, elevates and tones weakened or prolapsed structures, stimulates and protects the immune system.

INDICATIONS

• Spleen and Lung *qi* deficiency patterns with sinking *qi*. Improves muscle tone, elevates *yang qi* and lifts prolapsed organs; used for conditions where poor muscle tone and weak *qi* that is unable to resist the pull of gravity leads to various types of prolapse, including the eyelid (ptosis), hemorrhoids, rectum, uterus and bladder. Used for poor tone and weakness of smooth and skeletal muscles. Strengthens the Spleen and elevates *qi* to alleviate chronic diarrhea, recurrent miscarriage and bleeding disorders.

• Excellent for strengthening *wei qi* and boosting the immune system in those prone to frequent colds or infection, chronic fatigue syndrome and post-viral syndrome (of a pure deficiency type; for mixed patterns *see* **6.1 Xiao Chai Hu Tang Wan**).

• Protects and stimulates the immune system and bone marrow in patients undergoing chemotherapy or radiotherapy.

• Used for recurrent low grade fevers that occur in the morning, following exertion or when fatigued.

• With the appropriate identifying features, this formula may assist in the treatment of biomedical conditions such as first or second degree prolapse of the uterus, bladder or rectum, incompetent cervix, immune weakness, recurrent miscarriage, functional uterine bleeding, postpartum urinary incontinence, hypotension, hypoglycemia, post viral syndrome, chronic hepatitis, corneal ulcers, pernicious anemia, leucopenia, fever of unknown origin, myasthenia gravis and multiple sclerosis.

Pattern identifying features

- **Spleen & Lung *qi* deficiency with sinking *qi***
- **fatigue, debility**
- **immune weakness, frequent colds or infections**
- weakness, lack of vitality
- low grade fever
- symptoms initiated or aggravated when fatigued or with exertion

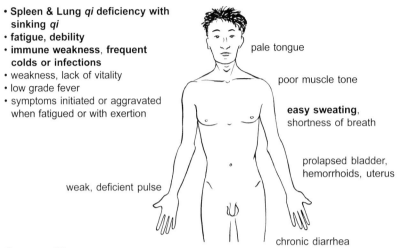

pale tongue

poor muscle tone

easy sweating, shortness of breath

prolapsed bladder, hemorrhoids, uterus

weak, deficient pulse

chronic diarrhea

Composition (each pill contains powdered)

Astragalus membranaceous (huang qi, astragalus) 42mg, *Glycyrrhiza uralensis* (gan cao, licorice) 21mg, *Codonopsis pilosula* (dang shen, codonopsis) 12.5mg, *Angelica sinensis* (dang gui) 12.5mg, *Atractylodes macrocephala* (bai zhu, atractylodes) 12.5mg, *Bupleurum falcatum* (chai hu, bupleurum) 12.5mg, *Cimicifuga foetida* (sheng ma, cimicifuga) 12.5mg, *Citrus reticulata* (chen pi, citrus) 12.5mg, *Zizyphus jujuba* (da zao, chinese dates) 5.6mg, *Zingiber officinalis* (sheng jiang, ginger) 2.8mg

Combinations

- With **7.26 Reishi Mushroom** as an adjunct to chemotherapy or radiotherapy.
- With **7.9 Fu Gui Ba Wei Wan** for prolapses with a degree of Kidney deficiency.

Dosage and method of administration

8-12 pills three times daily on an empty stomach. The dose may be taken in two lots of 12-18 pills, morning and evening. In severe cases or during the early stages of treatment (the first few weeks), a 50% increase in dose may be used, then reduced as the treatment takes effect. A double or treble dose is recommended for patients having chemotherapy or radiotherapy.

Cautions and contraindications

Contraindicated during the early phase of acute illness such as colds and flu or any other acute infection. This formula has an elevating tendency and in some patients can cause headaches and nausea. Some patients with Spleen deficiency (and hidden Damp) patterns may find symptoms initially aggravate while taking **2.11 Bu Zhong Yi Qi Wan**. A few weeks of **2.1 Xing Jun San** or **2.2 Huo Hsiang Cheng Chi Pien** may be used first to clear the Damp.

GIT

2.12 SHEN LING BAI ZHU WAN

参苓白术丸

Lanzhou Foci Pharmaceutical Factory (Gansu)
'Ginseng, Poria and Atractylodes Pills'
Shen Ling Bai Zhu Wan is packaged in bottles of 200 pills.
Also available in dissolvable granule form as: Absorbtion and
Digesion Pill (BE), Shen Ling Bai Zhu Pian (PF)

TCM actions
Supplements *qi* and strengthens the Spleen, transforms
and leaches out Dampness, stops diarrhea.

Biomedical actions
Tonic, stimulant, strengthens digestive function and absorption of fluids and
nutrients.

INDICATIONS

- Spleen *qi* deficiency with Dampness causing chronic loose stools or diarrhea.
  Also treats diarrhea associated with consumption of uncooked or otherwise
  hard to digest food and diarrhea during pregnancy or that precedes or
  accompanies menstruation. Also used to alleviate the diarrhea that complicates
  Spleen weakening orthodox therapy for chronic infection, such as antibiotics,
  anti-retroviral agents and protease inhibitors.

- Helps to regulate digestive function, insulin and blood glucose metabolism. Can
  be used for both high and low blood glucose problems.

- Copious watery or mucoid leukorrhea in Spleen deficient women (who are often
  overweight and edematous).

- Excellent to strengthen pale children over 5 years old (*see* **12.1 Bo Ying
  Compound** or **12.6 Healthy Child Tea** for children under 5), who tend to be
  picky eaters, prone to loose stools or chronic diarrhea, are underweight and
  lacking vitality.

- Indeterminate gnawing hunger (*see* glossary) from Spleen and Stomach *qi* and *yin*
  deficiency. This is a well balanced formula which gently strengthens Spleen *qi*
  and leaches out Dampness without drying and damaging *yin*.

- With the appropriate identifying features, this formula may be used to treat
  disorders such as chronic gastroenteritis, chronic colitis, gastritis, peptic ulcer
  disease, malabsorption syndrome, leaky gut syndrome, malnutrition,
  hypoglycemia, diabetes mellitus, chronic nephritis, coeliac disease and anemia.

Pattern identifying features

- **Spleen *qi* deficiency with Dampness & diarrhea**
- nausea, vomiting
- loss of appetite
- weight loss
- fatigue

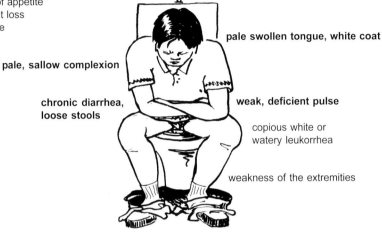

pale swollen tongue, white coat

pale, sallow complexion

chronic diarrhea, loose stools

weak, deficient pulse

copious white or watery leukorrhea

weakness of the extremities

Composition (each pill contains powdered)

Codonopsis pilosula (dang shen, codonopsis) 24mg, *Poria cocos* (fu ling, hoelen) 24mg, *Atractylodes macrocephala* (bai zhu, atractylodes) 24mg, *Dioscorea officinalis* (shan yao, dioscorea) 24mg, *Nelumbus speciosum* (lian zi, lotus seed) 16mg, *Coicis lachryma-jobi* (yi ren, coix) 14.4mg, *Dolichos lablab* (bian dou, hyacinth bean) 14.4mg, *Platycodon grandiflorum* (jie geng, platycodon) 9.6mg, *Glycyrrhiza uralensis* (gan cao, licorice) 4.8mg, *Amomum villosum* (sha ren, cardamon) 4.8mg

Combinations

- With **4.14 Chin So Ku Ching Wan** or **4.2 Wu Ling San Wan** for incessant diarrhea.
- With **2.23 Ping Wei San** or **4.5 Bi Xie Fen Qing Wan** for copious Cold Damp leukorrhea.
- With **4.2 Wu Ling San Wan** for pathological fluid accumulation and edema.

Dosage and method of administration

8-12 pills three times daily on an empty stomach. The dose may be spread out, or two lots of 12-18 pills may be taken, morning and evening. In severe cases or during the early stages of treatment (the first few weeks), a 50% increase in dose may be used, then reduced as the treatment takes effect.

Cautions and contraindications

Contraindicated during the early phase of acute illness such as colds and flu. Avoid all cold raw foods and dairy products while using this formula.

GIT

2.13 LI ZHONG WAN

理中丸

Lanzhou Foci Pharmaceutical Factory (Gansu)
'Regulate the Middle *Jiao* Pills'
Li Zhong Wan is packaged in bottles of 200 pills.

TCM actions
Supplements, strengthens and warms Spleen and Stomach *yang*, dispels Cold, relieves *tai yin* syndrome.

Biomedical actions
Tonic, digestive stimulant, strengthens digestive function.

INDICATIONS

- Spleen *yang* deficiency. Excellent for chronic digestive weakness and hypofunction with signs of cold. Particularly good for incessant abdominal distension, loss of appetite and persistent, frequent diarrhea. The diarrhea is characteristically watery, with undigested food material, and may wake the patient from sleep in the early hours of the morning. Also known as cockcrow or fifth watch diarrhea. All symptoms are aggravated by ingestion of cold or raw foods and iced fluids.
- Strengthens the Spleen and fluid metabolism, dries Dampness and transforms thin Phlegm to treat productive cough and chronic respiratory weakness with copious thin watery sputum. Also used for chronic drooling or hypersalivation.
- Chronic Spleen *yang* deficiency bleeding, particularly uterine bleeding, menorrhagia and rectal bleeding.
- Chronic or recurrent mouth ulcers of a cold or *yang* deficient type.
- Chronic childhood convulsions in a cold emaciated child.
- Can also be used for acute vomiting and diarrhea (a type of Sudden Turmoil Disorder, *see* glossary), that causes rapid deterioration and damage to *yang qi*.
- With the appropriate identifying features, this formula may be used to treat disorders such as chronic gastroenteritis, chronic colitis, chronic dysentery, gastritis, peptic ulcer disease, malabsorption syndromes, leaky gut syndrome, cholera, chronic bleeding disorders, apthous ulcer, oral herpes, irritable bowel syndrome and chronic bronchitis.

Composition
Codonopsis pilosula (dang shen, codonopsis) 40mg, *Zingiber officinale* (gan jiang, dry ginger) 40mg, *Atractylodes macrocephala* (bai zhu, atractylodes) 40mg, *Glycyrrhiza uralensis* (gan cao, licorice) 40mg

Pattern identifying features

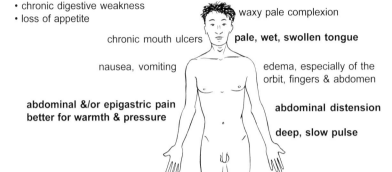

- **Spleen *yang* deficiency**
- fatigue, exhaustion
- chronic digestive weakness
- loss of appetite

waxy pale complexion

chronic mouth ulcers

pale, wet, swollen tongue

nausea, vomiting

edema, especially of the orbit, fingers & abdomen

abdominal &/or epigastric pain better for warmth & pressure

abdominal distension

deep, slow pulse

chronic uterine or rectal bleeding

chronic diarrhea with undigested food (or chronic atonic constipation)

cold intolerance, cold extremities

GIT

Combinations
- With **7.9 Fu Gui Ba Wei Wan** for Spleen and Kidney *yang* deficiency.
- With **2.33 Cong Rong Bu Shen Wan** for chronic atonic constipation from failure of *yang* movement through the Intestines.
- With **2.26 Xiang Lian Wan** for chronic dysenteric disorder.

Dosage and method of administration
8-12 pills three times daily on an empty stomach. The dose may be spread out, or two lots of 12-18 pills may be taken, morning and evening. In severe cases or during the early stages of treatment (the first few weeks), a 50% increase in dose may be used, then reduced as the treatment takes effect. When used for Sudden Turmoil Disorder, a dose may be taken every 2 hours until the symptoms subside, then discontinued.

Cautions and contraindications
Contraindicated during the early phase of acute illness such as colds and flu. It is essential that patients with Spleen *yang* deficiency patterns minimise or omit any raw or cold natured food from their diet.

2.14 LI CHUNG YUEN MEDICAL PILLS

(Fu Zi Li Zhong Wan)
Chan Li Chai Medical Factory (Hong Kong)
'Aconite Pills to Regulate the Middle'
Li Chung Yuen Medical Pills are packaged as large honey pills sealed in wax balls, 10 pills per box.
Also available as: Aconitum Compound Pills, Fu Tzu Li Chung Wan

TCM actions

Supplements, strengthens and warms Spleen and Stomach *yang*, powerfully dispels Cold, relieves *tai yin* syndrome.

Biomedical action

Tonic, digestive stimulant, strengthens digestive function.

INDICATIONS

- Spleen *yang* deficiency. This is a variation of **2.13 Li Zhong Wan**, with the addition of aconite to increase its *yang* warming and mobilising power. Similar in overall action and indications, but considerably warmer. An excellent formula for a range of chronic digestive problems associated with relatively severe weakness, coldness and hypofunction of the Spleen and Stomach.
- Especially good for chronic diarrhea, loss of appetite or anorexia, relentless abdominal distension, indigestion, severe cold intolerance, cramping abdominal pain that feels better for warmth and pressure, nausea and severe vomiting.
- Chronic respiratory problems with copious thin watery sputum.
- Chronic or recurrent mouth ulcers of a cold deficient type.
- Chronic childhood convulsions resulting from deficient *yang*.
- Can also be used for acute vomiting and diarrhea (a type of Sudden Turmoil disorder, *see* glossary), that causes rapid deterioration and damage to *yang qi*.
- With the appropriate identifying features, this formula may assist in the treatment of biomedical disorders such as chronic gastroenteritis, chronic colitis, chronic dysentery, gastritis, peptic ulcer disease, malabsorption syndromes, leaky gut syndrome, cholera, ascites, apthous ulcer, oral herpes, irritable bowel syndrome and chronic bronchitis.

Composition

Atractylodes macrocephala (bai zhu, atractylodes), *Codonopsis pilosula* (dang shen, codonopsis), *Zingiber officinale* (gan jiang, dry ginger), *Glycyrrhiza uralensis* (gan cao, licorice), *Aconite carmichaeli* (fu zi, aconite)

Pattern identifying features

- **Spleen *yang* deficiency**
- **cold intolerance**
- nausea, vomiting
- loss of appetite

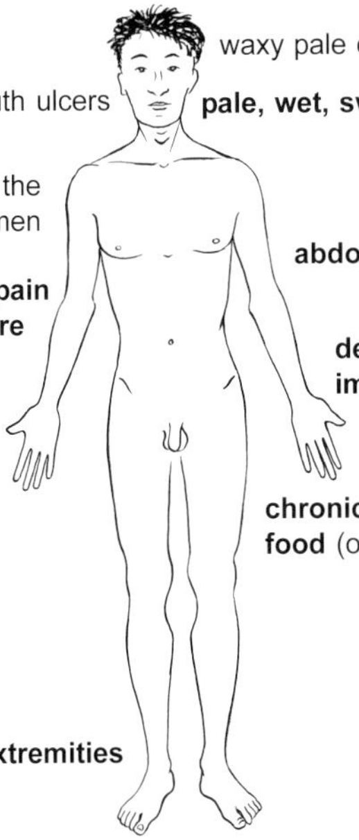

waxy pale complexion

chronic mouth ulcers

pale, wet, swollen tongue

edema, especially of the
orbit, fingers & abdomen

abdominal distension

**abdominal &/or epigastric pain
better for warmth & pressure**

**deep, slow or
imperceptible pulse**

**chronic diarrhea with undigested
food** (or chronic atonic constipation)

cold extremities

GIT

Combinations
- With **4.2 Wu Ling San Wan** for significant fluid retention.
- With **3.41 Xu Han Ting** for continuous sweating from deficient *yang*.

Dosage and method of administration
One or two pills per day, with warm water or ginger tea on an empty stomach. In general, two pills per day should be used at the start of treatment. These pills are often very hard and need to be softened in hot water before ingestion.

Once the patient begins to warm up the dose can be reduced. Be careful not to overheat the patient as this formula is very warming.

Cautions and contraindications
Contraindicated during pregnancy and during the early phase of acute illness such as colds and flu. This formula is hot and drying, and not suitable for any Heat pattern, or false Cold, true Heat pattern.

GMP ## 2.15 XIAO JIAN ZHONG WAN

 # 小建中丸

Available in the US, UK and Europe
See Note 1, p.xxi

Lanzhou Foci Pharmaceutical Factory (Gansu)
'Minor Strengthen the Middle [*Jiao*] Pills'
Xiao Jian Zhong Wan is packaged in bottles of 200 pills.
Available as: Minor Restore the Middle Teapills (PF)

TCM actions
Warms the Spleen and Stomach, supplements *qi*, alleviates abdominal spasm and pain.

Biomedical actions
Antispasmodic, digestive and energy stimulant.

INDICATIONS

• Spleen and Stomach *qi* and/or *yang* deficiency with Cold accumulation type epigastric and abdominal colicky pain. As a variation of **3.6 Gui Zhi Wan**, with the simple addition of malt sugar and increased proportion of white peony, the focus of this formula is shifted to warming and strengthening the digestive system and alleviating spasmodic pain. The pain tends to be dull and persistent, or colicky, initiated or aggravated by cold raw or hard to digest foods.
• As a gentle formula it is suitable for prolonged use and is popular for pale weak thin children with poor appetite and listlessness.
• Low grade fever associated with *yang* deficiency. This type of fever tends to be more apparent early in the day and is initiated or aggravated when the patient is overtired or fatigued.
• Assist convalescence in patients with Spleen *qi* deficiency, those recovering from a major illness or abdominal surgery.
• With the appropriate identifying features, this formula may be used to treat biomedical disorders such as gastric and duodenal ulcers, chronic atrophic gastritis, chronic hepatitis, chronic peritonitis, anemia, and fever of unknown origin.

Composition
Saccharum Granorum (yi tang, malt sugar) 35%, *Paeonia lactiflora* (bai shao, white peony) 21%, *Zizyphus jujuba* (da zao, chinese dates) 14%, *Cinnamomum cassia* (gui zhi, cinnamon twigs) 10%, *Zingiber officinale* (sheng jiang, ginger) 10%, *Glycyrrhiza uralensis* (zhi gan cao, honey fried licorice) 7%

Pattern identifying features

- **Spleen & Stomach *qi* &/or *yang* deficiency**
- possible low grade morning fevers
- drooling, hypersalivation

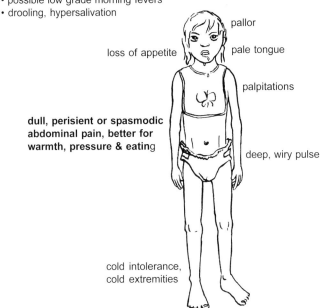

loss of appetite

pallor

pale tongue

palpitations

dull, perisient or spasmodic abdominal pain, better for warmth, pressure & eating

deep, wiry pulse

cold intolerance, cold extremities

GIT

Combinations
- With **10.22 Shao Yao Gan Cao Wan** for severe colicky pain.
- With **7.22 Shen Qi Da Bu Wan** for more severe *qi* deficiency.

Dosage and method of administration
8-12 pills, three times daily on an empty stomach. For children, reduce the dose by half to one third. The pills can also be crushed up, decocted and delivered as a slurry in an eye-dropper for children.

Cautions and contraindications
Contraindicated in *yin* deficiency patterns, *yin* deficient fevers and internal Heat patterns.

2.16 ZI SHENG WAN

資生丸

Lanzhou Foci Pharmaceutical Factory (Gansu)
'Aid Life Pills'
Zi Sheng Wan is packaged in bottles of 200 pills.
Also available as: Zi Sheng Stomachic Pills

TCM actions

Supplements Spleen *qi*, moves stagnant *qi*, dispels
Dampness, alleviates food stagnation, harmonises the
Stomach, stops diarrhea.

Biomedical actions

Tonic, digestive stimulant, improves digestive function and absorption of nutrients,
stomachic.

INDICATIONS

- Spleen deficiency and lingering Damp Heat in the Intestine type relapsing
  Dysenteric disorder. The patient will typically have had an acute gastric infection
  that has never been completely cleared and flares up when the patient is run
  down.
- Chronic diarrhea from Spleen deficiency with food stagnation. Also useful for
  the chronic diarrhea that occurs as a side effect of antibiotics, HIV anti-retroviral
  treatment or chemotherapy.
- Used for children over 5 years old with Spleen weakness, chronic diarrhea, poor
  appetite and lack of vitality. *See* **12.1 Bo Ying Compound** or **12.6 Healthy
  Child Tea** for children under 5.
- General digestive weakness with elements of Spleen deficiency and food
  stagnation.
- Morning sickness in Spleen *qi* deficient women with *qi* stagnation. Also threatened
  miscarriage from the same etiology.

Composition (each pill contains powdered)

Coix lachryma-jobi (yi ren, coix) 27.3mg, *Codonopsis pilosula* (dang shen, codonopsis)
21mg, *Atractylodes macrocephala* (bai zhu, atractylodes) 21mg, *Citrus reticulata* (chen pi,
citrus) 20.3mg, *Crategus pinnatifida* (shan zha, crategus) 20.3mg, *Dioscorea opposita*
(shan yao, dioscorea) 10.6mg, *Euryale ferox* (qian shi, euryale seed) 10.6mg, *Poria cocos*
(fu ling, hoelen) 10.6mg, *Glycyrrhiza uralensis* (gan cao, licorice) 9.7mg, *Dolichos lablab*

Pattern identifying features

- **Spleen *qi* deficiency with lingering Dampness & food stagnation**
- **morning sickness**
- fatigue
- weakness of the extremities
- weight loss

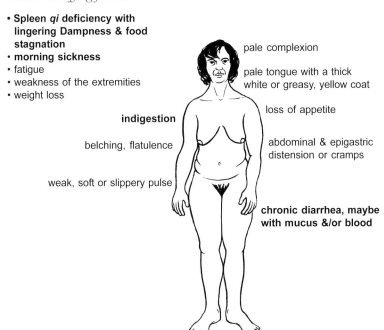

pale complexion

pale tongue with a thick white or greasy, yellow coat

loss of appetite

indigestion

belching, flatulence

abdominal & epigastric distension or cramps

weak, soft or slippery pulse

chronic diarrhea, maybe with mucus &/or blood

GIT

(bian dou, hyacinth bean) 7mg, *Nelumbus nucifera* (lian zi, lotus seed) 7mg, *Platycodon grandiflorum* (jie geng, platycodon) 3.5mg, *Pogostemon cablin* (huo xiang, agastache) 3.5mg, *Alisma orientale* (ze xie, alisma) 2.5mg, *Alpinia katsumadai* (cao dou kou, katsumadai cardamon) 2.5mg, *Coptis chinensis* (huang lian, coptis) 2.5mg

Dosage and method of administration

8-12 pills three times daily on an empty stomach. The dose may be spread out, or two lots of 12-18 pills may be taken, morning and evening. In severe cases or during the early stages of treatment (the first few weeks), a 50% increase in dose may be used, then reduced as the treatment takes effect.

Cautions and contraindications

Contraindicated during the early phase of acute illness such as colds and flu. Not suitable for acute gastroenteritis (*see* **2.1 Xing Jun San** or **2.2 Huo Hsiang Cheng Chi Pien**). The patient should avoid all cold natured or raw foods.

2.17 JIAN PI WAN

健脾丸

Lanzhou Foci Pharmaceutical Factory (Gansu)
'Strengthen the Spleen Pills'
Jian Pi Wan is packaged in bottles of 200 pills.
Also available as: Ginseng Stomachic Pills, Spleen Digest Aid Pill
(BE)

TCM actions
Alleviates food stagnation, strengthens the Spleen and
Stomach.

Biomedical actions
Enhances digestive functions, digestant, carminative, stomachic.

INDICATIONS

- Food stagnation with Spleen and Stomach deficiency. This formula is similar to **2.18 Bao He Wan** in its general action, with the main focus of this formula equally balanced between strengthening the Spleen and alleviating food stagnation. It is thus more suited to chronic cases of food stagnation complicated by digestive weakness.
- Heartburn and indigestion in late pregnancy.
- With the appropriate identifying features, this formula can be used to treat biomedical conditions such as chronic gastritis, peptic ulcer disease, chronic indigestion, dyspepsia, irritable bowel syndrome, autonomic dysfunction of the gastrointestinal tract, chronic colitis and Crohn's disease.

Composition (each pill contains powdered)
Citrus aurantium (zhi shi, aurantium) 22.1mg, *Codonopsis pilosula* (dang shen, codonopsis) 14.7mg, *Atractylodes macrocephala* (bai zhu, atractylodes) 14.7mg, *Crategus pinnatifida* (shan zha, crategus) 11mg, *Citrus reticulata* (chen pi, citrus) 14.7mg.
Note: There are several versions of this formula from the same factory, each with the same function and indications, but with minor variations in composition. Other herbs that may appear include *Hordeum vulgare* (mai ya, sprouted barley), *Coicis lachryma-jobi* (yi ren, coix) and *Amomum cardamomum* (bai dou kou, amomum).

Combinations
- With **2.22 Er Chen Wan** for severe rising *qi* causing nausea and vomiting.

Pattern identifying features

- **Spleen *qi* deficiency with food stagnation**
- gradual loss of appetite, or decrease in the amount of food that can be consumed before feeling bloated.
- fatigue

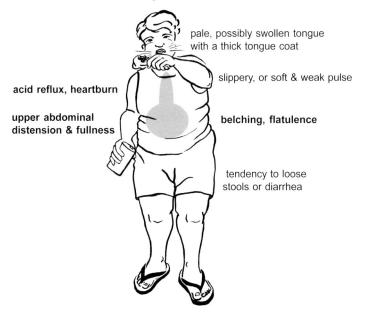

pale, possibly swollen tongue with a thick tongue coat

slippery, or soft & weak pulse

acid reflux, heartburn

upper abdominal distension & fullness

belching, flatulence

tendency to loose stools or diarrhea

GIT

- With **2.23 Ping Wei San** for patients with more Dampness and a very thick tongue coat.
- In small doses with any 'rich' supplementing formula that causes digestive upset.

Dosage and method of administration
8-12 pills three times daily on an empty stomach. In severe cases or during the early stages of treatment (the first few weeks), a 50% increase in dose may be used, then reduced to a maintenance dose as the condition settles down and the patient regulates his or her diet.

Cautions and Contraindications
Formulae that contain *Hordeum vulgare* (mai ya, sprouted barley) should be avoided while breast-feeding as this herb can reduce milk production.

2.18 BAO HE WAN

保和丸

Lanzhou Foci Pharmaceutical Factory (Gansu)
'Preserve Harmony Pills'
Bao He Wan is packaged in bottles of 200 pills.
Also available as: Preserve Harmony Pill (BE)

TCM actions
Alleviates food stagnation, harmonises the Stomach.

Biomedical actions
Enhances digestive functions, especially absorption of nutrients, digestant, carminative, stomachic.

INDICATIONS

• Acute or chronic indigestion, dyspepsia and gastric hyperacidity associated with food stagnation. This pattern is primarily related to overindulgence, excess food intake relative to energy output or irregular eating habits, such as eating too late at night, missing meals or eating while working or when stressed. *See* the glossary for more detail on food stagnation. Used for both acute episodes and chronic patterns of food stagnation.

• May be useful as an adjunct therapy for any condition induced by food consumption (often considered to be 'food allergies' or intolerances), such as asthma, skin rashes, sinus congestion, rhinitis and other mucus problems.

• Heartburn and indigestion in late pregnancy.

• For insomnia due to habitual late night snacking (Stomach Heat or Phlegm Heat).

• With the appropriate identifying features, this formula can be used to treat biomedical conditions such as chronic indigestion, dyspepsia, acute and chronic gastritis, peptic ulcer disease, autonomic dysfunction of the gastrointestinal tract and chronic cholecystitis.

Composition (each pill contains powdered)
Crataegus pinnatifida (shan zha, crataegus) 52.5mg, *Pinellia ternata* (ban xia, pinellia) 17.5mg, Massa Fermentata (shen qu) 17.5mg, *Poria cocos* (fu ling, hoelen) 17.5mg, *Hordeum vulgare* (mai ya, sprouted barley) 9.53mg, *Citrus reticulata* (chen pi, citrus) 8.75mg, *Forsythia suspensa* (lian qiao, forsythia) 8.75mg, *Raphanus sativus* (lai fu zi, radish seed) 8.75mg,

Pattern identifying features

- **Food stagnation**
- **indigestion, dyspepsia**
- halitosis

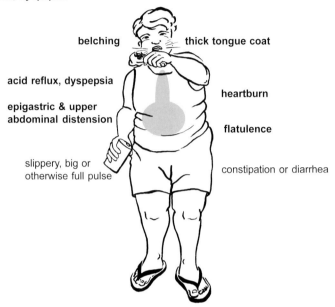

belching

thick tongue coat

acid reflux, dyspepsia

heartburn

epigastric & upper
abdominal distension

flatulence

slippery, big or
otherwise full pulse

constipation or diarrhea

GIT

Combinations
- With **14.2 Huang Lian Su Tablets** for concurrent Stomach Heat.
- With **2.23 Ping Wei San** for severe abdominal distension.
- With **2.26 Xiang Lian Wan** for severe reflux.
- In small doses with any 'rich' supplementing formula that causes digestive upset.

Dosage and method of administration
8-12 pills three times daily before or after a meal. In severe cases a 50% increase in dose may be used, then reduced to a maintenance dose (a few pills before or after a meal) as the condition settles down and the patient regulates his/her diet.

Cautions and Contraindications
Caution in patients with significant deficiency as this formula is quite dispersing to *qi* as well as stagnated food (*see* **2.17 Jian Pi Wan**).

2.19 SHEN CHU CHA

神曲茶

The United Pharmaceutical Manufactory (Guangzhou)
'Medicated Leaven Tea'
Shen Chu Cha is packaged in 38 gram blocks of
herbal material wrapped in paper. Eight blocks to a box.

TCM actions

Dispels Wind Cold and Summerdamp, alleviates food stagnation, regulates the
Spleen and Stomach.

Biomedical actions

Diaphoretic, stomachic, alleviates acute gastric conditions.

INDICATIONS

• This formula is a mixture of diaphoretic, Summerdamp clearing, *qi* moving and
Dampness draining herbs. It is designed to treat Wind Cold *gan mao* during the
humid weather of late Summer when Wind Cold exterior symptoms (chills,
myalgia, no sweating) are accompanied by digestive symptoms like nausea,
vomiting and diarrhea.

• For travellers diarrhea, or the digestive upsets that accompany changes in diet.
Used for biomedical conditions such as stomach flu, food poisoning, acute
gastroenteritis, indigestion, dyspepsia, recovery from hangover and the general
effects of an extended period of overindulgence.

• Often included in digestive formulae (or used to wash them down), to enhance
their resolving and Damp clearing action. Can be used to wash down rich
supplementing formulae in patients prone to digestive upset (especially the
rehmannia formulae).

Composition

Artemesia apiacea (qing hao, artemesia) 4.7%, *Scutellaria baicalensis* (huang qin, scute)
4.7%, *Amomum tsao-ko* (cao guo, tsaoko fruit) 4.7%, *Mosla chinensis* (xiang ru, madder)
4.7%, *Angelica pubescens* (du huo, Tu-huo) 4.7%, *Poria cocos* (fu ling, hoelen) 4.7%,
Glycyrrhiza uralensis (gan cao, licorice) 5%, *Dioscorea villosa* (shan yao, dioscorea) 5%,
Magnolia officinalis (hou po, magnolia bark) 4.7%, *Notopterygium incisum* (qiang huo,
notopterygium) 4.7%, *Citrus reticulata* (qing pi, blue citrus) 4.7%, *Platycodon
grandiflorum* (jie geng, platycodon) 4.7%, *Chaenomeles lagenaria* (mu gua, chinese
quince) 4.7%, *Triticum aestivum* (xiao mai, fermented wheat flour) 38%

Pattern identifying features

- **Summerdamp invasion; food stagnation**
- summer colds
- acute gastric upset

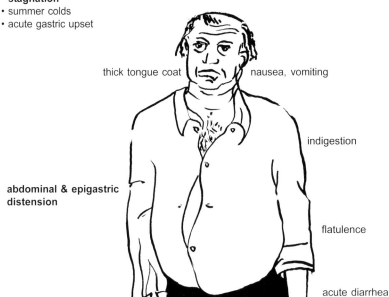

thick tongue coat

nausea, vomiting

indigestion

abdominal & epigastric distension

flatulence

acute diarrhea

GIT

Combinations
- In small doses to wash down any 'rich' supplementing formula that causes digestive upset. For this purpose, several blocks can be brewed at one time and the remainder stored in a plastic container in the fridge.

Dosage and method of administration
Simmer one block of **2.19 Shen Chu Cha** in 2 cups of water and reduce by one third. Discard the dregs and take in two doses. With chills or other signs of Wind Cold, add several thick slices of root ginger before simmering.

Cautions and Contraindications
Not suitable for patients with wheat intolerance or coeliac disease.

2.20 BOJENMI Chinese Tea

保健美

(Bao Jian Mei)
Fujian Provincial Medicines and Health Products.
'Protect Strength and Beauty Tea'
Bojenmi Chinese Tea is packaged in teabags,
twenty bags per box.

TCM actions
Alleviates food stagnation, harmonises the Stomach, promotes urination.

Biomedical actions
Enhances digestive functions, diuretic.

INDICATIONS

- Acute or chronic indigestion, dyspepsia and gastric hyperacidity associated with food stagnation (*see* glossary). This tea can be used as a digestive aid to treat acute and chronic indigestion.
- To improve general digestion, fat and fluid metabolism in those with a tendency to being overweight. In conjunction with an appropriate diet and exercise, **2.20 Bojenmi Chinese Tea** may aid in weight loss and improved absorption and metabolism of food. Can assist in lowering blood lipids and cholesterol.
- Fluid retention and edema from Spleen deficiency. May be useful for some patients with hypertension due to its diuretic action.

Composition
Crategus pinnatifida (shan zha, crategus) 9%, *Hordeum vulgare* (mai ya, sprouted barley) 3.5%, *Citrus reticulata* (chen pi, citrus) 3.5%, *Poria cocos* (fu ling, hoelen) 4%, *Alisma orientalis* (ze xie, alisma) 2.5%, Massa Fermentata (shen qu) 3.5%, *Pharbitis nil* (qian niu zi, pharbitis seed) 3%, *Phaseolus angularis* (chi xiao dou, adzuki bean) 4%, *Raphanus sativus* (lai fu zi, radish seed) 2%, *Prunella vulgaris* (xia ku cao, prunella) 8%, *Cassia tora* (jue ming zi, cassia seed) 3%, *Pogostemon cablin* (huo xiang, agastache) 4%, *Camellia sinensis* (cha ye, tea) 50%

Dosage and method of administration
Steep 1-2 teabags in a coffee mug of boiling water for 5 minutes, four times daily.

Cautions and Contraindications
Contraindicated during pregnancy. Avoid while breast-feeding as this product contains *Hordeum vulgare* (mai ya, sprouted barley), a herb that can reduce milk production.

2.21 KEEP FIT CAPSULE

清脂减肥丸

(Qing Zhi Jian Fei Wan)
Jing Xian Pharmaceutical Co. (Guangzhou)
'Clear Away Fats and Reduce Obesity Pills'
Keep Fit Capsules are packaged in bottles of 36 capsules.

KING TIM

**KEEP FIT
CAPSULE**

AUST L 91202
36 CAPSULES

MADE IN CHINA

TCM actions

Quickens Blood, alleviates food stagnation, transforms Phlegm, supplements *qi* and Blood.

Biomedical actions

Assists in lowering triglycerides and cholesterol, improves processing of fats, diuretic, strengthens digestive function.

INDICATIONS

- In concert with appropriate dietary modifications and a sensible exercise program, this formula may assist in weight loss by improving digestive function and the metabolism of fats.
- High blood cholesterol and triglycerides. This is a modern formulation constructed of herbs with a known action of lowering blood triglycerides and cholesterol.

GIT

Composition (each capsule contains herbal extracts equivalent to)

Crategus pinnatifida (shan zha, crategus) 428mg, *Astragalus membranaceous* (huang qi, astragalus) 285mg, *Salvia miltiorrhiza* (dan shen, salvia) 285mg, *Alisma orientalis* (ze xie, alisma) 285mg, *Panax notoginseng* (tian qi, pseudoginseng) 285mg, *Trichosanthes kirilowi* (tian hua fen, trichosanthes root) 285mg, *Polygonum multiflorum* (he shou wu, ho shou wu) 285mg, *Raphanus sativus* (lai fu zi, radish seed) 285mg, *Nelumbus speciosum* (he ye, lotus leaf) 142mg, *Panax ginseng* (ren shen, ginseng) 24mg

Dosage and method of administration

2 capsules, three times daily, 20 minutes before meals.

Cautions and contraindications

Contraindicated during pregnancy. Caution in patients who are also taking anticoagulant therapy (aspirin, warfarin, coumarin) as clotting time can be significantly reduced.

2.22 ER CHEN WAN

二陈丸

Lanzhou Foci Pharmaceutical Factory (Gansu)
'Two Aged Ingredients Pills'
Er Chen Wan is packaged in bottles of 200 pills.
Also available as: Pinellia Pachyma Pills, Erh Chen Wan

TCM actions
Dries Dampness and transforms Phlegm, regulates *qi*,
harmonizes the middle *jiao*.

Biomedical actions
Mucolytic, expectorant, anti-emetic.

INDICATIONS

- Phlegm Damp accumulation. Especially useful for Phlegm Damp in the gastro-intestinal system and Lungs, but can be used for all chronic mucus problems, regardless of location. **2.22 Er Chen Wan** is the base formula from which all Phlegm Damp resolving formulae are built. Used when Phlegm patterns are not complicated by significant Spleen deficiency (*see* **2.8 Liu Jun Zi Wan** for that problem).
- Common uses include productive cough with copious white sputum, mucus congestion in the ear ('glue ear'), nose and sinuses, and nausea and vomiting from Phlegm Damp accumulation in the Stomach, including morning sickness.
- Dizziness, palpitations and insomnia from Phlegm accumulation in the head and chest. This pattern may occur following an incompletely resolved upper respiratory tract infection, in which the heat has congealed body fluids into Phlegm. May also assist in Ménière's disease of a Phlegm type.
- Phlegm masses and nodules, such as ovarian and breast cysts, thyroid nodules and swollen lymph glands.
- Can be added to any rich supplementing formula to aid its digestion and absorption. Frequently combined with other constitutional formulae when enhanced Phlegm Damp transformation is desired.

Composition (each pill contains powdered)
Pinellia ternata (ban xia, pinellia) 51.5mg, *Citrus reticulata* (chen pi, citrus) 51.5mg,
Poria cocos (fu ling, hoelen) 31mg, *Zingiber officinale* (sheng jiang, ginger) 10.3mg,
Glycyrrhiza uralensis (gan cao, licorice) 15.5mg

Pattern identifying features

- **Phlegm Damp**
- **chronic mucus congestion**
- Phlegm nodules

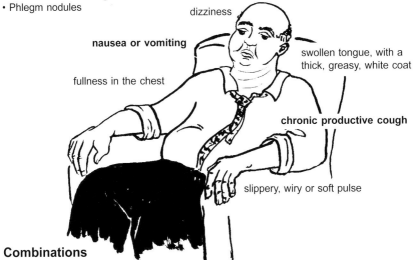

dizziness

nausea or vomiting

swollen tongue, with a thick, greasy, white coat

fullness in the chest

chronic productive cough

slippery, wiry or soft pulse

Combinations

- With **2.9 Xiang Sha Liu Jun Wan** to target the Phlegm in patients with Spleen deficiency and Phlegm Damp patterns. This is usually done in the early stages of treatment when the Phlegm aspects are prominent. As the Phlegm clears the proportion of **2.22 Er Chen Wan** can be reduced or omitted.
- With **1.33 Hai Zao Jing Wan** to enhance the Phlegm resolving effect when treating Phlegm type masses and nodules.
- With **6.1 Xiao Chai Hu Tang Wan** for residual productive cough and swollen glands in the aftermath of an upper respiratory tract infection.
- With **15.4 Tian Ma Gou Teng Wan** for Phlegm and Liver *yang* rising type vertigo (as in Ménière's syndrome).
- In small doses with any 'rich' supplementing formula that causes nausea.

Dosage and method of administration

8-12 pills three times daily on an empty stomach. The dose may be spread out, or two lots of 12-18 pills may be taken, morning and evening. In severe cases or during the early stages of treatment (the first few weeks), a 50% increase in dose may be used, then reduced to a maintenance dose as the Phlegm clears.

Cautions and Contraindications

Contraindicated in cough, nausea from dryness or *yin* deficiency. Not suitable unmodified for constitutionally *yin* deficient patients with Phlegm Damp accumulation. **2.22 Er Chen Wan** is quite drying and may cause dryness and thirst in some patients.

GIT

2.23 PING WEI SAN

平胃散

Lanzhou Foci Pharmaceutical Factory (Gansu)
'Stomach Calming Powder'.
Even though **Ping Wei San** is presented here in pill form, it
retains the name of the original well known form. Packaged in
bottles of 200 pills.
Also available as: Calm Stomach Teapills (PF)

TCM actions
Harmonises the Spleen and Stomach, dries Dampness,
regulates *qi* in the middle *jiao*.

Biomedical actions
Enhances digestive functions, digestant, antispasmodic, carminative, stomachic.

INDICATIONS

* Dampness or Cold Dampness accumulating in the Spleen and Stomach. This
  can be an acute pattern, following invasion of a Damp pathogen directly into
  the digestive system, or a chronic condition due to consumption of an excess of
  Damp producing foods. It can also be the result of poor Spleen function. The
  Dampness disrupts the *qi* mechanism (*see* glossary). *Qi* and Damp accumulate in
  the middle *jiao* causing pronounced distension. Symptoms are often worse first
  thing in the morning or after periods of inactivity as theDampness tends to
  settle and congeal when there is no movement.
* To hasten a reluctant labour.
* With the appropriate identifying features, this formula may be used to treat
  biomedical disorders such as acute and chronic gastroenteritis, chronic gastritis,
  nervous stomach, stomach flu, peptic ulcer disease, narcolepsy and somnolence.

Composition (each pill contains powdered)
Atractylodes lancea (cang zhu, red atractylodes) 48mg, *Magnolia officinalis* (hou po,
magnolia bark) 48mg, *Citrus reticulata* (chen pi, citrus) 32mg, *Zingiber officinale* (sheng
jiang, ginger) 16mg, *Glycyrrhiza uralensis* (gan cao, licorice) 16mg

Combinations
* With **14.1 Huang Lian Jie Du Wan** for Damp Heat in the Stomach.
* With **2.22 Er Chen Wan** for severe nausea.

Pattern identifying features

- **Cold Damp in the middle *jiao***
- heaviness in the body & limbs
- increased desire to sleep
- fatigue & lethargy
- symptoms worse in the morning
- decreased sense of taste

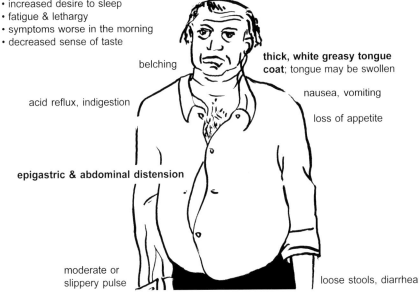

belching

thick, white greasy tongue coat; tongue may be swollen

nausea, vomiting

acid reflux, indigestion

loss of appetite

epigastric & abdominal distension

moderate or slippery pulse

loose stools, diarrhea

GIT

- With **4.2 Wu Ling San Wan** for diarrhea with fluid retention and scanty urine.
- With **6.1 Xiao Chai Hu Tang Wan** for acute infectious disorders characterised by alternating fever and chills, muscle aches, heaviness and lethargy, loss of appetite, nausea and vomiting and a soggy pulse. This is a Damp type of Malarial disorder (*see* glossary).

Dosage and method of administration

8-12 pills three times daily on an empty stomach. The dose may be spread out, or two lots of 12-18 pills may be taken, morning and evening. In severe cases or during the early stages of treatment (the first 7-10 days), a 50% increase in dosage may be used, then reduced to a maintenance dose as the treatment takes effect. To induce labour, use double the recommended dose.

Cautions and Contraindications

Caution during pregnancy (other than when used to induce an overdue labour), and in patients with *yin* and Blood deficiency patterns.

2.24 SHU GAN WAN

舒肝丸

Lanzhou Foci Pharmaceutical Factory (Gansu)
'Soothe the Liver Pills'
Shu Gan Wan is packaged in bottles of 200 pills.
Also available as: Soothe Liver Teapills (PF)

TCM actions

Invigorates Liver *qi* and Blood, breaks up stagnant *qi*, stops pain, harmonises the Liver and Stomach.

Biomedical actions

Antispasmodic, analgesic, benefits digestion, carminative.

INDICATIONS

- Liver *qi* stagnation and Liver invading the Spleen and Stomach patterns with pain as the main feature. The pain in this case may have elements of both *qi* and Blood stagnation–distending, as well as sharp and piercing. **2.24 Shu Gan Wan** can be used for a wide variety of pain conditions, including epigastric, abdominal, chest and hypochondriac pain, intercostal neuralgia, genital pain (*shan qi* and *qi lin* syndrome), fibromyalgia and chronic muscular pain.
- Useful for indigestion, dyspepsia, reflux and indeterminate gnawing hunger from Liver and Stomach disharmony.
- With the appropriate identifying features, this formula may be used to treat biomedical conditions such as peptic ulcer disease, chronic gastritis, nervous stomach, chronic cholecystitis, chronic hepatitis, gallstones, chronic pancreatitis, ulcerative colitis, Crohn's disease, irritable bowel syndrome, early hepatic cirrhosis, costochondritis, biliary and esophageal spasm, post herpetic neuralgia and intercostal neuralgia.

Composition (each pill contains powdered)

Cyperus rotundus (xiang fu, cyperus) 17mg, *Paeonia lactiflora* (bai shao, white peony) 17mg, *Amomum cardamomum* (bai dou kou, amomum) 14.9mg, *Paeonia suffruticosa* (mu dan pi, peony root bark) 11.3mg, *Citrus reticulata* (chen pi, citrus) 11.3mg, *Bupleurum falcatum* (chai hu, bupleurum) 11.3mg, *Citrus aurantium* (zhi shi, aurantium) 11.3mg, *Magnolia officinalis* (hou po, magnolia bark) 11.3mg, *Corydalis turtschaninovii* (yan hu suo, corydalis) 11.3mg, *Saussurea costus* (mu xiang, saussurea) 5.7mg, *Glycyrrhiza uralensis* (gan cao, licorice) 5.7mg, *Citrus medica* (xiang yuan, citron) 5.7mg, *Curcuma longa* (yu jin, curcuma) 4.2mg, *Aquilaria agallocha* (chen xiang, aquilaria) 3.5mg, *Santalum album* (tan xiang, sandalwood) 2.8mg

Pattern identifying features

- **Liver *qi* stagnation invading the Spleen & Stomach**
- **symptoms worse with emotion or stress**
- **pain syndromes**
- indigestion, nervous stomach
- wiry or paradoxical pulse
- irritability, easily angered

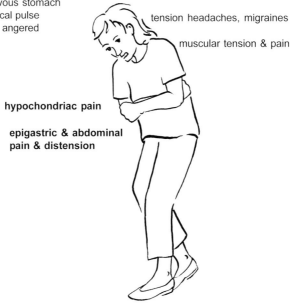

tension headaches, migraines

muscular tension & pain

hypochondriac pain

epigastric & abdominal pain & distension

GIT

Combinations
- With **2.26 Xiang Lian Wan** for epigastric pain and acid reflux. This combination can also be useful for bleeding and pain associated with ulcerative colitis and Crohn's disease.
- With **1.12 Shi Xiao Wan** or **5.7 Sunho Multi Ginseng Tablets** for concurrent Blood stagnation.
- With **6.11 Li Dan Tablets** or **6.10 Qing Gan Li Dan Tablets** for hypochondriac pain from gallstones.
- With **10.21 Yan Hu Suo Wan** for severe pain.

Dosage and method of administration
8-12 pills three times daily on an empty stomach. The dose may be spread out, or two lots of 12-18 pills may be taken, morning and evening. In severe cases or during the early stages of treatment, a 50% increase in dosage may be used, then reduced to a maintenance dose as the patient improves.

Cautions and Contraindications
Contraindicated during pregnancy.

GMP **2.25 TONG XIE YAO FANG WAN**

痛泻要方

Available in the US, UK and Europe See Note 1, p.xxi

Lanzhou Foci Pharmaceutical Factory (Gansu)
'Important Formula [Pills] for Painful Diarrhea'
Tong Xie Yao Wan is packaged in bottles of 200 pills.
Available as: Calm Wind Teapills (PF)

TCM actions

Harmonises the Liver and Spleen, strengthens the Spleen, softens the Liver and spreads Liver *qi*, eases spasm, stops pain and diarrhea.

Biomedical actions

Antispasmodic, carminative, benefits digestion.

INDICATIONS

- Liver invading the Spleen type diarrhea and abdominal pain. This pattern is also known as Wood overcontrolling Earth. The pathology at the basis of this pattern is very common, and involves the physiological response of the body to prolonged, repeated or severe emotional and psychological stress. Patients prone to this pattern tend to be easily stressed or under significant pressure. The key feature is the relationship of the main symptoms (cramping abdominal pain followed by explosive diarrhea, after which the pain subsides) to the emotional state of the patient. The pattern tends to be chronic and recurrent, exacerbating in tandem with the stress levels of the patient.
- This formula is very effective at dealing with the smooth muscle spasm in the gastrointestinal tract while gently harmonising the relationship between the Liver and Spleen. As its focus is primarily at the level of the symptoms, **2.25 Tong Xie Yao Fang Wan** is often combined with an appropriate constitutional formula to enhance the systemic *qi* regulating treatment.
- With the appropriate identifying features, this formula may be used to treat the diarrhea predominant presentation of irritable bowel syndrome, colitis and the general effects of stress on the gastro-intestinal tract.

Composition

Paeonia lactiflora (bai shao, white peony) 40%, *Atractylodes macrocephala* (chao bai zhu, dry fried atractylodes) 29%, *Citrus reticulata* (chen pi, citrus) 19%, *Ledebouriella divaricata* (fang feng, siler) 9%

Pattern identifying features

- **Liver *qi* invading the Spleen**
- symptoms worse with emotional upset & stress
- irritable bowel syndrome

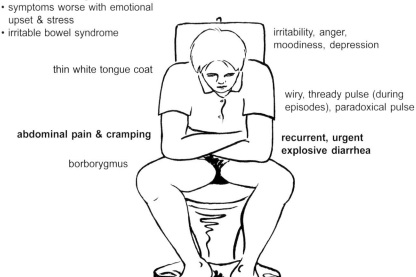

thin white tongue coat

irritability, anger, moodiness, depression

wiry, thready pulse (during episodes), paradoxical pulse

abdominal pain & cramping

borborygmus

recurrent, urgent explosive diarrhea

Combinations

- With **6.3 Chai Hu Shu Gan Wan** for Liver invading the Spleen patterns and irritable bowel syndrome in robust patients with little or no deficiency.
- With **6.4 Xiao Yao Wan** for Liver invading the Spleen patterns and irritable bowel syndrome in patients with Blood and *qi* deficiency.
- With **2.18 Bao He Wan** when there is significant abdominal distension and indigestion.
- With a degree of Damp Heat accumulation in the Large Intestine (the Primary Pathological Triad, *see* glossary), manifesting in a greasy yellow coat on the root of the tongue, a slippery pulse, tenesmus and burning diarrhea, combine with a small dose of **14.1 Huang Lian Jie Du Wan** or **2.30 Chen Xiang Hua Qi Wan**.

Dosage and method of administration

8-12 pills three times daily on an empty stomach. The dose may be spread out, or two lots of 12-18 pills may be taken, morning and evening. In severe cases or during the early stages of treatment, a 50% increase in dosage may be used, then reduced to a maintenance dose as the patient improves.

Cautions and Contraindications

None noted.

GIT

2.26 XIANG LIAN WAN
香连丸

Lanzhou Foci Pharmaceutical Factory (Gansu)
'Saussurea and Coptis Pills'
Xiang Lian Wan is packaged in bottles of 200 pills.
Also available as: Aucklandia and Coptis Teapills (PF)

TCM actions
Clears Toxic Heat, transforms Dampness, directs Stomach
qi downwards, regulates *qi*, harmonises the Stomach.

Biomedical actions
Alleviates indigestion, antacid, eases the intestines.

INDICATIONS

- Dysenteric disorder (*see* glossary) from accumulation of Damp Heat in the Large
  Intestine. This includes true infection (bacterial or amoebic dysentery, giardia,
  etc.), and disorders with blood and/or mucus in the stool, such as ulcerative
  colitis and Crohn's disease.
- Stomach Heat or Fire patterns with heartburn, acid reflux, gastro-esophageal
  reflux and dyspepsia. Very useful as an addition to a suitable constitutional
  formula. The coptis utilised in this formula is traditionally prepared with *Evodia
  rutaecarpae* (wu zhu yu, evodia). When combined, these two herbs are especially
  effective for heartburn.

Composition (each pill contains powdered)
Coptis japonica (huang lian, coptis) 128mg, *Saussurea lappa* (mu xiang, saussurea) 32mg

Combinations
- With **14.1 Huang Lian Jie Du Wan** for tenesmus in Dysenteric disorder arising
  from lingering Damp Heat.
- With **14.5 Chuan Xin Lian Antiphlogistic Tablets** for acute Dysenteric disorder
  or Intestinal abscess.
- With a large dose of **12.3 Baby Fat Powder** or **14.1 Huang Lian Jie Du Wan** for
  amebic dysentery.
- With **2.10 Xiang Sha Yang Wei Wan** for indigestion arising from Stomach *qi*
  stagnation with Damp accumulation.

Pattern identifying features

- **Damp Heat dysenteric disorder**
- Stomach Heat, rebellious Stomach *qi*

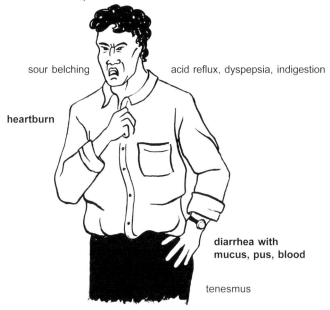

sour belching

acid reflux, dyspepsia, indigestion

heartburn

diarrhea with mucus, pus, blood

tenesmus

GIT

- With **6.3 Chai Hu Shu Gan Wan** or **2.24 Shu Gan Wan** for indigestion and reflux arising from Liver *qi* invading the Stomach. These combinations are also useful for some varieties of ulcerative colitis, Crohn's disease and irritable bowel syndrome.
- With **2.9 Xiang Sha Liu Jun Wan** for indigestion and reflux from Spleen and Stomach *qi* deficiency.

Dosage and method of administration

This pill is usually added to a suitable constitutional formula. The proportion will vary depending on the severity of the symptoms, however a 2:1 ratio of constitutional formula to **2.26 Xiang Lian Wan** is usual. *See also* p.xvii.

Cautions and Contraindications

Caution when used alone for patients with significant Spleen deficiency.

2.27 WEI TE LING

胃特灵

(Wei Te Ling Stomach Sedative)
Qingdao Medicine Works (Shandong)
'Stomach Especially Effective (Medicine)'
Wei Te Ling is packaged in bottles of 120 coated tablets.

TCM actions
Neutralises gastric acid, regulates *qi* and quickens
Blood in the Stomach, stops pain.

Biomedical actions
Antacid, analgesic.

INDICATIONS

- Gastric hyperacidity, acid reflux, heartburn, epigastric pain. May be used alone to provide quick relief from reflux, however it is usually combined with a constitutional formula.
- Can be used to assist in the treatment of peptic ulcers, acute and chronic gastritis and gastro-esophageal reflux disease (GERD).

Composition
Sepia esculenta (wu zei gu, cuttlefish backbone) 40%, *Corydalis turtschaninovii* (yan hu suo, corydalis) 30%, honey 30%

Combinations
- This medicine combines well with any appropriate constitutional formula, for example **6.3 Chai Hu Shu Gan Wan** for hyperacidity from Liver invading the Stomach, or **2.23 Ping Wei San** for accumulation of Phlegm Damp in the Stomach.
- With **2.24 Shu Gan Wan** for acid reflux with severe epigastric pain.
- With **2.10 Xiang Sha Yang Wei Wan** for Spleen and Stomach *qi* stagnation with Damp accumulation.
- With **9.8 Qing Wei Wan** for reflux associated with Heat in the Stomach.

Pattern identifying features

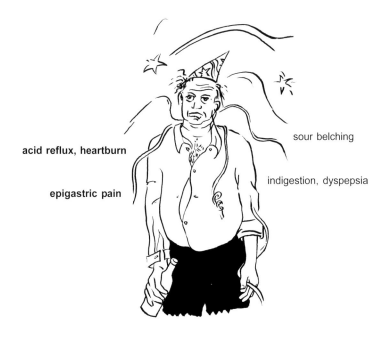

acid reflux, heartburn

sour belching

epigastric pain

indigestion, dyspepsia

Dosage and method of administration

4-6 pills three times daily on an empty stomach or during an episode of heartburn. In severe cases or the early stages of treatment (the first two weeks), the dose may be increased until the patient experiences relief, then reduced to a maintenance dose (a few pills before or after a meal) as the condition settles down.

Cautions and Contraindications

None noted.

2.28 WEI TONG DING

胃痛定

Guanghua Pharmaceutical Co. (Guangzhou)
'Calm Stomach Pain'
Wei Tong Ding is packaged in bottles of 36 tablets.

TCM actions

Warms the middle *jiao*, disperses Cold, regulates *qi* and corrects the *qi* mechanism, stops pain.

Biomedical actions

Analgesic, warms the stomach and assists digestion.

INDICATIONS

- Epigastric and abdominal pain or discomfort associated with accumulation of Cold, Cold and deficiency and/or *qi* stagnation. The pain is typically dull and persistent, and improved with the application of warmth from a hot water bottle or warm drink. If Cold is abundant, however, the pain may be acute, colicky and relatively severe.
- Can also assist in the alleviation of persistent hiccough, excessive salivation and drooling, indigestion, epigastric distension, acid reflux, heartburn, nausea, vomiting, from Cold accumulation or Spleen *qi* or *yang* deficiency.
- With the appropriate identifying features, this formula may assist in the treatment of gastric hyperacidity, dyspepsia, gastric and duodenal ulcers, chronic gastritis, hiccoughs and gastro-esophageal reflux disease (GERD).

Composition (each pill contains powdered)

Aquilaria sinensis (chen xiang, aquilaria) 60mg, *Cinnamomum cassia* (rou gui, cinnamon bark) 20mg, *Piper nigrum* (hu jiao, black pepper) 20mg, *Syzygium aromaticum* (ding xiang, cloves) 20mg, *Amomum villosum* (sha ren, cardamon) 20mg, *Citrus aurantium* (zhi shi, aurantium) 20mg, *Saussurea costus* (mu xiang, saussurea) 20mg, *Panax ginseng* (ren shen, ginseng) 20mg,

Combinations

- With **2.13 Li Zhong Wan** or **2.15 Xiao Jian Zhong Wan** for abdominal pain or hyperacidity from Spleen *yang* deficiency.

Pattern identifying features

- **Cold accumulation in the Stomach, Spleen *qi* / *yang* deficiency**
- vomiting of thin watery fluids
- poor appetite or anorexia
- hiccough
- indigestion, reflux

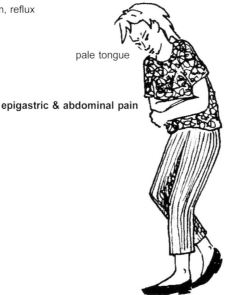

pale tongue

epigastric & abdominal pain

GIT

- With **2.10 Xiang Sha Yang Wei Wan** for *qi* stagnation distension and pain or chronic hiccough.
- With **2.7 Si Jun Zi Wan** for persistent hiccough from Spleen and Stomach *qi* deficiency.

Dosage and method of administration

One tablet, three times daily on an empty stomach.

Cautions and Contraindications

Contraindicated in patients with Stomach Heat, Fire or *yin* deficiency.

2.29 MU XIANG SHUN QI WAN

木香顺气丸

Lanzhou Foci Pharmaceutical Factory (Gansu)
'Saussurea *Qi* Promoting Pills'
Mu Xiang Shun Qi Wan is packaged in bottles of 200 pills.
Also available as: Aplotaxis Carminative Pills, Shun Qi Wan

TCM actions

Moves *qi* in the middle *jiao*, promotes the descent of
Stomach *qi,* relieves food and Damp stagnation.

Biomedical actions

Promotes peristalsis, gentle laxative, antispasmodic.

INDICATIONS

- Liver *qi* stagnation with food and/or Damp stagnation in the Intestines causing abdominal pain, bloating indigestion, flatulence and reflux.
- The main use of this formula is for patients with a tendency to sluggish bowel habits or habitual constipation associated with *qi* stagnation. This typically occurs in stressed and sedentary workers and is usually associated with a slowing down of peristalsis due to hypertonicity in the gastro-intestinal system, with secondary weakness of smooth muscle activity.
- Chronic Dysenteric disorder from lingering Damp Heat and *qi* stagnation, with tenesmus, discomfort preceding a bowel movement and diarrhea with mucus and/or blood.
- With the appropriate identifying features, this formula may be used to treat disorders such as chronic gastritis and colitis, habitual constipation, the constipation predominant presentation of irritable bowel syndrome, dyspepsia, cholecystitis, gallstones, chronic hepatitis and mild ascites.

Composition (each pill contains powdered)

Angelica sinensis (dang gui) 21.6mg, *Magnolia officinalis* (hou po, magnolia bark) 17.3mg, *Saussurea lappa* (mu xiang, saussurea) 13mg, *Alpinia katsumadai* (cao dou kou, katsumadai cardamon) 13mg, *Alpinia oxyphylla* (yi zhi ren, alpinia) 13mg, *Atractylodes lancea* (cang zhu, red atractylodes) 13mg, *Zingiber officinalis* (gan jiang, dried ginger) 8.6mg, *Pinellia ternata* (ban xia, pinellia) 8.6mg, *Evodia rutaecarpae* (wu zhu yu, evodia) 8.6mg, *Alisma orientalis* (ze xie, alisma) 8.6mg, *Citrus reticulata* (qing pi, immature citrus) 8.6mg, *Citrus reticulata* (chen pi, citrus) 8.6mg, *Poria cocos* (fu ling, hoelen)

Pattern identifying features

- **Liver *qi* stagnation with food & Damp stagnation**
- indigestion
- flatulence, belching
- acid reflux, heartburn
- borborygmus
- nausea, vomiting

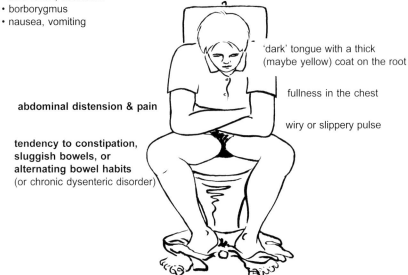

'dark' tongue with a thick (maybe yellow) coat on the root

fullness in the chest

abdominal distension & pain

wiry or slippery pulse

tendency to constipation, sluggish bowels, or alternating bowel habits (or chronic dysenteric disorder)

8.6mg, *Areca catechu* (bing lang, betel nut) 8.6mg, *Bupleurum falcatum* (chai hu, bupleurum) 4.3mg, *Cimicifuga foetida* (sheng ma, cimicifuga) 4.3mg

GIT

Combinations
- With a small dose (2-4 pills each time) of **2.30 Chen Xiang Hua Qi Wan** or **2.33 Da Huang Jiang Zhi Wan** in the early stages of treatment or in resistant cases, until the patient achieves a smooth bowel movement.
- With **2.26 Xiang Lian Wan** to treat chronic Dysenteric disorder from lingering Damp Heat with severe tenesmus.

Dosage and method of administration
Start with 8 pills three times daily on an empty stomach. The dose should be increased until a smooth bowel movement is achieved then reduced to the minimum required to give a result.

Cautions and contraindications
Caution in patients with significant *qi* or *yin* deficiency as this formula is quite dispersing.

2.30 CHEN XIANG HUA QI WAN

沉香化气丸

Lanzhou Foci Pharmaceutical Factory (Gansu)
'Aquilaria *Qi* Transforming Pills'
Chen Xiang Hua Qi Wan is packaged in bottles of 200 pills.
Also available as: Aquilaria Pills, Aquilaria Stomachic Pills

TCM actions

Regulates *qi* and supplements Spleen *qi*, clears Damp Heat, opens the bowels and alleviates food stagnation.

Biomedical actions

Improves digestive function, laxative.

INDICATIONS

• Spleen *qi* deficiency with *qi* blockage type constipation and indigestion. The deficiency leads to failure of Spleen *qi* to rise and Stomach *qi* to descend. *Qi* and incompletely digested food then accumulate in the middle and lower *jiao*. As a result of the accumulation, Damp Heat may be generated. The formula is composed of *qi* supplementing herbs to encourage the elevation of Spleen *qi*, and herbs to direct *qi* downwards and clear Damp Heat. The combination of these opposing actions corrects the *qi* mechanism (*see* glossary), re-establishing the correct flow and transformation of *qi*.

• May also be useful for chronic or recurrent diarrhea from lingering Damp Heat in the Intestines following an incompletely cleared infection. The role of the rhubarb here is to assist the scute in the expulsion of the Damp Heat, while the atractylodes and codonopsis protect the Spleen from further damage.

Composition (each pill contains powdered)

Atractylodes macrocephala (bai zhu, atractylodes) 45.7mg, *Codonopsis pilosula* (dang shen, codonopsis) 45.7mg, *Scutellaria baicalensis* (huang qin, scute) 30.5mg, *Rheum palmatum* (da huang, rhubarb) 30.5mg, *Aquilaria agallocha* (chen xiang, aquilaria) 7.6mg

Combinations

• With **2.29 Mu Xiang Shun Qi Wan** to enhance the laxative affect of that formula in the early stages of treatment.

• With **6.4 Xiao Yao Wan** for a few days before menstruation in women prone to premenstrual constipation.

• With **2.18 Bao He Wan** for severe food stagnation.

Pattern identifying features

- **Spleen *qi* deficiency, Damp Heat in
  the Intestines, obstruction to the *qi*
  mechanism**

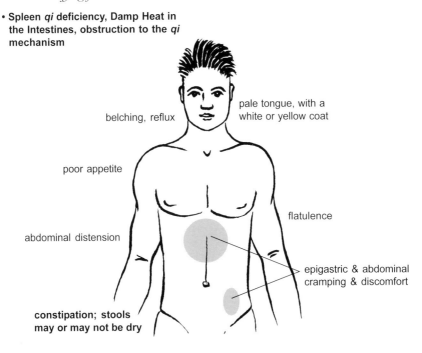

belching, reflux

pale tongue, with a
white or yellow coat

poor appetite

flatulence

abdominal distension

epigastric & abdominal
cramping & discomfort

**constipation; stools
may or may not be dry**

- With **6.3 Chai Hu Shu Gan Wan** for relatively severe *qi* stagnation and Liver
  invading the Spleen. This combination is useful for irritable bowel syndrome
  where constipation is the predominant feature.
- With **2.25 Tong Xie Yao Fang Wan** for cramping abdominal pain with alternating
  constipation and occasional explosive diarrhea from Liver invading the Spleen, with
  Damp Heat in the Intestines (the Primary Pathological Triad, *see* glossary).

Dosage and method of administration

4-8 pills three times daily on an empty stomach. Best to begin with a small dose and
increase it until a smooth bowel movement is achieved. The dose can then be
reduced to the minimum required to keep the bowels moving. Usually combined
with a constitutional formula and gradually withdrawn as the patient improves.
Generally not used for lengthy periods of time as patients can habituate to the
rhubarb. When used for recurrent diarrhea, discontinue once the symptoms subside.

Cautions and contraindications

Contraindicated during pregnancy.

2.31 RUN CHANG WAN

润肠丸

Lanzhou Foci Pharmaceutical Factory (Gansu)
'Lubricate the Intestines Pills'
Run Chang Wan is packaged in bottles of 200 pills.
Also available as: Peach Kernel Teapills (PF), Tao Ren Wan,
Fructus Persica Pills

TCM actions
Moistens and lubricates the bowel, promotes bowel movement.

Biomedical actions
Mild moistening laxative.

INDICATIONS

- Chronic constipation in Blood, fluid or *yin* deficient patients. This commonly occurs in the elderly and postpartum women, or following a febrile disease. Also used for constipation associated with chronic low grade Heat in the Intestines.
- This is a relatively gentle laxative formula, and is commonly added to other primary formulae where a mild laxative action is desired.

Composition (each pill contains powdered)
Prunus persica (tao ren, peach seed) 51.4mg, *Sesamum indicum* (hei zhi ma, black sesame seeds) 51.4mg, *Angelica polymorpha* (dang gui) 25.7mg, *Notopterygium inscisum* (qiang huo, notopterygium) 25.7mg, *Rheum palmatum* (da huang, rhubarb) 25.7mg

Combinations
- With **1.2 Si Wu Wan**, **1.9 Gui Pi Wan** or **1.1 Ba Zhen Wan** for postpartum or Blood deficiency type constipation.
- With **1.23 Zhi Bai Ba Wei Wan** or **8.1 Tian Wang Bu Xin Dan** for constipation in the elderly with a tendency to heat and dryness.

Dosage and method of administration
Usually start with a small dose (4 pills 2-3 times daily) and gradually increase until a smooth bowel movement is achieved. Once a satisfactory dose is found, it can be

Pattern identifying features

- **Dry Intestines; Blood,
  yin, fluid deficiency**

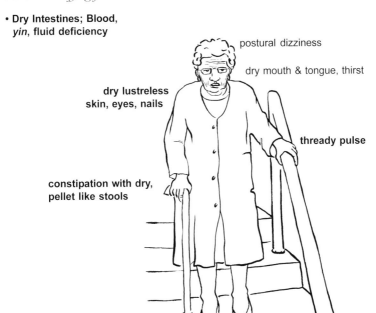

postural dizziness

dry mouth & tongue, thirst

**dry lustreless
skin, eyes, nails**

thready pulse

**constipation with dry,
pellet like stools**

GIT

adjusted from time to time to maintain effectiveness with the aim of gradually reducing the dose. If the patient is taking a constitutional formula to build Blood, *yin* or fluids, **2.31 Run Chang Wan** can be gradually withdrawn as the condition improves. This can take months in some patients.

Cautions and contraindications

Contraindicated during pregnancy. Caution in breast-feeding women as rhubarb can pass through the breast milk and affect the child causing colic and diarrhea. Some patients may habituate to the formula when taken alone, so should generally be combined with a constitutional formula. May cause mild abdominal cramping in sensitive patients. Not suitable for constipation from excess Heat (*see* **14.10 Liang Ge Wan**)

GMP **2.32 WU REN WAN**

五仁丸

Lanzhou Foci Pharmaceutical Factory (Gansu)
'Five Seed Pills'
Wu Ren Wan is packaged in bottles of 200 pills.
Available as: Five Seed Teapills (PF)

Available in the US,
UK and Europe
See Note 1, p.xxi

TCM actions

Moistens and lubricates the bowel, promotes bowel movement.

Biomedical actions

Mild moistening laxative.

INDICATIONS

* Chronic dry constipation in Blood, fluid or *yin* deficient patients. This commonly occurs in the elderly and postpartum women, or following a febrile disease.
* This is a gentle laxative formula, and is usually added to other primary formulae where a mild laxative action is desired. It is somewhat similar in action to **2.31 Run Chang Wan**, but is composed of oily seeds and does not have the purgative action of rhubarb root. It is suitable for prolonged use.

Composition

Citrus reticulata (chen pi, citrus) 25%, *Prunus armenica* (xing ren, apricot seed) 25%, *Prunus persica* (tao ren, peach seed) 15%, *Biota orientalis* (bai zi ren, biota seed) 15%, *Prunus japonica* (yu li ren, bush cherry seed) 10%, *Pinus massoniana* (song zi, pine nut) 8%

Combinations

* With **1.2 Si Wu Wan**, **1.9 Gui Pi Wan** or **1.1 Ba Zhen Wan** for postpartum constipation.
* With **7.1 Liu Wei Di Huang Wan** or **7.3 Zuo Gui Wan** for constipation in the elderly with a tendency to dryness and *yin* deficiency.

Dosage and method of administration

4-8 pills, three times daily on an empty stomach. The dose can be gradually increased until a smooth bowel movement is achieved, then adjusted from time to time to maintain effectiveness with the aim of gradually reducing the dose.

Cautions and contraindications

Contraindicated during pregnancy. Caution in patients with Phlegm of Dampness.

2.33 DA HUANG JIANG ZHI WAN

大黄降脂丸

Available in the US, UK and Europe See Note 1, p.xxi

GMP

Lanzhou Foci Pharmaceutical Factory (Gansu)
'Rhubarb Fat Reducing Pills'
Da Huang Jiang Zhi Wan is packaged in bottles of 200 pills.
Available as: Rhubarb Teapills (PF)

TCM actions
Purges the Intestines, promotes bowel movement, clears Heat, invigorates Blood.

Biomedical actions
Harsh laxative, febrifuge, antifungal.

INDICATIONS

- Constipation. Rhubarb is quite a powerful purgative herb and is used to open the bowels and stimulate peristalsis in patients with hard or dry impacted stools. It generally works within 6-8 hours following ingestion. Generally combined with a constitutional formula when a purgative action is desired.
- Fungal and bacterial infection of the Intestines. Rhubarb is a strong antifungal and antibiotic herb and is useful to assist in the treatment of *Candida*, *Shigella* and other infections of the Intestines.
- Used to reduce blood triglycerides.

Composition
Rheum palmatum (da huang, rhubarb) 39%, *Crategus pinnatifida* (jiao shan zha, baked crategus) 29%, *Hordeum vulgare* (chao mai ya, dry fried sprouted barley) 29%

Dosage and method of administration
2-4 pills, twice daily. When used as an antifungal agent, purgation is not desired, so 1-2 pills per day may be sufficient.

Cautions and contraindications
Contraindicated during pregnancy. Caution in breast-feeding women as rhubarb can pass through the breast milk and affect the child causing colic and diarrhea. Not suitable for prolonged use as patients may habituate to it and its bitter coldness can damage Spleen *yang*. Best combined with a constitutional formula. May cause mild abdominal cramping in sensitive patients.

GIT

2.34 CONG RONG BU SHEN WAN

苁蓉补肾丸

Lanzhou Foci Pharmaceutical Factory (Gansu)
'Cistanches Kidney Supplementing Pills'
Cong Rong Bu Shen Wan is packaged in bottles of 200 pills.

TCM actions
Supplements and warms Kidney *yang*, improves transformation of *qi* and bowel function.

Biomedical actions
Lubricates the bowel and enhances peristalsis.

INDICATIONS

- Chronic atonic constipation in a *qi* or *yang* deficient patient. The main feature is a lack of desire to defecate and stools that are not dry when voided. This type of constipation is usually seen in the elderly or post surgical patients.
- *Yang* deficiency type infertility, impotence, cold pains and weakness in the low back and knees, urinary frequency and uterine bleeding.

Composition
Cistanches deserticola (rou cong rong, cistanches) 66.3mg, *Rehmannia glutinosa* (shu di, processed rehmannia) 66.3mg, *Cuscuta chinensis* (tu su zi, cuscuta) 66.3mg, *Schizandra chinensis* (wu wei zi, schizandra) 1.1mg

Combinations
- Usually combined with a warming or *yang* strengthening formula such as **7.9 Fu Gui Ba Wei Wan**, **7.10 You Gui Wan**, **2.14 Li Chung Yuen Medical Pills**, or **2.13 Li Zhong Wan**.
- With **1.2 Si Wu Wan** or **1.1 Ba Zhen Wan** for postpartum constipation with Blood and Kidney deficiency symptoms. These combinations are also useful for infertility from Blood and *yang* deficiency.
- With **1.20 Cu Yun Yu Tai Capsule** or **1.21 Tiao Jing Cu Yun Wan** for infertility in a patient with severe *yang* deficiency, cold intolerance and copious vaginal discharge.
- With **1.9 Gui Pi Wan** for recurrent uterine bleeding from deficiency and Cold in the Uterus associated with *qi* and *yang* deficiency.

Pattern identifying features

- **Kidney *qi* &/or *yang* deficiency lack of propulsion**
- no urge to move bowels
- nocturia, frequent clear urination
- impotence, infertility

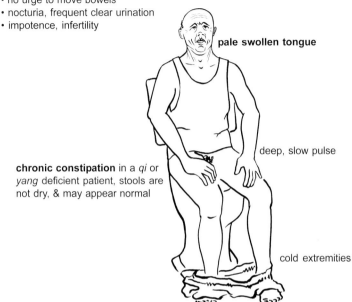

pale swollen tongue

chronic constipation in a *qi* or *yang* deficient patient, stools are not dry, & may appear normal

deep, slow pulse

cold extremities

GIT

Dosage and method of administration

8-12 pills three times daily, before meals. The dose may be spread out, or two lots of 12-18 pills may be taken, morning and evening. In severe cases or during the early stages of treatment (the first few weeks), a 50% increase in dose may be used, then reduced as the treatment takes effect. **2.34 Cong Rong Bu Shen Wan** needs to be used for prolonged periods to get a good result. When combined with a constitutional *yang* supplementing formula, a half dose may be sufficient.

Cautions and contraindications

Contraindicated during the early phase of acute illness such as colds and flu and in patients with diarrhea from Spleen deficiency.

GMP **2.35 YU QUAN WAN**

玉泉丸

Available in the US,
UK and Europe
See Note 1, p.xxi

Lanzhou Foci Pharmaceutical Factory (Gansu)
'Jade Spring Pills'
Yu Quan Wan is packaged in bottles of 200 pills.
Available as: Jade Spring Teapills (PF)

TCM actions

Nourishes *yin*, generates fluids, moistens dryness, stops thirst,
strengthens the Spleen and supplements *qi*.

Biomedical actions

Hypoglycemic, demulcent, energy stimulant.

INDICATIONS

- *Xiao ke* syndrome (*see* glossary). This is analogous to mature onset diabetes
  mellitus (type II), of a Kidney, Spleen and Stomach *yin* and *qi* deficient type.
  The herbs in this formula are selected on the basis of their action in enriching
  the *yin* and boosting *qi* as well as their known effects on reducing blood sugar
  levels.
- In many cases patients with diabetes or hyperglycemia will be medicated and
  the classical features, thirst, frequent copious urination, weight loss and
  hunger will be absent. In fact, many patients with adult onset diabetes tend to
  be overweight and overfed, with elements or Phlegm Damp (*see* **2.23 Ping
  Wei San**) or Phlegm Heat (*see* **8.8 Wen Dan Wan**), so care must be taken to
  differentiate patterns carefully and avoid supplementing when a reducing
  method is more appropriate.

Composition

Trichosanthes kirilowi (tian hua fen, trichosanthes root) 13%, *Pueraria lobata* (ge gen,
kudzu) 13%, *Codonopsis pilosula* (dang shen, codonopsis) 9%, *Astragalus membranaceous*
(huang qi, astragalus) 9%, *Poria cocos* (fu ling, hoelen)`9%, *Rehmannia glutinosa* (sheng
di, raw rehmannia) 9%, *Ophiopogon japonicus* (mai dong, ophiopogon) 9%, *Prunus
mume* (wu mei, black plum) 9%, *Glycyrrhiza uralensis* (gan cao, licorice) 9%, *Schizandra
chinensis* (wu wei zi, schizandra) 9%

Pattern identifying features

• **Kidney, Spleen, Stomach *qi* & *yin* deficiency**
• thirst
• hunger
• frequent urination

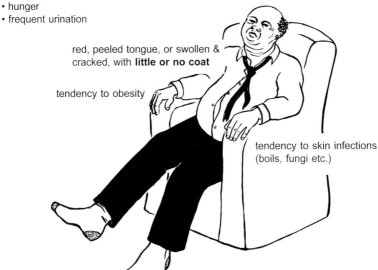

red, peeled tongue, or swollen & cracked, with **little or no coat**

tendency to obesity

tendency to skin infections (boils, fungi etc.)

Combinations
• With **2.36 Sugarid** to assist in reducing blood sugar.
• With **2.12 Shen Ling Bai Zhu Wan** for patients tending to more *qi* deficiency.

Dosage and method of administration
8-15 pills three times daily on an empty stomach. In severe cases or during the early stages of treatment, a 50% increase in dose may be used, then reduced to a maintenance dose (~8-12 pills three times daily) as the treatment takes effect.

Cautions and contraindications
Contraindicated in patients with Phlegm Damp, Phlegm Heat, or any other excess Heat pattern.

Medication alone is generally insufficient to control diabetes type II. Patent medicines should be one part of a comprehensive treatment plan involving diet and exercise. Over time, requirements for insulin (in those who require it) may decrease, however this must be allowed to occur naturally.

2.36 SUGARID

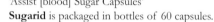
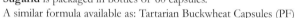

(Fu Tang Ping Jiao Nang)
Fu Yuan Tang Industrial Co. (Guangzhou)
'Assist [blood] Sugar Capsules'
Sugarid is packaged in bottles of 60 capsules.
A similar formula available as: Tartarian Buckwheat Capsules (PF)

TCM actions
Dries Dampness and transforms Phlegm, clears Heat, strengthens the Spleen.

Biomedical actions
Hypoglycemic, assists in lowering triglycerides and cholesterol, antioxidant, assists blood circulation.

INDICATIONS

• Hyperglycemia, diabetes mellitus. This formula is based on modern pharmacological studies. Bitter buckwheat has been shown to be an effective hypoglycemic, blood-lipid-reduction agent, and to have antioxidant effects. Andrographis reduces blood glucose and its extreme bitterness stimulates the digestive process, and in particular the digestion of fats, when used in relatively small doses.

Composition (each capsule contains herbal extracts equivalent to)
Fagopyrum esculentum (ku ji, bitter buckwheat) 11g, *Andrographis paniculata* (chuan xin lian, andrographis) 383mg, propolis 89mg

Combinations
• With **2.35 Yu Quan Wan** for diabetes.
• With **7.1 Liu Wei Di Huang Wan** for patients with Kidney *yin* deficiency.
• With **2.12 Shen Ling Bai Zhu Wan** for patients tending to more *qi* deficiency.

Dosage and method of administration
3-5 capsules, three times daily, 20 minutes before meals.

Cautions and contraindications
Contraindicated during pregnancy. Propolis may cause allergic reactions in some people. Contraindicated in patients with allergy to bee stings, atopic constitutions, and asthma.

2.37 HUAI JIAO WAN

槐角丸

Available in the US,
UK and Europe
See Note 1, p.xxi

GMP

Lanzhou Foci Pharmaceutical Factory (Gansu)
'Sophora Fruit Pills'
Huai Jiao Wan is packaged in bottles of 200 pills.
Available as: Sophora Japonica Teapills (PF)

TCM actions
Clears Damp Heat from the Large Intestine, stops bleeding, dispels Wind, nourishes the Blood.

Biomedical actions
Anti-inflammatory, analgesic, hemostatic.

INDICATIONS

• Intestinal Wind. This pattern is associated with bleeding of fresh blood prior to, or following, defecation, or with blood on the stool or on the toilet paper. Often there is no pain, itch, distension or swelling. This generally corresponds to the early stage of a first degree hemorrhoid. Also used for anal fissures and fistulae.

Composition
Sophora japonica (huai jiao, sophora fruit) 28%, *Sanguisorba officinalis* (di yu, sanguisorba) 16%, *Scutellaria baicalensis* (huang qin, scute) 14%, *Citrus aurantium* (zhi ke, aurantium 13%), *Ledebouriella divaricata* (fang feng, siler) 13%, *Angelica polymorpha* (dang gui, chinese angelica) 13%

Combinations
• With **2.11 Bu Zhong Yi Qi Wan** for bleeding hemorrhoids from *qi* deficiency.

Dosage and method of administration
8-12 pills three times daily on an empty stomach. The dose may be spread out, or two lots of 12-18 pills may be taken, morning and evening. In severe cases or the early stages of treatment, a 50% increase in dosage may be used, then reduced to a maintenance dose as the patient improves.

Cautions and contraindications
Contraindicated during pregnancy and in bleeding from *yin* deficiency.

GIT

2.38 HUA ZHI LING TABLET

强力化痔灵

(Qiang Li Hua Zhi Ling)
Jing Xian Pharmaceutical Co. (Guangzhou)
'Extra Strength Miraculous Hemorrhoid Transforming Tablets'
Hua Zhi Ling Tablets are packaged in bottles of 60 sugar coated tablets.

HUA ZHI
LING
TABLET

AUST L 82985
60 TABLETS

MADE IN CHINA

TCM actions

Clears Damp Heat from the Large Intestine, cools the Blood and stops bleeding, invigorates Blood and stops pain.

Biomedical actions

Anti-inflammatory, analgesic, hemostatic.

INDICATIONS

- Hemorrhoids. This formula treats internal or external, thrombosed, inflamed, painful or bleeding hemorrhoids arising from Damp Heat accumulation in the Large Intestine with Blood stagnation. The inclusion of the Blood regulating frankincense and myrrh increase the analgesic qualities of the formula. Good for the pain associated with a thrombosed hemorrhoid. There may or may not be systemic signs and symptoms of Damp Heat.
- Rectal bleeding associated with Damp Heat and/or Blood stagnation. This occurs in some inflammatory disorders of the Large Intestine.
- With the appropriate identifying features, this formula can be used to treat some biomedical conditions in addition to hemorrhoids, such as anal fissure, anal fistula, Crohn's disease and ulcerative colitis.

Composition (each tablet contains extracts equivalent to dry)

Angelica polymorpha (dang gui, chinese angelica) 390mg, *Sophora japonica* (huai hua, sophora flower bud) 300mg, *Agrimonia pilosa* (xian he cao, agrimony) 300mg, *Panax notoginseng* (tian qi, tian qi ginseng) 300mg, *Sanguisorba officinalis* (di yu, sanguisorba) 390mg, *Lonicera japonica* (jin yin hua, honeysuckle flower) 625mg, *Boswellia carteri* (ru xiang, frankincense) 12mg, *Commiphora myrrha* (mo yao, myrrh) 12mg

Combinations

- With **13.14 Ching Wan Hung** or **2.40 Hemorrhoids Ointment** topically for inflamed or thrombosed hemorrhoids.

Pattern identifying features

- **Damp Heat in the Intestine**
- tenesmus
- abdominal distension
- thirst
- concentrated urine
- tendency to constipation or
  sluggish loose stools

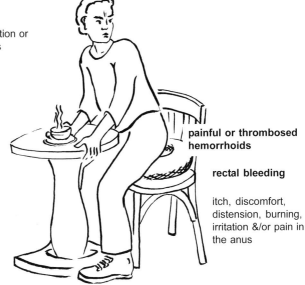

**painful or thrombosed
hemorrhoids**

rectal bleeding

itch, discomfort,
distension, burning,
irritation &/or pain in
the anus

- With **14.1 Huang Lian Jie Du Wan** for severe Damp Heat.
- With **14.5 Chuan Xin Lian Antiphlogistic Tablets** or **14.6 Fu Fang Nan Ban Lan Gen** for severe inflammation.
- With **10.1 Yunnan Paiyao** for severe bleeding.
- With **10.21 Yan Hu Suo Wan** for severe pain.
- With **10.5 Huo Luo Xiao Ling Dan** for severe Blood stagnation.
- With **6.3 Chai Hu Shu Gan Wan** for colitis, rectal bleeding and pain associated with Liver *qi* invading the Spleen and Intestines.

Dosage and method of administration

3-4 tablets three times daily on an empty stomach. One or two bottles is often enough to get a result, however in severe or very chronic cases, five or six bottles may be needed before a result is seen.

Cautions and contraindications

Contraindicated during pregnancy and in bleeding from *yin* deficiency.

2.39 FARGELIN FOR PILES

强力化痔灵

(Qiang Li Hua Zhi Ling)
Guangzhou Qixing Pharmaceutical Factory (Guangzhou)
'Extra Strength Miraculous Hemorrhoid Transforming Tablets'
Fargelin for Piles is packaged in bottles of 36 sugar coated
tablets.

TCM actions
Clears Damp Heat from the Large Intestine, cools the
Blood and stops bleeding, invigorates Blood and stops
pain.

Biomedical actions
Anti-inflammatory, analgesic, hemostatic.

INDICATIONS

• As for **2.38 Hua Zhi Ling Tablet**. This formula is similar in overall action to
2.38 Hua Zhi Ling Tablet, although it has slightly less Blood moving activity
and is slightly cooler.

Composition (each tablet contains extracts equivalent to dry)
Panax notoginseng (tian qi, tian qi ginseng) 400mg, *Scutellaria baicalensis* (huang qin,
scute) 300mg, *Sanguisorba officinalis* (di yu, sanguisorba) 200mg, *Sophora japonica* (huai
hua, sophora flower bud) 300mg, *Callicarpa pedunculata* (zi zhu cao, callicarpa)
300mg, *Corydalis turtschaninovii* (yan hu suo, corydalis) 100mg

Dosage and method of administration
3-4 tablets three times daily on an empty stomach. One or two bottles is often
enough to get a result, however in severe or very chronic cases, five or six bottles
may be needed before a result is seen.

Cautions and contraindications
Contraindicated during pregnancy and in bleeding from *yin* deficiency.

2.40 HEMORRHOIDS OINTMENT

特效痔疮膏

E

(Te Xiao Zhi Chuang Gao)
Jing Xian Pharmaceutical Co. (Guangzhou)
'Especially Effective Hemorrhoid Ointment'
Hemorrhoids Ointment is packaged in tubes of 20 grams.

TCM actions
Clears Damp Heat from the Large Intestine, invigorates Blood, stops bleeding, itch and pain.

Biomedical actions
Anti-inflammatory, analgesic, hemostatic.

INDICATIONS

• Applied topically for relief of the discomfort, pain and itching of internal or external, thrombosed, inflamed, painful or bleeding hemorrhoids arising from Damp Heat accumulation in the Large Intestine. Also used to relieve the discomfort and itching of anal lesions such as fissures and fistulae.

Composition (each 1 gram ointment contains extracts equivalent to dry)
Dryobalanops camphora (bing pian, borneol) 200mg, *Pinus massoniana* (hu po, amber) 840mg, *Sanguisorba officinalis* (di yu, sanguisorba) 840mg, *Sophora japonica* (huai jiao sophora fruit) 240mg, *Ostrea gigas* (mu li, oyster shell powder) 32mg

Dosage and method of administration
For external use only. Apply to the affected area, 3-4 times daily.

Cautions and contraindications
None noted.

GIT

3

Patent Medicines for Respiratory Disorders

肺病

Acute exterior disorders
3.1 Yin Chiao Chieh Tu Pien
3.2 Gan Mao Zhi Ke Chong Ji
3.3 Sang Ju Wan
3.4 Gan Mao Ling
3.5 Ma Huang Tang Wan
3.6 Gui Zhi Tang Wan
3.7 Su Zi Jiang Qi Wan
3.8 Xiao Qing Long Wan
3.9 Chuan Xiong Cha Tiao Wan
3.10 Jing Fang Bai Du Wan
3.11 Ge Gen Wan
3.12 Gan Mao Qing Re Chong Ji
3.13 Gan Mao Qing Re Ke Li
3.14 Ren Shen Bai Du Wan

Lung Heat
3.15 Qing Qi Hua Tan Wan
3.16 Ching Fei Yi Huo Pien
3.17 Pi Pa Cough Tea

Cough or wheezing

Phlegm
3.18 Tung Hsuan Li Fei Pien
3.19 Ding Chuan Wan
3.20 Qi Guan Yan Ke Sou Tan Chuan Wan

Phlegm Heat
3.21 She Dan Chuan Bei Ye
3.22 Orange Peel Powder
3.23 Tendrilleaf Fritillary Powder
3.24 She Dan Chuan Bei Pi Pa Gao
3.25 Nin Jiom Pei Pa Kao
3.26 Mi Lian Chuan Bei Pi Pa Gao
3.27 Fritillary & Loquat Leaf Mixture
3.28 Loquat Leaf Cough Syrup
3.29 African Sea Coconut Cough Syrup
3.30 Tong Xuan Li Fei Kou Fu Ye

Post acute
3.31 Zhi Sou Wan
3.32 Ning Sou Wan

Lung deficiency
3.33 Yang Yin Qing Fei Wan
3.34 Bai He Gu Jin Wan
3.35 Mai Wei Di Huang Wan
3.36 Luo Han Kuo Beverage
3.37 Sha Shen Mai Dong Wan
3.38 Sheng Mai San Wan
3.39 Yulin Bu Shen Wan
3.40 Bu Fei Wan
3.41 Xu Han Ting

3.1.1 YIN CHIAO CHIEH TU PIEN

银翘解毒片

(Yin Qiao Jie Du Pian)
Tianjin Drug Manufactory (Shandong)
'Lonicera and Forsythia Antitoxic Pills'
Yin Chiao Chieh Tu Pien is packaged
in vials of eight uncoated tablets, ten
vials to a box.

TCM actions
Dispels Wind Heat, clears Toxic Heat.

Biomedical actions
Antipyretic, diaphoretic, anti-inflammatory, antiviral.

INDICATIONS

- Wind Heat *gan mao*. This is the most important formula for the acute phase (the first few days) of a Wind Heat invasion, or Warm disease (*see* glossary). Biomedical conditions that may be classified as Wind Heat or Warm disease include acute upper respiratory tract infections, (viral or bacterial), the common cold, the early stage of influenza, tonsillitis, conjunctivitis, the acute phase of disorders such as otitis media and mumps, and the viral rash diseases of childhood, such as measles and chicken pox.
- For acute itchy red skin diseases such as urticaria, eczema and dermatitis. The rashes that may be treated by this formula usually affect the upper body and are characterised by redness, heat and itch which start suddenly and may move quickly from place to place.

Composition (each tablet contains extracts equivalent to dry)
Lonicera japonica (jin yin hua, lonicera) 1.33g, *Forsythia suspensa* (lian qiao, forsythia) 1.33g, *Arctium lappa* (niu bang zi, burdock seeds) 813mg, *Mentha haplocalyx* (bo he, mint) 739mg, *Lophatherum gracile* (dan zhu ye, bamboo leaves) 517mg, *Schizonepeta tenuifolia* (jing jie, schizonepeta) 517mg, *Glycine max* (dou chi, prepared soybean) 66mg, *Platycodon grandiflorum* (jie geng, platycodon) 65mg, *Glycyrrhiza uralensis* (gan cao, licorice) 53mg

Combinations
- With **9.9 Superior Sore Throat Powder** topically for acute sore throat.

Pattern identifying features

- **Wind Heat** *gan mao*
- fever, mild (or absent) chills

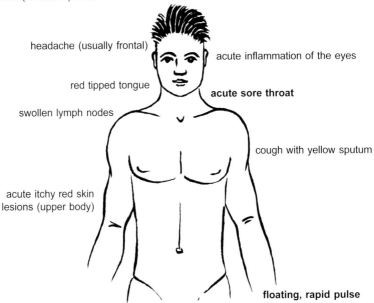

headache (usually frontal)

acute inflammation of the eyes

red tipped tongue

acute sore throat

swollen lymph nodes

cough with yellow sputum

acute itchy red skin
lesions (upper body)

floating, rapid pulse

- With **14.5 Chuan Xin Lian Antiphlogistic Tablets** for itchy chicken pox.
- With **2.2 Huo Hsiang Cheng Chi Pien** for Wind Heat sinus congestion or hayfever.
- With **13.2 Xiao Feng Wan** for very acute itchy urticaria or nettle rash.

Dosage and method of administration

The adult dose of **3.1.1 Yin Chiao Chieh Tu Pien** is eight tablets (one vial) 3-4 times daily, or in severe cases, every 2 hours. Not suitable for younger children due to the dimensions of the tablet. For Wind Heat *gan mao* in small children, see **12.7 Xiao Er Gan Mao Chong Ji.**

Cautions and contraindications

Not suitable for Wind Cold type colds or flu characterised by dominant chills, muscle aches and an absence of sweating (*see* **3.5 Ma Huang Tang Wan** or **3.9 Chuan Xiong Cha Tiao Wan** for that problem).

RESP

3.1.2 YIN CHIAO JIE DU PIAN

银翘解毒片

Tianjin Drug Manufactory (Shandong)
'Tianjin Lonicera and Forsythia Antitoxic Pills'
Yin Chiao Jie Du Pian is packaged in bottles of 120 coated pills.
Also available as: Tianjin Yin Chiao Plus

TCM actions
Dispels Wind Heat, clears Toxic Heat.

Biomedical actions
Antipyretic, diaphoretic, anti-inflammatory, antiviral.

INDICATIONS

• Same indications as for **3.1.1 Yin Chiao Chieh Tu Pien**. This formula includes the Heat clearing *Procaprea gutterosa pallas* (goat horn). This addition makes this version, **3.1.2 Yin Chiao Jie Du Pian**, slightly more cooling, even though the total amount of herb per dose is smaller.

Composition (each tablet contains)
Lonicera japonica (jin yin hua, lonicera) 1.04g, *Forsythia suspensa* (lian qiao, forsythia) 1.04g, *Mentha haplocalyx* (bo he, mint) 626mg, *Glycine max* (dou chi, prepared soybean) 520mg, *Schizonepeta tenuifolia* (jing jie, schizonepeta) 416mg, *Lophatherum gracile* (dan zhu ye, bamboo leaves) 416mg, *Platycodon grandiflorum* (jie geng, platycodon) 63mg, *Glycyrrhiza uralensis* (gan cao, licorice) 52mg, *Procaprea gutterosa pallas* (goat horn) 3.24mg

Combinations
• As for **3.1.1 Yin Chiao Chieh Tu Pien**.

Dosage and method of administration
The adult dose of **3.1.2 Yin Chiao Jie Du Pian** is 2-4 tablets 3-4 times daily; in severe cases take a dose every 2 hours. Take on an empty stomach. Half dose for children 8-12 years old. Not suitable for younger children due to the dimensions of the tablet. For Wind Heat patterns in small children, see **12.7 Xiao Er Gan Mao Chong Ji**.

Cautions and contraindications
• As for **3.1.1 Yin Chiao Chieh Tu Pien**.

3.1.3 YIN CHIAO JIE DU WAN

银翘解毒丸

Lanzhou Foci Pharmaceutical Factory (Gansu)
'Lonicera and Forsythia Antitoxic Pills'
Yin Chiao Jie Du Wan is packaged in bottles of 200 pills.

TCM actions
Dispels Wind Heat, clears Toxic Heat.

Biomedical actions
Antipyretic, diaphoretic, anti-inflammatory, antiviral.

INDICATIONS

• As for **3.1.1 Yin Chiao Chieh Tu Pien**.

Composition (each pill contains powdered)
Lonicera japonica (jin yin hua, lonicera) 28.5mg, *Forsythia suspensa* (lian qiao, forsythia) 28.5mg, *Arctium lappa* (niu bang zi, burdock seeds) 17.3mg, *Mentha haplocalyx* (bo he, mint) 17.3mg, *Platycodon grandiflorum* (jie geng, platycodon) 14.2mg, *Glycyrrhiza uralensis* (gan cao, licorice) 14.2mg, *Schizonepeta tenuifolia* (jing jie, schizonepeta) 11.4mg, *Lophatherum gracile* (dan zhu ye, bamboo leaves) 11.4mg

Combinations
• As for **3.1.1 Yin Chiao Chieh Tu Pien**.

Dosage and method of administration
8-12 pills three to five times daily on an empty stomach. Not suitable for younger children due to the number of pills required. For Wind Heat patterns in small children, see **12.7 Xiao Er Gan Mao Chong Ji**.

Cautions and contraindications
• As for **3.1.1 Yin Chiao Chieh Tu Pien**.

RESP

3.1.4 PEKING YIN CHIAO JIE DU PIAN

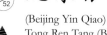

AUST L 77453
Improved Formula PEKING
YIN CHIAO JIE DU PIAN

(Beijing Yin Qiao)
Tong Ren Tang (Beijing)
'Beijing Lonicera and Forsythia Antitoxic Pills'
Peking Yin Chiao Jie Du Pian is packaged in bottles of 50 tablets.

TCM actions
Dispels Wind Heat, clears Toxic Heat.

Biomedical actions
Antipyretic, diaphoretic, anti-inflammatory, antiviral.

INDICATIONS

• As for **3.1.1 Yin Chiao Chieh Tu Pien**.

Composition (each tablet contains)
Lonicera japonica (jin yin hua, lonicera) 1.33g, *Forsythia suspensa* (lian qiao, forsythia) 1.2g, *Mentha haplocalycis* (bo he, mint) 600mg, *Schizonepeta tenuifolia* (jing jie, schizonepeta) 600mg, *Platycodon grandiflorum* (jie geng, platycodon) 600mg, *Procaprea gutterosa pallas* (goat horn) 1.2mg,

Combinations
• As for **3.1.1 Yin Chiao Chieh Tu Pien**.

Dosage and method of administration
2-4 tablets, twice daily. In severe cases, 2-4 tablets may be taken every 2-3 hours. Half dose for children 8-12 years old. Not suitable for younger children due to the dimensions of the tablet. For Wind Heat patterns in small children, see **12.7 Xiao Er Gan Mao Chong Ji**.

Cautions and contraindications
• As for **3.1.1 Yin Chiao Chieh Tu Pien**.

3.1.5 INFLUENZA AND COLD RELIEVER

银翘解毒片

Yin Qiao Jie Du Pian
Tong Ren Tang (Beijing)
'Lonicera and Forsythia Antitoxic Pills'
Influenza and Cold Reliever is packaged in bottles of 60 tablets.

TCM actions
Dispels Wind Heat, clears Toxic Heat.

Biomedical actions
Antipyretic, diaphoretic, anti-inflammatory, antiviral.

INDICATIONS

• As for **3.1.1 Yin Chiao Chieh Tu Pien**.

Composition (each tablet contains)
Lonicera japonica (jin yin hua, lonicera) 200g, *Forsythia suspensa* (lian qiao, forsythia) 200g, *Platycodon grandiflorum* (jie geng, platycodon) 120mg, *Arctium lappa* (niu bang zi, burdock seeds) 120mg, *Glycine max* (dou chi, prepared soybean) 100mg, *Lophatherum gracile* (dan zhu ye, bamboo leaves) 80.7mg, *Mentha haplocalyx* (bo he, mint essential oil) 1.1mg, *Schizonepeta tenuifolia* (jing jie, schizonepeta essential oil) 762µg

Combinations
• As for **3.1.1 Yin Chiao Chieh Tu Pien**.

Dosage and method of administration
4 tablets, 2-3 times daily. In severe cases, a dose may be taken every 2-3 hours. Half dose for children 8-12 years old. Not suitable for younger children due to the dimensions of the tablet. For Wind Heat patterns in small children, see **12.7 Xiao Er Gan Mao Chong Ji**.

Cautions and contraindications
• As for **3.1.1 Yin Chiao Chieh Tu Pien**.

RESP

3.2 GAN MAO ZHI KE CHONG JI

感冒止咳冲剂

Tong Ren Tang (Beijing)
'Cough and Cold Granules'
Gan Mao Zhi Ke Chong Ji is packaged in 10 gram sachets of dissolvable granules, six sachets per box.

TCM actions

Dispels Wind Heat, stops cough, harmonises *shao yang*.

Biomedical actions

Antipyretic, expectorant, diaphoretic.

INDICATIONS

- Acute Wind Heat *gan mao* with cough.
- *Shao yang* syndrome, or *tai yang/shao yang* overlap patterns. This type of disorder occurs in the post acute phase (around 3-7 days after onset) of an exterior syndrome as the pathogen begins to penetrate further into the body. The speed of change depends on the strength of the pathogen and the vitality of the patient. The symptoms in the *tai yang/shao yang* overlap pattern display a mixture of both levels.
- As an adjunct formula, combined with a constitutional formula, for any acute Heat disorder that exhibits alternating fever and chills. This may include conditions such as acute urinary tract infection, mastitis and pelvic inflammatory disease.

Composition

Bupleurum sinensis (chai hu, bupleurum) 19.99%, *Pueraria lobata* (ge gen, pueraria) 19.99%, *Scutellaria baicalensis* (huang qin, scute) 15%, *Forsythia suspensa* (lian qiao, forsythia) 15%, *Artemesia annua* (qing hao, artemesia) 10%, *Platycodon grandiflorum* (jie geng, platycodon) 10%, *Lonicera japonica* (jin yin hua, lonicera) 10%, Menthol 0.02%

Combinations

- With **9.9 Superior Sore Throat Powder** topically for severe sore throat.
- With **3.25 Nin Jiom Pei Pa Kao** for dry irritating cough.
- With **14.5 Chuan Xin Lian Antiphlogistic Tablets** for acute mastitis with alternating fever and chills.

Pattern identifying features

- **Wind Heat *gan mao*; *tai yang-shao yang* overlap patterns**
- mild fever, or **alternating fever & chills**
- acute or post acute phase of Wind Heat invasion
- fatigue

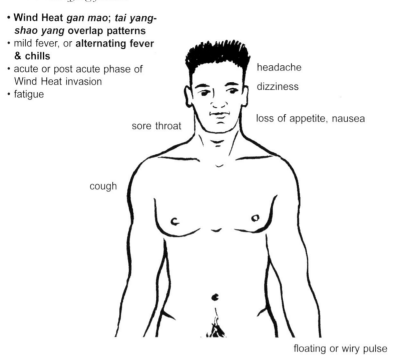

headache

dizziness

loss of appetite, nausea

sore throat

cough

floating or wiry pulse

- With **4.6 Ba Zheng San Wan** for acute urinary tract infection with alternating fever and chills.
- With **1.35 Fu Yan Qing Tablet** for acute pelvic infection with alternating fever and chills.

Dosage and method of administration

The recommended dose is one sachet dissolved in hot water 3-6 times daily depending on the severity of the symptoms. Half dose for children.

Cautions and contraindications

Not suitable for acute Wind Cold patterns (*see* **3.5 Ma Huang Tang Wan, 3.8 Xiao Qing Long Wan, 3.9 Chuan Xiong Cha Tiao Wan** or **3.7 Su Zi Jiang Qi Wan**).

RESP

3.3 SANG JU WAN

桑菊丸

Lanzhou Foci Pharmaceutical Factory (Gansu)
'Mulberry Leaf and Chrysanthemum Pills'
Sang Ju Wan is packaged in bottles of 200 pills.
Also available as: Clear Wind Heat Teapills (PF), Sang Ju Yin Wan–
Early Defence Formula (JD)

TCM actions
Dispels Wind Heat, cools and moistens the Lungs, stops
cough.

Biomedical actions
Antipyretic, antitussive, diaphoretic.

INDICATIONS

- Mild Wind Heat *gan mao* with cough. The main features are dry cough, slight fever, thirst, a white tongue coat and a floating, rapid pulse. Similar in action to **3.1.1 Yin Chiao Chieh Tu Pien** but with less diaphoretic and heat clearing action and more emphasis on stopping the cough. Also used to moisten the Lungs for cough associated with external dryness.
- Wind Heat eye disorders, with redness and pain.

Composition (each pill contains powdered)
Phragmites communis (lu gen, reed rhizome) 32.7mg, *Morus alba* (sang ye, mulberry leaf) 22.9mg, *Chrysanthemum sinense* (ju hua, chrysanthemum flower) 22.9mg, *Platycodon grandiflorum* (jie geng, platycodon) 22.9mg, *Forsythia suspensa* (lian qiao, forsythia) 22.9mg, *Prunus armeniaca* (xing ren, apricot seed) 19.6mg, *Glycyrrhiza uralensis* (gan cao, licorice) 8.2mg, *Mentha haplocalycis* (bo he, mint) 8.2mg

Dosage and method of administration
8-12 pills three to five times daily, on an empty stomach.

Cautions and contraindications
Not suitable for Wind Cold type colds or flu characterised by dominant chills, muscle aches and absence of sweating.

3.4 GAN MAO LING

Guangzhou Qixing Pharmaceutical Co. (Guangzhou)
'Miraculous Cold Pills'
Gan Mao Ling is packaged in bottles of 36 tablets.

TCM actions
Dispels Wind, clears Toxic Heat.

Biomedical actions
Antipyretic, antiviral.

INDICATIONS

- A good general formula for acute external Wind (and either Heat or mild Cold, but best for Heat, mixed or unclear) *gan mao* patterns. The herbs in this unusual formula are all Toxic Heat clearing and, in biomedical terms, antiviral.
- Can be used for the common cold, influenza, acute upper respiratory tract infections, mild bronchitis, tracheitis and tonsillitis.

Composition (each pill contains extracts equivalent to dry)
Ilex aquifolium (english holly) 1.2g, *Evodia lepta* (san jiao bie) 765mg, *Chrysanthemum indicum* (ye ju hua, wild chrysanthemum) 450.7mg, *Vitex negrundo* (mu jing ye, chinese vitex) 450.7mg, *Isatis tinctora* (ban lan gen, isatis) 450.7mg, *Lonicera japonica* (jin yin hua, lonicera) 166mg

Dosage and method of administration
The recommended dose is four tablets, three times daily, however in most cases the dose can be doubled or tripled for the best therapeutic effect. Take on an empty stomach.

Cautions and contraindications
Not suitable for severe Wind Cold patterns (*see* **3.5 Ma Huang Tang Wan**, **3.8 Xiao Qing Long Wan**, **3.9 Chuan Xiong Cha Tiao Wan** or **3.7 Su Zi Jiang Qi Wan**).

RESP

GMP 3.5 MA HUANG TANG WAN

Available in the US,
UK and Europe
See Note 1, p.xxi

麻黄汤丸

Lanzhou Foci Pharmaceutical Factory (Gansu)
'Ephedra Pills'
Ma Huang Tang Wan is packaged in bottles of 200 pills.
Available as: Ma Huang Tang Teapills (PF)

TCM actions

Dispels Wind Cold, directs Lung *qi* downwards, stops
wheezing.

Biomedical actions

Diaphoretic, anti-asthmatic, diuretic.

INDICATIONS

- Wind Cold induced wheezing and cough. A strong diaphoretic, **3.5 Ma Huang
  Tang Wan** is indicated for Wind Cold *gan mao* patterns with the Cold firmly
  lodged in the *tai yang* superficial layers of the body. This is described as 'Wind
  Cold with exterior excess' (*shang han biao shi*). The Cold, by 'freezing and
  constricting' shuts and locks the pores behind it, hence the key features of mild
  fever and more severe chills with no sweating, muscle and joint aches, occipital
  headache, cough and wheezing and a floating tight pulse.
- Acute Wind Cold edema. This occurs because the normal distribution of fluids
  is retarded by obstruction of Lung *qi* and closure of the pores by the Wind Cold
  pathogen. The edema comes on suddenly and first affects the orbits and face,
  and is accompanied by scanty urination and the Wind Cold pattern identifying
  features opposite.
- Cold induced urticaria. This occurs on parts of the body exposed to cold, such
  as the hands and forearms of those frequently in and out of fridges and freezers.
- Acute Wind Cold *bi* syndrome.
- With the appropriate identifying features this formula can assist in the treatment
  of biomedical conditions such as acute asthma, asthmatic bronchitis, the common
  cold, influenza, acute glomerulonephritis and urticaria.

Composition

Ephedra sinica (ma huang, ephedra), *Cinnamomum cassia* (gui zhi, cinnamon twigs),
Prunus armenica (xing ren, apricot seed), *Glycyrrhiza uralensis* (zhi gan cao, honey fried
licorice)

Pattern identifying features

- **Wind Cold *gan mao* (exterior excess);
  Cold dominant**
- chills > fever

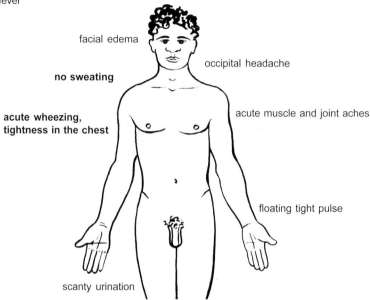

facial edema

occipital headache

no sweating

**acute wheezing,
tightness in the chest**

acute muscle and joint aches

floating tight pulse

scanty urination

RESP

Dosage and method of administration

For acute Wind Cold patterns the dose is 8-12 pills every two hours or so, on an empty stomach. The pills can be taken with hot soup or rice and ginger porridge to encourage sweating. It is also of benefit to follow a dose with a hot bath.

Cautions and contraindications

Contraindicated in Wind Cold patterns with sweating (*see* **3.6 Gui Zhi Tang Wan**), Wind Heat induced wheezing and in patients with frequent urination and general debility. Caution in patients with hypertension. May cause or aggravate insomnia in some patients due to presence of ephedra. Only suitable for short term use.

GMP **3.6 GUI ZHI TANG WAN**

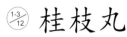

桂枝丸

Available in the US,
UK and Europe
See Note 1, p.xxi

Lanzhou Foci Pharmaceutical Factory (Gansu)
'Cinnamon Twig Pills'
Gui Zhi Tang Wan is packaged in bottles of 200 pills.
Available as: Gui Zhi Tang Teapills (PF)

TCM actions
Dispels Wind from the exterior, balances the relationship between nutritive *qi* (*ying qi*) and defensive *qi* (*wei qi*), harmonises the Spleen and Stomach.

Biomedical actions
Mild diaphoretic, antispasmodic.

INDICATIONS

• Wind Cold *gan mao* with predominant Wind that disperses *wei qi*. Also used for Wind Cold in a patient with pre-existing weak *wei qi* that is unable to keep the pores closed. In contrast to **3.5 Ma Huang Wan**, which is prefered for a *tai yang* invasion with exterior excess, this formula is for *tai yang* invasion with exterior deficiency (*zhong feng biao xu*). This manifests in mild or lingering upper respiratory tract disorders that are unrelieved by diaphoresis, and that are characterised by sweating or clamminess, aversion to wind, mild fever and chills, fatigue, nasal congestion, loss of appetite, dry retching and a floating moderate or weak pulse. Patients prone to this type of pattern are typically run down, convalescing or debilitated in some way.

• Itchy dry skin diseases that are initiated or aggravated by cold weather or exposure to cold water, or that recur each Winter, and that are not red or inflamed. Also indicated for the sensation of 'worms or insects crawling under the skin'.

• Cold type pain in the joints, extremities, epigastrium and abdomen; numbness in the extremities and skin.

• With the appropriate identifying features, this formula can assist in the treatment of biomedical conditions such as the common cold, the common cold in the debilitated, postpartum fever, postpartum colds, morning sickness, allergic rhinitis, eczema, urticaria, idiopathic pruritus, frostbite, neuralgia, sciatica and rheumatism.

Composition
Cinnamomum cassia (gui zhi, cinnamon twigs), *Paeonia lactiflora* (bai shao, white peony), *Zingiber officinale* (sheng jiang, ginger), *Zizyphus jujuba* (da zao, chinese dates), *Glycyrrhiza uralensis* (zhi gan cao, honey fried licorice)

Pattern identifying features

- **Wind Cold *gan mao* (exterior deficiency);
  Wind dominant**
- mild fever and chills
- sweating or clamminess
- aversion to wind
- no thirst

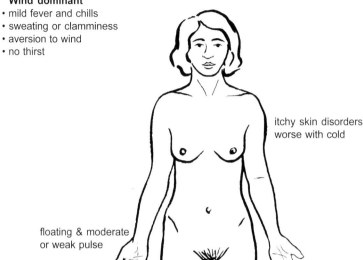

itchy skin disorders
worse with cold

floating & moderate
or weak pulse

Combinations
- With **10.22 Shao Yao Gan Cao Wan** for Wind invasion with more severe abdominal pain.
- With **6.1 Xiao Chai Hu Tang Wan** for *tai yang/ shao yang* overlap syndrome, abdominal pain due to Liver and Spleen disharmony, Wind Damp joint pain or creaking in the joints. This combination is also considered effective for epilepsy.

Dosage and method of administration
8-12 pills, three times daily on an empty stomach. The pills can be taken with hot soup or rice and ginger porridge to encourage mild sweating.

Cautions and contraindications
Contraindicated in exterior excess patterns (*see* **3.5 Ma Huang Tang Wan**, **3.8 Xiao Qing Long Wan**, or **3.9 Chuan Xiong Cha Tiao Wan**), external cold with internal Heat patterns, Wind Heat, acute Warm or Damp Heat patterns, internal Heat and *yin* deficiency.

RESP

3.7 SU ZI JIANG QI WAN
苏子降气丸

Lanzhou Foci Pharmaceutical Factory (Gansu)
'Perilla Seed Pills to Redirect *Qi* Downwards'
Su Zi Jiang Qi Wan is packaged in bottles of 200 pills.

TCM actions
Redirects Lung *qi* downwards, stops cough and wheezing, warms and transforms thin Phlegm.

Biomedical actions
Anti-asthmatic, antitussive, mucolytic, expectorant.

INDICATIONS

• Wind Cold *gan mao* with accumulation of Phlegm Damp or Cold Phlegm in the Lungs causing acute or chronic coughing and wheezing. Can be used for acute patterns with clear signs of exterior Wind Cold, and chronic patterns where the Phlegm Damp accumulation is primary. In either case, the sputum is copious and thin or watery. The formula is warming and drying in nature and its main focus is on transforming and expelling Phlegm, and encouraging the downward movement of Lung *qi*.

• With the appropriate identifying features, this formula can be used to treat disorders such as acute and chronic asthma, chronic bronchitis and emphysema.

Composition (each pill contains powdered)
Perilla frutescens (su zi, perilla seed) 24.24mg, *Pinellia ternata* (ban xia, pinellia) 24.24mg, *Prunus armenica* (xing ren, apricot seed) 21mg, *Peucedanum decursivum* (qian hu, peucedanum) 19.4mg, *Magnolia officinalis* (hou po, magnolia bark) 19.4mg, *Angelica polymorpha* (dang gui, chinese angelica) 16.2mg, *Ephedra sinica* (ma huang, ephedra) 12.9mg, *Aquilaria agallocha* (chen xiang, aquilaria) 12.9mg, *Glycyrrhiza uralensis* (gan cao, licorice) 9.7mg

Combinations
• With **3.30 Tong Xuan Li Fei Kou Fu Ye** for patients with severe dyspnea and copious sputum or obvious rattles and rales, until the sputum starts to break up.
• With **2.22 Er Chen Wan** for very thick or hard to expectorate sputum.

Pattern identifying features

• **Wind Cold *gan mao*; Phlegm Damp/Cold accumulation in the Lungs**
• **wheezing, dyspnea**
• breathlessness

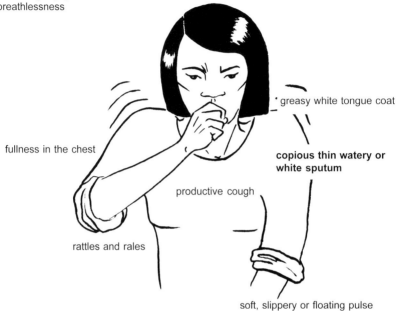

greasy white tongue coat

fullness in the chest

copious thin watery or white sputum

productive cough

rattles and rales

soft, slippery or floating pulse

RESP

Dosage and method of administration

8-12 pills three times daily on an empty stomach. Half dose for children. In severe cases or during the early stages of treatment (the first 7-10 days), a 50% increase in dose may be used, then reduced to a maintenance dose as the treatment takes effect.

Cautions and contraindications

Contraindicated in cases of wheezing, breathlessness and asthma from Heat in the Lungs or Lung *yin* deficiency. Caution in patients with hypertension. May cause or aggravate insomnia in some patients due to presence of ephedra.

3.8 XIAO QING LONG WAN

小青龙丸

Lanzhou Foci Pharmaceutical Factory (Gansu)
'Minor Blue Green Dragon Pills'
Xiao Qing Long Wan is packaged in bottles of 200 pills.
Also available as: Minor Blue Dragon Teapills (PF)

TCM actions
Dispels Wind Cold, warms the Lungs and transforms thin Phlegm, directs *qi* downward, stops wheezing.

Biomedical actions
Diaphoretic, anti-asthmatic, antitussive, expectorant.

INDICATIONS

- Wind Cold *gan mao* with congested thin fluids. The main feature of this formula is its ability to warm, dry and transform fluids, and improve fluid metabolism. The fluids are either pre-existing from Lung and Spleen weakness and stirred up by the Wind Cold, or are generated by blockage by the pathogen of Lung *qi's* natural descent.
- Acute episodes of hayfever and other atopic conditions characterised by copious discharge of thin watery fluids from the nasal sinuses, eyes or lungs.
- With the appropriate identifying features, this formula can be used to treat biomedical conditions such as the common cold, influenza, asthma, asthmatic bronchitis, acute exacerbation of chronic bronchitis or emphysema.

Composition
Paeonia lactiflora (bai shao, white peony) 21.4%, *Pinellia ternata* (zhi ban xia, processed pinellia) 21.4%, *Cinnamomum cassia* (gui zhi, cinnamon twigs) 14.4%, *Schizandra chinensis* (wu wei zi, schizandra) 14.3%, *Ephedra sinica* (ma huang, ephedra) 7%, *Zingiber officinale* (gan jiang, dry ginger) 7%, *Asarum seiboldi* (xi xin, asarum) 7%, *Glycyrrhiza uralensis* (gan cao, licorice) 7%

Note: The composition given here is the traditional formula from the *Shang Han Lun*, available outside Australia. The Australian version deletes asarum and ephedra.

Combinations
- With **3.30 Tong Xuan Li Fei Kou Fu Ye** for patients with severe dyspnea and copious sputum or obvious rattles and rales, until the sputum starts to break up.
- With **2.22 Er Chen Wan** for copious sputum and difficulty lying flat (orthopnea).

Pattern identifying features

- **Wind Cold** *gan mao* **with copious thin Phlegm**
- chills > fever
- **no sweating**

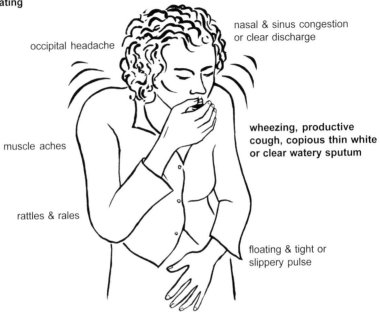

occipital headache

nasal & sinus congestion
or clear discharge

muscle aches

wheezing, productive
cough, copious thin white
or clear watery sputum

rattles & rales

floating & tight or
slippery pulse

RESP

Dosage and method of administration

8-15 pills three times daily on an empty stomach. For acute Wind Cold *gan mao* patterns the pills can be taken with hot soup or rice and ginger porridge to encourage sweating. It is also of benefit to follow a dose with a hot bath. In severe cases or during the early stages of treatment, a 50% increase in dose may be used, then reduced to a maintenance dose (~8-12 pills three times daily) as the treatment takes effect.

Cautions and contraindications

Not suitable for long term use. Contraindicated in cases of wheezing, breathlessness and asthma arising from *qi* or *yin* deficiency, or Heat in the Lungs. Contraindicated in Wind Cold exterior deficiency patterns with sweating (*see* **3.6 Gui Zhi Tang Wan**). Caution in patients with hypertension. May cause or aggravate insomnia in some patients due to presence of the ephedra.

3.9 CHUAN XIONG CHA TIAO WAN

川芎茶调丸

Lanzhou Foci Pharmaceutical Factory (Gansu)
'Cnidium and Tea Adjusting Pills'
Chuan Xiong Cha Tiao Wan is packaged in bottles of 200 pills.

TCM actions

Dispels Wind Cold, stops pain, invigorates the circulation of *qi* and Blood in the face and head.

Biomedical actions

Antipyretic, diaphoretic, analgesic.

INDICATIONS

- Acute Wind *gan mao* characterised by headache and neck stiffness. Generally considered to be best for Wind Cold patterns, this formula is quite well balanced and can be used for Wind Heat or Wind Damp patterns with headache, especially when combined with a specific Wind Heat or Damp formula.
- Also used for headaches (either acute, chronic or recurrent, including migraines) or facial pain set off by sudden exposure to cold, changes in weather or by going from a warm to a cold environment. Also used for acute frontal headaches associated with sinus congestion, sinusitis and rhinitis, as long as the nasal discharge is watery or white.
- With the appropriate identifying features, this formula can be used to treat biomedical conditions such as acute upper respiratory tract infection, the common cold, influenza, acute rhinitis, trigeminal neuralgia, migraine headaches, tension headaches, neurogenic headaches, acute torticollis and Bell's palsy.

Composition (each pill contains powdered)

Mentha haplocalycis (bo he, mint) 58.8mg, *Ligusticum wallici* (chuan xiong, cnidium) 29.4mg, *Schizonepeta tenuifolia* (jing jie, schizonepeta) 29.4mg, *Notopterygium incisum* (qiang huo, notopterygium) 14.7mg, *Angelica dahurica* (bai zhi, angelica) 14.7mg, *Glycyrrhiza uralensis* (gan cao, licorice) 14.7mg, *Ledebouriella divaricata* (fang feng, siler) 11mg, *Asarum seiboldi* (xi xin, asarum) 7.3mg

Combinations

- With **15.9 Headache and Dizziness Reliever** for severe occipital headache.

Pattern identifying features

- **Wind *gan mao* with headache**
- chills, mild fever
- no sweating

headache (usually occipital, but may be anywhere)

watery nasal discharge
or congestion

stiff painful neck

muscle aches

floating tight pulse

RESP

- With **9.18 Xin Yi San** for acute frontal headache, rhinitis or sinus congestion from Wind Cold invasion.
- With **3.4 Gan Mao Ling** or **3.3 Sang Ju Wan** for Wind Heat patterns.
- With **3.10 Jing Fang Bai Du Wan** for Wind Damp patterns.

Dosage and method of administration

For acute Wind Cold patterns the dose is 8-12 pills every two hours or so, on an empty stomach. The pills can be taken with hot soup or rice and ginger porridge to encourage sweating. When used for acute Wind Cold patterns, one week or less is usually sufficient treatment. When used for recurrent headaches the formula may be used continually for several months at a lower dose (8-12 pills three times daily).

Cautions and contraindications

Not suitable for headaches due to deficiency patterns.

GMP **3.10 JING FANG BAI DU WAN**

  荆防败毒丸

Available in the US, UK and Europe
See Note 1, p.xxi

Lanzhou Foci Pharmaceutical Factory (Gansu)
'Schizonepeta and Siler Pills to Overcome Toxin'
Jing Fang Bai Du Wan is packaged in bottles of 200 pills.
Available as: Release the Exterior Teapills (PF)

TCM actions
Dispels Wind Cold Damp, stops pain, expels Phlegm.

Biomedical actions
Antipyretic, diaphoretic, analgesic, expectorant.

INDICATIONS

- Acute Wind Cold Damp *gan mao*. A broad acting and relatively strong formula for dispelling strong pathogens from the surface. Particularly useful when Wind Cold Damp pathogens are on the edge of transforming into Heat, usually observed in a sore throat amidst clear Wind Cold signs and symptoms. The initial signs and symptoms are generally quite severe reflecting the intensity of the battle between the strong pathogens and the intact *zheng qi*.
- With the appropriate identifying features, this formula may be used to treat biomedical conditions such as the common cold, the early stage of superficial suppurative lesions, acute rheumatic joint pain, epidemic influenza, bronchitis, and epidemic parotitis (mumps).

Composition
Schizonepeta tenuifolia (jing jie, schizonepeta) 8.5%, *Ledebouriella divaricata* (fang feng, siler) 8.5%, *Bupleurum falcatum* (chai hu, bupleurum) 8.5%, *Peucedanum praeruptorum* (qian hu, peucedanum) 8.5%, *Ligusticum wallici* (chuan xiong, cnidium) 8.5%, *Notopterygium incisum* (qiang huo, notopterygium) 8.5%, *Angelica pubescens* (du huo, Tu-huo) 8%, *Poria cocos* (fu ling, hoelen) 8%, *Platycodon grandiflorum* (jie geng, platycodon) 8%, *Citrus aurantium* (zhi ke, aurantium) 8%, *Glycyrrhiza uralensis* (gan cao, licorice) 3.5%, *Zingiber officinale* (sheng jiang, ginger) 2%

Combinations
- With **9.7 Jie Geng Wan** for the beginnings of a sore throat from Heat transformation.
- With **15.9 Headache and Dizziness Reliever** for severe occipital headache.

Pattern identifying features

- **Wind Cold Damp** *gan mao*
- **acute simultaneous fever & chills, chills > fever**
- maybe high fever with shivering or rigors
- no sweating

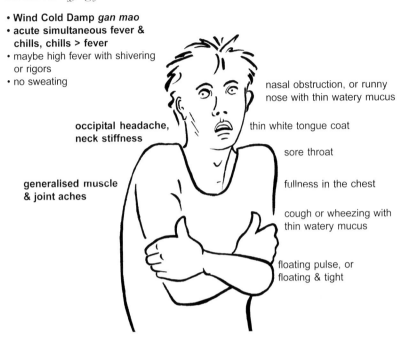

nasal obstruction, or runny nose with thin watery mucus

occipital headache, neck stiffness

thin white tongue coat

sore throat

generalised muscle & joint aches

fullness in the chest

cough or wheezing with thin watery mucus

floating pulse, or floating & tight

- With **9.18 Xin Yi San** for acute frontal headache, rhinitis or sinus congestion from Wind Cold invasion.
- With **3.30 Tong Xuan Li Fei Kou Fu Ye** for Wind Cold with copious watery sputum.

Dosage and method of administration

For acute Wind Cold Damp patterns the dose is 8-12 pills every two hours or so, on an empty stomach. The pills can be taken with hot soup or rice and ginger porridge to encourage sweating. It is also of benefit to follow a dose with a hot bath. When used for acute Wind Cold patterns, one week or less is usually sufficient treatment.

Cautions and contraindications

Not suitable for full blown Wind Heat patterns or Warm diseases.

GMP **3.11 GE GEN WAN**

葛根丸

Available in the US,
UK and Europe
See Note 1, p.xxi

Lanzhou Foci Pharmaceutical Factory (Gansu)
'Pueraria Pills'
Ge Gen Wan is packaged in bottles of 200 pills.
Available as: Kudzu Teapills (PF)

TCM actions
Dispels Wind Cold, eases the muscles, alleviates spasm, stops pain.

Biomedical actions
Diaphoretic, analgesic, muscle relaxant, calmative.

INDICATIONS

- Acute Wind Cold *gan mao*, the main feature of which is neck, upper back and shoulder stiffness and pain. This is the main formula for Wind Cold invasion into the *tai yang* channels of the upper back causing disruption to the circulation of *qi* and Blood and consequent stiffness and pain in that region. Even though the formula is designed for Wind Cold *gan mao* patterns, its use has been expanded to include stiff and painful neck, upper back and shoulders from a variety of causes as long as there is no significant Heat.
- With the appropriate identifying features, this formula may assist in the treatment of biomedical conditions such as the common cold, influenza, early stage of meningitis or encephalitis, acute torticollis, wry neck, cervical spondylosis, chronic pediatric diarrhea, early stage of Dysenteric disorder, early stage of measles, eczema and urticaria.

Composition
Pueraria lobata (ge gen, kudzu) 23%, *Ephedra sinica* (ma huang, ephedra) 17%, *Zingiber officinale* (sheng jiang, ginger) 17%, *Cinnamomum cassia* (gui zhi, cinnamon twigs) 11%, *Paeonia lactiflora* (bai shao, white peony) 11%, *Glycyrrhiza uralensis* (gan cao, licorice) 11%, *Zizyphus jujuba* (da zao, chinese dates) 8%

Combinations
- With **15.9 Headache and Dizziness Reliever** for severe occipital headache, stiff neck and upper back pain.
- With **10.30 Po Sum On Medicated Oil** topically for neck and upper back stiffness and pain.

Pattern identifying features

- **Wind Cold *gan mao* with neck & upper back pain**
- chills, mild fever
- no sweating

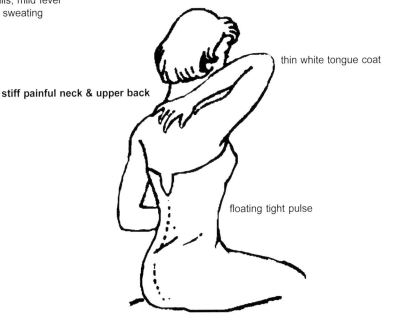

thin white tongue coat

stiff painful neck & upper back

floating tight pulse

Dosage and method of administration

For acute Wind Cold *gan mao* patterns the dose is 8-12 pills every two hours or so, on an empty stomach. The pills can be taken with hot soup or rice and ginger porridge to encourage sweating. It is also of benefit to follow a dose with a hot bath. When used for acute Wind Cold patterns, one week or less is usually sufficient treatment.

Cautions and contraindications

Contraindicated in Wind Cold exterior deficiency patterns with sweating (*see* **3.6 Gui Zhi Tang Wan**). Caution in patients with hypertension. May cause or aggravate insomnia in some patients due to presence of ephedra.

3.12 GAN MAO QING RE CHONG JI

感冒清热冲剂

(Colds and Flu Tea)
Tong Ren Tang (Beijing)
'Cold and Fever Clearing Granules'
Gan Mao Qing Re Chong Ji is packaged as dissolving
granules in single dose sachets, 10 sachets per box.

Tong Ren Tang
GANMAO QINGRE CHONGJI
感 冒 清 热 冲 剂

COLDS AND FLU TEA
AUST L 52415

TCM actions
Dispels Wind Cold, redirects Lung *qi* downward,
eases muscle aches.

Biomedical actions
Diaphoretic, antipyretic, analgesic.

INDICATIONS

- Wind Cold *gan mao* patterns, especially good when muscle aches and headaches are a prominent feature.
- There are two varieties, with and without sugar. The sugarless variety is quite bitter, but the sweet version is well tolerated by children and easily taken.
- With the appropriate identifying features, this formula can be used to treat biomedical conditions such as influenza and the common cold.

Composition (each sachet contains decoctions equivalent to fresh)
Corydalis turtschaninovii (yan hu suo, corydalis) 2.95g, *Phragmites communis* (lu gen, reed rhizome) 2.36g, *Bupleurum falcatum* (chai hu, bupleurum) 1.47g, *Ledebouriella divaricata* (fang feng, siler) 1.47g, *Pueraria lobata* (ge gen, pueraria) 1.47g, *Prunus armenica* (xing ren, apricot seed) 1.18g, *Angelica dahurica* (bai zhi, angelica) 880mg, *Platycodon grandiflorum* (jie geng, platycodon) 880mg, *Schizonepeta tenuifolia* (jing jie, schizonepeta essential oil) 17.6mcl, *Perilla frutescens* (zi su ye, perilla leaf essential oil) 0.09mcl, *Mentha haplocalycis* (bo he, mint oil) 3.5mcl

Dosage and method of administration
The recommended dose is one sachet dissolved in hot water twice daily, however to get the best therapeutic effect the dose should be doubled or trebled. Take one sachet every hour or two. Half dose for children.

Cautions and contraindications
Contraindicated during pregnancy.

3.13 GAN MAO QING RE KE LI

感冒清热颗粒

GMP

Tong Ren Tang (Beijing)
'Cold and Fever Clearing Granules'
Gan Mao Qing Re Ke Li is packaged as dissolving granules in single dose sachets, 10 sachets per box.

TCM actions
Dispels Wind Cold, clears Heat from the throat.

Biomedical actions
Diaphoretic, antipyretic, antiviral.

INDICATIONS

- A good general formula, primarily designed for acute Wind Cold *gan mao*. It may however, be used for mild Wind Heat patterns or Wind Cold patterns that are beginning to transform into Heat. Very similar to **3.12 Gan Mao Qing Re Chong Ji**, with the addition of *Viola yedoensis* (zi hua di ding, viola) to clear Toxic Heat.
- With the appropriate identifying features, this formula can be used to treat biomedical conditions such as influenza, the common cold, laryngitis and early tonsillitis.

Composition
Schizonepeta tenuifolia (jing jie sui, schizonepeta), *Mentha haplocalycis* (bo he, mint), *Ledebouriella divaricata* (fang feng, siler), *Bupleurum falcatum* (chai hu, bupleurum), *Perilla frutescens* (zi su ye, perilla leaf), *Pueraria lobata* (ge gen, pueraria), *Platycodon grandiflorum* (jie geng, platycodon), *Prunus armenica* (xing ren, apricot seed), *Angelica dahurica* (bai zhi, angelica), *Phragmites communis* (lu gen, reed rhizome), *Viola yedoensis* (zi hua di ding, viola)

Dosage and method of administration
The recommended dose is one sachet dissolved in hot water twice daily, however to get the best therapeutic effect the dose should be doubled or trebled. Take one sachet every hour or two. Half dose for children.

Cautions and contraindications
None noted.

RESP

GMP
3.14 REN SHEN BAI DU WAN

人参败毒丸

Available in the US,
UK and Europe
See Note 1, p.xxi

Lanzhou Foci Pharmaceutical Factory (Gansu)
'Ginseng Pills to Overcome Toxin'
Ren Shen Bai Du Wan is packaged in bottles of 200 pills.
Available as: Resilient Warrior Teapills (PF)

TCM actions
Dispels Wind Cold Damp, supplements *qi*, expels Phlegm.

Biomedical actions
Antipyretic, diaphoretic, analgesic, expectorant.

INDICATIONS

• Wind Cold Damp *gan mao* in patients with pre-existing, acquired or constitutional *qi* deficiency. This typically occurs in patients convalescing from a major or prolonged illness, in children and postpartum women, the elderly and debilitated. Wind Cold patterns such as this tend to drag on as the *zheng qi* is unable to expel the pathogen.

• The difference between this formula and **3.10 Jing Fang Bai Du Wan** is relatively small – replacement of two Wind expelling herbs, schizonepeta and siler, with mint and ginseng. This alteration subtly shifts the focus of the formula to expelling Wind Cold while supporting *zheng qi*. The overall pattern is the same as for **3.10 Jing Fang Bai Du Wan**. The pre-existing *qi* deficiency does, however, result in two phenomena that help differentiate the two formulae–the patient gets colds more easily and the symptoms are more subdued due to the relative weakness of the battle between the pathogen and the deficient *zheng qi*.

Composition
Notopterygium incisum (qiang huo, notopterygium) 10%, *Angelica pubescens* (du huo, Tu-huo) 10%, *Ligusticum wallici* (chuan xiong, cnidium) 10%, *Bupleurum falcatum* (chai hu, bupleurum) 10%, *Peucedanum praeruptorum* (qian hu, peucedanum) 10%, *Poria cocos* (fu ling, hoelen) 10%, *Platycodon grandiflorum* (jie geng, platycodon) 10%, *Citrus aurantium* (zhi ke, aurantium) 10%, *Mentha haplocalyis* (bo he, mint) 4.5%, *Panax ginseng* (ren shen, ginseng) 4.5%, *Glycyrrhiza uralensis* (gan cao, licorice) 4%, *Zingiber officinale* (sheng jiang, ginger) 4%

Pattern identifying features

- **Wind Cold Damp** *gan mao* with *qi* deficiency
- chills > fever
- no sweating

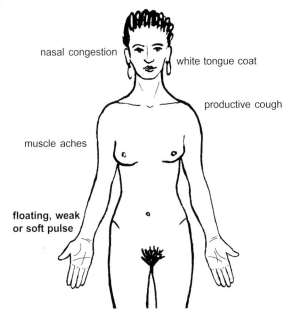

nasal congestion

white tongue coat

productive cough

muscle aches

floating, weak
or soft pulse

Combinations
- With a small dose of **3.5 Ma Huang Tang Wan** for wheezing and relatively severe Wind Cold with underlying *qi* deficiency.

Dosage and method of administration
8-12 pills every two hours or so, on an empty stomach. The pills can be taken with hot soup or rice and ginger porridge to encourage mild sweating. It is also of benefit to follow a dose with a hot bath.

Cautions and contraindications
Not suitable for Wind Heat patterns or Warm diseases.

3.15 QING QI HUA TAN WAN

清气化痰丸

Lanzhou Foci Pharmaceutical Factory (Gansu)
'Clear the *Qi* and Transform Phlegm Pills'
Qing Qi Hua Tan Wan is packaged in bottles of 200 pills.
Also available as: Clean Air Teapills (PF), Pinellia Root Teapills,
Pinellia Expectorant Pills, Clear Damp and Transform Phlegm Pill
(BE)

TCM actions
Clears Phlegm Heat from the Lungs, stops cough.

Biomedical actions
Expectorant, decongestant, febrifuge, antitussive.

INDICATIONS

• Acute and chronic Phlegm Heat in the Lungs. The main feature indicating the use of this formula is the nature and quantity of the sputum–copious, thick, sticky, yellow or green. Sometimes the sputum is so sticky that it can be hard to expectorate and so may not be immediately apparent. The patient will usually have difficulty breathing or have clear rattles and rales or wheezing. The cough tends to be loud and productive.

• For lingering or low grade Phlegm Heat patterns of the Lungs with chronic cough and sticky yellow or green sputum. Also useful for chronic Phlegm Heat congestion in the sinuses.

• With the appropriate identifying features, this formula can be used to treat biomedical conditions such as acute and chronic bronchitis, bronchiectasis, pneumonia, whooping cough, bronchial asthma and chronic sinusitis.

Composition (each pill contains powdered)
Scutellaria baicalensis (huang qin, scute) 26mg, *Poria cocos* (fu ling, hoelen) 26mg, *Trichosanthes kirilowi* (gua lou, trichosanthes) 25mg, *Pinellia ternata* (ban xia, pinellia) 21mg, *Prunus armenica* (xing ren, apricot seed) 20mg, *Arisaema cosanguinium* (dan nan xing, pig bile treated arisaema) 20mg, *Citrus aurantium* (zhi shi, aurantium) 17mg, *Citrus nobilis* (chen pi, citrus peel) 13mg

Combinations
• With **14.5 Chuan Xin Lian Antiphlogistic Tablets** or **3.16 Ching Fei Yi Huo Pien** for severe cases (the latter when there is constipation).

Pattern identifying features

- **Phlegm Heat in the Lungs**
- the cough is worse at night & early in the morning
- dry mouth, thirst, or an unpleasant sticky sensation in the mouth
- fever

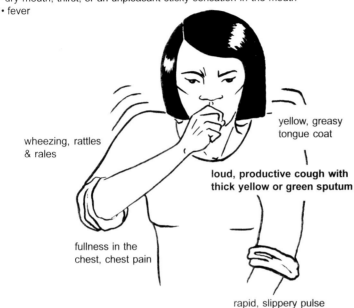

wheezing, rattles
& rales

yellow, greasy
tongue coat

loud, productive cough with
thick yellow or green sputum

fullness in the
chest, chest pain

rapid, slippery pulse

- With one or two vials of per day of **3.21 She Dan Chuan Bei Ye** for chronic Phlegm Heat in the Lungs with very sticky sputum.
- With **2.22 Er Chen Wan** for milder chronic cases with mixtures of yellow and white sticky sputum.

Dosage and method of administration

The recommended dose is 8 pills three times daily, however to get a good result in acute cases a much larger dose is generally required, 12-18 pills every 2 hours, to a maximum of around 80-100 pills per day. Therefore in acute cases one jar (200 pills) should only last 2-3 days. In chronic cases of lingering Phlegm Heat, 8-16 pills three times daily is usually sufficient. Take on an empty stomach.

Cautions and contraindications

Not suitable for hot dry cough, cough with thin watery sputum or cough from *yin* deficiency.

RESP

3.16 CHING FEI YI HUO PIEN

清肺抑火片

(Qing Fei Yi Huo Pian)
Tianjin Drug Manufactory (Shandong)
'Clear the Lungs and Restrain Fire Pills'
Ching Fei Yi Huo Pien is packaged in vials of eight pills, twelve vials per box.

TCM actions

Clears Heat and Fire from the Lungs, stops cough, promotes descent of Lung and Large Intestine *qi*.

Biomedical actions

Antipyretic, anti-inflammatory, antibiotic, laxative.

INDICATIONS

- Lung Heat or Lung Fire. This pattern is characterised by an acute loud, painful, barking cough, or wheezing with or without yellow sputum. It typically occurs a few days after an unresolved or severe Wind Cold or Wind Heat invasion. Patients will typically be prone to recurrent episodes, with the illness repeatedly lodging in the same part of the upper respiratory tract, the lungs, throat or sinuses.
- Also useful for acute sore throat (Toxic Heat in the throat) and acute sinusitis (Phlegm Heat or Fire in the sinuses).
- *Yang ming* organ syndrome with acute constipation, abdominal pain, fever and thirst. Because it can clear Heat (and Dampness) from the Intestines, it may also be used for the early stages of Dysenteric disorder.
- With the appropriate identifying features, this formula can be used to treat biomedical conditions such as acute upper respiratory tract infection, bronchitis, pneumonia, whooping cough, pleurisy, tonsillitis, pharyngitis, tracheitis, sinusitis, uncomplicated appendicitis, acute cholecystitis and acute pancreatitis.

Composition (each tablet contains extracts equivalent to dry)

Scutellaria baicalensis (huang qin, scute) 955mg, *Gardenia florida* (shan zhi zi, gardenia) 887mg, *Anemarrhena aspheloides* (zhi mu, anemarrhena) 665mg, *Sophora flavescentis* (ku shen, sophora root) 409mg, *Rheum palmatum* (da huang, rhubarb root) 106mg, *Trichosanthes kirilowi* (tian hua fen, trichosanthes root) 71mg, *Peucedanum praeruptorum* (qian hu, peucedanum) 318mg, *Platycodon grandiflorum* (jie geng, platycodon) 71mg

Pattern identifying features

• **Lung Heat or Fire**
• sore throat
• fever
• focal chest pain with cough

acute sinus infection

red tongue (or tongue tip),
dry yellow tongue coat

**hacking or barking painful
cough with little or no sputum,
or hard to expectorate sputum**

full, rapid, strong pulse,
especially the *cun* position

constipation

Combinations
• With **14.5 Chuan Xin Lian Antiphlogistic Tablets** for severe Heat in the Lungs, or the early stages of Dysenteric disorder.
• With **10.1 Yunnan Paiyao** for hemoptysis.
• With **3.15 Qing Qi Hua Tan Wan** for copious coloured sputum.
• With **9.9 Superior Sore Throat Powder** for sore throat.
• With **9.13 Pe Min Kan Wan** or **9.19 Cang Er Zi Wan** for acute sinus infection.

Dosage and method of administration
The recommended dose is 4 pills twice daily, but to be effective in severe acute Lung Fire patterns, one vial can be taken every 2 hours. Take on an empty stomach. Usually not necessary for more than 4-7 days. Patients should be advised that they may experience diarrhea.

Cautions and contraindications
Contraindicated during pregnancy and for acute cough from Wind Cold or cough due to Lung *yin* deficiency.

3.17 PI PA COUGH TEA

止咳川贝枇杷冲剂

(Zhi Ke Chuan Bei Pi Pa Chong Ji)
Jing Xian Pharmaceutical Co. (Guangzhou)
'Antitussive Fritillaria and Loquat Leaf Dissolvable
Granules'
Pi Pa Cough Tea is packaged in 5 gram sachets, 10
sachets per box.

TCM actions

Clears Heat from the Lungs, moistens the Lungs,
expels Phlegm, stops cough.

Biomedical actions

Antitussive, expectorant, febrifuge.

INDICATIONS

- Cough associated with Wind Heat, Lung Heat or Phlegm Heat. This Heat in this
  pattern may follow an acute Wind Heat or Wind Cold *gan mao*, or be the result of
  hot dry weather, or smoking. The main features are hacking dry or productive
  cough, with or without sticky yellow sputum. Coughing produces chest pain, a
  dry, sore throat, hoarse voice and fever. In some cases there will be constipation.
- With the appropriate identifying features, this formula may assist in the treatment
  of biomedical conditions such as upper respiratory tract infection, acute
  bronchitis, tonsillitis and pleurisy.

Composition (each sachet contains extracts equivalent to dry)

Fritillaria cirrhosa (chuan bei mu, fritillaria) 1.8g, *Eriobotria japonica* (pi pa ye, loquat
leaf) 1.8g, *Glycyrrhiza uralensis* (gan cao, licorice) 1.8g, *Lonicera japonica* (jin yin hua,
honeysuckle) 1.8g, *Platycodon grandiflorum* (jie geng, platycodon) 1.4g, *Scutellaria
baicalensis* (huang qin, scute) 900mg, *Morus alba* (sang bai pi, mulberry root bark)
900mg, *Mentha haplocalyx* (bo he, mint) 900mg, *Perilla frutescens* (su zi, perilla seed)
900mg, *Lepidium apetalum* (ting li zi, lepidium seed) 900mg, *Trichosanthis kirilowii* (gua
luo ren, trichosanthes seed) 900mg, *Peucedanum praeruptorum* (qian hu, peucedanum)

Pattern identifying features

• **Heat type cough**

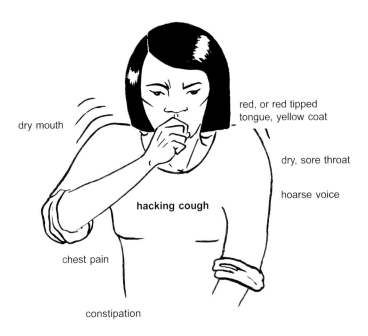

dry mouth

red, or red tipped
tongue, yellow coat

dry, sore throat

hoarse voice

hacking cough

chest pain

constipation

750mg, *Aster tataricus* (zi wan, aster) 750mg, *Stemona sessifolia* (bai bu, stemona) 750mg, *Lilium lancifolium* (bai he, lily), *Cynanchum stauntonii* (bai qian, cynanchum) 540mg

Dosage and method of administration

Adults: 1-2 sachets dissolved in hot water, three times daily.
Children over 4 years: 1 sachet dissolved in hot water, two or three times daily.
Children under 4 years *see* **12.1 Bo Ying Compound**.

Cautions and contraindications

Contains aspartame and phenylalanine. Not suitable for phenylketonurics.

RESP

3.18 TUNG HSUAN LI FEI PIEN

通宣理肺片

(Tong Xuan Li Fei Pian)
Tianjin Drug Manufactory (Shandong)
'Open and Benefit the Lung Pills'
Tung Hsuan Li Fei Pien is packaged in vials of eight pills, twelve vials per box.

TCM actions
Stops cough, benefits the throat, detoxifies and promotes healing.

Biomedical actions
Antitussive, antispasmodic, demulcent, anti-inflammatory.

INDICATIONS

- Cough from various etiologies. This formula has a broad application and can be used for acute or chronic cough, either from external or internal causes, with heat or cold, with or without Phlegm congestion. Good for smokers cough. Especially good for dryness and mild Heat patterns
- Sore throat from various etiologies. These include both acute and chronic sore throat, dry sore throat and sore throat with Phlegm congestion.
- May also be useful in the healing of gastric ulcers and in the treatment of chronic upper gastro-intestinal disorders, such as gastritis, with elements of both *qi* and *yin* deficiency. Disorders such as these are characterised by indeterminate gnawing hunger (*see* glossary), morning nausea, belching, epigastric fullness and pain and perhaps a peeled patch in the centre of the tongue (the Stomach area).

Composition (each pill contains extracts equivalent to dry)
Glycyrrhiza uralensis (gan cao, licorice) 2.07g, *Perilla frutescens* (zi su ye, perilla leaf) 1.18g, *Platycodon grandiflorum* (jie geng, platycodon) 665mg, *Peucedanum praeruptorum* (qian hu, peucedanum) 636mg, *Citrus aurantium* (zhi shi, aurantium) 591mg, *Citrus reticulata* (chen pi, citrus) 369mg, *Polygonatum odoratum* (yu zhu, polygonatum) 318mg, *Pueraria lobata* (ge gen, pueraria) 318mg, *Lilium lancifolium* (bai he, lily) 240mg

Combinations
- With **3.4 Gan Mao Ling** for acute cough from severe Wind Heat.
- With **2.27 Wei Te Ling** for epigastric pain and hyperacidity associated with peptic ulcer disease.
- With **9.9 Superior Sore Throat Powder** for sore throat from acute or chronic tonsillitis.

Pattern identifying features

• **Lung dryness and Heat**

persistent cough

acute or recurrent
sore throat

stomach ulcers,
epigastric pain

• With **3.33 Yang Yin Qing Fei Wan** or **3.35 Mai Wei Di Huang Wan** for recurrent sore throat from Lung *yin* deficiency.
• With **3.29 African Sea Coconut Cough Syrup** for persistent irritating tickle in the throat.

Dosage and method of administration

4 pills twice daily on an empty stomach. In severe cases, or during the early stages of treatment (the first week or so), the dose may be increased by 50%, then reduced as the treatment takes effect.

Cautions and contraindications

May aggravate digestive Dampness and cause abdominal distension and nausea in some patients. This can usually be relieved by reducing the dose. Licorice root has a sodium sparing and potassium leaching effect and when used in large doses can cause Sedema. Caution in patients with hypertension and fluid problems. May counteract spironolactone (Aldactone) and potentiate potassium depleting loop diuretics (like Lasix) leading to hypokalemia.

3.19 DING CHUAN WAN

定喘丸

Lanzhou Foci Pharmaceutical Factory (Gansu)
'Calm Wheezing Pills'
Ding Chuan Wan is packaged in bottles of 200 pills.
Also available as: Clear Mountain Air Teapills (PF)

TCM actions

Stops wheezing and cough, redirects Lung *qi* downwards, transforms Phlegm, clears Heat from the Lungs.

Biomedical actions

Anti-asthmatic, antitussive, expectorant.

INDICATIONS

- Acute, chronic or recurrent episodes of wheezing and asthma associated with Phlegm or mild Phlegm Heat congestion in the Lungs. The Phlegm is usually pre-existing, and is stirred up and mobilised by some trigger. Once mobilised, the Phlegm obstructs the bronchi causing difficulty in breathing. The trigger for the wheezing may be a Wind invasion, a sudden change in temperature or exposure to an allergen. The main focus of this formula is in transforming and expelling Phlegm, with directing Lung *qi* downward secondary.
- With the appropriate identifying features, this formula can be used to treat biomedical conditions such as asthma, asthmatic bronchitis, chronic bronchitis and emphysema.

Composition (each pill contains powdered)

Ginko biloba (yin xing, ginko seed) 22mg, *Morus alba* (sang bai pi, mulberry bark) 22mg, *Platycodon grandiflorum* (jie geng, platycodon) 18.4mg, *Perilla frutescens* (zi su ye, perilla leaf) 18.4mg, *Prunus armenica* (xing ren, apricot seed) 18.4mg, *Scutellaria baicalensis* (huang qin, scute) 18.4mg, *Pinellia ternata* (ban xia, pinellia) 18.4mg, *Stemona sessifolia* (bai bu, stemona) 14.7mg, *Glycyrrhiza uralensis* (gan cao, licorice) 14.7mg, *Aster tataricus* (zi wan, aster) 14.7mg

Combinations

- With **3.21 She Dan Chuan Bei Ye** for patients with copious sputum or obvious rattles and rales, until the sputum starts to break up.
- With **2.22 Er Chen Wan** for very thick or hard to expectorate sputum.

Pattern identifying features

- **Phlegm Heat accumulation in the Lungs**
- **dyspnea, wheezing**

wheeze, rattles & rales

**white or slightly
yellow sputum**

greasy white or yellow
tongue coat

slippery pulse

tightness & fullness in the chest

- With **3.15 Qing Qi Hua Tan Wan** for chronic deep rooted Phlegm Heat wheezing.

Dosage and method of administration

15 pills three times daily on an empty stomach. In severe cases or during the early stages of treatment (the first 7-10 days), a 50% increase in dose may be used, then reduced to a maintenance dose (~8-12 pills three times daily) as the treatment takes effect.

Cautions and contraindications

Contraindicated in cases of wheezing, breathlessness and asthma from *qi* or *yin* deficiency.

RESP

3.20 QI GUAN YAN KE SOU TAN CHUAN WAN

气管炎咳嗽痰喘丸

Tong Ren Tang (Beijing)
'Bronchitis, Cough, Phlegm and Wheezing Pills'
Qi Guan Yan Ke Sou Tan Chuan Wan is packaged in bottles of 300 pills.

TCM actions

Stops cough, redirects Lung *qi* downwards, transforms Phlegm.

Biomedical actions

Anti-asthmatic, antitussive, expectorant.

INDICATIONS

- Chronic cough from Phlegm congestion in the Lungs. Most suitable for chronic bronchitis with underlying Spleen deficiency.
- With the appropriate identifying features, this formula can be used to treat biomedical conditions such as chronic bronchitis, emphysema, asthmatic bronchitis and bronchiectasis.

Composition (30 pills contains powdered)

Codonopsis pilosula (dang shen, codonopsis) 570mg, *Platycodon grandiflorum* (jie geng, platycodon) 300mg, *Morus alba* (sang ye, mulberry leaf) 270mg, *Zingiber officinalis* (sheng jiang, ginger) 270mg, *Peucedanum praeruptorium* (qian hu, peucedanum) 180mg, *Cynanchum stauntonii* (bai qian, cynanchum) 180mg, *Pinellia ternata* (ban xia, pinellia) 180mg, *Fritillaria thunbergii* (zhe bei mu, fritillaria) 180mg, *Perilla frutescens* (zi su ye, perilla leaf) 180mg, *Aster tataricus* (zi wan, aster) 180mg, *Poria cocos* (fu ling, hoelen) 180mg, *Glycyrrhiza uralensis* (gan cao, licorice) 180mg, *Polygala sibiricum* (yuan zhi, polygala) 180mg, *Paeonia lactiflora* (bai shao, white peony) 180mg, *Stemona sessifolia* (bai bu, stemona) 180mg, *Belamcanda chinensis* (she gan, belamcanda) 180mg, *Allium macrostemon* (xie bai, allium bulb) 180mg, *Prunus armenica* (xing ren, apricot seed) 150mg, *Citrus reticulata* (chen pi, citrus) 120mg, *Schizandra chinensis* (wu wei zi, schizandra) 120mg, *Fritillaria cirrhosa* (chuan bei mu, Sichuan fritillaria) 90mg, *Scutellaria baicalensis* (huang qin, scute) 90mg, *Baphicacanthus cusia* (da qing ye) 90mg, *Cinnamomum cassia* (gui zhi, cinnamon twigs) 60mg, *Asarum seiboldi* (xi xin, wild ginger) 30mg, *Eriobotrya japonica* (pi pa ye, loquat leaf) 2.4mg

Pattern identifying features

- **Phlegm Damp accumulation in the Lungs**
- dyspnea, orthopnea
- breathlessness
- white or slightly yellow sputum

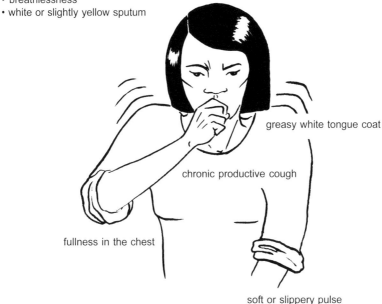

greasy white tongue coat

chronic productive cough

fullness in the chest

soft or slippery pulse

Combinations
- With **3.21 She Dan Chuan Bei Ye** or **3.30 Tong Xuan Li Fei Kou Fu Ye** for patients with very copious sputum or obvious rattles and rales, until the sputum starts to break up.
- With **2.22 Er Chen Wan** for very thick or hard to expectorate sputum.

Dosage and method of administration
The recommended dose for adults is 30 pills twice daily, before meals. Not suitable for children due to the number of pills required.

Cautions and contraindications
Contraindicated in cases of cough, wheezing, breathlessness and asthma arising from *yin* deficiency or Lung dryness.

3.21 SHE DAN CHUAN BEI YE

蛇胆川贝液

Guangzhou Pangaoshou Pharmaceutical Company
(Guangzhou)
'Snake Bile and Fritillaria Liquid'
She Dan Chuan Bei Ye is packaged in vials of liquid
extract, six vials to a box. The vials are pierced with a sharpened straw (supplied).

TCM actions
Breaks up, transforms and expels Phlegm, stops cough.

Biomedical actions
Mucolytic, expectorant, antitussive.

INDICATIONS

- Phlegm Damp congestion in the Lungs. Excellent for relief of persistent productive cough, or cough with deep lying and hard to expectorate sputum, especially continuing sputum in the convalescent phase of an upper respiratory tract infection.
- With the appropriate identifying features, this formula may be used to treat disorders such as persistent sputum in the convalescent phase of acute bronchitis or pneumonia, the tenacious sputum of whooping cough, bronchiectasis or chronic bronchitis.

Composition (each vial contains by volume)
Snake bile (she dan) 2.7%, *Fritillaria cirrhosa* (chuan bei mu, fritillaria) 10.13%, *Prunus armenica* (xing ren, apricot seed) 4.05%, menthol 0.01%, honey 0.5%, water, sucrose, benzoate as preservative

Combinations
- With **3.15 Qing Qi Hua Tan Wan** for chronic or residual Phlegm Heat in the Lungs in the post acute phase of an upper respiratory tract infection.
- With **3.19 Ding Chuan Wan** for wheezing from Phlegm Heat congestion.
- With **2.9 Xiang Sha Liu Jun Wan** for persistent productive cough in a patient with Spleen deficiency (often following repeated antibiotic treatment).

Pattern identifying features

• **Phlegm Damp in the Lungs**
• **persistent productive cough with either green or**
  white, hard to expectorate or tenacious sputum

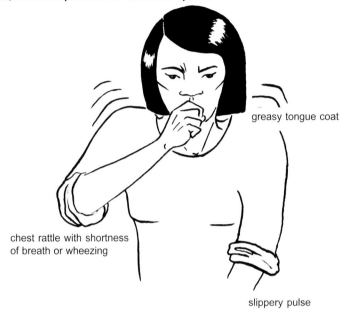

greasy tongue coat

chest rattle with shortness
of breath or wheezing

slippery pulse

Dosage and method of administration

In adults with severe cough and copious sputum, 4-6 vials per day may be used. For maintenance treatment, 1-3 vials per day is sufficient. For children over 4 years old 1-2 vials per day (for children below 4 years *see* **12.1 Bo Ying Compound**).

Cautions and contraindications

Not suitable during the acute stages of a lung infection (with fever and purulent sputum, *see* **3.15 Qing Qi Hua Tan Wan** or **3.16 Ching Fei Yi Huo Pien**), or for persistent unproductive cough (*see* **3.33 Yang Yin Qing Fei Wan**, **3.34 Bai He Gu Jin Wan**, **3.35 Mai Wei Di Huang Wan** or **3.31.1 Zhi Sou Wan**).

3.22 ORANGE PEEL POWDER

三蛇胆陈皮末

(San She Dan Chen Pi Mo)
Guangzhou Qixing Pharmaceutical Co. (Guangzhou)
'Three Snakes Bile and Orange Peel Powder'
Orange Peel Powder is packaged as a single dose powder in a plastic tube of 650mg.

TCM actions
Transforms and expels Phlegm, regulates *qi*, stops cough.

Biomedical actions
Expectorant, mucolytic.

INDICATIONS

- Phlegm Damp congestion in the Lungs. For relief of persistent productive cough or cough with deep lying and hard to expectorate sputum. Especially good for continuing sputum in the convalescent phase of an upper respiratory tract infection. The citrus assists in breaking up and transforming copious thick sputum. In contrast to **3.23 Tendrilleaf Fritillary Powder**, this formula is better when the cough is more productive.
- With the appropriate identifying features, this formula may assist in the treatment of disorders such as persistent sputum in the convalescent phase of acute bronchitis or pneumonia, the tenacious sputum of whooping cough, bronchiectasis or chronic bronchitis.

Composition (each vial contains by volume)
Citrus reticulata (chen pi, citrus) 600mg, Snake bile (she dan) 50mg

Dosage and method of administration
The adult dose is 1 vial mixed in warm water two or three times daily. In severe cases, the dose can be safely doubled for a few days. For children over 4 years old reduce the dose by half. For children below 4 years *see* **12.1 Bo Ying Compound**).

Cautions and contraindications
Not suitable for long term use. Caution during pregnancy.

3.23 TENDRILLEAF FRITILLARY POWDER

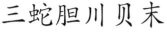 

(San She Dan Chuan Bei Mo)
Guangzhou Qixing Pharmaceutical Co. (Guangzhou)
'Three Snakes Bile and Fritillaria Powder'
Tendrilleaf Fritillary Powder is packaged as a single dose powder in a plastic tube of 650mg.

TCM actions
Transforms and expels Phlegm, moistens the Lungs, stops cough.

Biomedical actions
Expectorant, mucolytic.

INDICATIONS

- Phlegm Damp or residual Phlegm Heat congestion in the Lungs. For relief of persistent productive cough or cough with deep lying and hard to expectorate sputum, especially continuing sputum in the convalescent phase of an upper respiratory tract infection. The fritillaria is excellent for moistening and expelling dry or hard to expectorate sputum. In contrast to **3.22 Orange Peel Powder** this formula is better when there is a degree of Heat and the sputum is dryer, hidden and hard to shift.
- With the appropriate identifying features, this formula may be used to treat disorders such as persistent sputum in the convalescent phase of acute bronchitis or pneumonia, the tenacious sputum of whooping cough, bronchiectasis or chronic bronchitis.

Composition (each vial contains)
Fritillaria cirrhosa (chuan bei mu, fritillaria) 600mg, Snake bile (she dan) 50mg

Dosage and method of administration
The adult dose is 1 vial mixed in warm water two or three times daily. In severe cases, the dose can be safely doubled for a few days. For children over 4 years old reduce the dose by half. For children below 4 years *see* **12.1 Bo Ying Compound**).

Cautions and contraindications
Not suitable for long term use. Caution during pregnancy.

RESP

3.24 SHE DAN CHUAN BEI PI PA GAO

蛇胆川贝枇杷膏

Guangzhou Pangaoshou Pharmaceutical Company (Guangzhou)
'Snake Bile, Fritillaria and Loquat Syrup'
She Dan Chuan Bei Pi Pa Gao is packaged as a sweet syrup in
100ml bottles.

TCM actions
Breaks up, transforms and expels Phlegm, stops cough.

Biomedical actions
Antitussive, expectorant, mucolytic.

INDICATIONS

- Phlegm Damp in the Lungs. Relief of persistent productive cough or cough with deep lying and hard to expectorate sputum. This formula is similar in composition and action to **3.21 She Dan Chuan Bei Ye**. If anything, it is slightly stronger and more focused on alleviating the cough that accompanies persistent Phlegm congestion in the Lungs. Much used for persistent sputum in the convalescent phase of an upper respiratory tract infection.
- With the appropriate identifying features, this formula may be used to treat disorders such as persistent sputum in the convalescent phase of acute bronchitis or pneumonia, the tenacious sputum of whooping cough, bronchiectasis or chronic bronchitis.

Composition
Snake bile (she dan), *Fritillaria cirrhosa* (chuan bei mu, fritillaria), *Eriobotrya japonica* (pi pa ye, loquat leaf), *Platycodon grandiflorum* (jie geng, platycodon), *Pinellia ternata* (ban xia, pinellia), menthol, honey, sucrose, benzoate as preservative

Dosage and method of administration
The recommended adult dose is one tablespoon (~ 15ml) three times daily, although many people simply swig from the bottle every now and then with no untoward effects. For children, reduce the dose by half to a third (for children below 4 years *see* **12.1 Bo Ying Compound**).

Pattern identifying features

- **Phlegm Damp in the Lungs**
- **persistent productive cough with either green or white, hard to expectorate or tenacious sputum**

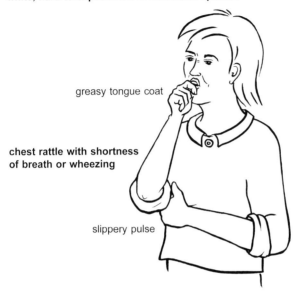

greasy tongue coat

chest rattle with shortness of breath or wheezing

slippery pulse

Cautions and contraindications

Not suitable during the acute stages of a lung infection (with fever and purulent sputum, *see* **3.15 Qing Qi Hua Tan Wan** or **3.16 Ching Fei Yi Huo Pien**), or for persistent unproductive cough (*see* **3.33 Yang Yin Qing Fei Wan**, **3.34 Bai He Gu Jin Wan**, **3.35 Mai Wei Di Huang Wan** or **3.31.1 Zhi Sou Wan**).

3.25 NIN JIOM PEI PA KAO

川贝枇杷膏

(Chuan Bei Pi Pa Gao)
Nin Jiom Manufactory (Hong Kong)
'Fritillaria and Loquat Leaf Syrup'
Nin Jiom Pei Pa Kao is packaged as a thick sweet syrup.

TCM actions

Transforms and expels Phlegm, clears Heat, moistens Lung *yin*, stops cough.

Biomedical actions

Antitussive, expectorant, mucolytic.

INDICATIONS

- Phlegm, Phlegm Heat, or Phlegm Heat in the Lungs, with mild damage to *yin* and Lung fluids. Especially good for persistent Phlegm Heat type cough that has begun to damage *yin* fluids in the Lungs. Sputum is sticky and hard to expectorate. Also good for persistent cough following an upper respiratory tract infection and smokers cough. Particularly good for children as they like the sweet taste. **3.25 Nin Jiom Pei Pa Kao** can be used for long periods for people who persist in smoking, perhaps acting to prevent some of the potential damage smoking can cause by helping break up Phlegm and by moistening and cooling the Lungs. Although tending to be cooling in general, this formula is mild enough to be used for Phlegm congestion without Heat.
- Also useful for hoarse voice, aphonia or sore throat from Phlegm, dryness or overuse. Helps soothe recurrent sore throat from Phlegm Heat congestion and mild dryness. This formula is particularly good for throat problems of this type because it is very viscous and adheres to and soothes the throat.

Composition (each 15ml contains)

Eriobotria japonica (pi pa ye, loquat leaf) 600mg, *Fritillaria cirrhosa* (chuan bei mu, fritillaria) 300mg, *Prunus armenica* (xing ren, apricot seed) 300mg, *Platycodon grandiflorum* (jie geng, platycodon) 300mg, *Polygala tenuifolia* (yuan zhi, polygala) 300mg, *Glycyrrhiza uralensis* (gan cao, licorice) 300mg, *Trichosanthis kirilowii* (gua luo ren, trichosanthes seed) 300mg, *Glehnia littoralis* (sha shen, glehnia) 150mg, *Citrus reticulata* (chen pi, citrus) 150mg, *Zingiber officinale* (sheng jiang, ginger) 150mg, *Mentha arvensis* (bo he, mint) 30mg, honey

Pattern identifying features

• **Phlegm or Phlegm Heat in the Lungs
with mild damage to *yin* fluids**

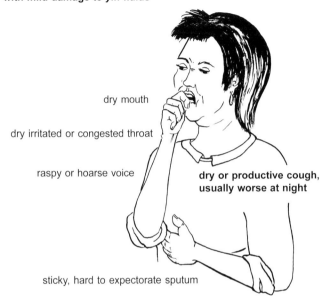

dry mouth

dry irritated or congested throat

raspy or hoarse voice

**dry or productive cough,
usually worse at night**

sticky, hard to expectorate sputum

Combinations
• With **3.1.1 Yin Chiao Chieh Tu Pien** for acute cough from Wind Heat.
• With **3.15 Qing Qi Hua Tan Wan** for acute cough from Phlegm Heat.
• With **3.35 Mai Wei Di Huang Wan**, **3.33 Yang Yin Qing Fei Wan** or **3.34 Bai
He Gu Jin Wan** for *yin* deficiency or dry cough with residual sticky sputum.
• With **9.11 Qing Yin Wan** for dry throat problems associated with overuse or
strain.

Dosage and method of administration
In chronic cases the dose for adults is one tablespoon (~15ml) three times daily
(half dose for children). In general, this dose can be doubled for acute or severe
cases.

Cautions and contraindications
Contraindicated in diabetic patients (due to sugar content).

RESP

3.26 MI LIAN CHUAN BE PI PA GAO

蜜炼川贝枇杷膏

Guangzhou Pangaoshou Pharmaceutical Company (Guangzhou)
'Fritillaria and Loquat Leaf Honey Syrup'
Mi Lian Chuan Bei Pi Pa Gao is packaged as a thick sweet syrup.

TCM actions

Transforms and expels Phlegm, clears Heat, moistens Lung
yin, stops cough.

Biomedical actions

Antitussive, expectorant, mucolytic.

INDICATIONS

• As for **3.25 Nin Jiom Pei Pa Kao**.

Composition (w/v)

Eriobotria japonica (pi pa ye, loquat leaf) 10%, *Platycodon grandiflorum* (jie geng,
platycodon) 3%, *Prunus armenica* (xing ren, apricot seed) 2%, *Adenophora tetraphylla*
(nan sha shen, adenophora) 2%, *Citrus reticulata* (chen pi, citrus) 2%, *Pinellia ternata*
(ban xia, pinellia) 2%, *Schizandra chinensis* (wu wei zi, schizandra) 0.5% *Mentha arvensis*
(bo he, mint oil) 0.02%, *Fritillaria cirrhosa* (chuan bei mu, fritillaria) 0.8%, honey,
sucrose, benzoate as preservative.

Dosage and method of administration

In chronic cases the dose for adults is one tablespoon (~15ml) three times daily
(half dose for children). In general, this dose can be doubled for acute or severe
cases.

Cautions and contraindications

Contraindicated in diabetic patients (due to sugar content).

3.27 FRITILLARY & LOQUAT LEAF MIXTURE

川贝枇杷糖浆

(Chuan Bei Pi Pa Tang Jiang)
Tong Ren Tang (Beijing)
Fritillary & Loquat Leaf Mixture is packaged in bottles of 150ml.

TCM actions
Transforms and expels Phlegm, clears Heat, moistens Lung *yin*, stops cough.

Biomedical actions
Antitussive, expectorant, mucolytic.

INDICATIONS

- Acute and chronic cough from Phlegm or Phlegm Heat accumulation in the Lungs. Can be used for coughs associated with acute Wind Heat and Lung Heat patterns, as well as more persistent coughs. This formula is rather thin in consistency and does not adhere to the throat on the way down, thus is best suited for cough without sore throat.

Composition (each 10ml contains extracts equivalent to dry)
Eriobotria japonica (pi pa ye, loquat leaf) 3g, *Fritillaria cirrhosa* (chuan bei mu, fritillaria) 450mg, *Platycodon grandiflorum* (jie geng, platycodon) 450mg

Dosage and method of administration
Shake well before use. In chronic cases the dose for adults is one tablespoon (~15ml) three times daily (half dose for children). In general, this dose can be doubled for acute cases.

Cautions and contraindications
None noted.

RESP

3.28 LOQUAT LEAF COUGH SYRUP

治咳川贝枇杷露

(Zhi Ke Chuan Bei Pi Pa Lu)
Guangzhou Pangaoshou Pharmaceutical Company (Guangzhou)
Loquat Leaf Cough Syrup is packaged in bottles of 150ml.

TCM actions

Transforms and expels Phlegm, clears Heat, moistens Lung *yin*, stops cough.

Biomedical actions

Antitussive, expectorant, mucolytic.

INDICATIONS

- Acute and chronic cough from Phlegm or Phlegm Heat accumulation in the Lungs. Similar to **3.27 Fritillary and Loquat Leaf Mixture**, with the addition of *Pinellia ternata* (ban xia, pinellia) to strengthen the mucolytic action. Can be used for productive coughs associated with acute Wind Heat and Lung Heat patterns, as well as more persistent coughs.

Composition (each 10ml contains extracts equivalent to dry)

Eriobotria japonica (pi pa ye, loquat leaf) 6.74g, *Pinellia ternata* (ban xia, pinellia) 1.98g, *Fritillaria cirrhosa* (chuan bei mu, fritillaria) 690mg, *Platycodon grandiflorum* (jie geng, platycodon) 590mg, sucrose, benzoic acid and ethyl hydroxybenzoate (as preservatives)

Dosage and method of administration

Shake well before use. Take the appropriate dose 3-5 times daily.

2-5 years 4ml
6-12 years 8ml
12+ years 10-20ml

Cautions and contraindications

Not suitable for children under 2 years of age without medical advice.

3.29 AFRICAN SEA COCONUT COUGH SYRUP

非洲海底椰

(Fei Zhou Hai Di Ye)
Luen Fook Medicine Co. (Malaysia)
'African Sea Coconut'
African Sea Coconut Cough Syrup is packaged in 177ml bottles of
flavoured syrup.

TCM actions
Transforms Phlegm and stops cough.

Biomedical actions
Antitussive, expectorant, mucolytic.

INDICATIONS

• Cough with Phlegm congestion. Good for loosening Phlegm and easing persistent
cough and wheezing associated with colds and flu, chronic bronchitis, asthma,
bronchiectasis and general mucus congestion.
• Soothes sore throat, dry throat and throat irritation from infection, overuse,
strain or smoking.

Composition (each 10ml contains)
Cephaelis ipecacuanha (tincture of ipecac) 0.224ml, *Drinia indica* (squill extract)
0.224ml, Wild Cherry Syrup 0.224ml, *Glycyrrhiza uralensis* (gan cao, licorice extract)
0.224ml, *Myroxylon balsamum* (tolu syrup) 0.448ml, sucrose, benzoate as preservative

Dosage and method of administration
Shake well before use. Take the appropriate dose 4-5 times daily mixed with an
equal volume of hot water.
Infants under one year old ... ½-1 teaspoon
Children one to two years ..... 1-2 teaspoons
Children 2-16 years .... 2-3 teaspoons
Adults .... 4 teaspoons

Cautions and contraindications
Not suitable for children under 2 years of age without medical advice.

RESP

3.30 TONG XUAN LI FEI KOU FU YE

通宣理肺口服液

Tong Ren Tang (Beijing)
'Open and Benefit the Lung Drink'
Tong Xuan Li Fei Kou Fu Ye is packaged in
10ml vials of liquid extract, ten vials to a box.
The vials are pierced with a sharpened straw
(supplied).

TCM actions
Stops cough and wheezing, redirects Lung *qi* downwards, transforms Phlegm
Damp.

Biomedical actions
Antitussive, expectorant.

INDICATIONS

- Phlegm Damp accumulation in the Lungs causing productive cough with sticky
  or frothy white or slightly yellow sputum. This formula is suitable for both acute
  and chronic patterns, as long as Phlegm Damp is present in the Lungs.
- Wind Cold *gan mao* with productive cough or wheezing, headache and stuffy
  nose.

Composition (each 10ml vial contains extracts equivalent to dry)
Peucedanum praeruptorum (qian hu, peucedanum) 192mg, *Perilla frutescens* (zi su ye,
perilla leaf) 164.8mg, *Platycodon grandiflorum* (jie geng, platycodon) 110.7mg, *Citrus
aurantium* (zhi shi, aurantium) 110.7mg, *Citrus reticulata* (chen pi, citrus) 110.7mg,
Scutellaria baicalensis (huang qin, scute) 110.7mg, *Poria cocos* (fu ling, hoelen) 110.7mg,
Glycyrrhiza uralensis (gan cao, licorice) 83.6mg, *Pinellia ternata* (ban xia, pinellia)
83.6mg, *Ephedra sinica* (ma huang, ephedra) 44mg, *Prunus armenica* (xing ren, apricot
seed) 2.5mg

Combinations
- With **3.9 Chuan Xiong Cha Tiao Wan** for Wind Cold patterns with productive
  cough.
- With **3.20 Qi Guan Yan Ke Sou Tan Chuan Wan** for chronic Phlegm Damp in
  the Lungs.

Pattern identifying features

- **Phlegm Damp accumulation in the Lungs**
- Wind Cold *gan mao*

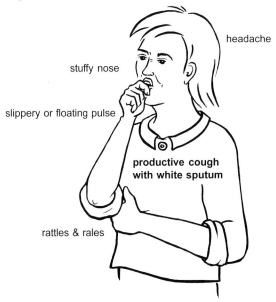

headache

stuffy nose

slippery or floating pulse

**productive cough
with white sputum**

rattles & rales

Dosage and method of administration

2 vials three times daily on an empty stomach (half dose for children).

Cautions and contraindications

Contraindicated in cases with little or no sputum, or with cough, wheezing, breathlessness and asthma from *yin* or *qi* deficiency, or dryness in the Lungs. Caution in patients with hypertension. May cause or aggravate insomnia in some patients due to presence of ephedra.

3.31.1 ZHI SOU WAN

止嗽丸

Lanzhou Foci Pharmaceutical Factory (Gansu)
'Antitussive Pills'
Zhi Sou Wan is packaged in bottles of 200 pills.

TRADE MARK

止嗽丸

ZHI SOU WAN

AUSTL 67309

200 PILLS

LANZHOU FOCI PHARMACEUTICAL FACTORY
LANZHOU CHINA

TCM actions

Stops cough, expels Wind from the Lungs, transforms Phlegm, aids the descent of Lung *qi*.

Biomedical actions

Antitussive, mildly mucolytic.

INDICATIONS

• Lingering persistent cough in the aftermath of an upper respiratory tract infection. This usually follows a Wind Cold or Wind Heat attack that was not completely cleared from the Lungs. This is a useful and broad acting antitussive formula for a range of persistent coughs in both adults and children. It can be combined with other patent formulae to deal with any complicating pathology (other than those noted under contraindications).

Composition (each pill contains powdered)

Schizonepeta tenuifolia (jing jie, schizonepeta) 30.6mg, *Aster tartaricus* (zi wan, aster) 30.6mg, *Stemona sessilifolia* (bai bu, stemona) 30.6mg, *Cynanchum stauntonii* (bai qian, cynanchum) 30.6mg, *Glycyrrhiza uralensis* (gan cao, licorice) 25.6mg, *Platycodon grandiflorum* (jie geng, platycodon) 20.9mg, *Citrus reticulata* (chen pi, citrus) 11.2mg

Combinations

• With **2.22 Er Chen Wan** for white sputum.
• With **3.25 Nin Jiom Pei Pa Kao** for a dry, irritated, ticklish throat.
• With **3.21 She Dan Chuan Bei Ye** for sticky, yellow, residual sputum.

Pattern identifying features

• **Residual cough unresolved following Wind invasion**

tickle in the throat, itchy throat

persistent irritating cough which may be worse at night

Dosage and method of administration

15 pills three times daily on an empty stomach (one third to one half dose for children over 8 years; for small children *see* **12.5 Gan Mao Tea**). In severe cases the dose can be increased by 50%. The dose should be spread out evenly, or may be taken every two hours. If the cough persists longer than 7-10 days, or at least shows no signs of improvement in that time, the patient should be reassessed.

Cautions and contraindications

Not suitable for acute cough from Wind Cold or cough due to Lung *yin* deficiency.

RESP

3.31.2 ZHI SOU SAN

止嗽散

Guandong Yifang Pharmaceutical Factory (Guandong)
'Antitussive Powder'
Zhi Sou San is packaged in bottles of 200 pills.

TCM actions
Stops cough, expels Wind from the Lungs, transforms
Phlegm, clears Heat, aids the descent of Lung *qi*.

Biomedical actions
Antitussive, mucolytic.

INDICATIONS

• As for **3.31.1 Zhi Sou Wan**. This formula is slightly stronger than **3.31.1 Zhi Sou Wan**, and includes herbs to clear Heat and Phlegm Heat from the Lungs, making it more suitable for residual cough with sticky yellow, or hard to expectorate, sputum.

Composition (each pill contains extracts equivalent to dry)
Platycodon grandiflorum (jie geng, platycodon) 127.5mg, *Peucedanum praeruptorum* (qian hu, peucedanum) 127.5mg, *Stemona sessilifolia* (bai bu, stemona) 127.5mg, *Aster tartaricus* (zi wan, aster) 102mg, *Trichosanthes kirilowi* (gua lou, trichosanthes) 102mg, *Glycyrrhiza uralensis* (gan cao, licorice) 76.5mg, *Citrus reticulata* (chen pi, citrus) 68mg, *Schizonepeta tenuifolia* (jing jie, schizonepeta) 68mg, *Eriobotrya japonica* (pi pa ye, loquat leaf) 51mg

Combinations
• With **3.25 Nin Jiom Pei Pa Kao** for a dry, irritated, ticklish throat.
• With **3.21 She Dan Chuan Bei Ye** for sticky, yellow, residual sputum.

Dosage and method of administration
8 pills three times daily on an empty stomach. In severe cases the dose can be increased by 50%. The dose should be spread out evenly, or may be taken every two hours. If the cough persists longer than 7-10 days, or at least shows no signs of improvement in that time, the patient should be reassessed.

Cautions and contraindications
Not suitable for acute cough from Wind Cold or coughs due to Lung *yin* deficiency.

3.32 NING SOU WAN

宁嗽丸

Available in the US, UK and Europe See Note 1, p.xxi

GMP

Lanzhou Foci Pharmaceutical Factory (Gansu)
'Calm Cough Pills'
Ning Sou Wan is packaged in bottles of 200 pills.
Available as: Quiet Cough Teapills (PF)

TCM actions
Transforms Phlegm, stops cough, moistens Lung *yin*.

Biomedical actions
Antitussive, mucolytic.

INDICATIONS

- Post acute or chronic cough associated with mild Lung Heat, dryness or mild *yin* deficiency. Best for lingering cough following an upper respiratory tract infection or Wind Heat *gan mao* that has not been cleared completely, and that has left a residue of Heat and dryness. The cough will be dry and hacking, worse at night, with small amounts of sticky or hard to expectorate sputum.

Composition
Platycodon grandiflorum (jie geng, platycodon) 10.5%, *Dendrobium nobile* (shi hu, dendrobium) 10.5%, *Fritillaria cirrhosa* (chuan bei mu, fritillaria) 10.5%, *Pinellia ternata* (jiang ban xia, ginger processed pinellia) 10.5%, *Perilla frutescens* (su zi, perilla seed) 10.5%, *Poria cocos* (fu ling, hoelen) 10.5%, *Morus alba* (sang bai pi, mulberry root bark) 7.5%, *Mentha arvensis* (bo he, mint) 7.5%, *Prunus armenica* (xing ren, apricot seed) 7.5%, *Citrus erythrocarpae* (ju hong, tangerine peel) 5%, *Oryza sativa* (gu ya, sprouted rice) 5%, *Glycyrrhiza uralensis* (gan cao, licorice) 2.5%

Combinations
- With **3.21 She Dan Chuan Bei Ye** for sticky, yellow sputum.

Dosage and method of administration
8-12 pills three times daily on an empty stomach. In severe cases or the early stages a 50% increase in dose may be used, then reduced to a maintenance dose as the treatment takes effect.

Cautions and contraindications
Not suitable for acute cough from Wind Cold (*see* **3.5 Ma Huang Tang Wan**), cough due to severe Phlegm Heat (*see* **3.15 Qing Qi Hua Tan Wan**) or Lung *yin* deficiency (*see* **3.33 Yang Yin Qing Fei Wan** or **3.34 Bai He Gu Jin Wan**).

RESP

3.33 YANG YIN QING FEI WAN

养阴清肺丸

Lanzhou Foci Pharmaceutical Factory (Gansu)
'Pills to Nourish *yin* and Clear (Heat from) the Lungs'
Yang Yin Qing Fei Wan is packaged in bottles of 200 pills.

TCM actions
Nourishes and moistens Lung *yin*, cools the Lungs, benefits the throat, moistens the Intestines.

Biomedical actions
Demulcent febrifuge, antitussive, mild laxative.

INDICATIONS

- Lung *yin* deficiency dry coughing or wheezing. Good for chronic respiratory illness resulting in Lung *yin* deficiency or for *yin* damage following an acute episode of Heat or Fire in the Lungs.
- Recurrent dry, sore or irritated throat.
- Dryness of the gastro-intestinal system. This includes constipation following a febrile illness that has damaged *yin* and fluids, and dryness of the oral cavity, either from a local pathology, the after effects of radiation treatment, or systemic pathology such as diabetes and Sjögren's syndrome.
- Useful for smokers of tobacco and other substances that introduce heat into the Lungs, damaging Lung *yin*. This formula can aid in repair and cooling of the Lungs, while clearing stubborn Phlegm accumulations.
- With the appropriate identifying features, this formula may be used to treat disorders such as the chronic dry cough of patients with lung cancer, tuberculosis and other chronic respiratory diseases, chronic tonsillitis, pharyngitis and smokers cough.
- This formula was originally designed to treat epidemic 'White Throat disorder' (*bai hou*), analogous to diptheria, with a white curd like membrane on the respiratory mucosa, swollen throat and fever. Diptheria is a life threatening illness that should be managed in hospital.

Composition (each pill contains powdered)
Rehmannia glutinosa (sheng di, rehmannia) 25.6mg, *Ophiopogon japonicus* (mai dong, ophiopogon) 25.6mg, *Scrophularia ningpoensis* (xuan shen, scrophularia) 25.6mg, *Paeonia suffruticosa* (mu dan pi, moutan) 25.6mg, *Paeonia lactiflora* (bai shao, white peony) 25.6mg, *Mentha haplocalycis* (bo he, mint) 11.2mg, *Glycyrrhiza uralensis* (gan cao, licorice) 11.2mg,

Pattern identifying features

• **Lung *yin* deficiency**
• low grade, afternoon or tidal fever

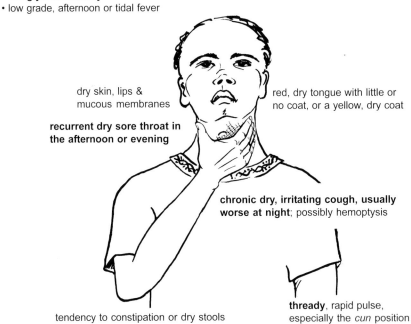

dry skin, lips & mucous membranes

red, dry tongue with little or no coat, or a yellow, dry coat

recurrent dry sore throat in the afternoon or evening

chronic dry, irritating cough, usually worse at night; possibly hemoptysis

tendency to constipation or dry stools

thready, rapid pulse, especially the *cun* position

Fritillaria cirrhosa (chuan bei mu, fritillaria) 9.6mg

Combinations
• With **10.1 Yunnan Paiyao** for blood streaked sputum or coughing blood.
• With **9.9 Superior Sore Throat Powder** for sore throat.
• With **1.33 Hai Zao Jing Wan** for the swollen rubbery cervical lymph nodes that sometimes occur in chronic Lung *yin* deficiency.
• With **7.1.1 Liu Wei Di Huang Wan** for *yin* deficient constipation.

Dosage and method of administration
8-12 pills three times daily on an empty stomach. In severe cases or during the early stages of treatment (the first few weeks), a 50% increase in dose may be used, then reduced to a maintenance dose as the treatment takes effect.

Cautions and contraindications
Contraindicated during pregnancy. Not suitable for acute cough from an external pathogenic invasion. This formula can be cloying, and may aggravate Dampness and Spleen deficiency in some patients. This can usually be alleviated by taking the pills with a small dose (3-6 pills at the same time) of **2.18 Bao He Wan**.

3.34 BAI HE GU JIN WAN

百合固金丸

Lanzhou Foci Pharmaceutical Factory (Gansu)
'Lily Pills to Strengthen Metal (Lungs)'
Bai He Gu Jin Wan is packaged in bottles of 200 pills.
Also available as: Lilium Teapills (PF)

TCM actions
Nourishes and moistens Lung and Kidney *yin*, cools the
Lungs, transforms Phlegm and stops cough, moistens the
Intestines.

Biomedical actions
Demulcent febrifuge, antitussive, mild laxative.

INDICATIONS

- Lung and Kidney *yin* deficiency. This formula is similar in action to **3.33 Yang Yin Qing Fei Wan**, but is more *yin* enriching. The indications are much the same–chronic Lung and Kidney *yin* deficiency causing dry coughing or wheezing and recurrent dry, sore throat. The cough tends to be worse at night and there may be sporadic hemoptysis or blood streaked sputum. The throat soreness is worse in the afternoon and towards the evening, and the throat is usually not especially red or inflamed.
- Dryness of the gastro-intestinal system, post febrile constipation, oral effects of radiation treatment, Sjögren's syndrome.
- Useful for patients with chronic respiratory disorders being treated by oral steroids. Rehmannia formulae have a steroid sparing effect.
- With the appropriate identifying features, this formula may be used to treat disorders such as the chronic dry cough of patients with lung cancer, tuberculosis, silicosis and other chronic respiratory diseases, chronic tonsillitis, pharyngitis and smokers cough.

Composition (each pill contains powdered)
Rehmannia glutinosa (shu di, cooked rehmannia) 25.8mg, *Rehmannia glutinosa* (sheng di, raw rehmannia) 20.6mg, *Scrophularia ningpoensis* (xuan shen, scrophularia) 20.6mg, *Ophiopogon japonicus* (mai dong, ophiopogon) 17.2mg, *Paeonia lactiflora* (bai shao, white peony) 17.2mg, *Lilium brownii* (bai he, lily) 17.2mg, *Fritillaria cirrhosa* (chuan bei mu, fritillaria), *Glycyrrhiza uralensis* (gan cao, licorice) 13.8mg, *Angelica polymorpha* (dang gui, chinese angelica) 12mg, *Platycodon grandiflorum* (jie geng, platycodon) 10.3mg

Pattern identifying features

- **Lung & Kidney *yin* deficiency**
- dry skin, lips & mucous membranes
- thirst, dry mouth & throat
- low grade, afternoon or tidal fever
- night sweats
- heat in the palms & soles

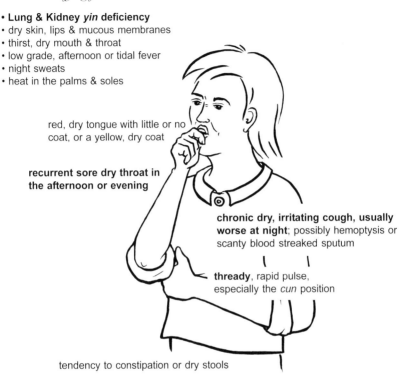

red, dry tongue with little or no coat, or a yellow, dry coat

recurrent sore dry throat in the afternoon or evening

chronic dry, irritating cough, usually worse at night; possibly hemoptysis or scanty blood streaked sputum

thready, rapid pulse, especially the *cun* position

tendency to constipation or dry stools

Dosage and method of administration

8-12 pills three times daily on an empty stomach. The dose may be spread out, or two lots of 12-18 pills may be taken, morning and evening. In severe cases or during the early stages of treatment (the first few weeks), a 50% increase in dose may be used, then reduced as the treatment takes effect.

Cautions and contraindications

Not suitable for acute cough from an external pathogenic invasion or Phlegm accumulation. This formula is quite rich and cloying, and can aggravate Dampness and Spleen deficiency in some patients. This can usually be alleviated by taking the pills with a small dose (3-6 pills at the same time) of **2.18 Bao He Wan**.

3.35 MAI WEI DI HUANG WAN

麦味地黄丸

Lanzhou Foci Pharmaceutical Factory (Gansu)
'Eight Immortal Pill for Longevity'
Mai Wei Di Huang Wan is packaged in bottles of 200 pills.
Also available as: Ba Xian Chang Shou Wan, Eight Immortals
Teapills (PF)

TRADE MARK

**MAI WEI
DI HUANG WAN**

AUSTL 69596
200 PILLS

LANZHOU FOCI PHARMACEUTICAL FACTORY
LANZHOU CHINA

TCM actions
Nourishes and moistens Lung and Kidney *yin*.

Biomedical actions
Demulcent febrifuge, antitussive, hematinic, hypoglycemic,
antihypertensive, improves kidney function, regulates adrenal cortex.

INDICATIONS

• Lung and Kidney *yin* deficiency respiratory disorders. This formula is a variation
of **7.1.1 Liu Wei Di Huang Wan**. The main indications are chronic Lung and
Kidney *yin* deficiency causing dry consumptive coughing, asthma, wheezing or
recurrent sore throat. The cough is worse at night and there may be sporadic
hemoptysis or blood streaked sputum. The throat soreness is worse in the
afternoon and towards the evening, and the throat is usually not especially red or
inflamed.

• Useful for patients with chronic respiratory disorders being treated by oral steroids.
Rehmannia formulae have a steroid sparing effect and can moderate the negative
effects of steroids.

• With the appropriate identifying features, this formula may be used to assist in
the treatment of disorders such as the chronic dry cough of patients with lung
cancer, tuberculosis, silicosis and other chronic respiratory diseases, chronic
tonsillitis, pharyngitis and smokers cough.

Composition (each pill contains powdered)
Rehmannia glutinosa (shu di, processed rehmannia) 42.7mg, *Cornus officinalis* (shan zhu
yu, cornus) 21.3mg, *Dioscorea opposita* (shan yao, dioscorea) 21.3mg, *Poria cocos* (fu
ling, hoelen) 16mg, *Alisma orientalis* (ze xie, alisma) 16mg, *Paeonia suffruticosa* (mu dan
pi, moutan) 16mg, *Ophiopogon japonicus* (mai dong, ophiopogon) 16mg, *Schizandra
chinensis* (wu wei zi, schizandra) 10.7mg

Pattern identifying features

- **Kidney & Lung *yin* deficiency**
- dry skin, lips & mucous membranes
- thirst, dry mouth & throat
- low grade, afternoon or tidal fever
- night sweats
- heat in the palms & soles
- weight loss

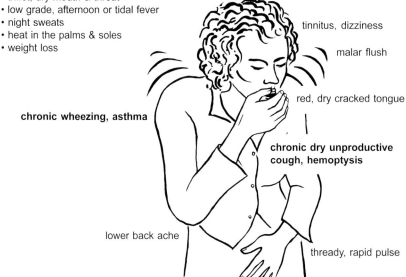

tinnitus, dizziness

malar flush

red, dry cracked tongue

chronic wheezing, asthma

chronic dry unproductive cough, hemoptysis

lower back ache

thready, rapid pulse

Combinations
- For chronic sore dry throat and hoarseness, combine with **9.11 Qing Yin Wan** or **3.36 Luo Han Kuo Beverage**.

Dosage and method of administration
8-12 pills three times daily on an empty stomach. The dose may be spread out, or two lots of 12-18 pills may be taken, morning and evening. In severe cases or during the early stages of treatment (the first few weeks), a 50% increase in dose may be used, then reduced as the treatment takes effect.

Cautions and contraindications
Not suitable for acute cough from an external pathogenic invasion. This formula is quite rich and cloying, and can aggravate Dampness and Spleen deficiency in some patients. This can usually be alleviated by taking the pills with a small dose (3-6 pills at the same time) of **2.18 Bao He Wan**.

RESP

3.36 LO HAN KUO BEVERAGE

罗汉果冲剂

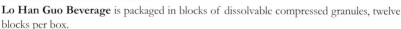

(Luo Han Guo Chong Ji)
Luo Han Kuo Products Manufactory (Guangxi)
'Momordica Dissolvable Granules'
Lo Han Guo Beverage is packaged in blocks of dissolvable compressed granules, twelve blocks per box.

TCM actions
Nourishes and moistens Lung *yin*, cools the Lungs, stops cough, moistens the Intestines.

Biomedical actions
Antitussive, demulcent.

INDICATIONS

- Lung Heat or Lung dryness cough, with generalised dryness in the respiratory system (lips, mucous membranes). Much used for stubborn, chronic dry cough following an upper respiratory tract infection. Also used for recurrent sore throat from Lung dryness. Useful as a Lung moistening agent for smokers.
- Hoarse voice or loss of voice from overuse, smoking, environmental dryness or following an upper respiratory tract infection.
- Constipation from dryness of the Intestines or following a febrile illness that damages Intestinal *yin* and fluids.
- With the appropriate identifying features, this medicine may assist in the treatment of disorders such as acute and chronic bronchitis, acute and chronic tonsillitis and pharyngitis, whooping cough and smoker's cough.

Composition
Momordica grosvenori (luo han guo, momordica fruit) 95%, sugar 5%

Dosage and method of administration
One block dissolved in a cup of boiling water 2-3 times daily.

Cautions and contraindications
Caution in patients with Spleen deficiency or diarrhea.

3.37 SHA SHEN MAI DONG WAN

沙参麦冬丸

Available in the US,
UK and Europe
See Note 1, p.xxi

GMP

Lanzhou Foci Pharmaceutical Factory (Gansu)
'Adenophora and Ophiopogon Pills'
Sha Shen Mai Dong Wan is packaged in bottles of 200 pills.
Available as: Autumn Rain Teapills (PF)

TCM actions
Moistens dryness, cools and nourishes Lung and Stomach *yin*.

Biomedical actions
Demulcent, antitussive.

INDICATIONS

- Dryness patterns of the Lungs and Stomach. Both these organs are prone to dry problems and are easily affected by the pathogenic Heat patterns, weather, habits such as smoking and diet. This formula assists in replenishing a healthy moist lining on dry or damaged tissues, and improves the functioning and health of mucus membranes. Typical features are dry cough, dry mouth and throat, thirst, a dry tongue with little or no coat and a thready, rapid pulse. Useful in alleviating the adverse effects of very dry climates.
- With the appropriate identifying features, this medicine may assist in the treatment of biomedical disorders such as residual dry cough following an upper respiratory tract infection, smokers cough, pharyngitis and gastritis.

Composition
Ophiopogon japonicus (mai dong, ophiopogon) 22%, *Polygonatum odoratum* (yu zhu, polygonatum) 15%, *Adenophora tetraphylla* (nan sha shen, adenophora) 11%, *Glehnia littoralis* (bei sha shen, glehnia) 11%, *Morus alba* (sang ye, mulberry leaf) 11%, *Trichosanthes kirilowi* (tian hua fen, trichosanthes root) 11%, *Dolichos lablab* (bian dou, hyacinth bean) 11%, *Glycyrrhiza uralensis* (gan cao, licorice) 6%

Dosage and method of administration
8-12 pills three times daily on an empty stomach. The dose may be spread out, or two lots of 12-18 pills may be taken, morning and evening. In severe cases or during the early stages of treatment, a 50% increase in dose may be used, then reduced as the treatment takes effect.

Cautions and contraindications
Contraindicated in Phlegm Damp patterns.

RESP

3.38 SHENG MAI SAN WAN

生脉散丸

Lanzhou Foci Pharmaceutical Factory (Gansu)
'Generate the Pulse Pills'
Sheng Mai San Wan is packaged in bottles of 200 pills.
Also available as: Great Pulse Teapills (PF)

TCM actions

Supplements *qi* and *yin* (especially of the Lungs, Heart and Stomach), moistens dryness, stops sweating.

Biomedical actions

Demulcent, energy stimulant, anhidrotic.

INDICATIONS

- Lung *qi* and *yin* deficiency type chronic respiratory disorders with coughing and wheezing.
- Convalescence following a severe febrile illness. High fevers, especially when the Lungs are involved, easily damage *qi* and *yin* and patients often experience nightsweats, insomnia and restlessness after the acute phase of an infection. This formula is ideal to replenish *qi* and *yin* during the convalescent phase.
- Cardiac disorders such as cardiac weakness, palpitations, cardiac arrhythmias (irregularity, tachycardia and bradycardia), and *shen* disturbances from Heart *qi* and *yin* deficiency.
- This elegant formula has a wide application, and as long as the basic pattern is one of *qi* and *yin* deficiency, it can be used to treat a variety of cardiac and respiratory disorders such as chronic asthma and persistent cough, cardiac arrhythmia, tachycardia, chronic obstructive airways disease (COAD), chronic bronchitis, post febrile weakness, debility following sunstroke, post coronary artery bypass debility, coronary artery disease and gastritis.

Composition (each pill contains powdered)

Codonopsis pilosula (dang shen, codonopsis) 80mg, *Ophiopogon japonicus* (mai dong, ophiopogon) 56mg, *Schizandra chinensis* (wu wei zi, schizandra) 24mg

Combinations

- With **7.23 Yu Ping Feng Wan** for spontaneous sweating and low immunity from *wei qi* deficiency.

Pattern identifying features

- **Lung, Heart & Stomach *qi* & *yin* deficiency**
- spontaneous sweating, night sweats
- breathlessness
- dry mouth & throat

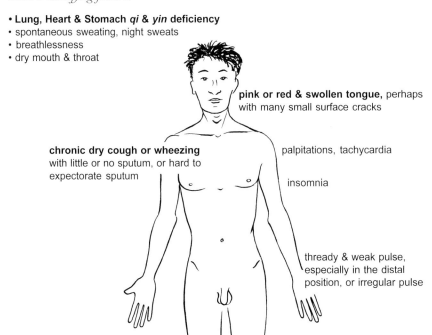

pink or red & swollen tongue, perhaps with many small surface cracks

chronic dry cough or wheezing with little or no sputum, or hard to expectorate sputum

palpitations, tachycardia

insomnia

thready & weak pulse, especially in the distal position, or irregular pulse

- With **7.1.1 Liu Wei Di Huang Wan** for chronic Lung and Kidney *qi* and *yin* deficiency respiratory weakness.

Dosage and method of administration

15-20 pills three times daily on an empty stomach, or two lots of 22-30 pills twice daily, morning and evening. Once the patient notices an effect, reduce the dose to a maintenance level (around 24-36 pills daily).

Cautions and contraindications

Contraindicated in the early stages of a febrile illness, or when there is residual pathogenic influence remaining in the Lungs.

RESP

3.39 YULIN BU SHEN WAN

玉林补肾丸

Yulin Pharmaceutical Factory (Guangxi)
'Supplement Kidney Pills from Yulin'
Yulin Bu Shen Wan is packaged in bottles of 50 capsules.
Also available as: Ge Jie Bu Shen Wan

TCM actions

Strengthens, warms and supports Kidney *yang*,
supplements *yuan qi* and *jing*, strengthens the Spleen.

Biomedical actions

Stimulant and tonic, strengthens adrenal function,
adaptogenic, warms the body, improves respiratory function.

INDICATIONS

- Lung and Kidney *yang qi* deficiency respiratory problems. Particularly good for chronic wheezing, asthma and shortness of breath. Useful to strengthen the Kidneys and their action of assisting inspiration for patients with a long history of respiratory weakness, asthma and emphysema.
- Urinary disorders associated with deficiency Kidney *yang*, including frequent urination, nocturia, incontinence of urine, broken stream or difficulty getting started.
- Useful for supporting *jing*. Used for all *jing* disorders in children and adults, including failure to thrive, slow development, learning problems, congenital disorders, loss of memory, weakening of the bones and teeth.
- Loss of libido, impotence, infertility.
- Generalised debility, convalescence from a debilitating, prolonged or serious illness or surgery. A very good general supplement for the elderly and excellent to build immunity in weak and immunocompromised patients with a tendency to *yang* deficiency.

Composition (each capsule contains powdered)

Gecko gecko (ge jie, gecko) 100mg, *Cervus japonicus* (lu rong, deer velvet) 25mg, *Panax ginseng* (ren shen, ginseng) 25mg, *Astragalus membranaceous* (huang qi, astragalus) 50mg, *Eucommia ulmoides* (du zhong, eucommia) 50mg, *Lycium chinensis* (gou qi zi, lycium) 50mg, *Cordyceps sinensis* (dong chong xia cao, cordyceps stroma) 25mg, *Poria cocos* (fu ling, hoelen) 85mg, *Atractylodes macrocephala* (bai zhu, atractylodes) 65mg

Pattern identifying features

- **Kidney failing to grasp Lung *qi*;
  Lung & Kidney *yang* deficiency**
- urinary disfunction
- fatigue, increased desire to sleep
- spontaneous sweating

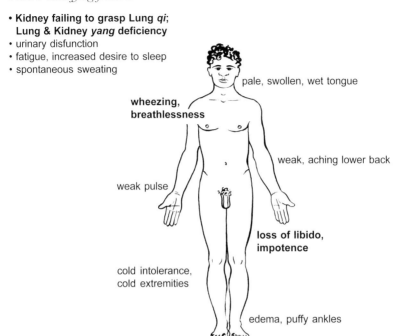

**wheezing,
breathlessness**

pale, swollen, wet tongue

weak, aching lower back

weak pulse

**loss of libido,
impotence**

cold intolerance,
cold extremities

edema, puffy ankles

Combinations
- With **7.23 Yu Ping Feng Wan** or **2.11 Bu Zhong Yi Qi Wan** for severe spontaneous sweating and immune deficiency.

Dosage and method of administration
3-4 capsules, two or three times daily on an empty stomach. Half dose for children 8-12 years old. For infants and small children, one or two capsules per day can be opened and mixed in with a suitable soft and disguising food.

Cautions and contraindications
Contraindicated during the early phase of acute illness such as colds and flu. This formula is quite warming, and may overheat some patients, especially if they are taking other warming medications, such as steroids. It is usually best to start with a smaller than standard dose for a week or two and gradually increase it until the desired level is achieved. If a patient overheats, reduce the dose.

GMP **3.40 BU FEI WAN**

补肺丸

Available in the US,
UK and Europe
See Note 1, p.xxi

Lanzhou Foci Pharmaceutical Factory (Gansu)
'Pills to Supplement the Lungs'
Bu Fei Wan is packaged in bottles of 200 pills.
Available as: Bu Fei Teapills (PF)

TCM actions
Supplements Lung *qi* and *wei qi*, nourishes *yin*, stops cough
and sweating.

Biomedical actions
Antitussive, energy stimulant, anhidrotic.

INDICATIONS

- Lung *qi* deficiency causing chronic cough, wheezing, breathlessness, sweating
  and fatigue. The cough is generally weak and persistent, tires the patient out, and
  is aggravated or initiated by exertion, fatigue or exposure to wind. Sputum, if
  present, is thin and mostly clear, frothy or white.
- With the appropriate identifying features this formula can assist in the treatment
  of biomedical conditions such as chronic asthma, persistent cough, chronic
  obstructive airways disease (COAD) and chronic bronchitis.

Composition
Astragalus membranaceous (huang qi, astragalus) 28%, *Rehmannia glutinosa* (shu di,
processed rehmannia) 28%, *Morus alba* (sang bai pi, mulberry root bark) 13%, *Aster
tataricus* (zi wan, aster) 11%, *Changium smyrnioides* (ming dang shen, changium) 8%,
Schizandra chinensis (wu wei zi, schizandra) 7%, *Panax ginseng* (ren shen, ginseng) 2%

Combinations
- With **7.23 Yu Ping Feng Wan** or **3.41 Xu Han Ting** for severe spontaneous
  sweating and low immunity from *wei qi* deficiency.
- With **2.8 Liu Jun Zi Wan** or **7.22 Shen Qi Da Bu Wan** for more severe Spleen *qi*
  deficiency.
- With **7.15 Yulin Da Bu Wan** if Kidney weakness is contributing to wheezing.
- With **3.22 Orange Peel Powder** for copious white sputum.

Pattern identifying features

- **Lung *qi* deficiency**
- weak low voice or a reluctance to speak
- frequent colds
- aversion to wind

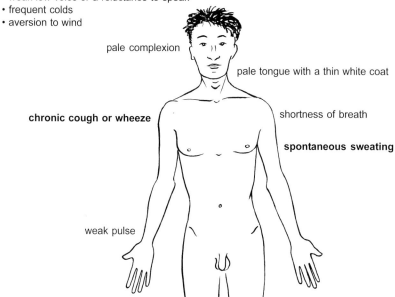

pale complexion

pale tongue with a thin white coat

chronic cough or wheeze

shortness of breath

spontaneous sweating

weak pulse

Dosage and method of administration

8-12 pills three times daily on an empty stomach. The dose may be spread out, or two lots of 12-18 pills may be taken, morning and evening. In severe cases or during the early stages of treatment (the first few weeks), a 50% increase in dose may be used, then reduced as the treatment takes effect.

Cautions and contraindications

Contraindicated in the early stages of a febrile illness, or when there is residual pathogenic influence remaining in the Lungs.

3.41 XU HAN TING

虚汗停

Jing Xian Pharmaceutical Co. (Guangzhou)
'Stop Deficient Sweating'
Xu Han Ting is packaged in 10 gram sachets of
dissolvable granules, ten sachets per box.

TCM actions
Supplements Spleen and Lung *qi*, strengthens *wei qi*,
stops sweating.

Biomedical actions
Astringent, anhidrotic, stimulates immunity.

INDICATIONS

- Sweating associated with *wei qi* deficiency. The focus of this astringent formula is on controlling the symptom of sweating, while secondarily strengthening the source of *wei qi*, the Spleen. Although it is targeted at *wei qi*, it can be used for any type of excessive sweating disorder when combined with the appropriate constitutional formula.
- Weakened immunity. Can be used alone for weak immunity. Especially good for children. May be used preventatively for those at risk of increased exposure to pathogens, such as children starting daycare or during influenza epidemics.
- Allergies. May be useful in hayfever, asthma and other atopic respiratory conditions, as these are often associated with *wei qi* deficiency and chronic retention of Wind in the nasal and respiratory mucus membranes.

Composition (each sachet contains extracts equivalent to dry)
Astragalus membranaceous (huang qi, astragalus) 2.97g, *Zizyphus jujuba* (da zao, chinese dates) 2.97g, *Oryza sativa* (nuo dao gen, glutinous rice root) 3.96g, *Triticum aestivum* (fu xiao mai, wheat) 3.96g, *Dioscorea opposita* (shan yao, dioscorea) 1.98g, *Atractylodes macrocephala* (bai zhu, atractylodes) 1.32g, *Pseudostellaria heterophylla* (tai zi shen, pseudostellaria) 1.32g, *Ostrea gigas* (mu li, oyster shell powder) 600mg

Combinations
- With **1.24 Er Xian Wan** or **1.23.1 Zhi Bai Ba Wei Wan** for severe or frequent nightsweats from *yin* deficiency.

Pattern identifying features

- **Wei qi deficiency**
- **nightsweats**
- frequent colds

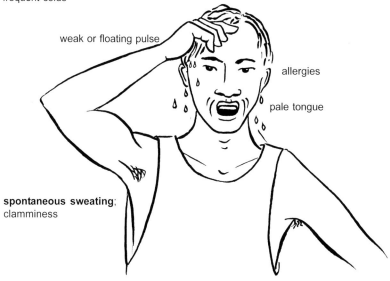

weak or floating pulse

allergies

pale tongue

spontaneous sweating;
clamminess

- With **2.11 Bu Zhong Yi Qi Wan** or **7.23 Yu Ping Feng Wan** for spontaneous sweating and frequent colds from *wei qi* deficiency.
- With **3.38 Sheng Mai San Wan** for sweating from *qi* and *yin* deficiency following a febrile illness.
- With **7.9 Fu Gui Ba Wei Wan** for copious sweating associated with *yang* deficiency.

Dosage and method of administration
Adults: 1-2 sachets dissolved in hot water, three times daily.
Children: ½-1 sachet, dissolved in hot water, once or twice daily.

Cautions and contraindications
Contraindicated in the early stages of a febrile or other acute upper respiratory tract illness (Wind Heat or Wind Cold *gan mao*), such as the common cold or flu.

RESP

4

Patent Medicines for Genito-urinary Disorders

Edema

Urinary Tract Infection (*Lin* syndrome)

Kidney & Bladder calculi

Frequency, nocturia, incontinence

See also

GMP 4.1 ZHEN WU TANG WAN

真武汤丸

Available in the US,
UK and Europe
See Note 1, p.xxi

Lanzhou Foci Pharmaceutical Factory (Gansu)
'True Warrior Pills'
Zhen Wu Tang Wan is packaged in bottles of 200 pills.
Available as: True Warrior Teapills (PF), Zhen Wu Tang (HT)

TCM actions
Warms the Kidney and Spleen, mobilises *yang* and activates
fluid metabolism, promotes urination.

Biomedical actions
Diuretic, cardiac stimulant.

INDICATIONS

- Edema associated with failure of Kidney *yang* to process and transform fluids.
  The edema is generally worse in the lower body, in particular the ankles and is
  usually pitting.
- *Shao yin* syndrome. This is *yang* deficiency affecting the Heart and Kidney. The
  typical features include palpitations, edema, poor circulation, cold extremities,
  bluish discoloration of the lips and tongue and a deep or imperceptible pulse.
- Abdominal pain, chronic diarrhea, weak digestion, poor fluid metabolism and
  dizziness from Spleen and Kidney *yang* deficiency.
- With the appropriate identifying features, this formula can be used to treat
  biomedical conditions such as congestive cardiac failure, cardiac edema, cor
  pulmonale, chronic nephritis, nephrotic syndrome, chronic hepatic disease
  resulting in ascites, Ménière's disease, hypothyroidism, chronic colitis and chronic
  arthritic pain.

Composition
Poria cocos (fu ling, hoelen) 24.5%, *Atractylodes macrocephala* (bai zhu, atractylodes)
24.5%, *Paeonia lactiflora* (bai shao, white peony) 19.5%, *Aconite carmichaeli* (shu fu zi,
processed aconite) 19.5%, *Zingiber officinale* (sheng jiang, ginger) 9.5%

Combinations
- With **4.2 Wu Ling San Wan** for severe edema.
- With **3.38 Sheng Mai San Wan** for cough or orthopnea with copious watery
  sputum.

Pattern identifying features

• **Kidney (& Spleen/Heart)** *yang* **deficiency**
• cold intolerance
• increased desire to sleep
• fatigue, exhaustion
• cough with thin watery sputum

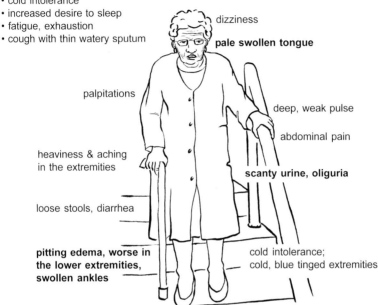

dizziness

pale swollen tongue

palpitations

deep, weak pulse

abdominal pain

heaviness & aching
in the extremities

scanty urine, oliguria

loose stools, diarrhea

**pitting edema, worse in
the lower extremities,
swollen ankles**

cold intolerance;
cold, blue tinged extremities

• With **7.1.1 Liu Wei Di Huang Wan** for nephrotic syndrome of a *yang* deficient
type.

Dosage and method of administration
8-12 pills three times daily on an empty stomach. The dose may be spread out, or
two lots of 12-18 pills may be taken, morning and evening or before bed. In severe
cases or during the early stages of treatment (the first few weeks), a 50% increase in
dose may be used, then reduced as the treatment takes effect.

Cautions and contraindications
Contraindicated during pregnancy. This is a very warming formula and is not
suitable for patients with swelling associated with Heat or Damp Heat patterns.

GMP **4.2 WU LING SAN WAN**

五苓散丸

Lanzhou Foci Pharmaceutical Factory (Gansu)
'Five *Ling* Powder Pills'
Wu Ling San Wan is packaged in bottles of 200 pills.
Available as: Wu Ling San Teapills (PF)

Available in the US,
UK and Europe
See Note 1, p.xxi

TCM actions
Promotes urination, strengthens the Spleen and benefits fluid metabolism.

Biomedical actions
Diuretic.

INDICATIONS

• Mild edema associated with Spleen deficiency and the accumulation of pathological fluids. **4.2 Wu Ling San Wan** is very useful as a general mild diuretic which can be used alone or combined with another constitutional formula. The edema tends to be more noticeable in the upper body, in particular around the eyes and in the fingers.

• Oliguria or anuria associated with an acute pathogenic invasion, characterised by fever, headache, thirst, vomiting and a floating pulse. This is a type of *tai yang* syndrome, in which the pathogen (usually Wind Cold) obstructs the *tai yang* channels and organs, blocking the passage of urine, which then backs up and contravects upwards through the *san jiao*.

• Summerdamp invasion or Sudden Turmoil disorder (*see* glossary) with acute vomiting and diarrhea. In this case, promoting urination provides an alternative outlet for the pathogen.

• With the appropriate identifying features, this formula can be used to treat biomedical conditions such as edema, nephritic edema, acute gastroenteritis, post surgical urinary inhibition or difficulty, paralysis of the bladder sphincter, mild ascites and neurogenic bladder syndrome.

Composition
Alisma orientalis (ze xie, alisma) 26.5%, *Poria cocos* (fu ling, hoelen) 20%, *Polyporus umbellatus* (zhu ling, polyporus) 20%, *Atractylodes macrocephala* (bai zhu, atractylodes) 20%, *Cinnamomum cassia* (gui zhi, cinnamon twigs) 13.5%

Pattern identifying features

- ***Tai yang fu* syndrome; Spleen *qi* deficiency**
- **edema**

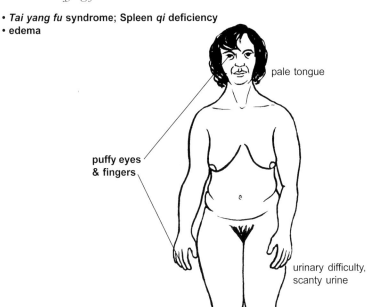

pale tongue

puffy eyes
& fingers

urinary difficulty,
scanty urine

Combinations
- With **2.7 Si Jun Zi Wan** for edema associated with Spleen *qi* deficiency.
- With **6.4 Xiao Yao Wan** for premenstrual fluid retention.
- With **2.23 Ping Wei San** for accumulation of pathological fluids and Dampness in the Spleen and Stomach.
- With **4.1 Zhen Wu Tang Wan** for relatively severe edema associated with Spleen and Kidney *yang* deficiency.
- With **1.2 Si Wu Wan** for edema during pregnancy.

Dosage and method of administration
8-12 pills three times daily on an empty stomach. The dose may be spread out, or two lots of 12-18 pills may be taken, morning and evening or before bed.

Because this is a mild formula, the dose required to effect a result may be higher than recommended, so the patient may increase the dose until urinary output increases.

Cautions and contraindications
Even though this is a mild formula, overuse of diuretic herbs can damage *qi* and *yin*, so prolonged use of this formula alone is not recommended. When overused it may cause symptoms such as dizziness and loss of appetite. Contraindicated in difficult urination associated with *yin* deficiency.

GU

GMP **4.3 WU PI YIN**

 五皮饮

Available in the US,
UK and Europe
See Note 1, p.xxi

Lanzhou Foci Pharmaceutical Factory (Gansu)
'Five Peel Drink'
Wu Pi Yin is packaged in bottles of 200 pills.
Available as: Five Peel Teapills (PF)

TCM actions
Promotes urination.

Biomedical actions
Diuretic.

INDICATIONS

- A broad acting diuretic formula for mild and generalised edema, especially when superficial or interstitial. It is suitable for edema resulting from dysfunction of any of the organs of fluid metabolism–Lungs, Spleen and Kidney. It is typically combined with a constitutional formula aimed at correcting the underlying cause of the edema.
- With the appropriate identifying features, this formula can be used to treat biomedical conditions such as edema during pregnancy, protein deficiency edema, premenstrual fluid retention, edema associated with menopause and chronic nephritis.

Composition (each pill contains powdered)
Poria cocos (fu ling pi, hoelen skin) 19.5%, *Alisma orientalis* (ze xie, alisma) 19.5%, *Morus alba* (sang bai pi, mulberry root bark) 19.5%, *Citrus reticulata* (chen pi, citrus) 19.5%, *Zingiber officinale* (sheng jiang pi, ginger skin) 19.5%

Combinations
- With **1.2 Si Wu Wan** for edema during pregnancy.
- With **4.2 Wu Ling San Wan** for relatively severe generalized edema.
- With **2.7 Si Jun Zi Wan** for edema associated with Spleen *qi* deficiency.
- With **6.4 Xiao Yao Wan** for premenstrual fluid retention.
- With **2.23 Ping Wei San** for accumulation of pathological fluids and Dampness in the Spleen and Stomach.

Pattern identifying features

• **Edema**

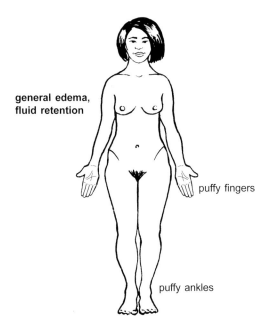

general edema,
fluid retention

puffy fingers

puffy ankles

• With **4.1 Zhen Wu Tang Wan** for relatively severe edema associated with Spleen and Kidney *yang* deficiency.

Dosage and method of administration

8-12 pills three times daily on an empty stomach. The dose may be spread out, or two lots of 12-18 pills may be taken, morning and evening or before bed. In severe cases or during the early stages of treatment (the first few weeks), a 50% increase in dose may be used, then reduced as the treatment takes effect.

Cautions and contraindications

Even though this is a mild formula, overuse of diuretic herbs can damage *qi* and *yin*, thus prolonged use of this formula alone is not recommended.

GU

GMP **4.4 FANG JI HUANG QI WAN**

防己黄芪丸

Available in the US, UK and Europe
See Note 1, p.xxi

Lanzhou Foci Pharmaceutical Factory (Gansu)
'Stephania and Astragalus Pills'
Fang Ji Huang Qi Wan is packaged in bottles of 200 pills.
Available as: Stephania and Astragalus Teapills (PF)

TCM actions
Strengthens the Spleen and supplements *qi*, promotes
urination, dispels Wind Damp, stops pain.

Biomedical actions
Diuretic, analgesic.

INDICATIONS

- Wind edema (*see* glossary). This is an acute condition due to invasion of the superficial tissues by Wind Dampness in patients with a constitutional or relative *wei qi* deficiency.
- Wind Damp *bi* syndrome, mostly in the lower limbs and especially the knees, in patients with acquired or constitutional *qi* deficiency. A commonly used formula for swelling and pain in the knees in clammy, overweight, fatigued individuals.
- With the appropriate identifying features, this formula can be used to treat biomedical conditions such as osteo-arthritis or rheumatoid arthritis of the knees, chronic nephritis, post streptococcal glomerulonephritis, and edema associated with malnutrition and protein deficiency. May assist in alleviating lymphedema following mastectomy.

Composition
Astragalus membranaceous (huang qi, astragalus) 38%, *Stephania tetrandra* (fang ji, stephania) 20%, *Atractylodes macrocephala* (bai zhu, atractylodes) 13%, *Zizyphus jujuba* (da zao, chinese dates) 9%, *Zingiber officinale* (sheng jiang, ginger) 9%, *Glycyrrhiza uralensis* (gan cao, licorice) 8%

Combinations
- With **4.2 Wu Ling San Wan** for severe swelling in the knees or chronic nephritis.
- With **10.22 Shao Yao Gan Cao Wan** for Wind edema with abdominal pain.
- With **3.5 Ma Huang Tang Wan** for wheezing or breathlessness and edema.

Pattern identifying features

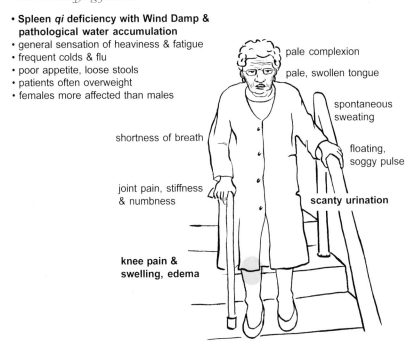

- **Spleen *qi* deficiency with Wind Damp & pathological water accumulation**
- general sensation of heaviness & fatigue
- frequent colds & flu
- poor appetite, loose stools
- patients often overweight
- females more affected than males

pale complexion

pale, swollen tongue

spontaneous sweating

shortness of breath

floating, soggy pulse

joint pain, stiffness & numbness

scanty urination

knee pain & swelling, edema

- With **1.17 Gui Zhi Fu Ling Wan** for edema, joint pain and palpitations following rheumatic heart disease.
- With **7.22 Shen Qi Da Bu Wan** for relatively severe *qi* deficiency.

Dosage and method of administration

8-12 pills three times daily on an empty stomach. The dose may be spread out, or two lots of 12-18 pills may be taken, morning and evening or before bed. In severe cases or during the early stages of treatment (the first few weeks), a 50% increase in dose may be used, then reduced as the treatment takes effect.

Cautions and contraindications

Contraindicated in edema or ascites from pure excess patterns, such as Damp Heat or Blood stagnation.

GU

4.5 BI XIE FEN QING WAN

萆薢分清丸

Lanzhou Foci Pharmaceutical Factory (Gansu)
'*Dioscorea hypoglauca* Pills to Separate and Clear'
Bi Xie Fen Qing Wan is packaged in bottles of 200 pills.
Also available as: Bi Xie Fen Qing Teapills (PF)

TCM actions
Promotes urination and leaches out Dampness, warms the
Kidneys, separates the turbid from the clear.

Biomedical actions
Diuretic.

INDICATIONS

- Kidney *qi* or *yang* deficiency with accumulation of Damp in the lower *jiao* causing cloudy or turbid *lin* syndrome, copious watery or white leukorrhea and white or mucoid discharges.
- With the appropriate identifying features, this formula can be used to treat biomedical conditions such as vaginal thrush (candidiasis), leukorrhea, chronic or recurrent urinary tract infections, chronic cystitis, chronic prostatitis or urinary discomfort with chyluria, albuminuria or urinary sediment, chronic nephritis and nephrotic syndrome.

Composition (each pill contains powdered)
Dioscorea hypoglauca (bei xie, fish poison yam) 35mg, *Alpinia oxyphylla* (yi zhi ren, alpinia) 35mg, *Lindera strychnifolia* (wu yao, lindera) 35mg, *Poria cocos* (fu ling, hoelen) 32mg, *Glycyrrhiza uralensis* (gan cao, licorice) 20.4mg

Combinations
- With **7.9 Fu Gui Ba Wei Wan** for prostate swelling and significant Kidney *yang* deficiency.
- With **2.23 Ping Wei San** for severe Dampness.
- With **2.13 Li Zhong Wan** for Spleen *yang* deficiency and Dampness sinking downward.
- With **2.12 Shen Ling Bai Zhu Wan** for copious Cold Damp leukorrhea with Spleen *qi* deficiency.

Pattern identifying features

• **Kidney *qi* deficiency with Damp accumulation**

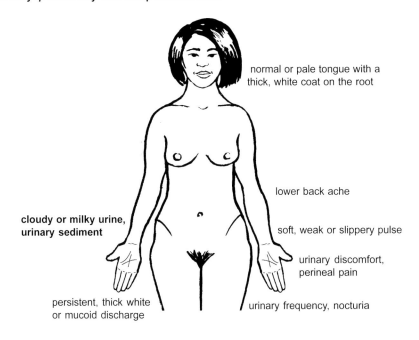

normal or pale tongue with a thick, white coat on the root

lower back ache

cloudy or milky urine, urinary sediment

soft, weak or slippery pulse

urinary discomfort, perineal pain

persistent, thick white or mucoid discharge

urinary frequency, nocturia

• With **11.1 Qian Lie Xian Capsule** or **11.2 Prostate Gland Pills** for Damp accumulation in the prostate causing chronic swelling, perineal discomfort and discharge.

Dosage and method of administration

8-12 pills three times daily on an empty stomach. The dose may be spread out, or two lots of 12-18 pills may be taken, morning and evening. In severe cases or during the early stages of treatment (the first few weeks), a 50% increase in dose may be used, then reduced as the treatment takes effect.

Cautions and contraindications

Not suitable unmodified for patients with lingering Damp Heat.

GU

4.6 BA ZHENG SAN WAN

八正散丸

Lanzhou Foci Pharmaceutical Factory (Gansu)
'Eight (herbs to) Correct Pills'
Ba Zheng San Wan is packaged in bottles of 200 pills.
Also available as: Eight Righteous Teapills (PF)

TCM actions
Clears Damp Heat from the Urinary Bladder.

Biomedical actions
Diuretic, anti-inflammatory, urinary antiseptic.

INDICATIONS

- Damp Heat in the Urinary Bladder causing acute pain and burning with urination. The Damp Heat may be from an external invasion, or generated internally. This is the classical formula for Damp Heat *lin* syndrome.
- With the appropriate identifying features, this formula may be used to treat such biomedical conditions as acute urinary tract infection, cystitis and urethritis, prostatitis, urinary calculi, pyelonephritis and glomerulonephritis.

Composition (each tablet contains powdered)
Lysimachia christina (jin qian cao, golden coin grass) 28.8mg, *Clematis armandii* (mu tong, akebia) 22.4mg, *Gardenia florida* (shan zhi zi, gardenia fruit) 22.4mg, *Plantago asiatica* (che qian zi, plantago) 19.2mg, *Polygonum aviculare* (bian xu, knotweed) 19.2mg, *Lopatherum gracile* (dan zhu ye, bamboo leaf) 16mg, *Juncus effusus* (deng xin cao, juncus) 12.8mg, *Rheum palmatum* (da huang, rhubarb root) 9.6mg, *Glycyrrhiza uralensis* (gan cao, licorice) 9.6mg

Combinations
- With **14.1 Huang Lian Jie Du Wan** for severe pain with urination.
- With **6.1 Xiao Chai Hu Tang Wan** for acute cystitis with alternating fever and chills.
- With **10.1 Yunnan Paiyao** for dysuria with bleeding.
- With **4.10 Shi Lin Tong** for stone *lin* syndrome with Damp Heat.

Pattern identifying features

• **Damp Heat in the Urinary Bladder**
• may be fever, or alternating fever & chills

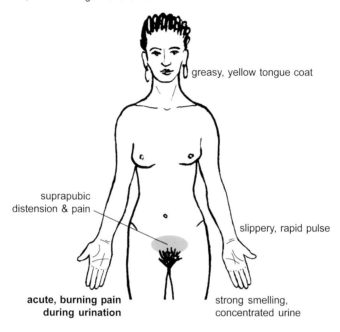

greasy, yellow tongue coat

suprapubic
distension & pain

slippery, rapid pulse

**acute, burning pain
during urination**

strong smelling,
concentrated urine

Dosage and method of administration

The recommended dose is 8-12 pills three times daily. However in acute or severe disorders a higher dose is required to be effective, in general, 16-24 pills three times daily (or about 12 pills every two hours), on an empty stomach.

Cautions and contraindications

Contraindicated during pregnancy.

4.7 QING RE QU SHI TEA

清热去湿冲剂

(Qing Re Qu Shi Chong Ji)
Jing Xian Pharmaceutical Co. (Guangzhou)
'Heat clearing, Dampness Expelling Granules'
Qing Re Qu Shi Tea is packaged in 10 gram sachets of dissolvable granules, ten sachets per box.

TCM actions

Clears Damp Heat and Toxic Heat, promotes urination.

Biomedical actions

Diuretic, anti-inflammatory, urinary antiseptic.

INDICATIONS

- Damp Heat and/or Toxic Heat in the genito-urinary system. This is quite a strong formula for acute infection and inflammation of the reproductive system, urinary bladder and kidneys. The main focus of the formula is on clearing Toxic Heat, with diuresis secondary. Suitable for acute and relatively severe patterns. The main characteristics are thick colored malodorous discharges, redness, swelling and burning pain.
- Damp Heat lodged in the skin, red, itchy vesicular rashes, especially in the lower body.
- With the appropriate identifying features, this formula may assist in the treatment of biomedical conditions such as acute urinary tract infection, acute cystitis and urethritis, acute prostatitis, pyelonephritis, glomerulonephritis, pelvic inflammatory disease, salpingitis, vaginitis, shingles, eczema, genital eczema, Bartholin's cyst and acute genital herpes.

Composition (each sachet contains extracts equivalent to dry)

Chrysanthemum indicum (ye ju hua, wild chrysanthemum) 7.2g, *Coix lachryma-jobi* (yi ren, coix) 4.8g, *Lonicera japonica* (jin yin hua, lonicera) 4.3g, *Plantago asiatica* (che qian zi, plantago) 3.8g, *Lysimachia christina* (jin qian cao, golden coin grass) 3.2g, *Taraxacum mongolicum* (pu gong ying, dandelion) 3g, *Gardenia florida* (shan zhi zi, gardenia fruit) 3g, *Atractylodes lancea* (cang zhu, red atractylodes) 2.6g

Combinations

- With **14.1 Huang Lian Jie Du Wan** for severe pain with urination.

Pattern identifying features

- **Damp Heat &/or Toxic Heat in the genito-urinary system**
- infection of the genito-urinary system
- fever, or fever & chills
- colored discharges

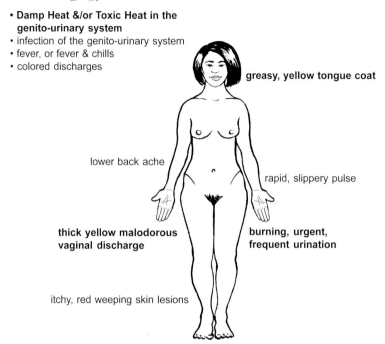

greasy, yellow tongue coat

lower back ache

rapid, slippery pulse

thick yellow malodorous vaginal discharge

burning, urgent, frequent urination

itchy, red weeping skin lesions

- With **6.1 Xiao Chai Hu Tang Wan** for acute cystitis with alternating fever and chills.
- With **10.1 Yunnan Paiyao** for dysuria with bleeding.
- With **4.10 Shi Lin Tong** for stone *lin* syndrome with Damp Heat.
- With **14.5 Chuan Xin Lian Antiphlogistic Tablets** for severe pelvic infection.
- With **6.6 Long Dan Xie Gan Wan** for genito-urinary infections, eczema or herpes associated with Liver Fire or Damp Heat in the Liver channel.

Dosage and method of administration

1-2 sachets dissolved in hot water, three times daily. In severe cases, the dose may be safely doubled.

Cautions and contraindications

Not suitable in the absence of Damp or Toxic Heat, for Cold Damp discharges, or for prolonged use.

GU

4.8 TAO CHIH PIEN

导赤片

(Dao Chi Pian)
Tianjin Drug Manufactory (Shandong)
'Guide out the Red Pills'
Tao Chih Pien is packaged in vials of
eight small tablets, twelve vials per box.
Also available as: Red Door Teapills (PF)

TCM actions
Clears Heat, promotes urination, eases *lin* syndrome.

Biomedical actions
Diuretic, anti-inflammatory, urinary antiseptic.

INDICATIONS

- Acute urinary tract infection or dark, scanty, strong smelling urine with burning
  or irritation. Specifically designed for conditions associated with Heart Fire
  invading the Small Intestine, but can be used for any Heat or Damp Heat pattern
  with dysuria.
- Heart Fire patterns with sleep disturbances, insomnia, mouth ulcers, stomatitis,
  gingivitis, irritability, thirst and a red tipped tongue.

Composition (each tablet contains extracts equivalent to dry)
Gardenia florida (shan zhi zi, gardenia) 1.16g, *Rehmannia glutinosa* (sheng di,
rehmannia) 773mg, *Glycyrrhiza uralensis* (gan cao, licorice) 394mg, Calcium sulphate
163mg, *Rheum palmatum* (da huang, rhubarb root) 87mg, *Poria cocos* (fu ling, hoelen)
23mg, *Alsima orientale* (ze xie, alisma) 23mg

Dosage and method of administration
The adult dose is 4-8 tablets every 2-3 hours.
For children   1-2 years .... one tablet 2-3 times daily
                3-5 years .... one tablet 3-4 times daily
                6-10 years ...... one to two tablets 4 times daily.

Pattern identifying features

- **Heart Fire transmitting to the Small Intestine**
- **urinary tract infection**, cystitis, urethritis
- insomnia, restlessness
- night crying, nightmares

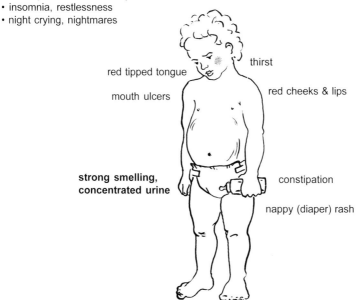

red tipped tongue

mouth ulcers

thirst

red cheeks & lips

strong smelling, concentrated urine

constipation

nappy (diaper) rash

Note: This product is noted on the packaging 'for babies', but the tablet size is too large for children under 6 years old. The tablets can, however, be ground up and mixed with hot water or other liquid to create a suspension that can be delivered to a small child in an eye-dropper. For infants and small children *see also* **12.9 Xiao Er Qi Xing Cha Chong Ji**.

Cautions and contraindications

Contraindicated during pregnancy. The tablets must be crushed before giving to children to avoid choking. May cause diarrhea.

GU

GMP **4.9 DBD CAPSULE**

大败毒胶囊

(Da Bai Du Jiao Nang)
Tong Ren Tang (Beijing)
'Great Toxin Relieving Capsules'
DBD Capsule is packaged in gelatine capsules on blister
sheets, twenty capsules per box.

TCM actions
Clears Toxic Heat, cools the Blood, reduces swelling, stops pain.

Biomedical actions
Antibiotic, anti-inflammatory, detoxicant.

INDICATIONS

• Internal excess Heat and Toxic Heat patterns, especially of the genito-urinary
system. This formula utilises cane toad venom, a powerful detoxicant substance
when used in small doses. Also used for suppurative swellings and superficial
sores, ulcers and carbuncles.
• With the appropriate identifying features, this formula can be used to treat
disorders such as urinary tract infection, cystitis, hematuria, pyelonephritis,
syphillis, abscesses, carbuncles and furuncles.

Composition
Taraxacum mongolicum (pu gong ying, dandelion), *Lonicera japonica* (jin yin hua,
lonicera), *Rheum palmatum* (da huang, rhubarb root), *Bufo bufo* (chan su, cane toad
venom), *Angelica sinensis* (dang gui), Snake skin slough (she tui)

Combinations
• With **10.1 Yunnan Paiyao** for hematuria.

Dosage and method of administration
For acute disorders, the recommended dose is five capsules, 4 times daily and the
length of treatment is usually no more than a few days. For syphillis, the length of
treatment is longer and the dose reduced by 50-75%.

Cautions and contraindications
Contraindicated during pregnancy.

4.10 SHI LIN TONG

石林通

Swatow United Medicinal Factory
'Open (and clear) Stone Painful Urination'
Shi Lin Tong is packaged in bottles of 200 pills.

TCM actions
Clears Damp Heat, promotes urination, dissolves stones and small calculi.

Biomedical actions
Diuretic.

INDICATIONS

- Kidney and Bladder calculi. This formula utilises the main herb for urinary stones, and is quite effective in dissolving and easing the passage of small stones. Generally not effective for large or staghorn calculi. Usually needs to be taken for 3-6 months to be effective. The patient must increase water intake during therapy. Gallstones associated with Damp, Damp Heat or *qi* stagnation. May also be useful for sialoliths.

Composition (each tablet contains extracts equivalent to)
Desmodium styracifolium (guang jin qian cao, desmodium) 3.125g

Combinations
- With **1.23.1 Zhi Bai Ba Wei Wan** for Kidney *yin* deficiency.
- With **4.6 Ba Zheng San Wan** for Damp Heat in the Bladder.
- With **1.15 Tong Jing Wan** for stones with Blood stagnation causing back pain.
- With **6.11 Li Dan Tablets** for gallstones from Damp Heat.
- With **6.3 Chai Hu Shu Gan Wan** for gallstones associated with Liver *qi* stagnation.

Dosage and method of administration
6-10 tablets two or three times daily on an empty stomach.

Cautions and contraindications
This herb can leach potassium from the body when used long term causing palpitations and dizziness. This can be remedied by increasing potassium intake in the form of bananas or potassium replacement pills. Caution in patients with large stones.

GU

4.11 BA JI YIN YANG WAN

巴戟阴阳丸

Lanzhou Foci Pharmaceutical Factory (Gansu)
'Morinda Pills to Balance *yin* and *yang*'
Ba Ji Yin Yang Wan is packaged in bottles of 200 pills.
Also available as: Ba Ji Yin Yang Teapills (PF)

TCM actions

Warms and supplements Kidney *yang*, strengthens the
Spleen, benefits fluid metabolism, secures *jing* and
astringes leakage of fluids.

Biomedical action

Stimulant, strengthens adrenal function, improves fluid metabolism.

INDICATIONS

- Kidney *yang* deficiency. This formula focuses on strengthening the Kidneys' role of governing fluid metabolism. Excellent for warming and astringing the Kidneys to benefit transformation of fluids and alleviate excessive urination. Particularly indicated for leakage of fluids–urinary frequency, nocturia or incontinence. Also useful for chronic cockcrow diarrhea.
- Used to strengthen the Lung Kidney axis for alleviation of chronic or congenital respiratory weakness or hypersensitivity. This manifests as conditions such as allergic rhinitis, atopic asthma and atopic eczema.
- Impotence, infertility, premature ejaculation, copious watery leukorrhea.
- With the appropriate identifying features, this formula can be used to treat other biomedical conditions such as benign prostatic hypertrophy, chronic nephritis, infertility, impotence, chronic colitis, chronic cystitis and chronic pelvic inflammatory disease.

Composition (each pill contains powdered)

Morinda officinalis (ba ji tian, morinda) 19.7mg, *Epimedium brevicornu* (xian ling pi, epimedium) 19.7mg, *Rehmannia glutinosa* (shu di, processed rehmannia) 19.7mg, *Dioscorea opposita* (shan yao, dioscorea) 13.6mg, *Paeonia lactiflora* (bai shao, white peony root) 13.6mg, *Nelumbium speciosum* (lian zi, lotus seed) 10.7mg, *Cornus officinalis* (shan zhu yu, cornus) 10.7mg, *Rosa laevigata* (jin ying zi, chinese rose) 9.1mg, *Dipsacus asper* (xu duan, dipsacus) 9.1mg, *Cibotium barometz* (gou ji, cibotium fern) 9.1mg, *Eucommia ulmoides* (du zhong, eucommia) 9.1mg, *Lycium barbarum* (gou qi zi, lycium fruit) 9.1mg, *Angelica sinensis* (dang gui, chinese angelica) 6.9mg

Pattern identifying features

- **Kidney *yang* deficiency with weakness of fluid metabolism**
- fatigue, lassitude
- cold intolerance

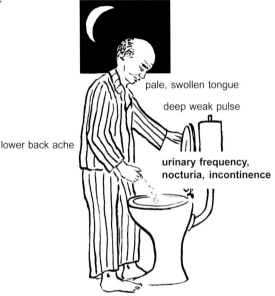

pale, swollen tongue

deep weak pulse

lower back ache

urinary frequency, nocturia, incontinence

Combinations
- With **4.14 Chin So Ku Ching Wan** or **4.15 Sang Piao Xiao Wan** for severe urinary frequency or nocturia.
- With **2.13 Li Zhong Wan** for cockcrow, or persistent Spleen and Kidney *yang* deficient, diarrhea.
- With a course or two of **11.8 Kang Wei Ling Wan** for impotence from *yang* weakness and Blood stagnation.
- With **9.18 Xin Yi San** for congenital Lung and Kidney deficiency allergy and hayfever.

Dosage and method of administration
8-12 pills three times daily on an empty stomach. The dose may be spread out, or two lots of 12-18 pills may be taken, morning and evening. In severe cases or during the early stages of treatment (the first two weeks), a 50% increase in dose may be used, then reduced as the treatment takes effect.

Cautions and contraindications
Contraindicated during the early phase of acute illness such as colds and flu. This formula is generally well tolerated and rarely causes any digestive problems.

GU

GMP **4.12 SAN YUEN MEDICAL PILLS**

宁心补肾丸

(Ning Xin Bu Shen Wan)
Chan Li Chai Medical Factory (Hong Kong)
'Pills to Calm the Heart, Supplement the Kidneys'
San Yuen Medical Pills are packaged as large honey pills sealed in
yellow wax balls.

TCM actions
Supplements and warms Kidney *yang*, strengthens the Spleen
and benefits *qi*, secures *jing* and restrains leakage of fluids.

Biomedical actions
Astringent.

INDICATIONS

* Kidney *qi* and *yang* deficiency patterns with frequent urination, enuresis or nocturia, or watery leukorrhea.
* Weak Kidneys leading to recurrent miscarriage, impotence or infertility. May also be useful for premature ejaculation or anxiety associated with sexual dysfunction.
* Fearfulness, anxiety, easy fright or emotional timidity associated with weakness of the Kidneys and *zhi*.
* Weakness of the eyes from Liver and Kidney deficiency.
* Sperm motility disorder, low sperm count, high proportion of abnormal sperm forms.

Composition
Codonopsis pilosula (dang shen, codonopsis) 25.6%, *Psoralea corylifolia* (bu gu zhi, psoralea) 12.8%, *Polygonum multiflorum* (he shou wu, ho shou wu) 10.24%, *Euryale ferox* (qian shi, euryale) 10.24%, *Eucommia ulmoides* (du zhong, eucommia bark) 10.24%, *Rosa laevigata* (jin ying zi, rose fruit) 7.82%, *Cuscuta japonica* (tu si zi, cuscuta) 7.7%, *Rubus coreanus* (fu pen zi, rubus) 5.12%, *Poria cocos* (fu shen, hoelen) 5.12%, *Allium odorum* (jiu zi, chinese chive seed) 5.12%

Combinations
* With **7.9 Fu Gui Ba Wei Wan** for severe cold.
* With **7.1.1 Liu Wei Di Huang Wan** for *yin* deficiency urinary disorders.

Pattern identifying features

• Kidney *qi/yang* deficiency

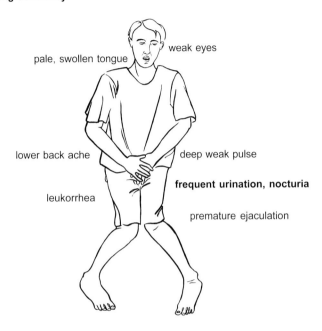

weak eyes

pale, swollen tongue

lower back ache

deep weak pulse

frequent urination, nocturia

leukorrhea

premature ejaculation

• With **8.1 Tian Wang Bu Xin Dan** for Heart and Kidney *yin* and *yang* deficiency anxiety states, premature ejaculation and insomnia.
• With **10.41 Gou Pi Gao** plaster topically on the key acupoints of the lower abdomen (such as Ren.6 *qi hai* and Ren.4 *guan yuan*) to warm the Kidneys and invigorate lower *jiao qi.*

Dosage and method of administration

The recommended dose is one pill twice daily before meals. These pills tend to be quite hard and can be soaked in hot water for ten minutes or so to soften them before ingestion.

Cautions and contraindications

Not suitable for Kidney deficiency patterns with oliguria and edema.

4.13 ZI SHEN DA BU CAPSULE

滋肾大补丸

(Zi Shen Da Bu Wan)
Jing Xian Pharmaceutical Co. (Guangzhou)
'Pills to Nourish and Powerfully Supplement the Kidneys'
Zi Shen Da Bu Capsule is packaged in bottles of 36 capsules.

ZI SHEN DA BU
CAPSULE

AUST L 91203
36 CAPSULES
MADE IN CHINA

TCM actions
Warms and supplements Kidney *yang*, strengthens the Spleen, benefits fluid metabolism, secures *jing* and astringes leakage of fluids.

Biomedical actions
Astringent.

INDICATIONS

- Kidney *qi* and/or *yang* deficiency. This formula is effective for leakage or loss of fluids, in particular urine, and is used to treat urinary frequency, nocturia, incontinence or enuresis. Also treats loss or leakage of other fluids that should be secured by Kidney *yang*. This manifests in problems such as premature ejaculation and copious watery leukorrhea.
- Used for male infertility, impotence and sperm disorders such as low sperm count, poor quality sperm or a high proportion of abnormal forms.
- With the appropriate identifying features, this formula can be used to treat biomedical conditions such as benign prostatic hypertrophy, chronic nephritis, prolapsed bladder, infertility and impotence.

Composition (each capsule contains extracts equivalent to dry)
Epimedium brevicornu (xian ling pi, epimedium) 500mg, *Dioscorea opposita* (shan yao, dioscorea) 240mg, *Rosa laevigata* (jin ying zi, chinese rose) 175mg, *Cuscuta hygrophila* (tu su zi, cuscuta) 150mg, *Nelumbium speciosum* (lian zi, lotus seed) 140mg, *Alpinia oxyphylla* (yi zhi ren, alpinia) 140mg, *Rehmannia glutinosa* (shu di, processed rehmannia) 140mg, *Paeonia lactiflora* (bai shao, white peony) 125mg, *Curculigo orchioides* (xian mao, curculigo) 125mg, *Euryale ferox* (qian shi, euryale seed) 100mg

Combinations
- With **2.11 Bu Zhong Yi Qi Wan** for urinary frequency from Spleen and Kidney deficiency with urinary bladder prolapse, or uterine prolapse that presses on the bladder.
- With **4.14 Chin So Ku Ching Wan** for severe incontinence of urine.

Pattern identifying features

- **Kidney *qi/yang* deficiency**
- **clear copious urine**
- premature ejaculation
- fatigue, lack of vitality
- cold intolerance
- easy sweating

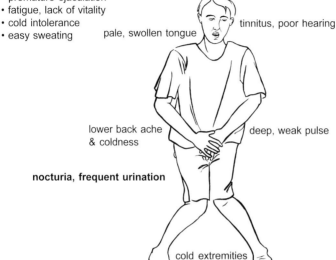

tinnitus, poor hearing

pale, swollen tongue

lower back ache & coldness

deep, weak pulse

nocturia, frequent urination

cold extremities

Dosage and method of administration

3-4 capsules, three times daily on an empty stomach.

Cautions and contraindications

Contraindicated during the early phase of acute illness such as colds and flu, and in urinary dysfunction or other patterns associated with lingering Damp Heat or other pathogen that requires expulsion.

4.14 CHIN SO KU CHING WAN

金锁固精丸

(Jin Suo Gu Jing Wan)
Lanzhou Foci Pharmaceutical Factory (Gansu)
'Golden Lock Pills to Contain the Essence'
Chin So Ku Ching Wan is packaged in bottles of 200 pills.

TCM actions
Consolidates the Kidney, secures *jing* and prevents leakage of fluids.

Biomedical actions
Astringent.

INDICATIONS

- Chronic leakage of fluids associated with Spleen and Kidney deficiency. This is an stringent and thermally neutral formula that simply restrains fluids. It is usually combined with an appropriate constitutional formula to deal with the underlying cause of the fluid leakage. Most commonly used for urinary frequency, nocturia, enuresis, incontinence of urine, premature ejaculation or copious watery or white mucoid leukorrhea.
- Can also assist in astringing excessive sweating and chronic diarrhea.
- With the appropriate identifying features, this formula may be used to treat biomedical conditions such as benign prostatic hypertrophy, childhood enuresis, bladder prolapse, chronic nephritis, chronic nephritic albuminuria, chyluria and chronic pelvic inflammatory disease.

Composition (each pill contains powdered)
Nelumbium speciosum (lian zi, lotus seed) 60mg, *Nelumbium speciosum* (lian xu, lotus stamen) 30mg, *Euryale ferox* (qian shi, euryale seed) 30mg, *Astragalus complanatus* (sha yuan ji li, astragalus seed) 30mg, *Ostrea gigas* (mu li, oyster shell) 15mg, Calcium sulphate 15mg

Combinations
- With **7.9 Fu Gui Ba Wei Wan, 4.11 Ba Ji Yin Yang Wan** or **4.13 Zi Shen Da Bu Capsule** for nocturia, urinary frequency or incontinence arising from Kidney *yang* deficiency.
- With **7.1.1 Liu Wei Di Huang Wan** for nocturia, urinary frequency or incontinence in patients with a tendency to Kidney *yin* deficiency.

Pattern identifying features

• **Kidney *qi* deficiency**
• leakage of fluids

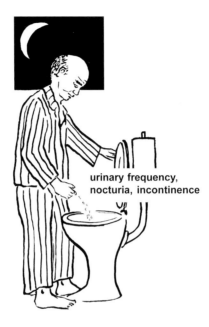

urinary frequency,
nocturia, incontinence

• With **2.11 Bu Zhong Yi Qi Wan** for prolapsed bladder causing incontinence and *wei qi* deficiency excessive sweating.
• With **4.5 Bi Xie Fen Qing Wan** for chyluria and copious leukorrhea.

Dosage and method of administration

The recommended dose if used alone is 12 pills three times daily before meals. However, this formula is usually combined with a constitutional formula, in which case the dose can be reduced by 25-50%

Cautions and contraindications

Contraindicated during the early phase of acute illness such as colds and flu, and in urinary dysfunction or other patterns associated with lingering Damp Heat or other pathogen that requires expulsion.

GU

GMP **4.15 SANG PIAO XIAO WAN**

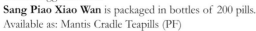

Available in the US,
UK and Europe
See Note 1, p.xxi

Lanzhou Foci Pharmaceutical Factory (Gansu)
'Mantis Egg Case Pills'
Sang Piao Xiao Wan is packaged in bottles of 200 pills.
Available as: Mantis Cradle Teapills (PF)

TCM actions
Regulates and supplements Heart and Kidney *qi*, astringes
leakage of fluids, restrains urine and secures *jing*.

Biomedical actions
Astringent.

INDICATIONS

• Urinary frequency, incontinence of urine, nocturia and enuresis associated with
Heart and Kidney *qi* deficiency. The urinary frequency or enuresis may fluctuate
with the patient's anxiety levels, and, in children especially, the bed-wetting is
often found to be associated with night-time fearfulness or fear of the dark. The
pathology is common in feeble or timid children with weak Kidney energy that
is unable to support the *shen* sufficiently. The focus of this formula is primarily
on astringing the leakage and secondarily on supplementing the deficiency, so it
combines well with more supplementing formulae for long term results.

• With the appropriate identifying features, this formula can be used to assist in
the treatment of biomedical conditions such as diabetes mellitus and insipidus,
and neurogenic bladder dysfunction.

Composition
Os draconis (long gu, dragon bone) 28%, *Chinemys reevesii* (gui ban, turtle shell) 14%,
Ootheca Mantidis (sang piao xiao, mantis egg case) 11%, *Panax ginseng* (ren shen,
ginseng) 11%, *Poria cocos* (fu shen, hoelen spirit) 11%, *Angelica sinensis* (dang gui,
chinese angelica) 8%, *Acorus gramineus* (shi chang pu, acorus) 8%, *Polygala sibirica*
(yuan zhi, polygala) 6%

Combinations
• With **7.1.1 Liu Wei Di Huang Wan** for diabetes associated with Kidney *yin*
deficiency.
• With **2.15 Xiao Jian Zhong Wan** for *qi* deficiency urinary problems in children.

Pattern identifying features

• **Heart & Kidney *qi* deficiency**
• cloudy urine
• nocturia, incontinence of urine
• anxiety, dream disturbed sleep, insomnia
• tendency to timidity or fearfulness
• memory problems

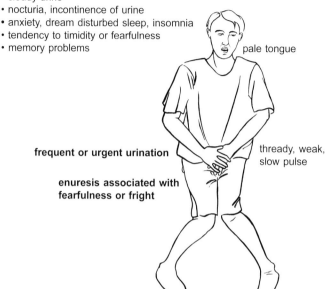

pale tongue

frequent or urgent urination

thready, weak, slow pulse

enuresis associated with fearfulness or fright

• With **2.35 Yu Quan Wan** for diabetes.
• With **7.9 Fu Gui Ba Wei Wan**, **4.11 Ba Ji Yin Yang Wan** or **4.13 Zi Shen Da Bu Capsule** for nocturia, urinary frequency or incontinence from Kidney *yang* deficiency.

Dosage and method of administration

In adults, the dose is 8-12 pills three times daily on an empty stomach. The dose may be spread out, or two lots of 12-18 pills may be taken, morning and evening or before bed. In severe cases or during the early stages of treatment (the first few weeks), a 50% increase in dose may be used, then reduced as the treatment takes effect. Reduce the dose by 50-75% for children depending on their age and weight. Not suitable in pill form for children under 5 years.

Cautions and contraindications

Contraindicated in frequent urination patterns associated with Heat or Damp Heat.

GU

5

Patent Medicines for Cardiovascular Disorders

5.1 XUE FU ZHU YU WAN

血府逐瘀丸

Lanzhou Foci Pharmaceutical Factory (Gansu)
'Remove Stagnant Blood from the Blood Palace Pills'
Xue Fu Zhu Yu Wan is packaged in bottles of 200 pills.
Also available as: Stasis in the Mansion of Blood Teapills (PF)

TRADE MARK

血府逐瘀丸
XUE FU ZHU YU WAN

AUSTL 67229

200 PILLS

LANZHOU FOCI PHARMACEUTICAL FACTORY
LANZHOU CHINA

TCM actions

Invigorates the circulation of *qi* and Blood, quickens Blood, disperses stagnant Blood.

Biomedical actions

Vasodilator, antispasmodic, anti-platelet action.

INDICATIONS

- *Qi* and Blood stagnation patterns, both acute and chronic. This formula is one of the most useful and broad spectrum Blood stagnation movers, incorporating significant *qi* moving capacity as well. Excellent for chronic *qi* stagnation patterns that are complicated by Blood stagnation.
- Especially good for chronic Blood stagnation patterns of the upper body, head, chest and Liver organ system (including reproductive system and channel pathway), but is effective for systemic problems as well.
- Being such a broad acting formula, this formula can assist in the treatment of many biomedical conditions, as long as the appropriate identifying features are present. In the following selection, those considered most amenable to treatment are in bold type.
  - Cardiovascular: **coronary artery disease**, **angina**, sequelae of rheumatic fever, peripheral vascular insufficiency, varicose veins, Raynaud's syndrome, Buerger's disease, vasculitis, phlebitis, hypertension, thrombocytemia, hemochromatosis
  - Liver: **chronic hepatitis**, early stage **hepatic cirrhosis**
  - Head: post-concussion or head trauma syndrome, **migraine headaches**, trigeminal neuralgia, cerebrovascular insufficiency
  - Chest: **post herpetic neuralgia**, intercostal neuralgia, post traumatic chest wall pain, costochondritis
  - Gastrointestinal: peptic ulcer disease, diverticulosis, abdominal masses
  - Gynecological: **dysmenorrhea**, **endometriosis**, painful fibroids, ovarian cysts, uterine bleeding with dark clotted blood, infertility, interstitial cystitis
  - Psychiatric: **chronic depression**, bipolar mood disorder, schizophrenia, chronic recalcitrant insomnia, memory problems
  - Connective tissue: lupus, scleroderma, mixed connective tissue disease

Pattern identifying features

- **Qi & Blood** stagnation
- fixed sharp pain anywhere in the body
- purple discoloration or broken vessels on the skin; purple lips; dark circles around the eyes
- masses
- low grade hectic fevers
- dry, scaly skin
- insomnia

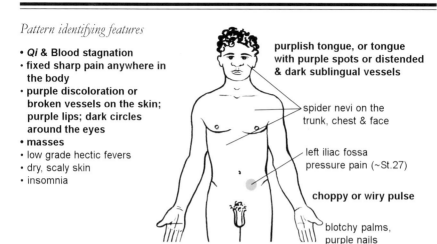

purplish tongue, or tongue with purple spots or distended & dark sublingual vessels

spider nevi on the trunk, chest & face

left iliac fossa pressure pain (~St.27)

choppy or wiry pulse

blotchy palms, purple nails

Composition (each pill contains powdered)

Prunus persica (tao ren, peach seed) 25.6, *Angelica sinensis* (dang gui, chinese angelica) 19.2mg, *Rehmannia glutinosa* (sheng di, raw rehmannia) 19.2mg, *Carthamus tinctorius* (hong hua, carthamus) 19.2mg, *Achyranthes bidentata* (niu xi, achyranthes) 19.2mg, *Citrus aurantium* (zhi ke, aurantium) 14.4mg, *Paeonia lactiflora* (bai shao, white peony) 14.4mg, *Ligusticum wallici* (chuan xiong, cnidium) 9.6mg, *Bupleurun falcatum* (chai hu, bupleurum) 6.4mg, *Glycyrrhiza uralensis* (gan cao, licorice) 6.4mg, *Platycodon grandiflorum* (jie geng, platycodon) 6.4mg

Combinations

- With **6.9 Jigucao Wan** for chronic hepatitis or early cirrhosis.
- With **5.7 Sunho Multi Ginseng Tablets** for chronic depression and insomnia. This combination is also useful for fixed headaches or migraines.
- With **15.8 Fu Fang Jiang Ya Capsule** for chronic essential hypertension associated with Blood stagnation.

Dosage and method of administration

8-12 pills three times daily on an empty stomach. The dose may be spread out, or two lots of 12-18 pills may be taken, morning and evening. In severe cases or during the early stages of treatment, a 50% increase in dose may be used, then reduced as the treatment takes effect.

Cautions and contraindications

Contraindicated during pregnancy, in women with menorrhagia, and in patients with bleeding disorders. Caution in patients on anticoagulant therapy (aspirin, warfarin, coumarin). Watch for bruising or increased tendency to bleeding.

Prolonged use may deplete *qi* and Blood, so a break every 2-3 months, with a change to a simple *qi* and Blood supplementing formula for a few weeks, is recommended.

CV

5.2 DAN SHEN PILL

复方丹参片

(Fu Fang Dan Shen Pian)
China National Chemicals Corp. (Shanghai)
'Salvia Compound Pills'
Dan Shen Pills are packaged in bottles of 50 pills.

TCM actions
Invigorates Blood circulation in the chest, quickens Blood, disperses stagnant Blood and Phlegm, fragrantly opens the vessels, regulates *qi* and stops pain.

Biomedical actions
Anti-platelet action, vasodilator, lowers cholesterol and triglycerides, improves coronary circulation.

INDICATIONS

- Blood stagnation patterns of the heart and chest, in particular angina pectoris, cardiovascular disease and atherosclerotic and arteriosclerotic heart disease.
- Can be used to lower blood cholesterol and triglycerides.
- With the appropriate identifying features, this formula can assist in the treatment of biomedical conditions such as the early stage of coronary heart disease, angina pectoris, hypercholesterolemia, cerebrovascular insufficiency, transient ischemic attacks, carotid stenosis, peripheral vascular disease, Raynaud's syndrome and Buerger's disease.

Composition
Salvia miltiorrhiza (dan shen, salvia) 59%, *Panax notoginseng* (tian qi, tianqi ginseng) 39%, Borneol (bing pian) 2%

Combinations
- With **5.1 Xue Fu Zhu Yu Wan** for cardiac disease and cerebrovascular insufficiency.
- With **7.16 Shi Quan Da Bu Wan** and **13.14 Ching Wan Hung** topically for chronic non-healing ulcers and sores on the legs associated with *qi* and Blood deficiency.
- With **2.18 Bao He Wan** for hypercholesterolemia in an overweight, Damp patient.

Pattern identifying features

- **Blood stagnation in the chest**
- **cardiovascular disease**
- **angina**
- **stuffy sensation in the chest, chest oppression**
- palpitations

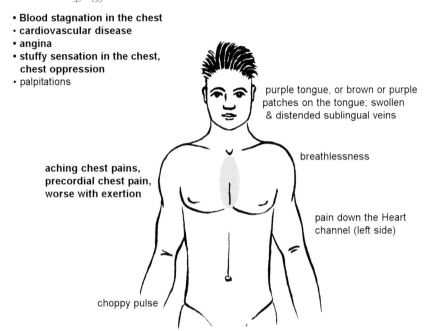

purple tongue, or brown or purple patches on the tongue; swollen & distended sublingual veins

breathlessness

aching chest pains, precordial chest pain, worse with exertion

pain down the Heart channel (left side)

choppy pulse

Dosage and method of administration

3 pills, three times daily on an empty stomach. Patients should expect to see some improvement within 1-3 months.

Cautions and contraindications

Contraindicated during pregnancy. Caution in patients who are also taking anticoagulant therapy (aspirin, warfarin, coumarin) as clotting time can be significantly reduced.

CV

GMP 5.3 DAN SHEN YIN WAN

丹参饮丸

Available in the US,
UK and Europe
See Note 1, p.xxi

Lanzhou Foci Pharmaceutical Factory (Gansu)
'Salvia Pills'
Dan Shen Yin Wan is packaged in bottles of 200 pills.
Available as: Salvia Teapills (PF), Dan Shen Wan (HT)

TCM actions

Invigorates the circulation of *qi* and Blood circulation in the chest and Stomach, quickens Blood, disperses stagnant Blood and stops pain.

Biomedical actions

Anti-platelet action, vasodilator, lowers cholesterol and triglycerides, improves coronary circulation.

INDICATIONS

- Blood and *qi* stagnation patterns of the Heart and Stomach. A simple and elegant formula that utilises a high proportion of salvia to invigorate the Blood and disperse Blood stasis, it is best used in chronic, yet relatively mild, patterns with focal pain, but without severe systemic signs and symptoms of stagnant Blood. Also useful for mild *qi* and Blood stagnation patterns affecting the Liver causing hypochondriac pain.
- With the appropriate identifying features, this formula can assist in the treatment of biomedical conditions such as the early stage of coronary heart disease, angina pectoris, atherosclerosis, arteriosclerosis, chronic gastritis, peptic ulcer disease, chronic hepatitis, early hepatic cirrhosis and dysmenorrhea.

Composition

Salvia miltiorrhiza (dan shen, salvia) 69%, *Santalum album* (tan xiang, sandalwood) 13%, *Amomum villosum* (sha ren, cardamon) 13%, *Glycyrrhiza uralensis* (gan cao, licorice) 2%

Combinations

- With **5.1 Xue Fu Zhu Yu Wan** for cardiac disease and cerebrovascular insufficiency.
- With **10.21 Yan Huo Suo Wan** for relatively severe pain.

Pattern identifying features

• **Mild Blood stagnation in Heart or Stomach**

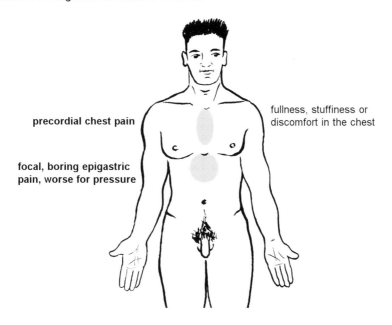

precordial chest pain

focal, boring epigastric pain, worse for pressure

fullness, stuffiness or discomfort in the chest

Dosage and method of administration

8-12 pills three times daily on an empty stomach. The dose may be spread out, or two lots of 12-18 pills may be taken, morning and evening. In severe cases or during the early stages of treatment, a 50% increase in dose may be used, then reduced as the treatment takes effect.

Cautions and contraindications

Contraindicated in patients with bleeding disorders. Caution in patients who are also taking anticoagulant therapy (aspirin, warfarin, coumarin) as clotting time can be significantly reduced. Caution during pregnancy.

CV

5.4 XIN MAI LING

心脉灵

Guanghua Pharmaceutical Co. (Guangzhou)
'Miraculously Effective Pills for Coronary Circulation'
Xin Mai Ling is packaged in bottles of 36 capsules.

TCM actions
Invigorates Blood circulation in the chest, quickens Blood, disperses stagnant Blood, opens the vessels, clears Toxic Heat.

Biomedical actions
Anti-platelet action, vasodilator, lowers cholesterol and triglycerides, improves coronary circulation.

INDICATIONS

- Blood stagnation patterns of the heart, chest and periphery. The main herb, Ilex, is bitter and cooling, and widely used in China to treat cardiac and peripheral Blood stagnation patterns. It is considered especially useful to help restore circulation into hemiplegic limbs following Wind stroke, and when peripheral Blood stagnation is complicated by Heat.
- Used to lower blood cholesterol and triglycerides. Also useful as a preventative against cardiovascular and cerebrovascular disease for those at risk.
- With the appropriate identifying features, this formula can be used to assist in the treatment of biomedical conditions such as the early stage of coronary heart disease, **angina pectoris**, hypercholesterolemia, cerebrovascular insufficiency, transient ischemic attacks, **hemiplegia**, carotid stenosis, **thrombophlebitis**, peripheral vascular disease, diabetic vascular disease and ulcers, Raynaud's syndrome, Buerger's disease and central retinitis.

Composition (each capsule contains extracts equivalent to dry)
Ilex pubescens (mao dong qing, ilex) 3.75g, *Salvia miltiorrhiza* (dan shen, salvia) 315mg, *Panax notoginseng* (tian qi, tianqi ginseng) 50mg

Combinations
- With **5.1 Xue Fu Zhu Yu Wan** for cardiac disease, cerebrovascular insufficiency and peripheral vascular disease associated with stagnation of *qi* and Blood.
- With **7.16 Shi Quan Da Bu Wan** and **13.14 Ching Wan Hung** topically for chronic non-healing ulcers and sores on the legs.

Pattern identifying features

• **Blood stagnation (with Heat) in the chest & extremities**

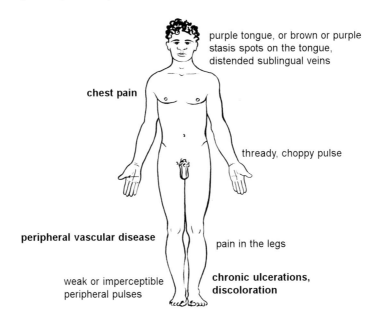

purple tongue, or brown or purple
stasis spots on the tongue,
distended sublingual veins

chest pain

threading, choppy pulse

peripheral vascular disease

pain in the legs

weak or imperceptible
peripheral pulses

**chronic ulcerations,
discoloration**

Dosage and method of administration

3 capsules three times daily on an empty stomach. In severe cases the dose can be increase to 4-5 capsules three times daily. In general, quite a large dose of Ilex is required for a satisfactory therapeutic effect.

Cautions and contraindications

Contraindicated during pregnancy. Caution in patients who are also taking anticoagulant therapy (aspirin, warfarin, coumarin) as clotting time can be significantly reduced. This formula is quite cooling and thus not recommended alone for patients with deficient Cold patterns accompanying Blood stagnation. Although Ilex is generally considered a very safe herb, some patients do experience side effects such as nausea, dizziness and abdominal pain. These can usually be alleviated by reducing the dose.

CV

GMP **5.5 ZHI GAN CAO WAN**

炙甘草丸

Available in the US,
UK and Europe
See Note 1, p.xxi

Lanzhou Foci Pharmaceutical Factory (Gansu)
'Honey Fried Licorice Pills'
Zhi Gan Cao Wan is packaged in bottles of 200 pills.
Available as: Zhi Gan Cao Teapills (PF)

TCM actions
Supplements Heart *qi*, Blood and *yin*, promotes circulation
of Heart *yang*, restores the pulse, calms the *shen*.

Biomedical actions
Anti-arrhythmic, improves cardiac function, sedative and tranquillizer.

INDICATIONS

- Palpitations and cardiac arrhythmia associated with Heart *qi*, Blood and/or *yin* deficiency. The palpitations or arrhythmias are initiated or aggravated by exertion and when fatigued. The specific arrhythmia referred to here is an irregularly irregular beat, that is, beats are dropped at irregular intervals. The formula can, however, also be used for heart beats dropped at regular intervals, as well as tachycardia and bradycardia.
- Consumptive Lung disease (*fei lao* or *fei wei*), characterised by chronic dry cough, or cough with blood streaked sputum, weight loss, breathlessness, low grade fever, nightsweats and spontaneous sweating and generalised dryness.
- With the appropriate identifying features, this formula may assist in the treatment of biomedical conditions such as supraventricular arrhythmia, sick sinus syndrome, premature ectopic asystole, bradycardia, hyperthyroidism, cardiomyopathy, viral myocarditis, sequelae of rheumatic heart disease, coronary artery disease, and pulmonary tuberculosis.

Composition
Rehmannia glutinosa (sheng di, raw rehmannia) 26%, *Glycyrrhiza uralensis* (zhi gan cao, honey fried licorice) 12%, *Ophiopogon japonicus* (mai dong, ophiopogon) 9.5%, *Cannabis sativa* (huo ma ren, cannabis seeds) 9.5%, *Cinnamomum cassia* (gui zhi, cinnamon twigs) 9.5%, *Zingiber officinale* (sheng jiang, ginger) 9.5%, *Zizyphus jujuba* (da zao, chinese dates) 9.5%, *Panax ginseng* (ren shen, ginseng) 6%, *Equus asinus* (e jiao, donkey skin gelatin) 6%

Pattern identifying features

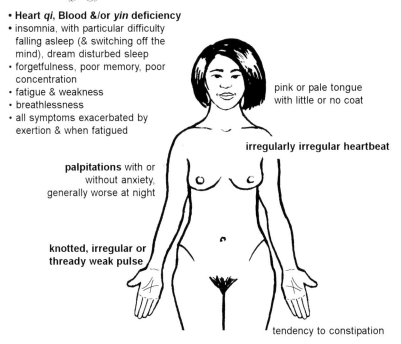

- **Heart *qi*, Blood &/or *yin* deficiency**
- insomnia, with particular difficulty falling asleep (& switching off the mind), dream disturbed sleep
- forgetfulness, poor memory, poor concentration
- fatigue & weakness
- breathlessness
- all symptoms exacerbated by exertion & when fatigued

pink or pale tongue with little or no coat

irregularly irregular heartbeat

palpitations with or without anxiety, generally worse at night

knotted, irregular or thready weak pulse

tendency to constipation

Combinations
- With **2.7 Si Jun Zi Wan** for patients with a greater degree of *qi* deficiency.
- With **1.2 Si Wu Wan** for patients with a greater degree of Blood deficiency.
- With **1.16 Tao Hong Si Wu Wan** for elements of mild Blood stagnation.

Dosage and method of administration
8-12 pills three times daily on an empty stomach. The dose may be spread out, or two lots of 12-18 pills may be taken, morning and evening. In severe cases or during the early stages of treatment, a 50% increase in dose may be used, then reduced as the treatment takes effect.

Cautions and contraindications
Caution in patients with loose bowels or diarrhea, and where prescribed alone for patients with significant Heat generated by deficiency. Caution in patients with hypertension and fluid problems due to the large proportion of licorice. May counteract spironolactone (Aldactone) and potentiate potassium depleting loop diuretics, such as Lasix, leading to hypokalemia.

CV

5.6 GUAN XIN AN KOU FU YE

冠心安口服液

Tong Ren Tang (Beijing)

'Calm Coronary Artery Drink'

Guan Xin An Kou Fu Ye is packaged as liquid extract in small vials, ten vials per box.

TCM actions

Invigorates Blood circulation in the chest, quickens Blood, benefits Heart *qi*.

Biomedical actions

Improves cardiac circulation, anti-platelet action.

INDICATIONS

- Blood stagnation affecting the Heart causing chest pain, atherosclerotic and arteriosclerotic heart disease, angina pectoris.
- Cerebrovascular insufficiency, transient ischemic attacks, cerebrovascular spasm.
- Also used for poor peripheral circulation.

Composition (each vial contains extracts equivalent to dry)

Bupleurum falcatum (chai hu, bupleurum) 2.91g, *Ligusticum wallichi* (chuan xiong, cnidium) 2.31g, *Chrysanthemum indicum* (ye ju hua, wild chrysanthemum) 2.01g, *Poria cocos* (fu ling, hoelen) 1.89g, *Dalbergia odorifera* (jiang xiang, dalbergia wood) 1.79g, *Polygonum multiflorum* (he shou wu, ho shou wu) 1.51g, *Zizyphus jujuba* (da zao, chinese dates) 1.47g, *Achyranthes bidentata* (niu xi, achyranthes) 1.41g, *Glycyrrhiza uralensis* (gan cao, licorice) 803mg, *Panax notoginseng* (tian qi, tian qi ginseng) 616mg, *Cinnamomum cassia* (gui zhi, cinnamon twigs) 411mg

Combinations

- With **5.2 Dan Shen Pill** or **5.7 Sunho Multi Ginseng Tablets** for frequent angina.
- With **13.14 Ching Wan Hung** for venous ulcers in a patient with Blood stagnation and Cold accumulation.

Pattern identifying features

• **Blood stagnation in the chest & Heart**

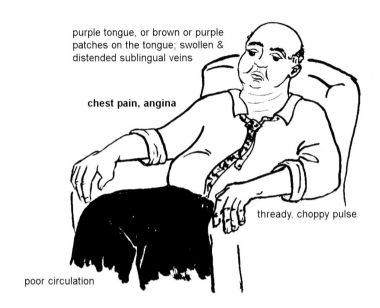

purple tongue, or brown or purple patches on the tongue; swollen & distended sublingual veins

chest pain, angina

thready, choppy pulse

poor circulation

Dosage and method of administration
One vial, 2-3 times daily.

Cautions and contraindications
Contraindicated during pregnancy and for patients with low platelet count, internal bleeding (as in a bleeding gastric ulcer) or heavy menstrual periods. Caution in patients who are also taking anticoagulant therapy (aspirin, warfarin, coumarin) as clotting time may be reduced.

CV

5.7 SUNHO MULTI GINSENG TABLETS

三参健康丸

(San Shen Jian Kang Wan)
Sunho Traditional Medicine Co. (Australia)
'Health [Promoting] Pills Composed of Three Roots'
Sunho Multi Ginseng Tablets are packaged in bottles of 80 tablets.

TCM actions

Quickens Blood, disperses stagnant Blood, supplements *qi* and *yin*.

Biomedical actions

Anti-platelet action, vasodilator, lowers cholesterol and triglycerides, improves coronary circulation.

INDICATIONS

- Blood stagnation and *qi* deficiency. Improves and strengthens cardiac function, dilates coronary arteries. Useful for preventative maintenance of healthy cardiovascular and cerebrovascular circulation. Can be used to alleviate mild angina.
- For maintenance of peripheral circulation and treatment of Blood stasis in the extremities. This includes disorders such as varicose veins, spider vessels or discoloration around the ankles and mild peripheral vascular disease. Useful for peripheral or diabetic neuropathy.
- Supplements Lung and Spleen *qi* and calms the *shen*. A useful energy supplement to improve endurance and stamina, or for the treatment of fatigue and lack of vitality.
- Various types of pain associated with Blood stagnation, including epigastric, hypochondriac and cardiac.
- Chronic liver disease, such as hepatitis and mild cirrhosis.
- Can lower blood cholesterol and reduce high blood pressure.

Composition (each tablet contains powdered)

Panax quinquefolium (xi yang shen, american ginseng) 120mg, *Panax notoginseng* (tian qi, tianqi ginseng) 120mg, *Salvia miltiorrhiza* (dan shen, salvia) 60mg

Combinations

- With **5.1 Xue Fu Zhu Yu Wan** for cardiac disease and cerebrovascular insufficiency. This combination is also useful for chronic liver disease with mild cirrhosis.

Pattern identifying features

- **Blood stagnation; *qi* deficiency**
- fixed recurrent pain

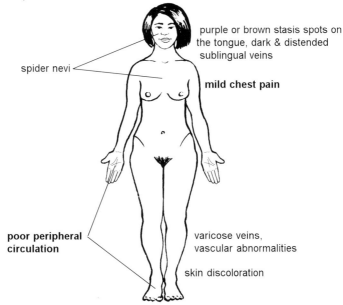

spider nevi

purple or brown stasis spots on the tongue, dark & distended sublingual veins

mild chest pain

poor peripheral circulation

varicose veins, vascular abnormalities

skin discoloration

- With **6.1 Xiao Chai Hu Tang Wan** for chronic hepatitis C with elements of Blood stagnation.
- With **3.18 Tung Hsuan Li Fei Pien** for gastric ulcers with fixed, boring pain.
- With **2.18 Bao He Wan** for hypercholesterolemia.
- With **15.7 Yang Yin Jiang Ya Wan** for resistant hypertension.
- With **7.26 Reishi Mushroom** as an adjunct treatment for lung cancer.
- With **5.8 Bu Yang Huan Wu Wan** for hemiplegia following a stabilised Wind stroke.

Dosage and method of administration

The dose for general cardiovascular maintenance is two tablets twice daily. In the early stages of treatment for disease, the dose may be doubled until results are noticed, then reduced to the maintenance dose.

Cautions and contraindications

Contraindicated during pregnancy. Caution in patients who are also taking anticoagulant therapy (aspirin, warfarin, coumarin) as clotting time may be significantly reduced.

5.8 BU YANG HUAN WU WAN

补阳还五丸

Lanzhou Foci Pharmaceutical Factory (Gansu)
'Pills to Supplement *yang* and Restore the Other Half'
Bu Yang Huan Wu Wan is packaged in bottles of 200 pills.
Also available as: Great Yang Restoration Teapills (PF)

TCM actions
Supplements *qi*, invigorates and quickens Blood, unblocks the channels.

Biomedical actions
Improves circulation to the periphery, anti-platelet action.

INDICATIONS

- Sequelae of Wind-stroke in patients with *qi* and/or *yang* deficiency complicated by Blood stagnation. The typical features of this pattern are hemiplegia, facial paralysis, slurred speech, drooling, incontinence, exhaustion and wasting. This is a widely used and quite effective formula for convalescence from a stabilised Wind-stroke. Also useful for loss of function, weakness and wasting following surgery on the brain.
- Sequelae of poliomyelitis and other *wei* syndrome disorders with wasting and weakness of the peripheral muscles (*see* glossary), such as myasthenia gravis and multiple sclerosis.
- Peripheral or diabetic neuropathy with altered sensation, paresthesia or loss of sensation in the extremities, usually the lower limbs.
- Peripheral vascular disease and insufficiency, deep venous thrombosis, diabetic and stasis ulcers, varicose veins.

Composition (each pill contains powdered)
Astragalus membranaceous (huang qi, astragalus) 54mg, *Spatholobus suberectus* (ji xue teng, spatholobus) 27mg, *Prunus persica* (tao ren, peach seed) 27mg, *Crocus sativus* (xi hong hua, crocus stamen) 23.4mg, *Paeonia rubra* (chi shao, red peony) 18mg, *Angelica sinensis* (dang gui, chinese angelica) 18mg, *Ligusticum wallichii* (chuan xiong, cnidium) 12.6mg

Combinations
- With **5.1 Xue Fu Zhu Yu Wan** or **5.7 Sunho Multi Ginseng Tablets** to enhance the Blood moving action in chronic or resistant cases.

Pattern identifying features

- **Blood stagnation & *qi* deficiency**
- sequelae of stroke
- wei syndrome
- easy sweating
- fatigue, breathlessness

facial paralysis

pale purplish complexion, tongue, lips

hemiplegia

thready pulse

wasting of the limbs

poor peripheral circulation

peripheral neuropathy

- With **10.11 Shu Jin Huo Xue Wan** for paralysis and pain that is worse in the lower limbs from Wind Damp and Blood stagnation.
- With **2.22 Er Chen Wan** for complication by residual Phlegm (thick greasy tongue coat, dizziness).
- With **11.8 Kang Wei Ling Wan** for pronounced or difficult facial paralysis.
- With **2.11 Bu Zhong Yi Qi Wan** or **7.17 Hua Tuo Shi Quan Da Bu Jiu** for *wei* syndrome patterns associated with *qi* deficiency.
- With **10.16 Zhuang Yao Jian Shen** or **10.18 Jian Bu Qiang Shen Wan** for *wei* syndrome patterns associated with Kidney deficiency.

Dosage and method of administration

12-15 pills three times daily on an empty stomach. The dose may be spread out, or two lots of 18-22 pills may be taken, morning and evening. In severe cases or during the early stages of treatment (the first few weeks), a 50% increase in dose may be used, then reduced as the treatment takes effect. The pills may need to be softened and mashed to a slurry with hot water before ingestion.

Cautions and contraindications

Contraindicated during pregnancy, and in the first two weeks following a stroke. This is to avoid any possibility of aggravating bleeding from a cerebral hemorrhage. The patient must be stable before beginning this treatment. Contraindicated in patients with residual Liver *yang* rising (*see* **15.4 Tian Ma Gou Teng Wan** or **15.6 Zhen Gan Xi Feng Wan**).

CV

GMP
5.9 DANG GUI SI NI WAN

当归四逆丸

Available in the US,
UK and Europe
See Note 1, p.xxi

Lanzhou Foci Pharmaceutical Factory (Gansu)
'Dang Gui Pills for Frigid Extremities'
Dang Gui Si Ni Wan is packaged in bottles of 200 pills.
Available as: Dang Gui Si Ni Teapills (PF)

TCM actions
Warms and opens the channels, dispels Cold, nourishes Blood
and unblocks the Blood vessels.

Biomedical actions
Vasodilator, promotes circulation to the extremities.

INDICATIONS

- Cold obstructing and congealing circulation of *qi* and Blood in channels,
  collaterals, and Blood vessels of the periphery. This manifests primarily as chronic,
  icy cold hands and feet that may be pale or purple pale. There may also be
  cramping and pain in the affected limbs. The focus of the pathology, the Cold,
  is mostly confined to the hands and feet, thus this pattern differs from that in
  which *yang* is systemically weak and unable to reach the limbs (*see* **7.9 Fu Gui Ba
  Wei Wan** and **2.14 Li Chung Yuen Medical Pills**), in which case the whole
  limb is cold and there are systemic signs of *yang* deficiency.
- Can also be used for joint pain, lower back pain, abdominal pain and dysmenorrhea
  from Blood deficiency and Cold accumulation.
- With the appropriate identifying features, this formula can be used to assist in
  the treatment of biomedical conditions such as Raynaud's syndrome, frostbite,
  sciatica, scleroderma, thrombophlebitis and intestinal adhesions.

Composition
Angelica sinensis (dang gui, chinese angelica) 17.5%, *Paeonia lactiflora* (bai shao, white
peony) 17.5%, *Cinnamomum cassia* (gui zhi, cinnamon twigs) 17.5%, *Asarum seiboldi* (xi
xin, asarum) 11.5%, *Glycyrrhiza uralensis* (zhi gan cao, honey fried licorice) 11.5%,
Clematis armandi (chuan mu tong, clematis mu tong) 11.5%, *Zizyphus jujuba* (da zao,
chinese dates) 10%

Pattern identifying features

- **Cold accumulation in the channels & vessels**
- pain & cramping in the limbs, aggravated by exposure to cold, better for heat

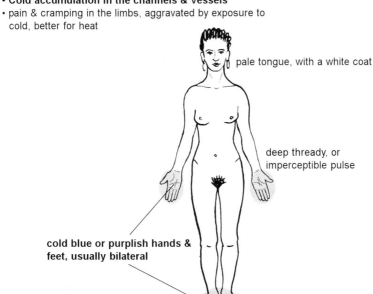

pale tongue, with a white coat

deep thready, or imperceptible pulse

cold blue or purplish hands & feet, usually bilateral

Combinations
- With **5.7 Sunho Multi Ginseng Tablets** or **10.2 Raw Tienchi Tablets** to enhance the Blood moving action in chronic or resistant cases.

Dosage and method of administration
8-12 pills three times daily on an empty stomach. The dose may be spread out, or two lots of 12-18 pills may be taken, morning and evening. In severe cases or the early stages of treatment (the first few weeks), a 50% increase in dose may be used, then reduced as the treatment takes effect.

Cautions and contraindications
Contraindicated in patients with *yin* deficiency or internal Heat causing cold extremities (*see* **6.2 Si Ni San Wan**).

CV

GMP 5.10 XIAO SHUAN ZAI ZAO WAN

消栓再造丸

Tong Ren Tang (Beijing)
'Pills to Remove the Plug and Give a New
Lease on Life'

Xiao Shuan Zai Zao Wan is packaged as 55
small pills inside a sealed wax ball, ten balls per box.

TCM actions

Invigorates and quickens Blood, disperses stagnant Blood, dispels Wind and opens
the channels, supplements *qi* and Blood.

Biomedical actions

Improves circulation, anti-cholesterol, anti-thrombus, anti-platelet action.

INDICATIONS

- Sequelae of Wind-stroke–hemiplegia, slurred speech, drooling, facial paralysis etc. This is a broad spectrum formula, designed to address a variety of pathological conditions that may occur in the aftermath of a stabilised stroke.
- Acute facial paralysis, Bell's palsy.
- *Wei* syndrome (*see* glossary).

Composition (each dose contains powdered)

Astragalus membranaceous (huang qi, astragalus) 231mg, *Angelica polymorpha* (dang gui, chinese angelica) 198mg, *Atractylodes macrocephala* (bai zhu, atractylodes) 137.5mg, *Achyranthes bidentata* (niu xi, achyranthes) 121mg, *Citrus aurantium* (zhi ke, aurantium) 121mg, *Clematis sinensis* (wei ling xian, chinese clematis) 110mg, *Ophiopogon japonicus* (mai dong, ophiopogon) 99mg, *Ligusticum wallici* (chuan xiong, cnidium) 93.5mg, *Poria cocos* (fu ling, hoelen) 93.5mg, *Panax notoginseng* (tian qi, tian qi ginseng) 82.5mg, *Curcum longa* (yu jin, curcuma) 71.5mg, *Salvia miltiorrhiza* (dan shen, salvia) 71.5mg, *Schizandra chinensis* (wu wei zi, schizandra) 71.5mg, *Stephania tetrandra* (fang ji, stephania) 71.5mg, *Drynaria fortunei* (gu sui bu, drynaria rhizome) 71.5mg, *Gastrodia elata* (tian ma, gastrodia) 71.5mg, *Cinnamomum cassia* (rou gui, cinnamon bark) 66mg, *Sophora japonica* (huai hua mi, sophora seed) 44mg, *Ammomum cardamomum* (bai dou kou, amomum) 44mg, *Daemonorops draco* (xue jie, dragons blood) 44mg, *Crategus pinnatifida* (shan zha, crategus) 44mg, *Commiphora myrrha* (mo yao, myrrh) 44mg, *Paeonia veitchii* (chi shao, red peony) 44mg, *Panax ginseng* (ren shen, ginseng) 38.5mg, *Aquilaria sinensis* (chen xiang, aquilaria wood) 38.5mg, *Chaenomeles speciosa* (mu gua, chinese quince) 22mg, *Styrax tonkinensis* (an xi xiang, styrax resin) 22mg, *Bungarus*

Pattern identifying features

• **sequelae of Wind-stroke**

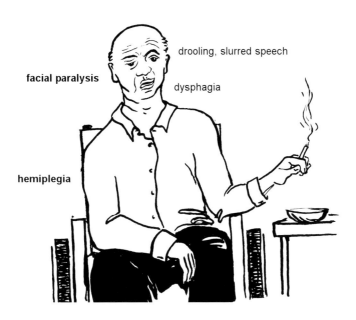

drooling, slurred speech

facial paralysis

dysphagia

hemiplegia

parvus (bai hua she, golden coin snake) 11mg, *Liquidamber orientalis* (su he xiang, liquidamber resin) 11mg, Borneol 5.5mg, honey

Dosage and method of administration

The recommended dose is one ball (55 pills) twice daily with warm water or a little alcohol (vodka or sherry is good). Take for one month, then stop for one week, then repeat. A course of treatment is 1-3 months, although patients should notice some improvement after one month. Physical therapy must be maintained during the treatment period.

Cautions and contraindications

Contraindicated during pregnancy. The patient must be stable before beginning this treatment. Contraindicated in patients with residual Liver *yang* rising (*see* **15.4 Tian Ma Gou Teng Wan** or **15.6 Zhen Gan Xi Feng Wan**).

CV

5.11 HUA TUO ZAI ZAO WAN

华佗再造丸

Guangzhou Qixing Pharmaceutical Co. (Guangzhou)
'Hua Tuo's Restorative Pills'
Hua Tuo Zai Zao Wan is packaged in bottles of 500 small
pills with a slotted measuring spoon.

TCM actions
Supplements *qi, yin* and Blood, dispels Wind Damp,
warms and stimulates circulation of *qi* and Blood
through the channels.

Biomedical actions
Tonic, circulatory stimulant.

INDICATIONS

- *Wei* syndromes with spastic or flaccid paralysis and hemiplegia. This formula is
  used for patterns associated with *qi* and *yin* deficiency following Wind-stroke or
  associated with a variety of wasting disorders.
- Used for chronic or persistent tremors, tics, spasms and cramps resulting from
  yin and Blood deficiency.
- Poor circulation in the extremities in a patient with deficient *qi, yang* and *yin*.
- With the appropriate identifying features, this formula can assist in the treatment
  of biomedical conditions such as post stroke hemiplegia, dysphagia and aphasia,
  Bell's palsy, peripheral neuropathy, fibromyalgia, Raynaud's syndrome, chilblains
  and frostbite. Also for chronic headaches or migraines that are worse with
  exposure to cold, facial pain, chronic trigeminal neuralgia, coldness and discomfort
  in the external genitals and chronic neck pain. May assist in conditions such as
  Amyotrophic Lateral Sclerosis (ALS), multiple sclerosis and Parkinson's disease.

Composition (each pill contains extracts equivalent to dry)
Gentiana macrophylla (qin jiao, gentiana chin chiu) 89.6mg, *Panax ginseng* (ren shen,
ginseng) 89.6mg, *Ophiopogon japonicus* (mai dong, ophiopogon) 89.6mg, *Schizandra
chinensis* (wu wei zi, schizandra) 89.6mg, *Sophora japonica* (huai hua, sophora flower)
89.6mg, *Angelica dahurica* (bai zhi, angelica) 35.2mg, *Ligusticum wallichi* (chuan xiong,
cnidium) 35.2mg, *Angelica polymorpha* (dang gui, chinese angelica) 35.2mg,
Cinnamomum cassia (rou gui, cinnamon bark) 19.2mg, *Evodia rutaecarpa* (wu zhu yu,
evodia) 19.2mg

Pattern identifying features

- ***Qi & yin* deficiency, Wind Damp**
- cold intolerance
- poor peripheral circulation
- wasting & weakness of the extremities
- dysphagia, aphasia

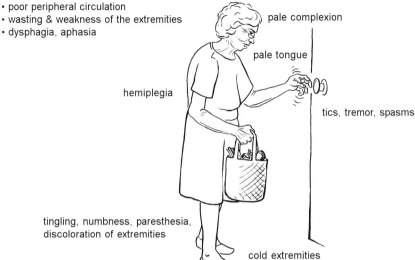

pale complexion

pale tongue

hemiplegia

tics, tremor, spasms

tingling, numbness, paresthesia, discoloration of extremities

cold extremities

Combinations

- With **15.9 Headache and Dizziness Reliever** for chronic neck and upper back pain from fibromyalgia.
- With **2.11 Bu Zhong Yi Qi Wan** or **2.12 Shen Ling Bai Zhu Wan** for *wei* syndrome from Spleen *qi* and *yin* deficiency with Dampness.
- With **10.18 Jian Bu Qiang Shen Wan** or **10.16.2 Zhuang Yao Jian Shen Tablet** for *wei* syndrome from Kidney *qi* and *yin* deficiency.
- With **1.2 Si Wu Wan** or **7.16 Shi Quan Da Bu Wan** for *wei* syndrome with significant muscle spasm, fasiculations and tics.
- With **5.7 Sunho Multi Ginseng Tablets** for concurrent Blood stagnation.

Dosage and method of administration

The recommended dose is fifty (50) pills twice daily for ten days (the equivalent of two jars), then break for a day, then repeat twice for a total of six jars. Alternatively, fewer pills, to a total of 100, can be consumed over the course of a day. This formula comes with a neat slotted spoon device that takes 12 pills, so four spoons is close enough to a single dose. After the first six jars, or when an improvement is noticed, reduce the dose by half. The pills can be soaked in hot water and mashed to ease ingestion.

Cautions and contraindications

Contraindicated during the early phase of acute illness such as colds and flu.

CV

6

Patent Medicines for the Liver and Gallbladder Systems

肝

胆

疾

病

6.1 XIAO CHAI HU TANG WAN

小柴胡汤丸

Lanzhou Foci Pharmaceutical Factory (Gansu)
'Minor Bupleurum Decoction Pills'
Xiao Chai Hu Tang Wan is packaged in bottles of 200 pills.

TCM actions

Harmonises *shao yang*, supplements *qi*, transforms Phlegm, spreads Liver *qi*, clears Heat.

Biomedical actions

Hepatoprotective, enhances digestive function, strengthens immunity, aids clearance of residual pathogens.

INDICATIONS

- *Shao yang* syndrome (*see* glossary). This is the classical formula for *shao yang* syndrome, and is extensively used to treat chronic or persistent viral, parasitic, or otherwise mysterious low grade infections of a *shao yang* type.
- Used for gastro-intestinal disorders associated with Liver *qi* stagnation, Spleen deficiency and Damp Heat (the primary pathological triad, *see* glossary).
- With the appropriate identifying features, this formula can assist in the treatment of biomedical conditions such as post viral syndrome, chronic fatigue syndrome, post acute Ross River fever and glandular fever, symptoms that occur in the post acute stage of a febrile illness or upper respiratory tract infection, acute and chronic hepatitis, acute mastitis, recurrent glue ear, otitis media, malaria, postpartum fever and *gan mao*, bronchitis, pleurisy, acute pyelonephritis and cystitis, intercostal neuralgia, pleurisy, gallstones, cholecystitis and menstrual disorders.

Composition (each pill contains powdered)

Bupleurum falcatum (chai hu, bupleurum) 40.3mg, *Pinellia ternata* (ban xia, pinellia) 23mg, *Scutellaria baicalensis* (huang qin, scute) 23mg, *Codonopsis pilosula* (dang shen, codonopsis) 23mg, *Zizyphus jujuba* (da zao, chinese dates) 23mg, *Glycyrrhiza uralensis* (gan cao, licorice) 15.3mg, *Zingiber officinalis* (sheng jiang, ginger) 12.3mg

Combinations

- With **1.2 Si Wu Wan** for acute or lingering colds and flu in menstruating or run down women.
- With either **14.5 Chuan Xin Lian Antiphlogistic Tablets, 14.8 Wu Wei Xiao Du Wan** or **13.1 Lien Chiao Pai Tu Pien** for acute mastitis or ear infections.

Pattern identifying features

- **shao yang** syndrome
- never well since a severe flu, gastroenteritis or other infection
- alternating fever & chills (or 'flu like' feelings, especially when fatigued)
- fatigue
- irritability

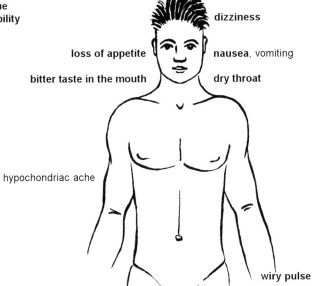

loss of appetite

bitter taste in the mouth

dizziness

nausea, vomiting

dry throat

hypochondriac ache

wiry pulse

- With **6.9 Jigucao Wan** for chronic hepatitis.
- With **7.22 Shen Qi Da Bu Wan** for pronounced *qi* deficiency.
- With **3.2 Gan Mao Zhi Ke Chong Ji** to assist in rooting out deeply buried or hidden pathogens.

Dosage and method of administration

8-12 pills three times daily on an empty stomach. The dose may be spread out, or two lots of 12-18 pills may be taken, morning and evening. In severe cases or during the early stages of treatment (the first few weeks), a 50% increase in dose may be used, then reduced as the treatment takes effect.

Cautions and contraindications

Contraindicated for patients taking interferon. In general **6.1 Xiao Chai Hu Tang Wan** is a very safe and well tolerated formula, but can cause energy to rise in some patients causing headaches or dizziness, especially when used long term. Any side effects cease when the formula is stopped. Patients with chronic fatigue or post viral patterns may experience a temporary recurrence of the initial disorder as the pathogen is eliminated from the body.

LIV GB

GMP ## 6.2 SI NI SAN WAN

四逆散丸

Available in the US,
UK and Europe
See Note 1, p.xxi

Lanzhou Foci Pharmaceutical Factory (Gansu)
'Frigid Extremities Powder Pills'
Si Ni San Wan is packaged in bottles of 200 pills.
Available as: Four Pillars Teapills (PF)

TCM actions
Spreads Liver *qi*, softens the Liver, harmonises the Liver and
Spleen, corrects the *qi* mechanism.

Biomedical actions
Antispasmodic, benefits digestion, carminative, alleviates
depression.

INDICATIONS

• Liver *qi* stagnation. This is the base formula on which all other Liver *qi* moving
formulae are built. Its main focus is on moving *qi* in the Liver and gastro-intestinal
system, and ensuring correct distribution of *qi* and Blood to the extremities.
One of the main features pointing to the use of this formula reflects this unequal
distribution–stagnant *qi* and pent up Heat from the stagnation trapped in the
interior obstruct the movement of *qi* and Blood to the tips of the extremities so
the that fingers and toes are quite cold while the trunks feels quite warm–hence
the name Frigid Extremities Pills.

• For Liver invading Spleen and Stomach patterns with hypochondriac, abdominal
and epigastric pain and distension. The combination of honey fried licorice and
white peony is especially good at alleviating smooth muscle spasm and pain,
while the ascending action of bupleurum and the descending action of aurantium
create a dynamic flow through the middle *jiao* and effectively restore the *qi*
mechanism (*see* glossary).

• Can otherwise be used in a similar fashion to **6.3 Chai Hu Shu Gan Wan**.

Composition
Paeonia alba (bai shao, white peony) 34.5%, *Bupleurum falcatum* (chai hu, bupleurum)
24.5%, *Citrus aurantium* (zhi shi, aurantium) 24.5%, *Glycyrrhiza uralensis* (zhi gan cao,
honey fried licorice) 14%

Combinations
• With **2.26 Xiang Lian Wan** for heartburn from Liver invading the Spleen.

Pattern identifying features

- **Liver *qi* stagnation**
- **symptoms worse with emotion or stress**
- **irritability, depression, mood swings**
- cyclical symptoms in an otherwise robust patient
- premenstrual syndrome
- tooth grinding

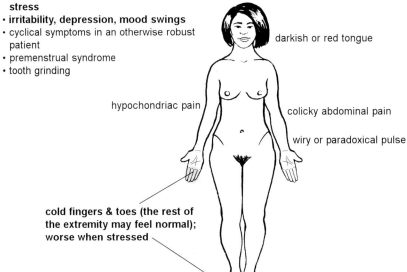

darkish or red tongue

hypochondriac pain

colicky abdominal pain

wiry or paradoxical pulse

cold fingers & toes (the rest of the extremity may feel normal); worse when stressed

- With **6.11 Li Dan Tablets** for gallstones or chronic cholecystitis from *qi* stagnation and Damp Heat.
- With **4.10 Shi Lin Tong** for gallstones from *qi* stagnation.
- With **2.18 Bao He Wan** for irritable bowel syndrome characterised by abdominal bloating and indigestion.
- With **2.38 Hua Zhi Ling Tablet** for rectal bleeding or colitis from *qi* stagnation.
- With **1.33 Hai Zao Jing Wan** or **1.32 Ru Jie Xiao** for breast and ovarian cysts.
- With **2.30 Chen Xiang Hua Qi Wan** for constipation.

Dosage and method of administration

8-12 pills three times daily on an empty stomach. The dose may be spread out, or two lots of 12-18 pills may be taken, morning and evening. In severe cases, premenstrually, or during the early stages of treatment a 50% increase in dosage may be used, then reduced as the treatment takes effect.

Cautions and contraindications

Contraindicated for cold extremities associated with *yang* or Blood deficiency. Not suitable for very weak or deficient patients.

LIV GB

6.3 CHAI HU SHU GAN WAN

柴胡疏肝丸

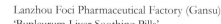

Lanzhou Foci Pharmaceutical Factory (Gansu)
'Bupleurum Liver Soothing Pills'
Chai Hu Shu Gan Wan is packaged in bottles of 200 pills.
Also available as: Bupleurum Soothe Liver Teapills (PF)

TCM actions

Spreads Liver *qi*, quickens Blood, softens the Liver, harmonises the Liver and Spleen, corrects the *qi* mechanism.

Biomedical actions

Antispasmodic, benefits digestion, carminative, alleviates depression.

INDICATIONS

- Liver *qi* stagnation problems with little or no deficiency, especially those with pain or distension. A variation of **6.2 Si Ni San Wan**, with the addition of three herbs to enhance *qi* and Blood regulating activity. This makes the current formula more popular while retaining similar overall action and indications.
- Liver *qi* stagnation and Liver invading the Spleen or Stomach patterns causing gastro-intestinal pain, distension and spasm, gas buildup or ulceration.
- Gynecological disorders when Liver *qi* stagnation is the primary component. Can also be useful following lumpectomy or mastectomy to prevent complications and future stagnation.
- Painful conditions with an emotional component (especially those along the Liver or Gallbladder channel pathways), including intercostal neuralgia, hypochondriac pain, genital pain (*shan qi* and *qi lin* syndrome, *see* glossary), tension and migraine headaches.
- Poor peripheral circulation associated with *qi* stagnation–usually only the fingers and toes are cold and the body is warm.
- Depression, mood swings, irritability from Liver *qi* stagnation. This includes disorders like 'plum stone throat' (globus hystericus).
- With the appropriate identifying features, this formula may be used to treat irritable bowel syndrome, gastritis, nervous stomach, peptic ulcers, bruxism, TMJ dysfunction, chronic cholecystitis, gallstones, biliary spasm, hepatitis, fibrocystic breast disease and lumps associated with the menstrual cycle, ovarian cysts, irregular menstruation, premenstrual syndrome, premenstrual headaches and dysmenorrhea.

Pattern identifying features

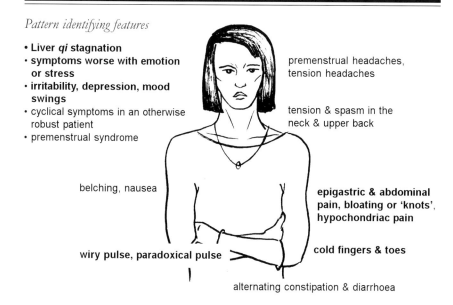

- **Liver *qi* stagnation**
- **symptoms worse with emotion or stress**
- **irritability, depression, mood swings**
- cyclical symptoms in an otherwise robust patient
- premenstrual syndrome

premenstrual headaches, tension headaches

tension & spasm in the neck & upper back

belching, nausea

epigastric & abdominal pain, bloating or 'knots', hypochondriac pain

wiry pulse, paradoxical pulse

cold fingers & toes

alternating constipation & diarrhoea

Composition (each pill contains powdered)
Bupleurum falcatum (chai hu, bupleurum) 33mg, *Paeonia alba* (bai shao, white peony) 33mg, *Cyperus rotundus* (xiang fu, cyperus) 33mg, *Citrus aurantium* (zhi shi, aurantium) 23mg, *Ligusticum wallichi* (chuan xiong, cnidium) 23mg, *Citrus reticulata* (qing pi, immature citrus) 23mg, *Glycyrrhiza uralensis* (gan cao, licorice) 16mg

Combinations
- With **2.26 Xiang Lian Wan** for heartburn from Liver invading the Spleen.
- With **6.11 Li Dan Tablets** for gallstones or chronic cholecystitis from *qi* stagnation and Damp Heat.
- With **2.23 Ping Wei San** for mild ascites from *qi* and Damp stagnation.
- With **10.22 Shao Yao Gan Cao Wan** for severe colicky abdominal or epigastric pain.
- With **1.33 Hai Zao Jing Wan** or **1.32 Ru Jie Xiao Tablet** for breast lumps.
- With **2.30 Chen Xiang Hua Qi Wan** for dry constipation.
- With **2.38 Hua Zhi Ling Tablet** for rectal bleeding and colitis from stress.

Dosage and method of administration
8-12 pills three times daily on an empty stomach. The dose may be spread out, or two lots of 12-18 pills may be taken, morning and evening. In severe cases, premenstrually, or during the early stages of treatment a 50% increase in dosage may be used, then reduced as the treatment takes effect.

Cautions and contraindications
Not suitable for very weak or deficient patients.

LIV GB

6.4 XIAO YAO WAN

逍遥丸

Lanzhou Foci Pharmaceutical Factory (Gansu)
'Free and Easy Wanderer Pills', 'Rambling Pills'
Xiao Yao Wan is packaged in bottles of 200 pills.
Also available as: Free and Easy Wanderer Teapills (PF), Hsiao Yao
Wan, Liv-Ease Pill (BE)

TCM actions
Softens the Liver, regulates Liver *qi*, nourishes Blood,
strengthens the Spleen, harmonises the Liver and Spleen.

Biomedical actions
Regulates the hormones that influence the menstrual cycle, emmenagogue, relieves
depression and emotional stress.

INDICATIONS

- Liver *qi* stagnation with Liver Blood and Spleen *qi* deficiency. This is a common
  mix of pathology, especially in women. The balance and effectiveness of this
  formula makes it one of the most popular of all Chinese herbal formulae.
- An important formula for all menstrual disorders with an emotional component.
  Specifically used for irregular menstruation, late periods, **premenstrual
  syndrome**, **breast tenderness** or lumps, fibrocystic breast disease, premenstrual
  irritability, headaches, depression, constipation and insomnia, dysmenorrhea and
  chronic pelvic inflammatory disease.
- For the effects of stress on the body in general, and in particular on the gastro-
  intestinal system. Liver and Spleen disharmony.
- In addition to the gynecological conditions noted above, with the appropriate
  identifying features, this formula can be used to treat irritable bowel syndrome,
  chronic gastritis, peptic ulcers, chronic tension in the gastro-intestinal system,
  biliary spsam, **chronic hepatitis**, the early stages of liver cirrhosis, anemia,
  neurasthenia, **depression**, tension headaches and migraines, bruxism, **chronic
  neck and upper back pain** and globus hystericus ('plum stone' throat).

Composition (each pill contains powdered)
Bupleurum falcatum (chai hu, bupleurum) 27mg, *Angelica sinensis* (dang gui, chinese angelica)
27mg, *Paeonia alba* (bai shao, white peony) 27mg, *Atractylodes macrocephala* (bai zhu,
atractylodes) 27mg, *Poria cocos* (fu ling, hoelen) 27mg, *Zingiber officinalis* (sheng jiang, ginger)
27mg, *Glycyrrhiza uralensis* (gan cao, licorice) 21mg, *Mentha haplocalycis* (bo he, mint) 5mg

Pattern identifying features

- **Liver *qi* stagnation, Spleen & Blood deficiency**
- **symptoms worse with stress or emotional upset**
- **premenstrual syndrome**
- **irritability, depression, mood swings**
- vague nonspecific aches & pains
- variable energy levels
- frequent sighing
- tooth grinding

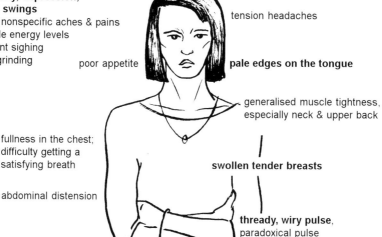

tension headaches

poor appetite

pale edges on the tongue

generalised muscle tightness, especially neck & upper back

fullness in the chest; difficulty getting a satisfying breath

abdominal distension

swollen tender breasts

thready, wiry pulse, paradoxical pulse

variable bowel habits

Combinations

- As part of a cyclical treatment (*see* glossary) with a *qi* and Blood supplement like **1.1 Ba Zhen Wan** or **1.9 Gui Pi Wan** from the end of the period to midcycle to nourish Blood and *yin*, then **6.4 Xiao Yao Wan** from midcycle to menstruation.
- With **1.32 Ru Jie Xiao Tablet** for breast cysts and thyroid nodules.
- With **1.2 Si Wu Wan** for irregular menstruation from Blood deficiency and *qi* stagnation.
- With **4.2 Wu Ling San Wan** for premenstrual fluid retention.

Dosage and method of administration

8-12 pills three times daily on an empty stomach. The dose may be spread out, or two lots of 12-18 pills may be taken, morning and evening. In severe cases or during the early stages of treatment (the first few weeks), a 50% increase in dose may be used, then reduced as the treatment takes effect.

Cautions and contraindications

Contraindicated during the early phase of acute illness such as colds and flu. Very occasionally a sensitive patient may experience mild nausea or loose stools in the early days of treatment. This can be alleviated by reducing the dose or by adding a few pills of **2.9 Xiang Sha Liu Jun Wan**.

LIV GB

6.5 JIA WEI XIAO YAO WAN

加味逍遥丸

Lanzhou Foci Pharmaceutical Factory (Gansu)
'Augmented Free and Easy Wanderer Pills'
Jia Wei Xiao Yao Wan is packaged in bottles of 200 pills.
Also available as: Free and Easy Wanderer Plus Teapills (PF), Dan
Zhi Xiao Yao Wan, Liv-Ease Plus Pill (BE)

TCM actions
Softens the Liver, regulates Liver *qi*, nourishes the Blood and
strengthens the Spleen, clears stagnant Heat from the Liver.

Biomedical actions
Regulates the hormones that influence the menstrual cycle, relieves depression and
emotional stress, cools the body.

INDICATIONS

- Liver *qi* stagnation with stagnant Heat. This is a variation of **6.4 Xiao Yao Wan**,
  the addition simply being two herbs to clear away stagnant heat. The key feature
  for the use of this formula (and others used to treat Liver *qi* stagnation), is the
  clear relationship between the initiation or aggravation of symptoms and the
  emotional state of the patient.
- Used for menstrual disorders from *qi* stagnation with signs of heat. These include
  irregular menstruation, especially shortened cycles, menorrhagia or abnormal
  uterine bleeding, premenstrual syndrome with Heat symptoms (fever, flushing,
  redness), bruxism, migraine headaches, rashes, acne, red, sore eyes, mouth ulcers,
  galactorrhea and nonspecific vaginitis.
- An important formula for inflammatory skin disorders with an emotional
  component, such as premenstrual acne or rashes, eczema, dermatitis, psoriasis.
- Chronic sinus congestion and headaches (including migraines) that are worse
  with stress.

Composition (each pill contains powdered)
Bupleurum falcatum (chai hu, bupleurum) 29mg, *Paeonia suffruticosa* (mu dan pi,
moutan) 29mg, *Gardenia jasminoides* (shan zhi zi, gardenia) 19mg, *Angelica sinensis*
(dang gui, chinese angelica) 19mg, *Paeonia lactiflora* (bai shao, white peony) 19mg,
Atractylodes macrocephala (bai zhu, atractylodes) 19mg, *Poria cocos* (fu ling, hoelen)
19mg, *Glycyrrhiza uralensis* (gan cao, licorice) 15mg, *Zingiber officinalis* (sheng jiang,
ginger) 6mg, *Mentha haplocalycis* (bo he, mint) 4mg

Pattern identifying features

- **Liver *qi* stagnation with stagnant Heat**
- **cyclical symptoms with heat signs, aggravated by stress**
- **irritability, anger outbursts**
- premenstrual syndrome
- tooth grinding

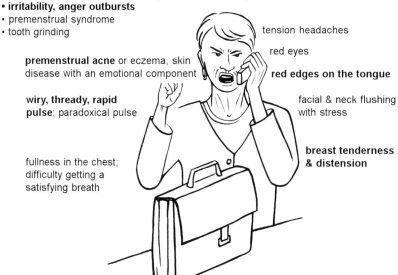

tension headaches

red eyes

premenstrual acne or eczema, skin disease with an emotional component

red edges on the tongue

wiry, thready, rapid pulse; paradoxical pulse

facial & neck flushing with stress

breast tenderness & distension

fullness in the chest; difficulty getting a satisfying breath

Combinations
- With **10.1 Yunnan Paiyao** for uterine bleeding or menorrhagia from *qi* stagnation with stagnant Heat.
- With **13.2 Xiao Feng Wan** for psoriasis, eczema or dermatitis worse for stress or premenstrually.
- With **14.2 Huang Lian Su Tablets** for stubborn pustular acne in teenagers.
- With **9.17 Qian Bai Bi Yan Pian** for chronic sinusitis.
- With **1.12 Shi Xiao Wan** for mild Blood stagnation.
- With **13.11 Dan Shen Huo Xue Wan** for chronic *qi* and Blood stagnation and Hot Blood type skin diseases.

Dosage and method of administration
8-12 pills three times daily on an empty stomach. The dose may be spread out, or two lots of 12-18 pills may be taken, morning and evening. In severe cases or during the early stages of treatment (the first few weeks), a 50% increase in dose may be used, then reduced as the treatment takes effect.

Cautions and contraindications
Caution during pregnancy. Very occasionally a sensitive patient may experience mild nausea, diarrhoea or loose stools in the early days of treatment. This can be alleviated by reducing the dose or by adding a few pills of **2.9 Xiang Sha Liu Jun Wan**.

LIV GB

6.6 LONG DAN XIE GAN WAN

龙胆泻肝丸

Lanzhou Foci Pharmaceutical Factory (Gansu)
'Gentiana Drain the Liver Pills'
Long Dan Xie Gan Wan is packaged in bottles of 200 pills.
Also available as: Snake and Dragon Teapills (PF), Lung Tan Hsieh
Kan Wan, Wetness Heat Pill, Gentiana Liver-Drain Pill (BE)

TCM actions
Clears Damp Heat from the Liver system (Heat greater
than Damp), cools Liver Fire.

Biomedical actions
Bitter tonic, depurative, anti-inflammatory, detoxicant, cholagogue.

INDICATIONS

- Liver Fire or Liver and Gallbladder Damp Heat affecting those areas that are controlled by the Liver and Gallbladder systems–the ears, eyes, flanks and urogenital system.
- With the appropriate identifying features, this formula can be used to treat the following biomedical conditions:
  - **Liver Fire rising through the Liver and GB channel**: acute otitis media and externa, conjunctivitis, glaucoma, uveitis, corneal ulcers, migraine headache, ocular or aural herpes, acute sinusitis, hypertension and hyperthyroidism.
  - **Damp Heat or Fire in the flanks**: hepatobiliary infections (acute cholecystitis and hepatitis), jaundice, abscess and other swellings associated with infection, intercostal neuralgia, shingles.
  - **Damp Heat in the lower *jiao***: acute genital herpes, acute cystitis or urethritis, pyelonephritis, pelvic inflammatory disease, vulvitis, Bartholin's cyst, acute prostatitis, orchitis, epididymitis, genital eczema and pruritus. (but *see also* **1.36 Bi Xie Sheng Shi Wan** for similar patterns with Damp greater than Heat)

Composition (each pill contains powdered)
Gentiana scabra (long dan cao, gentiana) 29mg, *Bupleurum falcatum* (chai hu, bupleurum) 29mg, *Alisma plantago-aquatica* (ze xie, alisma) 29mg, *Rehmannia glutinosa* (sheng di, raw rehmannia) 29mg, *Gardenia jasminoides* (shan zhi zi, gardenia) 14mg, *Scutellaria baicalensis* (huang qin, scute) 14mg, *Plantago asiatica* (che qian zi, plantago) 14mg, *Akebia trifolata* (mu tong, akebia) 14mg, *Angelica sinensis* (dang gui, chinese angelica) 14mg, *Glycyrrhiza uralensis* (gan cao, licorice) 14mg

Pattern identifying features

- **Liver Fire, Damp Heat in the Liver & Gallbladder**
- Redness, swelling, pain or yellow mucopurulent discharges in a hot, strong or otherwise relatively robust patient.
- pounding headaches, migraines
- jaundice

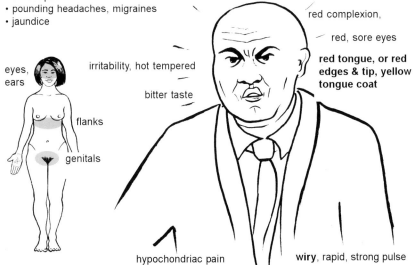

eyes, ears

irritability, hot tempered

bitter taste

flanks

genitals

red complexion,

red, sore eyes

red tongue, or red edges & tip, yellow tongue coat

hypochondriac pain

wiry, rapid, strong pulse

Combinations
- With **9.9 Superior Sore Throat Powder** topically for otitis or shingles.
- With **6.11 Li Dan Tablets** for Damp Heat jaundice (acute hepatitis).
- With **14.5 Chuan Xin Lian Antiphlogistic Tablets** or **14.6 Fu Fang Nan Ban Lan Gen** for herpes zoster or simplex.
- With **1.2 Si Wu Wan** for nonspecific vaginitis or genital eczema with a component of Liver Fire and Blood deficiency.
- With **1.37 Yu Dai Wan** for yellow vaginal discharge from Liver Fire or Damp Heat.

Dosage and method of administration
The recommended dose is 8-12 pills three or four times daily on an empty stomach, however in most acute cases this needs to be doubled or trebled. The dose should be spread out evenly, and in very acute cases may be taken every two hours. Generally not recommended for use longer than a few weeks (two weeks optimum), except in constitutional cases at a lower dose.

Cautions and contraindications
Caution during pregnancy. Can weaken the Spleen and damage *yin* and *yang* when overused.

LIV GB

GMP **6.7 DA CHAI HU WAN**

大柴胡丸

Available in the US,
UK and Europe
See Note 1, p.xxi

Lanzhou Foci Pharmaceutical Factory (Gansu)
'Major Bupleurum Pills'
Da Chai Hu Wan is packaged in bottles of 200 pills.
Available as: Major Bupleurum Teapills

TCM actions
Harmonises *shao yang*, spreads Liver *qi*, purges Heat and
stagnation from *yang ming*.

Biomedical actions
Hepatoprotective, aids clearance of residual pathogens,
laxative, cholagogue.

INDICATIONS

- *Shao yang/yang ming* overlap syndrome. This is an acute pattern characterised by relatively severe fever and gastro-intestinal symptoms which follow a few days (or slightly longer) of malaise and flu like (*tai yang*) symptoms. The main features are alternating fever and chills, nausea and vomiting, abdominal and epigastric pain and constipation or urgent diarrhea. There may be jaundice.
- Chronic Damp Heat and *qi* stagnation in the Liver and Gallbladder causing accumulation and congealing of Dampness into gallstones. This is a particularly good formula for gradually improving gall bladder function and assisting in the breakdown and expulsion of small gallstones. Some of the main features may be absent in chronic cases, but the practitioner would still expect to see constipation, intermittent hypochondriac and abdominal pain, nausea, aversion to fats and oils, a strong wiry pulse and greasy, yellow tongue coat.
- With the appropriate identifying features, this formula can be used to treat biomedical conditions such as acute and chronic **cholecystitis**, **acute pancreatitis**, **hepatitis**, dysentery, **gallstones**, malaria, migraine headaches and hypertension.

Composition
Zingiber officinalis (sheng jiang, ginger) 19%, *Bupleurum falcatum* (chai hu, bupleurum) 12%, *Pinellia ternata* (zhi ban xia, processed pinellia) 12%, *Scutellaria baicalensis* (huang qin, scute) 12%, *Citrus aurantium* (zhi shi, aurantium) 12%, *Paeonia alba* (bai shao, white peony) 12%, *Zizyphus jujuba* (da zao, chinese dates) 10%, *Rheum palmatum* (da huang, rhubarb) 9%

Pattern identifying features

- **Shao yang / yang ming overlap syndrome; Damp Heat/excess Heat in the Gallbladder & Stomach**
- **alternating fever & chills**
- irritability, manic behaviour
- bitter taste in the mouth
- jaundice

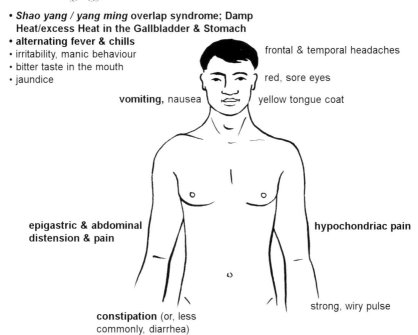

frontal & temporal headaches

red, sore eyes

yellow tongue coat

vomiting, nausea

epigastric & abdominal distension & pain

hypochondriac pain

strong, wiry pulse

constipation (or, less commonly, diarrhea)

Combinations
- With **6.10 Qing Gan Li Dan Tablets** or **4.10 Shi Lin Tong** for gallstones.
- With **14.5 Chuan Xin Lian Antiphlogistic Tablets** or **14.8 Wu Wei Xiao Du Wan** for acute infectious hepatitis or cholecystitis.
- With **2.26 Xiang Lian Wan** for severe vomiting, both formulae crushed and decocted together, then sipped slowly through a straw to facilitate ingestion.

Dosage and method of administration
The recommended dose is 8-12 pills three or four times daily on an empty stomach, however in most acute cases this needs to be doubled or trebled. The dose should be spread out evenly, and in very acute cases may be taken every two hours. When treating chronic problems such as gallstones, the dose is 4-6 pills three times daily, or sufficient to cause a smooth bowel movement with no abdominal cramping. After a month or two the patient should be rested off the formula for a few weeks as they can become habituated to the rhubarb.

Cautions and contraindications
Contraindicated during pregnancy and for patients taking interferon. Can weaken the Spleen and damage *yin* when overused.

LIV GB

GMP **6.8 YI GUAN JIAN WAN**

一贯煎丸

Lanzhou Foci Pharmaceutical Factory (Gansu)
'Linking Decoction Pills'
Yi Guan Jian Wan is packaged in bottles of 200 pills.
Available as: Linking Decoction Teapills (PF)

Available in the US,
UK and Europe
See Note 1, p.xxi

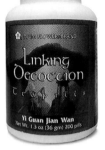

TCM actions

Supplements Liver *yin*, nourishes Liver Blood, spreads and
regulates Liver *qi*, benefits the Stomach.

Biomedical actions

Demulcent febrifuge, antispasmodic.

INDICATIONS

• Liver *yin* and Blood deficiency with Liver *qi* stagnation; Liver *qi* invading the
Stomach damaging Stomach *yin*. Blood and *yin* deficiency with *qi* stagnation is a
common combination of pathology. The physiology of the Liver is such that
deficiency of the *yin* aspects of the Liver (the *yin* and Blood) lead to a relative
excess of Liver *yangness*, in this case stasis and accumulation of Liver *qi*, which in
turn can affect the Stomach. Strong *qi* moving herbs are not indicated as they
can further deplete the already damaged *yin*. This is a popular and versatile formula
for a variety of chronic Liver and digestive complaints, in particular those with
an upper gastro-intestinal focus.

• With the appropriate identifying features, this formula can assist in the treatment
of biomedical conditions such as **chronic hepatitis**, early hepatic cirrhosis, fatty
liver, peptic ulcer disease, chronic gastritis, gastric neurosis, **gastro-esophageal
reflux** (GERD), intercostal neuralgia, essential hypertension and preeclampsia.

Composition

Rehmannia glutinosa (sheng di, raw rehmannia) 37%, *Lycium barbarum* (gou qi zi,
lycium fruit) 16%, *Glehnia littoralis* (bei sha shen, glehnia) 13%, *Ophiopogon japonicus*
(mai dong, ophiopogon) 13%, *Angelica sinensis* (dang gui, chinese angelica) 13%,
Melia toosendan (chuan lian zi, melia fruit) 5.5%

Combinations

• With **10.22 Shao Yao Gan Cao Wan** for more intense cramping abdominal pain.
• With **3.38 Sheng Mai San Wan** for chronic hepatitis from *yin* and *qi* deficiency.
• With **2.26 Xiang Lian Wan** for severe heartburn.

Pattern identifying features

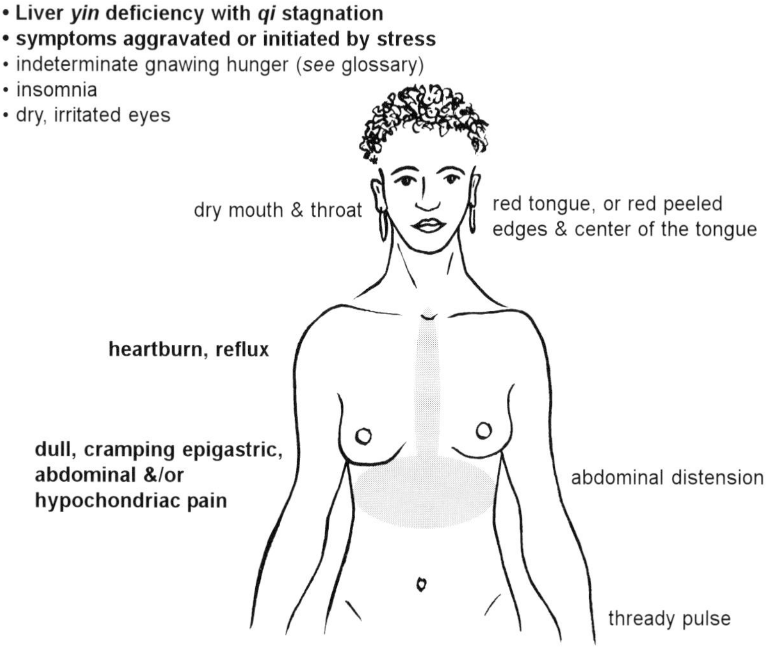

- **Liver *yin* deficiency with *qi* stagnation**
- **symptoms aggravated or initiated by stress**
- indeterminate gnawing hunger (*see* glossary)
- insomnia
- dry, irritated eyes

dry mouth & throat

red tongue, or red peeled edges & center of the tongue

heartburn, reflux

dull, cramping epigastric, abdominal &/or hypochondriac pain

abdominal distension

thready pulse

- With **5.7 Sunho Multiginseng Tablets** for early cirrhosis with mild Blood stagnation.
- With a small dose of **2.31 Run Chang Wan** or **2.32 Wu Ren Wan** for constipation.
- With **2.18 Bao He Wan** for distension and food stagnation.
- With **15.7 Yang Yin Jiang Ya Wan** or **15.8 Fu Fang Jiang Ya Capsule** for hypertension.
- With **8.6 Suan Zao Ren Wan** for insomnia and restlessness.

Dosage and method of administration

8-12 pills three times daily on an empty stomach. The dose may be spread out, or two lots of 12-18 pills may be taken, morning and evening. In severe cases or during the early stages of treatment (the first few weeks), a 50% increase in dose may be used, then reduced as the treatment takes effect.

Cautions and contraindications

Contraindicated during the early phase of acute illness such as colds and flu, and in Phlegm Damp patterns.

Caution in patients with elevated liver enzyme (AST/ALT) levels, as the melia, even though the dose is small, can occasionally cause irritation of the liver and cause elevation of AST/ALT levels.

LIV GB

6.9 JIGUCAO WAN

鸡骨草丸

Yulin Pharmaceutical Factory (Guangxi)
'Abrus Pills'
Jigucao Wan is packaged in bottles of 50 capsules.
Also available as: Ji Gu Cao Pian (PF)

TCM actions

Cools the Liver and benefits the Gallbladder, nourishes
yin and Blood, quickens the Blood.

Biomedical actions

Hepatoprotective, cholagogue.

INDICATIONS

- Acute and chronic Liver and Gallbladder disease from smouldering Damp Heat.
  This is a relatively mild formula suited to both acute and chronic problems, but
  best for chronic conditions. Excellent for chronic hepatitis, especially hepatitis
  C infection. Suitable for prolonged use.
- With the appropriate identifying features, this formula can assist in the treatment
  of biomedical conditions such as acute and chronic hepatitis, cholecystitis and
  jaundice.

Composition (each capsule contains)

Abrus cantoniensis (ji gu cao, abrus) 160mg, pearl powder (zhen zhu fen) 72mg, *Lycium chinensis* (gou qi zi, lycium fruit) 68mg, *Salvia miltorrhiza* (dan shen, salvia) 60mg, Bovine gallstone (niu huang) 40mg

Combinations

- With **6.1 Xiao Chai Hu Tang Wan** for chronic hepatitis (especially chronic
  asymptomatic hepatitis C).
- With **14.5 Chuan Xin Lian Antiphogistic Tablets** for acute viral hepatitis.
- With **6.3 Chai Hu Shu Gan Wan**, **6.4 Xiao Yao Wan** or **6.5 Jia Wei Xiao Yao
  Wan** for chronic hepatitis of a Liver *qi* stagnation type.
- With **2.12 Shen Ling Bai Zhu Wan**, **2.16 Zi Sheng Wan** or **2.13 Li Zhong Wan**
  for hepatitis patients with significant Spleen deficiency.

Pattern identifying features

- **Liver/Gallbladder Damp Heat, Blood stagnation**
- acute & **chronic liver disease**
- malaise, fatigue, lack of vitality
- jaundice

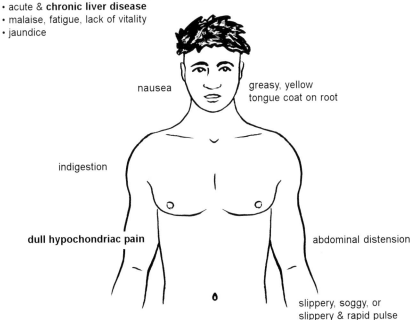

nausea

greasy, yellow
tongue coat on root

indigestion

dull hypochondriac pain

abdominal distension

slippery, soggy, or
slippery & rapid pulse

- With **2.24 Shu Gan Wan** for chronic hepatic disease and abdominal pain from *qi* stagnation.
- With **6.6 Long Dan Xie Gan Wan** for acute or symptomatic hepatitis associated with Liver Fire or severe Damp Heat.

Dosage and method of administration

4 pills, three times daily on an empty stomach.

Cautions and Contraindications

Contraindicated during pregnancy. Not suitable unmodified for Cold Damp patterns, with dull or sallow skin, 'dirty' yellow jaundice and significant digestive weakness. Caution in patients who are also taking anticoagulant therapy (aspirin, warfarin, coumarin) as clotting time can be significantly reduced.

LIV GB

6.10 QING GAN LI DAN TABLETS

清肝利胆片

(Qing Gan Li Dan Pian)
'Cool the Liver and Benefit the Gallbladder Pills'
Qing Gan Li Dan Tablets are packaged in bottles of 60 tablets.

TCM actions

Clears Damp Heat from the Liver and Gallbladder,
regulates *qi* and quickens Blood, promotes urination,
assists in expulsion of minor gall stones, opens the bowels.

Biomedical actions

Diuretic, cholagogue, laxative.

INDICATIONS

• Damp Heat (Dampness greater than Heat) and *qi* stagnation affecting the Gallbladder and Liver. Used for gallstones (usually those less than 10mm diameter), sludge in the gallbladder, colicky hypochondriac pain, indigestion, aversion to, or intolerance of, fats and oils and constipation or pasty stools. This formula is similar in overall action to **6.11 Lidan Tablets** but with less emphasis on cooling Heat, and more on draining Dampness and descending and regulating *qi*. It is more focused on the gastro-intestinal symptoms that accompany gall bladder disease, such as abdominal distension and bloating, indigestion and nausea. Useful for chronic indigestion and gastro-intestinal upsets from poor gall bladder or liver function, for biliousness in those who overindulge and for chronic gall bladder disorders in obese patients.

• Can also be used to aid in the treatment of chronic gallbladder congestion and irritation, which in TCM terms can affect not only the Gallbladder organ, but also structures along the course of the Gallbladder channel. A patient with this type of problem may not necessarily have symptoms localised in the Gallbladder, instead the symptoms may be reflected along the course of the Gallbladder channel, manifesting as vague temporomandibular, jaw, hip or shoulder pain, ear problems or headaches.

• With the appropriate identifying features, this formula can be used to treat biomedical conditions such as **gallstones**, chronic **cholecystitis**, biliary spasm, hepatitis and early hepatic cirrhosis.

Composition (each tablet contains extracts equivalent to dry)

Plantago asiatica (che qian zi, plantago) 576mg, *Salvia miltorrhiza* (dan shen, salvia)

Pattern identifying features

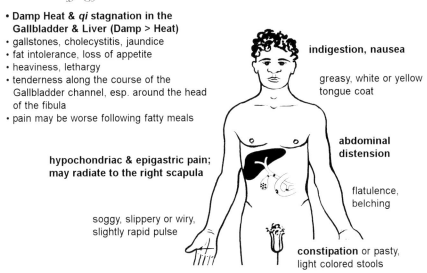

- **Damp Heat & *qi* stagnation in the Gallbladder & Liver (Damp > Heat)**
- gallstones, cholecystitis, jaundice
- fat intolerance, loss of appetite
- heaviness, lethargy
- tenderness along the course of the Gallbladder channel, esp. around the head of the fibula
- pain may be worse following fatty meals

indigestion, nausea

greasy, white or yellow tongue coat

abdominal distension

hypochondriac & epigastric pain; may radiate to the right scapula

flatulence, belching

soggy, slippery or wiry, slightly rapid pulse

constipation or pasty, light colored stools

576mg, *Citrus aurantium* (zhi shi, aurantium) 576mg, *Curcuma longa* (yu jin, curcuma) 480mg, *Lysimachia christina* (jin qian cao, lysimachia) 480mg, *Magnolia officinalis* (hou po, magnolia bark) 480mg, *Scutellaria baicalensis* (huang qin, scute) 432mg, *Areca catechu* (da fu pi, betel husk) 432mg, *Rheum officinale* (da huang, rhubarb) 40mg

Combinations
- With **6.4 Xiao Yao Wan** for chronic hypochondriac ache and gallbladder irritation (particularly in women) from *qi* and/or Damp stagnation.
- With **2.23 Ping Wei San** for severe distension or Dampness. A good combination for obese patients.
- With **6.7 Da Chai Hu Wan** for gallstones from lingering Damp Heat.
- With **4.10 Shi Lin Tong** to reinforce the stone dissolving action.

Dosage and method of administration
3-5 tablets, three times daily on an empty stomach. When treating gall stones, long term administration is usually required (3-6 months), in association with appropriate dietary modifications. The patient should be advised to expect diarrhea. The dose can be adjusted until a smooth bowel movement is achieved.

Cautions and Contraindications
Contraindicated during pregnancy. Not suitable unmodified for Cold Damp patterns. Caution in patients who are also taking anticoagulant therapy (aspirin, warfarin, coumarin) as clotting time can be significantly reduced.

LIV GB

6.11 LIDAN TABLETS

利胆片

(Li Dan Pian)
Qingdao Traditional Chinese Medicine Co. (Qingdao)
'Benefit the Gallbladder Pills'
Lidan Tablets are packaged in bottles of 120 tablets.

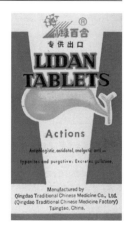

TCM actions

Clears Damp and Toxic Heat from Liver and Gallbladder,
alleviates jaundice, assists in expulsion of minor gall
stones, opens the bowels.

Biomedical actions

Cholagogue, diuretic, anti-inflammatory, antipyretic, laxative.

INDICATIONS

- Damp Heat in the Liver and Gallbladder with inflammation and gallstones. This
  formula is quite cooling and is best suited to acute conditions with clear signs of
  Heat such as fever, red eyes and a yellow tongue coat. It can, however, be used
  for chronic conditions with lingering Heat. In general, similar in overall action
  to **6.10 Qing Gan Li Dan Tablets**, with a greater emphasis on cooling Heat.
- With the appropriate identifying features, this formula can be used to treat
  biomedical conditions such as **gallstones**, acute and chronic **cholecystitis**,
  cholangitis, inflammation of the bile duct, **jaundice**, acute **hepatitis** and early
  hepatic cirrhosis.

Composition

Scutellaria baicalensis (huang qin, scute) 30%, *Plantago asiatica* (che qian zi, plantago)
16%, *Bupleurum falcatum* (chai hu, bupleurum) 10%, *Artemesia capillaris* (yin chen,
capillaris) 10%, *Lysimachia christina* (jin qian cao, lysimachia) 10%, *Isatis tinctora* (da
qing ye, isatis) 10%, *Lonicera japonica* (jin yin hua, honeysuckle) 10%, *Rheum palmatum*
(da huang, rhubarb) 4%

Combinations

- With **2.24 Shu Gan Wan** or **10.21 Yan Hu Suo Zhi Tong Wan** for severe
  hypochondriac pain.
- With **6.6 Long Dan Xie Gan Wan** for acute hepatitis with jaundice.

Pattern identifying features

- **Damp Heat in the Liver & Gallbladder (Heat > Damp)**
- **fever**
- irritability
- malaise
- pain may be worse following fatty or rich meals

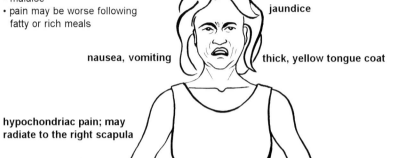

jaundice

nausea, vomiting

thick, yellow tongue coat

hypochondriac pain; may radiate to the right scapula

slippery, rapid pulse

constipation or pasty, light colored stools

- With **14.5 Chuan Xin Lian Antiphlogistic Tablets** to enhance the Toxic Heat clearing action for acute viral hepatitis or cholecystitis.
- With **6.1 Xiao Chai Hu Tang Wan** for acute cholecystitis with alternating fever and chills.

Dosage and method of administration
4-6 tablets three times daily on an empty stomach. The patient should be advised to expect diarrhea. The dose can be adjusted until a smooth bowel movement is achieved.

Cautions and contraindications
Contraindicated during pregnancy. Not suitable for Cold Damp patterns.

LIV GB

GMP **6.12 GE XIA ZHU YU WAN**

膈下逐瘀丸

Lanzhou Foci Pharmaceutical Factory (Gansu)
'Remove Stagnant Blood from Beneath the Diaphragm Pills'
Ge Xia Zhu Yu Wan is packaged in bottles of 200 pills.
Available as: Stasis in the Lower Chamber Teapills

Available in the US,
UK and Europe
See Note 1, p.xxi

TCM actions

Invigorates the circulation of *qi* and Blood, breaks up and disperses stagnant Blood, resolves masses, stops pain.

Biomedical actions

Vasodilator, analgesic, anti-platelet action, softens and resolves masses.

INDICATIONS

* Masses and swelling in the upper abdomen as a result of chronic Liver *qi* and Blood stagnation. This variation of the classic **5.1 Xue Fu Zhu Yu Wan** is specifically targeted at painful masses or swellings of the Liver and Spleen.
* Being a powerful *qi* and Blood 'breaking' formula, it can also be used for painful Blood stagnation type masses in other locations within the abdomen, such as endometriosis and fibroids (but *see also* **1.18 Shao Fu Zhu Yu Wan**).
* With the appropriate identifying features, this formula may assist in the treatment of biomedical conditions such as hepatic cirrhosis, chronic malaria, liver abscess, hepatosplenomegaly, ascites secondary to liver disease, benign gynecological masses. Also uses for splenomegaly secondary to glandular fever, bacteraemia, portal hypertension, systemic lupus erythematosus, leukaemia, cysts or hemolytic anemia.

Composition

Trogopterus xanthipes (wu ling zhi, flying squirrel feces) 11.5%, *Angelica sinensis* (dang gui, chinese angelica) 11.5%, *Prunus persica* (tao ren, peach seed) 11.5%, *Carthamus tinctorius* (hong hua, carthamus) 11.5%, *Lindera strychnifolia* (wu yao, lindera) 11.5%, *Ligusticum wallici* (chuan xiong, cnidium) 7%, *Paeonia suffruticosa* (mu dan pi, moutan) 7%, *Paeonia veitchii* (chi shao, red peony) 7%, *Cyperus rotundus* (xiang fu, cyperus) 6%, *Citrus aurantium* (zhi ke, aurantium) 6%, *Corydalis turtschaninovii* (yan hu suo, corydalis) 4%, *Glycyrrhiza uralensis* (gan cao, licorice) 3%

Pattern identifying features

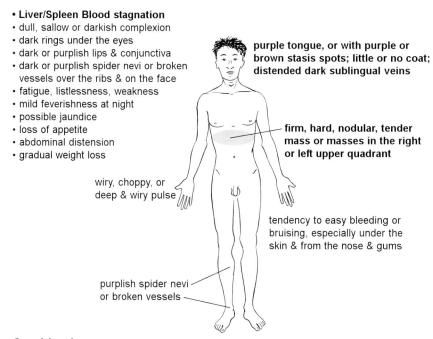

- **Liver/Spleen Blood stagnation**
- dull, sallow or darkish complexion
- dark rings under the eyes
- dark or purplish lips & conjunctiva
- dark or purplish spider nevi or broken vessels over the ribs & on the face
- fatigue, listlessness, weakness
- mild feverishness at night
- possible jaundice
- loss of appetite
- abdominal distension
- gradual weight loss

purple tongue, or with purple or brown stasis spots; little or no coat; distended dark sublingual veins

firm, hard, nodular, tender mass or masses in the right or left upper quadrant

wiry, choppy, or deep & wiry pulse

tendency to easy bleeding or bruising, especially under the skin & from the nose & gums

purplish spider nevi or broken vessels

Combinations
- With **1.33 Hai Zao Jing Wan** for rubbery Phlegm and Blood stagnation masses.
- With **1.2 Si Wu Wan** for patients with a greater degree of Blood deficiency.

Dosage and method of administration
8-12 pills three times daily on an empty stomach. The dose may be spread out, or two lots of 12-18 pills may be taken, morning and evening. In severe cases or during the early stages of treatment, a 50% increase in dose may be used, then reduced as the treatment takes effect.

Cautions and contraindications
Contraindicated during pregnancy, in women with menorrhagia, and in patients with bleeding disorders. Caution in patients on anticoagulant therapy (aspirin, warfarin, coumarin). Watch for bruising or increased tendency to bleeding.

Prolonged use may deplete *qi* and Blood, so a break every 2-3 months, with a change to a simple *qi* and Blood supplementing formula for a few weeks, is recommended.

The conditions for which this formula are indicated are serious and TCM treatment will generally be supportive in the context of orthodox medical management.

LIV GB

6.13 HERBA ABRI FRUTICULOSI BEVERAGE

鸡骨草精

(Ji Gu Cao Jing)
Guangdong Medicines and Health
Products Co.
'Essence of *Abrus fruticulosus*'
Herba Abri Fruticulosi Beverage is
packaged in 15 gram sachets of
dissolvable granules, ten sachets per box.

TCM actions
Clears Damp Heat from the Liver and Gallbladder, promotes urination, alleviates
jaundice.

Biomedical actions
Hepatoprotective, diuretic, cholagogue.

INDICATIONS

• Acute and chronic hepatitis. This formula has both preventive effects (for those
in epidemic areas or in high risk) and therapeutic effects in cases of acute and
chronic disease.

Composition
Abrus cantoniensis (ji gu cao, abrus), *Hypericum japonicum* (di er cao, hypericum),
Artemesia capillaris (yin chen, capillaris), Radix Rhodomyrti (tao jin tui gen), *Artemesia
anomala* (ya tui ai), *Zanthoxylum avicennae* (ying bu bo)

Dosage and method of administration
The recommended dose is one sachet, 2-3 times daily. In acute cases the dose may
be increase 50-100%.

Cautions and contraindications
Contraindicated during pregnancy.

6.14 XI HUANG CAO

溪黄草

(Xi Huang Cao Hu Gan Chong Ji)
Wuzhou Traditional Medicine
Factory (Guangxi)
'Rabdosia Liver Protecting Granules'
Xi Huang Cao is packaged in 10 gram sachets of dissolvable granules, twenty to a box.

TCM actions
Clears Damp Heat from the Liver and Gallbladder, clears Toxic Heat, strengthens the Liver and Spleen.

Biomedical actions
Hepatoprotective, antipyretic, immunomodulating.

INDICATIONS

- Acute and chronic hepatitis. This formula has both preventive effects for those in epidemic areas or at high risk, and therapeutic effects in cases of acute and chronic disease. It is slightly more supplementing than **6.13 Herba Abri Fruticulosi Beverage** and good for chronic hepatitis with some *qi* deficiency.

Composition (each 10 gram sachet)
Rabdosia lophanthoides (xi huang cao, rabdosia) 40%, *Abrus cantoniensis* (ji gu cao, abrus) 15%, *Oldenlandia diffusa* (bai hua she she cao, oldenlandia) 15%, *Codonopsis pilosula* (dang shen, codonopsis) 15%, *Poria cocos* (fu ling, hoelen) 15%

Dosage and method of administration
The recommended dose is one or two sachets, 2-3 times daily. In acute cases the dose may be increased by 50%.

Cautions and contraindications
None noted.

LIV GB

7

Patent Medicines for Supplementing
Qi, Blood, *Yin* and *Yang*

Kidney Supplements

Yin supplements

7.1.1 Liu Wei Di Huang Wan
7.1.2 Liu Wei Di Huang Wan
7.1.3 Tinnitus Herbal Treatment
7.1.4 Liu Wei Di Huang Pills
7.2.1 Qi Ju Di Huang Wan
7.2.2 Qi Ju Di Huang Wan
7.3 Zuo Gui Wan
7.4 Da Bu Yin Wan
7.5 Gu Ben Wan

Yin and Blood supplements

7.6 Yang Xue Sheng Fa Capsule
7.7 Qi Bao Mei Ran Dan
7.8 Shou Wu Chih

Yang supplements

7.9 Fu Gui Ba Wei Wan
7.10 You Gui Wan
7.11 Deer Velvet
7.12 Lu rong Jiao
7.13 Huan Shao Dan
7.14 Deer Antler & Ginseng
7.15 Yulin Da Bu Wan

Qi and Blood supplements

7.16.1 Shi Quan Da Bu Wan
7.16.2 Shi Quan Da Bu Wan
7.17 Hua Tuo Shi Quan Da Bu Jiu
7.18 Yang Ying Wan
7.19 Shou Wu Pian
7.20 Cordyceps Essence of Chicken
7.21 American Ginseng Essence of Chicken
7.22 Shen Qi Da Bu Wan
7.23 Yu Ping Feng Wan
7.24 Panax Ginseng Extractum
7.25 Peking Ginseng Royal Jelly
7.26 Reishi Mushroom

7.1.1 LIU WEI DI HUANG WAN

六味地黄丸

Lanzhou Foci Pharmaceutical Factory (Gansu)
'Six Flavour Pills with Rehmannia'
Liu Wei Di Huang Wan is packaged in bottles of 200 pills.
Also available as: Six Flavor Teapills (PF)

TCM actions
Supplements Kidney and Liver *yin*.

Biomedical actions
Demulcent febrifuge, hematinic, hypoglycemic, antihypertensive, improves kidney function, regulates adrenal cortex.

INDICATIONS

• Kidney and Liver *yin* deficiency. The base from which almost all other Kidney *yin* and *yang* supplements are built and one of the most important formulae of Chinese medicine. It is used for a wide variety of problems associated with Kidney *yin* deficiency in both adults and children. Excellent as a general Kidney support in the elderly or in those at risk of Kidney *yin* depletion such as the chronically overworked, night shift workers, flight attendants and steroid users. This formula has a steroid sparing effect, and can help to minimise and alleviate the unwanted effects of prolonged corticosteroid use.

• Used as a support for patients with *Xiao Ke* syndrome (*see* glossary). This formula has been shown to have a significant regulatory effect on blood glucose levels.

• With the appropriate identifying features, this formula can be used to treat biomedical conditions such as hypertension, anovulation, amenorrhea, delayed development in children, hyperthyroidism, arteriosclerosis, impotence, diabetes mellitus, optic neuritis and optic nerve atrophy. Also used for chronic disorders of the biomedical kidney–chronic nephritis, glomerulonephritis, cystitis, polycystic kidneys and various *yin* deficiency type urinary disturbances.

Composition (each pill contains powdered)
Rehmannia glutinosa (shu di, processed rehmannia) 51.5mg, *Cornus officinalis* (shan zhu yu, cornus) 27.5mg, *Dioscorea opposita* (shan yao, dioscorea) 27.5mg, *Poria cocos* (fu ling, hoelen) 20.6mg, *Alisma orientalis* (ze xie, alisma) 20.6mg, *Paeonia suffruticosa* (mu dan pi, moutan) 20.6mg

Pattern identifying features

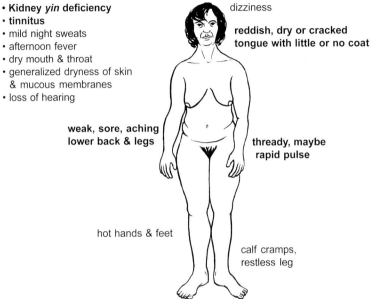

- **Kidney *yin* deficiency**
- **tinnitus**
- mild night sweats
- afternoon fever
- dry mouth & throat
- generalized dryness of skin
  & mucous membranes
- loss of hearing

dizziness

reddish, dry or cracked
tongue with little or no coat

weak, sore, aching
lower back & legs

thready, maybe
rapid pulse

hot hands & feet

calf cramps,
restless leg

Combinations
- With **7.11 Deer Velvet** or **7.12 Lu Rong Jiao** for failure to thrive, developmental delay or bone growth problems in children.
- With **2.35 Yu Quan Wan** or **2.36 Sugarid** for diabetes.
- With **7.22 Shen Qi Da Bu Wan** for concurrent Spleen *qi* deficiency.
- With **4.10 Shi Lin Tong** for urinary calculi.
- With **3.33 Yang Yin Qing Fei Wan** or **2.32 Wu Ren Wan** for chronic *yin* deficient constipation.

Dosage and method of administration
8-12 pills three times daily on an empty stomach. The dose may be spread out, or two lots of 12-18 pills may be taken, morning and evening. In severe cases or during the early stages of treatment (the first few weeks), a 50% increase in dose may be used, then reduced as the treatment takes effect.

Cautions and contraindications
Contraindicated during the early phase of acute illness such as colds and flu. Care should be taken in patients with a tendency to abdominal distension, loose stools or Phlegm Damp. This is a cooling formula and overuse can cool and weaken digestion. This can usually be alleviated by taking **7.1 Liu Wei Di Huang Wan** with a small dose (3-6 pills at the same time) of **2.18 Bao He Wan** or **2.9 Xiang Sha Liu Jun Wan**, or by taking the pills after food.

SUPP

7.1.2 LIU WEI DI HUANG WAN

六味地黄丸

Tong Ren Tang (Beijing)
'Six Flavour Pills with Rehmannia'
Liu Wei Di Huang Wan is packaged in bottles of 360 little water honey pills.

TCM actions
Supplements Kidney and Liver *yin*.

Biomedical actions
Demulcent febrifuge, hematinic, hypoglycemic, antihypertensive, improves kidney function, regulates adrenal cortex.

INDICATIONS

• As for 7.1.1 Liu Wei Di Huang Wan.

Composition (each dose [30 pills] contains powdered)
Rehmannia glutinosa (shu di, processed rehmannia) 1.6mg, *Cornus officinalis* (shan zhu yu, cornus) 810mg, *Dioscorea opposita* (shan yao, dioscorea) 810mg, *Poria cocos* (fu ling, hoelen) 600mg, *Alisma orientalis* (ze xie, alisma) 600mg, *Paeonia suffruticosa* (mu dan pi, moutan) 600mg

Dosage and method of administration
30 pills twice daily on an empty stomach.

Cautions and contraindications
As for **7.1.1 Liu Wei Di Huang Wan**.

7.1.3 TINNITUS HERBAL TREATMENT

六味地黄丸

(Liu Wei Di Huang Wan)
Tong Ren Tang (Beijing)
'Six Flavour Pills with Rehmannia'
Tinnitus Herbal Treatment is packaged in bottles of 200 pills.

TCM actions
Supplements Kidney and Liver *yin*.

Biomedical actions
Demulcent febrifuge, hematinic, hypoglycemic, antihypertensive, improves kidney function, regulates adrenal cortex.

INDICATIONS

- As for **7.1.1 Liu Wei Di Huang Wan**.

Composition (each dose [8 pills] contains extracts equivalent to dry)
Rehmannia glutinosa (shu di, processed rehmannia) 960mg, *Cornus officinalis* (shan zhu yu, cornus) 480mg, *Dioscorea opposita* (shan yao, dioscorea) 480mg, *Poria cocos* (fu ling, hoelen) 360mg, *Alisma orientalis* (ze xie, alisma) 360mg, *Paeonia suffruticosa* (mu dan pi, moutan) 360mg

Dosage and method of administration
8 pills twice daily on an empty stomach.

Cautions and contraindications
As for **7.1.1 Liu Wei Di Huang Wan**.

SUPP

7.1.4 LIU WEI DI HUANG PILLS

六味地黄丸

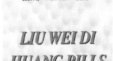

(Liu Wei Di Huang Wan)
Jing Xian Pharmaceutical Co. (Guangzhou)
'Six Flavour Pills with Rehmannia'
Liu Wei Di Huang Pills are packaged in bottles of 200 pills.

LIU WEI DI
HUANG PILLS

AUST L 91205
200 PILLS

MADE IN CHINA

TCM actions
Supplements Kidney and Liver *yin*.

Biomedical actions
Demulcent febrifuge, hematinic, hypoglycemic, antihypertensive, improves kidney function, regulates adrenal cortex.

INDICATIONS

• As for **7.1.1 Liu Wei Di Huang Wan**.

Composition (each pill contains extracts equivalent to dry)
Rehmannia glutinosa (shu di, processed rehmannia) 473mg, *Cornus officinalis* (shan zhu yu, cornus) 218mg, *Dioscorea opposita* (shan yao, dioscorea) 218mg, *Poria cocos* (fu ling, hoelen) 164mg, *Alisma orientalis* (ze xie, alisma) 164mg, *Paeonia suffruticosa* (mu dan pi, moutan) 164mg

Dosage and method of administration
8 pills, three times daily on an empty stomach.

Cautions and contraindications
As for **7.1.1 Liu Wei Di Huang Wan**.

7.2.1 QI JU DI HUANG WAN

杞菊地黄丸

Tong Ren Tang (Beijing)
'Rehmannia Pills with Lycium Fruit and Chrysanthemum Flowers'
Qi Ju Di Huang Wan is packaged in bottles of 200 pills.

TCM actions
Supplements Liver and Kidney *yin* and brightens the eyes.

Biomedical actions
Demulcent febrifuge, hematinic, hypoglycemic, antihypertensive, improves kidney function, regulates adrenal cortex.

INDICATIONS

• As for **7.2.2 Qi Ju Di Huang Wan**.

Composition
Rehmannia glutinosa (shu di, processed rehmannia) 27.7%, *Cornus officinalis* (shan zhu yu, cornus) 13.8%, *Dioscorea opposita* (shan yao, dioscorea) 13.8%, *Poria cocos* (fu ling, hoelen) 10.3%, *Alisma orientalis* (ze xie, alisma) 10.3%, *Paeonia suffruticosa* (mu dan pi, moutan) 10.3%, *Lycium barbarum* (gou qi zi, lycium fruit) 6.9%, *Chrysanthemun morifolium* (ju hua, chrysanthemum flower) 6.9%

Dosage and method of administration
30 pills, twice daily on an empty stomach.

Cautions and contraindications
Contraindicated during the early phase of acute illness such as colds and flu. Care should be taken in patients with a tendency to abdominal distension, loose stools or Phlegm Damp. This is a cooling formula and overuse can cool and weaken digestion. This can usually be alleviated by taking the formula with a small dose (3-6 pills at the same time) of **2.18 Bao He Wan** or **2.9 Xiang Sha Liu Jun Wan**, or by taking the pills after food.

SUPP

7.2.2 QI JU DI HUANG WAN

杞菊地黄丸

Lanzhou Foci Pharmaceutical Factory (Gansu)
'Rehmannia Pills with Lycium Fruit and Chrysanthemum Flowers'
Qi Ju Di Huang Wan is packaged in bottles of 200 pills.
Also available as: Lycium Rehmannia Teapills (PF)

TCM actions
Supplements Liver and Kidney *yin* and brightens the eyes.

Biomedical actions
Demulcent febrifuge, hematinic, hypoglycemic, antihypertensive, improves kidney function, regulates adrenal cortex.

INDICATIONS

• Liver and Kidney *yin* deficiency patterns. This is a variation of **7.1 Liu Wei Di Huang Wan**, with the addition of chrysanthemum flower and lycium fruit to shift the focus of the formula towards the Liver. This formula is prefered for more Liver *yin* specific disorders such as visual weakness and eye disorders, headaches, chronic liver disease and tightness or stiffness of the tendons and muscles.

• With the appropriate identifying features, this formula can assist in the treatment of biomedical conditions such as keratitis sicca, chronic glaucoma, optic neuritis, optic nerve atrophy, essential hypertension, chronic migraine headaches, hyperthyroidism, diabetes mellitus and chronic hepatitis.

Composition (each pill contains powdered)
Rehmannia glutinosa (shu di, processed rehmannia) 49.7mg, *Cornus officinalis* (shan zhu yu, cornus) 24.8mg, *Dioscorea opposita* (shan yao, dioscorea) 24.6mg, *Poria cocos* (fu ling, hoelen) 18.6mg, *Alisma orientalis* (ze xie, alisma) 18.6mg, *Paeonia suffruticosa* (mu dan pi, moutan) 18.6mg, *Lycium barbarum* (gou qi zi, lycium fruit) 12.4mg, *Chrysanthemun morifolium* (ju hua, chrysanthemum flower) 12.4mg

Combinations
• With **15.4 Tian Ma Gou Teng Wan** or **15.7 Yang Yin Jiang Ya Wan** for Liver and Kidney *yin* deficiency with *yang* rising type hypertension, headaches, dizziness, transient ischemic attacks.
• With **13.19 Pearl Powder** for *yin* deficient eye disorders.

Pattern identifying features

- **Liver & Kidney *yin* deficiency visual weakness**
- irritability, anger, tinnitus, dizziness
- dull hypochondriac pain
- reddish tongue with little or no coat

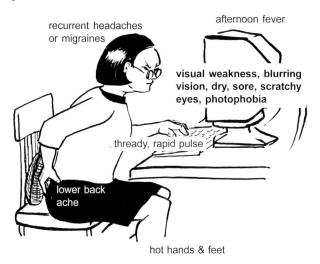

recurrent headaches or migraines

afternoon fever

visual weakness, blurring vision, dry, sore, scratchy eyes, photophobia

thready, rapid pulse

lower back ache

hot hands & feet

SUPP

Dosage and method of administration

8-12 pills three times daily on an empty stomach. The dose may be spread out, or two lots of 12-18 pills may be taken, morning and evening. In severe cases or during the early stages of treatment (the first few weeks), a 50% increase in dose may be used, then reduced as the treatment takes effect.

Cautions and contraindications

Contraindicated during the early phase of acute illness such as colds and flu. Care should be taken in patients with a tendency to abdominal distension, loose stools or mucus accumulation. This is a cooling formula and overuse can cool and weaken digestion. This can usually be alleviated by taking the formula with a small dose (3-6 pills at the same time) of **2.18 Bao He Wan** or **2.9 Xiang Sha Liu Jun Wan**, or by taking the pills after food.

7.3 ZUO GUI WAN

左归丸

Lanzhou Foci Pharmaceutical Factory (Gansu)
'Right Returning Pills'
Zuo Gui Wan is packaged in bottles of 200 pills.
Also available as: Left Side Replenishing Teapills (PF)

TCM actions
Supplements Kidney *yin*, nourishes *jing*.

Biomedical actions
Demulcent febrifuge, hematinic, hypoglycemic, antihypertensive, improves kidney function, regulates adrenal cortex.

INDICATIONS

• Kidney *yin* and *jing* deficiency. Similar in action to **7.1 Liu Wei Di Huang Wan**, however, this formula lacks the 'draining' components that are used to clear Heat from deficiency, substituting additional supplementing herbs. This variation makes this formula a slightly richer *yin* supplement suitable for relatively pure *yin* deficiency patterns with little deficient Heat. Excellent as a general Kidney *yin* support in the elderly or in those at risk of Kidney *yin* depletion.

• With the appropriate identifying features, this formula can be used to treat biomedical conditions such as hypertension, delayed development in children, anovulation, amenorrhea, impotence, diabetes mellitus, chronic nephritis, glomerulonephritis, cystitis, polycystic kidneys and various *yin* deficiency type urinary disturbances and consumptive disorders.

Composition (each pill contains powdered)
Rehmannia glutinosa (shu di, processed rehmannia) 55.1mg, *Cornus officinalis* (shan zhu yu, cornus) 29.4mg, *Dioscorea opposita* (shan yao, dioscorea) 29.4mg, *Lycium barbarum* (gou qi zi, lycium fruit) 22mg, *Cuscuta hygrophilae* (tu si zi, cuscuta) 22mg, *Achyranthes bidentata* (niu xi, achyranthes) 22mg

Combinations
• With powdered **7.11 Deer Velvet** or **7.12 Lu Rong Jiao** for failure to thrive, learning difficulties or developmental delay in children with weak *jing*.
• With **1.2 Si Wu Wan** for the pre-ovulation phase of a cyclical infertility treatment.

Pattern identifying features

- **Kidney *yin* deficiency**
- fatigue, lack of vitality

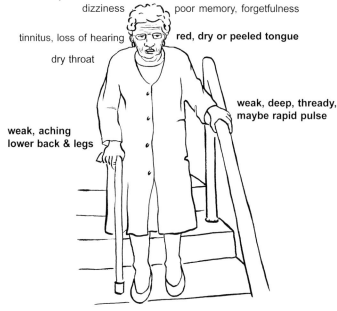

dizziness

poor memory, forgetfulness

tinnitus, loss of hearing

red, dry or peeled tongue

dry throat

weak, deep, thready, maybe rapid pulse

weak, aching lower back & legs

- With **3.38 Sheng Mai San Wan** for *qi* and *yin* deficiency (dry, cracked tongue, easy sweating, breathlessness).
- With **7.19 Shou Wu Pian, 7.7 Qi Bao Mei Ran Dan** or **7.6 Yang Xue Sheng Fa Capsule** for prematurely greying or falling hair from Kidney *jing* deficiency.

Dosage and method of administration

8-12 pills three times daily on an empty stomach. The dose may be spread out, or two lots of 12-18 pills may be taken, morning and evening. In severe cases or during the early stages of treatment (the first few weeks), a 50% increase in dose may be used, then reduced to maintenance as the treatment takes effect.

Cautions and contraindications

Contraindicated during the early phase of acute illness such as colds and flu. Care should be taken in patients with a tendency to abdominal distension, loose stools or mucus accumulation. Any digestive upset can usually be alleviated by taking the pills with a small dose (3-6 pills at the same time) of **2.18 Bao He Wan** or **2.9 Xiang Sha Liu Jun Wan**, or taking after food.

GMP **7.4 DA BU YIN WAN**

大补阴丸

Lanzhou Foci Pharmaceutical Factory (Gansu)
'Great Tonify the *Yin* Pills'
Da Bu Yin Wan is packaged in bottles of 200 pills.
Also available as: Abundant *Yin* Teapills (PF)

TCM actions
Deeply enriches and supplements Kidney *yin*, clears deficient Heat, cools the Blood, alleviates bone steaming.

Biomedical actions
Demulcent febrifuge, hematinic, hypoglycemic, regulates adrenal cortex.

INDICATIONS

- Liver and Kidney *yin* deficiency patterns with abundant deficient Heat causing **bone streaming fever**, afternoon or tidal fever, heat in the palms and soles, nightsweats and facial flushing. The main focus of this formula is to cool the Blood and alleviate the Heat generated by the deficiency, with *yin* nourishing secondary. It combines well with other constitutional formulae when a more profound *yin* supplementing and Blood cooling effect is desired.
- Bleeding disorders associated with *yin* deficiency patterns. Especially indicated for hemoptysis.
- With the appropriate identifying features, this formula can assist in the treatment of biomedical conditions such as fever of unknown origin, menopausal syndrome, chronic consumptive or wasting diseases with fever (such as tuberculosis and AIDS), interstitial cystitis, bronchiectasis, hyperthyroidism, and diabetes mellitus.

Composition
Rehmannia glutinosa (shu di, processed rehmannia) 30%, *Chinemys reevesii* (gui ban, turtle shell) 30%, *Anemarrhena aspheloides* (zhi mu, anemarrhena) 20%, *Phellodendron amurense* (huang bai, phellodendron) 20%

Combinations
- With **3.34 Bai He Gu Jin Wan** for hemoptysis associated with Lung and Kidney *yin* deficiency. Add **10.1 Yunnan Paiyao** when bleeding is persistent or severe.

Pattern identifying features

- **Liver & Kidney *yin* deficiency with deficient Heat**
- **bone streaming, nightsweats**
- **afternoon or tidal fever**
- insomnia
- irritability
- hemoptysis

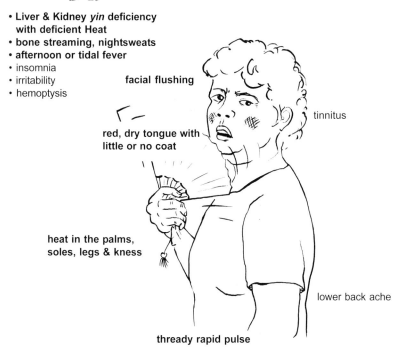

facial flushing

tinnitus

red, dry tongue with little or no coat

heat in the palms, soles, legs & kness

lower back ache

thready rapid pulse

- With **7.1 Liu Wei Di Huang Wan** or **7.3 Zuo Gui Wan** for Kidney *yin* deficiency patterns with bone steaming fever and nightsweats.
- With **3.41 Xu Han Ting** for severe sweating.

Dosage and method of administration

8-12 pills three times daily on an empty stomach. The dose may be spread out, or two lots of 12-18 pills may be taken, morning and evening. In severe cases or during the early stages of treatment (the first few weeks), a 50% increase in dose may be used, then reduced to maintenance as the treatment takes effect.

Cautions and contraindications

Contraindicated during the early phase of acute illness such as colds and flu. Care should be taken in patients with a tendency to abdominal distension, loose stools or mucus accumulation. Any digestive upset can usually be alleviated by taking the pills with a small dose (3-6 pills at the same time) of **2.18 Bao He Wan** or **2.9 Xiang Sha Liu Jun Wan**, or taking after food.

SUPP

7.5 GU BEN WAN

固本丸

Lanzhou Foci Pharmaceutical Factory (Gansu)
'Strengthen the Root Pills'
Gu Ben Wan is packaged in bottles of 200 pills.

TCM actions
Nourishes Kidney, Lung and Stomach *yin*, supplements *qi*, generates body fluids.

Biomedical actions
Demulcent, hematinic, hypoglycemic anti-inflammatory.

INDICATIONS

- Dryness or *yin* deficiency of the Lungs, Stomach and Kidney. Used for symptoms such as dry cough, thirst and dry mouth and throat, low grade fever, dry constipation and indeterminate gnawing hunger (*see* glossary). Especially good for Lung and Stomach *yin* deficiency. Can be combined with a constitutional or targeting formula to enhance the *yin* nourishing, fluid generating action of that formula.
- With the appropriate identifying features, this formula can assist in the treatment of biomedical conditions such as diabetes mellitus, persistent dry cough following an upper respiratory tract or febrile illness, chronic gastritis, dryness of the oral cavity following radiation treatment to the head and neck, dysphagia from dryness of the esophagus, glossitis, stomatitis, Sjögren's syndrome and xerostomia.

Composition
Rehmannia glutinosa (shu di, processed rehmannia) 35.5mg, *Rehmannia glutinosa* (sheng di, raw rehmannia) 35.5mg, *Asparagus lucidius* (tian dong, asparagus) 35.5mg, *Ophiopogon japonicus* (mai dong, ophiopogon) 35.5mg, *Codonopsis pilosula* (dang shen, codonopsis) 17.8mg

Combinations
- With **7.1 Liu Wei Di Huang Wan** or **7.3 Zuo Gui Wan** for patients with Kidney *yin* deficiency type diabetes.
- With **3.35 Mai Wei Di Huang Wan** for chronic dry cough from Lung *yin* deficiency.

Pattern identifying features

- **Lung & Stomach *yin* & fluid deficiency**
- dryness of the Lungs, Stomach & Intestines
- dryness of mucous membranes
- indeterminate gnawing hunger

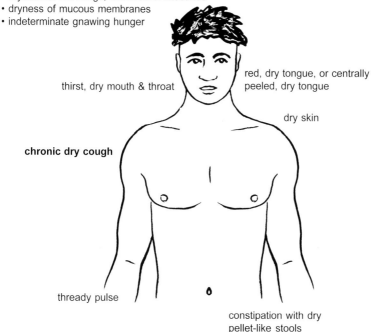

red, dry tongue, or centrally peeled, dry tongue

thirst, dry mouth & throat

dry skin

chronic dry cough

threadly pulse

constipation with dry pellet-like stools

- With **2.11 Bu Zhong Yi Qi Wan** for chronic atrophic gastritis associated with Stomach *qi* and *yin* deficiency.

Dosage and method of administration

When used alone, the recommended dose is 8-12 pills three times daily on an empty stomach. When used to augment another formula, 12-15 pills per day is usually sufficient.

Cautions and contraindications

Contraindicated during the early phase of acute illness such as colds and flu. Care should be taken in patients with a tendency to abdominal distension, loose stools or mucus accumulation as rehmannia may aggravate these problems. Any digestive upset can usually be alleviated by taking the pills with a small dose (3-6 pills at the same time) of **2.18 Bao He Wan** or **2.9 Xiang Sha Liu Jun Wan**, or taking after food.

7.6 YANG XUE SHENG FA CAPSULE

养血生发胶囊

(Yang Xue Sheng Fa Jiao Nang)
Tianjin Drug Manufactory (Shandong)
'Blood Nourishing, Hair Generating Capsules'
Yang Xue Sheng Fa Capsules are packaged in bottles of 40 capsules.

TCM actions
Supplements and nourishes Kidney *yin* and Liver Blood, promotes hair growth.

Biomedical actions
Hematinic, antioxidant.

INDICATIONS

- Liver and Kidney *yin, jing* and Blood deficiency patterns with loss of hair or prematurely greying of hair.
- Liver and Kidney deficiency patterns with dizziness, weak or blurring vision, numbness in the extremities, chronic lower back weakness and ache, memory problems, poor hearing and fatigue. In women there may be menstrual disorders such as scanty periods or amenorrhea, long cycles and infertility.
- With the appropriate identifying features, this formula may assist in the treatment of biomedical conditions such as alopecia areata, postpartum alopecia, alopecia totalis, and hair loss following chemotherapy or radiation therapy.

Composition (each capsule contains)
Polygonum multiflorum (he shou wu, ho shou wu) 160mg, *Rehmannia glutinosa* (shu di, processed rehmannia) 160mg, *Angelica polymorpha* (dang gui, chinese angelica) 80mg, *Chaenomeles lagenaria* (mu gua, chinese quince) 50mg, *Ligusticum wallichi* (chuan xiong, cnidium) 35mg, *Cuscuta hygrophilae* (tu si zi, cuscuta) 15mg

Combinations
- With **13.2 Xiao Feng Wan** or **13.3 Dang Gui Yin Zi Wan** for itchy skin diseases with underlying Blood deficiency.
- With **7.3 Zuo Gui Wan** or **7.1 Liu Wei Di Huang Wan** for falling or prematurely greying hair from Kidney *jing* deficiency or following radiation therapy.
- With **1.2 Si Wu Wan** or **7.12 Lu Rong Jiao** for severe Blood deficiency.

Pattern identifying features

- **Liver & Kidney *yin* & Blood deficiency**
- visual weakness
- lower back ache

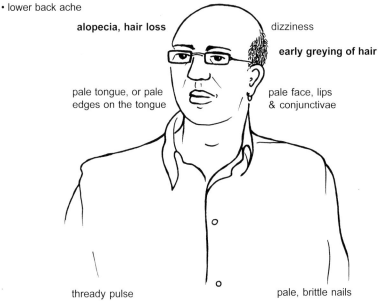

alopecia, hair loss   dizziness

early greying of hair

pale tongue, or pale
edges on the tongue   pale face, lips
& conjunctivae

threatdy pulse   pale, brittle nails

- With **7.10 You Gui Wan** for early greying or loss of hair in patients with a tendency to *yang* deficiency.

Dosage and method of administration

4 capsules, twice daily on an empty stomach. The dose may be increased by 50% for the first week or two to get the treatment started. To nourish Blood and assist the hair in cases with hair loss, **7.6 Yang Xue Sheng Fa Capsules** usually need to be taken for a minimum of 6 months.

Cautions and contraindications

Contraindicated during the early phase of acute illness such as colds and flu. Care should be taken in patients with a tendency to abdominal distension, loose stools or mucus accumulation as rehmannia and chinese angelica may aggravate these problems. Any digestive upset can usually be alleviated by taking the pills with a small dose (3-6 pills at the same time) of **2.18 Bao He Wan** or **2.9 Xiang Sha Liu Jun Wan**, or taking after food.

GMP **7.7 QI BAO MEI RAN DAN**

七宝美髯丹

Available in the US,
UK and Europe
See Note 1, p.xxi

Lanzhou Foci Pharmaceutical Factory (Gansu)
'Seven Treasure Special Pill for Beautiful Whiskers'
Qi Bao Mei Ran Dan is packaged in bottles of 200 pills.
Available as: Seven Treasures for Beautiful Hair Teapills

TCM actions
Supplements and nourishes Kidney *yin* and Liver Blood,
promotes hair growth, strengthens tendons and bones.

Biomedical actions
Hematinic, antioxidant.

INDICATIONS

• Liver Blood and Kidney *yin* deficiency patterns with hair loss from the head or
  body, or premature greying of the hair.
• With the appropriate identifying features, this formula may assist in the treatment
  of biomedical conditions such as alopecia areata, postpartum alopecia, alopecia
  totalis, and hair loss following chemotherapy or radiation therapy. Also used for
  loose teeth, or loss of teeth associated with Kidney deficiency.

Composition
Polygonum multiflorum (he shou wu, ho shou wu) 30%, *Angelica polymorpha* (dang gui,
chinese angelica) 10%, *Lycium chinense* (gou qi zi, lycium fruit) 10%, *Achyranthes
bidentata* (niu xi, achyranthes) 10%, *Poria cocos* (fu ling, hoelen) 10%, *Cuscuta
hygrophilae* (tu si zi, cuscuta) 10%, *Psoralea corylifolia* (bu gu zhi, psoralea) 10%,
Sesamum indicum (hei zhi ma, sesame seed) 10%

Combinations
• With **1.16 Tao Hong Si Wu Wan** for hair loss associated with a mild degree of
  Blood stagnation, or following a significant emotional trauma or shock.
• With **7.3 Zuo Gui Wan** or **7.1 Liu Wei Di Huang Wan** for falling or prematurely
  greying hair from Kidney *jing* deficiency or following radiation therapy.
• With **1.2 Si Wu Wan** or **7.12 Lu Rong Jiao** for severe Blood deficiency.
• With **7.10 You Gui Wan** for early greying or loss of hair in patients with a
  tendency to *yang* deficiency.

Pattern identifying features

- **Liver Blood & Kidney *yin* deficiency**
- poor memory & concentration
- loose teeth

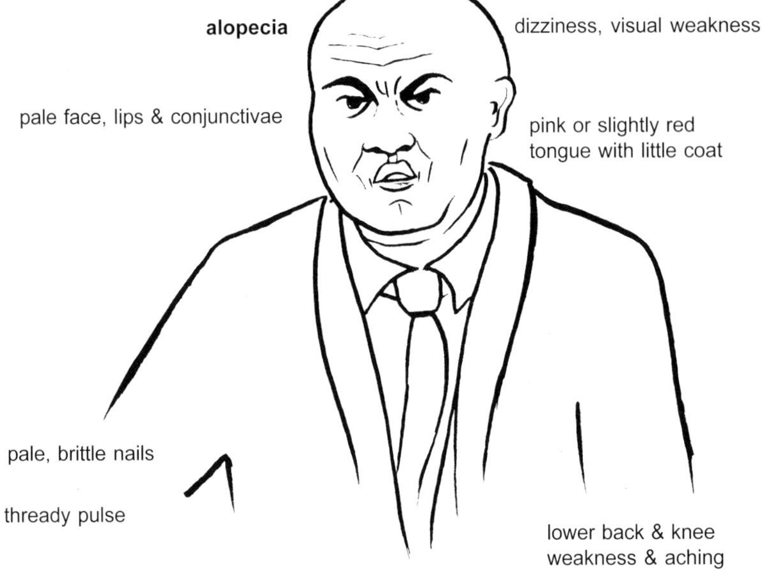

alopecia

dizziness, visual weakness

pale face, lips & conjunctivae

pink or slightly red
tongue with little coat

pale, brittle nails

thready pulse

lower back & knee
weakness & aching

SUPP

Dosage and method of administration

8-12 pills three times daily on an empty stomach. The dose may be spread out, or
two lots of 12-18 pills may be taken, morning and evening. In severe cases or during
the early stages of treatment (the first few weeks), a 50% increase in dose may be
used, then reduced to maintenance as the treatment takes effect.

Cautions and contraindications

Contraindicated during the early phase of acute illness such as colds and flu. Care
should be taken in patients with a tendency to abdominal distension, loose stools or
Phlegm Damp.

7.8 SHOU WU CHIH

首乌汁

(Shou Wu Zhi)
United Pharmaceutical Manufactory (Guangzhou)
'*Polygonum multiflorum* Drink'
Shou Wu Chih is packaged as a liquid in bottles of about 600ml.

TCM actions
Supplements and nourishes Kidney *yin* and Liver Blood, regulates *qi*, promotes hair growth.

Biomedical actions
Hematinic, antioxidant.

INDICATIONS

- Liver and Kidney *yin* and Blood deficiency. Used for generalized and postpartum weakness and deficiency, anemia, menstrual disorders, convalescence from surgery or serious illness. Contains digestive *qi* regulating herbs (cardamon, cloves and finger citron) to improve absorption and digestibility of the richer supplementing herbs. Accordingly, this formula is particularly good for patients requiring Blood supplementation but who have Spleen deficiency or a tendency to *qi* or Damp stagnation in the Spleen.
- Excellent as a general supplement for the elderly, and for periods when demands on *qi* and Blood are higher then normal.
- Menstrual disorders associated with *qi* and Blood deficiency, including irregular menstruation, infertility, scanty periods or amenorrhea, premenstrual syndrome or post menstrual fatigue.
- Used to treat or prevent premature greying or loss of head hair.

Composition
Polygonum multiflorum (he shou wu, ho shou wu) 25%, *Angelica sinensis* (dang gui, chinese angelica) 25%, *Polygonatum chinensis* (huang jing, polygonatum) 20%, *Rehmannia glutinosa* (sheng di, raw rehmannia) 10%, *Ligusticum wallichi* (chuan xiong, cnidium) 10%, *Angelica dahurica* (bai zhi, angelica) 6.7%, *Ammomum villosum* (sha ren, cardamon) 1.6%, *Eugenia caryophyllata* (ding xiang, cloves) 0.85%, *Citrus medica* (fo shou, finger citron) 0.85%, rice or sorghum wine

Pattern identifying features

- **Liver & Kidney *yin* & Blood deficiency**
- memory problems

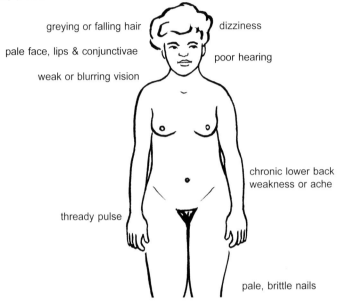

greying or falling hair

dizziness

pale face, lips & conjunctivae

poor hearing

weak or blurring vision

chronic lower back
weakness or ache

thready pulse

pale, brittle nails

SUPP

Combinations
- With **1.2 Si Wu Wan** for severe Blood deficiency.

Dosage and method of administration
2-3 tablespoons, three times daily on an empty stomach.

Cautions and contraindications
Contraindicated during the early phase of acute illness such as colds and flu.
Generally very well tolerated but care should be taken in patients with a tendency to
abdominal distension, loose stools or Phlegm Damp.

7.9 FU GUI BA WEI WAN

附桂八味丸

Lanzhou Foci Pharmaceutical Factory (Gansu)
'Eight Flavoured Rehmannia Pills with Aconite and Cinnamon'
Fu Gui Ba Wei Wan is packaged in bottles of 200 pills.
Also available as: Jin Kui Shen Qi Wan (HT, BE), Golden Book
Teapills (PF), Sexoton Pills, Ba Wei Di Huang Wan

TCM actions
Supplements and warms Kidney *yang*.

Biomedical actions
Stimulates metabolism, strengthens and regulates adrenal
function, improves fluid metabolism, hypoglycemic, antihypertensive, improves kidney
function.

INDICATIONS

- Kidney *yang* deficiency. Excellent for general hypofunction of Kidney *yang* with
  cold intolerance, poor circulation, fatigue and disturbances of fluid metabolism.
  Much prized as a strengthening supplement for the elderly.
- Urinary disorders characterised by frequency or difficulty. This includes nocturia,
  daytime frequency, broken stream, or terminal dribbling. The flip side of weak
  fluid metabolism however, may be the opposite–scanty urine or oliguria with
  ankle or generalised edema.
- Sexual dysfunction, low libido, impotence, infertility, lower back ache.
- With the appropriate identifying features, this formula can assist in the treatment
  of biomedical conditions such as benign prostatic hypertrophy, chronic nephritis,
  chronic asthma, diabetes mellitus, chronic arthritis, amenorrhea, senile cataracts
  and hypothyroidism.

Composition (each pill contains powdered)
Rehmannia glutinosa (shu di, processed rehmannia) 38mg, *Cornus officinalis* (shan zhu yu,
cornus) 19mg, *Dioscorea opposita* (shan yao, dioscorea) 19mg, *Poria cocos* (fu ling, hoelen)
14mg, *Alisma orientalis* (ze xie, alisma) 14mg, *Paeonia suffruticosa* (mu dan pi, moutan)
14mg, *Cinnamomum cassia* (rou gui, cinnamon bark) 5mg; and either *Pinellia ternata* (ban
xia, pinellia), *Codonopsis pilosula* (dang shen, codonopsis) or *Cyperus rotundus* (xiang fu,
cyperus) depending on the batch.
Note: The original formulation (found in US and other non TGA listed products)
contains *Aconite carmicaheli* (fu zi, processed aconite).

Pattern identifying features

- **Kidney yang deficiency**
- **cold intolerance, cold extremities**
- fatigue, listlessness
- digestive weakness

pale, swollen, wet tongue

deep, slow, weak pulse

lower back ache,
coldness & weakness

**clear copious urine, urinary frequency,
nocturia**, or oliguria & edema

edema below the waist,
especially ankles

weakness & cold in
the legs & knees

Combinations

- With **1.33 Hai Zao Jing Wan** or **1.17 Gui Zhi Fu Ling Wan** for gynecological masses (like fibroids or endometriosis, etc.) arising from Kidney *yang* deficiency.
- With **11.5 Wu Zi Yan Zong Wan** for sperm disorders from *yang* deficiency.
- With **2.13 Li Zhong Wan** for Spleen and Kidney *yang* deficiency.
- With **2.34 Cong Rong Bu Shen Wan** for cold atonic constipation.
- With **2.11 Bu Zhong Yi Qi Wan** for uterine or bladder prolapse.
- With **4.14 Chin So Ku Ching Wan** or **4.11 Ba Ji Yin Yang Wan** for severe nocturia, frequency or incontinence of urine.
- With **3.41 Xu Han Ting** for copious sweating from *yang* and *wei qi* deficiency.

Dosage and method of administration

8-12 pills three times daily on an empty stomach. The dose may be spread out, or two lots of 12-18 pills may be taken, morning and evening. In severe cases or during the early stages of treatment (the first two weeks), a 50% increase in dose may be used, then reduced as the treatment takes effect.

Cautions and contraindications

Contraindicated during pregnancy and during the early phase of acute illness such as colds and flu. Some patients may experience digestive upset or diarrhea which can be alleviated with a small dose of **2.13 Li Zhong Wan**.

SUPP

7.10 YOU GUI WAN

右归丸

Lanzhou Foci Pharmaceutical Factory (Gansu)
'Left Returning Pills'
You Gui Wan is packaged in bottles of 200 pills.
Also available as: Right Side Replenishing Teapills (PF)

TCM actions

Warms and supplements Kidney *yang*, nourishes *jing*,
supplements Blood, strengthens tendons and bones.

Biomedical actions

Stimulant and supplement, strengthens adrenal function,
adaptogenic, hematinic, warms the body.

INDICATIONS

- Kidney *yang* and *jing* deficiency patterns with exhaustion and debility. Similar to **7.9 Fu Gui Ba Wei Wan**. This formula, however, lacks the 'draining' components, substituting additional *yang* supplementing herbs. This variation makes this formula a slightly stronger *yang* and *jing* supplement suitable for relatively more severe deficiency patterns. Widely used in the elderly as a general Kidney support. The overall indications are similar to those of **7.9 Fu Gui Ba Wei Wan**.
- Congenital weakness of the Kidneys causing failure to thrive, learning difficulties and slow development. This may manifest as late descent of the testicles, delayed or absent menarche, or any of a series of disorders present from birth. Severe *jing* or *yang* deficiency may also follow severe or prolonged illness.
- For *wei* syndromes (*see* glossary) associated with *jing* deficiency.
- With the appropriate identifying features, this formula can assist in the treatment of biomedical conditions such as leukopenia, anemia, diabetes mellitus, chronic nephritis, chronic asthma, benign prostatic hypertrophy, infertility, declining sexual function, progressive muscular dystrophy and multiple sclerosis.

Composition (each pill contains powdered)

Rehmannia glutinosa (shu di, processed rehmannia) 38.8mg, *Cornus officinalis* (shan zhu yu, cornus) 28.6mg, *Dioscorea opposita* (shan yao, dioscorea) 28.6mg, *Lycium barbarum* (gou qi zi, lycium fruit) 22.4mg, *Eucommia ulmoides* (du zhong, eucommia) 22.4mg, *Cuscuta hygrophilae* (tu si zi, cuscuta) 22.4mg, *Angelica polymorpha* (dang gui, chinese angelica) 22.4mg, *Cinnamomun cassia* (rou gui, cinnamon bark) 14.2mg
Note: Other patent medicine versions of this formula include *Aconite carmichaeli* (fu zi, processed aconite) and *Cervus nippon* (lu jiao, deerhorn).

Pattern identifying features

- **Kidney *yang* deficiency**
- **cold intolerance, cold extremities**
- exhaustion, lassitude
- impotence, infertility
- urinary frequency; or scanty urine & edema

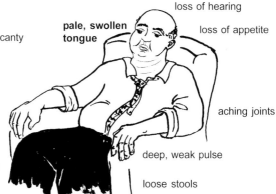

loss of hearing

loss of appetite

pale, swollen tongue

aching joints

deep, weak pulse

aching & weakness of the lower back & legs

loose stools

Combinations
- With **7.12 Lu Rong Jiao** or **7.11 Deer Velvet** to enhance the overall impact of this formula.
- With a small dose (around 2-4 pills per day) of **10.8 Xiao Huo Luo Dan** for those with severe cold signs and cold intolerance.
- With **11.5 Wu Zi Yan Zong Wan** for sperm disorders from *jing* deficiency.
- With **2.13 Li Zhong Wan** for Spleen and Kidney *yang* deficiency.
- With **10.16 Zhuang Yao Jian Shen** for chronic back, leg or joint ache and weakness.

Dosage and method of administration
8-12 pills three times daily on an empty stomach. The dose may be spread out, or two lots of 12-18 pills may be taken, morning and evening. In severe cases or during the early stages of treatment (the first two weeks), a 50% increase in dose may be used, then reduced to maintenance as the treatment takes effect.

Cautions and contraindications
Contraindicated during the early phase of acute illness such as colds and flu. May occasionally cause digestive upset in sensitive individuals. This can usually be alleviated by taking the formula with a small dose (3-6 pills at the same time) of **2.13 Li Zhong Wan**.

SUPP

7.11 DEER VELVET

鹿茸

(Lu Rong)
Tong Ren Tang (Australia)
'Deer Velvet'
Deer Velvet is packaged in bottles of 60 capsules,
500mg per capsule.

100% TOP QUALITY (Grade A)
Australian *Natural*
Deer Velvet.
Aust L 81014
60 粒膠囊
每粒 500 毫克
CONTENTS: 60 Capsules (each 500 mg)
PURE CHINESE MEDICINE
Made in Australia

TCM actions

Warms and supplements Kidney *yang* and *jing*, nourishes Blood, strengthens tendons
and bones.

Biomedical actions

Adaptogenic, stimulant, increases metabolism, promotes hemopoiesis.

INDICATIONS

- The most important substance for supporting *jing*. Essential for all *jing* disorders
  in children and adults. Used to strengthen Kidney *yang* and nourish *jing* and
  Blood in the treatment of premature greying of the hair or hair loss, lower back
  ache, general debility, impotence, primary infertility, amenorrhea, anovulation,
  sperm abnormalities and low sperm count, hearing disorders and other signs
  and symptoms of *yang* deficiency.
- The most important substance for *jing* deficiency problems such as failure to
  thrive, slow or retarded development, poor tooth development, failure of the
  fontanel to close, learning problems and other congenital problems.
- For joint pain associated with osteo-arthritis. Recent research has shown that
  Deer Velvet and related deer horn products can stimulate the growth of cartilage
  in degenerate joints.
- Chronic non-healing ulcerations and sores, such as diabetic ulcers, bedsores or
  tropical ulcers.
- Useful to enhance Blood production in patients with severe or resistant Blood
  deficiency.

Composition (each capsule contains)

Cervus nippon (lu rong, deer velvet) 500mg

Combinations

- With **7.9 Fu Gui Ba Wei Wan** for patients tending to *yang* deficiency.
- With **7.16 Shi Quan Da Bu Wan** for non healing ulcers and sores.

Pattern identifying features

- **yang, jing & Blood deficiency**
- learning difficulties
- failure to thrive
- joint pain

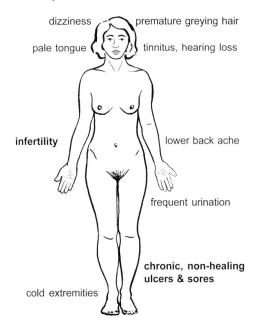

dizziness

premature greying hair

pale tongue

tinnitus, hearing loss

infertility

lower back ache

frequent urination

chronic, non-healing ulcers & sores

cold extremities

- With **7.1 Liu Wei Di Huang Wan** for children with *jing* deficiency developmental problems and women with *yang* deficiency infertility (used in the post-ovulation phase of the cycle).
- With **1.1 Ba Zhen Wan** or **1.9 Gui Pi Wan** for resistant Blood deficiency patterns.
- With **11.5 Wu Zi Yan Zong Wan** for sperm disorders.

Dosage and method of administration

2 capsules per day. In severe cases the dose can be doubled to 4 capsules daily. Quarter to half dose for children. Generally best to begin with a small dose (1 capsule per day) and gradually increase it. **7.11 Deer Velvet** is quite heating and some people are easily overheated by it. Usually combined with a constitutional formula. Good for children as the capsules can be opened and the contents mixed with food to aid ingestion.

Cautions and contraindications

Contraindicated during the early phase of acute illness such as colds and flu. Not suitable for *yin* deficiency with deficient Heat patterns, or excess Heat patterns. Keep an eye on the patient when beginning therapy with **7.11 Deer Velvet** to make sure the patient doesn't overheat. Symptoms of overheating include facial flushing, nosebleeds and dizziness.

7.12 LU RONG JIAO

鹿茸胶 [鹿角胶]

(also packaged as **Lu Jiao Jiao**)
Tong Fu Tang, Henan Lao Jun Tang Pharmaceutical Factory
'Deer Horn Resin'
Lu Rong Jiao is packaged in hard resinous blocks
which can be pulverised to a fine powder in a coffee
grinder and added to a liquid, or just taken as is.

TCM actions

Warms and supplements Kidney *yang* and *jing*,
nourishes Blood, strengthens tendons and
bones.

Biomedical actions

Adaptogenic, stimulant, increases metabolism, promotes hemopoiesis.

INDICATIONS

• As for **7.11 Deer Velvet**. The difference between this product and deer velvet is
the concentration and price. **7.11 Deer Velvet** is generally considered to be
superior to **7.12 Lu Rong Jiao** for supplementing *jing* and Blood, but is
considerably more expensive, although less is used. **7.12 Lu Rong Jiao** is not as
strong and more must be used, but is considered an affordable yet effective
compromise.

Composition

Cervus nippon (lu jiao, deerhorn) boiled down to a hard resin.

Dosage and method of administration

5-10 grams per day. Generally best to begin with a small dose (2-3 grams per day) and
gradually increase it. **7.12 Lu Rong Jiao** is quite warming and some people are easily
overheated by it. Usually combined with a constitutional formula.

Cautions and contraindications

Contraindicated during the early phase of acute illness such as colds and flu. Not
suitable for *yin* deficiency with deficient Heat patterns, or excess Heat patterns. Keep
an eye on the patient when beginning therapy with **7.12 Lu Rong Jiao** to make sure
the patient doesn't overheat. Symptoms of overheating include facial flushing,
nosebleeds and dizziness.

7.13 HUAN SHAO DAN

还少丹

Available in the US, UK and Europe
See Note 1, p.xxi

GMP

Lanzhou Foci Pharmaceutical Factory (Gansu)
'Miraculous Pills for the Recovery of Youth'
Available as: Return to Spring Teapills (PF)

TCM actions
Supplements the Liver and Kidneys, nourishes *yin*, warms *yang*, strengthens the Spleen, nourishes the Heart, benefits and calms the mind.

Biomedical actions
Strengthens digestion, memory, kidney and adrenocortical function.

INDICATIONS

- Heart and Kidney *qi* and *yang* deficiency patterns with chronic lower back ache, *shen* disturbances and memory problems, loss of hearing acuity, loss of appetite, weight loss, impotence, urinary frequency and loss of teeth.
- Prized in China for strengthening and invigorating the elderly, infirm or debilitated. Can assist in the treatment and prevention of the confusion and memory problems of old age, such as the early stages of Alzheimer's disease. Also used for infertility from Spleen and Kidney deficiency.

Composition
Zizyphus jujuba (da zao, chinese dates) 20%, *Rehmannia glutinosa* (shu di, processed rehmannia) 6%, *Lycium chinensis* (gou qi zi, lycium) 6%, *Poria cocos* (fu ling, hoelen) 6%, *Cistanche deserticola* (rou cong rong, cistanches) 6%, *Eucommia ulmoides* (du zhong, eucommia) 6%, *Morinda officinalis* (ba ji tian, morinda) 6%, *Foeniculum vulgarae* (xiao hui xiang, fennel seed) 6%, *Broussonetia papyrifera* (chu shi zi, broussonetia) 6%, *Achyranthes bidentata* (niu xi, achyranthes) 6%, *Polygala sibiricum* (yuan zhi, polygala) 6%, *Cornus officinalis* (shan zhu yu, cornus) 6%, *Schizandra chinensis* (wu wei zi, schizandra) 6%, *Dioscorea opposita* (shan yao, dioscorea) 6%

Dosage and method of administration
8-12 pills three times daily on an empty stomach. In severe cases or during the early stages of treatment (the first few weeks), a 50% increase in dose may be used, then reduced as the treatment takes effect.

Cautions and contraindications
Contraindicated during the early phase of acute illness such as colds and flu.

SUPP

7.14 DEER ANTLER AND GINSENG

ADP Pharmaceuticals Pty. Ltd (Australia)
Deer Antler and Ginseng is packaged in 350mg capsules, in jars of 25 or 50 capsules.

TCM actions
Strengthens and supplements the Spleen and Kidneys, supplements *qi* and *yang*, nourishes *jing*.

Biomedical actions
Adaptogenic, stimulant, increases metabolism, immunomodulating.

INDICATIONS

- A good supplement for all *qi* deficiency patterns with fatigue, lack of energy, vitality and stamina. Can assist in maintaining strength and well being and augment the immune system in many situations where energy demands are high. These include chronic or serious illness and post surgical recovery.
- Useful for supporting *jing*. Used for all *jing* disorders in children and adults, including failure to thrive, poor tooth development, slow development, failure of the fontanel to close, learning problems and other congenital problems.
- To strengthen Kidney *yang* and nourish Blood for premature greying of the hair or hair loss, lower back ache, general debility, impotence, hearing disorders.
- For joint pain associated with osteo-arthritis. Recent research has shown that deer antler and related deer horn products can stimulate the growth of cartilage in degenerate joints.
- Chronic non-healing sores, such as bedsores or tropical ulcers.
- Also useful in enhancing Blood production in patients with severe or resistant Blood deficiency.

Composition (each capsule contains)
Cervus nippon (lu jiao, deer antler cartilage) 245mg, *Panax ginseng* (ren shen, ginseng) 105mg

Combinations
- With **7.9 Fu Gui Ba Wei Wan** or **7.10 You Gui Wan** for patients tending to *yang* or *jing* deficiency.
- With **7.1 Liu Wei Di Huang Wan** for children with *yin* and *jing* deficiency type developmental problems, and for women with *yang* deficiency infertility (post-ovulation).

Pattern identifying features

- **yang & *jing* deficiency**
- lack of stamina & vitality
- failure to thrive
- non healing sores
- fatigue

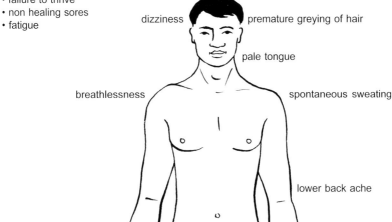

dizziness   premature greying of hair

pale tongue

breathlessness   spontaneous sweating

lower back ache

weak pulse   cold extremities

- With **1.1 Ba Zhen Wan** or **1.9 Gui Pi Wan** for resistant Blood deficiency patterns.
- With **11.5 Wu Zi Yan Zong Wan** for sperm disorders.

SUPP

Dosage and method of administration

The adult dose is 1-4 capsules daily; for children ½-2 capsules daily. Usually best to begin with one capsule per day and build up gradually, as deer antler is very warming and can cause patients to overheat. Good for children as the capsules can be opened and the contents mixed with food to aid ingestion.

Cautions and contraindications

Contraindicated during the early phase of acute illness such as colds and flu, in patients with Heat, *yang* rising or *yin* deficiency patterns, and in the absence of *qi* or *yang* deficiency. Contraindicated (without modification) in patients with a tendency to hypertension, and those with gastric ulcers. Overdose can lead to side effects such as headaches, insomnia, palpitations, hypertension, tremors, nervousness and anxiety. Concurrent consumption of other stimulants (e.g. coffee) can exacerbate the negative effects.

Keep an eye on the patient when beginning therapy with **7.14 Deer Antler and Ginseng** to make sure the patient doesn't overheat. Symptoms of overheating include facial flushing, nosebleeds and dizziness.

7.15 YULIN DA BU WAN

玉林大补丸

Yulin Pharmaceutical Factory (Guangxi)
'Great Supplementing Pills from Yulin'
Yulin Da Bu Wan is packaged in bottles of 50 capsules.
Also available as: Gecko Tonic Teapills (PF), Ge Jie Da Bu Wan

TCM actions

Warms and supplements Kidney *yang, yuan qi* and Blood,
strengthens the Spleen and Lungs.

Biomedical actions

Energy supplement and stimulant, promotes metabolism,
improves respiratory, digestive and renal functions.

INDICATIONS

- Kidney, Spleen and Lung *qi* and *yang* deficiency. Used for loss of libido, infertility, impotence, urinary dysfunction, urinary frequency or nocturia, generalised weakness, fatigue and exhaustion from Kidney *yang* deficiency.
- Spleen and Kidney *yang* deficiency causing early morning diarrhea (cock crow), diarrhea with undigested food, abdominal distension, loss of appetite, fluid metabolism problems and edema.
- Lung and Kidney deficiency and Kidney failure to grasp Lung *qi* type respiratory weakness causing chronic wheezing, asthma, shortness of breath, frequent colds and chronic cough. Used for emphysema and other chronic respiratory illnesses.
- A good general supplementing formula for the elderly, and for those convalescing from a prolonged illness or surgical procedure that has damaged *yang qi*.

Composition (each capsule contains)

Gecko gecko (ge jie, gecko) 107.5mg, *Poria cocos* (fu ling, hoelen) 50mg, *Rehmannia glutinosa* (shu di, processed rehmannia) 34mg, *Polygonatum sibiricum* (huang jing, solomon seal rhizome) 28.5mg, *Dioscorea batatas* (shan yao, dioscorea) 26.5mg, *Ligustrum lucidum* (nu zhen zi, privet fruit) 26mg, *Dipsacus asper* (xu duan, dipsacus) 24mg, *Chaenomeles lagenaria* (mu gua, chinese quince) 23.5mg, *Astragalus membranaceous* (huang qi, astragalus) 21.5mg, *Atractylodes macrocephala* (bai zhu, atractylodes) 21.5mg, *Morinda officinalis* (ba ji tian, morinda) 21.5mg, *Eucommia ulmoides* (du zhong, eucommia) 21.5mg, *Codonopsis pilosula* (dang shen, codonopsis) 21.5mg, *Lycium barbarum* (gou qi zi, lycium fruit) 20.5mg, *Drynaria fortunei* (gu sui bu, drynaria) 20mg,

Pattern identifying features

- **Kidney, Spleen & Lung *yang qi* deficiency**
- wheezing, chronic cough, respiratory weakness
- fatigue, exhaustion

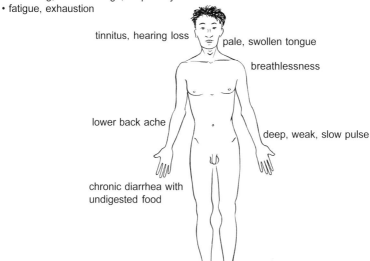

tinnitus, hearing loss

pale, swollen tongue

breathlessness

lower back ache

deep, weak, slow pulse

chronic diarrhea with
undigested food

cold extremities

Angelica polymorpha (dang gui, chinese angelica) 19mg, *Glycyrrhiza uralensis* (gan cao, licorice) 14mg

Combinations
- With **3.40 Bu Fei Wan** for chronic wheezing and cough from Lung and Kidney *qi* deficiency.
- With **7.11 Deer Velvet** to enhance the *yang* warming action of the formula.

Dosage and method of administration
3-5 capsules twice daily on an empty stomach.

Cautions and contraindications
Contraindicated during the early phase of acute illness such as colds and flu. Contraindicated in patients with wheezing or other respiratory patterns associated with external pathogens or Heat.

This formula can be quite warming and may overheat some patients. Lowering the dosage usually alleviates the problem.

7.16.1 SHI QUAN DA BU WAN

十全大补丸

Lanzhou Foci Pharmaceutical Factory (Gansu), Tong Ren Tang (Beijing)
'Ten Ingredient Pills for Complete Supplementation'
Shi Quan Da Bu Wan is packaged in bottles of 200 pills.
Also available as: Ten Flavour Teapills (PF)

TCM actions

Warms and supplements *qi* and Blood, supports *yang*, strengthens *wei qi*.

Biomedical actions

Energy supplement and stimulant, promotes metabolism, nourishes Blood and regulates menstruation, promotes circulation to the extremities.

INDICATIONS

- *Qi* and Blood deficiency with Cold accumulation. This popular and widely used formula is a variation of **1.1 Ba Zhen Wan**, with astragalus to increase *wei qi* supplementation, and cinnamon bark to warm the Kidneys and channels, and stimulate transformation of *qi* into Blood.
- With the appropriate identifying features, **7.16 Shi Quan Da Bu Wan** can be used to assist in conditions such as convalescent weakness and exhaustion, consumptive disorders, **post surgical, post partum or post hemorrhage weakness**, chronic debility, malnutrition associated with deprivation or anorexia, **anemia**, chronic leukemia, scanty menstrual periods or amenorrhea, **infertility**, habitual miscarriage, abnormal uterine bleeding, long menstrual cycle or irregular menstruation, postpartum weakness or insufficient lactation, weakness during pregnancy and thrombocytopenic purpura.
- An important formula for chronic *yin* sores or ulcers that are slow to heal, such as bedsores and tropical ulcers.
- Used for benign gynecological tumors, such as fibroids and ovarian cysts associated with weak movement of *yang qi* and Blood deficiency in the lower *jiao*.

Composition (each pill contains powdered)

Rehmannia glutinosa (shu di, processed rehmannia) 21mg, *Angelica sinensis* (dang gui, chinese angelica) 21mg, *Codonopsis pilosula* (dang shen, codonopsis) 14mg, *Paeonia alba* (bai shao, white peony) 14mg, *Atractylodes macrocephala* (bai zhu, atractylodes) 14mg, *Poria cocos* (fu ling, hoelen) 14mg, *Astragalus membranaceous* (huang qi,

Pattern identifying features

- ***Qi* & Blood deficiency with Cold**
- fatigue, weakness
- loss of appetite
- palpitations
- poor appetite
- cold intolerance
- poor concentration

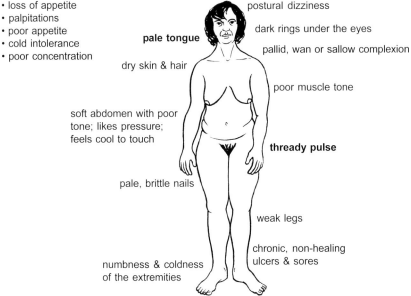

postural dizziness

dark rings under the eyes

pale tongue

pallid, wan or sallow complexion

dry skin & hair

poor muscle tone

soft abdomen with poor tone; likes pressure; feels cool to touch

thready pulse

pale, brittle nails

weak legs

chronic, non-healing ulcers & sores

numbness & coldness of the extremities

astragalus) 14mg, *Ligusticum wallichi* (chuan xiong, cnidium) 14mg, *Glycyrrhiza uralensis* (gan cao, licorice) 7mg, *Cinnamomum cassia* (rou gui, cinnamon bark) 3mg

Combinations
- With **13.14 Ching Wan Hung** topically for chronic ulcers and bed sores.

Dosage and method of administration
8-12 pills three times daily on an empty stomach. The dose may be spread out, or two lots of 12-18 pills may be taken, morning and evening. In severe cases or during the early stages of treatment (the first few weeks), a 50% increase in dose may be used, then reduced as the treatment takes effect.

Cautions and contraindications
Contraindicated during the early phase of acute illness such as colds and flu. Care should be taken in patients with a tendency to abdominal distension, loose stools or general digestive weakness. Some patients may find **7.16 Shi Quan Da Bu Wan** aggravates these symptoms. This can usually be alleviated by taking it with a small dose (3-6 pills at the same time) of **2.18 Bao He Wan** or **2.9 Xiang Sha Liu Jun Wan**.

SUPP

7.16.2 SHI QUAN DA BU WAN

十全大补丸

Tong Ren Tang (Beijing)
'Ten Ingredient Pills for Complete Supplementation'
Shi Quan Da Bu Wan is packaged in bottles of 300 pills

TCM actions

Warms and supplements *qi* and Blood, supports *yang*, strengthens *wei qi*.

Biomedical actions

Energy supplement and stimulant, promotes metabolism, nourishes Blood and regulates menstruation, promotes circulation to the extremities.

INDICATIONS

• As for **7.16.1 Shi Quan Da Bu Wan**.

Composition (each dose of 30 pills contains powdered)

Rehmannia glutinosa (shu di, processed rehmannia) 696mg, *Angelica polymorpha* (dang gui, chinese angelica) 696mg, *Codonopsis pilosula* (dang shen, codonopsis) 462mg, *Paeonia alba* (bai shao, white peony) 462mg, *Atractylodes macrocephala* (bai zhu, atractylodes) 462mg, *Poria cocos* (fu ling, hoelen) 462mg, *Astragalus membranaceous* (huang qi, astragalus) 462mg, *Ligusticum wallichi* (chuan xiong, cnidium) 234mg, *Glycyrrhiza uralensis* (gan cao, licorice) 234mg, *Cinnamomum cassia* (rou gui, cinnamon bark) 114mg, sucrose

Dosage and method of administration

30 pills, twice daily on an empty stomach. In severe cases or during the early stages of treatment (the first few weeks), a 50% increase in dose may be used, then reduced as the treatment takes effect.

Cautions and contraindications

Contraindicated during the early phase of acute illness such as colds and flu. Care should be taken in patients with a tendency to abdominal distension, loose stools or general digestive weakness. Although generally well tolerated, some patients may find **7.16.2 Shi Quan Da Bu Wan** aggravates these symptoms. This can usually be alleviated by taking it with a small dose (3-6 pills at the same time) of **2.18 Bao He Wan** or **2.9 Xiang Sha Liu Jun Wan**.

7.17 HUA TUO SHI QUAN DA BU JIU

华佗十全大补酒

Shanghai Guanshengyuan Huaguang Brewing and Medicine Company (Shanghai)

'Hua Tuo's Ten Ingredient Wine for Complete Supplementation'
Hua Tuo Shi Quan Da Bu Jiu is packaged in 445ml bottles.

TCM actions

Warms and supplements *qi* and Blood, supports *yang*, strengthens *wei qi*.

Biomedical actions

Energy supplement and stimulant, opens the channels, nourishes Blood and regulates menstruation, promotes circulation to the extremities.

INDICATIONS

- This famous and popular medicinal wine is identical in composition and action to **7.16 Shi Quan Da Bu Wan**. It can be used for the same conditions. The wine makes this version a little warmer and more invigorating to the Blood. It is thus ideal for *bi* syndrome (*see* glossary) and general aches and pains associated with *qi* and Blood deficiency, as well as chronic ulcers, post-operative sores, bedsores and other non-healing wounds.
- An excellent restorative and preventative supplement for elderly patients and those recovering from a serious illness or surgery.

Composition

Rehmannia glutinosa (shu di, processed rehmannia), *Angelica sinensis* (dang gui, chinese angelica), *Codonopsis pilosula* (dang shen, codonopsis), *Paeonia alba* (bai shao, white peony), *Atractylodes macrocephala* (bai zhu, atractylodes), *Poria cocos* (fu ling, hoelen), *Astragalus membranaceus* (huang qi, astragalus), *Ligusticum wallichi* (chuan xiong, cnidium), *Glycyrrhiza uralensis* (gan cao, licorice), *Cinnamomum cassia* (rou gui, cinnamon bark), *Shao Xing Jiu* (sorghum or rice wine) 24.5% (v/v)

Dosage and method of administration

50-80mls (2 small cups, supplied), daily.

Cautions and contraindications

As for **7.16 Shi Quan Da Bu Wan**, but in general very well tolerated.

GMP **7.18 YANG YING WAN**

养营丸

Lanzhou Foci Pharmaceutical Factory (Gansu)
'Nutritive Pills'
Yang Ying Wan is packaged in bottles of 200 pills.

TCM actions
Warms and supplements *qi* and Blood, supports *yang*, strengthens *wei qi*, calms the shen.

Biomedical actions
Energy supplement and stimulant, promotes metabolism, nourishes Blood and regulates menstruation, promotes circulation to the extremities, sedative, tranquilizer.

INDICATIONS

- Similar in actions and indications to **7.16.1 Shi Quan Da Bu Wan**, with the addition of herbs to calms the Heart and *shen*. Used for *qi* and Blood deficiency patterns with *shen* disturbances, insomnia, palpitations, shortness of breath, chronic debility, exhaustion and loss of appetite. Also useful for convalescence from serious illness, surgery or pregnancy, as well as all chronic disorders of a *qi* and Blood deficiency type. Good for chronic Hepatitis C infection of a *qi* and Blood deficiency type.

Composition
Codonopsis pilosula (dang shen, codonopsis) 8%, *Atractylodes macrocephala* (bai zhu, atractylodes) 8%, *Poria cocos* (fu ling, hoelen) 6%, *Astragalus membranaceous* (huang qi, astragalus) 8%, *Glycyrrhiza uralensis* (gan cao, licorice) 8%, *Zizyphus jujuba* (da zao, chinese dates) 8%, *Angelica sinensis* (dang gui, chinese angelica) 8%, *Rehmannia glutinosa* (shu di, processed rehmannia) 6%, *Paeonia lactiflora* (bai shao, white peony) 8%, *Cinnamomum cassia* (rou gui, cinnamon bark) 8%, *Polygala sibiricum* (yuan zhi, polygala) 4%, *Citrus reticulata* (chen pi, citrus) 8%, *Schizandra chinensis* (wu wei zi, schizandra) 6%, *Zingiber officinale* (sheng jiang, ginger) 4%

Dosage and method of administration
8-12 pills three times daily, on an empty stomach. Two lots of 12-18 pills may be taken, morning and evening. In the early stages of treatment (the first few weeks), a 50% increase in dose may be used, then reduced as the treatment takes effect.

Cautions and contraindications
Contraindicated during the early phase of acute illness such as colds and flu.

7.19 SHOU WU PIAN

首乌片

Lanzhou Foci Pharmaceutical Factory (Gansu)
'*Polygonum multiflorum* Pills'
Shou Wu Pian is packaged in bottles of 100 coated tablets.

TCM actions
Supplements the Liver and Kidneys, benefits *jing* and nourishes Blood and hair.

Biomedical actions
Hematinic, antioxidant.

INDICATIONS

- Liver and Kidney *yin* and Blood deficiency patterns with dizziness, weak or blurring vision, chronic lower back weakness or ache, memory problems and poor hearing, premature greying or loss of head hair, brittle nails and numbness in the extremities.
- Chronic itchy skin diseases and Wind rash. Especially good when there is a component of Blood deficiency.

Composition (each pill contains powdered)
Polygonum multiflorum (he shou wu, ho shou wu) 160mg

Combinations
- With **13.2 Xiao Feng Wan** for itchy skin diseases with underlying Blood deficiency.
- With **7.3 Zuo Gui Wan** for falling or prematurely greying hair from Kidney *jing* deficiency.

Dosage and method of administration
4-5 pills, three times daily on an empty stomach. The dose may be increased by 50% for the first week or two to get the treatment started.

Cautions and contraindications
Contraindicated during the early phase of acute illness such as colds and flu. Care should be taken in patients with a tendency to abdominal distension, loose stools or Phlegm Damp.

7.20 CORDYCEPS ESSENCE OF CHICKEN

虫草鸡精

(Chong Cao Ji Jing)
Cerebos Thailand Ltd (Thailand)
Cordyceps Essence of Chicken is packaged in
68ml jars of liquid extract, six jars to a box.

TCM actions
Supplements the Kidneys and Lungs and
fortifies *yang*, strengthens and supplements Lung *qi* and *yin*.

Biomedical actions
Nutritive to build energy and improve athletic performance, strengthens lung and
kidney function, stimulates and protects the immune system.

INDICATIONS

- Lung and Kidney *yang, yin* and *qi* deficiency. A broad spectrum and well balanced
  nutritive supplement suitable to patients with elements of general deficiency,
  with an emphasis towards warming *yang* and thus general hypofunction. An
  excellent general supplement for the debilitated, elderly and those recovering
  from prolonged or severe illness, including major surgery and the after effects
  of radiotherapy of chemotherapy. Powerfully builds immunity in weak and
  immunocompromised patients. Useful in conditions such as leukopenia and
  thrombocytopenia, as well as HIV.
- Strengthens the Lungs and improves Lung function to assist in the treatment of
  chronic consumptive pulmonary diseases of a *qi* and *yin* deficiency type, such as
  pulmonary tuberculosis, sarcoidosis and silicosis, as well as emphysema and
  chronic asthma.
- Warms Kidney *yang* to assist in urinary and sexual disorders of a *yang* deficient
  type.
- Assists in the improvement of physical endurance, maintenance of peak
  performance and recovey time in athletes and others with high physical and
  stress demands.

Composition (Each jar contains extracts equivalent to dry)
Black foot chicken, *Cordyceps sinensis* (dong chong xia cao, cordyceps stroma) 6.8g,
Rehmannia glutinosa (shu di, processed rehmannia) 950mg, *Polygonatum officinale* (yu
zhu, polygonatum) 950mg, *Cistanches deserticola* (rou cong rong, cistanches) 815mg,
Astragalus membranaceous (huang qi, astragalus) 540mg

Pattern identifying features

- **Lung & Kidney *yang qi* & *yin* deficiency**
- **general debility, weakness & frailty**
- spontaneous sweating, nightsweats
- breathlessness, dyspnea
- poor appetite
- loss of libido, impotence

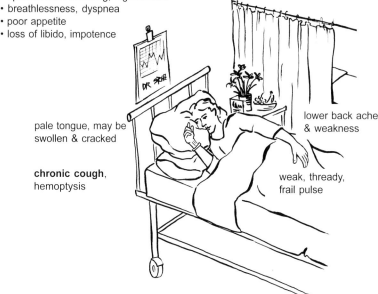

pale tongue, may be
swollen & cracked

lower back ache
& weakness

chronic cough,
hemoptysis

weak, thready,
frail pulse

SUPP

Combinations

- With **3.35 Mai Wei Di Huang Wan** or **3.34 Bai He Gu Jin Wan** for chronic respiratory disorders from Lung *yin* deficiency.
- With **7.23 Yu Ping Feng Wan**, **2.11 Bu Zhong Yi Qi Wan** or **3.41 Xu Han Ting** for severe spontaneous sweating and immune deficiency.
- With **3.18 Tung Hsuan Li Fei Pien** for a persistent cough.

Dosage and method of administration

In the early days of treatment, 1-2 jars may be taken daily, diluted with warm water or straight, or used in cooking. As energy and symptoms improve, one jar every second or third day is usually sufficient.

Cautions and contraindications

Contraindicated during the early phase of acute illness such as colds and flu. Care should be taken in those patients with a tendency to abdominal distension, loose stools or nausea. Some patients may find **7.20 Cordyceps Essence of Chicken** aggravates these symptoms. This can usually be alleviated by dilution with a strong ginger root tea.

7.21 AMERICAN GINSENG ESSENCE OF CHICKEN

花旗参鸡精

(Hua Qi Shen Ji Jing)
Cerebos Thailand Ltd (Thailand)
American Ginseng Essence of Chicken is
packaged in 68ml jars of liquid extract, six jars to a
box.

TCM actions
Supplements *qi* and *yin*, generates fluids, strengthens the Lungs.

Biomedical action
Tonic to build energy, strengthens the lungs, stimulates and protects the immune system.

INDICATIONS

- Lung *qi* and *yin* deficiency. Used for chronic respiratory weakness or disease of a *qi* and *yin* deficient type. Useful for chronic respiratory irritation in smokers or others exposed to respiratory irritants that dry and damage Lung fluids.
- Used to support patients recuperating from a severe febrile or other illness (including surgery, *see* glossary) that has damaged *qi* and *yin*. Also used for those with significant loss of appetite or enhanced nutritional needs, such as patients with cancer or other severe illness. Also used for persistent low grade fever associated with chronic illnesses such as AIDS.
- Can assist in alleviating the side effects of chemotherapy or radiotherapy, especially dryness and damage to mucous membranes, oral ulceration, decreased salivation and fatigue.
- May be useful as an adjunct in the treatment of *Xiao Ke* syndrome (*see* glossary).

Composition (Each jar contains extracts equivalent to dry)
Black foot chicken, *Panax quinquefolium* (xi yang shen, american ginseng) 6.8g

Combinations
- With **7.1 Liu Wei Di Huang Wan** or **7.5 Gu Ben Wan** for *Xiao Ke* syndrome.
- With **3.33 Yang Yin Qing Fei Wan** or **3.36 Luo Han Kuo Beverage** for severe or chronic dryness of the oral cavity.

Pattern identifying features

- **Lung *qi* & *yin* deficiency**
- **fatigue, exhaustion**
- high stress
- convalescence following
  febrile illness

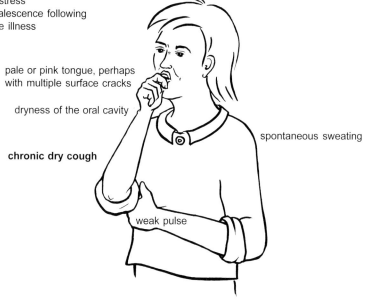

pale or pink tongue, perhaps
with multiple surface cracks

dryness of the oral cavity

chronic dry cough

spontaneous sweating

weak pulse

- With **6.1 Xiao Chai Hu Tang Wan** for post febrile fatigue and loss of appetite with mild alternating fever and chills.

Dosage and method of administration

For recovery following illness, surgery, chemotherapy or radiotherapy, one jar may be taken daily, diluted with warm water. As energy improves, one jar every second or third day is sufficient. For general maintenance of health, one jar every 2-3 days is sufficient.

Cautions and contraindications

Contraindicated during the early phase of acute illness such as colds and flu.

7.22 SHEN QI DA BU WAN

参芪大补丸

Lanzhou Foci Pharmaceutical Factory (Gansu)
'Codonopsis and Astragalus Big Supplement Pills'
Shen Qi Da Bu Wan is packaged in bottles of 200 pills.
Also available as: Shen Qi Wan

TCM actions
Supplements Spleen and Lung *qi*, strengthens *wei qi*.

Biomedical actions
Energy supplement, immune stimulant, anhidrotic.

INDICATIONS

- A general formula to strengthen Spleen and Lung *qi* and *wei qi*. Can be used alone for this purpose, but more frequently is combined with another constitutional formula when an enhanced *qi* supplementation effect is desired.

Composition (each pill contains powdered)
Astragalus membranaceous (huang qi, astragalus) 80mg, *Codonopsis pilosula* (dang shen, codonopsis) 80mg

Combination examples
- With **2.9 Xiang Sha Liu Jun Wan** for patients with significant deficiency, to enhance the *qi* supplementing and *wei qi* consolidating effect.
- With **7.1 Liu Wei Di Huang Wan** for Kidney *yin* deficiency with elements of Spleen *qi* deficiency.
- With **1.2 Si Wu Wan** for patients with elements of *qi* deficiency within predominant Blood deficiency.
- With **11.1 Qian Lie Xian Capsule** or **11.2 Prostate Gland Pills** for prostate swelling that is worse when fatigued, and following sex, in patients with Kidney *qi* deficiency.
- With **5.8 Bu Yang Huan Wu Wan** to enhance that formula's ability to penetrate through obstructions in the channels and relieve hemiplegia.

Pattern identifying features

- **Lung & Spleen *qi* deficiency**
- frequent colds, low immunity

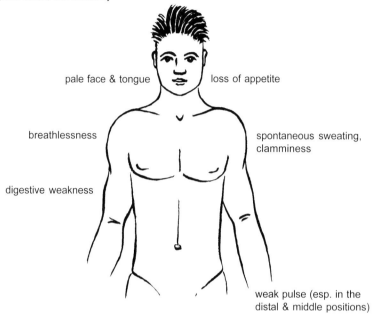

pale face & tongue

loss of appetite

breathlessness

spontaneous sweating, clamminess

digestive weakness

weak pulse (esp. in the distal & middle positions)

SUPP

- With **7.23 Yu Ping Feng Wan** or **3.41 Xu Han Ting** for children with significant immune weakness, tendency to allergies and loss of appetite.

Dosage and method of administration

When used alone, the recommended dose is 8-12 pills three times daily on an empty stomach. When used to augment another formula, 12-15 pills per day is usually sufficient.

Cautions and contraindications

Contraindicated during the early phase of acute illness such as colds and flu.

7.23 YU PING FENG WAN

玉屏风丸

玉屏風丸
YU PING FENG WAN

(AUST L 11742)

200粒

Lanzhou Foci Pharmaceutical Factory (Gansu)
'Jade Screen Wind Pills'
Yu Ping Feng Wan is packaged in bottles of 200 pills.
Also available as: Jade Screen Teapills (PF)

中國　蘭州
蘭州佛慈製藥廠
Product of People's Republic of china
LANZHOU FOCI PHARMACEUTICAL FACTORY

TCM actions
Strengthens *wei qi*, supplements the Spleen, strengthens the surface and stops sweating.

Biomedical actions
Immune stimulant, strengthens digestion, tones the mucous membranes, anhidrotic.

INDICATIONS

- Lung *qi* and *wei qi* deficiency with chronic retention of Wind on the surface. **7.23 Yu Ping Feng Wan** strengthens *qi* and disperses pathogens at the same time. It is an important formula to strengthen *wei qi* and improve the body's resistance to pathogenic invasion. Widely used for patients prone to frequent colds and upper respiratory tract infection, or patients unable to shake off the last of a lingering cold. Mostly used in between infections. This is an important formula for children.
- Chronic retention of Wind in the respiratory system, mucous membranes and skin. This manifests as respiratory allergies–allergic and perennial rhinitis, atopic asthma and a tendency to allergic skin rashes, urticaria and itch.
- Excessive sweating from *qi* deficiency that occurs at rest and during the day.

Composition (each pill contains powdered)
Astragalus membranaceous (huang qi, astragalus) 103mg, *Atractylodes macrocephala* (bai zhu, atractylodes) 33mg, *Ledebouriella divaricata* (fang feng, siler) 33mg

Combinations
- With **9.18 Xin Yi San** for chronic or allergic rhinitis in a patient with *qi* deficiency.
- With a Kidney *yang* supplementing formula such as **4.11 Ba Ji Yan Yang Wan** to strengthen the Lung Kidney axis for patients with an atopic constitution.
- With **6.1 Xiao Chai Hu Tang Wan** to strengthen immunity in children prone to middle ear infection.

Pattern identifying features

- **Lung *qi* & *wei qi* deficiency**
- **frequent colds & flu**
- chronic respiratory allergies
- weak immunity
- fatigue, run down
- sensitivity to wind
- breathlessness

waxy, pale complexion   pale tongue

spontaneous sweating

weak, deficient pulse

- With **3.38 Sheng Mai San Wan** for hypotension.
- With **3.41 Xu Han Ting** for persistent sweating.
- With **7.22 Shen Qi Da Bu Wan** or **2.7 Si Jun Zi Wan** for pronounced Spleen *qi* deficiency.

Dosage and method of administration

8-12 pills three times daily, before meals. The dose may be spread out, or two lots of 12-18 pills may be taken, morning and evening. In severe cases or during the early stages of treatment (the first few weeks), a 50% increase in dose may be used, then reduced as the treatment takes effect. One third to one half dose for children.

Cautions and contraindications

Contraindicated during the early phase of acute illness such as colds and flu, such as a full on Wind Cold or Wind Heat invasion.

7.24 PANAX GINSENG EXTRACTUM

人参精

(Ren Shen Jing)
China National Native Produce and
Animal By Products Import Export
Corporation (Tianjin)
'Essence of Ginseng'

Panax Ginseng Extractum is packaged in 10ml vials of liquid extract, ten vials per box.

TCM actions

Supplements *yuan qi*, strengthens the Spleen and Lungs, generates fluids and stops thirst, calms the *shen*.

Biomedical actions

Immune stimulant, immunomodulating, adaptogenic, regulates adrenal function, lowers blood glucose.

INDICATIONS

- Lung and Spleen *qi* deficiency. A good supplement for all *qi* deficiency patterns with fatigue, lack of energy, vitality and stamina. Can assist in maintaining strength and well being and augment the immune system in many situations where energy demands are high. These include chronic or serious illness (cancer, auto-immune disorders) and post surgical recovery.
- Used to help moderate the negative effects of prolonged or severe stress; helps people adapt to changing conditions and stresses.
- Can help to better regulate and lower blood glucose in patients with hyperglycemia. Useful as an adjunct in the treatment of *Xiao Ke* syndrome (*see* glossary).
- May be useful following a severe shock or emotional trauma that has dispersed *qi*, leading to shortness of breath, anxiety, insomnia, mood swings and lethargy.

Composition (each vial contains)

Panax ginseng (ren shen, ginseng) 1200mg

Combinations

- Can be added to any appropriate supplementing prescription if an enhanced *qi* supplementing effect is desired.

Pattern identifying features

- **Lung & Spleen** *qi* **deficiency**
- **fatigue, lack of stamina**
- poor appetite
- hypotension
- immune weakness

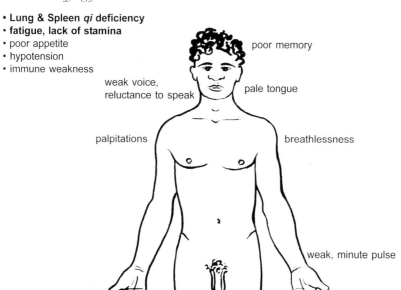

poor memory

weak voice,
reluctance to speak

pale tongue

palpitations

breathlessness

weak, minute pulse

Dosage and method of administration

In the early stages of treatment, three or four vials per day may be used. As the symptoms improve, the dose can be reduced to a maintenance dose of one or two vials per day. The major benefits of ginseng are observed after prolonged and regular use, usually a minimum of two months.

Cautions and contraindications

Contraindicated during the early phase of acute illness such as colds and flu, in patients with Heat, *yang* rising or *yin* deficiency patterns and in the absence of *qi* deficiency. Also contraindicated when used alone for patients with a tendency to hypertension, and those with gastric ulcers. Overdose can lead to side effects such as headaches, insomnia, palpitations, hypertension, tremors, nervousness and anxiety. Concurrent consumption of other stimulants (e.g. coffee) can exacerbate the negative effects. Caution in patients on anticoagulant therapy as ginseng can decrease the effectiveness of warfarin. Caution prior to surgical procedures, as in some patients ginseng can inhibit clotting.

Ginseng products are seriously abused, both in China and the West, particularly by already fit and healthy individuals looking for some sort of super health. Inappropriate use of ginseng by young and otherwise healthy individuals can generate excessive Heat and damage *yin*.

SUPP

7.25 PEKING GINSENG ROYAL JELLY

北京人参蜂王精

(Bei Jing Ren Shen Feng Wang Jing)
Laboratory de Tonique de Pekin (Beijing)
Peking Ginseng Royal Jelly is packaged
in 10ml vials of liquid extract, ten vials per
box.

TCM actions
Supplements *yuan qi*, warms and strengthens the Spleen, Lungs and Liver, generates
fluids and stops thirst, calms the *shen*.

Biomedical actions
Immune stimulant, immunomodulating, adaptogen, regulates adrenal function,
lower blood glucose.

INDICATIONS

• A general supplementing formula, with warming B vitamins combined with
ginseng and royal jelly. Similar in action and indications to **7.24 Panax Ginseng
Extractum**, but more warming. There are numerous varieties of royal jelly with
and without additional herbs. Their functions are all quite similar. Royal jelly
supplements *qi* and Blood, and strengthens the Liver and Spleen.

Composition (each vial contains)
Fresh Royal Jelly 2000mg, *Panax ginseng* (ren shen, ginseng) 1000mg, *Schizandra
chinensis* (wu wei zi, schizandra) 100mg, Nicotinamide 10mg, Thiamine
hydrochloride (Vit B1) 3mg, Pyridoxine hydrochloride (Vit B6) 200μg, Benzyl
alcohol 100mg, Citric acid monohydrate 8mg, Agar 10mg, Caramel 200mg

Combinations
• Can be combined with any appropriate formula where an enhanced *qi* and Blood
supplementing effect is desired.

Dosage and method of administration
One vial daily.

Pattern identifying features

- **fatigue, lack of stamina**
- cold intolerance
- poor appetite
- convalescence
- immune weakness

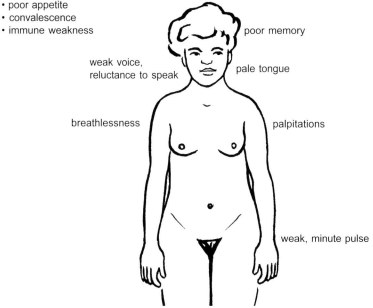

poor memory

weak voice,
reluctance to speak

pale tongue

breathlessness

palpitations

weak, minute pulse

SUPP

Cautions and contraindications

Contraindicated in patients with allergy to bee stings, atopic constitutions, and asthma. Although rare, there have been reported deaths from anaphylactic shock following use of royal jelly. Contraindicated during the early phase of acute illness such as colds and flu, in patients with Heat *yang* rising or *yin* deficiency patterns and in the absence of *qi* deficiency. Caution in those on anticoagulant therapy as ginseng can decrease the effectiveness of warfarin. Caution prior to surgical procedures, as in some cases when large doses are used, ginseng can inhibit clotting.

Overdose can lead to headaches, insomnia, palpitations, hypertension, tremors, nervousness and anxiety. Concurrent consumption of other warming stimulants (e.g. coffee) can exacerbate the negative effects.

7.26 REISHI MUSHROOM

(Ling Zhi)
Various manufacturers in Australia, Japan, Korea and
China.

TCM actions

Nourishes the Heart and calms the *shen*, stops cough and alleviates
wheezing, supplements *qi* and Blood.

Biomedical actions

Immune stimulant, adaptogen, immunomodulating, anti-platelet
action, antitussive, sedative.

INDICATIONS

- Reishi mushroom extract has been shown to exert many beneficial effects consistent with its reputation as an adaptogen. An adaptogen is defined as a substance which increases the resistance to stress and improves the general tone of the body and mind.
- Used to improve immune surveillance as an adjunct treatment for patients with cancer and chronic viral or auto-immune diseases. Well designed studies have shown that reishi mushroom appears to improve not only quality of life for those undergoing chemotherapy or radiotherapy, but also can enhance survival and reduce the likelihood of metastasis, as well as help to prevent recurrence.
- May also be useful for connective tissue diseases such as rheumatoid arthritis, lupus (SLE), Beçhet's syndrome and scleroderma.
- Also used for insomnia, high altitude sickness, sleep apnea, high cholesterol, chronic hepatitis, chronic cough and asthma, allergies and hypersensitive or weakened immune system problems, such as Chronic Fatigue Syndrome (CFS) or HIV.

Composition

Ganoderma lucidum or *G. japonicum* (ling zhi, reishi)
Note: Not all available brands are listed with the TGA.

Combinations

- With **6.1 Xiao Chai Hu Tang Wan** to assist in maintaining the immune system in patients with HIV or chronic hepatitis.
- With **7.1 Liu Wei Di Huang Wan** for patients on high dose steroid treatment.

Pattern identifying features

- **immune weakness or hypersensitivity**
- adjunct to cancer therapy
- lack of vitality, malaise
- general weakness
- sleep apnea

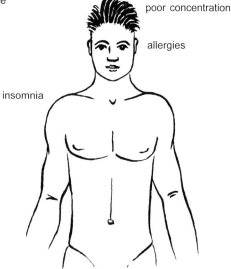

poor concentration

allergies

insomnia

- With **2.11 Bu Zhong Yi Qi Wan** for patients undergoing chemotherapy or radiotherapy.
- With **3.38 Sheng Mai San Wan** for chronic respiratory diseases of a *qi* and *yin* deficient type.
- With **7.23 Yu Ping Feng Wan** or **3.41 Xu Han Ting** for atopic individuals with allergies, eczema and weak immunity.
- May be useful when combined with **11.5 Wu Zi Yan Zong Wan** for antisperm antibodies or to enhance low sperm count.

Dosage and method of administration

The manufacturers recommended dose is usually sufficient. Absorption and utilisation of reishi mushroom is improved if taken with a dose of vitamin C (500mg is sufficient).

Cautions and contraindications

Reishi mushroom can induce some side effects including dizziness, dry mouth and throat, nose bleeds and abdominal upset; these rare effects may develop with continuous use over three to six months. As it may increase bleeding time, reishi mushroom is not recommended immediately prior to surgical procedures, or for those taking anticoagulant medications including non steroidal anti-inflammatories, warfarin or aspirin.

SUPP

8

Patent Medicines for Shen Disorders

8.1 TIAN WANG BU XIN DAN

天王补心丹

Lanzhou Foci Pharmaceutical Factory (Gansu)
'Heavenly King Heart Supplementing Special Pills'
Tian Wang Bu Xin Dan is packaged in bottles of 200 pills.
Also available as: Emperor's Teapills (PF), Tian Wang Pu Hsin Tan

TCM actions
Supplements Heart and Kidney *yin*, nourishes Blood, calms the *shen*, clears deficient Heat.

Biomedical actions
Sedative and tranquilizer, nervine, calmative.

INDICATIONS

- Heart and Kidney *yin* deficiency; also described as Heart and Kidney not communicating. This marvellous formula treats *shen* disturbances and dryness Heat patterns from *yin* deficiency and deficient Fire affecting the Kidney and Heart. An important formula for chronic insomnia accompanied by emotional disturbances, anxiety states and phobias. Especially good for patients who have taken sedatives or tranquillizing drugs for so long the drugs have become ineffective. Also good for the physical and psychological damage inflicted by long term stimulant use (such as amphetamines and cocaine)–paranoia, agitation, anxiety, insomnia. Suitable when *yin* deficiency patterns are complicated by a degree of Phlegm or Phlegm Heat.
- For chronic or recurrent oral ulcerations from *yin* deficiency with Phlegm accumulation.
- With the appropriate identifying features, this formula can be used to treat biomedical conditions such as acute and chronic anxiety states, panic attacks, chronic insomnia, memory problems, palpitations, tachycardia, cardiac arrhythmias, menopausal syndrome, chronic urticaria, chronic or recurrent apthous ulcers, stomatitis, Beçhet's syndrome and neurasthenia.

Composition (each pill contains powdered)
Rehmannia glutinosa (sheng di, rehmannia) 60mg, *Angelica sinensis* (dang gui, chinese angelica) 15mg, *Schizandra chinensis* (wu wei zi, schizandra) 15mg, *Zizyphus spinoza* (suan zao ren, zizyphus) 15mg, *Biota orientalis* (bai zi ren, biota) 15mg, *Asparagus lucidius* (tian dong, asparagus) 15mg, *Ophiopogon japonicus* (mai dong, ophiopogon) 15mg, *Scrophularia*

Pattern identifying features

- **Heart & Kidney *yin* deficiency**
- waking feeling hot, night sweats, hot hands and feet, dry skin and hair
- patients tend to be thin, dry and nervy or agitated, mostly women >40yrs
- irritability, poor concentration, forgetfulness
- chronic or recurrent mouth ulcers
- physical contact with the skin (massage, acupuncture) leaves large red marks

insomnia; frequent waking, waking feeling anxious; vivid dreaming

palpitations

anxiety, panic attacks,

tendency to dry stools or constipation

red, dry tongue, or cracked, or very red at the tip of the tongue

threadly, rapid pulse

ningpoensis (xuan shen, scrophularia) 15mg, *Salvia miltorrhiza* (dan shen, salvia) 7mg, *Codonopsis pilosula* (dang shen, codonopsis) 7mg, *Poria cocos* (fu ling, hoelen) 7mg, *Platycodon grandiflorum* (jie geng, platycodon) 7mg, *Polygala sibirica* (yuan zhi, polygala) 7mg

Combinations
- With **9.10 Sanjin Watermelon Frost** for recurrent mouth ulcers.

Dosage and method of administration
8-12 pills three times daily on an empty stomach. The dose may be spread out, or two lots of 12-18 pills may be taken, morning and evening or before bed. In severe cases or during the early stages of treatment (the first few weeks), a 50% increase in dose may be used, then reduced as the treatment takes effect.

Cautions and contraindications
Contraindicated during the early phase of acute illness such as colds and flu. Generally well tolerated, but care should be taken in patients with a tendency to abdominal distension, loose stools or general digestive weakness. Digestive upsets can usually be alleviated by taking this formula with a small dose (3-6 pills at the same time) of **2.18 Bao He Wan** or **2.9 Xiang Sha Liu Jun Wan**.

SHEN

8.2 BAI ZI YANG XIN WAN

柏子养心丸

Lanzhou Foci Pharmaceutical Factory (Gansu)
'Biota Pills to Nourish the Heart'
Bai Zi Yang Xin Wan is packaged in bottles of 200 pills.
Also available as: Pai Tzu Yang Hsin Wan

TCM actions

Supplements Heart Blood and *yin*, clears Heat, calms the *shen*.

Biomedical actions

Sedative, tranquilizer.

INDICATIONS

- Heart Blood and/or *yin* deficiency causing *shen* disturbances, in particular anxiety. Also useful for nightsweats from *yin* deficiency. Although tending to be somewhat cooling, this formula is mild enough to be used for Heat or thermally neutral presentations, and combines well with other constitutional formulae when additional *shen* calming action is desired.
- With the appropriate identifying features, this formula can be used to treat conditions such as neurasthenia, chronic anxiety states and insomnia, loss of memory, recurrent nightmares, palpitations, tachycardia and arrhythmias. Also useful for anxiety or insomnia that can occur in the aftermath of a febrile illness that has damaged *yin* and fluids.

Composition

Rehmannia glutinosa (shu di, prepared rehmannia) 25mg, *Scrophularia ningpoensis* (xuan shen, scrophularia) 23mg, *Polygala sibirica* (yuan zhi, polygala) 20mg, *Poria cocos* (fu ling, hoelen) 20mg, *Lycium chinensis* (gou qi zi, lycium fruit) 20mg, *Biota orientalis* (bai zi ren, biota seed) 17mg, *Ophiopogon japonica* (mai dong, ophiopogon) 17mg, *Angelica sinensis* (dang gui, chinese angelica) 17mg, *Glycyrrhiza uralensis* (gan cao, licorice) 13mg
Note: Other versions of this formula from the same factory substitute *Acorus gramineus* (shi chang pu, acorus) for *Polygala sibirica* (yuan zhi, polygala).

Combinations

- With **1.2 Si Wu Wan** for patients with a greater degree of Blood deficiency.
- With **1.9 Gui Pi Wan** for Heart Blood and Spleen *qi* deficiency.

Pattern identifying features

- **Heart Blood &/or *yin* deficiency**
- **insomnia, nightmares, vivid or disturbing dreams**
- nightsweats

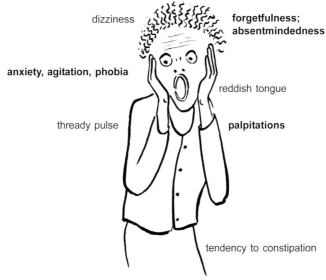

dizziness

forgetfulness; absentmindedness

anxiety, agitation, phobia

reddish tongue

thready pulse

palpitations

tendency to constipation

- With **8.1 Tian Wang Bu Xin Dan** for Heart *yin* deficiency.
- With **3.41 Xu Han Ting** for nightsweats, insomnia and anxiety.

Dosage and method of administration

8-12 pills three times daily on an empty stomach. In severe cases or during the early stages of treatment (the first few weeks), a 50% increase in dose may be used, then reduced as the treatment takes effect.

Cautions and contraindications

Contraindicated during the early phase of acute illness such as colds and flu. Generally well tolerated, but care should be taken in patients with a tendency to abdominal distension, loose stools or general digestive weakness. Digestive upsets can usually be alleviated by taking this formula with a small dose (3-6 pills at the same time) of **2.18 Bao He Wan** or **2.9 Xiang Sha Liu Jun Wan**.

8.3 AN SHEN DING ZHI WAN

安神定志丸

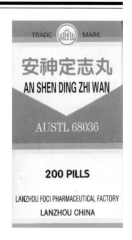

Lanzhou Foci Pharmaceutical Factory (Gansu)
'Calm the *Shen* and Settle the *Zhi* Pills'
An Shen Ding Zhi Wan is packaged in bottles of 200 pills.

TCM actions
Supplements *yin*, *qi* and Blood, calms the *shen* and *zhi*, transforms Phlegm.

Biomedical actions
Sedative for anxiety and mild neurosis, nervine.

INDICATIONS

• A thermally neutral and general *shen* calming formula suitable for *qi*, Blood and/or *yin* deficiency, with insubstantial Phlegm misting the Heart type *shen* disturbances and anxiety states. Because this formula is quite broad and general in action, it can be combined with an appropriate constitutional formula where an increased *shen* calming effect is desired.

Composition (each pill contains powdered)
Zizyphus jujuba (da zao, chinese dates) 20.2mg, *Poria cocos* (fu ling, hoelen) 17.2mg, *Paeonia alba* (bai shao, white peony) 17.2mg, *Polygonum multiflorum* (ye jiao teng, ho shou wu stem) 17.2mg, *Glycyrrhiza uralensis* (gan cao, licorice) 16.1mg, *Ophiopogon japonica* (mai dong, ophiopogon) 13.7mg, *Zizyphus spinoza* (suan zao ren, zizyphus) 13.7mg, *Biota orientalis* (bai zi ren, biota seed) 13mg, *Curcuma longa* (yu jin, curcuma) 13mg, *Pinellia ternata* (ban xia, pinellia) 13mg, *Polygala sibirica* (yuan zhi, polygala) 9.6mg, *Chrysanthemum sinensis* (ju hua, chrysanthemum) 9.6mg, *Schizandra chinensis* (wu wei zi, schizandra) 6.4mg

Combinations
• With **1.9 Gui Pi Wan** for Spleen and Heart deficiency anxiety states and insomnia.
• With **8.1 Tian Wang Bu Xin Dan** for Heart and Kidney *yin* deficiency anxiety states and insomnia.
• With **6.4 Xiao Yao Wan** for anxiety and insomnia associated with Liver *qi* stagnation.

Pattern identifying features

- **Blood, *qi* & *yin* deficiency;
  Phlegm misting the Heart**
- **insomnia**
- dream disturbed sleep, nightmares
- racing mind at night; difficulty
  settling to sleep

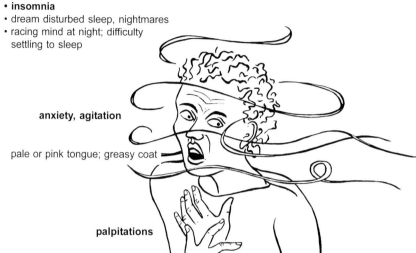

anxiety, agitation

pale or pink tongue; greasy coat

palpitations

weak or slightly slippery or wiry pulse

SHEN

Dosage and method of administration

8-12 pills three times daily on an empty stomach, but when combining **8.3 An Shen Ding Zhi Wan** with a constitutional formula, a half dose is usually sufficient. In severe cases or during the early stages of treatment (the first few weeks), a 50% increase in dose may be used, then reduced to a maintenance dose as the treatment takes effect.

Cautions and contraindications

Contraindicated during the early phase of acute illness such as colds and flu.

GMP ## 8.4 AN SHEN BU XIN WAN

 # 安神补心丸

 Lanzhou Foci Pharmaceutical Factory (Gansu)
'Calm the *Shen* and Supplement the Heart Pills'
An Shen Bu Xin Wan is packaged in bottles of 200 pills.

TCM actions
Subdues *yang*, calms the *hun* and *shen*, supplements *yin*
and Blood, regulates *qi* and quickens Blood.

Biomedical actions
Sedative, tranquilizer.

INDICATIONS

- Heart and Liver *yin* and Blood deficiency patterns with rising *yang* and relatively severe *shen* and/or *hun* disturbance. This formula utilises a high proportion of the heavy mineral sedative, mother of pearl, to weigh down and anchor the *hun* and *shen*. Similar in general action to **8.1 Tian Wang Bu Xin Dan**, the main focus of the formula is to quickly sedate and calm, while secondarily supplementing the underlying deficiency. Being able to sedate *yang* and regulate *qi* and Blood, it is also good for *shen* and *hun* disturbances as a result of stress or emotional trauma.
- Used for irritability, restlessness, resistant insomnia or nightmare disturbed sleep, stress induced insomnia or palpitations, insomnia or panic attacks following trauma, post traumatic stress disorder, hypertension, sleepwalking, palpitations and anxiety.

Composition
Pteria martensii (zhen zhu mu, mother of pearl) 44%, *Polygonum multiflorum* (ye jiao teng, ho shou wu stem) 11%, *Ligustrum lucidum* (nu zhen zi, privet fruit) 9%, *Eclipta prostrata* (han lian cao, eclipta) 7%, *Salvia miltiorrhiza* (dan shen, salvia) 7%, *Cuscuta chinensis* (tu su zi, cuscuta) 7%, *Albizzia julibrissin* (he huan pi, albizzia) 7%, *Rehmannia glutinosa* (shu di, processed rehmannia) 4%, *Schizandra chinensis* (wu wei zi, schizandra) 3%, *Acorus gramineus* (shi chang pu, acorus) 2%

Combinations
- With **6.4 Xiao Yao Wan** or **8.7 An Shen Jie Yu Capsule** for anxiety and insomnia associated with Liver *qi* stagnation.

Pattern identifying features

- **Yin & Blood deficiency with unsettled *hun* & *shen*, & yang excess**
- **insomnia, dream disturbed sleep, nightmares**
- **irritability, restlessness**
- heat intolerance
- facial flushing
- emotional instability

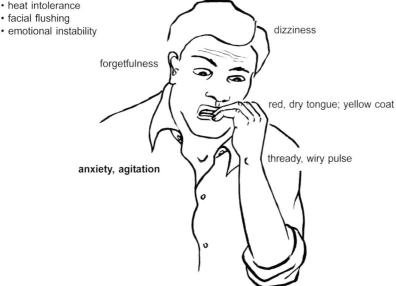

forgetfulness

dizziness

red, dry tongue; yellow coat

thready, wiry pulse

anxiety, agitation

SHEN

Dosage and method of administration

8-12 pills three times daily on an empty stomach, best towards the end of the day or before bedtime. In severe cases or during the early stages of treatment (the first few weeks), a 50% increase in dose may be used, then reduced to a maintenance dose as the treatment takes effect. Generally only used for a few weeks, or until the *shen* and *hun* have settled, after which a more constitutional approach may be phased in.

Cautions and contraindications

Contraindicated during pregnancy. Caution in patients on anticoagulant therapy (aspirin, warfarin, coumarin). Watch for bruising or increased tendency to bleeding.

8.5 SHUIAN CAPSULE

睡安胶囊

(Shui An Jiao Nang)
Yulin Drug Manufactory (Guangxi)
'Peaceful Sleep Capsules'
Shuian Capsules are packaged in bottles of 30 capsules.

TCM actions
Nourishes Blood, settles the Heart, calms the *shen*.

Biomedical actions
Mild sedative, tranquilizer.

INDICATIONS

• A mild and gentle formula for Blood and *yin* deficiency insomnia, nervous tension and mild anxiety. Similar in action and indications to **8.6 Suan Zao Ren Wan**. May be used alone for mild patterns or added to a constitutional formula when enhanced *shen* calming action is desired.

Composition (each capsule contains extracts equivalent to)
Zizyphus spinoza (suan zao ren, zizyphus) 125mg, *Poria cocos* (fu ling, hoelen) 100mg, *Polygonum multiflorum* (ye jiao teng, ho shou wu stem) 100mg, *Schizandra chinensis* (wu wei zi, schizandra) 95mg, *Polygala sibirica* (yuan zhi, polygala) 80mg

Combinations
• With **1.9 Gui Pi Wan** for Spleen and Heart deficiency anxiety states and insomnia.
• With **8.1 Tian Wang Bu Xin Dan** for relatively severe Heart and Kidney *yin* deficiency anxiety states and insomnia.
• With **6.4 Xiao Yao Wan** or **6.5 Jia Wei Xiao Yao Wan** for anxiety and insomnia associated with Liver *qi* stagnation.

Dosage and method of administration
3 capsules, three times daily, preferably later in the day or close to bedtime.

Cautions and contraindications
Contraindicated during the early phase of acute illness such as colds and flu.

8.6 SUAN ZAO REN TANG PIAN

酸枣仁汤片

Available in the US,
UK and Europe
See Note 1, p.xxi

GMP

Guangzhou Qixing Pharmaceutical Co. (Guangzhou)
'*Zizyphus spinoza* Pills'
Suan Zao Ren Wan is packaged in bottles of 50 tablets.

TCM actions
Nourishes Liver Blood, calms the *shen*, clears Heat, alleviates irritability.

Biomedical actions
Sedative, tranquilizer.

INDICATIONS

- Liver Blood deficiency *shen* and sleep disturbances. The bulk of this formula is composed of zizyphus, a gentle and effective sedative herb that nourishes the Liver and Heart, and is suitable for mild *shen* disturbances. On balance, this formula is cooling, and is considered best for patterns with a degree of Heat, although it can also be for patterns without Heat. When the deficiency does generate some Heat, there may also be nightsweats, irritability, dryness of the mouth and throat and a red tongue. Commonly used for menopausal syndrome with sleep disturbances and irritability. Can be added to a constitutional formula when enhanced *shen* calming and sedative action is required.

Composition
Zizyphus spinoza (suan zao ren, zizyphus) 78%, *Poria cocos* (fu ling, hoelen) 6%, *Ligusticum wallichi* (chuan xiong, cnidium) 6%, *Anemarrhena aspheloides* (zhi mu, anemarrhena) 6%, *Glycyrrhiza uralensis* (gan cao, licorice) 3%

Combinations
- With **1.24 Er Xian Wan** or **1.23 Zhi Bai Ba Wei Wan** for anxiety in menopause.
- With **6.4 Xiao Yao Wan** for anxiety and insomnia associated with Liver *qi* stagnation.

Dosage and method of administration
2-3 pills three times daily on an empty stomach, preferably towards the end of the day or close to bedtime. In severe cases a 50% increase in dose may be used, then reduced as the treatment takes effect.

Cautions and contraindications
None noted.

SHEN

8.7 AN SHEN JIE YU CAPSULE

安神解郁丸

(An Shen Jie Yu Wan)
Jing Xian Pharmaceutical Co. (Guangzhou)
'Calm the *Shen* and alleviate [*Qi*] Stagnation Pills'
An Shen Jie Yu Capsules are packaged in bottles of 36
capsules.

TCM actions

Regulates Liver *qi* and soothes the Liver, calms the *shen*
and settles the *hun*.

Biomedical actions

Sedative, tranquilizer.

INDICATIONS

- *Shen* disturbances associated with Liver *qi* stagnation. Liver *qi* stagnation
  influences the Heart and *shen* via the generating cycle (*sheng* cycle), and this
  type of *shen* disturbance typically occurs during periods of stress or emotional
  tension, or in the premenstrual period. The main features are insomnia,
  palpitations, dizziness, stress headaches, fullness in the chest and difficulty
  getting a full breath. The patient typically wakes during the Liver time, around
  1-3am. Because the Liver and therefore the *hun* is involved, some patients may
  experience sleepwalking.
- With the appropriate identifying features, this formula can be used to treat
  conditions such as bruxism, stress induced sleep disturbances and
  premenstrual insomnia.

Composition (each capsule contains extracts equivalent to)

Schizandra chinensis (wu wei zi, schizandra) 765mg, *Polygala sibirica* (yuan zhi, polygala)
382mg, *Lycium barbarum* (gou qi zi, lycium fruit) 382mg, *Atractylodes macrocephala* (bai
zhu, atractylodes) 340mg, *Bupleurum falcatum* (chai hu, bupleurum) 306mg, *Zizyphus
spinoza* (suan zao ren, zizyphus) 306mg, *Poria cocos* (fu shen, hoelen spirit) 306mg

Pattern identifying features

- ***Shen* disturbance associated with Liver *qi* stagnation**
- insomnia, easy waking (especially around 1-3am), vivid dreaming
- irritability, anger outbursts, depression
- frequent sighing

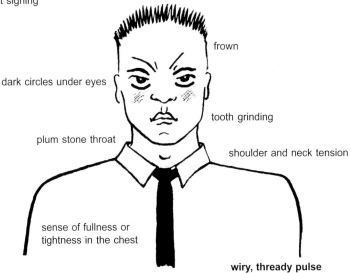

frown

dark circles under eyes

tooth grinding

plum stone throat

shoulder and neck tension

sense of fullness or tightness in the chest

wiry, thready pulse

Combinations
- With **6.4 Xiao Yao Wan** for more severe Liver *qi* stagnation.
- With **6.5 Jia Wei Xiao Yao Wan** for more severe insomnia and restlessness due to *qi* stagnation with stagnant Heat

Dosage and method of administration
3 capsules, three times daily. The days dose may also be taken later in the day, close to bedtime.

Cautions and contraindications
None noted.

8.8 WEN DAN WAN

温胆丸

Lanzhou Foci Pharmaceutical Factory (Gansu)
'Warm the Gallbladder Pills'
Wen Dan Wan is packaged in bottles of 200 pills.
Also available as: Rising Courage Teapills (PF)

TCM actions
Clears and transforms Phlegm Heat, regulates *qi*,
harmonises the Stomach and Gallbladder, calms the *shen*.

Biomedical actions
Sedative, tranquilizer, expectorant.

INDICATIONS

- Phlegm Heat. An important formula for Phlegm Heat affecting the Heart and *shen*, Gallbladder and Stomach. Used for a wide variety of mental emotional complaints of a Phlegm Heat type, especially those characterised by anxiety and insomnia.
- Stomach and Gallbladder disharmony with Phlegm Heat clogging the digestion. This is a common pattern of nausea, vomiting and morning sickness, indigestion and indeterminate gnawing hunger.
- Phlegm Heat in the head causing dizziness, vertigo, fuzzy head and poor concentration. In severe cases, Phlegm Heat in the head can contribute to tremor and convulsion patterns, as well as epilepsy or absences.
- Used for residual fatigue, insomnia, restlessness, depression and anxiety states that can occur in the aftermath of a serious febrile illness that has consumed *yin* and congealed fluids into Phlegm. Also for residual cough or wheezing from Phlegm Heat following an upper respiratory tract infection.
- With the appropriate identifying features, this formula can be used to treat Ménière's disease, the early stages of schizophrenia and other mental disorders, anxiety states, arrhythmias, acute and chronic gastritis, hypertension, post febrile insomnia and anxiety and chronic bronchitis.

Composition (each pill contains powdered)
Bambusa textilis (zhu ru, bamboo shavings) 24.8mg, *Citrus aurantium* (zhi shi, aurantium) 24.8mg, *Pinellia ternata* (ban xia, pinellia) 24.8mg, *Citrus reticulata* (chen pi, citrus) 24.8mg, *Poria cocos* (fu ling, hoelen) 24.8mg, *Zingiber officinale* (sheng jiang, ginger) 12mg, *Zizyphus jujuba* (da zao, chinese dates) 12mg

Pattern identifying features

- **Phlegm Heat**
- **insomnia, waking early in the morning**
- restlessness, irritability
- bitter taste in the mouth
- indeterminate gnawing hunger (*see* glossary)
- tinnitus

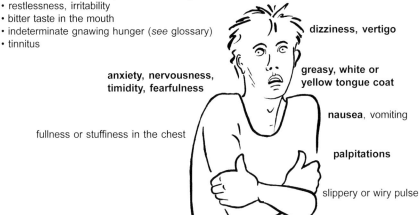

dizziness, vertigo

anxiety, nervousness, timidity, fearfulness

greasy, white or yellow tongue coat

fullness or stuffiness in the chest

nausea, vomiting

palpitations

slippery or wiry pulse

Combinations
- With a small dose of **14.2 Huang Lian Su Tablets** for severe Phlegm Heat.
- With **7.22 Shen Qi Da Bu Wan** for *qi* deficiency.
- With **15.4 Tian Ma Gou Teng Wan** for severe vertigo.
- With **3.21 She Dan Chuan Bei Ye** for residual cough from Phlegm Heat congestion in the Lungs.
- With **8.3 An Shen Ding Zhi Wan** for severe insomnia or anxiety.

Dosage and method of administration
8-12 pills three times daily on an empty stomach. The dose may be spread out, or two lots of 12-18 pills may be taken, morning and evening. In severe cases or during the early stages of treatment (the first few weeks), a 50% increase in dose may be used, then reduced as the treatment takes effect.

Cautions and contraindications
Contraindicated in *yin* or Blood deficiency type *shen* disturbances.

SHEN

GMP **8.9 CHAI HU LONG GU MU LI WAN**

柴胡龙骨牡蛎丸

Available in the US,
UK and Europe
See Note 1, p.xxi

Lanzhou Foci Pharmaceutical Factory (Gansu)
'Bupleurum, Dragon Bone and Oyster Shell Pills'
Chai Hu Long Gu Mu Li Wan is packaged in bottles of 200 pills.
Available as: Bupleurum, Dragon Bone and Oystershell Teapills (PF)

TCM actions

Harmonises *shao yang*, clears Heat from the Liver and Intestines, *yang*, transforms Phlegm, clears Phlegm Heat, calms the *shen*.

Biomedical actions

Sedative for anxiety, agitation and neurosis, nervine, sedates the sympathetic nervous system.

INDICATIONS

• Liver *qi* stagnation, Phlegm Heat, Liver *yang* rising and Liver and Heart Fire. A very useful and broad acting *shen* calming formula for conditions associated with *qi* stagnation, Heat and Phlegm. Patients are usually relatively robust, and display clear signs of excess. Traditionally used for simultaneous pathology of the three *yang* levels of the Six Level disease differentiation system (*see* glossary) following iatrogenic purgation of a superficial pathogen.

• Effective for the symptoms associated with drug withdrawal (including tobacco, narcotics and stimulants), such as insomnia, anxiety, irritability and palpitations or tachycardia.

• Palpitations or cardiac arrhythmia that occur at rest.

• Relatively severe emotional or psychological pathology, manifesting as severe irritability, agitation or manic behaviour.

• Mild epilepsy, seizures or tremors associated with Liver Fire and Phlegm accumulation.

• With the appropriate identifying features, this formula can be used to treat biomedical conditions such as hypertension, hyperthyroidism, epilepsy, cardiac arrhythmia, withdrawal from narcotics and other drugs of addiction, post traumatic stress disorder, schizophrenia and manic depressive psychosis.

Composition

Bupleurum falcatum (chai hu, bupleurum) 17%, *Pinellia ternata* (ban xia, pinellia) 13.5%, *Poria cocos* (fu ling, hoelen) 10%, *Cinnamomum cassia* (gui zhi, cinnamon twigs) 10%, *Scutellaria baicalensis* (huang qin, scute) 8%, *Zizyphus jujuba* (da zao, chinese dates) 8%,

Pattern identifying features

- **Liver *qi* stagnation, Phlegm Heat, Liver *yang* rising, Liver and Heart Fire**
- insomnia, restlessness
- anxiety, agitation
- heaviness in the body

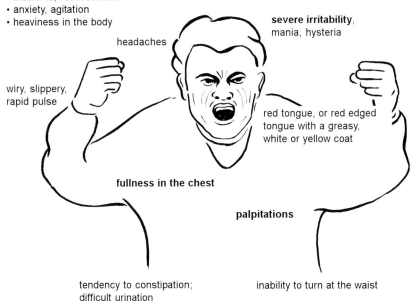

headaches

severe irritability, mania, hysteria

wiry, slippery, rapid pulse

red tongue, or red edged tongue with a greasy, white or yellow coat

fullness in the chest

palpitations

tendency to constipation; difficult urination

inability to turn at the waist

Codonopsis pilosula (dang shen, codonopsis) 8%, Os Draconis (long gu, dragon bone) 8%, *Ostrea gigas* (mu li, oyster shell) 8%, *Zingiber officinale* (sheng jiang, ginger) 3.5%, *Rheum palmatum* (da huang, rhubarb) 3.5%

Combinations
- With **6.2 Si Ni San Wan** for relatively severe Liver *qi* stagnation.
- With **6.6 Long Dan Xie Gan Wan** for relatively severe Liver Fire.
- With **8.8 Wen Dan Wan** for relatively severe Phlegm Heat.

Dosage and method of administration
8-12 pills three times daily on an empty stomach. The dose may be spread out, or two lots of 12-18 pills may be taken, morning and evening or before bed. In severe cases or during the early stages of treatment (the first few weeks), a 50% increase in dose may be used, then reduced as the treatment takes effect.

Cautions and contraindications
Contraindicated during pregnancy. Caution in patients with significant Spleen weakness as this formula can be hard on the digestion.

SHEN

8.10 CEREBRAL TONIC PILLS

补脑丸

(Bu Nao Wan)
Xian C.P Pharmaceutical Co. (Shanxi)
'Brain Supplementing Pills'
Cerebral Tonic Pills are packaged in bottles of 300 pills.
Also available as: Bu Nao Wan (PF)

TCM actions

Calms the *shen*, transforms Phlegm, extinguishes Wind, strengthens the Kidneys, nourishes Blood, benefits and clears the brain, opens the bowels.

Biomedical actions

Sedative and tranquilizer, nervine, sedates the sympathetic nervous system, mild laxative.

INDICATIONS

- Phlegm misting the mind and obscuring the clear perception of the *shen*. This is a complex formula that supplements Kidney *yang* and Blood, while transforming and dispersing Phlegm and extinguishing Wind. Particularly useful for absentminded, confused or disoriented elderly, Kidney deficient or weakened patients with elements of Phlegm accumulation and *shen* disturbance. Suitable for anxiety, nervousness, memory disorders, difficulty concentrating, palpitations, insomnia and mental agitation from the same etiology. The cistanches and walnut play a dual role in this formula–they supplement the Kidneys and thus strengthen the basis of fluid metabolism, and encourage bowel movement thereby providing an outlet for the Phlegm in the upper body.
- May be useful for mild manic states where Phlegm Heat obstructs the clear expression of the *shen*.

Composition

Schizandra chinensis (wu wei zi, schizandra), *Zizyphus spinoza* (suan zao ren, zizyphus), *Biota orientalis* (bai zi ren, biota seed), *Angelica sinensis* (dang gui, chinese angelica), *Lycium barbarum* (gou qi zi, lycium fruit), *Alpinia oxyphylla* (yi zhi ren, alpinia), *Acorus gramineus* (shi chang pu, acorus), *Polygala sibirica* (yuan zhi, polygala), *Gastrodia elata* (tian ma, gastrodia), *Arisaema cosanguinium* (dan nan xing, bile treated arisaema), *Bambusa textilis* (tian zhu huang, tabasheer), Os Draconis (long gu, dragon bone), Amber (hu po), *Juglans regia* (hu tao ren, walnut), *Cistanches deserticola* (rou cong rong, cistanches)

Pattern identifying features

- **Phlegm misting the mind, senses & *shen***
- **dull sensorum; lack of *jing shen*; forgetfulness, poor concentration; absentmindedness**
- confusion, disorientation
- insomnia, dream disturbed sleep
- anxiety, nervousness

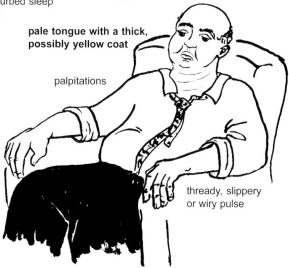

foggy headedness

pale tongue with a thick, possibly yellow coat

palpitations

thready, slippery or wiry pulse

SHEN

Combinations
- With **8.8 Wen Dan Wan** for severe Phlegm Heat.
- With **1.9 Gui Pi Wan** for Spleen and Heart deficiency anxiety states and insomnia with a degree of Phlegm accumulation.
- With **8.1 Tian Wang Bu Xin Dan** for Heart and Kidney *yin* deficiency anxiety states and insomnia with Phlegm accumulation.

Dosage and method of administration
2-3 pills two or three times daily on an empty stomach. In the early stages of treatment (the first two weeks or so) the dose can be increased by 50% until results are noticed, then reduced to the maintenance dose.

Cautions and contraindications
None noted.

8.11 JIAN NAO YI ZHI CAPSULE

健脑益智丸

(Jian Nao Yi Zhi Wan)
Guanghua Pharmaceutical Co. (Guangzhou)
'Strengthen the Brain and Benefit the Mind Pills'
Jian Nao Yi Zhi Capsules are packaged in bottles of 36 capsules.

TCM actions
Supplements *qi*, nourishes the Heart, strengthens the brain
and benefits the mind, quickens Blood, calms the *shen*.

Biomedical actions
Improves circulation, mild sedative, energy stimulant.

INDICATIONS

- Forgetfulness and memory problems. Improves concentration and sharpens the
  mind for periods of intensive brain and memory work such as periods of intensive
  study at exam time. Also used for mental exhaustion and burn out following
  periods of intensive mental activity.
- Used as a preventive against the memory problems of the elderly.

Composition (each capsule contains extracts equivalent to dry)
Panax ginseng (ren shen, ginseng) 556mg, *Poria cocos* (fu shen, hoelen spirit) 556mg,
Polygala sibirica (yuan zhi, polygala) 371mg, *Salvia miltorrhiza* (dan shen, salvia) 371mg

Combinations
- With **7.10 You Gui Wan** or **7.13 Huan Shao Dan** for memory problems in
  elderly patients arising from Kidney *yang* deficiency.
- With **7.3 Zuo Gui Wan** for memory problems in elderly patients arising from
  Kidney *yin* or *jing* deficiency.

Dosage and method of administration
2-3 capsules, two or three times daily on an empty stomach.

Cautions and contraindications
Contraindicated during the early phase of acute illness such as colds and flu, in
patients with Heat, *yang* rising or *yin* deficiency patterns. Caution in patients with
hypertension, those with gastric ulcers, and patients on anticoagulant therapy.

8.12 ZAO REN AN SHEN YE

枣仁安神液

Tong Ren Tang (Beijing)
'Zizyphus Drink to Calm the *Shen*'
Zao Ren An Shen Ye is packaged as a liquid extract in 10 ml vials, ten vials per box

TCM actions

Calms the *shen* and *hun*, nourishes the Heart and Liver.

Biomedical actions

Sedative, tranquilizer, mild astringent.

INDICATIONS

- A mild *shen* calming sedative for insomnia, dream disturbed sleep and neurasthenia associated with Heart and Liver Blood deficiency. The main advantage of this formula is its ease of use and mild taste. Gentle enough for restless infants and children.
- May be of assistance in sweating disorders.

Composition (each 10 ml contains)

Zizyphus spinoza (suan zao ren, zizyphus) 500mg, *Schizandra chinensis* (wu wei zi, schizandra) 250mg, *Salvia miltorrhiza* (dan shen, salvia) 250mg

Combinations

- Can be combined with any other *shen* calming formula to enhance the sedative effect.
- With **1.23 Zhi Bai Ba Wei Wan** for insomnia and nightsweats from *yin* deficiency.

Dosage and method of administration

One or two vials before bed or upon waking during the night.

Cautions and contraindications

Caution in patients on anticoagulant therapy.

SHEN

GMP 8.13 GAN MAI DA ZAO WAN

甘麦大枣丸

Available in the US, UK and Europe See Note 1, p.xxi

Lanzhou Foci Pharmaceutical Factory (Gansu)
'Licorice, Wheat and Chinese Date Pills'
Gan Mai Da Zao Wan is packaged in bottles of 200 pills.
Available as: Calm Spirit Teapills (PF)

TCM actions
Nourishes the Heart, calms the *shen* and *hun*, harmonises the middle *jiao*, strengthens the Spleen.

Biomedical actions
Sedative, tranquilizer.

INDICATIONS

• *Zang zao* syndrome. This is a type of emotional disorder associated with Heart and Spleen deficiency, characterised by paroxysmal depression, hysteria, mood swings, behavioural changes, anxiety, hypersensitivity and sleep disturbances. Considered to be most common in women and frequently associated with hormonal changes, it can be applied to any situation where emotional or physical trauma has led to emotional instability. Commonly combined with other constitutional formulae for disorders such as menopausal syndrome, postpartum depression, premenstrual syndrome, post traumatic stress disorder and neurosis.

Composition
Polygonum multiflorum (ye jiao teng, ho shou wu stem) 18%, *Triticum aestivum* (fu xiao mai, wheat) 15%, *Zizyphus jujuba* (da zao, chinese dates) 15%, *Poria cocos* (fu shen, hoelen spirit) 15%, *Lilium brownii* (bai he, lily) 15%, *Glycyrrhiza uralensis* (zhi gan cao, honey fried licorice) 10%, *Albizzia julibrissin* (he huan pi, albizzia) 10%

Combinations
• With **1.9 Gui Pi Wan** for severe anxiety from Heart and Spleen deficiency.
• With **1.23 Zhi Bai Ba Wei Wan** or **1.24 Er Xian Wan** for agitation, insomnia and nightsweats from *yin* deficiency.

Dosage and method of administration
8-12 pills three times daily on an empty stomach. In severe cases or the early stages of treatment a 50% increase in dose may be used, reduced as the treatment takes effect.

Cautions and contraindications
None noted.

9

Patents Medicines for Ear, Nose, Throat and Eye Disorders

9.1 ER LONG ZUO CI WAN

耳聾左慈丸

Lanzhou Foci Pharmaceutical Factory (Gansu)
'Deafness Left Supporting Pills'
Er Long Zuo Ci Wan is packaged in bottles of 200 pills.
Also available as: Er Ming Zuo Ci Wan, Tso-Tzu Otic Pills

TCM actions

Supplements Kidney *yin*, regulates *qi* and restrains exuberant *yang*.

Biomedical actions

Demulcent febrifuge, hematinic, hypoglycemic, antihypertensive, improves kidney function, regulates adrenal cortex.

INDICATIONS

- Kidney *yin* deficiency with hearing problems, specifically tinnitus and gradual loss of hearing acuity. This formula is a variation of **7.1 Liu Wei Di Huang Wan**. Most frequently used for chronic tinnitus with a high pitch that is worse with fatigue, exertion and at night.
- For Liver and Kidney *yin* deficiency patterns with a degree of Liver *qi* stagnation. This may include some visual problems like optic neuritis, optic nerve atrophy and central retinitis.
- With the appropriate identifying features, this formula can assist in the treatment of biomedical conditions such as tinnitus in the elderly, chronic labyrinthitis, Ménière's disease and hypertension.

Composition (each pill contains powdered)

Rehmannia glutinosa (shu di, processed rehmannia) 30mg, *Dioscorea opposita* (shan yao, dioscorea) 28mg, *Poria cocos* (fu ling, hoelen) 23mg, *Paeonia suffruticosa* (mu dan pi, moutan) 21mg, *Bupleurum chinensis* (chai hu, bupleurum) 21mg, *Cornus officinalis* (shan zhu yu, cornus) 17mg, *Alisma orientalis* (ze xie, alisma) 17mg, *Schizandra chinensis* (wu wei zi, schizandra) 12mg
Note: Other versions of this formula (from the same factory) contain Magnetite (ci shi).

Combinations

- With **15.4 Tian Ma Gou Teng Wan** if there is a significant component of Liver *yang* rising.

Pattern identifying features

- **Liver and Kidney *yin* deficiency hearing disorders**

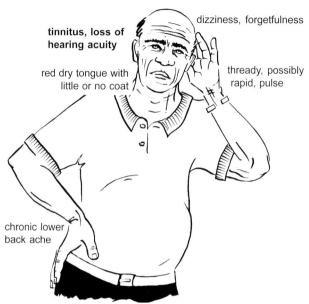

tinnitus, loss of hearing acuity

dizziness, forgetfulness

red dry tongue with little or no coat

thready, possibly rapid, pulse

chronic lower back ache

- With **8.1 Tian Wang Bu Xin Dan** if the tinnitus keeps the patient awake at night.
- It is useful to use ear candles one or twice a week for patients with ear problems from Kidney *yin* deficiency.

Dosage and method of administration

8-12 pills three times daily on an empty stomach. The dose may be spread out, or two lots of 12-18 pills may be taken, morning and evening. In severe cases or during the early stages of treatment (the first few weeks), a 50% increase in dose may be used, then reduced as the treatment takes effect.

Cautions and contraindications

Contraindicated during the early phase of acute illness such as colds and flu. Care should be taken in patients with a tendency to abdominal bloating, loose stools or Phlegm Damp. This is a cooling formula and overuse can cool and weaken digestion. This can usually be alleviated by taking a small dose (3-6 pills at the same time) of **2.18 Bao He Wan** or **2.9 Xiang Sha Liu Jun Wan**.

ENT

GMP **9.2 TONG QIAO HUO XUE WAN**

通窍活血丸

Lanzhou Foci Pharmaceutical Factory (Gansu)
'Blood Regulating, Orifice Opening Pills'
Tong Qiao Huo Xue Wan is packaged in bottles of 200 pills.
Available as: Tong Qiao Huo Xue Teapills

Available in the US,
UK and Europe
See Note 1, p.xxi

TCM actions
Invigorates Blood and disperses stagnant Blood, opens the sensory orifices.

Biomedical actions
Vasodilator, antispasmodic, anti-platelet action.

INDICATIONS

• Blood stagnation affecting the Head. Particularly useful for Blood stagnation patterns affecting the ears and other sensory structures. The Blood stasis may be associated with chronic pathology or traumatic injury to the head. Direct injury to the ear includes etiology such as exposure to loud noise or sudden pressure changes when flying or scuba diving. The resulting tinnitus and/or hearing loss is persistent, and may be associated with pain and a dark or black discharge from the ear, or dark matter mixed in with the ear wax.

• Acute or chronic focal headaches including migraine and cluster headaches, post surgical, post traumatic and headache associated with drug reaction.

• Purple discoloration of the face and nose, 'brandy nose', hair and eyebrow loss and dark rings around the eyes.

• With the appropriate identifying features, this formula may assist in the treatment of disorders such as post concussion headache and dizziness, migraine and cluster headaches, vitiligo, epilepsy or seizures following head trauma, somnolence, memory loss, dizziness and vertigo.

Composition
Prunus persica (tao ren, peach seed) 20%, *Carthamus tinctorius* (hong hua, carthamus) 20%, *Paeonia veitchii* (chi shao, red peony) 10%, *Ligusticum wallici* (chuan xiong, cnidium) 10%, *Acorus gramineus* (shi chang pu, acorus) 9.5%, *Angelica dahurica* (bai zhi, angelica) 9.5%, *Zingiber officinale* (sheng jiang, ginger) 9.5%, *Zizyphus jujuba* (da zao, chinese dates) 9%

Pattern identifying features

- **Blood stagnation in the head**
- dry, scaly skin
- swollen, purple nose
- purple or dark complexion
- vitiligo

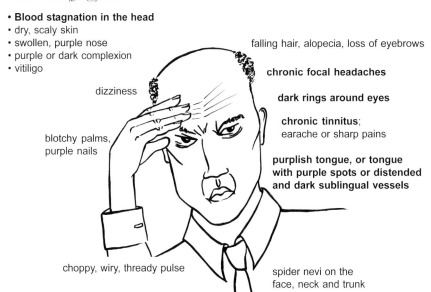

falling hair, alopecia, loss of eyebrows

chronic focal headaches

dizziness

dark rings around eyes

chronic tinnitus;
earache or sharp pains

blotchy palms,
purple nails

**purplish tongue, or tongue
with purple spots or distended
and dark sublingual vessels**

choppy, wiry, thready pulse

spider nevi on the
face, neck and trunk

Dosage and method of administration

8-12 pills three times daily on an empty stomach. The dose may be spread out, or two lots of 12-18 pills may be taken, morning and evening. In severe cases or during the early stages of treatment, a 50% increase in dose may be used, then reduced as the treatment takes effect.

Cautions and contraindications

Contraindicated during pregnancy, in women with menorrhagia, and in patients with bleeding disorders. Caution in patients on anticoagulant therapy (aspirin, warfarin, coumarin). Watch for bruising or increased tendency to bleeding.

Prolonged use may deplete *qi* and Blood, so a break every 2-3 months, with a change to a simple *qi* and Blood supplementing formula for a few weeks is recommended.

ENT

9.3 PEKING NIU HUANG JIE DU PIAN

北京牛黄解毒片

(Beijing Niu Huang Jie Di Pian)
Tong Ren Tang (Beijing)
'Cow Gallstone Anti-Toxic Pills'
Peking Niu Huang Jie Du Pian is packaged in bottles of 20 coated tablets and in vials of 8 uncoated pills, 12 vials to a box.
Also available as: Niu Huang Jie Du Pian

TCM actions

Clears Heat and Toxic Heat from the head and upper body and the *yang ming* organs, dispels Wind, stops pain and opens the bowels.

Biomedical actions

Anti-inflammatory, detoxicant, antibiotic, antiviral, laxative.

INDICATIONS

- Toxic Heat type infections, both bacterial and viral, of the head and upper body. An important formula for acute suppurative and febrile disorders, **9.3 Peking Niu Huang Jie Du Pian** is especially good for infection of the oral cavity, throat, ear and facial skin, including conditions such as tonsillitis, strep throat, acne and boils on the face and neck, folliculitis, herpes simplex, acute otitis media and externa, acute sinusitis, conjunctivitis, stye, gingivitis, dental abscess, toothache and mouth ulcers. May also be useful for acne rosacea.
- Acute Wind Heat, Warm disease (*wen bing*, see glossary) or Toxic Heat type fevers, especially when accompanied by constipation. Can be used for disorders such as mumps, scarlet fever, measles and chicken pox.

Composition (each tablet contains extracts equivalent to)

Bovine gallstone (niu huang) 13.8mg, *Lonicera japonica* (jin yin hua, honeysuckle) 726mg, *Forsythia suspensa* (lian qiao, forsythia) 726mg, *Mentha haplocalycis* (bo he, mint) 240mg, *Schizonepeta tenuifolia* (jing jie, schizonepeta) 240mg, *Platycodon grandiflorum* (jie geng, platycodon) 360mg, *Glycyrrhiza uralensis* (gan cao , licorice) 240mg, *Gardenia florida* (shan zhi zi, gardenia) 360mg, *Siler divaricum* (fang feng, siler) 180mg, *Ligusticum wallichi* (chuan xiong, cnidium) 240mg, *Inula britannica* (xuan fu hua, inula flower) 360mg, *Rheum officinale* (da huang, rhubarb) 492mg, *Chrysanthemum sinense* (ju hua, chrysanthemum flower) 492mg, *Angelica dahurica* (bai zhi, angelica) 306mg, *Vitex trifolia* (man jing zi, vitex fruit) 180mg, Gypsum (shi gao) 36mg

Pattern identifying features

- **Toxic Heat in the head and upper body**
- **localised suppuration, redness, swelling & pain**
- acute heat & inflammation
  in the head & upper body
- constipation

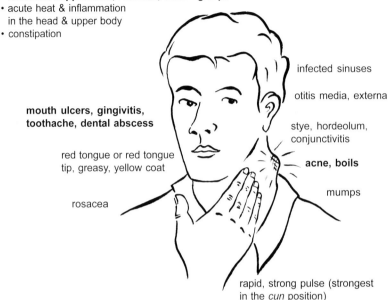

infected sinuses

otitis media, externa

**mouth ulcers, gingivitis,
toothache, dental abscess**

stye, hordeolum,
conjunctivitis

red tongue or red tongue
tip, greasy, yellow coat

acne, boils

mumps

rosacea

rapid, strong pulse (strongest
in the *cun* position)

Combinations
- With topical **9.10 Sanjin Watermelon Frost** for mouth ulcers.
- With **9.9 Superior Sore Throat Powder** topically for tonsillitis or otitis media or externa.
- With **3.1.1 Yin Chiao Chieh Tu Pien** for the early stage of an acute seasonal febrile illness.
- With a saline eyewash or wash of decocted chrysanthemum flowers for acute conjunctivitis.

Dosage and method of administration
2 pills twice daily on an empty stomach (1 pill twice daily crushed for children). This may be safely doubled in adults and in severe cases. May cause diarrhea. For rosacea, **9.3 Peking Niu Huang Jie Du Pian** may be used for 1-3 months at a half or quarter dose. Do not take within one hour of eating rich or oily foods.

Cautions and contraindications
Contraindicated during pregnancy. Not suitable for prolonged use (except as noted above) or for deficient patients without Toxic Heat.

9.4.1 HUANG LIEN SHANG CHING PIEN

黄连上清片

(Huang Lian Shang Qing Pian)
Tianjin Drug Manufactory (Shandong)
'Coptis Pill to Clear [Heat from] the Upper Body'
Huang Lien Shang Ching Pien is packaged in
vials of eight uncoated pills, twelve vials per box.

TCM actions
Dispels Wind Heat, and clears Toxic Heat, Fire and Damp Heat from the upper
body, cools the Blood, clears Heat from *yang ming*, opens the bowels.

Biomedical actions
Antipyretic, anti-inflammatory, antibiotic, laxative.

INDICATIONS

- Wind Heat, Toxic Heat and Damp Heat type focal infections of the head and
  upper body. Especially good for infection and inflammation of the eyes associated
  with Wind Heat, Fire or Heat in the Liver channel. With the appropriate identifying
  features, this may include such biomedical disorders as acute conjunctivitis,
  hordeolum, stye, blepharitis, excessive lacrimation and orbital cellulitis.
- Wind Heat or Toxic Heat affecting the throat causing acute sore throat, tonsillitis
  and laryngitis.
- Inflammatory or suppurative skin disorders of the head and upper body, including
  eczema, urticaria, pityriasis rosea, dermatitis, acne, abscesses, boils and cellulitis.
- Heat in the Stomach and *yang ming* channel and organ system causing constipation,
  halitosis, gingivitis, ulcerations of the oral cavity, tooth infection or dental abscess.
- Headache, dizziness and tinnitus from Wind Heat or Liver Fire rising up through
  the Liver/Gallbladder channel.

Composition (each tablet contains extracts equivalent to dry)
Chrysanthemum sinense (ju hua, chrysanthemum flower) 1.1g, *Vitex trifolia* (man jing zi,
vitex fruit) 773mg, *Platycodon grandiflorum* (jie geng, platycodon) 591mg, *Schizonepeta
tenuifolia* (jing jie, schizonepeta) 507mg, *Coptis chinensis* (huang lian, coptis) 364mg,
Scutellaria baicalensis (huang qin, scute) 273mg, *Ledebouriella divaricata* (fang feng, siler)
253mg, *Rheum palmatum* (da huang, rhubarb) 148mg, *Angelica dahurica* (bai zhi,
angelica) 53mg, *Glycyrrhiza uralensis* (gan cao, licorice) 18mg, Calcium sulphate 18mg

Pattern identifying features

- **Wind Heat & Toxic Heat in the head & upper body**
- inflammatory & suppurative disorders of the oral cavity, eyes, head & face
- mouth ulcers, gingivitis, toothache, dental abscess
- fever

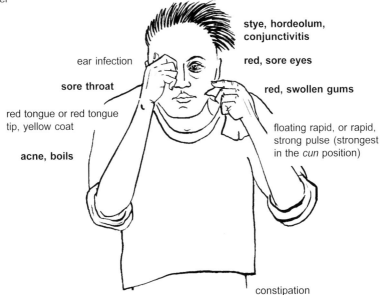

ear infection

sore throat

red tongue or red tongue tip, yellow coat

acne, boils

stye, hordeolum, conjunctivitis

red, sore eyes

red, swollen gums

floating rapid, or rapid, strong pulse (strongest in the *cun* position)

constipation

Combinations
- With topical **9.10 Sanjin Watermelon Frost** for mouth ulcers.
- With **9.9 Superior Sore Throat Powder** topically for tonsillitis or otitis media or otitis externa.

Dosage and method of administration
The recommended dose is 4 pills twice daily, on an empty stomach. In severe cases the dose may be increased by 50%. Usually not necessary for more than 4-7 days. Generally not recommended for children under 5 years old. May cause diarrhea.

Cautions and contraindications
Contraindicated during pregnancy. This formula is bitter and cold and can easily damage the Spleen and Stomach, and consume *yin*. It should only be used for the duration of the acute excess Heat pattern. Overdose can cause dizziness and vomiting.

ENT

9.4.2 HUANG LIAN SHANG QING TABLET

黄连上清片

(Huang Lian Shang Qing Pian)
Jing Xian Pharmaceutical Co. (Guangzhou)
'Coptis Pill to Clear [Heat from] the Upper Body'
Huang Lian Shang Qing Tablets are packaged in bottles of 60 tablets.

KING TIM®

HUANG LIAN
SHANG QING
TABLET

AUST L 79824
60 TABLETS

MADE IN CHINA

TCM actions

Dispels Wind Heat and clears Toxic Heat, Fire and Damp Heat from the upper body, cools the Blood, clears Heat from *yang ming*, opens the bowels.

Biomedical actions

Antipyretic, anti-inflammatory, antibiotic, laxative.

INDICATIONS

• As for **9.4.1 Huang Lien Shang Ching Pien**.

Composition (each tablet contains extracts equivalent to dry)

Chrysanthemum sinense (ju hua, chrysanthemum flower) 949mg, *Phellodendron amurense* (huang bai, phellodendron) 474mg, *Forsythia suspensa* (lian qiao, forsythia) 474mg, *Angelica dahurica* (bai zhi, angelica) 474mg, *Platycodon grandiflorum* (jie geng, platycodon) 474mg, *Scutellaria baicalensis* (huang qin, scute) 474mg, *Gardenia florida* (shan zhi zi, gardenia) 474mg, *Siler divaricum* (fang feng, siler) 238mg, *Rheum palmatum* (da huang, rhubarb) 20mg, *Coptis chinensis* (huang lian, coptis) 6.6mg, *Mentha haplocalycis* (bo he, mint) 26.4mg

Dosage and method of administration

3-5 tablets, three times daily, on an empty stomach.

Cautions and contraindications

As for **9.4.1 Huang Lien Shang Ching Pien**.

9.5 PU JI XIAO DU WAN

普济消毒丸

Available in the US, UK and Europe
See Note 1, p.xxi

GMP

Lanzhou Foci Pharmaceutical Factory (Gansu)
'Universal Benefit Pills to Eliminate Toxin'
Available as: Universal Benefit Teapills (PF)

TCM actions
Clears Toxic Heat and Fire, benefits the throat.

Biomedical actions
Antipyretic, anti-inflammatory, antibiotic.

INDICATIONS

- Acute Warm diseases (*see* glossary). Used for acute and relatively severe infection of the throat and/or other structures of the head–the parotid and salivary glands, subcutaneous connective tissues etc. The main features are acute high fever and chills or rigors, redness, swelling and burning pain of the throat, head or face, thirst, a red or red tipped tongue with dry coat and a rapid floating pulse.
- With the appropriate identifying features, this formula may assist in the treatment of disorders such as infectious parotitis (mumps), erysipelas or cellulitis of the face and head, streptococcal tonsillitis, measles, infectious meningitis, scarlet fever, lymphadenitis and otitis media.

Composition
Coptis chinensis (huang lian, coptis) 19%, *Scutellaria baicalensis* (huang qin, scute) 19%, *Scrophularia ningpoensis* (xuan shen, scrophularia) 7.5%, *Platycodon grandiflorum* (jie geng, platycodon) 7.5%, *Citrus reticulata* (chen pi, citrus) 7%, *Bupleurum falcatum* (chai hu, bupleurum) 7%, *Glycyrrhiza uralensis* (gan cao, licorice) 6.5%, *Arctium lappa* (niu bang zi, burdock seeds) 4%, *Forsythia suspensa* (lian qiao, forsythia) 4%, *Mentha haplocalyx* (bo he, mint) 4%, *Lasiosphaera femslii* (ma bo, puffball) 4%, *Isatis tinctora* (ban lan gen, isatis root) 4%, *Cimicifuga foetida* (sheng ma, cimicifuga) 2%, *Bombyx mori* (jiang can, silkworm) 2%

Dosage and method of administration
The recommended dose is 8-12 pills three times daily, however to get a good result in acute cases a much larger dose usually needs to be taken–8-15 pills every 2 hours depending on severity and size of patient.

Cautions and contraindications
Reserved for relatively severe Heat patterns. Being very bitter and cold, this formula can easily damage Spleen *yang* if overused.

ENT

9.6 BAN LAN GEN CHONG JI

板蓝根冲剂

Tong Ren Tang (Beijing)
'Isatis granules'
Ban Lan Gen Chong Ji is packaged in 12 gram sachets
of dissolvable granules, ten sachets per box.
Also available as: Ban Lan Gen Ke Li

TCM actions

Clears Toxic Heat, dispels Wind Heat.

Biomedical actions

Anti-inflammatory, detoxicant, antibiotic, antiviral.

INDICATIONS

- Acute throat and upper respiratory tract infections, especially viral, such as sore throat, tonsillitis and pharyngitis.
- Also used for disorders that may be classified as Warm diseases (*see* glossary), such as mumps, measles, infectious meningitis, scarlet fever and hepatitis.
- Effective for skin diseases such as herpes zoster (shingles), herpes simplex (cold sores), warts, pityriasis rosea and acne rosacea.
- Used preventatively against hepatitis and meningitis during outbreaks.

Composition (each sachet contains extract equivalent to)

Isatis tinctoria (ban lan gen, isatis root) 12.5g, sucrose

Combinations

- With **9.9 Superior Sore Throat Powder** for tonsillitis or otitis. This combination is also effective for shingles.
- With **3.1.1 Yin Chiao Chieh Tu Pien** or **3.4 Gan Mao Ling** for the early stage of an acute seasonal febrile illness or Warm disease.
- With **6.6 Long Dan Xie Gan Wan** for shingles from Liver Fire or Damp Heat.

Dosage and method of administration

4-6 sachets per day, dissolved in hot water. Halve the dose for children.

Cautions and contraindications

Not suitable for use in the absence of Heat or Toxic Heat symptoms.

9.7 JIE GENG WAN

桔梗丸

Lanzhou Foci Pharmaceutical Factory (Gansu)
'*Platycodon grandiflorum* Pills'
Jie Geng Wan is packaged in bottles of 200 pills.

TCM actions
Expels Phlegm and stops cough, eases the throat, aids in the discharge of pus, directs other herbs to the upper body.

Biomedical actions
Expectorant, antitussive.

INDICATIONS

- An important herb for sore throat from any cause, including Heat, Phlegm Heat and *yin* deficiency.
- For a variety of productive coughs from both excess and deficient causes.
- Helps to discharge pus. Used for suppurative disorders such as Lung abscess and throat abscess.
- Usually added to a targeting formula to enhance its throat easing or cough stopping effect.

Composition (each pill contains powdered)
Platycodon grandiflorum (jie geng, platycodon) 169mg

Combinations
- With **3.31 Zhi Sou Wan** for persistent cough following unresolved Wind invasion.
- With **3.15 Qing Qi Hua Tan Wan** for acute cough from severe Phlegm Heat.

Dosage and method of administration
8 pills three times daily, on an empty stomach.

Cautions and contraindications
Contraindicated for patients with hemoptysis. Caution in nauseous patients as the elevating nature of platycodon can cause Stomach *qi* to rise.

ENT

GMP **9.8 QING WEI SAN WAN**

清胃散丸

Available in the US, UK and Europe See Note 1, p.xxi

Lanzhou Foci Pharmaceutical Factory (Gansu)
'Stomach Cooling Pills'
Qing Wei San Wan is packaged in bottles of 200 pills.
Available as: Qing Wei San Teapills (PF)

TCM actions
Clears Heat and cools the Stomach, cools, nourishes and regulates the Blood.

Biomedical actions
Anti-inflammatory.

INDICATIONS

- Stomach Heat type oral disorders. Typical features include acute, chronic or recurrent inflammation, ulceration and pain of the oral cavity. Ulcers may be single, or more usually, multiple and tend to be concentrated on the gums or buccal cavity which, in severe cases, may coalesce into a large ulcerated area. The ulcers are burning and painful, with a yellow or white floor and a red, swollen margin. They are often initiated or aggravated by overindulgence in heating foods and substances, and alleviated somewhat by the application of ice.
- Toothache and facial pain or swelling from Heat in the Stomach channel.
- Epigastric pain from Stomach Heat.
- With the appropriate identifying features, this formula can assist in the treatment of biomedical conditions such as apthous stomatitis, post radiation stomatitis, ulcerative stomatitis, dental caries, periodontal disease, acute episode of Beçhet's syndrome or Reiter's syndrome, trigeminal neuralgia, glossitis and gingivitis.

Composition
Cimicifuga foetida (sheng ma, cimicifuga) 36%, *Coptis chinensis* (huang lian, coptis) 21.5%, *Paeonia suffruticosa* (mu dan pi, moutan) 18.5%, *Rehmannia glutinosa* (sheng di, raw rehmannia) 10.5%, *Angelica sinensis* (dang gui, chinese angelica) 10.5%

Combinations
- With **9.10 Sanjin Watermelon Frost** or **9.9 Superior Sore Throat Powder** topically on ulcerated areas.
- With **7.1 Liu Wei Di Huang Wan** for post radiation stomatitis.

Pattern identifying features

- **Stomach Heat/Fire**
- frequent hunger
- tendency to constipation or dry stools
- thirst, desire for cold drinks
- dry mouth and lips
- belching, heartburn, reflux

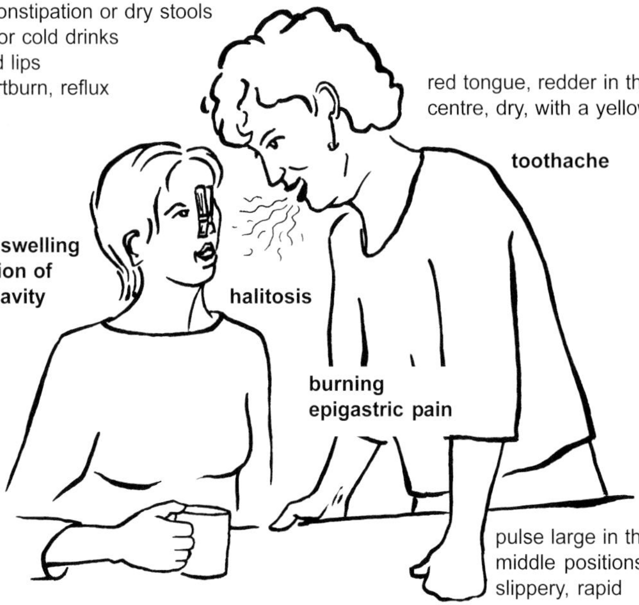

red tongue, redder in the centre, dry, with a yellow coat

toothache

redness, swelling & ulceration of the oral cavity

halitosis

burning epigastric pain

pulse large in the middle positions, slippery, rapid

- With **14.2 Huang Lian Su Tablets** for intense Stomach Fire with bleeding.
- With **10.21 Yan Hu Suo Wan** for facial pain from Heat.

Dosage and method of administration

The recommended dose for chronic or recurrent cases is 8-12 pills three times daily, however, in acute or severe disorders a higher dose is required to be effective, in general, 16-24 pills three times daily (or about 12 pills every two hours), on an empty stomach.

Cautions and contraindications

Contraindicated in oral disorders associated with deficient Heat or without excess Heat. In patients with constipation, *see* **14.10 Liang Ge Wan**.

ENT

9.9 SUPERIOR SORE THROAT POWDER

双料喉风散

(Shuang Liao Hou Feng San)
Meichou Medicine Factory (Guandong)
'Superior Throat Wind Powder'

Superior Sore Throat Powder is packaged in 2.2 gram bottles of powder to be puffed onto the affected area.

TCM actions

Clears Toxic Heat and Damp Heat from the throat and skin, relieves inflammation and stops pain.

Biomedical actions

Anti-inflammatory, vulnerary, promotes healing.

INDICATIONS

- Topical application for inflammation and Toxic Heat patterns of the mouth and throat, especially tonsillitis, pharyngitis, mouth ulcers and gingivitis. Can be applied with a clean finger to the mouths of babies and infants with mouth ulcers.
- Can be applied to other sites of infection and inflammation. Can be blown up the nose for acute sinusitis or into the ear for suppurative otitis media and externa. Applied topically to ulcerative dermatitis or other open suppurative lesions, as well as the lesions of shingles and other viral infections of the skin.

Composition

Coptis chinensis (huang lian, coptis) 30%, Borneol (bing pian) 25%, *Glycyrrhiza uralensis* (gan cao, licorice) 15%, *Sophora subprostrata* (shan dou gen, sophora) 15%, Bovine gallstone (niu huang) 5%, Pearl (zhen zhu) 5%, *Indigo Pulverata Levis* (qing dai, indigo) 5%

Combinations

- With **9.3 Peking Niu Huang Jie Du Pian, 9.4.1 Huang Lien Shang Ching Pien** or **14.6 Fu Fang Nan Ban Lan Gen** for tonsillitis with suppuration.
- With **3.1 Yin Chiao Chieh Tu Pien** for tonsillitis without suppuration.
- With **6.6 Long Dan Xie Gan Wan** or **9.3 Peking Niu Huang Jie Du Pian** for acute otitis.
- With **6.6 Long Dan Xie Gan Wan** for shingles from Damp Heat in the Liver.

Pattern identifying features

- **Toxic Heat in the throat & mouth**
- inflammation, suppuration and pain in the **mouth, throat**, ear, sinus or skin

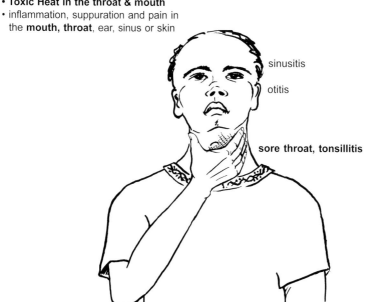

sinusitis

otitis

sore throat, tonsillitis

ulcerative dermatitis, shingles

ENT

Dosage and method of administration

Spray on to the affected area 3-5 times daily. For mouth ulcers in infants, the powder can be rubbed over the affected area with a clean finger. For suppurative skin lesions, wash the affected area with strong black tea first, then spray. For otitis, rinse the ear with 3% hydrogen peroxide solution first, then spray. Only used for a short time during the acute phase (usually 5-7 days).

Cautions and contraindications

None noted.

9.10 SANJIN WATERMELON FROST

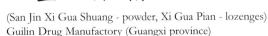

(San Jin Xi Gua Shuang - powder, Xi Gua Pian - lozenges)
Guilin Drug Manufactory (Guangxi province)
Sanjin Watermelon Frost is packaged either in powder form to be sprayed on directly or in blister packs of lozenges that can be dissolved slowly in the mouth.

TCM actions

Clears Heat and Toxic Heat from the mouth, stops pain and bleeding, promotes healing.

Biomedical actions

Anti-inflammatory, antibiotic, analgesic, soothing to mucous membranes, demulcent, vulnerary, promotes healing.

INDICATIONS

- Inflammation and/or ulceration of the mouth and throat, especially mouth ulcers, apthous stomatitis, gingivitis and toothache. Even though the powder is cooling, it can be used topically for ulcers associated with deficient and cold patterns. Also useful to soothe a sore throat, laryngitis and tonsillitis.
- Can be sprayed onto open wounds to stop bleeding.
- Topically for burns and scalds (*see also* **13.14 Ching Wan Hung** and **13.17 Xiao Yan Tang Shang Cream**), and insect stings and bites.

Composition (each gram of powder contains)

Citrullus vulgaris (xi gua shuang, watermelon frost) 510mg, *Fritillaria cirrhosa* (chuan bei, fritillaria) 150mg, *Belamcanda chinensis* (she gan, belamcanda) 60mg, *Sophora subprostrata* (shan dou gen, sophora) 60mg, *Siraitia grosvenorii* (luo han guo, momordica fruit) 60mg, *Scutellaria baicalensis* (huang qin, scute) 60mg, *Indigo Pulverata Levis* (qing dai, indigo) 40mg, *Dryobalanops camphora* (bing pian, borneol) 30mg, Menthol (bo he, mint oil) 30mg

Combinations

- With **9.3 Peking Niu Huang Jie Du Pian** for acute Hot type mouth ulcers or tonsillitis.
- With **8.1 Tian Wang Bu Xin Dan** for chronic or recurrent mouth ulcers from Heart and Kidney *yin* deficiency.

Pattern identifying features

- Toxic Heat in the mouth and throat
- inflammation, pain and ulceration of the
  mouth, gums, tongue and throat

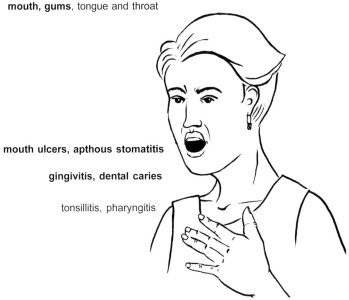

mouth ulcers, apthous stomatitis

gingivitis, dental caries

tonsillitis, pharyngitis

- With **2.13 Li Zhong Wan** or **2.14 Li Chung Yuen Medical Pills** for chronic mouth ulcers arising from Spleen *yang* deficiency.
- With **7.1 Liu Wei Di Huang Wan** or **3.33 Yang Yin Qing Fei Wan** for mouth ulcers as a result of chemotherapy or radiotherapy.
- With **12.7 Xiao Er Gan Mao Chong Ji** for acute febrile illness with mouth ulcers in babies.
- With **10.1 Yunnan Paiyao** (internally) for bleeding from trauma.

Dosage and method of administration

Powder: For problems in the throat and nose, spray a puff of powder directly onto the affected area. For gum disease the powder can be massaged into the area with a clean finger. Repeat every 2-4 hours. For burns and scalds mix some powder with an oil (olive or apricot) and apply to the affected area. For bleeding, wash away excess blood and spray on the affected area, bind lightly with sterile gauze.

Lozenges: For throat disorders and mouth ulcers, dissolve one tablet in the mouth at a time.

Cautions and contraindications

None noted.

ENT

9.11 QING YIN WAN

清音丸

Tong Ren Tang (Beijing)
'Pure Sound Pills'
Qing Yin Wan is packaged in 3 gram
honey pills sealed in wax balls, ten pills per box.

TCM actions

Clears Heat from the throat and Lungs, benefits the throat, generates fluids and saliva, moistens dryness and stops thirst.

Biomedical actions

Demulcent, soothes and lubricates the throat.

INDICATIONS

- Hoarse or raspy voice, or loss of voice following an upper respiratory tract infection, overuse or smoking. Much used for the voice strain or discomfort of singers, teachers and public speakers. May be useful in the prevention or alleviation of discomfort from polyps on the vocal cords.
- Recurrent or chronic soreness and irritation of the throat.
- Dryness of the oral cavity, either from a local pathology, the after effects of radiation treatment or systemic pathology such as diabetes and Sjögren's syndrome.

Composition (each pill contains powdered)

Pueraria lobata (ge gen, pueraria) 228mg, *Fritillaria cirrhosa* (chuan bei mu, fritillaria) 228mg, *Trichosanthes kirilowii* (tian hua fen, trichosanthes root) 114mg, *Terminalia chebula* (he zi rou, terminalia) 114mg, *Poria cocos* (fu ling, hoelen) 114mg, *Prunus mume* (wu mei, umeboshi plum) 114mg, *Glycyrrhiza uralensis* (gan cao, licorice), honey

Combinations

- With **3.33 Yang Yin Qing Fei Wan**, **7.5 Gu Ben Wan** or **3.35 Mai Wei Di Huang Wan** for chronic hoarse or raspy voice from Lung *yin* deficiency.
- With **3.38 Sheng Mai San Wan** for lingering throat problems following an upper respiratory tract infection.
- With a large dose of **7.2.2 Qi Ju Di Huang Wan**, or **9.22 Ming Mu Di Huang Wan** for systemic dryness (especially affecting the eyes and mouth) from Liver and Kidney *yin* deficiency (in conditions such as Sjögren's syndrome).

Pattern identifying features

- **Heat & dryness of the throat & Lungs**
- chronic Heat and dryness in the throat
- discomfort associated with nodules or polyps

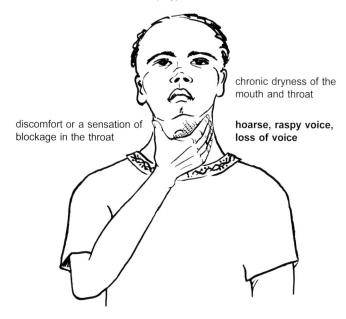

chronic dryness of the mouth and throat

discomfort or a sensation of blockage in the throat

hoarse, raspy voice, loss of voice

ENT

Dosage and method of administration

1-2 pills dissolved slowly in the mouth and run over the throat and vocal cords, two or three times daily.

Cautions and contraindications

Avoid spicy or excessively greasy foods and other obvious irritants, such as cigarettes and other inhaled substances, while using this formula.

GMP

9.12 BAN XIA HOU PO WAN

半夏厚朴丸

Lanzhou Foci Pharmaceutical Factory (Gansu)
'Pinellia and Magnolia Pills'
Ban Xia Hou Po Wan is packaged in bottles of 200 pills.
Available as: Pinellia and Magnolia Teapills (PF)

TCM actions

Invigorates *qi*, transforms Phlegm, directs *qi* downwards and dissipates nodules.

Biomedical actions

Sedative, mucolytic, anti-emetic.

INDICATIONS

- *Qi* and Phlegm stagnation affecting the throat and esophagus, known as 'Plum Stone *qi*' (also known as Plum Stone throat). The characteristic feature of Plum Stone *qi* is the sensation that something is lodged in the throat and it can neither be swallowed nor cleared. The sensation has an emotional component, appearing and disappearing in concert with the emotional state of the patient. The pattern is associated with dysfunction of the Liver and Spleen. Typically, Liver *qi* stagnation invades and weakens the Spleen creating the conditions for accumulation of Dampness and Phlegm, which are then carried via the Liver channel to catch in the throat. The *qi* stagnation may have its roots in an inability to express or vocalise feelings of anger or frustration–this especially affects the area of the larynx and throat. Similarly, difficulty in accepting (or swallowing) change or a new situation can create *qi* stagnation in the throat. Patients may be stressed and under pressure; they may be fed up with various elements of their lives–'I can't swallow any more!'.
- With the appropriate identifying features, this formula can be used to treat biomedical conditions such as globus hystericus, neurosis, assertiveness issues, anxiety, esophageal spasm, chronic laryngitis or pharyngitis.

Composition

Poria cocos (fu ling, hoelen) 30%, *Pinellia ternata* (jiang ban xia, ginger processed pinellia) 20%, *Magnolia officinalis* (hou po, magnolia bark) 20%, *Perilla frutescens* (zi su ye, perilla leaf) 15%, *Zingiber officinale* (sheng jiang, ginger) 15%

Pattern identifying features

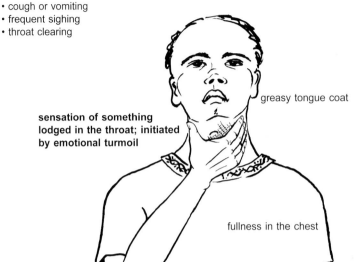

- *Qi* & **Phlegm stagnation**
- cough or vomiting
- frequent sighing
- throat clearing

sensation of something lodged in the throat; initiated by emotional turmoil

greasy tongue coat

fullness in the chest

wiry, slippery pulse

Combinations
- With **6.3 Chai Hu Shu Gan Wan** or **6.2 Si Ni San Wan** for relatively severe *qi* stagnation.
- With **2.22 Er Chen Wan** for relatively predominant Phlegm.

Dosage and method of administration
8-12 pills three times daily on an empty stomach. The dose may be spread out, or two lots of 12-18 pills may be taken, morning and evening. In severe cases or the early stages of treatment (the first few weeks), a 50% increase in dose may be used, then reduced as the treatment takes effect.

Cautions and contraindications
Contraindicated in *yin* deficiency and dryness patterns.

ENT

9.13 PE MIN KAN WAN

鼻敏感丸

(Bi Min Gan Wan)
Guandong Shaoqing Pharmaceutical Factory
'Nasal Allergy Pills'
Pi Min Kan Wan is packaged in bottles of 50 pills.

TCM actions
Dispels Wind, dries Dampness, unblocks the nasal passages.

Biomedical actions
Anti-inflammatory, mucolytic.

INDICATIONS

- Allergic rhinitis, hayfever, perennial rhinitis. This formula is basically symptomatic, and used for acute attacks of sneezing, nasal congestion and discharge with non specific heat or cold signs, that is, acute Wind in the nasal passages.

Composition
Magnolia liliflora (xin yi hua, magnolia flower), *Xanthium sibiricum* (cang er zi, xanthium), *Paeonia suffruticosa* (mu dan pi, moutan), *Agastache rugosa* (huo xiang, agastache), *Schizonepeta tenuifolia* (jing jie, schizonepeta), *Angelica dahurica* (bai zhi, angelica)

Combinations
- With **7.9 Fu Gui Ba Wei Wan**, **4.11 Ba Ji Yin Yang Wan** or **7.10 You Gui Wan** for patients with a lifetime history of allergic rhinitis (indicating a congenital Lung and Kidney *qi* or *yang* weakness). Add **7.11 Deer Velvet** or **7.12 Lu Rong Jiao** for *jing* deficiency patterns.
- With **7.23 Yu Ping Feng Wan** for *wei qi* deficiency.
- With **2.11 Bu Zhong Yi Qi Wan** for failure of Spleen *qi* to rise to the nasal mucous membranes, with chronic recurrent allergy and weak immunity.

Pattern identifying features

- **Wind in the nasal passages**
- **sneezing**
- hypersensitive mucous
  membranes

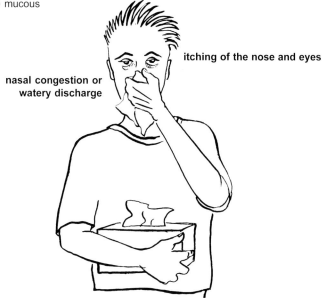

itching of the nose and eyes

**nasal congestion or
watery discharge**

Dosage and method of administration

3 pills three times daily, on an empty stomach. In severe cases the dose may be increased by 50%. For chronic cases, the dose should be reduced as the patient improves, to a level that maintains a clear airway. For chronic cases some weeks of treatment may be necessary. Better and faster results are obtained when combined with a sinus wash. Generally not used for children.

Cautions and contraindications

9.13 Pe Min Kan Wan is quite drying and may dry out the nasal mucous membranes excessively in some patients. May occasionally cause headache or nausea (xanthium is slightly toxic).

ENT

9.14 BI YE NING CAPSULE

鼻咽宁

(Bi Yan Ning)
Guangxi Medicines and Health Corporation (Guangxi)
'Calm the Nose and Throat'
Bi Ye Ning Capsule is packaged in bottles of 30 capsules.

TCM actions
Clears Heat, unblocks the nasal passages, reduces swelling
and stops pain.

Biomedical actions
Anti-inflammatory, mucolytic, antibacterial.

INDICATIONS

• Heat or Phlegm Heat accumulation in the nose and sinuses. Similar in action to
9.15 Pe Min Kan Wan (Nasal Clear), but this formula is cooler and slightly
stronger. Used for acute and chronic sinusitis and rhinitis. Particularly good for
chronic and stubborn sinus congestion with Heat signs.

Composition
Xanthium sibiricum (cang er zi, xanthium), *Magnolia liliflora* (xin yi hua, magnolia
flower), *Suis domesticus* (zhu dan zhi, pig bile), *Centipeda minima* (e bu shi cao,
centipeda), *Cryptotympana atrata* (chan tui, cicada shell), *Agastache rugosa* (huo xiang,
agastache), Borneol (bing pian), *Scutellaria baicalensis* (huang qin, scute), *Angelica
sinensis* (dang gui, chinese angelica), *Astragalus membranaceous* (huang qi, astragalus)

Combinations
• With **6.5 Jia Wei Xiao Yao Wan** for sinus congestion or sinusitis which is initiated
or aggravated by stress. Continue the **6.5 Jia Wei Xiao Yao Wan** after the sinus
has resolved to prevent recurrence.
• With **6.6 Long Dan Xie Gan Wan** for acute sinus infection of a Liver Fire type.
• With **3.16 Ching Fei Yi Huo Pien** or **9.3 Peking Niu Huang Jie Du Pian** for
acute sinusitis.
• With **2.18 Bao He Wan** for chronic Phlegm Heat in the sinuses associated with
food allergies or intolerances. The sinus congestion is worse with certain foods,
especially alcohol and rich or greasy foods.

Pattern identifying features

• **Heat, Phlegm Heat in the sinuses**

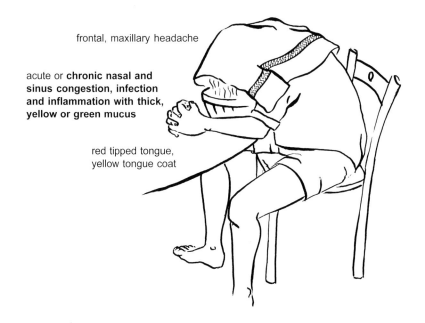

frontal, maxillary headache

acute or **chronic nasal and sinus congestion, infection and inflammation with thick, yellow or green mucus**

red tipped tongue, yellow tongue coat

• The long term results of sinus treatments are definitely improved by combining any herbal or acupuncture treatment with regular rinsing of the nasal cavity and sinuses with warm salty water.

Dosage and method of administration

2 capsules three times daily, on an empty stomach. In severe cases the dose may be increased by 50%. For chronic cases, the dose should be reduced as the patient improves, to a level that maintains a clear airway. For chronic cases some weeks of treatment may be necessary. Better and faster results are obtained when combined with a sinus wash. Generally not used for children.

Cautions and contraindications

Only used when there is coloured mucus or chronic congestion. **9.14 Bi Ye Ning Capsule** is quite drying and excess use, or use unmodified in between episodes of sinus, can dry out the mucous membranes. May occasionally cause headache or nausea (xanthium is slightly toxic).

ENT

9.15 PE MIN KAN WAN (Nasal Clear)

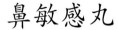

(Bi Min Gan Wan)
Wild Plants Research Centre, PRC
'Nasal Allergy Pills'
Pi Min Kan Wan is packaged in bottles of 50 pills.

TCM actions
Clears Heat, unblocks the nasal passages, reduces swelling and stops pain.

Biomedical actions
Anti-inflammatory, antibacterial, mucolytic.

INDICATIONS

- Acute and chronic sinusitis and rhinitis. Particularly good for chronic and stubborn sinus congestion with Heat signs. The nasal mucus will be sticky, yellow or green and hard to eliminate, or the patient may simply be more or less permanently congested.

Composition
Scutellaria baicalensis (huang qin, scute) 26%, *Xanthium sibiricun* (cang er zi, xanthium) 25%, *Agastache rugosa* (huo xiang, agastache) 25%, *Epates australis* (e bu shi cao, centipeda) 14%, *Angelica sinensis* (dang gui, chinese angelica) 10%

Dosage and method of administration
2-3 pills three times daily on an empty stomach. In acute or severe cases the dose may be increased by 50%. For chronic cases, the dose should be reduced after the first few weeks or as the patient improves, to a level that maintains a clear airway. For chronic cases some months of treatment are usually necessary. Better and faster results are obtained when combined with a sinus wash and constitutional formula. Generally not used for children.

Cautions and contraindications
Only used when there is coloured mucus or chronic congestion. **9.15 Pe Min Kan Wan** is quite drying and excessive use or use alone between episodes of sinus, can dry out the mucous membranes. May occasionally cause headache or nausea (xanthium is slightly toxic).

9.16 HAY FEVER TABLET

鼻敏感片

(Bi Min Gan Pian)
Jing Xian Pharmaceutical Co. (Guangzhou)
'Nasal Allergy Pills'
Hay Fever Tablets are packaged in bottles of 60 pills.

HAY FEVER
TABLET

AUST L 76471
60 TABLETS

MADE IN CHINA

TCM actions
Clears Heat, unblocks the nasal passages, reduces swelling and stops pain.

Biomedical actions
Anti-inflammatory, antibacterial, mucolytic.

INDICATIONS

- Acute and chronic sinusitis and rhinitis with Heat signs. The nasal mucus will be sticky, yellow or green and hard to eliminate, or the patient may simply be more or less permanently congested.

Composition (each tablet contains extracts equivalent to dry)
Lonicera japonica (jin yin hua, honeysuckle) 830mg, *Xanthium sibiricum* (cang er zi, xanthium) 830mg, *Chrysanthemum indicum* (ye ju hua, wild chrysanthemum) 415mg, *Angelica dahurica* (bai zhi, angelica) 415mg, *Centipeda minima* (e bu shi cao, centipeda) 332mg, *Mentha haplocalycis* (bo he, mint) 83mg

Dosage and method of administration
3-5 tablets, three times daily on an empty stomach. For chronic cases, the dose should be reduced after the first few weeks or as the patient improves, to a level that maintains a clear airway. For chronic cases some months of treatment are usually necessary. Better and faster results are obtained when combined with a sinus wash and constitutional formula. Generally not used for children.

Cautions and contraindications
Only used when there is coloured mucus or chronic congestion. **9.16 Hay Fever Tablets** are quite drying and excessive use or use alone between episodes of sinus, can dry out the mucous membranes. May occasionally cause headache or nausea (xanthium is slightly toxic).

ENT

9.17 QIAN BAI BI YAN PIAN

千柏鼻炎片

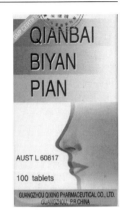

Guangzhou Qixing Pharmaceutical Co. (Guangzhou)
'*Senecio and Selaginella* Sinusitis Pills'
Qian Bai Bi Yan Pian is packaged in bottles of 30 capsules.

TCM actions
Dispels Wind, clears Toxic Heat, cools the Liver, dries Phlegm Damp, unblocks the nasal passages, stops pain.

Biomedical actions
Anti-inflammatory, analgesic, antibacterial, mild laxative.

INDICATIONS

• Heat in the sinuses and nasal cavity. Used for acute and chronic sinusitis and rhinitis, with nasal and sinus congestion, sinus pain and headaches. This formula is focused primarily on the pain and inflammation associated with sinus congestion. Even though primarily targeted at Heat patterns, it can be combined with appropriate targeting formulae to treat sinus pain and frontal headaches from Cold or thermally neutral patterns.

Composition (each tablet contains extracts equivalent to dry)
Senecio scandens (qian li guang, senecio) 140mg, *Selaginella tamariscana* (juan bai, selaginella) 100mg, *Notopterygium incisum* (qiang huo, notopterygium) 76mg, *Ligusticum sinense* (gao ben, ligusticum) 53.6mg, *Angelica dahurica* (bai zhi, angelica) 50.8mg, *Cassia tora* (jue ming zi, cassia seed) 23mg

Combinations
• With **6.5 Jia Wei Xiao Yao Wan** for sinus congestion and pain which is initiated or aggravated by stress.
• With **6.6 Long Dan Xie Gan Wan** for acute sinus infection of a Liver Fire type.
• With **3.15 Qing Qi Hua Tan Wan** for chronic Phlegm Heat congestion in the sinuses.
• With **3.9 Chuan Xiong Cha Tiao Wan** for acute frontal headaches from Wind Cold congesting the sinuses.
• With **2.9 Xiang Sha Liu Jun Wan** for chronic sinus congestion and frontal headaches associated with Spleen *qi* deficiency and Phlegm accumulation.

Pattern identifying features

- **Heat, Phlegm Heat in the sinuses**

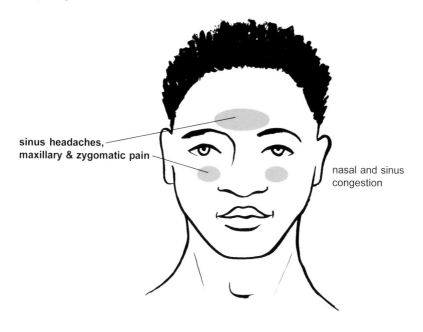

sinus headaches,
maxillary & zygomatic pain

nasal and sinus
congestion

ENT

- The long term results of sinus treatments are definitely improved by combining any herbal or acupuncture treatment with regular rinsing of the nasal cavity and sinuses with warm salty water.

Dosage and method of administration
4 tablets three times daily on an empty stomach. After the condition begins to improve, the dose can be decreased to maintenance.

Cautions and contraindications
None noted.

9.18 XIN YI SAN

辛夷散

Lanzhou Foci Pharmaceutical Factory (Gansu)
'Magnolia Flower Powder'
Xin Yi San is packaged in bottles of 200 pills.
Also available as: Magnolia Flower Teapills (PF)

TCM actions
Dispels Wind Cold, dries Dampness, unblocks the nasal passages and stops pain.

Biomedical actions
Diaphoretic, anti-inflammatory, analgesic.

INDICATIONS

• Wind Cold invasion or persistent Cold lingering in the sinus cavity causing acute or chronic sinus congestion, sinusitis or rhinitis. Particularly good for chronic and stubborn sinus congestion with no heat signs, or with white or watery nasal discharge and postnasal drip.
• Sinus or frontal headaches.

Composition (each pill contains powdered)
Magnolia liliflora (xin yi hua, magnolia flower) 25.2mg, *Atractylodes macrocephala* (bai zhu, atractylodes) 21.6mg, *Ledebouriella divaricata* (fang feng, siler) 18mg, *Cimicifuga heraclefolia* (sheng ma, cimicifuga) 18mg, *Clematis armandii* (mu tong, akebia) 18mg, *Ligusticum wallici* (chuan xiong, cnidium) 18mg, *Asarum heterotropoides* (xi xin, asarum) 16.2mg, *Ligusticum sinense* (gao ben, ligusticum) 16.2mg, *Glycyrrhiza uralensis* (gan cao, licorice) 14.4mg, *Notopterygium incisum* (qiang huo, notopterygium) 14.4mg

Combinations
• With **3.9 Chuan Xiong Cha Tiao Wan** for acute frontal headache and sinus congestion from a Wind Cold attack.
• With **2.9 Xiang Sha Liu Jun Wan** for chronic sinus congestion from Phlegm Damp accumulation in the sinuses.
• With **7.23 Yu Ping Feng Wan** for perennial rhinitis and sinusitis from *wei qi* deficiency.

Pattern identifying features

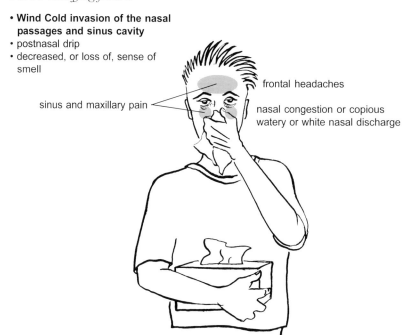

- **Wind Cold invasion of the nasal passages and sinus cavity**
- postnasal drip
- decreased, or loss of, sense of smell

sinus and maxillary pain

frontal headaches

nasal congestion or copious watery or white nasal discharge

- With **4.11 Ba Ji Yin Yang Wan** for lifetime atopic rhinitis from congenital deficiency of Lung and Kidney *qi*.
- The long term results of sinus treatments are definitely improved by combining any herbal or acupuncture treatment with regular rinsing of the nasal cavity and sinuses with warm salty water.

ENT

Dosage and method of administration

The recommended dose is 8-15 pills three times daily, on an empty stomach. Once the symptoms are controlled, the dose can be reduced until a comfortable maintenance level is reached.

Cautions and contraindications

Contraindicated in sinus congestion from Heat.

GMP

9.19 CANG ER ZI WAN

 苍耳子丸

Available in the US, UK and Europe See Note 1, p.xxi

Lanzhou Foci Pharmaceutical Factory (Gansu)
'*Xanthium sibiricum* Pills'
Cang Er Zi Wan is packaged in bottles of 200 pills.
Available as: Upper Chamber Teapills (PF)

TCM actions
Dispels Wind, clears Heat, unblocks the nasal passages.

Biomedical actions
Diaphoretic, anti-inflammatory, analgesic.

INDICATIONS

- Wind Heat lingering in the nose and sinuses, causing sinus and nasal congestion, pain and discharge. This pattern typically follows an acute invasion of Wind Heat (or Cold that transforms into Heat) that congeals physiological fluids to Phlegm Heat or stirs up existing Phlegm. Although **9.19 Cang Er Zi Wan** is best for Heat patterns, it can be combined with other formulae not specifically for Heat when enhanced nasal and sinus decongestion is desired.
- With the appropriate identifying features, this formula may be used to treat conditions such as acute and chronic sinusitis and rhinitis, perennial and allergic rhinitis.

Composition
Xanthium sibiricum (cang er zi, xanthium) 34%, *Angelica dahurica* (bai zhi, angelica) 34%, *Magnolia liliflora* (xin yi hua, magnolia flower) 19%, *Mentha arvensis* (bo he, mint) 10%

Combinations
- With **2.11 Bu Zhong Yi Qi Wan** for chronic sinus congestion from retention of Wind in a patient with *qi* deficiency.
- With **7.1.1 Liu Wei Di Huang Wan** for sinus congestion in patients with a tendency to *yin* deficiency.
- With **6.5 Jia Wei Xiao Yao Wan** for sinus congestion or sinusitis which is initiated or aggravated by stress. Continue the **6.5 Jia Wei Xiao Yao Wan** after the sinus has resolved to prevent recurrence.
- With **3.16 Ching Fei Yi Huo Pien** or **9.3 Peking Niu Huang Jie Du Pian** for acute sinusitis.

Pattern identifying features

- **Wind Heat & Phlegm Heat in the sinuses**
- reduction or loss of sense of smell, nasal voice
- inflamed and swollen nasal mucous membranes
- cough with yellow sputum
- in the early stages there may be fever, or fever and chills
- thirst

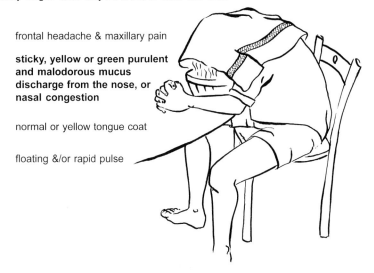

frontal headache & maxillary pain

**sticky, yellow or green purulent
and malodorous mucus
discharge from the nose, or
nasal congestion**

normal or yellow tongue coat

floating &/or rapid pulse

- With **2.18 Bao He Wan** for chronic Phlegm Heat in the sinuses associated with food allergies or intolerances. The sinus congestion is worse with certain foods, especially alcohol and rich or greasy foods.
- The long term results of sinus treatments are definitely improved by combining any herbal or acupuncture treatment with regular rinsing of the nasal cavity and sinuses with warm salty water.

Dosage and method of administration

8-12 pills three times daily on an empty stomach. The dose may be spread out, or two lots of 12-18 pills may be taken, morning and evening. In severe cases or during the early stages of treatment (the first few weeks), a 50% increase in dose may be used, then reduced as the treatment takes effect.

Cautions and contraindications

9.19 Cang Er Zi Wan is quite drying and excess use or use alone in between episodes of sinus, can dry out the mucous membranes. May occasionally cause headache or nausea (xanthium is slightly toxic).

ENT

9.20 HAY FEVER RELIEVING TEA

过敏鼻炎茶

(Guo Min Bi Yan Cha)
Tong Ren Tang (Beijing)
Hay Fever Relieving Tea is packaged
in boxes of 20 teabags.

TCM actions
Clears Phlegm Heat, dries Dampness
and transforms Phlegm, stops cough

Biomedical actions
Decongestant, expectorant, antitussive.

INDICATIONS

- Sinus and nasal congestion or sticky, yellow nasal discharge associated with Phlegm Heat congestion in the sinus cavity.
- Cough and wheezing from acute and chronic Phlegm Heat in the Lungs.
- With the appropriate identifying features, this formula can assist in the treatment of biomedical conditions such as acute and chronic sinusitis, hayfever, bronchitis, bronchiectasis, mild pneumonia and bronchial asthma.

Composition (each teabag [3g] contains extracts equivalent to dry)
Fritillaria thunbergii (zhe bei mu, fritillaria) 1.23g, *Scutellaria baicalensis* (huang qin, scute) 1.05g, *Eriobotrya japonica* (pi pa ye, loquat leaf) 877mg, *Cynanchum stauntonii* (bai qian, cynanchum) 877mg, *Morus alba* (sang bai pi, mulberry root bark) 877mg, *Perilla frutescens* (zi su ye, perilla) 877mg, *Glycyrrhiza uralensis* (gan cao, licorice) 877mg, *Poria cocos* (fu ling, hoelen) 877mg, *Citrus reticulata* (chen pi, citrus) 702mg, *Peucedanum praeruptorum* (qian hu, peucedanum) 526mg, *Angelica dahurica* (bai zhi, angelica) 351mg, *Xanthium sibiricun* (cang er zi, xanthium) 351mg, *Pinellia ternata* (ban xia, pinellia) 526mg, *Ephedra sinica* (ma huang, ephedra) 3mg

Combinations
- With **9.17 Qian Bai Bi Yan Pian** for severe cases with frontal headache.
- The long term results of sinus treatments are definitely improved by combining any herbal or acupuncture treatment with regular rinsing of the nasal cavity and sinuses with warm salty water.

Pattern identifying features

- **Phlegm Heat accumulation in the Lung system**
- sinus congestion
- sneezing

frontal headache, sinus pain

sticky, white or yellow nasal discharge

greasy, yellow tongue coat

productive cough, with sticky, yellow or green sputum

Dosage and method of administration

The adult dose is 1-2 teabags steeped for 5 minutes in a cup of boiling water. More water may be added to the teabag until all taste is gone. In severe cases, up to six teabags may be used daily.

Cautions and contraindications

Not suitable for Wind Cold type cough or sinus congestion, with thin watery Phlegm, or cough from *yin* deficiency. Caution in patients with hypertension. May cause or aggravate insomnia in some patients due to presence of ephedra.

9.21 MING MU SHANG CHING PIEN

明目上清片

(Ming Mu Shang Qing Pian)
Tianjin Drug Manufactory (Shandong)
'Brighten the Eyes, Clear (Heat from) the
Upper (body) Pills'
Ming Mu Shang Ching Pien is packaged
in vials of eight uncoated pills, twelve vials
per box.

TCM actions
Clears Heat and Damp Heat from the Liver and Liver channel, dispels Wind Heat,
brightens the eyes, benefits vision.

Biomedical action
Anti-inflammatory, antibiotic, diuretic.

INDICATIONS

- Wind Heat, Damp Heat, Toxic Heat, Heat in the Liver channel or Liver *yang*
  rising type inflammatory eye disorders. These patterns are generally acute and
  may be associated with infection, eyestrain, stress and diet (especially alcohol).
  They may be diagnosed as biomedical conditions such as acute conjunctivitis,
  blepharitis, uveitis, glaucoma, dacryocystitis, urticaria, hordeolum, stye, pterygia
  and orbital cellulitis.
- Also useful for other infections of the head, including skin, ear and oral infection
  and inflammation from Liver and Gallbladder Heat, Damp Heat or Heart Fire.
- Heat or Damp Heat type *lin* syndrome, or Heart Fire invading the Small Intestine.
  Useful for urinary tract infection, cystitis, urethritis or prostatitis from Heat.
- Damp Heat or Toxic Heat in the skin, causing itchy, inflamed or suppurative
  skin disorders such as boils, acne, eczema, urticaria and dermatitis.

Composition (each tablet contains extract equivalent to dry)
Gardenia florida (shan zhi zi, gardenia) 2.22g, *Angelica polymorpha* (dang gui, chinese
angelica) 909mg, *Chrysanthemum sinense* (ju hua, chrysanthemum flower) 443mg,
Forsythia suspensa (lian qiao, forsythia) 369mg, *Tribulus terrestris* (bai ji li, tribulus)
296mg, *Lophatherum elatum* (dan zhu ye, bamboo leaves) 296mg, *Ophiopogon japonicus*
(mai dong, ophiopogon) 296mg, *Coptis chinensis* (huang lian, coptis) 273mg, *Scutellaria
baicalensis* (huang qin, scute) 273mg, *Plantago asiatica* (che qian zi, plantago) 182mg,
Rheum palmatum (da huang, rhubarb root) 36mg, Calcium sulphate 30mg

Pattern identifying features

- **Wind Heat, Liver Heat, Damp
  Heat or Toxic Heat eye disorders**
- fever

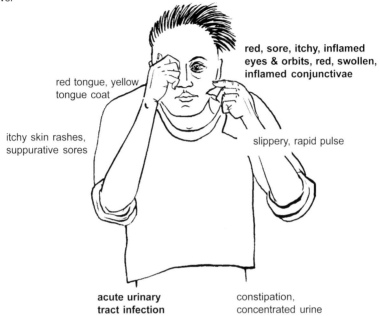

red tongue, yellow
tongue coat

**red, sore, itchy, inflamed
eyes & orbits, red, swollen,
inflamed conjunctivae**

itchy skin rashes,
suppurative sores

slippery, rapid pulse

**acute urinary
tract infection**

constipation,
concentrated urine

Combinations
- With **13.19 Pearl Powder** for cataracts or inflamed pterygium from Liver Fire.
- With **7.2 Qi Ju Di Huang Wan** for red, sore, irritated eyes from Liver *yin* deficiency and *yang* rising.
- With **6.6 Long Dan Xie Gan Wan** for acute exacerbation of glaucoma from Liver Fire.

Dosage and method of administration
4-8 pills twice daily. In acute or severe cases, take one vial every 2-3 hours. May cause diarrhea.

Cautions and contraindications
Contraindicated during pregnancy.

9.22 MING MU DI HUANG WAN
明目地黄丸

Lanzhou Foci Pharmaceutical Factory (Gansu)
'Rehmannia Pills to Brighten the Eyes'
Ming Mu Di Huang Wan is packaged in bottles of 200 pills.
Also available as: Ming Mu Di Huang Teapills (PF)

TCM actions
Supplements Liver and Kidney *yin* and Blood, restrains
Liver *yang*, brightens the eyes and improves vision.

Biomedical actions
Demulcent febrifuge, hematinic, hypoglycemic,
antihypertensive, improves kidney function.

INDICATIONS

• Liver and Kidney *yin* and Blood deficiency type chronic visual and eye disorders.
These include weakness of vision, floaters, chronically sore dry irritated eyes,
bloodshot eyes, photophobia, excessive lacrimation, night blindness, opacity of
the vitreous humour, Sjögren's syndrome, keratitis sicca, non-acute glaucoma,
optic neuritis, retinitis, retinal degeneration, myopia and atrophy of the optic
nerve. May also be useful for strengthening the eyes in patients prone to
conjunctivitis when used in between episodes of infection, or degenerative visual
disorders.
• Dizziness, vertigo or hypertension from *yin* deficiency with *yang* rising.

Composition (each pill contains powdered)
Rehmannia glutinosa (shu di, processed rehmannia) 33.47mg, *Cornus officinalis* (shan
zhu yu, cornus) 17.08mg, *Dioscorea opposita* (shan yao, dioscorea) 12.25mg, *Poria cocos*
(fu ling, hoelen) 12.25mg, *Alisma orientalis* (ze xie, alisma) 12.25mg, *Paeonia suffruticosa*
(mu dan pi, moutan) 12.25mg, *Lycium barbarum* (gou qi zi, lycium fruit) 12.25mg,
Chrysanthemum morifolium (ju hua, chrysanthemum flower) 12.25mg, *Paeonia lactiflora*
(bai shao, white peony) 12.25mg, *Tribulus terrestris* (bai ji li, tribulus) 12.25mg, *Uncaria
rhyncophylla* (gou teng, gambir) 12.25mg, *Angelica polymorpha* (dang gui, chinese
angelica) 8.28mg, *Glycyrrhiza uralensis* (gan cao, licorice) 3.44mg

Combinations
• With **13.19 Pearl Powder** for cataracts.
• With **1.2 Si Wu Wan** for *yin* and Blood deficient eye disorders.

Pattern identifying features

- **Liver and Kidney *yin* and Blood deficiency visual disorders**
- heat, flushing, nightsweats
- vision worse with overuse of the eyes
- red, thread like capillaries in otherwise normal looking conjunctivae

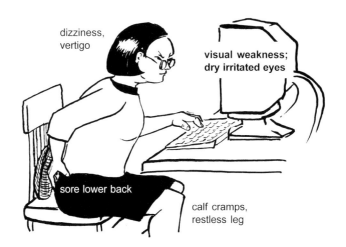

dizziness, vertigo

visual weakness; dry irritated eyes

sore lower back

calf cramps, restless leg

- With **15.4 Tian Ma Gou Teng Wan** for severe dizziness, vertigo or headaches from Liver *yin* deficiency with *yang* rising.
- With **15.7 Yang Yin Jiang Ya Wan** for severe or resistant hypertension from Liver *yin* deficiency with *yang* rising.
- With **9.11 Qing Yin Wan** or **7.21 American Ginseng Essence of Chicken** for the oral and ocular dryness associated with Sjögren's syndrome or other systemic patterns producing dryness of the mucous membranes.

Dosage and method of administration

8-12 pills three times daily before meals. The dose may be spread out, or two lots of 12-18 pills may be taken, morning and evening. In severe cases or during the early stages of treatment (the first few weeks), a 50% increase in dose may be used, then reduced as the treatment takes effect.

Cautions and contraindications

Not suitable for acute inflammatory eye disorders. Contraindicated during the early phase of acute illness such as colds and flu. Care should be taken in patients with a tendency to abdominal bloating, loose stools or mucus accumulation. This can usually be alleviated by taking the formula with a small dose (3-6 pills at the same time) of **2.18 Bao He Wan** or **2.9 Xiang Sha Liu Jun Wan**.

ENT

9.23 MING MU CAPSULE

明目丸

(Ming Mu Wan)
'Eye Brightening Capsules'
Jing Xian Pharmaceutical Co. (Guangzhou)
Ming Mu Capsule is packaged in bottles of 200 pills.
A similar formula is available as: Shi Hu Ye Guang Wan (PF)

TCM actions

Supplements the Liver and Kidneys, nourishes *yin* and Blood, clears Heat, brightens the eyes and improves vision.

Biomedical actions

Anti-inflammatory, improves kidney function, antihypertensive.

INDICATIONS

• Visual disorders associated with Liver and Kidney *yin* and Blood deficiency. This includes conditions such as loss of visual acuity, blurring vision following reading, eyestrain, photophobia, floaters, dry irritated eyes, excessive lacrimation and cataracts. Similar in scope and action to **9.22 Ming Mu Di Huang Wan**
• Hypertension associated with Liver *yin* deficiency with *yang* rising.

Composition (each capsule contains extracts equivalent to dry)

Rehmannia glutinosa (shu di, processed rehmannia) 440mg, *Dendrobium nobile* (shi hu, dendrobium) 440mg, *Paeonia lactiflora* (bai shao, white peony) 365mg, *Schizandra chinensis* (wu wei zi, schizandra) 365mg, *Cornus officinalis* (shan zhu yu, cornus) 260mg, *Chrysanthemum sinense* (ju hua, chrysanthemum flower) 125mg, *Lycium barbarum* (gou qi zi, lycium fruit) 80mg, *Cuscuta hygrophila* (tu su zi, cuscuta) 80mg, *Achyranthes bidentata* (niu xi, achyranthes) 80mg, *Astragalus complanatus* (sha yuan ji li, astragalus seed) 80mg, *Angelica polymorpha* (dang gui, chinese angelica) 80mg, *Lycium chinense* (di gu pi, lycium root bark) 80mg

Dosage and method of administration

3-4 capsules, three times daily on an empty stomach.

Cautions and contraindications

Not suitable for acute inflammatory eye disorders. Caution in patients with digestive weakness and Spleen deficiency.

10

Patent Medicines for Pain and Trauma

Trauma

10.1 Yunnan Paiyao
10.2 Raw Tienchi Tablets
10.3 Die Da Zhi Tong Capsule
10.4 Chin Gu Tie Shang Wan
10.5 Huo Luo Xiao Ling Wan

Wind Cold Damp *bi* syndrome

10.6 Juan Bi Wan
10.7 Qu Feng Zhen Tong Capsule
10.8 Xiao Huo Luo Dan

Wind Damp Heat *bi* syndrome

10.9 Xuan Bi Tang Wan
10.10 Guan Jie Yan Wan

Blood stagnation *bi* syndrome

10.11 Shu Jin Huo Xue Wan
10.12 Shen Tong Zhu Yu Wan

***Bi* syndrome with Kidney deficiency**

10.13 Da Huo Luo Dan
10.14 San Bi Wan
10.15 Du Huo Ji Sheng Wan
10.16.1 Zhuang Yao Jian Shen
  10.16.2 Zhuang Yao Jian Shen Tablet
10.17 Tong Luo Zhi Tong Tablet
10.18 Jian Bu Qiang Shen Wan
10.19 Kang Gu Zeng Sheng Pian

General

10.20 Tian Ma Tou Tong Capsule
10.21 Yan Hu Suo Zhi Tong Wan
10.22 Shao Yao Gan Cao Wan

Liniments and plasters

10.23 Zheng Gu Shui
10.24 Zheng Gu Ging
10.25 Die Da Tian Qi Yao Jiu
10.26 Min Jak Gosok
10.27 Zhi Tong You
10.28 Wong Lop Kong Medicated Oil
10.29 White Flower Embrocation
10.30 Po Sum On Medicated Oil
10.31 Trans Wood Lock Liniment
10.32 Die Da Jiu
10.33 Wood Lock Medicated Balm
10.34 Imada Red Flower Oil
10.35 Eagle Brand Medicated Oil
10.36 Kung Fu Oil
10.37 Tiger Balm
10.38 Plaster for Bruise & Analgesic
10.39 Die Da Feng Shi Plaster
10.40 Porous Capsicum Plaster
10.41 Gou Pi Gao

跌

打

风

湿

10.1 YUNNAN PAIYAO
云南白药

(Yun Nan Bai Yao)
Yunnan Paiyao Factory (Yunnan)
'White Powder from Yun Nan Province'

Yunnan Paiyao is packaged in two different forms, blister sheets of 16 x 250mg capsules, and small bottles of 4 grams loose powder. Both have a single peppercorn sized red pill reserved for serious hemorrhage and shock.

TCM actions
Stops bleeding, quickens Blood and disperses stagnant Blood.

Biomedical actions
Hemostatic, invigorates local circulation, analgesic.

INDICATIONS

- Bleeding. An important first aid remedy for all types of bleeding, regardless of etiology. Used to arrest internal and external bleeding from trauma, as well as conditions such as bleeding gastric ulcers and gums, hematemesis, hematuria, hemoptysis, epistaxis, rectal bleeding, bronchiectasis and purpura. Can be applied topically as well as taken internally for traumatic hemorrhage.
- Gynecological conditions with Blood stagnation or bleeding, including menorrhagia and dysmenorrhea from fibroids, amenorrhea, postpartum or post termination Blood stagnation and hemorrhage, placental retention and painful gynecological masses.
- Suppurative skin infections such as abscesses, boils, carbuncles and ulcers, both acute and chronic non-healing.
- May be useful in alleviating bleeding and pain associated with certain types of neoplasm, such as those of the bladder and prostate.
- Used post-operatively to reduce keloid scarring, arrest bleeding, accelerate hemolysis and promote healing (*see* Surgery and the use of patent medicines, in the glossary).

Composition (each capsule [250mg] contains)

Panax notoginseng (tian qi, tian qi ginseng) 99mg, *Arjuga reptans* (jin gu cao, common bugle) 42.08mg, *Dioscorea batatas* (shan yao, dioscorea) 32.92mg, *Dioscorea japonica* (chuan shan long, japanese dioscorea) 24.75mg, *Erodium stephanianum* (lao guan cao, cranebill) 17.82mg, *Diospyros kaki* (shi shu gen, persimmon root) 14.85mg, *Inula cappa* (bai niu dan, inula) 12.38mg, *Cinnamomum camphora* (zhang nao, camphor) 3.71mg

Pattern identifying features

- **all types of bleeding–**
  uterine, hematemesis,
  hemoptysis, rectal, etc.

localised bruising & pain from trauma;
damage to ligaments & tendons

suppurative sores

Note: The ingredient listed, supplied by the manufacturer on application for listing with the TGA, are those in the powder. The contents of the red pill remains undisclosed at the time of printing.

Combinations
- With **10.23 Zheng Gu Shui** rubbed externally for the bruising of traumatic injury.
- With **1.9 Gui Pi Wan** for uterine bleeding or menorrhagia of a deficient type.
- With **14.1 Huang Lian Jie Du Wan** for sudden bleeding due to Hot Blood.
- With **2.37 Huai Jiao Wan** or **2.38 Hua Zhi Ling Tablet** and **13.14 Ching Wan Hung** topically for painful bleeding hemorrhoids.
- With **1.16 Tao Hong Si Wu Wan** following dilatation and curette.

Dosage and method of administration
The recommended dose is 2 capsules four times daily; for children 2-5 years old half a capsule four times daily; for children 5-12 years old one capsule four times daily. In serious cases the dose can be safely doubled for a few days to a week. A capsule can be broken and the wound sprinkled with the powder, then held closed until bleeding ceases.

For bleeding take with water; for Blood stagnation take with a little alcohol such as vodka or sherry.

The red pill is reserved for serious wounds and is used for patients about to go into shock.

Cautions and contraindications
Contraindicated during pregnancy. Avoid broad beans, fish, crustaceans and sour and cold foods while using this product.

PAIN

GMP **10.2 RAW TIENCHI TABLETS**

生田七片

(Sheng Tian Qi Pian)
Yunnan Medicines & Health Products Corp. (Yunnan)
Tienchi Tablets are packaged in blister sheets, 36
tablets per box.
A similar product available as: Tian Qi Teapills (PF), Pseudoginseng Capsules (Raw)

TCM actions
Quickens Blood, disperses stagnant Blood and stops bleeding.

Biomedical actions
Hemostatic, dilates coronary arteries, lower cholesterol and triglycerides, improves microcirculation.

INDICATIONS

- Bleeding and stagnant Blood. Has the unique property of being able to arrest bleeding without causing blood stasis, and disperse Blood stagnation without causing potential bleeding problems. An important herb for a variety of traumatic and cardiovascular problems. The subject of considerable research in China, tian qi ginseng has been shown to dilate coronary arteries and stimulate new microcirculation thus improving cardiac function. It is also able to decrease blood lipids. May be used post surgically to improve healing.
- Used in large doses for a few days to a few weeks for hemorrhagic disorders and acute trauma with bruising and hemorrhage, both internally and topically.
- Used in small doses over long periods of time for the prevention and treatment of ischemic cardiovascular and cerebrovascular disease, transient ischemic attacks, angina, hyperlipidemia, hypertension, retinal hemorrhage, sequelae of cerebrovascular hemorrhage, hemiplegia, thrombophlebitis and deep venous thrombosis.

Composition (each tablet contains)
Panax notoginseng (tian qi, tian qi ginseng) 500mg

Dosage and method of administration
Cardiovascular and cerebrovascular disease, hyperlipidemia: 2-4 tablets, 3 times daily. Bleeding and trauma: 4-8 tablets three times daily. The crushed tablet can be applied topically to a bleeding wound.

Cautions and contraindications
Contraindicated during pregnancy.

10.3 DIE DA ZHI TONG CAPSULE

跌打止痛丸

(Die Da Zhi Tong Wan)
Jing Xian Pharmaceutical Co. (Guangzhou)
'Trauma and Analgesic Pills'
Die Da Zhi Tong Capsules are packaged in bottles of 36
capsules.

TCM actions

Invigorates circulation of *qi* and Blood, disperses stagnant
Blood, alleviates swelling and stops pain.

Biomedical actions

Analgesic, dissipates bruising, enhances circulation, promotes healing.

INDICATIONS

- Pain, swelling, bruising and soft tissue damage from traumatic injury. Usually only used for a few weeks to disperse stagnant Blood. In the case of bone fractures, this formula can be followed by **1.29 Bu Gai Zhuang Gu Capsule** or similar once bruising has subsided. This is quite a strong Blood invigorating formula, and in conjunction with a topical liniment can significantly alleviate pain and swelling, and accelerate healing and recovery.

Composition (each capsule contains)

Salvia miltiorrhiza (dan shen, salvia) 90mg, *Paeonia lactiflora* (bai shao, white peony) 78mg, *Panax notoginseng* (tian qi, tian qi ginseng) 50mg, *Angelica polymorpha* (dang gui, chinese angelica) 35mg, *Corydalis turtschaninovii* (yan hu suo, corydalis) 35mg, *Dalbergia odorifera* (jiang xiang, dalbergia wood) 35mg, *Sparganium stoloniferum* (san leng, sparganium) 32mg, *Curcuma zedoaria* (e zhu, curcuma) 32mg, *Boswellia carterii* (ru xiang, frankincense) 25mg, *Rheum officinale* (da huang, rhubarb root) 15mg

Combinations

- With **10.23 Zheng Gu Shui** or **10.32 Die Da Jiu** topically for bruising and pain.

Dosage and method of administration

2-3 capsules, three times daily on an empty stomach. May cause diarrhea.

Cautions and contraindications

Contraindicated during pregnancy and where there is continuing bleeding or open wounds. Caution in patients who are also taking anticoagulant therapy (aspirin, warfarin, coumarin) as clotting time can be significantly reduced.

PAIN

10.4 CHIN GU TIE SHANG WAN

筋骨跌伤丸

(Jin Gu Die Shang Wan)
Tianjin Lerentang Pharmaceutical Factory
'Tendon and Bone Trauma Pills'
Chin Gu Tie Shang Wan is packaged in bottles of 120 pills.
A similar formula is available as: Great Mender Teapills (PF)

TCM actions
Invigorates circulation of *qi* and quickens Blood,
disperses stagnant Blood, alleviates swelling and stops
pain.

Biomedical actions
Analgesic, dissipates bruising, enhances circulation, promotes healing.

INDICATIONS

- Pain, swelling, spasm and bruising from traumatic injury. May be used for soft
  tissue injury, sprains, strains, ligamentous damage, bruising and fracture.
- Especially good in encouraging the healing of slow to heal fractures. Similar in
  most respects to **10.3 Die Da Zhi Tong Capsule** but more suited to prolonged
  use and better for bony lesions.
- Also used for internal Blood stagnation patterns with pain, including chest and
  epigastric pain, dysmenorrhea and pelvic pain.
- May be useful for chronic skin diseases with purple or dark discoloration from
  Blood stagnation, including chronic abscesses and ulcers, psoriasis and rosacea.

Composition (each pill contains powdered)
Panax notoginseng (tian qi, tian qi ginseng) 30mg, *Angelica polymorpha* (dang gui, chinese
angelica) 22.5mg, *Boswellia carterii* (ru xiang, frankincense) 22.5mg, *Daemonorops draco*
(xue jie, dragons blood) 22.5mg, *Dipsacus asper* (xu duan, dipsacus) 22.5mg, *Commiphora
myrhha* (mo yao, myrrh) 15mg, *Carthamus tinctorius* (hong hua, carthamus) 15mg

Combinations
- With **10.23 Zheng Gu Shui** topically for the bruising and pain of traumatic injury.
- With **10.11 Shu Jin Huo Xue Wan** or **5.1 Xue Fu Zhu Yu Wan** for chronic non-
  healing or slow healing fractures in patients with significant Blood stagnation.
  These combinations are also useful for severe pain in the joints and muscles from
  Blood stagnation following trauma.

Pattern identifying features

- **Blood stagnation; bruising, sprains & fractures from traumatic injury**

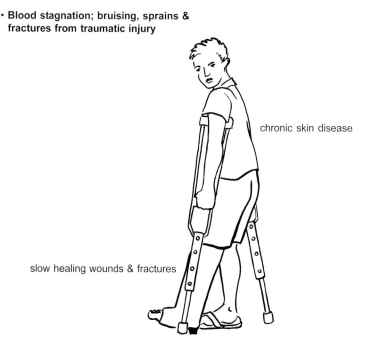

chronic skin disease

slow healing wounds & fractures

- With **1.29 Bu Gai Zhuang Gu Capsule** for slow healing fractures with minor residual Blood stasis.
- With **7.16.1 Shi Quan Da Bu Wan** for chronic non-healing of fractures in patients with *qi* and Blood deficiency.
- With **1.15 Tong Jing Wan**, **1.13 Woo Garm Yuen Medical Pills** or **1.18 Shao Fu Zhu Yu Wan** for severe dysmenorrhea.
- With **13.2 Xiao Feng Wan** for bleeding or chronic non-healing eczema and dermatitis.

Dosage and method of administration

8 pills three times daily on an empty stomach. The dose may be spread out, or two lots of 12 pills may be taken, morning and evening.

Cautions and contraindications

Contraindicated during pregnancy.

PAIN

GMP **10.5 HUO LUO XIAO LING WAN**

 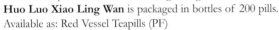 活络效灵丸

Lanzhou Foci Pharmaceutical Factory (Gansu)
'Miraculously Effective Collateral Regulating Pill'
Huo Luo Xiao Ling Wan is packaged in bottles of 200 pills.
Available as: Red Vessel Teapills (PF)

Available in the US, UK and Europe See Note 1, p.xxi

TCM actions
Invigorates circulation of *qi* and quickens Blood, disperses stagnant Blood, alleviates swelling and stops pain.

Biomedical actions
Analgesic, dissipates bruising, enhances circulation, promotes healing.

INDICATIONS

- *Qi* and Blood stagnation patterns with pain. This formula is effective for both acute and chronic Blood stagnation type pain, regardless of the location. Being a versatile formula, it can be added to other targeting formulae when an extra analgesic or Blood stasis dispersing action is desired.
- Fixed and painful abdominal masses.
- Purple or dark skin lesions associated with Blood stagnation, including internal and external suppurative lesions that may be acute and inflamed, or chronic and non-healing, chronic psoriasis and dermatitis, and rosacea.
- With the appropriate identifying features, this formula can assist in the treatment of biomedical conditions such as acute traumatic injury and bruising, angina pectoris, endometriosis, fibroids and cysts, hepatic abscess, hepatic cirrhosis, hepatosplenomegaly, chronic appendicitis, chronic abscess, chronic osteomyelitis, diverticulosis, diabetic ulcers, chronic fixed pain, post-herpetic, intercostal or trigeminal neuralgia, 'fifty year shoulder' and sciatica.

Composition
Angelica polymorpha (dang gui, chinese angelica) 24.5%, *Salvia miltiorrhiza* (dan shen, salvia) 24.5%, *Commiphora myrrha* (mo yao, myrrh) 24%, *Boswellia carteri* (ru xiang, frankincense) 24%

Combinations
- With **1.16 Tao Hong Si Wu Wan** for dysmenorrhea and endometriosis.
- With **5.4 Xin Mai Ling** for diabetic ulcers and peripheral vascular disease.

Pattern identifying features

- **Blood stagnation type pain**
- **abdominal, chest, peripheral pain**
- fixed masses

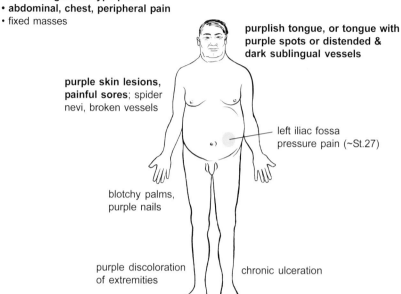

purplish tongue, or tongue with purple spots or distended & dark sublingual vessels

purple skin lesions, painful sores; spider nevi, broken vessels

left iliac fossa pressure pain (~St.27)

blotchy palms, purple nails

purple discoloration of extremities

chronic ulceration

- With **5.1 Xue Fu Zhu Yu Wan** for focal Blood stagnation type pain in the chest or head, such as post herpetic neuralgia, migraine or angina. Also used for abdominal masses, especially hepatic cirrhosis.
- With **10.23 Zheng Gu Shui** topically for pain and bruising from trauma.
- With **13.2 Xiao Feng Wan** for chronic non-healing eczema, dermatitis or psoriasis with stubborn, purplish lesions.
- With **7.12 Lu Rong Jiao** or **7.16.1 Shi Quan Da Bu Wan** for deeply rooted *yin* type chronic abscesses or ulcerations.
- With **10.12 Shen Tong Zhu Yu Wan** for chronic Blood stagnation *bi* syndrome.
- With **14.8 Wu Wei Xiao Du Wan** for acute superficial painful abscesses and sores.

Dosage and method of administration

8 pills three times daily on an empty stomach. The dose may be spread out, or two lots of 12 pills may be taken, morning and evening. When used to augment another formula, 4-6 pills three times daily is usually sufficient.

Cautions and contraindications

Contraindicated during pregnancy and in patients with bleeding disorders. Caution in patients who are also taking anticoagulant therapy (aspirin, warfarin, coumarin) as clotting time can be significantly reduced.

PAIN

GMP

10.6 JUAN BI WAN

蹻痹丸

Lanzhou Foci Pharmaceutical Factory (Gansu)
'Remove Painful Obstruction Pills'
Juan Bi Wan is packaged in bottles of 200 pills.
Available as: Clear Channels Teapills (PF)

Available in the US, UK and Europe
See Note 1, p.xxi

TCM actions

Dispels Wind Cold Damp, warms and unblocks the channels and collaterals, stops pain.

Biomedical actions

Analgesic, anti-arthritic, anti-inflammatory, enhances circulation.

INDICATIONS

- Wind Cold Damp *bi* syndrome. This formula is best for the early stages of a *bi* syndrome pattern, when pain and stiffness are intermittent and relatively mild and there is little or no underlying deficiency. Pain of this type is characterised by its responsiveness to changes in weather (generally worse on wet, cold or humid days), aggravation with lack of movement, alleviation with the application of heat, and by its mobile nature, appearing in different parts of the body at different times.
- With the appropriate identifying features, this formula can be used to treat osteoarthritis, bursitis, spondylosis, fibromyalgia and sciatic pain.

Composition

Morus alba (sang zhi, mulberry twig) 20%, *Piper futokadsura* (hai feng teng, kadsura stem) 20%, *Angelica sinensis* (dang gui, chinese angelica) 12.5%, *Notopterygium incisum* (qiang huo, notopterygium) 6.5%, *Angelica pubescens* (du huo, Tu-huo) 6.5%, *Gentiana macrophylla* (qin jiao, chin chiu) 6.5%, *Ligusticum wallichi* (chuan xiong, cnidium) 6%, *Saussurea lappa* (mu xiang, saussurea) 6%, *Cinnamomum cassia* (gui zhi, cinnamon twigs) 6%, *Boswellia carteri* (ru xiang, frankincense) 4.5%, *Glycyrrhiza uralensis* (zhi gan cao, honey fried licorice) 2.5%

Combinations

- With **10.38 Plaster for Bruise and Analgesic** topically for localised pain.

Pattern identifying features

- **Wind Cold Damp** *bi* **syndrome**
- worse with changes of weather &
  lack of activity
- better for heat & movement
- relatively robust patient with little or
  no contributing deficiency

thick white tongue coat

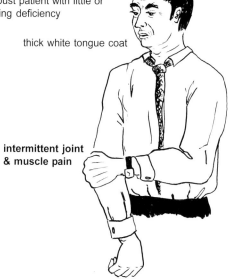

intermittent joint
& muscle pain

heaviness & numbness
in the extremities

- With **10.40 Porous Capsicum Plaster** for relatively severe pain with cold
  predominant.

Dosage and method of administration

8-12 pills three times daily on an empty stomach. The dose may be spread out, or two
lots of 12-18 pills may be taken, morning and evening. In severe cases or during the
early stages of treatment, a 50% increase in dose may be used, then reduced as the
treatment takes effect.

Cautions and contraindications

Contraindicated during pregnancy and in pain patterns associated with redness and
heat in joints or muscles.

PAIN

10.7 QU FENG ZHEN TONG CAPSULE

祛风镇痛丸

(Qu Feng Zhen Tong Wan)
Jing Xian Pharmaceutical Co. (Guangzhou)
'Expel Wind, Suppress Pain Pills'
Qu Feng Zhen Tong Capsules are packaged in bottles of 36 capsules.

TCM actions
Dispels Wind Damp, warms and unblocks the channels and collaterals, stops pain.

Biomedical actions
Analgesic, anti-arthritic, enhances circulation.

INDICATIONS

- Wind Cold Damp *bi* syndrome. Especially good for pain in the upper body–neck, shoulders, thoracic region and arms–but can be used for Wind Cold Damp *bi* pain anywhere in the body. Quite pungent, dispersing and warm, this formula is best for Cold Damp patterns with localised pain and swelling in patients with little or no significant underlying deficiency.
- With the appropriate identifying features, this formula may be used to treat the pain of osteo-arthritis, rheumatoid arthritis, fibromyalgia, osteophytes and spurs, cervical spondylosis, sciatica, migraine headache and tendinitis.

Composition (each capsule contains extracts equivalent to dry)

Notopterygium incisum (qiang huo, notopterygium) 500mg, *Angelica pubescens* (du huo, Tu-huo) 500mg, *Paeonia lactiflora* (bai shao, white peony) 500mg, *Chaenomeles speciosa* (mu gua, chinese quince) 500mg, *Spatholobus suberectus* (ji xue teng, spatholobus) 500mg, *Angelica polymorpha* (dang gui, chinese angelica) 500mg, *Morus alba* (sang zhi, mulberry twig) 400mg, *Clematis sinensis* (wei ling xian, chinese clematis) 400mg, *Curcuma longa* (jiang huang, turmeric rhizome) 400mg, *Gentiana macrophylla* (qin jiao, chin chiu) 400mg, *Achyranthes bidentata* (niu xi, achyranthes) 400mg

Pattern identifying features

• **Wind Cold Damp *bi* syndrome**

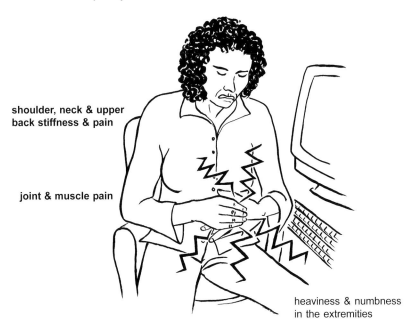

shoulder, neck & upper
back stiffness & pain

joint & muscle pain

heaviness & numbness
in the extremities

Dosage and method of administration
3-4 capsules, three times daily, on an empty stomach.

Cautions and contraindications
Contraindicated during pregnancy.

PAIN

10.8 XIAO HUO LUO DAN

小活络丹

Lanzhou Foci Pharmaceutical Factory (Gansu)
'Smaller Invigorate the Channel (Flow) Special Pill'
Xiao Huo Luo Dan is packaged in bottles of 100 pills.
Also available as: Xiao Huo Luo Dan Teapills (PF)

TCM actions
Powerfully warms and dispels Cold, dries Damp, transforms Phlegm and disperses stagnant Blood, unblocks the channels and collaterals, stops pain.

Biomedical actions
Analgesic, anti-arthritic, enhances circulation.

INDICATIONS

- Chronic Cold Damp *bi* syndrome with Phlegm and Blood stasis and relatively severe joint pain and stiffness. The pain is generally excruciating, fixed, worse with cold weather and associated with stiffness, spasm, numbness and paresthesia in the extremities. This is an important and powerful formula for chronic pain, but must be used cautiously because it is very hot, pungent and dispersing, and can easily damage *yin*.
- Numbness and loss of function in the extremities following a Wind-stroke in a patient tending to cold or *yang* deficiency. Also used for *wei* syndrome from Cold, Phlegm and Blood stagnation in the channels.
- With the appropriate identifying features, this formula may assist in the treatment of biomedical conditions such as hemiplegia following a stroke, chronic rheumatoid or osteo-arthritis, degenerative joint disease, sciatica, peripheral neuropathy, post herpetic neuralgia, cervical and lumbar spondylosis and numbness and wasting in the extremities.

Composition (each pill contains powdered)
Aconitium carmichaeli (chuan wu, aconite) 21.25%, *Aconitium kusnezoffii* (cao wu, wild aconite) 21.25%, *Arisaema consanguinum* (dan nan xing, bile treated arisaema) 21.25%, *Pheretima asiatica* (di long, earthworm) 21.25%, *Boswellia carterii* (ru xiang, frankincense) 7.5%, *Commiphora myrrha* (mo yao, myrrh) 7.5%

Combinations
- With **7.1.1 Liu Wei Di Huang Wan** for Kidney *yang* deficiency and Cold *bi* syndrome.

Pattern identifying features

- **Cold Damp *bi* syndrome**
- **pain is worse for cold**
- **no heat signs**
- cold intolerance

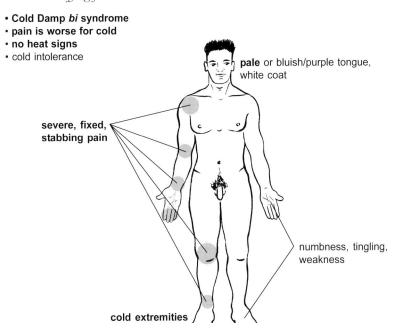

pale or bluish/purple tongue, white coat

severe, fixed, stabbing pain

numbness, tingling, weakness

cold extremities

- With **10.15 Du Huo Ji Sheng Wan** for chronic or stubborn Wind Damp *bi* pain.
- With **10.11 Shu Jin Huo Xue Wan** for chronic pain with Blood and Phlegm stagnation.

Dosage and method of administration

4 pills two or three times daily (maximum dose), on an empty stomach. May be taken with a shot of alcohol (vodka or sherry) to enhance the channel opening effect. It is important to keep to the recommended dose of this medicine as it is very hot and can easily cause overheating and damage *yin*. It is best to begin with a small dose (1-2 pills each time), see how the patient responds and then gradually increase the dose. Signs of overheating are usually flagged first by insomnia and restlessness, wild dreaming, facial flushing, sweats and thirst.

Cautions and contraindications

Contraindicated during pregnancy, in *yin* deficiency patterns and when there is any sign of heat at all (red tongue, warm joints, etc.). Only suitable unmodified for patients with a relatively robust constitution or severe Cold accumulation.

PAIN

10.9 XUAN BI TANG WAN

宣痹汤丸

Lanzhou Foci Pharmaceutical Factory (Gansu)
 Drain Away Obstruction Pills'
Xuan Bi Tang Wan is packaged in bottles of 200 pills.
Also available as: Xuan Bi Teapills (PF)

TCM actions
Clears Damp Heat from the joints, unblocks the channels and collaterals, promotes urination and stops pain.

Biomedical actions
Analgesic, diuretic, anti-inflammatory, enhances circulation.

INDICATIONS

• Heat or Damp Heat *bi* syndrome. When Damp Heat accumulates in the joints it causes heat, swelling, redness and pain. This is usually an acute disorder, or an acute flare-up of a chronic disorder, but may be chronic, in which case the Heat signs tend to be lower grade. Similar in overall action to **10.10 Guan Jie Yan Wan**, the main difference being that this formula is cooler and preferred for more acute Damp Heat *bi* patterns.
• With the appropriate identifying features, this formula can assist in the treatment of biomedical conditions such as inflammatory joint disorders, inflammatory phase of osteo-arthritis and rheumatoid arthritis, rheumatic fever, gouty arthritis, gout and connective tissue disorders.

Composition (each pill contains powdered)
Coix lachryma-jobi (yi ren, coix) 24.5mg, *Stephania tetrandra* (fang ji, stephania) 19.6mg, *Prunus armeniaca* (xing ren, apricot seed) 19.6mg, *Achyranthes bidentata* (niu xi, achyranthes) 16.3mg, *Scutellaria baicalensis* (huang qin, scute) 16.3mg, *Forsythia suspensa* (lian qiao, forsythia fruit) 16.3mg, *Atractylodes lancea* (cang zhu, red atractylodes) 13.1mg, *Gardenia florida* (shan zhi zi, gardenia fruit) 13.1mg, *Pinellia ternata* (ban xia, pinellia) 11.4mg, *Clematis armandii* (mu tong, akebia) 9.8mg

Combinations
• With **10.37 White Tiger Balm** topically for localised pain and inflammatory arthritis.
• With **14.1 Huang Lian Jie Du Wan** for severe acute gout.

Pattern identifying features

- **Damp Heat *bi* syndrome**
- may be fever & chills
- heaviness & aching in the joints & limbs, worse during hot humid weather

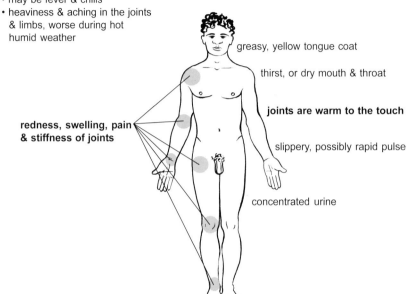

greasy, yellow tongue coat

thirst, or dry mouth & throat

joints are warm to the touch

redness, swelling, pain & stiffness of joints

slippery, possibly rapid pulse

concentrated urine

Dosage and method of administration

8-15 pills three times daily on an empty stomach. The dose may be spread out, or two lots of 12-22 pills may be taken, morning and evening. In severe cases or during the early stages of treatment (the first two weeks), a 50% increase in dose may be used, then reduced as the treatment takes effect.

Cautions and contraindications

Contraindicated in Wind Cold *bi* patterns. Caution in patients with a tendency to mucus production or Spleen Damp.

PAIN

GMP **10.10 GUAN JIE YAN WAN**

关节炎丸

Available in the US,
UK and Europe
See Note 1, p.xxi

Lanzhou Foci Pharmaceutical Factory (Gansu)
'Joint Inflammation Pills'
Guan Jie Yan Wan is packaged in bottles of 200 pills.
Available as: Joint Inflammation Teapills (PF)

TCM actions
Clears Damp Heat from the joints, unblocks the channels
and collaterals, stops pain.

Biomedical actions
Analgesic, diuretic, anti-inflammatory, enhances circulation.

INDICATIONS

- Damp Heat *bi* syndrome. Especially good for chronic Damp Heat affecting the
  lower body–hips, knees, ankles and toes. Even though the formula contains a
  few warming herbs, these serve to open up the channels to enable Dampness
  and Heat to be dissipated. The thermal nature of the formula overall is cooling,
  although not quite as cooling as **10.9 Xuan Bi Tang Wan**, which also varies
  from this formula by being preferred for more acute patterns of Damp Heat *bi*
  syndrome.
- With the appropriate identifying features, this formula can assist in the treatment
  of inflammatory joint disorders, inflammatory phase of osteo-arthritis and
  rheumatoid arthritis, rheumatic fever, gouty arthritis and connective tissue
  disorders.

Composition
Coix lachryma-jobi (yi ren, coix) 21%, *Stephania tetrandra* (fang ji, stephania) 14%,
Atractylodes lancea (cang zhu, red atractylodes) 9%, *Erythrina variegata* (hai tong pi,
erythrina bark) 9%, *Cinnamomum cassia* (gui zhi, cinnamon twigs) 7%, *Periploca sepium*
(xiang jia pi, periploca) 7%, *Achyranthes bidentata* (niu xi, achyranthes) 7%, *Gentiana
macrophylla* (qin jiao, chin chiu) 7%, *Evodia rutacarpae* (wu zhu yu, evodia) 7%,
Scutellaria baicalensis (huang qin, scute) 3%, *Angelica pubescens* (du huo, Tu-huo) 3%,
Zingiber officinale (sheng jiang, ginger) 3%

Pattern identifying features

- **Damp Heat *bi* syndrome**
- heaviness & aching in the joints & limbs, worse during hot humid weather

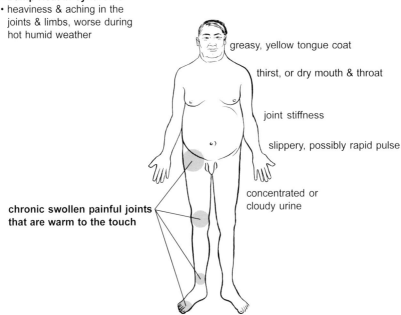

greasy, yellow tongue coat

thirst, or dry mouth & throat

joint stiffness

slippery, possibly rapid pulse

concentrated or cloudy urine

chronic swollen painful joints that are warm to the touch

Combinations
- With **10.37 White Tiger Balm** topically for localised pain and inflammatory arthritis.

Dosage and method of administration
8-15 pills three times daily on an empty stomach. The dose may be spread out, or two lots of 12-22 pills may be taken, morning and evening. In severe cases or during the early stages of treatment (the first two weeks), a 50% increase in dose may be used, then reduced as the treatment takes effect.

Cautions and contraindications
Contraindicated in Wind Cold *bi* patterns. Caution in patients with a tendency to mucus production or Spleen Damp.

PAIN

10.11 SHU JIN HUO XUE WAN

舒筋活血丸

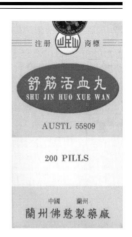

Lanzhou Foci Pharmaceutical Factory (Gansu)
'Soothe the Tendons and Invigorate Blood Pills'
Shu Jin Huo Xue Wan is packaged in bottles of 200 pills.

TCM actions
Dispels Wind Damp, invigorates *qi* and quickens Blood, unblocks the channels and collaterals, transforms Phlegm, stops pain.

Biomedical actions
Analgesic, anti-arthritic, anti-inflammatory, enhances circulation.

INDICATIONS

• Wind Cold Damp *bi* syndrome with *qi*, Blood and Phlegm stagnation in the channels causing chronic joint and muscle pain, spasm and paresthesia. This formula is used for predominantly excess patterns with little or no underlying deficiency. The main focus is on pain and stiffness in the lower body–lower back, hips, legs and knees–but it can be used for pain in any location. There may be a degree of bony deformity, osteophytosis or tissue change, such as wasting, discoloration or distended or broken vessels over the affected tissues or joints.

• With the appropriate identifying features, this formula may be used for biomedical conditions such as cervical and lumbar spondylosis, osteo-arthritis, arthritis following trauma, prolapsed intervertebral discs, sciatica, and slow healing of bone fractures.

Composition (each pill contains powdered)

Acanthopanax gracilistylus (wu jia pi, acanthopanax) 23.5mg, *Cinnamomun cassia* (gui zhi, cinnamon twig) 23.5mg, *Siegesbeckia orientalis* (xi xian cao, siegesbeckia) 15.7mg, *Angelica pubescens* (du huo, Tu-huo) 15.7mg, *Achyranthes bidentata* (niu xi, achyranthes) 15.7mg, *Angelica sinensis* (dang gui, chinese angelica) 15.7mg, *Chaenomeles speciosa* (mu gua, chinese quince) 15.7mg, *Clematis sinensis* (wei ling xian, chinese clematis) 15.7mg, *Notopterygium inscisum* (qiang huo, notopterygium) 15.7mg, *Angelica dahurica* (bai zhi, angelica) 7.8mg, *Illicium verum* (di feng pi, illicium bark) 7.8mg, *Pinellia ternata* (ban xia, pinellia) 7.8mg

Pattern identifying features

- **Wind Cold Damp *bi* with stagnant *qi*, Blood & Phlegm**
- slow healing of fractures

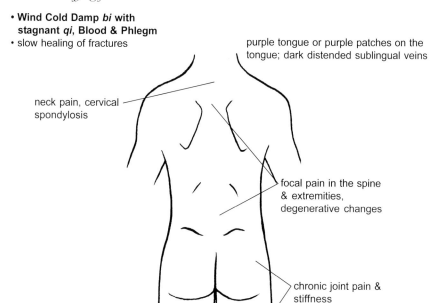

neck pain, cervical spondylosis

purple tongue or purple patches on the tongue; dark distended sublingual veins

focal pain in the spine & extremities, degenerative changes

chronic joint pain & stiffness

Combinations
- With **5.8 Bu Yang Huan Wu Wan** for severe numbness, loss of sensation or other paresthesia in the limbs with discoloration.
- With **10.4 Chin Gu Tie Shang Wan** for slow knitting of bones.
- With **5.1 Xue Fu Zhu Yu Wan** for severe Blood stagnation.
- With **10.5 Huo Luo Xiao Ling Wan** for severe pain.
- With **10.23 Zheng Gu Shui** rubbed externally for chronic fixed joint pain.

Dosage and method of administration
8-12 pills three times daily on an empty stomach. The dose may be spread out, or two lots of 12-18 pills may be taken, morning and evening. In severe cases or during the early stages of treatment (the first few weeks), a 50% increase in dose may be used, then reduced as the treatment takes effect.

Cautions and contraindications
Contraindicated during pregnancy. Not suitable for use in very deficient or run down patients without modification.

PAIN

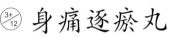

GMP **10.12 SHEN TONG ZHU YU WAN**

Available in the US,
UK and Europe
See Note 1, p.xxi

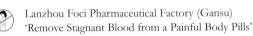

身痛逐瘀丸

Lanzhou Foci Pharmaceutical Factory (Gansu)
'Remove Stagnant Blood from a Painful Body Pills'
Shen Tong Zhu Yu Wan is packaged in bottles of 200 pills.
Available as: Great Invigorator Teapills (PF)

TCM actions
Invigorates the circulation of *qi* and Blood, breaks up and
disperses stagnant Blood, unblocks the channels and
collaterals, stops pain.

Biomedical actions
Analgesic, antispasmodic, vasodilator, anti-platelet action.

INDICATIONS

• Blood stagnation in the joints, channels and collaterals causing chronic and
relatively severe and persistent joint or muscular pain. This is a type of *bi* syndrome
that typically follows long standing Wind Cold Damp *bi* syndrome or trauma
that has impeded the circulation of *qi* and Blood. The pain is generally fixed and
focal, worse with pressure and deep seated. It may, however, be diffuse or widely
distributed. In some cases there may be associated bony deformity or tissue
changes, such as wasting, discoloration or distended or broken vessels over the
affected tissues or joints.

• With the appropriate identifying features, this formula may be used for biomedical
conditions such as fibromyalgia, tendonitis, osteo-arthritis and chronic rheumatoid
arthritis, traumatic arthritis, pain following trauma, post surgical pain, sciatica,
post-herpetic neuralgia, phantom limb pain, dysmenorrhea and painful abdominal
masses such as endometriosis.

Composition
Prunus persica (tao ren, peach seed) 12%, *Carthamus tinctorius* (hong hua, carthamus)
12%, *Angelica sinensis* (dang gui, chinese angelica) 12%, *Cyathula officinalis* (chuan niu
xi, cyathula) 12%, *Ligusticum wallici* (chuan xiong, cnidium) 8%, *Glycyrrhiza uralensis*
(gan cao, licorice) 6%, *Commiphora myrrha* (mo yao, myrrh) 8%, *Trogopterus xanthipes*
(wu ling zhi, flying squirrel feces) 8%, *Pheretima asiatica* (di long, earthworm) 8%,
Gentiana macrophylla (qin jiao, chin chiu) 4%, *Notopterygium incisum* (qiang huo,
notopterygium) 3.5%, *Cyperus rotundus* (xiang fu, cyperus) 3.5%

Pattern identifying features

- **Chronic *bi* syndrome with Blood stagnation**
- purple discoloration of face, lips, conjunctiva, nails
- purple tongue, or brown or purple spots on the tongue, dark, distended sublingual veins

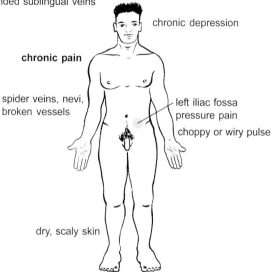

chronic depression

chronic pain

spider veins, nevi, broken vessels

left iliac fossa pressure pain

choppy or wiry pulse

dry, scaly skin

Combinations
- With **10.23 Zheng Gu Shui** rubbed externally for chronic fixed joint pain.
- With **10.5 Huo Luo Xiao Ling Wan** for severe pain.
- With **5.4 Xin Mai Ling** or **5.2 Dan Shen Pill** for Blood stagnation *bi* syndrome with signs of mild Heat.
- With a small dose of **10.8 Xiao Huo Luo Dan** for patients with signs of Cold complicating the Blood stagnation.
- With **10.41 Gou Pi Gao plasters** topically for severe pain.
- With **1.16 Tao Hong Si Wu Wan** for patients with a degree of Blood deficiency.

Dosage and method of administration
8-12 pills three times daily on an empty stomach. The dose may be spread out, or two lots of 12-18 pills may be taken, morning and evening. In severe cases or during the early stages of treatment, a 50% increase in dose may be used, then reduced as the treatment takes effect.

Cautions and contraindications
Contraindicated during pregnancy, in women with menorrhagia, and with bleeding disorders. Caution in patients on anticoagulant therapy (aspirin, warfarin, coumarin). Watch for bruising or increased tendency to bleeding.

Prolonged use may deplete *qi* and Blood, so a break every 2-3 months, with a change to a simple *qi* and Blood supplementing formula for a few weeks, is recommended.

PAIN

10.13 DA HUO LUO DAN

大活络丹

Tong Ren Tang (Beijing)
'Great Invigorate the Channels Special Pill'
Da Huo Luo Dan is packaged as 3.6 gram
honey pills sealed inside a wax ball, ten balls per box.

TCM actions
Dispels Wind Cold Damp, eases the Tendons, stops pain, supplements *qi* and Blood.

Biomedical actions
Analgesic, anti-arthritic, enhances circulation.

INDICATIONS

- Wind Cold Damp *bi* syndrome with underlying weakness of the Kidneys and *qi*
  and Blood deficiency. This large and famous formula is used for chronic pain
  and paralysis patterns. Especially esteemed in China by the elderly with joint
  stiffness and pain, mobility disorders, general debility and the sequelae of Wind-
  stroke causing hemiplegia, facial paralysis, aphasia and dysphagia.
- Used as a general supplement for the elderly to promote vitality and protect
  against cerebrovascular disease.

Composition (each pill contains extracts equivalent to)
Panax ginseng (ren shen, ginseng) 30mg, *Siler divaricum* (fang feng, siler) 27mg,
Saussurea lappa (mu xiang, saussurea) 27mg, *Agkistrodon acutus* (qi she, tiger snake)
24mg, *Rehmannia glutinosa* (shu di, processed rehmannia) 19.5mg, *Cinnamomun cassia*
(rou gui, cinnamon bark) 19.5mg, *Glycyrrhiza uralensis* (gan cao, licorice) 19.5mg,
Osmunda japonica (guan zhong, shield fern) 19.5mg, *Agastache rugosa* (huo xiang,
agastache) 19.5mg, *Rheum palmatum* (da huang, rhubarb root) 19.5mg, *Polygonum
multiflorum* (he shou wu, ho shou wu) 19.5mg, *Coptis chinensis* (huang lian, coptis)
19.5mg, *Gastrodia elata* (tian ma, gastrodia) 19.5mg, *Notopterygium forbesii* (qiang huo,
notopterygium) 19.5mg, *Lindera strychnifolia* (wu yao, lindera) 19.5mg, *Clematis sinensis*
(wei ling xian, chinese clematis) 19.5mg, *Angelica polymorpha* (dang gui, chinese
angelica) 15mg, *Scrophularia ningpoensis* (xuan shen, scrophularia) 15mg, *Citrus
reticulata* (qing pi, immature citrus) 10.5mg, *Zaocys dhumnades* (wu shao she, black
striped snake) 10.5mg, *Eugenia caryophyllata* (ding xiang, cloves) 10.5mg, *Asarum
seiboldi* (xi xin, asarum) 10.5mg, *Boswellia carteri* (ru xiang, frankincense) 10.5mg,

Pattern identifying features

- **Chronic pain & hemiplegia, Kidney &
  qi & Blood deficiency**

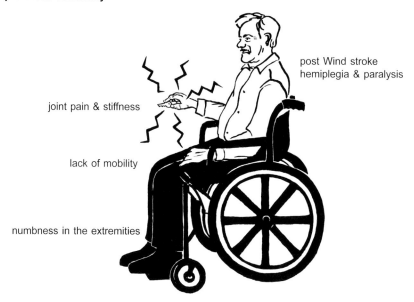

joint pain & stiffness

lack of mobility

numbness in the extremities

post Wind stroke
hemiplegia & paralysis

Commiphora myrrha (mo yao, myrrh) 10.5mg, *Poria cocos* (fu ling, hoelen) 10.5mg,
Scutellaria baicalensis (huang qin, scute) 10.5mg, *Paeonia veitchii* (chi shao, red peony)
10.5mg, *Atractylodes macrocephala* (bai zhu, atractylodes) 10.5mg, *Cyperus rotundus*
(xiang fu, cyperus) 10.5mg, *Styrax tonkinensis* (an xi xiang, benzoinum) 10.5mg,
Drynaria fortunei (gu sui bu, drynaria) 10.5mg, *Elettaria cardamomum* (bai dou kou,
amomum) 10.5mg, *Pueraria lobata* (ge gen, kudzu) 7.5mg, Bovine gallstone (niu
huang) 1.5mg, *Arisaema cosanguinium* (tian nan xing, arisaema) 1mg, honey

Dosage and method of administration
One pill twice daily on an empty stomach. For patients with difficulty swallowing,
the ball can be decocted and mashed into a slurry for ingestion.

Cautions and contraindications
Contraindicated during pregnancy.

PAIN

GMP

10.14 SAN BI WAN

三痹丸

Available in the US,
UK and Europe
See Note 1, p.xxi

Lanzhou Foci Pharmaceutical Factory (Gansu)
'Three Obstructions Decoction Pill'
San Bi Wan is packaged in bottles of 200 pills.
Available as: San Bi Tang Teapills (PF)

TCM actions
Supplements *qi* and Blood, strengthens the Liver and Kidney,
warms *yang*, dispels Wind Damp and stops pain.

Biomedical actions
Analgesic, anti-arthritic, anti-inflammatory, enhances circulation.

INDICATIONS

- Wind Damp *bi* syndrome with deficiency of Kidney *qi* and *yang* and Liver Blood causing chronic joint and muscle pain, stiffness, spasm, cramp, numbness and paresthesia. Especially good for pain in the lower body–lower back, hips, knees, ankles and feet. This formula is very similar in composition and action to **10.15 Du Huo Ji Sheng Wan**. The only difference between them is that the current formula is slightly more supplementing to *qi*.
- Also used to treat mild tremors of the head, hands and feet from internal Wind generated by the deficiency.
- With the appropriate identifying features, this formula can assist in the treatment of chronic arthritic conditions, osteo-arthritis, rheumatism, joint pain in the elderly, debilitated and postpartum women, benign familial tremor and Parkinson's disease.

Composition
Dipsacus asper (xu duan, dipsacus) 7%, *Eucommia ulmoides* (du zhong, eucommia) 7%, *Ledebouriella divaricata* (fang feng, siler) 7%, *Cinnamomun cassia* (rou gui, cinnamon bark) 7%, *Asarum seiboldi* (xi xin, asarum) 7%, *Panax ginseng* (ren shen, ginseng) 7%, *Poria cocos* (fu ling, hoelen) 7%, *Angelica sinensis* (dang gui, chinese angelica) 7%, *Paeonia lactiflora* (bai shao, white peony) 7%, *Astragalus membranaceous* (huang qi, astragalus) 7%, *Achyranthes bidentata* (niu xi, achyranthes) 7%, *Glycyrrhiza uralensis* (zhi gan cao, honey fried licorice) 4%, *Gentiana macrophylla* (qin jiao, chin chiu) 4%, *Rehmannia glutinosa* (sheng di, raw rehmannia) 4%, *Angelica pubescens* (du huo, Tu-huo), *Ligusticum wallichi* (chuan xiong, cnidium) 4%

Pattern identifying features

- **Wind Cold Damp *bi* syndrome with Kidney *qi* & *yang* & Liver Blood deficiency**
- cold intolerance
- pain worse in cold wet weather & with fatigue

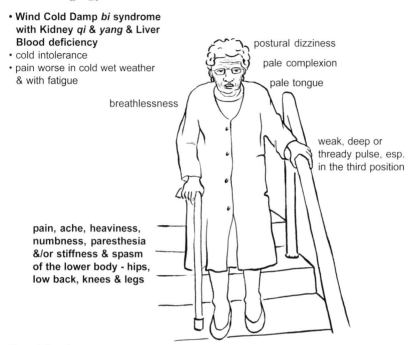

postural dizziness

pale complexion

pale tongue

breathlessness

weak, deep or thready pulse, esp. in the third position

pain, ache, heaviness, numbness, paresthesia &/or stiffness & spasm of the lower body - hips, low back, knees & legs

Combinations

- With **7.9 Fu Gui Ba Wei Wan** for pain and spasm associated with coldness, hypofunction and Kidney *yang* deficiency.
- With **10.16 Zhuang Yao Jian Shen** to enhance the general Kidney strengthening effect.
- With a small dose (1-2 pills twice daily) of **10.8 Xiao Huo Luo Dan** or **10.41 Gou Pi Gao** (topically on the affected area) for relatively severe cold symptoms with debilitating fixed pain.
- With **10.38 Plaster for Bruise and Analgesic** topically for localised pain.

Dosage and method of administration

8-12 pills three times daily on an empty stomach. The dose may be spread out, or two lots of 12-18 pills may be taken, morning and evening. In severe cases or during the early stages of treatment, a 50% increase in dose may be used, then reduced as the treatment takes effect.

Cautions and contraindications

Contraindicated during the early stage of colds and flu, or other acute pathogenic disorder.

PAIN

10.15 DU HUO JI SHENG WAN

独活寄生丸

Lanzhou Foci Pharmaceutical Factory (Gansu)
'*Angelica pubescens* and *Viscum coloratum* Pills'
Du Huo Ji Sheng Wan is packaged in bottles of 200 pills.
Also available as: Solitary Hermit Teapills (PF), Tu Huo Ji
Sheng Wan

TCM actions
Dispels Wind Damp, supplements *qi* and Blood,
strengthens the Liver and Kidneys, stops pain.

Biomedical actions
Analgesic, anti-arthritic, anti-inflammatory, enhances circulation.

INDICATIONS

- Chronic joint and muscle pain, stiffness, spasm, cramp, numbness and
  paresthesia associated with osteo-arthritis and/or sciatica in patients with
  Wind Dampness, Kidney weakness and deficiency of *qi* and Blood. Especially
  good for pain in the lower body–lower back, hips, knees, ankles and feet.
  Slightly more dispersing, yet quite similar in action to, and interchangeable
  with, **10.14 San Bi Wan**.
- With the appropriate identifying features, this formula can assist in the
  treatment of chronic arthritic conditions, osteo-arthritis, degenerative joint
  disease, rheumatism, joint pain in the elderly and debilitated, chronic lower
  back ache and sciatica.

Composition (each pill contains powdered)
Angelica pubescens (du huo, Tu-huo) 15.8mg, *Viscum coloratum* (sang ji sheng, mistletoe)
15.8mg, *Spatholobus suberectus* (ji xue teng, spatholobus) 10.3mg, *Gentiana macrophylla*
(qin jiao, chin chiu) 10.3mg, *Ledebouriella divaricata* (fang feng, siler) 10.3mg, *Asarum
seiboldi* (xi xin, asarum) 10.3mg, *Eucommia ulmoides* (du zhong, eucommia) 10.3mg,
Paeonia lactiflora (bai shao, white peony) 10.3mg, *Angelica dahurica* (bai zhi, angelica)
10.3mg, *Rehmannia glutinosa* (shu di, prepared rehmannia) 10.3mg, *Angelica sinensis*
(dang gui, chinese angelica) 10.3mg, *Cyathula officinalis* (chuan niu xi) 10.3mg,
Codonopsis pilosula (dang shen, codonopsis) 10.3mg, *Poria cocos* (fu ling, hoelen)
10.3mg, *Glycyrrhiza uralensis* (gan cao, licorice) 10.3mg, *Zingiber officinalis* (sheng jiang,
ginger), *Cinnamomun cassia* (rou gui, cinnamon bark) 10.3mg

Pattern identifying features

- **Wind Cold Damp *bi* syndrome with
  Kidney *qi*& *yang* & Liver Blood deficiency**
- cold intolerance
- pain worse in cold wet weather
- fatigue
- breathlessness

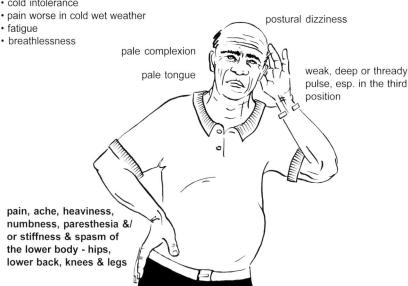

postural dizziness

pale complexion

pale tongue

weak, deep or thready
pulse, esp. in the third
position

pain, ache, heaviness,
numbness, paresthesia &/
or stiffness & spasm of
the lower body - hips,
lower back, knees & legs

Combinations

With **7.9 Fu Gui Ba Wei Wan** for pain and spasm associated with coldness,
hypofunction and Kidney *yang* deficiency.

- With **10.16.1 Zhuang Yao Jian Shen** to enhance the general Kidney strengthening
  effect.
- With a small dose (1-2 pills twice daily) of **10.8 Xiao Huo Luo Dan** or **10.41 Gou
  Pi Gao** (topically on the affected area) for relatively severe cold symptoms with
  debilitating fixed pain.
- With **10.38 Plaster for Bruise and Analgesic** topically for localised pain.

Dosage and method of administration

8-12 pills three times daily on an empty stomach. The dose may be spread out, or
two lots of 12-18 pills may be taken, morning and evening. In severe cases or during
the early stages of treatment (the first two weeks), a 50% increase in dose may be
used, then reduced as the treatment takes effect.

Cautions and contraindications

Contraindicated during the early stage of colds and flu, or other acute pathogenic
disorder.

PAIN

10.16.1 ZHUANG YAO JIAN SHEN

壮腰健肾

Guangzhou Qixing Pharmaceutical Co. (Guangzhou)
'Strengthen the Lower Back and Benefit the Kidney'
Zhuang Yao Jian Shen is packaged in bottles of 100 tablets.

TCM actions
Supplements, strengthens and warms the Kidneys,
benefits and secures *jing*, dispels Wind Damp, stops pain.

Biomedical actions
Tonic, astringent, strengthens Kidney function.

INDICATIONS

• Chronic Wind Damp *bi* syndrome with Kidney *yang* deficiency causing lower
back, spine and lower limb pain, stiffness and heaviness. Good for weakness or
pain in the hips, knees or ankles associated with osteo-arthritis, sciatica, chronic
lumbago, scoliosis and rheumatism. Although in general tending to be warm,
this formula is mild enough to be used for patients with lower back pain tending
to heat, cold or neither. It combines well with other more constitutional Kidney
supplementing formulae. Suitable for prolonged use to strengthen Kidney
function.
• Urinary frequency, nocturia or incontinence from Kidney *qi* or *yang* deficiency.
• Kidney weakness and *jing* deficiency causing premature ejaculation and sperm
disorders such as low sperm count, poor motility and poor sperm quality.

Composition (each pill contains extract equivalent to dry)
Cibotium barometz (gou ji, cibotium fern) 525.7mg, *Schizandra chinensis* (wu wei zi,
schizandra) 280mg, *Spatholobus suberectus* (ji xue teng, spatholobus) 280mg, *Cuscuta
hygropilae* (tu su zi, cuscuta) 208.6mg, *Viscum coloratum* (sang ji sheng, mistletoe)
197.1mg, *Rosa laevigata* (jin ying zi, chinese rose fruit) 157.1mg, *Ligustrum lucidum* (nu
zhen zi, privet fruit) 22.9mg

Combinations
• With **7.9 Fu Gui Ba Wei Wan** for pain and spasm associated with more profound
Kidney *yang* deficiency. This combination is also used for nocturia or urinary
frequency from *yang* or *qi* deficiency.

Pattern identifying features

- **Kidney *qi* & *yang* deficiency lower back & leg pain**
- aches & pains worse with cold wet weather

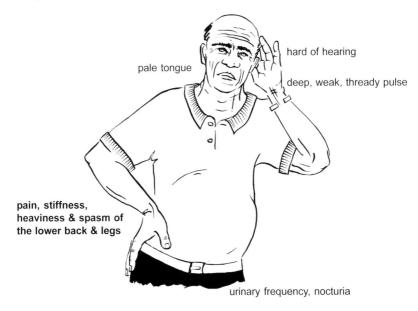

pale tongue

hard of hearing

deep, weak, thready pulse

pain, stiffness, heaviness & spasm of the lower back & legs

urinary frequency, nocturia

- With **10.15 Du Huo Ji Sheng Wan** for chronic Wind Damp *bi* pain with Kidney *qi* and Liver Blood deficiency.
- With **7.1.1 Liu Wei Di Huang Wan** for *bi* syndrome in those prone to Kidney *yin* deficiency.
- With **5.1 Xue Fu Zhu Yu Wan** or **10.11 Shu Jin Huo Xue Wan** for chronic stubborn fixed pain associated with Blood stagnation and Kidney *yang* deficiency.

Dosage and method of administration

4 pills three times daily on an empty stomach; doubled in the early stages of treatment (first two weeks) then reduced as the treatment takes effect. When combined with a constitutional formula, four pills twice daily is usually sufficient.

Cautions and contraindications

Contraindicated during the early stage of colds and flu, or other acute pathogenic disorder.

PAIN

10.16.2 ZHUANG YAO JIAN SHEN TABLET

壮腰健肾片

(Zhuang Yao Jian Shen Pian)
Jing Xian Pharmaceutical Co. (Guangzhou)
'Strengthen the Lower Back and Benefit the Kidney Pills'
Zhuang Yao Jian Shen Tablet is packaged in bottles of 60 tablets.

TCM actions
Supplements, strengthens and warms the Kidneys, benefits and secures *jing*, dispels Wind Damp, stops pain.

Biomedical actions
Tonic, astringent, strengthens Kidney function.

INDICATIONS

- As for **10.16.1 Zhuang Yao Jian Shen**. With basically the same action and indications, the only difference between these formulae is that this version has slightly more Kidney supplementing activity with the inclusion of prepared rehmannia, solomon seal rhizome and ho shou wu. Achyranthes is added to direct the action of the formula to the lower body.

Composition (each pill contains extract equivalent to dry)
Rehmannia glutinosa (shu di, prepared rehmannia) 333mg, *Spatholobus suberectus* (ji xue teng, spatholobus) 333mg, *Polygonum multiflorum* (he shou wu, ho shou wu) 222mg, *Polygonatum sibiricum* (huang jing, solomon seal rhizome) 178mg, *Rosa laevigata* (jin ying zi, chinese rose fruit) 178mg, *Cibotium barometz* (gou ji, cibotium fern) 167mg, *Achyranthes bidentata* (niu xi, achyranthes) 114mg, *Dipsacus asper* (xu duan, dipsacus) 68mg, *Ligustrum lucidum* (nu zhen zi, privet fruit) 68mg

Dosage and method of administration
3-5 tablets, three times daily on an empty stomach; may be doubled during the early stages of treatment (first two weeks), then reduced as the treatment takes effect.

Cautions and contraindications
Contraindicated during the early stage of colds and flu, or other acute pathogenic disorder.

10.17 TONG LUO ZHI TONG TABLET

通络止痛片

(Tong Luo Zhi Tong Pian)
Jing Xian Pharmaceutical Co. (Guangzhou)
'*Luo Mai* Opening, Analgesic Tablets'
Tong Luo Zhi Tong Tablets are packaged in bottles of 36 tablets.

TCM actions
Quickens and supplements Blood, stimulates circulation in the channels and collaterals, eases the tendons.

Biomedical actions
Analgesic, anti-inflammatory.

INDICATIONS

- A modern formulation utilising the channel opening and Blood regulating effects of spatholobus with the hematinic and relaxing effects of B group vitamins.
- Can stimulate production of leukocytes in patients with low white blood cell counts and following chemotherapy or radiotherapy.
- This formula can assist in the treatment of neurological and vascular pain such as sciatica, trigeminal neuralgia, intercostal neuralgia and migraine headache, as well as facial paralysis, numbness and paresthesia in the extremities, hemiplegia following Wind-stroke, dysmenorrhea, irregular menstruation and premenstrual syndrome.

Composition (each tablets contains)
Spatholobus suberectus (ji xue teng, spatholobus) 550mg, Thiamine hydrochloride (Vitamin B1) 100mg, Pyridoxine hydrochloride (Vitamin B6) 10mg, Cyanocobalamin (Vitamin B12) 50µg

Dosage and method of administration
1-2 tablets, three times daily on an empty stomach to a maximum of 5 tablets per day.

Cautions and contraindications
Contraindicated in patients with bleeding disorders or menorrhagia.

PAIN

10.18 JIAN BU QIANG SHEN WAN
健步强身丸

(Aches and Pains Relief Pill)
Tong Ren Tang (Beijing)
'Walking with Vigour, Body Strengthening Pills'
Jian Bu Qiang Shen Wan is packaged in bottles of 600 very small pills.

TCM actions
Dispels Wind Damp, supplements *qi* and Blood, strengthens the Liver and Kidneys, stops pain.

Biomedical actions
Analgesic, anti-arthritic, anti-inflammatory, enhances circulation.

INDICATIONS

- Kidney *qi* or *yang* deficiency type lower back pain, general muscular aches, pains, stiffness, cramps, spasms and weakness, especially in the lower body and legs. This formula is similar in action to **10.15 Du Huo Ji Sheng Wan**.
- Useful as a general Kidney supplement for chronic problems such as lack of vitality, infertility, low libido, sperm disorders or urinary disorders.
- With the appropriate identifying features, this formula may assist in the treatment of biomedical conditions such as chronic osteo-arthritis and rheumatoid arthritis, weakness of the lower back and legs, sciatic pain, numbness and paresthesia of the legs and recurrent ankle sprain or low back pain.

Composition (each dose of 60 pills [6 grams] contains)
Lycium barbarum (gou qi zi, lycium fruit) 360mg, *Chaenomeles lagenaria* (mu gua, chinese quince) 360mg, *Achyranthes bidentata* (niu xi, achyranthes) 336mg, *Dipsacus asper* (xu duan, dipsacus) 270mg, *Ledebouriella divaricata* (fang feng, siler) 240mg, *Poria cocos* (fu ling, hoelen) 210mg, *Notopterygium incisum* (qiang huo, notopterygium) 168mg, *Paeonia lactiflora* (bai shao, white peony) 168mg, *Astragalus membranaceous* (huang qi, astragalus) 168mg, *Cynomorium songariorum* (suo yang, cynomorium) 168mg, *Angelica pubescens* (du huo, Tu-huo) 168mg, *Rehmannia glutinosa* (shu di, prepared rehmannia) 168mg, *Angelica polymorpha* (dang gui, chinese angelica) 168mg, *Schizandra chinensis* (wu wei zi, schizandra) 168mg, *Psoralea corylifolia* (bu gu zhi, psoralea) 168mg, *Gentiana macrophylla* (qin jiao, chin chiu) 168mg, *Anemarrhena aspheloides* (zhi mu, anemarrhena) 168mg, *Panax ginseng* (ren shen, ginseng) 42mg, *Eucommia ulmoides* (du zhong, eucommia) 42mg, honey

Pattern identifying features

• **Kidney deficiency lower back & leg pain**

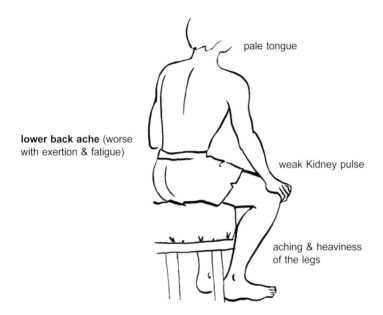

pale tongue

lower back ache (worse with exertion & fatigue)

weak Kidney pulse

aching & heaviness of the legs

Combinations
• With **7.9 Fu Gui Ba Wei Wan** for pain and spasm associated with coldness, hypofunction and Kidney *yang* deficiency.
• With **10.41 Gou Pi Gao** topically over the lower back for chronic back ache.

Dosage and method of administration
The recommended dose is 60 pills twice daily, before meals. In most cases, this is rather inconvenient as counting the right dose can be extremely tedious and lead to poor compliance. The best way to take it is not to worry about getting exactly the right dose each time, instead aim to finish a jar in 5 days. Patients can simply estimate the dose by taking as many pills as fit into the lid of the bottle, which is close enough to 60.

Cautions and contraindications
Contraindicated during the early stages of colds and flu, and other acute pathogenic invasion.

PAIN

GMP

10.19 KANG GU ZENG SHENG PIAN

抗骨增生片

Available in the US, UK and Europe See Note 1, p.xxi

Guangzhou Qixing Pharmaceutical Co. (Guangzhou)
'Inhibit Bony Proliferation Pill'
Kang Gu Zeng Sheng Pian is packaged in bottles of 100 pills.
Also available as: Kang Gu Zeng Sheng Wan

TCM actions
Supplements the Liver and Kidneys, strengthens tendons and bones, invigorates *qi* and quickens Blood, stops pain.

Biomedical actions
Analgesic, encourages bony matrix remodelling, enhances circulation.

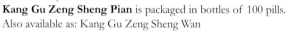

INDICATIONS

- Proliferative bone disorders such as osteophytosis, vertebral calcification, ankylosing spondylitis, vertebral and cervical spondylitis, heel spurs, bony deformity consequent upon chronic rheumatoid arthritis, Kashin-Beck disease, traumatic arthritis and Heberden's nodes.

Composition
Os Felis (mao gu, cat bone) 23%, *Rehmannia glutinosa* (shu di, processed rehmannia) 15%, *Cistanche deserticola* (rou cong rong, cistanches) 12%, *Pyrola rotundifolia* (lu xian cao, pyrola) 10%, *Liquidamber taiwaniana* (lu lu tong, sweetgum fruit) 10%, *Hedera nepalensis* (chang chun teng, hedera) 10%, *Dioscorea nipponica* (chuan shan long, japanese dioscorea) 8%, *Geranium wilfordii* (lao guan cao, geranium) 8%, *Epimedium brevicornu* (xian ling pi, epimedium) 3.5%

Dosage and method of administration
6-8 pills, three times daily, on an empty stomach.

Cautions and contraindications
Contraindicated during pregnancy.

10.20 TIAN MA TOU TONG CAPSULE

天麻头痛丸

(Tian Ma Tou Tong Wan)
Jing Xian Pharmaceutical Co. (Guangzhou)
'Gastrodia Headache Pills'
Tian Ma Tou Tong Capsules are packaged in bottles of 36
capsules.

TCM actions
Dispels Wind Cold, extinguishes internal Wind, restrains
Liver *yang*.

Biomedical actions
Analgesic, enhances circulation.

INDICATIONS

- Headaches, including tension headaches, cluster headaches and migraines associated with Wind Cold *gan mao*, Liver *yang* rising, Liver Wind or mild Blood stagnation.
- Dizziness or vertigo from Liver *yang* rising.

Composition (each capsule contains extracts equivalent to dry)
Gastrodia elata (tian ma, gastrodia) 540mg, *Angelica dahurica* (bai zhi, angelica) 540mg,
Ligusticum sinense (gao ben, ligusticum) 540mg, *Schizonepeta tenuifolia* (jing jie,
schizonepeta) 360mg, *Angelica polymorpha* (dang gui, chinese angelica) 360mg,
Boswellia carteri (ru xiang, frankincense) 45mg

Combinations
- With **15.4 Tian Ma Gou Teng Wan** for Liver *yang* rising.
- With **15.9 Headache and Dizziness Reliever** for occipital headache.

Dosage and method of administration
3-4 capsules, three times daily, on an empty stomach.

Cautions and contraindications
None noted.

PAIN

GMP **10.21 YAN HU SUO ZHI TONG WAN**

延胡索止痛丸

Lanzhou Foci Pharmaceutical Factory (Gansu)
'*Corydalis turtschaninovii* Pills'
Yan Hu Suo Zhi Tong Wan is packaged in bottles of 200 pills.
Available as: Great Corydalis Teapills (PF)

Available in the US,
UK and Europe
See Note 1, p.xxi

TCM actions
Invigorates *qi* and quickens Blood, stops pain.

Biomedical actions
Analgesic.

INDICATIONS

- For all types of pain associated with *qi* and/or Blood stagnation. An excellent formula to add to a constitutional or targeting formula when enhanced analgesia is desired. Generally considered best for pain associated with the Liver and Heart organ systems and channels.
- Because both herbs are quite dispersing, this formula can also be used for the generalised muscle aches that accompany a Wind Cold *gan mao*.

Composition
Corydalis turtschaninovii (yan hu suo, corydalis) 65%, *Angelica dahurica* (bai zhi, angelica) 32.5%

Combinations
- With **5.1 Xue Fu Zhu Yu Wan** for migraine headache, facial pain or post-herpetic neuralgia from stagnant *qi* and Blood.
- With **10.9 Xuan Bi Tang Wan** for acute joint pain from Damp Heat *bi* syndrome.
- With **1.18 Shao Fu Zhu Yu Wan** for severe dysmenorrhea.
- With **10.5 Huo Luo Xiao Ling Wan** for severe pain from trauma.
- With **11.4 Tian Tai Wu Yao Wan** for testicular or inguinal pain from Cold in the Liver channel.
- With **5.2 Dan Shen Pill** for angina.

Dosage and method of administration
8-12 pills, three times daily used alone. When combined with a targeting formula, 4-8 pills, three times daily may be sufficient.

Cautions and contraindications
Contraindicated during pregnancy.

10.22 SHAO YAO GAN CAO WAN

芍药甘草丸

Available in the US, UK and Europe
See Note 1, p.xxi

GMP

Lanzhou Foci Pharmaceutical Factory (Gansu)
'*Paeonia lactiflora* and *Glycyrrhiza uralensis* Pills'
Shao Yao Gan Cao Wan is packaged in bottles of 200 pills.
Available as: Peony and Licorice Teapills (PF)

TCM actions
Softens the Liver, benefits *yin*, eases cramps, stops pain.

Biomedical actions
Antispasmodic, analgesic.

INDICATIONS

- Pain associated with spasm and cramping of smooth and skeletal muscles. Primarily used for muscle spasm from Liver *yin* or Blood deficiency failing to moisten and nourish the tendons, this formula can be used for any pattern where smooth or skeletal muscle spasm is a problem. This includes spasmodic epigastric and abdominal pain from Liver invading the Spleen and Stomach, neck and upper back pain from *qi* stagnation, calf cramps and restless leg syndrome, writers cramp, post febrile and dehydration muscle spasm, intercostal and trigeminal neuralgia, generalised muscle spasm, urinary bladder and gallbladder colic, spasm of the uterus and vasospasm.
- Polycystic ovarian disease. The combination of sour (peony) and sweet (licorice) helps creates physiological *yin* to replace pathological *yin*, here in the form of Phlegm cysts on the ovaries.

Composition
Paeonia lactiflora (bai shao, white peony) 48.5%, *Glycyrrhiza uralensis* (zhi gan cao, honey fried licorice) 48.5%

Combinations
- With **6.3 Chai Hu Shu Gan Wan** for abdominal pain from Liver Spleen disharmony.
- With **7.1.1 Liu Wei Di Huang Wan** for nocturnal calf cramps and restless leg.

Dosage and method of administration
8-12 pills, three times daily used alone. When combined with a targeting formula, 4-8 pills, three times daily may be sufficient.

Cautions and contraindications
None noted.

PAIN

10.23 ZHENG GU SHUI

正骨水

Yulin Drug Manufactory (Guangxi)
'Correct (or mend) Bone Water'
Zheng Gu Shui is packaged in several forms with different applicators, including roll on (pictured), spray packs, aerosols and small and large bottles.

E

TCM actions

Quickens Blood and disperses stagnant Blood, stops pain, promotes healing.

Biomedical actions

Anodyne, rubefacient.

INDICATIONS

- Blood stagnation type pain, associated with trauma, sprains, strains, uncomplicated fractures and bruising. Excellent for all injuries, especially those with bruising. Alcohol based and thus absorbed quickly. Stimulates local circulation and metabolism, accelerates osteoblast activity. Significantly reduces recovery time for all types of closed trauma.
- Used extensively to aid the healing of simple fractures (such as greenstick), or to encourage non-healing bones to knit.
- For relief of the chronic pain of Wind Damp *bi* syndrome, osteo-arthritis or rheumatoid arthritis and old injuries.

Composition (each ml contains)

Cinnamomum camphora (zhang nao, camphor) 500mg, *Panax notoginseng* (tian qi, tianqi ginseng) 220mg, *Paeonia suffruticosa* (mu dan pi, moutan) 220mg, *Dalbergia odorifera* (jiang xiang, dalbergia wood) 209mg, *Zanthoxylum nitidum* (liang mian zhen, zanthoxylum root) 176mg, *Angelica dahurica* (bai zhi, angelica root) 143mg, *Polygonum cuspidatum* (hu zhang, bushy knotweed) 121mg, *Moghania macrophylla* (qian jin ba, moghania) 121mg, menthol 50mg

Combinations

- With **10.4 Chin Gu Tie Shang Wan** or **1.29 Bu Gai Zhuang Gu Capsule** to encourage the healing of slow knitting fractures and broken bones.
- With **10.3 Die Da Zhi Tong Capsules** for pain and bruising from trauma.

Pattern identifying features

- **all types of traumatic injury**
- chronic pain from stagnant Blood

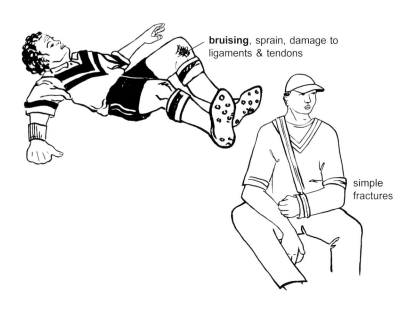

bruising, sprain, damage to ligaments & tendons

simple fractures

Dosage and method of administration

Rub liberally and firmly into the affected area as often as practical, or apply on cotton wool and bandage for up to 2 hours at a time.

Cautions and contraindications

Contraindicated during pregnancy, for children under 5 years, when there is skin disease such as eczema, and for patients with acute inflammation where RICE (rest, ice, compression, elevation) is the appropriate treatment. Not suitable for use on broken skin. For external use only. Keep out of reach of children.

May irritate the skin of some patients causing redness and itch, especially those with fair skin. Avoid contact with the eyes, mucous membranes and other sensitive areas.

PAIN

10.24 ZHENG GU GING

正骨精

(Zheng Gu Jing)

Hua Tuo Chinese Herbal Co. (Australia)

'Correct (or mend) Bone Alcohol Extract'

Zheng Gu Ging is packaged in bottles of 100 ml.

E

TCM actions

Quickens Blood and disperses stagnant Blood, stops pain, promotes healing.

Biomedical actions

Anodyne, rubefacient.

INDICATIONS

- Similar in action to **10.23 Zheng Gu Shui**. For Blood stagnation type pain from trauma, sprains, strains and uncomplicated fractures. Stimulates local circulation and metabolism, accelerates osteoblast activity.
- Wind Damp *bi* syndrome or Blood stagnation type chronic joint pain, spasm and stiffness associated with arthritic conditions.

Composition (each bottle contains)

Menthol 5.5g, Camphor 4.5g, *Panax notoginseng* (tian qi, tianqi ginseng) 2.2g, *Rheum palmatum* (da huang, rhubarb root) 1.8g, *Angelica dahurica* (bai zhi, angelica) 1g, *Angelica pubescens* (du huo, Tu-huo) 1g, *Commiphora myrrha* (mo yao, myrrh) 1g, *Pistocia lentiscus* (mastic) 1g, *Angelica sinensis* (dang gui, chinese angelica) 0.8g, ethanol

Dosage and method of administration

Rub liberally and firmly into the affected area as often as practical, or apply on cotton wool and bandage for up to 2 hours at a time.

Cautions and contraindications

Contraindicated during pregnancy, for children under 5 years, when there is skin disease such as eczema, and for patients with acute inflammation where RICE (rest, ice, compression, elevation) is the appropriate treatment. Not suitable for use on broken skin. For external use only. Keep out of reach of children.

May irritate the skin of some patients causing redness and itch, especially those with fair skin. Avoid contact with the eyes, mucous membranes and other sensitive areas.

10.25 DIE DA TIAN QI YAO JIU
跌打田七药酒

Wu Xiang Brand (Hong Kong)
'Pseudoginseng Alcohol Extract for Traumatic Injury'
Die Da Tian Qi Yao Jiu is packaged in bottles of 198 ml.

E

TCM actions
Quickens Blood and disperses stagnant Blood, stops pain, promotes healing.

Biomedical actions
Anodyne, rubefacient.

INDICATIONS

- Similar in action to **10.23 Zheng Gu Shui**. For Blood stagnation type pain from trauma, sprains, strains and uncomplicated fractures. Stimulates local circulation and metabolism, accelerates osteoblast activity. This formula is particularly popular amongst martial arts enthusiasts.
- Wind Damp *bi* syndrome or Blood stagnation type chronic joint pain, spasm and stiffness associated with arthritic conditions.

Composition
Panax notoginseng (tian qi, tianqi ginseng) 20%, *Angelica sinensis* (dang gui, chinese angelica) 20%, *Daemonorops draco* (xue jie, dragons blood) 15%, *Typhae augustifolia* (pu huang, bulrush pollen) 15%, *Carthamus tinctorius* (hong hua, carthamus) 10%, *Paeonia veitchii* (chi shao, red peony) 10%, *Boswellia carterii* (ru xiang, frankincense) 5%, *Commiphora myrrha* (mo yao, myrrh) 5%, ethanol

Dosage and method of administration
Rub liberally and firmly into the affected area as often as practical, or apply on cotton wool and bandage for up to 2 hours at a time.

Cautions and contraindications
Contraindicated during pregnancy, for children under 5 years, when there is skin disease such as eczema, and for patients with acute inflammation where RICE (rest, ice, compression, elevation) is the appropriate treatment. Not suitable for use on broken skin. For external use only. Keep out of reach of children.

May irritate the skin of some patients causing redness and itch, especially those with fair skin. Avoid contact with the eyes, mucous membranes and other sensitive areas.

PAIN

E

10.26 MINJAK GOSOK

莪术油

Wu Xiang Brand (Sulawesi)
'Curcuma Oil'
Min Jak Gosok is packaged in 50 ml bottles.

TCM actions

Quickens Blood and disperses stagnant Blood, dispels Wind Cold Damp, stops pain, promotes healing.

Biomedical actions

Anodyne, rubefacient.

INDICATIONS

- Chronic pain, stiffness, numbness and paresthesia from Wind Cold Damp *bi* syndrome or Blood stagnation. Also for acute pain following trauma. This liniment is quite warming and best for cold type pain.
- Can also be applied to the lower abdomen for dysmenorrhea and for gynecological pain from Blood stagnation or masses.

Composition

Curcuma zeodoria (e zhu, curcuma ezhu)

Dosage and method of administration

Rub liberally and firmly into affected area as often as practical. Good as an invigorating and heating massage oil.

Cautions and contraindications

Contraindicated during pregnancy, for children under 5 years, when there is skin disease such as eczema, and for patients with acute inflammation where RICE (rest, ice, compression, elevation) is the appropriate treatment. Not suitable for use on broken skin. For external use only. Keep out of reach of children.

May irritate the skin of some patients causing redness and itch, especially those with fair skin. Avoid contact with the eyes, mucous membranes and other sensitive areas.

10.27 ZHI TONG YOU

止痛油

Jing Xian Pharmaceutical Co. (Guangzhou)
'Analgesic Oil'
Zhi Tong You is packaged in 198 ml bottles.

TCM actions
Dispels Wind Cold Damp, quickens Blood, disperses stagnant Blood, stops pain.

E

Biomedical actions
Anodyne, rubefacient.

INDICATIONS

- Temporary relief of pain associated with rheumatic conditions, arthritis, sciatica, fibrositis, neuralgia, traumatic injury, sprains and bruising.
- Relief of muscular pain, spasm and cramp, tension headache.

Composition (each 100ml contains extracts equivalent to)
Gaultheria procumbens (wintergreen oil) 35g, *Pinus massoniana* (turpentine oil) 18g, *Cinnamomum cassia* (rou gui, cinnamon bark oil) 18g, *Mentha haplocalyx* (peppermint oil) 12.5g, *Panax notoginseng* (tian qi, tianqi ginseng) 250mg, *Angelica polymorpha* (dang gui, chinese angelica) 250mg

Dosage and method of administration
Massage 3-5 drops onto the affected area several times daily.

Cautions and contraindications
Contraindicated during pregnancy, for children under 5 years, when there is skin disease such as eczema, and for patients with acute inflammation where RICE (rest, ice, compression, elevation) is the appropriate treatment. Not suitable for use on broken skin. For external use only. Keep out of reach of children.

May irritate the skin of some patients causing redness and itch, especially those with fair skin. Avoid contact with the eyes, mucous membranes and other sensitive areas.

PAIN

10.28 WONG LOP KONG MEDICATED OIL

祛风止痛油

(Qu Feng Zhi Tong You)

Wong Lap Kwong Medicine Co. (Hong Kong)

'Expel Wind Stop Pain Oil'

Wong Lop Kong Medicated Oil is packaged in 30 ml bottles.

E

TCM actions

Invigorates *qi* and quickens Blood, disperses stagnant Blood, dispels Wind Cold Damp, stops pain.

Biomedical actions

Anodyne, rubefacient.

INDICATIONS

- Used for a variety of minor muscular and joint aches and pains associated with simple backache, strains, bruising, trauma and overuse. Arthritic pain. As with all oils, this is slowly absorbed and long acting.
- Alleviates itching and irritation from insect bites and stings.

Composition (w/v)

Camphor oil 34%, *Camellia oleifera* (tea oil) 30%, *Pinus massoniana* (turpentine oil) 12%, *Daemonorops draco* (xue jie, dragons blood oil) 4%, *Mentha haplocalyx* (peppermint oil) 4%, *Angelica sinensis* (dang gui, chinese angelica) 4%, *Carthamus tinctorius* (hong hua, carthamus) 4%, *Commiphora myrrha* (mo yao, myrrh) 4%, *Boswellia carterii* (ru xiang, frankincense) 4%

Dosage and method of administration

Massage 3-5 drops into the affected area several times daily.

Cautions and contraindications

Contraindicated during pregnancy, for children under 5 years and for patients with acute inflammation where RICE (rest, ice, compression, elevation) is the appropriate treatment. Not suitable for use on broken skin. For external use only. Keep out of reach of children.

May irritate the skin of some patients causing redness and itch, especially those with fair skin. Avoid contact with the eyes, mucous membranes and other sensitive areas.

10.29 WHITE FLOWER EMBROCATION

白花油

E

(Bai Hua You)
'White Flower Oil'
Hoe Hin Pak Fah Yeow Manufactory (Hong Kong)
White Flower Embrocation is packaged in bottles of 10 and 20ml.

TCM actions
Stimulates and moves *qi* and eases the muscles, transforms and disperses Phlegm and opens the orifices.

Biomedical actions
Anodyne, rubefacient.

INDICATIONS

- For temporary relief of minor muscular aches and pains from fatigue and exertion, minor muscular strains and minor arthritic pain. Also useful for tension headaches and epigastric pain.
- Stops the itch and irritation from insect bites and stings.
- Relieves chest, nasal and sinus congestion associated with colds and flu. Can also clear stuffiness in the head. May assist in alleviating motion sickness.

Composition (w/v)
Gaultheria procumbens (wintergreen oil) 40%, Menthol crystal 30%, Eucalyptus Oil 18%, Camphor 6%, Lavender Oil 6%

Dosage and method of administration
Rub a few drops into the affected area. If necessary, repeat every two hours. Can be mixed with a carrier oil if too strong. A few drops in hot water as a steam inhalation can relieve nasal and sinus congestion associated with colds and flu. Can also be rubbed on the chest for congestion and mucus buildup. A few drops can be inhaled on a tissue to alleviate motion sickness.

Cautions and contraindications
Contraindicated during pregnancy. May cause skin irritation in some patients. Avoid contact with the eyes and mucous membranes. Not suitable for use on broken skin. Keep out of reach of children.

PAIN

10.30 PO SUM ON MEDICATED OIL

保心安

(Bao Xin An)

Po Sum On Medicine Factory (Hong Kong)
'Protect and Calm the Heart'
Po Sum On Medicated Oil is packaged in small bottles of 30ml.

TCM actions
Stimulates movement of *qi* and quickens Blood, regulates Liver *qi*,
eases the muscles and stops pain.

Biomedical actions
Relaxes muscles, anodyne, rubefacient.

INDICATIONS

- Regulates and disperses stagnant *qi*. Used as a massage oil for tight muscles, especially good on the neck and shoulders. Excellent for very tense or uptight patients and those with chronic Liver *qi* stagnation, as it fairly powerfully moves stagnant *qi* in the muscles of the Liver and Gallbladder channel pathways, easing and soothing muscular tension and stress.
- Nasal and sinus congestion and tension headaches. A little on a tissue can clear blocked sinuses and a dab rubbed on the temples can ease tension and stress headaches. Can assist in relieving chest congestion associated with colds and flu. Can also clear stuffiness in the head.

Composition
Mentha haplocalyx (peppermint oil) 57.3% v/v, *Camelia sinensis* (tea oil) 39.4% v/v, *Daemonorops draco* (xue jie, dragons blood) 2.07% w/v, *Scutellaria baicalensis* (huang qin, scute) 0.58% w/v, *Cinnamon cassia* (rou gui, cinnamon bark) 0.32% w/v, *Glycyrrhiza uralensis* (gan cao, licorice) 0.32% w/v

Combinations
- With **6.4 Xiao Yao Wan** or **6.5 Jia Wei Xiao Yao Wan** for constitutionally stressed and uptight patients with chronic neck and upper back spasm and pain.
- With **15.4 Tian Ma Gou Teng Wan** for frontal or temporal headaches or migraines from Liver *qi* stagnation with *yang* rising.
- With **3.9 Chuan Xiong Cha Tiao Wan** for headache from Wind Cold.

Pattern identifying features

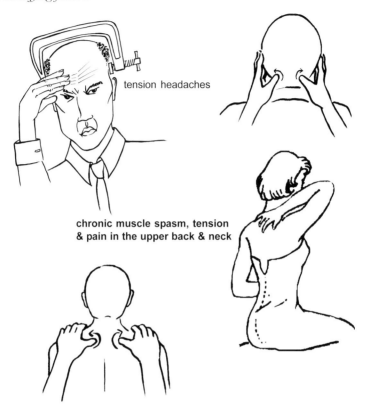

tension headaches

chronic muscle spasm, tension
& pain in the upper back & neck

Dosage and method of administration

Rub a few drops into the affected area and massage gently. If necessary, repeat
every two hours. Can be mixed with a carrier oil if too strong. A few drops in hot
water as a steam inhalation can relieve nasal and sinus congestion associated with
colds and flu. Can also be rubbed on the chest for congestion and mucus buildup. A
few drops can be inhaled on a tissue to alleviate motion sickness.

Cautions and contraindications

Contraindicated during pregnancy. Not recommended in very run down individuals,
as being quite pungent the oil can disperse *qi* and cause fatigue and dizziness. Keep
out of reach of children. May irritate the skin in some patients, especially those with
fair skin, causing redness and itch. Avoid contact with the eyes, mucous membranes
and other sensitive areas.

PAIN

10.31 TRANS WOOD LOCK LINIMENT

鸸鹋活络油

(Er Miao Huo Luo You)
Sunho Traditional Medicine Company (Australia)
'Emu Oil to Invigorate (circulation in) the Channels'
Trans Wood Lock Liniment is packaged in 50 ml bottles.

TCM actions
Dispels Wind Cold Damp, warms the channels, stops pain.

Biomedical actions
Anodyne, rubefacient.

INDICATIONS

- A very warming liniment for Wind Cold Damp *bi* syndrome, rheumatic pain, musculoskeletal aches and pains, chronic heaviness, aching and pain of joints and muscles, stiffness and spasm of muscles and tendons. Emu oil is absorbed quite slowly, so **10.31 Trans Wood Lock Liniment** is useful for prolonged relief of the pain associated with osteo-arthritis and rheumatoid arthritis, muscular and joint sprain, trauma and overuse, lumbago and sciatica.
- Itching and pain of insect bites and stings.

Composition (per 100ml)
Australian Emu Oil 20ml, Menthol 25g, Methyl Salicylate 25ml, Camphor 10g, Turpentine oil 15ml, Oleoresin Capsicum 0.5ml

Dosage and method of administration
Apply generously to the affected area and gently massage into the skin 1-2 times daily and before bed. Because emu oil is slowly absorbed, it takes a while for the full effects to be felt, and they last a relatively long time. It is usual to wait for at least 30-60 minutes before assuming that insufficient liniment was applied because the patient does not feel the effect. If too much is applied, it can become uncomfortably hot.

Cautions and contraindications
Contraindicated during pregnancy, for children under 5 years, when there is skin disease such as eczema, and for patients with acute inflammation where RICE (rest, ice, compression, elevation) is the appropriate treatment. Not suitable for use on broken skin. For external use only. Keep out of reach of children. May irritate the skin of some patients causing redness and itch, especially those with fair skin. Avoid contact with the eyes, mucous membranes and other sensitive areas.

10.32 DIE DA JIU

特效跌打酒

(Te Xiao Die Da Jiu)
Wu Min Pharmaceutical Co. (Guangzhou)
'Specially Effective Trauma [Alcohol based] Liniment'
Die Da Jiu is packaged in 100ml bottles.

E

TCM actions
Quickens Blood and disperses stagnant Blood, stops pain, promotes healing.

Biomedical actions
Anodyne, rubefacient.

INDICATIONS

- Similar in action to **10.23 Zheng Gu Shui**. For Blood stagnation type pain from sports injuries and trauma, sprains, strains and uncomplicated fractures. Stimulates local circulation and metabolism, accelerates osteoblast activity.
- Wind Damp *bi* syndrome or Blood stagnation type chronic joint pain, spasm and stiffness associated with arthritic conditions.

Composition (per 100ml)
Panax notoginseng (tian qi, tianqi ginseng) 250mg, *Angelica dahurica* (bai zhi, angelica) 250mg, *Angelica pubescens* (du huo, Tu-huo) 250mg, *Ligusticum wallichi* (chuan xiong, cnidium) 250mg, *Boswellia carterii* (ru xiang, frankincense) 250mg, *Angelica polymorpha* (dang gui, chinese angelica) 250mg, ethanol

Dosage and method of administration
Rub liberally and firmly into the affected area as often as practical, or apply on cotton wool and bandage for up to 2 hours at a time.

Cautions and contraindications
Contraindicated during pregnancy, for children under 5 years, when there is skin disease such as eczema, and for patients with acute inflammation where RICE (rest, ice, compression, elevation) is the appropriate treatment. Not suitable for use on broken skin. For external use only. Keep out of reach of children. May irritate the skin of some patients causing redness and itch, especially those with fair skin. Avoid contact with the eyes, mucous membranes and other sensitive areas.

PAIN

10.33 WOOD LOCK MEDICATED BALM

黄道益活络油

(Huang Dao Yi Huo Luo You)
China Medical Laboratory (Hong Kong)
'Huang Dao Yi's Invigorate (circulation in) the Channels Oil'
Wood Lock Medicated Balm is packaged in bottles of 50ml.

TCM actions
Moves *qi* and eases the muscles, transforms and disperses Phlegm and opens the orifices.

Biomedical actions
Anodyne, rubefacient.

INDICATIONS

- For temporary relief of the pain of arthritis and rheumatism; relief of muscular aches and pains, cramps and spasms.
- Symptoms of influenza, nasal, sinus and chest congestion.
- Can relieve tension headache and neuralgia. Good for tightness in the muscles of the neck and shoulders.

Composition (each gram contains)
Mentha haplocalyx (peppermint oil) 350mg, *Gaultheria procumbens* (wintergreen oil) 240mg, Turpentine oil 225mg, Lavender oil 130mg, Camphor oil 25mg; liquid extracts equivalent to dry *Angelica polymorpha* (dang gui, chinese angelica) 55mg, *Eucommia ulmoides* (du zhong, eucommia) 55mg

Dosage and method of administration
Rub a few drops into the affected area. If necessary, repeat every two hours. Can be mixed with a carrier oil if too strong. A few drops in hot water as a steam inhalation can relieve nasal and sinus congestion associated with colds and flu. Can also be rubbed on the chest for congestion and mucus buildup. A few drops can be inhaled on a tissue to alleviate motion sickness.

Cautions and contraindications
Contraindicated during pregnancy. For external use only. Do not massage too vigorously or the skin may become irritated. Avoid contact with eyes and mucous membranes. Not suitable for use on open wounds or skin diseases. Not suitable for children under 3 years old.

10.34 IMADA RED FLOWER OIL

正红花油

(Zheng Hong Hua You)
Imada Pharmaceutical Co. (Hong Kong)
'True Carthamus Oil'
Imada Red Flower Oil is packaged in bottles of 50ml.

E

TCM actions

Invigorates *qi* and quickens Blood, dispels Cold, stops pain.

Biomedical actions

Anodyne, rubefacient.

INDICATIONS

- Temporary relief of pain associated with rheumatic conditions, arthritis, sciatica, fibrositis, neuralgia, traumatic injury, sprains and bruising.
- Relief of muscular pain, spasms and cramps.
- Insect bites and stings.

Composition

Methyl Salicylate, Cinnamon leaf oil, *Eugenia caryophyllata* (ding xiang, clove oil), Citronella oil, *Daemonorops draco* (xue jie, dragons blood), *Carthamus tinctorius* (hong hua, carthamus)

Dosage and method of administration

Apply to the affected area and massage gently. Repeat every four hours as necessary.

Cautions and contraindications

Contraindicated during pregnancy. For external use only. Do not massage too vigorously or the skin may become irritated. Avoid contact with eyes and mucous membranes. Not suitable for use on open wounds or skin diseases. Not suitable for children under 3 years old.

PAIN

E

10.35 EAGLE BRAND MEDICATED OIL

德国风油精

(De Guo Feng You Jing)
Borden Co. Pte Ltd (Singapore)
'German Wind Essential Oil'
Eagle Brand Medicated Oil is packaged in bottles of 24ml.

TCM actions
Stimulates and regulates Liver *qi*, eases the muscles and stops pain.

Biomedical actions
Relaxes muscles, anodyne, rubefacient.

INDICATIONS

- Temporary relief of minor muscular aches and pains associated with simple backache, rheumatic conditions, osteo-arthritis, strains and sprains. Also used for stress and tension headaches. Especially good on the neck and upper back. The relatively high proportion of menthol makes this oil quite good for regulating and invigorating stagnant *qi* in the superficial muscles.

Composition
Menthol 28.5% w/w, Methyl Salicylate 18.6% w/w, Eucalyptus oil 1.56% w/w, ethanol

Dosage and method of administration
Rub a few drops into the affected area and massage gently. If necessary, repeat every two hours. Maximum application is four times daily. Can be mixed with a carrier oil if too strong.

Cautions and contraindications
Caution during pregnancy. For external use only. Do not massage too vigorously or the skin may become irritated. Avoid contact with eyes and mucous membranes. Not suitable for use on open wounds or skin diseases. Not suitable for children under 3 years old.

10.36 KUNG FU OIL

功夫油

(Gong Fu You)
Run Cheng Tang Herbal Remedies Co. (Australia)
'Gong Fu [Martial Arts] Oil'
Kung Fu Oil is packaged in bottles of 50ml.

TCM actions

Stimulates and regulates Liver *qi*, eases the muscles, dispels Wind Cold Damp, warms the channels, stops pain.

Biomedical actions

Anodyne, rubefacient.

INDICATIONS

- Temporary relief of minor muscular aches and pains associated with sporting injuries, overuse syndromes, rheumatic conditions, osteo-arthritis, strains and sprains.
- Particularly useful as an adjunct treatment for chronic Wind Cold Damp *bi* syndrome due to the inclusion of the Wind Damp expelling Tu-huo, and the *yang* warming asarum and clove oil.

Composition (w/v)

Mentha haplocalyx (peppermint oil) 40%, *Eugenia caryophyllata* (ding xiang, clove oil) 6%, *Gaultheria procumbens* (wintergreen oil) 10%, Paraffin oil 24%, *Angelica pubescens* (du huo, Tu-huo) 1.5%, *Asarum seiboldi* (xi xin, asarum) 1.7%, ethanol 16.8%

Dosage and method of administration

Apply 3-6 drops to the affected area and massage gently. Maximum application is three times daily.

Cautions and contraindications

Contraindicated during pregnancy. For external use only. Do not massage too vigorously or the skin may become irritated. Avoid contact with eyes and mucous membranes. Not suitable for use on open wounds or skin diseases. Not suitable for children under 3 years old.

PAIN

E

10.37 TIGER BALM

虎標万金油

(Hu Piao Wan Jin You)
Haw Par Corporation (Singapore)
Tiger Balm is packaged in small jars or flat tins of ointment.
There are two types, red and white.

E

TCM actions

Stimulates and moves *qi* and eases the muscles, transforms
and disperses Phlegm and opens the orifices.

Biomedical actions

Relaxes muscles, improves local circulation, analgesic.

INDICATIONS

- For temporary relief of muscular aches, pain and spasm, arthritic or
  rheumatic pain, sprains, headaches, nasal, sinus and chest congestion, insect
  bites, itch and flatulence. Useful for the pain of gout (White Tiger balm).
- For quick relief of cramps and spasms in the muscles, especially the calf.
- Useful as a pre-workout warm up on the leg muscles to enhance endurance.
- **Red Tiger Balm** contains cinnamon oil and thus is hotter and better for Wind
  Cold Damp *bi* syndrome and pain associated with poor circulation or exposure
  to cold.
- **White Tiger Balm** is more cooling and better at moving stuck *qi* locally–ideal
  for cramps and spasms, and warmer injuries or inflammatory pain such as gout.

Composition
Tiger Balm Red
Camphor 25%, Menthol 10%, *Melaleuca cajuputi* (cajuput teatree oil) 7%, dementholised
mint oil 6%, *Eugenia caryophyllata* (ding xiang, clove oil) 5%, *Cinnamon cassia* (rou gui,
cinnamon bark oil) 5%, paraffin and petroleum jelly to 100%

Tiger Balm White
Camphor 25%, dementholised mint oil 16%, *Melaleuca cajuputi* (cajuput teatree oil)
13%, Menthol 8%, *Eugenia caryophyllata* (ding xiang, clove oil) 1.5%, yellow soft paraffin
10.5%, hard paraffin to 100%

Pattern identifying features

• temporary relief of aches & pains,
  spasms, cramps & congestion

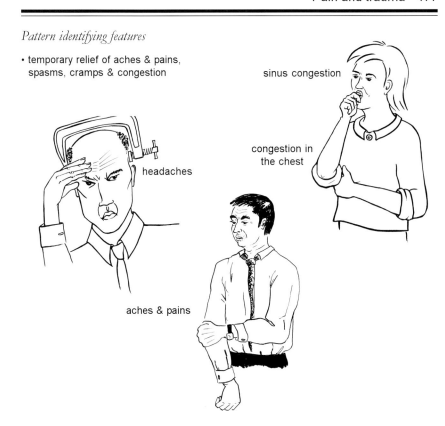

sinus congestion

congestion in
the chest

headaches

aches & pains

Dosage and method of administration
Apply gently to the affected area.

Cautions and contraindications
Contraindicated during pregnancy and for children under three years old. Keep out
of reach of children. For external use only. Avoid contact with the eyes, mucous
membranes and broken skin. May irritate the skin of some patients, especially those
with fair skin, causing redness and itch. **Red Tiger Balm** can stain clothes.

PAIN

10.38 PLASTER FOR BRUISE AND ANALGESIC

跌打止痛膏

(Die Da Zhi Tong Gao)
Guangzhou Medicine and Health Products Import Export
Corp. (Guangzhou)
'Analgesic Trauma Plaster'
Plaster for Bruise and Analgesic is packaged as sticky herb
lined cloth sheet, ten sheets per box.

E

TCM actions

Quickens Blood, disperses stagnant Blood, stops pain.

Biomedical actions

Invigorates local circulation, anti-inflammatory, anodyne.

INDICATIONS

- Excellent applied topically for all acute injuries, including sprains and strains, bruising, and traumatic injury where the skin is unbroken. Can significantly accelerate resolution of bruising and healing of damaged tissues.
- Good for chronic osteo-arthritis, rheumatoid arthritic and other Wind Cold Damp *bi* pain conditions. Especially good for chronic lower back ache.
- May also assist in the relief of neuralgic pain, such as intercostal and post-herpetic neuralgia.

Composition

Lonicera japonica (jin yin hua, lonicera) 20%, *Os draconis* (long gu, dragon bone) 10.42%, *Eupolyphaga sinensis* (di bie chong, field cockroach) 10.42%, *Carthamus tinctorius* (hong hua, carthamus) 9.17%, *Rheum palmatum* (da huang, rhubarb) 8.33%, *Gardenia jasminoides* (shan zhi zi, gardenia) 8.32%, *Taraxacum mongolicum* (pu gong ying, dandelion) 8.33%, *Daemonorops draco* (xue jie, dragons blood) 4.17%, *Acacia catechu* (hai er cha, catechu) 6.25%, *Commiphora myrrha* (mo yao, myrrh) 6.25%, *Drynaria fortunei* (gu sui bu, drynaria) 4.17%, *Dipsacus asper* (xu duan, dipsacus) 4.17%

Combinations

- With **10.1 Yunnan Paiyao** or **10.3 Die Da Zhi Tong Capsule** for pain and bruising from trauma.
- With **10.15 Du Huo Ji Sheng Wan** for Kidney deficiency aches and pains.
- With **7.9 Fu Gui Ba Wei Wan** for Kidney *yang* deficiency pain and stiffness.

Pattern identifying features

- **Blood stagnation**
- Wind Cold Damp *bi* pain

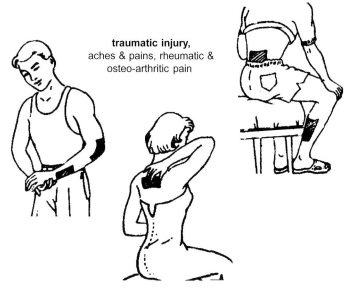

traumatic injury,
aches & pains, rheumatic &
osteo-arthritic pain

- With **5.1 Xue Fu Zhu Yu Wan** for post-herpetic neuralgia associated with
  stagnant Blood.

Dosage and method of administration

Cut a sheet to the desired size and apply to the affected area after removal of the
transparent backing plastic. Mobile or hairy areas may need to be bound with a
bandage or thermoskin to keep the plaster in place. Good at night when movement
is less. Effective for 24 hours.

Cautions and Contraindications

Contraindicated during pregnancy, on skin disease and during acute inflammation
following trauma where RICE (rest, ice, compression, elevation) is the appropriate
treatment (usually the first 24-48 hours). Not suitable for use on broken skin and on
young children. May cause skin irritiation in some patients, usually those with fair
skin. Any irritation usually subsides quickly once the patch is removed.

PAIN

10.39 DIE DA FENG SHI PLASTER

跌打风湿膏

Guangzhou Jingxiutang Pharmaceutical Co. (Guangzhou)
Trauma and Arthritis Plaster'
Die Da Feng Shi Plasters are packaged in boxes of five small sheets.

E

TCM actions
Dispels Wind Damp, stops pain.

Biomedical actions
Invigorates local circulation, anti-inflammatory, anodyne.

INDICATIONS

- For temporary relief of Wind Cold Damp *bi* pain, osteo-arthritic or rheumatic pain and musculo-tendonous aches and pains associated with sprains and strains, sports injury, trauma and overexertion.

Composition (each plaster contains)
Dryobalanops aromatica (bing pian, borneol) 137mg, *Nardostachys chinensis* (gan song, nardostachys) 360mg, *Zanthoxylum nitidum* (liang mian zhen) 159mg, *Eucalyptus globus* (eucalyptus oil) 80mg, *Ilex chinensis* (chinese holly seed oil) 69mg, *Kaempferia galanga* 36mg, *Schizonepeta tenuifolia* (jing jie, schizonepeta) 32mg, *Impatiens balsamina* (ji xing zi, impatiens) 32mg, *Angelica dahurica* (bai zhi, angelica) 30mg, *Zingiber officinalis* (sheng jiang, ginger) 26mg, *Ledebouriella divaricata* (fang feng, siler) 24mg, *Drynaria fortunei* (gu sui bu, drynaria) 20mg, *Cinnamomum cassia* (rou gui, cinnamon oil) 20mg, *Syzygium aromaticum* (ding xiang, clove oil) 14mg

Dosage and method of administration
Applied to the affected area after removal of the transparent plastic backing. Mobile or hairy areas may need to be bound with a bandage or thermoskin to keep the plaster in place. Good at night when movement is less. Effective for 24 hours.

Pattern identifying features

• **Wind Cold Damp** *bi* **syndrome**

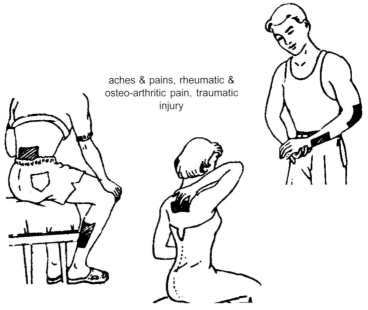

aches & pains, rheumatic &
osteo-arthritic pain, traumatic
injury

Cautions and Contraindications

Contraindicated over the lower abdomen and lower back during pregnancy, on skin disease and during acute inflammation following trauma where RICE (rest, ice, compression, elevation) is the appropriate treatment (usually the first 24-48 hours). Not suitable for use on broken skin and or on children under six years old. May cause skin irritation in some patients, usually those with fair skin. Any irritation usually subsides quickly once the patch is removed.

PAIN

10.40 POROUS CAPSICUM PLASTER

(La Jiao Gao)
Vorwerk & Sohn (Germany)
Porous Capsicum Plasters are packaged as large and small rubber backed sheets lined with the sticky herbal extract.

E

TCM actions
Warms the channels and dispels Cold, stops pain.

Biomedical actions
Invigorates local circulation, counter-irritant, dilates capillaries, anodyne.

INDICATIONS

• A very hot plaster for pain associated with cold conditions. Excellent for Wind Cold Damp *bi* syndrome, cold type dysmenorrhea, osteo-arthritis and generalised musculoskeletal aches and pains that are worse in cold weather.

Composition
Pinus massoniana (turpentine oil) 27%, *Capsicum oleoresin* (la jiao, chilli) 3%, Zinc oxide 14%, Ferric oxide 1%, rubber 55%

Combinations
• With **10.8 Xiao Huo Luo Dan** for severe Cold *bi* pain.
• With **10.15 Du Huo Ji Sheng Wan** for Kidney deficiency aches and pains.
• With **7.9 Fu Gui Ba Wei Wan** for Kidney *yang* deficiency pain and stiffness.
• With **10.18 Jian Bu Qiang Shen Wan** for lower back ache from Kidney *yang* deficiency with Wind Damp.

Dosage and method of administration
Wash the skin with soap and dry well. Apply the sticky side to the affected area after removal of the backing sheet. Mobile or hairy areas may need to be bound with a bandage or thermoskin to keep the plaster in place. Good at night when movement is less. Effective for 24-48 hours. Rest the area for a few days before applying another plaster. The large plasters are good for big areas, but can be cut to fit on small areas such as the fingers and toes. Any residue left after removal of the plaster can be removed with alcohol.

Pattern identifying features

• Cold *bi* syndrome

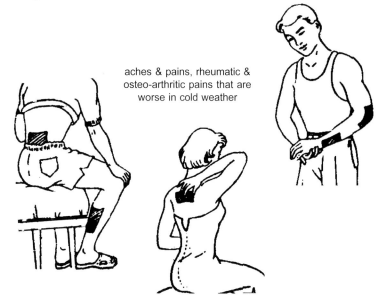

aches & pains, rheumatic &
osteo-arthritic pains that are
worse in cold weather

Cautions and Contraindications

Contraindicated over the lower abdomen and lower back during pregnancy, on skin diseases, and during acute inflammation where RICE (rest, ice, compression, elevation) is the appropriate treatment (usually the first 24-48 hours). Not suitable for use on broken skin or on young children. These plasters are very hot and will often cause skin irritation or blistering in fair skinned patients if left too long. Be careful with the elderly and with those who may have reduced sensation in the skin.

PAIN

GMP **10.41 GOU PI GAO**

 狗皮膏

E

Tong Ren Tang (Beijing)
'Dog Skin Plaster'
Gou Pi Gou is packaged as a 15 gram
mass of herbs on a cloth square.

TCM actions
Warms the channels and powerfully dispels Cold, stops pain.

Biomedical actions
Invigorates local circulation, counter-irritant, dilates capillaries, anodyne.

INDICATIONS

- Localised joint or muscle pain, numbness, paresthesia or compromised circulation associated with chronic Cold Damp *bi* syndrome, arthritic conditions or trauma. The pain is fixed, worse with cold, damp weather and significantly improved with warmth.
- Can also be used locally or on selected acupuncture points for *yang* deficient or Cold type disorders such as dysmenorrhea, chronic lower back ache, impotence, lung disease with copious thin watery sputum (e.g. chronic bronchitis), and abdominal masses from Cold accumulation.

Composition
Aconitium carmichaeli (chuan wu, aconite), *Aconitium kusnezoffii* (cao wu, wild aconite), *Angelica pubescens* (du huo, Tu-huo), *Notopterygium incisum* (qiang huo, notopterygium), *Periploca sepium* (xiang jia pi), *Clematis chinensis* (wei ling xian, chinese clematis), *Dipsacus asper* (xu duan, dipsacus), *Angelica sinensis* (dang gui, chinese angelica)

Combinations
- With **10.8 Xiao Huo Luo Dan** for severe or chronic Cold arthritic pain.
- With **1.13 Woo Garm Yuen Medical Pills, 1.18 Shao Fu Zhu Yu Wan** or **1.14 Wen Jing Tang Wan** for severe Cold type dysmenorrhea.
- With **10.15 Du Huo Ji Sheng Wan** for Kidney deficiency aches and pains.
- With **7.9 Fu Gui Ba Wei Wan** for Kidney *yang* deficiency lower back and joint pain and stiffness.

Pattern identifying features

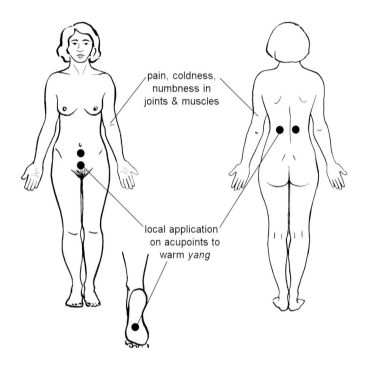

pain, coldness, numbness in joints & muscles

local application on acupoints to warm *yang*

Dosage and method of administration

The mass of herbs is quite hard and must be softened before use. To do this, it can be placed in an oven or microwave and gently warmed, or steamed over a boiling jug until soft. While still warm (not hot), apply to the affected area. If no irritation occurs it can be left in place for a several days at a time. The same plaster can be gently removed and reused a few times.

Cautions and Contraindications

Contraindicated during pregnancy, on skin diseases, and during acute inflammation where RICE (rest, ice, compression, elevation) is the appropriate treatment (usually the first 24-48 hours). Not suitable for use on broken skin or on young children. These plasters are very hot and will often cause skin irritation or blistering in fair skinned patients if left too long. Be careful with the elderly and with those who may have reduced sensation in the skin.

PAIN

Patent Medicines for Men's Health

男科病

11.1 QIAN LIE XIAN CAPSULE

特效前列腺丸

(Te Xiao Qian Lie Xian Wan)
Jing Xian Pharmaceutical Co. (Guangzhou)
'Especially Effective Prostate Gland Pills'
Qian Lie Xian Capsules are packaged in bottles of 36 capsules.

TCM actions

Clears residual and lurking Damp and Toxic Heat from
the prostate and lower *jiao*, quickens Blood, transforms
Phlegm, warms Kidney *yang*, stops pain.

Biomedical actions

Conditions and improves the functional activity of the prostate gland, reduces
inflammation and swelling, stops pain, improves fluid metabolism, diuretic.

INDICATIONS

- Chronic prostatitis. An excellent formula for residual or lurking Damp Heat and
  stagnant Blood in the prostate. Also supports Kidney *yang* and the transformation
  and processing of pathological fluids that tend to accumulate in the prostate
  gland. The combination of vaccaria seed and astragalus assists in 'opening up'
  the prostate gland to facilitate access by herbs or drugs.
- Also used for prostatic hypertrophy, elevated prostate specific antigen (PSA),
  testicular swelling and pain, urinary tract infection, epididymitis, hematuria and
  inguinal pain due to chronic Damp Heat and/or Blood stagnation.

Composition (each capsule contains extracts equivalent to dry)

Phellodendron amurense (huang bai, phellodendron) 340mg, *Polygonum cuspidatum*
(hu zhang, bushy knotweed) 306mg, *Raphanus sativus* (lai fu zi, radish seed) 306mg, *Cuscuta hygrophila*
(tu su zi, cuscuta) 306mg, *Hedyotis diffusa* (bai hua she she cao, oldenlandia) 306mg,
Vaccaria segetalis (wang bu liu xing, vaccaria seed) 306mg, *Epimedium brevicornu* (xian ling
pi, epimedium) 306mg, *Poria cocos* (fu ling, hoelen) 306mg, *Plantago asiatica* (che qian zi,
plantago) 230mg, *Lycium barbarum* (gou qi zi, lycium fruit) 230mg, *Astragalus
membranaceous* (huang qi, astragalus) 230mg, *Schizandra chinensis* (wu wei zi, schizandra)
230mg, *Glycyrrhiza uralensis* (gan cao, licorice) 191mg

Combinations

- With **4.10 Shi Lin Tong** for urinary calculi and to improve the overall diuretic
  action of the formula.

Pattern identifying features

- **Damp Heat & Blood stagnation affecting the prostate gland**
- difficulty starting urination, broken or weak urinary stream, dribbling, nocturia

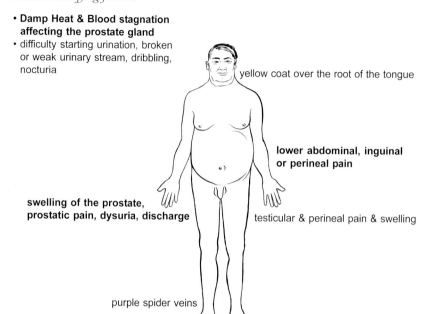

yellow coat over the root of the tongue

lower abdominal, inguinal or perineal pain

swelling of the prostate, prostatic pain, dysuria, discharge

testicular & perineal pain & swelling

purple spider veins

MEN

- With **2.24 Shu Gan Wan** or **11.4 Tian Tai Wu Yao Wan** for *qi* stagnation type *shan qi* or *lin* syndrome.
- With **1.34 Nei Xiao Luo Li Wan** or **11.3 Ji Sheng Ju He Wan** for persistent prostate swelling and elevated prostate specific antigen (PSA) arising from chronic Damp Heat or Phlegm Heat.
- With **7.9 Fu Gui Ba Wei Wan** or **4.11 Ba Ji Yin Yang Wan** for patients tending to relatively severe *yang* deficiency and prostate swelling.
- With **1.17 Gui Zhi Fu Ling Wan** (mild) or **1.18 Shao Fu Zhu Yu Wan** for sharp or stabbing prostatic or perineal pain.

Dosage and method of administration

3-4 capsules, three times daily on an empty stomach. In severe cases, the dose may be increased by 50% until results are noted, then scaled back to the recommended dose. For best results, combine with prostate drainage massage.

Cautions and contraindications

None noted.

11.2 PROSTATE GLAND PILLS

前列腺丸

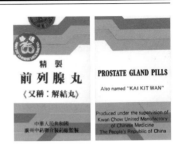

(Qian Lie Xian Wan)
United Manufactory of Chinese Medicine
(Guangzhou)
'Prostate Gland Pills'
Prostate Gland Pills are packaged in bottles of 90 pills.
Also available as: Kai Kit Wan

TCM actions

Clears residual and lurking Damp and Toxic Heat from the prostate and lower *jiao*, quickens Blood, stops pain.

Biomedical actions

Conditions and improves the functional activity of the prostate gland, reduces inflammation and swelling, stops pain.

INDICATIONS

- Chronic prostatitis. Very similar in scope and action to **11.1 Qian Lie Xian Capsule**, the main difference being the absence of Kidney *yang* support in this formula, making it better for patients with a tendency to *yin* deficiency.
- Can also be used for prostatic hypertrophy, elevated prostate specific antigen (PSA), testicular swelling and pain, urinary tract infection, hematuria and inguinal pain due to chronic Damp Heat and/or Blood stagnation.

Composition

Vaccaria segetalis (wang bu liu xing, vaccaria seed), *Paeonia suffruticosa* (mu dan pi, moutan), *Paeonia rubra* (chi shao, red peony), *Astragalus membranaceous* (huang qi, astragalus), *Patrinia villosa* (bai jiang cao, patrinia), *Corydalis turtschaninovii* (yan hu suo, corydalis), *Codonopsis pilosula* (dang shen, codonopsis), *Glycyrrhiza uralensis* (gan cao, licorice), *Akebia trifoliata* (mu tong, akebia)

Combinations

- With **4.10 Shi Lin Tong** for urinary calculi and to improve the overall diuretic action of the formula.
- With **2.24 Shu Gan Wan** or **11.4 Tian Tai Wu Yao Wan** for *qi* stagnation type *shan qi* or *lin* syndrome (*see* glossary).

Pattern identifying features

- **Damp Heat & Blood stagnation affecting the prostate gland**

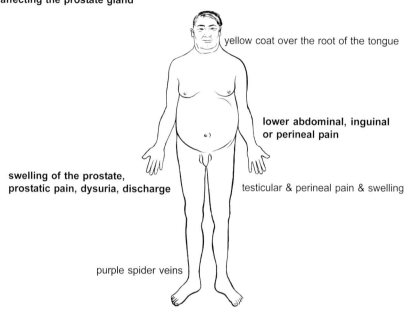

yellow coat over the root of the tongue

lower abdominal, inguinal or perineal pain

swelling of the prostate, prostatic pain, dysuria, discharge

testicular & perineal pain & swelling

purple spider veins

- With **1.34 Nei Xiao Luo Li Wan** or **11.3 Ji Sheng Ju He Wan** for persistent prostate swelling and elevated prostate specific antigen (PSA) arising from chronic Damp Heat or Phlegm Heat.
- With **7.9 Fu Gui Ba Wei Wan** or **4.11 Ba Ji Yin Yang Wan** for men tending to relatively severe *yang* deficiency and prostate swelling.
- With **1.17 Gui Zhi Fu Ling Wan** (mild) or **1.18 Shao Fu Zhu Yu Wan** for sharp or stabbing prostatic or perineal pain.
- With **1.23.1 Zhi Bai Ba Wei Wan** for patients with *yin* deficiency and chronic or residual Damp Heat in the lower *jiao*.

Dosage and method of administration

6 pills, three times daily on an empty stomach. **11.2 Prostate Gland Pills** need to be taken for some months to achieve a satisfactory result. For best results, combine with prostate drainage massage.

Cautions and contraindications

None noted.

GMP 11.3 JI SHENG JU HE WAN

济生橘核丸

Lanzhou Foci Pharmaceutical Factory (Gansu)
'Tangerine Seed Pills [from Formulas to Aid the Living])'
Ji Sheng Ju He Wan is packaged in bottles of 200 pills.
Also available as: Citrus Aurantium Compound Pills, Citrus
Seed Pills

TCM actions
Regulates *qi* and quickens Blood, transforms and
disperses Phlegm, softens hardness, reduces swelling
and dissipates nodules, stops pain.

Biomedical actions
Reduces swelling, stops pain.

INDICATIONS

- Testicular swellings that are relatively firm and rubbery to palpation and may or
may not be tender or painful. Swellings such as these are usually associated with
chronic accumulation of Cold and Damp in the Liver channel, compounded by
Liver *qi* stagnation and the eventual congealing of Phlegm and Blood stagnation.
This is a type of *shan qi* disorder (*see* glossary).
- Phlegm and *qi* stagnation type masses, such as thyroid nodules, breast, benign
ovarian and uterine tumours, fibroids, ovarian cysts and other Phlegm type
swellings.
- With the appropriate identifying features, this formula can assist in the treatment
of biomedical conditions such as varicocele, hydrocele, chronic orchitis,
epididymitis, uterine fibroids, breast and ovarian cysts and thyroid swellings.

Composition
Citrus reticulata (ju he, citrus seed) 13.3%, *Melia toosendan* (chuan lian zi, melia fruit)
13.3%, *Ecklonia kurome* (kun bu, kelp) 13.3%, *Laminaria japonica* (hai dai, laminaria)
13.3%, *Sargassum pallidum* (hai zao, sargassum seaweed) 13.3%, *Prunus persica* (tao ren,
peach seed) 13.3%, *Corydalis turtschaninovii* (yan hu suo, corydalis) 3.3%, *Cinnamomum
cassia* (rou gui, cinnamon bark) 3.3%, *Magnolia officinalis* (hou po, magnolia bark)
3.3%, *Saussurea lappa* (mu xiang, saussurea) 3.3%, *Akebia trifoliata* (mu tong, akebia)
3.3%, *Citrus aurantium* (zhi shi, aurantium) 3.3%

Pattern identifying features

- **Cold Damp, Phlegm & *qi* stagnation in the Liver channel & testicles**
- Phlegm nodules & masses

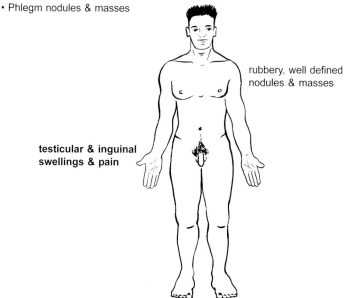

rubbery, well defined nodules & masses

testicular & inguinal swellings & pain

Combinations
- With **6.6 Long Dan Xie Gan Wan** for acute redness and swelling.

Dosage and method of administration
8-12 pills three times daily on an empty stomach. The dose may be spread out, or two lots of 12-18 pills may be taken, morning and evening. In severe cases or during the early stages of treatment (the first few weeks), a 50% increase in dose may be used, then reduced as the treatment takes effect.

Cautions and contraindications
Contraindicated during pregnancy.

GMP

11.4 TIAN TAI WU YAO WAN

天台乌药丸

Available in the US,
UK and Europe
See Note 1, p.xxi

Lanzhou Foci Pharmaceutical Factory (Gansu)
'Top Quality Lindera Pills'
Tian Tai Wu Yao Wan is packaged in bottles of 200 pills.
Available as: Lindera Combination Teapills (PF)

TCM actions
Regulates and invigorates Liver *qi*, warms and dispels Cold
from the Liver channel, stops pain.

Biomedical actions
Analgesic, improves circulation.

INDICATIONS

- Liver *qi* stagnation and/or Cold accumulation in the Liver channel causing pain in the lower abdomen, inguinal region or testicles, and testicular swelling, contracture or coldness. When affected, the scrotum is bilaterally or unilaterally swollen and distended, with distension or pain radiating from or to the lower abdomen and/or the lumbar region; the condition is aggravated or initiated by anger, stress and exposure to cold, and is alleviated by relaxation and warmth. This is a type of *shan qi* (*see* glossary).
- Can also be used for dysmenorrhea associated with Cold and *qi* stagnation in the Liver channel, and epigastric and abdominal pain from Cold and *qi* stagnation in the Spleen and Intestines.
- With the appropriate identifying features this formula can be used to treat biomedical conditions such as the discomfort and pain of inguinal hernia, orchitis, epididymitis and dysmenorrhea.

Composition
Lindera strychnifolia (wu yao, lindera) 18.5%, *Foeniculum vulgarae* (xiao hui xiang, fennel seed) 12%, *Alpinia officinarum* (gao liang jiang, galangal) 12%, *Saussurea lappa* (mu xiang, saussurea) 12%, *Citrus reticulata* (qing pi, immature citrus) 12%, *Melia toosendan* (chuan lian zi, melia fruit) 12%, *Areca catechu* (bing lang, betel nut) 12%, *Evodia rutacarpae* (wu zhu yu, evodia) 6.5%

Combinations
- With **11.3 Ji Sheng Ju He Wan** for hard painful swellings of the testicles.
- With **1.2 Si Wu Wan** or **1.14 Wen Jing Tang Wan** for Cold type dysmenorrhea.

Pattern identifying features

- **Cold & *qi* stagnation in the Liver channel**
- pain aggravated by stress & exposure to cold

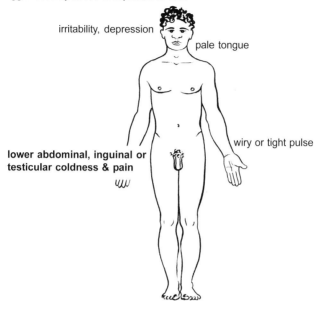

irritability, depression

pale tongue

wiry or tight pulse

lower abdominal, inguinal or testicular coldness & pain

Dosage and method of administration

8-12 pills three times daily, on an empty stomach or with a warm drink (a little warm red wine or ginger tea is ideal). The dose may be spread out, or two lots of 12-18 pills may be taken, morning and evening. In severe cases or during the early stages of treatment (the first few weeks), a 50% increase in dose may be used, then reduced as the treatment takes effect.

Cautions and contraindications

None noted.

MEN

11.5 WU ZI YAN ZONG WAN

五子衍宗丸

Tong Ren Tang (Beijing)
'Pills of Five Seeds to Bring Forth Offspring'
Wu Zi Yan Zong Wan is packaged in bottles of 600 small pills.
Also available as: Five Ancestors Teapills

TCM actions
Strengthens and benefits the Liver and Kidneys, nourishes
jing and *yin*, benefits the eyes.

Biomedical actions
Improves sperm quality and motility, tonic, may aid in
counteracting antisperm antibody formation, elevates levels of superoxide
dismutase, antioxidant.

INDICATIONS

- *Jing* deficiency type sperm disorders, including motility disorders, oligospermia,
  poor sperm quality, seminal abnormalities and sperm viscosity or liquifaction
  disorders. Also useful as preparation for, and convalescence from, vasectomy
  reversal. May assist in reducing the tendency to develop antisperm antibodies
  for patients who have had vasectomy.
- Visual disorders such as spots, loss of visual acuity and weakening vision associated
  with Liver or Kidney weakness.
- Also used to assist in Kidney deficient conditions such as premature ejaculation,
  impotence and lower back ache.
- This formula is fairly neutral in temperature and so can be, and usually is,
  combined with any other formula aimed at correcting the primary constitutional
  imbalance.

Composition (each pill contains powdered)
Lycium chinensis (gou qi zi, lycium) 1.38g, *Cuscuta chinensis* (tu su zi, cuscuta) 1.38g,
Rubus chingii (fu pen zi, rubus) 660mg, *Plantago asiatica* (che qian zi, plantago) 5.6%,
Schizandra chinensis (wu wei zi, schizandra) 2.8%, honey

Combinations
- With **7.9 Fu Gui Ba Wei Wan** or **7.10 You Gui Wan** for patients tending to *yang*
  deficiency; add **7.11 Deer Velvet** or **7.12 Lu Rong Jiao** for severe cases.

Pattern identifying features

• **Liver & Kidney deficiency, insufficient *jing***

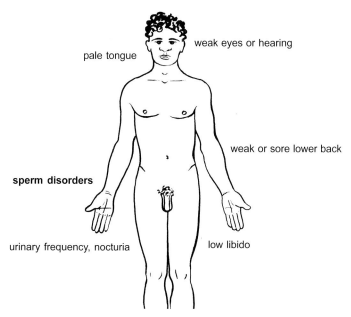

weak eyes or hearing

pale tongue

weak or sore lower back

sperm disorders

urinary frequency, nocturia

low libido

- With **2.11 Bu Zhong Yi Qi Wan** for patients with *qi* deficiency.
- With **1.9 Gui Pi Wan** for patients prone to anxiety and nervousness.
- With **1.23.1 Zhi Bai Ba Wei Wan**, **7.1.1 Liu Wei Di Huang Wan** or **7.3 Zuo Gui Wan** for patients tending to *yin* deficiency. These combinations are also useful for sperm liquifaction disorders.
- With **7.8 Shou Wu Chih** for Blood deficiency.
- With **1.2 Si Wu Wan** for Liver Blood deficiency visual disorders.
- With **7.2 Qi Ju Di Huang Wan** or **9.23 Ming Mu Capsule** for visual disorders associated with Liver *yin* deficiency.

Dosage and method of administration
The recommended dose is rather large at 30-40 (very small) pills three times daily before meals. The pills may be soaked in boiling water first, but are best just eaten by the handful. For practical purposes, one jar should be consumed every 4-5 days.

Cautions and contraindications
Contraindicated during the early phase of acute illness such as colds and flu, and in patients with sperm disorders associated with lingering Damp Heat (*see* **11.1 Qian Lie Xian Capsule** or **1.36 Bi Xie Sheng Shi Wan**).

MEN

11.6 GU BEN FU ZHENG CAPSULE

固本扶正丹

(Gu Ben Fu Zheng Dan)
'Secure the Base and Support the True [*Qi*] Special Pills'
Gu Ben Fu Zheng Capsule is packaged in bottles of 36 capsules.

**GU BEN FU
ZHENG**
CAPSULE

AUST L 76473
36 CAPSULES
MADE IN CHINA

TCM actions
Strengthens and warms Kidney *yang*, nourishes Blood, supplements *qi*.

Biomedical actions
Stimulant and tonic, strengthens adrenal function, adaptogenic, warms the body and stimulates the libido.

INDICATIONS

- A good general Kidney *yang* supplementing formula for *yang* deficiency type sexual dysfunction, impotence, loss of libido, premature ejaculation, infertility associated with poor sperm motility. This formula is quite warming and stimulating, and so is also good for the general lack of *yang* motivation typical of *yang* deficiency and Cold accumulation, such as is found in elderly patients.
- Lack of energy, vitality and motivation; tendency to sleep too much or desire to sleep too much, cold intolerance, patient feels cold to the touch, urinary frequency or nocturia, lower back ache.
- Warms *yang* and supplements *jing* to treat male infertility and sperm disorders such as low sperm count and poor sperm motility.

Composition (each capsule contains extracts equivalent to dry)
Epimedium brevicornu (xian ling pi, epimedium) 455mg, *Angelica polymorpha* (dang gui, chinese angelica) 455mg, *Curculigo orchioides* (xian mao, curculigo) 364mg, *Allium odorum* (jiu zi, chinese chive seed) 364mg, *Paeonia lactiflora* (bai shao, white peony) 364mg, *Panax ginseng* (ren shen, ginseng) 364mg, *Psoralea corylifolia* (bu gu zhi, psoralea) 364mg, *Eucommia ulmoides* (du zhong, eucommia) 364mg, *Cynomorium songaricum* (suo yang, cynomorium) 364mg, *Lycium barbarum* (gou qi zi, lycium fruit) 364mg, *Morinda officinalis* (ba ji tian, morinda) 364mg, *Glycyrrhiza uralensis* (gan cao, licorice) 364mg

Pattern identifying features

- **Kidney *yang* deficiency**
- impotence, loss of libido
- lethargy, lack of vitality

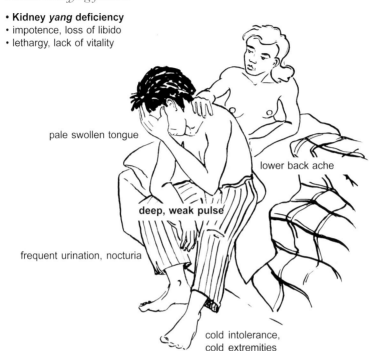

pale swollen tongue

lower back ache

deep, weak pulse

frequent urination, nocturia

cold intolerance, cold extremities

MEN

Combinations
- With **4.14 Chin So Ku Ching Wan** for nocturia or urinary frequency.
- With **11.5 Wu Zi Yan Zong Wan** for sperm disorders from Kidney *yang* deficiency.

Dosage and method of administration
3-4 capsules, three times daily, on an empty stomach.

Cautions and contraindications
Contraindicated during the early phase of acute illness such as colds and flu, and in *yin* deficiency or internal excess Heat patterns.

11.7 NAN BAO CAPSULES

男宝

(Nan Bao)
Tianjin Lisheng Pharmaceutical Factory (Shandong)
'Male Treasure'
Nan Bao Capsules are packaged on blister sheets
of ten capsules, two sheets per box.

TCM actions
Strengthens and tones the Kidneys, warms and supports *yang*.

Biomedical actions
Stimulant and tonic, strengthens adrenal function, adaptogenic, warms the body and
stimulates the libido.

INDICATIONS

- Kidney *qi* and *yang* deficiency type impotence, loss of libido, premature ejaculation.
  A very general and broad acting formula with almost every *yang* warming and
  supplementing herb in the materia medica, at quite low doses.
- General Kidney *yang* weakness patterns with lack of vitality and drive, fatigue,
  lower back ache, weakness in the legs, fearfulness and timidity and cold intolerance.

Composition (each capsule contains)
Panax ginseng (ren shen, ginseng) 33.25mg, *Angelica sinensis* (dang gui, chinese angelica)
33.25mg, *Astragalus membranaceous* (huang qi, astragalus) 33.25mg, *Rehmannia glutinosa*
(shu di, processed rehmannia) 33.25mg, *Epimedium brevicornu* (xian ling pi, epimedium)
33.25mg, *Lycium barbarum* (gou qi zi, lycium fruit) 33.25mg, *Poria cocos* (fu ling, hoelen)
33.25mg, *Eucommia ulmoides* (du zhong, eucommia) 16.75mg, *Psoralea corylifolia* (bu gu
zhi, psoralea) 16.75mg, *Morinda officinalis* (ba ji tian, morinda) 16.75mg, *Cistanches deserticola*
(rou cong rong, cistanches) 16.75mg, *Cuscuta chinensis* (tu su zi, cuscuta) 16.75mg, *Cornus
officinalis* (shan zhu yu, cornus) 16.75mg, *Atractylodes macrocephala* (bai zhu, atractylodes)
16.75mg, *Rubus chingii* (fu pen zi, rubus) 16.75mg, *Trigonella foenum-graecum* (hu lu ba,
fenugreek seed) 16.75mg, *Ophiopogon japonicum* (mai dong, ophiopogon) 16.75mg,
Cynomorium songaricum (suo yang, cynomorium) 16.75mg, *Scrophularia ningpoensis* (xuan
shen, scrophularia) 16.75mg, *Cinnamomum cassia* (rou gui, cinnamon bark) 13.25mg,
Paeonia suffruticosa (mu dan pi, peony root bark) 8.25mg, *Dipsacus asper* (xu duan, dipsacus)
8.25mg, *Achyranthes bidentata* (niu xi, achyranthes) 8.25mg

Pattern identifying features

- **Kidney *qi* & *yang* deficiency**
- inability to maintain an erection
- low libido
- premature ejaculation
- fatigue, lack of vitality
- cold intolerance

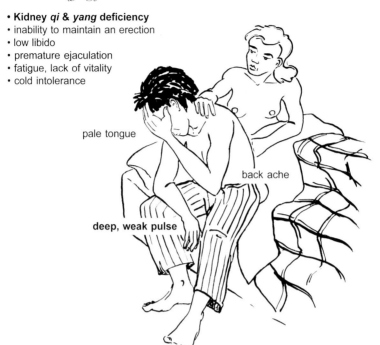

pale tongue

back ache

deep, weak pulse

Combinations
- With **7.9 Fu Gui Ba Wei Wan** or **7.10 You Gui Wan** for patients tending to *yang* deficiency; add **7.12 Lu Rong Jiao** for severe cases.
- With **2.11 Bu Zhong Yi Qi Wan** or **7.22 Shen Qi Da Bu Wan** for severe *qi* deficiency.
- With **1.9 Gui Pi Wan** for those with Spleen and Heart deficiency and a tendency to anxiety and nervousness.

Dosage and method of administration
2 capsules twice daily, on an empty stomach.

Cautions and contraindications
Contraindicated during the early phase of acute illness such as colds and flu.

11.8 KANG WEI LING WAN

抗痿灵

Kuan Chiu Medical Company (Hong Kong)
'Marvellous Pills to Combat Impotence'
Kang Wei Ling Wan is packaged in bottles of 120 pills.

TCM actions
Supplements *qi*, Blood and *yang*, regulates Blood and disperses stagnant Blood to open up circulation through the channels to nourish and revitalise the tendons and ligaments (especially the ancestral ligament of the Liver).

Biomedical actions
Improves circulation, hematinic, stimulant.

INDICATIONS

- Blood stagnation with *yang* and Blood deficiency type impotence. This formula contains a powerful Blood moving substance and works by improving the circulation to the penis, while at the same time strengthening *yang*. May help in impotence associated with reduced blood circulation to the penis, chronic prostatitis or other genital stagnation syndromes.
- The main ingredient, scolopendra centipede, is a strong substance used to 'burrow' through obstructions and also extinguish Wind, so this formula may be useful as an adjunct treatment for facial paralysis or Bell's palsy, hemiplegia, facial pain and neuralgia, severe chronic migraines or trigeminal neuralgia.

Composition
Paeonia alba (bai shao, white peony) 30%, *Cervus nippon* (lu jiao, deer antler cartilage) 16%, *Panax ginseng* (ren shen, ginseng) 15%, *Angelica sinensis* (dang gui) 15%, *Scolopendra subspinipes* (wu gong, centipede) 12%, *Glycyrrhiza uralensis* (gan cao, licorice) 12%

Combinations
- With **7.9 Fu Gui Ba Wei Wan** or **7.10 You Gui Wan** for patients tending to *yang* deficiency.
- With **5.1 Xue Fu Zhu Yu Wan** for patients with systemic signs of *qi* and Blood stagnation.

Pattern identifying features

- **Blood stagnation, *qi*, Blood & *yang* deficiency**
- **inability to achieve erection**

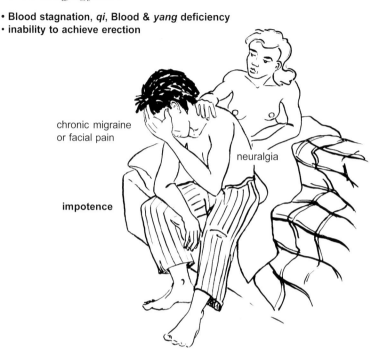

chronic migraine
or facial pain

neuralgia

impotence

MEN

- With **6.4 Xiao Yao Wan** or **6.5 Jia Wei Xiao Yao Wan** for stressed out patients with performance anxiety.
- With **3.9 Chuan Xiong Cha Tiao Wan** for severe migraine headaches associated with exposure to cold.
- With **5.8 Bu Yang Huan Wu Wan** for chronic facial paralysis.

Dosage and method of administration

The recommended dose is 10-15 pills twice daily for fifteen to thirty days, ideally with a shot of vodka or sherry to open the vessels and promote circulation. Usually given in two courses of 15 days each, with a break of a few days in between courses.

Cautions and contraindications

Contraindicated during pregnancy. Not suitable for prolonged use (usually no more than 2-3 courses).

12

Patent Medicines for Infants and Children

12.1 Bo Ying Compound
12.2 King Fung Powder
12.3 Baby Fat Powder
12.4 Hua Ji Xiao Zhi Oral Liquid
12.5 Gan Mao Tea
12.6 Healthy Child Tea
12.7 Xiao Er Gan Mao Chong Ji
12.8 Qi Xing Tea
12.9 Xiao'er Qi Xing Cha Chong Ji

See also

GMP

12.1 BO YING COMPOUND

保嬰丹

(Bao Ying Dan)
Eu Yan Sang (Hong Kong)
'Protect Children Special Pills'
Bo Ying Compound is packaged as a fine powder in small vials of 0.33g powder, six vials to a box.

TCM actions

Strengthens the Spleen, transforms Phlegm, extinguishes Wind, clears Heat.

Biomedical actions

Strengthens digestion and immunity, mucolytic.

INDICATIONS

- Accumulation disorder (*see* glossary). An excellent and popular formula for childhood fevers and restlessness, mucus congestion and digestive problems from accumulation. Only used for children up to 5 years old.
- For children with a tendency to mucus production, digestive weakness and poor appetite. This includes so called 'colicky babies'. Widely used for children with a general tendency to mucus, including problems such as 'glue ear', chronic productive cough, tummy ache, tendency to reflux, vomiting or diarrhoea, constant dribbling in toddlers, chronic or recurrent tonsillitis, and children prone to frequent colds or other upper respiratory tract or ear infections.
- Also used for skin diseases associated with accumulation disorder, such as childhood eczema, dermatitis and nappy (diaper) rash.
- Useful for dispelling latent pathogens introduced by vaccination, with chronic swollen tonsils, low grade fever and swelling at the site of the vaccination. Excellent for infants that have not been well since a vaccination.

Composition

Bambusa textillis (tian zhu huang, bamboo sap) 7%, *Bombyx mori* (jiang can, silkworm) 8%, Borax (peng sha) 4%, Bovine gallstone (niu huang) 3%, Borneol (bing pian) 4%, *Cryptotympana atrata* (chan tui, cicada shell) 7%, *Fritillaria cirrhosa* (chuan bei mu, fritillaria) 7%, Mica (meng shi) 5%, *Uncaria rhynchophylla* (gou teng, gambir) 8%, Pearl (zhen zhu) 4%, *Mentha haplocalyis* (bo he, mint) 6%, *Curcuma longa* (yu jin, curcuma) 3%, *Gastrodia elata* (tian ma, gastrodia) 4%, *Buthus martensi* (quan xie, scorpion) 8%, *Siler divaricum* (fang feng, siler) 8%, Amber (hu po) 3%, *Zingiber officinale* (sheng jiang, ginger) 2%

Pattern identifying features

- **accumulation disorder, food stagnation**
- **poor appetite, picky eater**
- **general tendency to mucus production**
- irritability, bad temper
- the child is generally robust & will cry loudly & with vigor
- insomnia, heat & sweating at night
- eczema along Stomach channel
- chronic or recurrent swollen, pea like lymph nodes
- constantly runny or snotty nose
- sweet cravings
- fevers
- post nasal drip
- snoring

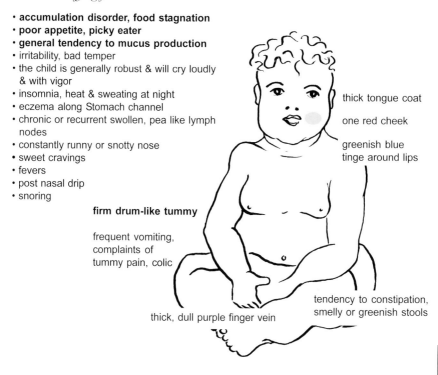

thick tongue coat

one red cheek

greenish blue tinge around lips

firm drum-like tummy

frequent vomiting, complaints of tummy pain, colic

tendency to constipation, smelly or greenish stools

thick, dull purple finger vein

PED

Dosage and method of administration

- In the early stages of treatment ¼-1 vial can be given daily mixed in with food such as apple sauce, or a fluid until the appetite improves or the mucus starts to clear. The dose is then tapered off over a couple of weeks to a maintenance dose. Very mucus prone children may need longer treatment (up to three months).

Maintenance dose

- Infants to one month .... ½-1 vial per week dissolved in hot water and administered by an eye-dropper or a warm bottle of liquid
- 1 month to 2 years .... 1-2 vials per week
- 2-5 years .... 2-3 vials per week

Cautions and contraindications

While dispensing this formula, parents or carers should eliminate or minimise mucus producing foods from the child's diet. These include raw or greasy foods, peanut butter, excess sugar and dairy products. Avoid overfeeding the child.

12.1 Bo Ying Compound is a very safe and reliable formula, and suitable for prolonged use in children with a constitutional tendency to mucus production.

12.2 KING FUNG POWDER

惊风散

(Jing Feng San)
Ho Hei Ming Pharmaceutical Company (Hong Kong)
'Convulsion Powder'
King Fung Powder is packaged as a fine powder in small plastic jars,
ten jars to a box.

TCM actions
Dispels and extinguishes Wind, stops spasms, clears Heat,
transforms Phlegm.

Biomedical actions
Antipyretic, febrifuge, antispasmodic, mucolytic.

INDICATIONS

- Childhood fevers from Heat or Phlegm Heat. The fever may be moderate or high, and associated with common childhood infections such as upper respiratory tract infection (with yellow sputum) and cystitis, or may have no obvious cause. Also useful for febrile convulsions or mild seizures associated with Phlegm Heat.
- Red, itchy skin diseases, such as eczema and dermatitis in infants.
- Restlessness, difficulty settling babies at night (night crying), easy fright and frequent waking associated with accumulation of Heat and Phlegm.
- For children with a tendency to poor appetite, chronic productive cough, tummy ache, tendency to vomiting, diarrhoea or constipation, reflux, colic, mucus production and digestive weakness associated with accumulation disorder (*see* glossary).

Composition
Tribulus terrestris (bai ji li, tribulus) 15%, *Cryptotympana atrata* (chan tui, cicada shell) 15%, *Bambusa textillis* (tian zhu huang, bamboo sap) 15%, *Buthus martensi* (quan xie, scorpion) 15%, *Bombyx mori* (jiang can, silkworm) 15%, *Uncaria rhynchophylla* (gou teng, gambir) 10%, *Glycyrrhiza uralensis* (gan cao, licorice) 5%, Borneol (bing pian) 4%, *Fritillaria cirrhosa* (chuan bei mu, fritillaria) 3%, *Trichosanthes kirilowii* (tian hua fen, trichosanthes root) 3%

Pattern identifying features

- **Phlegm, Phlegm Heat**
- **fevers, convulsions**
- accumulation disorder with heat
- restlessness, night crying
- easy fright, nightmares, night terrors

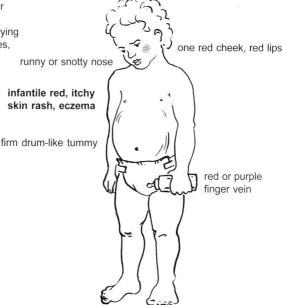

one red cheek, red lips

runny or snotty nose

infantile red, itchy skin rash, eczema

firm drum-like tummy

red or purple finger vein

PED

Dosage and method of administration

Infants to 1 year .... 1 jar per day in small doses (about every 4 hours) dissolved in warm water and administered by an eye-dropper or bottle.

1-3 years .... 1 jar three times daily

3-6 years .... 2 jars three times daily

Take with water, breast milk or apple sauce.

Cautions and contraindications

While dispensing this formula, parents or carers should eliminate or minimise mucus producing foods from the child's diet. These include raw or greasy foods, peanut butter, excess sugar and dairy products. Avoid overfeeding the child.

12.3 BABY FAT POWDER

肥仔散

(Fei Zi San)
United Pharmaceutical Manufactory
(Guangzhou)
'Fat Baby Powder'
Baby Fat Powder is packaged as a fine powder in plastic vials, six vials to a box.

TCM actions
Kills intestinal parasites.

Biomedical actions
Broad spectrum antihelminthic.

INDICATIONS

- Intestinal parasites, such as threadworm, tapeworm and roundworm. This is a very useful broad spectrum antiparasitic agent, and may be of assistance in conditions like *gu* syndrome (*see* glossary) in combination with other constitutional formulae. The name of this formula derives from the fact that children with parasites are likely to be thin or emaciated, thus its use will 'fatten up the baby'.

Composition
Quisqualis indica (shi jun zi, rangoon creeper fruit) 14.8%, *Areca catechu* (bing lang, betel nut) 14.8%, *Osmunda japonica* (guan zhong) 13.4%, *Poria cocos* (fu ling, hoelen) 9%, *Pharbitis nil* (qian niu zi, morning glory seed) 9%, *Glycyrrhiza uralensis* (gan cao, licorice) 7.5%, *Omphalia lapidescens* (lei wan, omphalia puffball) 7.5%, *Punica granatum* (shi liu pi, pomegranate skin) 6%, *Dioscorea opposita* (shan yao, dioscorea) 6%, *Saussurea lappa* (mu xiang, saussurea) 6%, *Stemona sessilifolia* (bai bu, stemona) 6%

Dosage and method of administration
3 months-2 years old .... ¼ jar twice daily
3-5 years old .... ½ jar twice daily
6-10 years old .... 1 jar twice daily
10-14 years old .... 1-3 jars twice daily
Adults .... 4 jars daily

Pattern identifying features

- **intestinal parasites**
- loss of appetite or ravenous appetite, eating unusual things (dirt, sand etc.), craving for unusual foods
- restless sleep, easy fright
- fatigue, malaise, restlessness
- dull, lifeless hair
- dark rings under the eyes

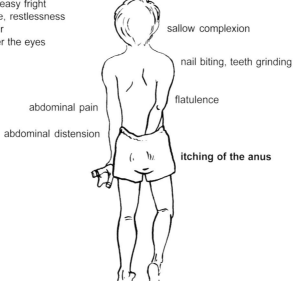

sallow complexion

nail biting, teeth grinding

flatulence

abdominal pain

abdominal distension

itching of the anus

Cautions and contraindications

None noted. Generally only used for short periods of time (~2 weeks), then followed by a formula to strengthen the digestive system, such as **2.9 Xiang Sha Liu Jun Wan** for older children or adults, or **12.6 Healthy Child Tea** for children under three years old.

12.4 HUA JI XIAO ZHI ORAL LIQUID

小儿化积消滞口服液

(Xiao Er Hua Ji Xiao Zhi Kou Fu Ye)
Jing Xian Pharmaceutical Co. (Guangzhou)
'Children's Digestive Accumulation Drink'
Hua Ji Xiao Zhi Oral Liquid is packaged
in vials of 10ml, 10 vials per box.

TCM actions
Strengthens the Spleen and harmonises
the Stomach, kills intestinal parasites.

Biomedical actions
Antihelminthic, strengthens digestion.

INDICATIONS

- Childhood accumulation disorder, indigestion and gastro-intestinal weakness
  associated with parasitic infestation by threadworm, tapeworm or roundworm.
  Similar to **12.3 Baby Fat Powder**, with a larger proportion of the Spleen
  strengthening hoelen, this formula is more strengthening to the digestion, with
  fewer antiparasitic herbs. The indications are much the same, although milder.
  This formula is for children only.

Composition (each 10ml dose contains extracts equivalent to dry)
Poria cocos (fu ling, hoelen) 2.33g, *Crategus pinnatifida* (shan zha, crategus) 830mg,
Carthamus tinctorius (hong hua, carthamus) 632mg, *Carpesium abrotanoides* (he shi,
carpesium fruit) 500mg, *Quisqualis indica* (shi jun zi, rangoon creeper fruit) 500mg,
Areca catechu (bing lang, betel nut) 500mg, *Sparganium stoloniferum* (san leng,
sparganium) 500mg, *Omphalia lapidescens* (lei wan, omphalia puffball) 500mg,
Raphanus sativus (lai fu zi, radish seed) 500mg

Dosage and method of administration
Infants to 2 years .... 5ml, twice daily
2-5 years .... 10ml, twice daily
5 years + ... 10ml three times daily

Cautions and contraindications
None noted.

12.5 GAN MAO TEA

小儿感冒退热冲剂

(Xiao Er Gan Mao Liang Re Chong Ji)
Jing Xian Pharmaceutical Co. (Guangzhou)
'Children's Cold and Fever Relieving Dissolvable
Granules'
Gan Mao Tea is packaged in 10 gram sachets of
dissolvable granules, ten sachets per box.

AUST L 90968
10x10g granules

MADE IN CHINA

TCM actions

Dispels Wind Heat, stops cough, supports *yin*.

Biomedical actions

Antipyretic, diaphoretic, antiviral.

INDICATIONS

- Wind Heat *gan mao* and upper respiratory tract infections with fever, sore throat, headache, stomach upset, nausea, vomiting and productive cough with yellow sputum. Very similar in composition and action to **12.7 Xiao Er Gan Mao Chong Ji**.

Composition (each sachet contains extracts equivalent to dry)

Platycodon grandiflorum (jie geng, platycodon) 1.25g, *Morus alba* (sang ye, mulberry leaf) 1.25g, *Agastache rugosa* (huo xiang, agastache) 752mg, *Chrysanthemum sinense* (ju hua, chrysanthemum flower) 752mg, *Forsythia suspensa* (lian qiao, forsythia) 752mg, *Rehmannia glutinosa* (sheng di, raw rehmannia) 752mg, *Lycium chinensis* (di gu pi, lycium root bark) 752mg, *Scutellaria baicalensis* (huang qin, scute) 752mg, *Cynanchum atratum* (bai wei, cynanchum) 752mg, *Mentha haplocalycis* (bo he, mint) 504mg

Dosage and method of administration

Dissolve the granules in a little hot water. For infants, the resulting warm liquid can be delivered by eye-dropper.

1-2 years .... ¼-½ sachet twice daily
2-3 years .... ½-1 sachet twice daily
4-7 years .... 1 sachet 2-3 times daily

Cautions and contraindications

None noted.

PED

12.6 HEALTHY CHILD TEA

肥仔散*

(Fei Zi San)

Jing Xian Pharmaceutical Co. (Guangzhou)

'Fat Baby Powder' (*Note: Even though the Chinese name of this formula is the same as that of **12.3 Baby Fat Powder**, their compositions and mode of action are quite different.)

Healthy Child Tea is packaged in 10 gram sachets of dissolvable granules, ten sachets per box.

HEALTHY CHILD TEA

AUST L 90970
10x10g GRANULES

MADE IN CHINA

TCM actions

Strengthens the Spleen and Stomach, supplements *qi*, improves digestion.

Biomedical actions

Digestive stimulant.

INDICATIONS

- Spleen and Stomach *qi* deficiency type weak digestion and indigestion. In contrast to the pathology treated by **12.1 Bo Ying Compound** and **12.8 Qi Xing Tea**, where a robust child suffers from food accumulation from overfeeding or inappropriate feeding, the main problem here is the underlying weakness of the Spleen and Stomach which fail to process food and extract sufficient nutrition from it. Children with digestive weakness of this type lack the normal vitality of childhood, tend to be thin, are very picky eaters or lacking in appetite, look pale and wan and lack the sparkle of *jing shen* in the eyes.
- For constitutionally weak children and premature babies who fail to thrive.
- Excellent to rebuild a child's Spleen *qi* following a protracted or severe illness.

Composition (each sachet contains extracts equivalent to dry)

Coicis lachryma-jobi (yi ren, coix) 1.5g, *Paeonia lactiflora* (bai shao, white peony) 1.5g, *Nelumbus speciosum* (lian zi, lotus seed) 1.5g, *Hordeum vulgare* (mai ya, sprouted barley) 1.5g, *Prunus mume* (wu mei, black plum) 1.5g, *Poria cocos* (fu ling, hoelen) 1.5g, *Dioscorea opposita* (shan yao, dioscorea) 1.25g, *Atractylodes macrocephala* (bai zhu, atractylodes) 1.25g, *Pseudostellaria heterophylla* (tai zi shen, pseudostellaria) 1g

Pattern identifying features

- **Spleen & Stomach *qi* deficiency**
- weak, thin child
- listlessness, lack of vitality
- lack of hair & nail growth
- spontaneous sweating, night sweats
- restless sleep
- teeth grinding
- poor appetite, picky eater
- tends to be clingy & shy
- translucent skin

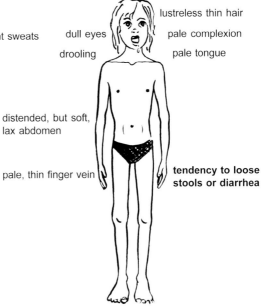

lustreless thin hair

dull eyes

pale complexion

drooling

pale tongue

distended, but soft, lax abdomen

pale, thin finger vein

tendency to loose stools or diarrhea

PED

Combinations
- Good combined with nutritious rice porridge (*zhou*) for children with very weak digestions.
- With **3.41 Xu Han Ting** for spontaneous sweating and weakened immunity.

Dosage and method of administration
Dissolve the granules in a little hot water. For infants, the resulting warm liquid can be delivered by eye-dropper.

1-2 years .... ¼-½ sachet twice daily
2-3 years .... ½-1 sachet twice daily
4-7 years .... 1 sachet 2-3 times daily

Cautions and contraindications
None noted. In addition to any herbal therapy, an appropriate diet is essential for success, avoid raw whole foods, juices, sweets and dairy products.

12.7 XIAO ER GAN MAO CHONG JI

小儿感冒冲剂

Tong Ren Tang (Beijing)
'Children's Cold Dissolvable Granules'
Xiao Er Gan Mao Chong Ji is packaged as dissolvable granules
in single dose sachets of 12 grams, ten sachets per box.

TCM actions
Dispels Wind Heat, clears Toxic Heat, benefits the throat.

Biomedical action
Antipyretic, diaphoretic, anti-inflammatory, antiviral.

INDICATIONS

• Wind Heat *gan mao* causing fever, sore throat, and cough. Used for colds, influenza, tonsillitis and early stage of upper respiratory tract infection in children. Especially good for sore throat.
• Also useful for Wind or Toxic Heat patterns affecting the ears and eyes of small children, causing disorders such as otitis media and conjunctivitis.
• May be useful for acute inflammatory rashes and eczema in small children, including impetigo and hand, foot and mouth disease.

Composition (each sachet contains extracts equivalent to dry)
Isatis tinctoria (da qing ye, isatis leaf) 1.6g, *Rehmannia glutinosa* (sheng di, raw rehmannia) 986mg, *Cynanchum atratum* (bai wei, cynanchum) 986mg, *Lycium chinensis* (di gu pi, lycium root bark) 986mg, *Chrysanthemum chinensis* (ju hua, chrysanthemum flower) 986mg, *Isatis tinctoria* (ban lan gen, isatis root) 986mg, *Forsythia suspensa* (lian qiao, forsythia ess. oil) 4.4mg, *Pogostemon cablin* (huo xiang, agastache ess. oil) 2.95mg, *Mentha haplocalycis* (bo he, mint ess. oil) 2.63mg, sugar 5.3g

Combinations
• With **9.10 Sanjin Watermelon Frost** for mouth ulcers or gum inflammation.
• With **9.9 Superior Sore Throat Powder** for acute tonsillitis and otitis.
• With pear juice for cough.

Pattern identifying features

- **Wind Heat** *gan mao*
- **acute colds & flu**
- early upper respiratory tract infection
- fever

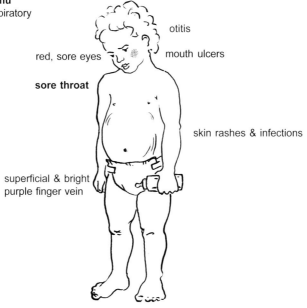

red, sore eyes

otitis

mouth ulcers

sore throat

skin rashes & infections

superficial & bright purple finger vein

PED

Dosage and method of administration

Dissolve the granules in a little hot water. Allow to cool before use. For small children, the resulting liquid can be delivered by eye-dropper.

1-2 years .... ½ sachet 2-3 times daily
2-3 years .... 1-1½ sachets 2-3 times daily
4-7 years .... 1-1½ sachets every 2-4 hours
7-10 years .... 2 sachets every 2-4 hours

Cautions and contraindications

None noted.

12.8 QI XING TEA

七星茶

(Qi Xing Cha)
Jing Xian Pharmaceutical Co. (Guangzhou)
'Seven Star Tea'
Qi Xing Tea is packaged in 10 gram sachets of
dissolvable granules, ten sachets per box.

AUST L 82986
10x10g SACHETS

MADE IN CHINA

TCM actions

Alleviates food stagnation, strengthens the Spleen,
clears Heat and Damp Heat, extinguishes internal
Wind and calms the *shen*.

Biomedical action

Digestive, tonic, calmative.

INDICATIONS

• A mild formula for indigestion, poor feeding, colic and accumulation disorder
in babies and small children. In contrast to **12.1 Bo Ying Compound**, which is
good for accumulation disorder causing Phlegm buildup, this formula is good
for accumulation disorder leading to Heat. The main focus of the formula is in
clearing out accumulation in the digestive system. Can be applied to infants who
aren't digesting milk well, or suffer from repeated reflux.

• Restlessness, insomnia, gum pain and nappy (diaper) rash associated with teething.

• Urinary tract infection, mouth ulcers or other infection from Heat or Heart
Fire; acute gastroenteritis.

• General restlessness, night crying, insomnia or restless sleep, fearfulness and
irritability associated with Heat or accumulation disorder. In some cases there
may be mild convulsions, muscular spasms or seizures.

• Useful for acute rashes and eczema in small children, especially those associated
with food intolerance, poor diet or overeating.

Composition (each sachet contains extracts equivalent to dry)

Crategus pinnatifida (shan zha, crategus) 5.4g, *Uncaria rhynchophylla* (gou teng, gambir)
5.4g, *Setaria italica* (gu ya, sprouted rice) 4.8g, *Hordeum vulgare* (mai ya, sprouted
barley) 4.8g, *Lophatherum elatum* (dan zhu ye, bamboo leaves) 3.2g, *Coicis lachryma-jobi*
(yi ren, coix) 3.2g, *Juncus effusus* (deng xin cao, juncus) 3.2g, *Glycyrrhiza uralensis* (gan
cao, licorice) 1.9g, sucrose

Pattern identifying features

- **Accumulation disorder**
- **infantile colic**
- **insomnia, night crying**, restlessness, fractiousness
- the child is generally robust & will cry loudly & with vigor
- clammy, night sweats
- bad breath
- reflux

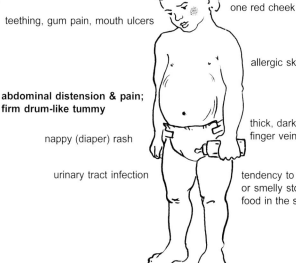

poor appetite

one red cheek

teething, gum pain, mouth ulcers

allergic skin rash

abdominal distension & pain; firm drum-like tummy

thick, dark, red or purple finger vein

nappy (diaper) rash

urinary tract infection

tendency to constipation, dry or smelly stools; undigested food in the stools

PED

Combinations

- With **9.10 Sanjin Watermelon Frost** for mouth ulcers, teething or gum pain and inflammation.

Dosage and method of administration

Dissolve the granules in a little hot water. For infants, the resulting warm liquid can be delivered by eye-dropper.

1-2 years .... ¼-½ sachet twice daily
2-3 years .... ½-1 sachet twice daily
4-7 years .... 1 sachet 2-3 times daily

Cautions and contraindications

None noted.

12.9 XIAO'ER QI XING CHA CHONG JI

小儿七星茶冲剂

Zhongshan City Pharmaceutical Factory (Guangdong)
'Children's Seven Star Dissolvable Granules'
Xiao'er Qi Xing Cha Chong Ji is packaged as
dissolvable granules in plastic jars shaped like panda bears.
Seven grams per jar, 12 jars to a box.

TCM actions
Alleviates food stagnation, strengthens the Spleen, clears Heat and Damp Heat,
extinguishes internal Wind and calms the *shen*.

Biomedical action
Digestive, tonic, calmative.

INDICATIONS

- Very similar in most respects to **12.8 Qi Xing Tea**, with less emphasis on
  accumulation disorder and more on internal Wind resulting from Heat. Good
  for allergic eczema that occurs in the child that eats too much sugar and starts
  scratching. Also used as a mild digestive stimulant for children that lack appetite
  or pick at food, or who complain of abdominal pain after eating.

Composition
Coicis lachryma-jobi (yi ren, coix), *Uncaria rhynchophylla* (gou teng, gambir), *Lophatherum elatum* (dan zhu ye, bamboo leaves), *Cryptotympana atrata* (chan tui, cicada shell), *Crategus pinnatifida* (shan zha, crategus), *Glycyrrhiza uralensis* (gan cao, licorice), *Oryza sativa* (dao ya, sprouted rice)

Dosage and method of administration
Dissolve the granules in a little hot water. For infants, the resulting warm liquid can
be delivered by eye-dropper.
1-2 years .... 1 jar twice daily
2-3 years .... 1 jar three times daily
4-7 years .... 1-2 jars three times daily

Cautions and contraindications
None noted.

13

Patent Medicines for Skin Disorders

Pills

Topical

See also

13.1 LIEN CHIAO PAI TU PIEN

连翘败毒片

(Lian Qiao Bai Du Pian)
Tianjin Drug Manufactory (Shandong)
'Forsythia Antitoxic Pills'

Lien Chiao Pai Tu Pien is packaged in vials of eight uncoated pills, twelve vials per box.

TCM actions
Dispels Wind Heat, clears Toxic Heat, relieves itch.

Biomedical actions
Diaphoretic, antibiotic, detoxicant, antipruritic, laxative.

INDICATIONS

- Toxic Heat and Wind Heat type skin disorders, including–
  - The early stage of suppurative skin disorders, such as boils, carbuncles, acne, folliculitis, abscess, paronychia, cellulitis, erysipelas, mastitis, shingles, lymphangitis, lymphadenitis, impetigo and hand foot and mouth disease.
  - Acute or chronic itchy inflamed skin disorders such as eczema, dermatitis, psoriasis, pityriasis rosea and lichen sclerosis.
  - Allergic skin eruptions such as contact dermatitis, urticaria and poison ivy.
  - Viral skin disorders and rashes, such as herpes zoster and simplex, measles and chicken pox.
- Severe Wind Heat type *gan mao* or Warm disease (*see* glossary).

Composition (each pill contains)
Lonicera japonica (jin yin hua, lonicera) 1.03g, *Forsythia suspensa* (lian qiao, forsythia) 1.03g, *Gardenia jasminoides* (shan zhi zi, gardenia) 739mg, **Carum carvi* (carraway seed) 739mg, *Lophatherum gracile* (dan zhu ye, bamboo leaves) 517mg, *Scutellaria baicalensis* (huang qin, scute) 455mg, *Dictamnus desycarpus* (bai xian pi, dictamnus) 455mg, *Rheum palmatum* (da huang, rhubarb root) 83mg, *Paeonia lactiflora* (bai shao, white peony) 65mg

Note: *One version of this formula (from the same factory) substitutes cicada shell (chan tui, Periostracum Cicadae) for this herb.

Pattern identifying features

- **Wind Heat & Toxic Heat in the skin**
- **acute & chronic red, itchy skin lesions**
- fever, headache, sore, dry throat
- red tipped tongue, yellow coat

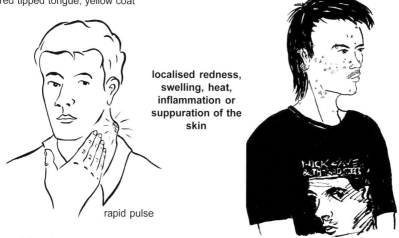

localised redness, swelling, heat, inflammation or suppuration of the skin

rapid pulse

Combinations
- With **1.2 Si Wu Wan** for chronic or stubborn skin diseases with a degree of Blood deficiency.
- With **13.13 Fu Yin Tai Liniment** topically for dermatitis and eczema.
- With **14.5 Chuan Xin Lian Antiphlogistic Tablets** for lymphangitis or pityriasis.
- With **9.9 Superior Sore Throat Powder** for suppurative tonsillitis or pharyngeal abscess.
- With **6.1 Xiao Chai Hu Tang Wan** for acute mastitis.

Dosage and method of administration
The recommended dose is 2-4 pills twice daily on an empty stomach. In acute or severe cases, take one vial every 2-3 hours for a few days. When used for chronic disorders the recommended dose, or less, can be taken over several months. The patient should be advised that he or she may experience diarrhoea initially, and the dose may be adjusted until the diarrhoea is alleviated.

Cautions and contraindications
Contraindicated during pregnancy. The patient should be advised to avoid all drying, greasy or heating food or substances, especially seafood and shellfish, coffee, alcohol, spicy foods and tobacco.

SKIN

13.2 XIAO FENG WAN

消风丸

Lanzhou Foci Pharmaceutical Factory (Gansu)
'Disperse Wind Pills'
Xiao Feng Wan is packaged in bottles of 200 pills.
Also available as: Great Windkeeper Teapills (PF)

TCM actions
Dispels Wind, clears Dampness and Heat, nourishes Blood, stops itch.

Biomedical actions
Anti-inflammatory, diaphoretic, antipruritic.

INDICATIONS

- Wind Heat or Wind Damp in the skin causing itchy, red skin diseases. This formula is widely used for the itch and inflammation of acute and chronic skin diseases. Can be used for both wet and dry skin disorders.
- With the appropriate identifying features, this formula can be used to treat biomedical disorders such as eczema, contact dermatitis, neurodermatitis, psoriasis, tinea infection, lichen simplex, nappy (diaper) rash, urticaria and generalised idiopathic pruritus.

Composition (each pill contains powdered)
Rehmannia glutinosa (sheng di, raw rehmannia) 25.5mg, *Paeonia lactiflora* (bai shao, peony root) 20.4mg, *Saponaria officinalis* 18.7mg, *Clematis armandii* (mu tong, akebia) 18.7mg, *Sesamum indicum* (hei zhi ma, sesame seed) 13.6mg, *Anemarrhena asphendoides* (zhi mu, anemarrhena) 13.6mg, *Arctium lappa* (niu bang zi, arctium) 13.6mg, *Schizonepeta tenuifolia* (jing jie, schizonepeta) 13.6mg, *Angelica sinensis* (dang gui, chinese angelica) 11.9g, *Glycyrrhiza uralensis* (gan cao, licorice) 10.2g

Combinations
- With **1.2 Si Wu Wan** for chronic eczema or dermatitis or other itchy dry skin disorder arising from Blood deficiency. This combination is also good for dry skin disorders that are worse in cold or dry weather.
- With **13.19 Pearl Powder** topically (mixed in a little sorbolene) for moist eczema or other weeping itchy lesions.

Pattern identifying features

• **Wind Heat or Wind Damp in the skin**

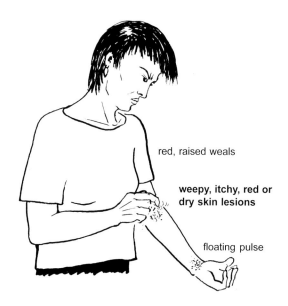

red, raised weals

weepy, itchy, red or dry skin lesions

floating pulse

• With **5.1 Xue Fu Zhu Yu Wan** or **13.11 Dan Shen Huo Xue Wan** for chronic purplish lesions with itchy, dry, scaly skin, the itch worse at night.
• With **13.4 Ke Yin Wan** for severe itch, weeping lesions, or very stubborn cases. This combination is useful for psoriasis and nummular dermatitis.
• With **6.5 Jia Wei Xiao Yao Wan** for dermatitis or eczema that is worse when the patient is stressed.

Dosage and method of administration

12-15 pills three times daily on an empty stomach. The dose may be spread out, or two lots of about 20 pills may be taken, morning and evening. In severe cases or during the early stages of treatment (the first few weeks), a 50% increase in dose may be used, then reduced as the treatment takes effect.

Cautions and contraindications

Not suitable for use alone for patients with significant Blood deficiency. The patient should be advised to avoid all drying, greasy or heating food and substances, especially seafood and shellfish, coffee, alcohol, spicy foods and tobacco.

SKIN

GMP **13.3 DANG GUI YIN ZI WAN**

当归饮子丸

Lanzhou Foci Pharmaceutical Factory (Gansu)
'*Angelica sinensis* Decoction Pills'
Dang Gui Yin Zi Wan is packaged in bottles of 200 pills.
Available as: Nourish the Surface Teapills (PF)

Available in the US,
UK and Europe
See Note 1, p.xxi

TCM actions

Nourishes and cools the Blood, supplements *qi* and strengthens *wei qi*, dispels Wind, stops itch.

Biomedical actions

Hematinic, diaphoretic, antipruritic.

INDICATIONS

• Chronic Blood deficiency with Wind in the skin. The main features of this type of skin disorder is dryness, itch and chronicity. The skin is often thickened due to prolonged irritation and from relentless scratching. Itching and irritation are typically aggravated following menstruation or when fatigued and are worse during dry or windy weather. Frequently, the upper body, especially chest, neck and face are most affected.

• This formula is a variation **1.2 Si Wu Wan**, with the addition of herbs to dispel Wind and supplement *qi*. The main focus of the formula is to replenish Blood so as to nourish the skin–when the Blood is abundant in the skin, any existing Wind is expelled and new pathogens cannot get a foothold.

• With the appropriate identifying features, this formula can be used to treat biomedical disorders such as chronic eczema or dermatitis, neurodermatitis, psoriasis, idiopathic pruritus, Winter itch and senile pruritus.

Composition

Angelica sinensis (dang gui, chinese angelica) 18%, *Rehmannia glutinosa* (sheng di, raw rehmannia) 18%, *Ligusticum wallichi* (chuan xiong, cnidium) 10%, *Ledebouriella divaricata* (fang feng, siler) 10%, *Paeonia lactiflora* (bai shao, peony root) 10%, *Tribulus terrestris* (bai ji li, tribulus) 10%, *Polygonum multiflorum* (he shou wu, ho shou wu) 8%, *Astragalus membranaceous* (huang qi, astragalus) 5%, *Schizonepeta tenuifolia* (jing jie, schizonepeta) 5%, *Glycyrrhiza uralensis* (gan cao, licorice) 5%

Combinations

• With **3.6 Gui Zhi Wan** for itch and skin rashes that are worse in cold weather.

Pattern identifying features

- **Blood deficiency with chronic Wind in the skin**
- scanty menstruation
- spots before eyes, blurring vision, dry eyes

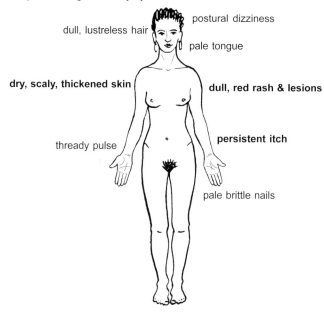

dull, lustreless hair

postural dizziness

pale tongue

dry, scaly, thickened skin

dull, red rash & lesions

thready pulse

persistent itch

pale brittle nails

- With **1.16 Tao Hong Si Wu Wan** for patients with a greater degree of Blood deficiency with elements of mild Blood stagnation.
- With **6.4 Xiao Yao Wan** or **6.5 Jia Wei Xiao Yao Wan** for chronic dermatitis or eczema that is worse when the patient is stressed.

Dosage and method of administration

8-12 pills three times daily on an empty stomach. The dose may be spread out, or two lots of about 12-18 pills may be taken, morning and evening. In severe cases or during the early stages of treatment (the first few weeks), a 50% increase in dose may be used, then reduced as the treatment takes effect.

Cautions and contraindications

Care should be taken in patients with a tendency to abdominal distension, loose stools or general digestive weakness. Some patients may find **13.3 Dang Gui Yin Zi Wan** aggravates these symptoms. This can usually be alleviated by taking the pills with a small dose (3-6 pills at the same time) of **2.18 Bao He Wan** or **2.9 Xiang Sha Liu Jun Wan**.

SKIN

13.4 KE YIN WAN

克银丸

Tong Ren Tang (Beijing)
'Overcome Psoriasis Pills'
Ke Yin Wan is packaged in bottles of 300 small pills.

TCM actions
Clears Toxic Heat and drains Dampness, dispels Wind,
promotes urination, stops itch.

Biomedical actions
Anti-inflammatory, diaphoretic, diuretic, antipruritic.

INDICATIONS

- Stubborn Toxic Heat or Damp Heat skin conditions. Mainly used for psoriasis,
  but can also be useful for eczema, dermatitis and other difficult and persistent
  wet or dry, itchy skin diseases. The main herb, smilax root, is traditionally used
  for syphillitic skin lesions. Often added to a targeting formula when enhanced
  Toxic and Damp Heat clearing action is desired.
- Also used to clear Damp Heat from the lower *jiao* to treat conditions such as
  acute urinary tract infection, cystitis, urethritis, Heat or Damp Heat *lin* syndrome,
  vaginal pruritus and vulvitis.

Composition
Smilax glabra (tu fu ling, smilax root), *Dictamnus desycarpus* (bai xian pi, dictamnus)

Combinations
- With **5.1 Xue Fu Zhu Yu Wan** for very chronic or purplish and thickened lesions
  from Blood stagnation.
- With **13.1 Lien Chiao Pai Tu Pien** for cases with Heat.
- With **1.2 Si Wu Wan** for patients with a degree of Blood deficiency.
- With **4.8 Tao Chih Pien**, **6.6 Long Dan Xie Gan Wan** or **14.5 Chuan Xin Lian
  Antiphlogistic Tablets** for urinary tract infection.
- With **14.1 Huang Lian Jie Du Wan** for recurrent boils and sores.
- With **6.5 Jia Wei Xiao Yao Wan** for psoriasis, neurodermatitis or lichen simplex
  that is worse when the patient is stressed.

Pattern identifying features

- **Chronic Damp Heat**
- **stubborn, chronic, itchy skin diseases**

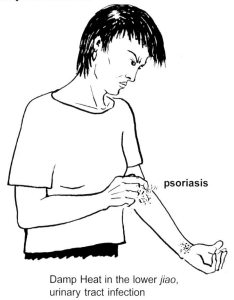

psoriasis

Damp Heat in the lower *jiao*,
urinary tract infection

- With **1.36 Bi Xie Sheng Shi Wan** for acute vulvitis and severe moist, itchy skin diseases of the lower limbs.
- With **1.38 Chien Chin Chih Tai Wan** for chronic or recurrent pelvic infections.

Dosage and method of administration

The recommended dose is 100 pills twice daily, but this is obviously impractical for all but the most fastidious patient. The practical way to use the formula is to direct the patient to consume two bottles every 2-3 days without regard for how many pills are taken at any one time. This may appear to be a huge dose, but a large amount of these herbs is required for satisfactory results.

Cautions and contraindications

None noted.

SKIN

13.5 SHI DU QING CAPSULE

湿毒清胶囊

(Shi Du Qing Jiao Nang)
Yulin Drug Manufactory (Guangxi)
'Capsules to Clear Damp Toxin'
Shi Du Qing Capsules are packaged in bottles of 30 capsules.

TCM actions
Clears Dampness and dispels Wind from the skin, nourishes *yin* and Blood, stops itch.

Biomedical actions
Anti-inflammatory, antipruritic.

INDICATIONS

- Itchy skin conditions. This general antipruritic formula is suitable for skin conditions where itch is the main feature, including idiopathic pruritus, eczema, psoriasis and dermatitis. Most beneficial for lesions that tend to weep and are very itchy. Being a small and essentially symptomatic formula, it is best when added to a more complete constitutional formula where enhanced antipruritic action is desired.

Composition (each capsule contains)
Rehmannia glutinosa (di huang, rehmannia) 150mg, *Sophora angustifolia* (ku shen, sophora) 95mg, *Xanthium sibiricum* (cang er zi, xanthium) 95mg, *Paeonia veitchii* (chi shao, red peony) 85mg, *Dictamnus desycarpus* (bai xian pi, dictamnus) 75mg

Combinations
• With **13.2 Xiao Feng Wan** for severe itch in eczema.

Dosage and method of administration
3 capsules three times daily, on an empty stomach.

Cautions and contraindications
This formula is quite drying and excessive use can dry the skin and mucous membranes. May occasionally cause headache or nausea as xanthium is slightly toxic and powerfully dispersing to both Wind and *zheng qi*.

13.6 SHI DU QING

湿毒清

Jing Xian Pharmaceutical Co. (Guangzhou)
'Clear Damp Toxin'
Shi Du Qing is packaged in bottles of 36 capsules.

TCM actions

Nourishes *yin* and Blood, cools and quickens the Blood, dispels Wind and clears Heat and Dampness from the skin, stops itch.

Biomedical actions

Anti-inflammatory, antipruritic.

INDICATIONS

- Stubborn, itchy, dry skin conditions associated with Blood deficiency, Blood stagnation and chronic Wind and Dampness in the skin. Even though the name of this formula is similar to **13.5 Shi Du Qing Capsule**, it's composition and actions are quite different. The main focus of this formula is on treating chronic dry and stubborn skin disorders—it has slightly more *yin* and Blood supplementing activity, and a stronger Heat clearing action. The combination of salvia to regulate the Blood and smilax to leach Damp and clear stubborn Heat, makes this especially good for difficult and chronic conditions such as psoriasis, eczema and allergic dermatitis. Also used for acne, nettle rash, urticaria, tinea and vulvitis.

Composition (each capsule contains extracts equivalent to dry)

Smilax glabra (tu fu ling, smilax) 630mg, *Dictamnus desycarpus* (bai xian pi, dictamnus) 490mg, *Rehmannia glutinosa* (di huang, rehmannia) 378mg, *Sophora angustifolia* (ku shen, sophora) 350mg, *Glycyrrhiza uralensis* (gan cao, licorice) 315mg, *Angelica polymorpha* (dang gui, chinese angelica) 252mg, *Salvia miltiorrhiza* (dan shen, salvia) 252mg, *Scutellaria baicalensis* (huang qin, scute) 252mg

Dosage and method of administration

3-4 capsules three times daily, on an empty stomach.

Cautions and contraindications

Caution in patients who are also taking anticoagulant therapy (aspirin, warfarin, coumarin) as clotting time can be significantly reduced.

SKIN

13.7 ECZEMA HERBAL FORMULA

皮肤病血毒丸

(Pi Fu Bing Xue Du Wan)
Tong Ren Tang (Beijing)
'Skin Disease Toxic Blood Pills'
Eczema Herbal Formula is packaged in bottles of 200 pills.

TCM actions
Clears Toxic Heat and Damp Heat from the skin, nourishes, quickens and cools the Blood, dispels Wind, drains Dampness and stops itch.

Biomedical actions
Anti-inflammatory, diaphoretic, antipruritic.

INDICATIONS

• Chronic eczema, neurodermatitis, contact dermatitis and psoriasis. Also used for pustular and cystic acne. This is a broad acting 'shotgun' formula with just about every herb you could think of for the skin combined with herbs to move stagnant Blood, nourish Blood, clear Toxic Heat and stop itch.

Composition (10 pills contain powdered)
Paeonia lactiflora (bai shao, peony root) 129mg, *Imperata cylindrica* (bai mao gen, imperata) 88mg, *Rehmannia glutinosa* (sheng di, raw rehmannia) 83mg, *Paeonia veitchii* (chi shao, red peony) 63mg, *Ledebouriella divaricata* (fang feng, siler) 63mg, *Arctium lappa* (niu bang zi, arctium) 63mg, *Ligusticum wallici* (chuan xiong, cnidium) 63mg, *Rubia cordifolia* (qian cao gen, rubia) 41mg, *Juglans regia* (hu tao ren, walnut) 41mg, *Schizonepeta tenuifolia* (jing jie, schizonepeta) 41mg, *Angelica sinensis* (dang gui, chinese angelica) 41mg, *Kochia scoparia* (di fu zi, kochia) 41mg, *Xanthium sibiricum* (cang er zi, xanthium) 41mg, *Lonicera japonica* (jin yin hua, lonicera flower) 41mg, *Lonicera japonica* (ren dong teng, lonicera stem) 41mg, *Forsythia suspensa* (lian qiao, forsythia) 41mg, *Smilax glabra* (tu fu ling, smilax) 41mg, *Gleditsia australis* (zao jiao ci, gleditsia thorn) 41mg, *Platycodon grandiflorum* (jie geng, platycodon) 41mg, *Leonurus sibiricus* (yi mu cao, motherwort) 41mg, *Paeonia suffruticosa* (mu dan pi, moutan) 41mg, *Dictamnus desycarpus* (bai xian pi, dictamnus) 41mg, *Rheum palmatum* (da huang, rhubarb root) 41mg, *Glycyrrhiza uralensis* (gan cao, licorice) 41mg, *Angelica dahurica* (bai zhi, angelica) 41mg, *Spatholobus suberectus* (ji xue teng, spatholobus) 41mg, *Sempervivum tectorum* 41mg, *Arnebia euchroma* 21mg, *Carthamus tinctorius* (hong hua, carthamus) 21mg, *Spiroldela polyrrhiza* (fu ping, duckweed) 21mg

Pattern identifying features

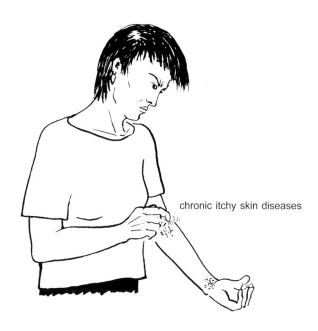

chronic itchy skin diseases

Combinations
• With **13.4 Ke Yin Wan** for stubborn skin diseases.
• With **13.5 Shi Du Qing Capsule** for severe itch.

Dosage and method of administration
The recommended dose is 10-20 pills twice daily. The dose may be reduced to a maintenance dose (~50-75% of recommended dose) after about one month or when the patient sees significant improvement.

Cautions and contraindications
Contraindicated during pregnancy.

SKIN

13.8 FANG FENG TONG SHENG WAN

防风通圣丸

Lanzhou Foci Pharmaceutical Factory (Gansu)
'Ledebouriella Pills to Sagely Unblock'
Fang Feng Tong Sheng Wan is packaged in bottles of 200 pills.
Also available as: Ledebouriella Sagely Unblocks Teapills (PF)

TCM actions
Clears external and internal Heat, dispels Wind, opens the bowels.

Biomedical actions
Anti-inflammatory, detoxicant, laxative.

INDICATIONS

• Internal and external Heat patterns causing skin diseases such as rashes, contact dermatitis, hypersensitive or allergic dermatitis, urticaria, recurrent boils and sores, otitis externa or eczema. Most commonly used in young or robust patients with these features. The internal Heat is typically located in the Stomach and Intestines, affecting the skin through the Intestines' relationship with the Lungs. The Heat usually has a dietary component.

• Acute Wind Heat *gan mao* in a patient with pre-existing internal Heat. The signs and symptoms include strong fever and chills, headache, dizziness, red, sore eyes, nasal congestion with thick, colored mucus, thirst, constipation, concentrated urine and a slippery rapid pulse. Similar to a *tai yang* / *yang ming* simultaneous pattern.

• Obesity in a robust or otherwise excess patient with a strong constitution and a tendency to heat and constipation. These patients are quite *yang* in nature, and may suffer from disorders such as arteriosclerosis, gallbladder disease, hypertension or gout. **13.8 Fang Feng Tong Sheng Wan** is useful as an adjunct 'clearing' formula in such patients trying to lose weight as they modify their diets and increase exercise.

• Chronic *bi* syndrome of a heat type, characterized by pain, redness, heat and swelling of joints, the pain worse in warm weather or with heat.

Composition
Glycyrrhiza uralensis (gan cao, licorice) 36.6mg, *Scutellaria baicalensis* (huang qin, scute) 18.3mg, *Platycodon grandiflorum* (jie geng, platycodon) 18.3mg, *Schizonepeta tenuifolia* (jing jie, schizonepeta) 13.7mg, *Ledebouriella divaricata* (fang feng, siler) 9.1mg, *Paeonia*

Pattern identifying features

- **Simultaneous internal & external excess
  Heat patterns**
- robust, overweight, large frame
- general tendency to heat

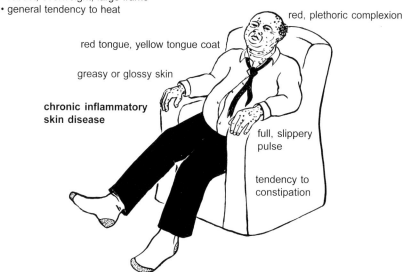

red, plethoric complexion

red tongue, yellow tongue coat

greasy or glossy skin

**chronic inflammatory
skin disease**

full, slippery
pulse

tendency to
constipation

lactiflora (bai shao, white peony) 9.1mg, *Rheum palmatum* (da huang, rhubarb) 9.1mg, *Ligusticum wallichi* (chuan xiong, cnidium) 9.1mg, *Mentha haplocalycis* (bo he, mint) 9.1mg, *Angelica sinensis* (dang gui, chinese angelica) 9.1mg, *Forsythia suspensa* (lian qiao, forsythia) 9.1mg, *Gardenia jasminoides* (shan zhi zi, gardenia) 4.6mg, *Atractylodes macrocephala* (bai zhu, atractylodes) 4.6mg

SKIN

Combinations
• With **13.4 Ke Yin Wan** for stubborn skin diseases.

Dosage and method of administration
8-12 pills three times daily on an empty stomach. The dose may be spread out, or two lots of 12-18 pills may be taken, morning and evening. In severe cases or during the early stages of treatment (the first few weeks), a 50% increase in dose may be used, then reduced as the treatment takes effect.

Cautions and contraindications
Contraindicated during pregnancy.

13.9 QING RE AN CHUANG PIAN

清热暗疮片

Yang Cheng Pharmaceutical Stock Co. (Guangzhou)
'Heat Clearing Acne Pills'
Qing Re An Chuang Pian is packaged in bottles of 90 pills.

TCM actions
Cools the Blood, clears Toxic Heat from the skin, Lungs
and Stomach.

Biomedical actions
Anti-inflammatory, antibiotic, detoxicant.

INDICATIONS

- Toxic Heat and Hot Blood skin lesions. Used for a variety of suppurative skin
  infections, but in particular conditions such as teenage acne, acne vulgaris,
  abscesses, boils and sores, folliculitis and impetigo herpetiformis. The lesions
  are pustular, inflamed, angry and may be painful.

Composition
Andrographis paniculata (chuan xin lian, andrographis), *Taraxacum mongolicum* (pu gong
ying, dandelion), *Lonicera japonica* (jin yin hua, lonicera), *Rheum palmatum* (da huang,
rhubarb root), *Gardenia jasminoides* (shan zhi zi, gardenia), *Sophora tonkinensis* (shan
dou gen, sophora), Synthetic Bovine Gallstone (ren gong niu huang), pearl powder
(zhen zhu)

Combinations
- With **14.5 Chuan Xin Lian Antiphlogistic Tablets**, **14.6 Fu Fang Nan Ban
  Lan Gen** or **14.1 Huang Lian Jie Du Wan** for severe or resistant cases.
- With **6.5 Jia Wei Xiao Yao Wan** for premenstrual acne.

Dosage and method of administration
2-4 pills three times daily on an empty stomach. One course of treatment is 15 days,
and usually 1-2 courses are needed to see a reasonable result. The patient should
refrain from all greasy, spicy and excessively sweet foods, in particular junk food and
fast food. In addition, alcohol should be avoided. This formula may cause diarrhea.

Cautions and contraindications
Contraindicated during pregnancy.

13.10 ZHEN ZHU AN CHUANG TABLET

珍珠暗疮片

(Zhen Zhu An Chuang Pian)
Jing Xian Pharmaceutical Co. (Guangzhou)
'Pearl Acne Pills'
Zhen Zhu An Chuang Tablets are packaged in bottles of 60 tablets. A similar formula available as: Margarite Acne Pills

TCM actions
Cools the Blood, clears Toxic Heat from the skin, Lungs and Stomach.

Biomedical actions
Anti-inflammatory, antibiotic, detoxicant.

INDICATIONS

- Toxic Heat and Damp Heat in the skin. Used for acne, both cystic acne and with whiteheads. The characteristic feature is small red or white lumps and pimples on the skin of the face, neck and upper back that may or may not be painful. Suitable for teenage acne, acne vulgaris, boils and sores and folliculitis.

Composition (each tablet contains extracts equivalent to dry)
Lonicera japonica (jin yin hua, lonicera) 864mg, *Taraxacum mongolicum* (pu gong ying, dandelion) 864mg, *Gardenia florida* (shan zhi zi, gardenia) 864mg, *Sophora japonica* (huai hua, sophora flower bud) 648mg, *Rheum officinale* (da huang, rhubarb root), *Ostrea gigas* (mu li, oyster shell) 30mg, sucrose

Combinations
- With **14.5 Chuan Xin Lian Antiphlogistic Tablets, 14.6 Fu Fang Nan Ban Lan Gen** or **14.1 Huang Lian Jie Du Wan** for severe or resistant cases.
- With **6.5 Jia Wei Xiao Yao Wan** for premenstrual acne.

Dosage and method of administration
3-5 tablets, three times daily on an empty stomach. The patient should refrain from all greasy, spicy and excessively sweet foods, in particular junk food and fast food. In addition, alcohol should be avoided. This formula may cause diarrhea.

Cautions and contraindications
Contraindicated during pregnancy.

GMP **13.11 DAN SHEN HUO XUE WAN**

丹参活血丸

Available in the US,
UK and Europe
See Note 1, p.xxi

Lanzhou Foci Pharmaceutical Factory (Gansu)
'*Salvia miltiorrhiza* Pills to Regulate Blood'
Dan Shen Huo Xue Wan is packaged in bottles of 200 pills.
Available as: Quell the Surface Teapills (PF)

TCM actions
Quickens, cools and nourishes Blood, regulates *qi*, clears
Heat, stops itch.

Biomedical actions
Anti-inflammatory, vasodilator, antipruritic.

INDICATIONS

• Blood and *qi* stagnation with Heat in the Blood type skin disorders. Skin disorders
of this type are generally chronic, recurrent and stubborn, and are characterised
by the dull red or purplish colour of the lesion. The lesions tends to be fairly
fixed in location or to recur in the same place, often along the course of the
upper Liver channel–face, neck, chest. There will often be an emotional
component to inititiation or aggravation of the lesion, and they are frequently
extremely itchy. The genesis of this pattern is typically in the Liver, as prolonged
Liver *qi* stagnation is commonly the precursor to both Heat in the Blood (via
stagnant Heat) and stagnant Blood. In some cases there will be a dietary
component as well–alcohol and heating spicy food in particular.

• The salvia serves a dual purpose here–not only does it cool and regulate the
Blood, it also calms the *shen* to assist in moderating the patients response to the
intense itching.

• With the appropriate identifying features, this formula can assist in the treatment
of biomedical conditions such as psoriasis, psoriatic arthritis, chronic eczema,
systemic lupus erythematosus, rosacea and pityriasis rosea.

Composition
Salvia miltiorrhiza (dan shen, salvia) 12%, *Rehmannia glutinosa* (sheng di, raw
rehmannia) 12%, *Rubia cordifolia* (qian cao gen, rubia) 10%, *Paeonia veitchii* (chi shao,
red peony) 8%, *Carthamus tinctorius* (hong hua, carthamus) 8%, *Lycopus lucidus* (ze lan,
bugleweed) 8%, *Dictamnus desycarpus* (bai xian pi, dictamnus) 8%, *Angelica sinensis*
(dang gui wei, tail of chinese angelica) 8%, *Tribulus terrestris* (bai ji li, tribulus) 8%,
Paris polyphylla (cao he che, paris) 6%, *Sophora subprostrata* (shan dou gen, sophora)
6%, *Citrus reticulata* (qing pi, immature citrus) 6%

Pattern identifying features

- **Blood stagnation & Hot Blood**
- chronic skin rash or disease with a stress component
- itch worse at night
- thickened, dry, scaly skin

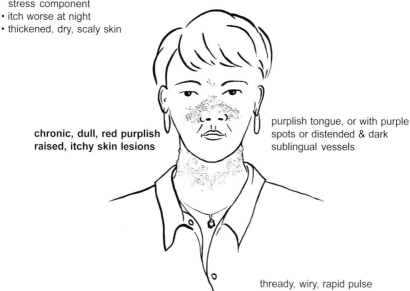

chronic, dull, red purplish raised, itchy skin lesions

purplish tongue, or with purple spots or distended & dark sublingual vessels

thready, wiry, rapid pulse

Combinations
- With **13.4 Ke Yin Wan** for stubborn psoriasis.
- With **13.5 Shi Du Qing Capsule** for relentless itching.

Dosage and method of administration
8-12 pills three times daily on an empty stomach. The dose may be spread out, or two lots of about 12-18 pills may be taken, morning and evening. In severe cases or during the early stages of treatment (the first few weeks), a 50% increase in dose may be used, then reduced as the treatment takes effect.

Cautions and contraindications
Contraindicated during pregnancy, for women with menorrhagia, and for patients with bleeding disorders. Caution in patients on anticoagulant therapy (aspirin, warfarin, coumarin). Watch for bruising or increased tendency to bleeding.

Prolonged use may deplete *qi* and Blood, so a break every 2-3 months, perhaps with a change to a simple clearing or Wind expelling formula for a few weeks, is recommended.

SKIN

13.12 CHUAN XIN LIAN CREAM

穿心莲消炎膏

(Chuan Xin Lian Xiao Yan Gao)

Jing Xian Pharmaceutical Co. (Guangzhou)

'Andrographis Anti-inflammatory Ointment'

Chuan Xin Lian Cream is packaged in tubes of 20 grams of ointment.

TCM actions

Clears Toxic Heat and Damp Heat from the skin, reduces swelling.

Biomedical actions

Anti-inflammatory, antibiotic, detoxicant.

INDICATIONS

• Damp Heat and Toxic Heat in the skin. Used for inflammatory and suppurative skin disorders with redness, swelling and pain. Used topically on abscesses and boils, carbuncles and furuncles, acne, cellulitis, erysipelas, Bartholin's cyst, impetigo, eczema, dermatitis and other inflamed skin conditions. may also be useful in some cases of warts.

Composition (each 1 gram contains extracts equivalent to dry)

Andrographis paniculata (chuan xin lian, andrographis) 600mg, *Scutellaria baicalensis* (huang qin, scute) 300mg, *Coptis chinensis* (huang lian, coptis) 300mg

Combinations

• With **14.1 Huang Lian Jie Du Wan** or **14.8 Wu Wei Xiao Du Wan** for abscesses and boils from Damp or Toxic Heat.

• With **6.6 Long Dan Xie Gan Wan** for Bartholin's cyst from Damp Heat affecting the Liver.

Dosage and method of administration

Apply locally to affected area 3-4 times daily.

Cautions and Contraindications

Avoid contact with the eyes and broken skin. For external use only.

13.13 FU YIN TAI LINIMENT

肤阴泰

(Fu Yin Tai)
Jing Xian Pharmaceutical Co. (Guangzhou)
'Protect the Skin of the External *Yin* [Vulva]'
Fu Yin Tai Liniment is packaged in bottles of 120ml.

FU YIN TAI

LINIMENT

E

AUST L 91204
120ml

MADE IN CHINA

TCM actions

Clears Toxic Heat, dispels Wind, dries Dampness, kills parasites, stops itch.

Biomedical actions

Anti-inflammatory, antipruritic, antifungal, detoxicant.

INDICATIONS

- Applied topically for a variety of itchy skin conditions, including bacterial, viral, and fungal infections, and pruritic skin diseases.
- Vulval and vaginal infections by pathogens such as *Trichomonas*, cervical inflammation, vulval eczema and pruritus, yellow malodorous leukorrhea.
- Also useful for painful and itching hemorrhoids, anal itch, stubborn itchy eczema and dermatitis, fungal infections of the skin, tinea, onychomycosis, tinea versicolour and prickly heat.

Composition (each 1 ml dose contains extracts equivalent to dry)

Cnidium monneri (she chuang zi, cnidium seed) 1.1g, *Eucalyptus globus* (an you, eucalyptus oil) 720mg, *Pinus massoniana* (song you, turpentine oil) 720mg, *Kochia scoparia* (di fu zi, kochia) 540mg, *Cinnamomum camphora* (zhang nao, camphor) 624mg, *Coptis chinensis* (huang lian, coptis) 72mg

Dosage and method of administration

For external use only. Apply 1ml of liniment to the affected areas, or dilute 15ml of liniment in 1 litre of water and wash the affected area, once or twice daily.

Cautions and contraindications

Avoid contact with the eyes and broken skin. For external use only.

SKIN

GMP **13.14 CHING WAN HUNG**

京万红

E

(Jing Wan Hong)
Tianjin Drug Manufactory (Shandong)
'Capital Ten Thousand Reds'
Ching Wan Hung is packaged in tubes of red ointment
and in large tubs (pictured).

TCM actions

Stops pain, clears Heat, quickens Blood, disperses stagnant Blood, promotes healing.

Biomedical actions

Anodyne, anti-inflammatory, bacteriocidal, vulnerary.

INDICATIONS

- An excellent topical ointment for all types of burns and scalds, including electrical, chemical, solar and radiation. Can be used to relieve mild burns such as sunburn, and encourage the repair of tissues subject to severe burns or scalding, with blistering, redness, necrosis and pain.
- Can be applied to ulcerated or open skin lesions to accelerate granulation and healing, including painful, thrombosed or inflamed hemorrhoids, anal fissure, chronic diabetic or tropical ulcers and bedsores. Also can be applied to eczema, psoriasis and dermatitis.
- Essential for the acupuncturist who uses lots of moxa. Very useful for dabbing under rice grain moxa pellets to hold them on and to prevent blistering.

Composition

Lobelia chinensis (ban bian lian, lobelia) 28%, *Commiphora myrrha* (mo yao, myrrh) 18%, *Angelica sinensis* (dang gui, chinese angelica) 12%, *Dryobalanops camphora* (bing pian, borneol) 12%, *Chaenomelas sinensis* (mu gua, chinese quince) 9%, *Sanguisorba officinalis* (di yu, sanguisorba) 9%, *Boswellia carteri* (ru xiang, frankincense) 6%, *Carthamus tinctorius* (hong hua, carthamus) 6%,

Combinations

- With **1.1 Ba Zhen Wan** or **7.16 Shi Quan Da Bu Wan** for chronic ulcers and bed sores.
- With **2.38 Hua Zhi Ling Tablet** or **2.39 Fargelin for Piles** for inflamed or painful hemorrhoids or anal fissure.

Pattern identifying features

- **burns & scalds**
- non-healing ulcers & sores

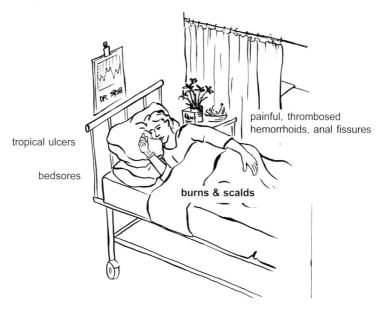

tropical ulcers

bedsores

painful, thrombosed
hemorrhoids, anal fissures

burns & scalds

- With **2.11 Bu Zhong Yi Qi Wan** for Spleen *qi* deficiency hemorrhoids.
- With **5.1 Xue Fu Zhu Yu Wan** for inflamed venous or tropical ulcers. This combination is also useful for chronic Blood stagnation type anal fissures that refuse to heal.

Dosage and method of administration

For mild scalds and burns, **13.14 Ching Wan Hung** can be applied directly to the affected area after the wound is cleaned. The area may be covered with a piece of sterile gauze, changed daily. For deep wounds and full thickness burns, a thick layer can be applied daily and covered with sterile gauze. The wound should be cleaned and debrided daily, as necessary. Apply locally for hemorrhoids and anal lesions.

Cautions and contraindications

For external use only. Avoid contact with the eyes. May stain clothes.

13.15 TUJIN LINIMENT

E 土槿皮酊

(Tu Jin Pi Ding)
The United Pharmaceutical Manufactory (Guangzhou)
'Hibiscus Bark Extract'
Tujin Liniment is packaged as a liquid extract in small plastic bottles.

INDICATIONS:
For scabies,
itch of toes
and skin, etc.

TCM actions
Dries Dampness, stops itching.

Biomedical actions
Antiparasitic, antifungal, disinfectant, antipruritic.

INDICATIONS

* Localised fungal infections, including various manifestations of tinea (corporis, pedis, unguium, capitis etc.), jock itch, and scabies.
* May be useful for small areas of psoriasis and stubborn dermatitis.

Composition
Hibiscus syricus (mu jin pi, hibiscus bark), benzoic acid, salicylic acid, ethanol

Combinations
* With **2.23 Ping Wei San, 1.38 Chien Chin Chih Tai Wan** or **1.36 Bi Xie Sheng Shi Wan** for Damp or recurrent Damp Heat accumulation in the lower body affecting the feet.
* With **14.1 Huang Lian Jie Du Wan** for Damp Heat pouring downwards.
* With **2.9 Xiang Sha Liu Jun Wan** for patients with Spleen Damp.

Dosage and method of administration
Rub a few drops on the affected area as often as practical. Good if left overnight beneath a covering bandage.

Cautions and Contraindications
For external use only. Avoid contact with the eyes. May stain clothes.

13.16 HUA TUO GAO

华佗膏

Shanghai Chinese Drug Pharmaceutical Works
'Hua Tuo's (famous doctor) Ointment'
Hua Tuo Gao is packaged in 20 gram jars of ointment.

E

TCM actions
Dries Dampness, stops itching.

Biomedical actions
Antiparasitic, antifungal, disinfectant, antipruritic.

INDICATIONS

- Scabies.
- Localised fungal infections, including various manifestations of tinea (corporis, pedis, unguium, capitis etc.), jock itch, Hong Kong foot, ringworm.
- Moist eczema, dermatitis with vesicles, crusting and itch, including pompholyx.

Composition
Benzoic acid 10%, Salicylic acid 5%, *Cera chinensis* 2%, Camphor 2%, *Chimonanthus praecox* (la mei) 1%, in a vaseline base

Combinations
- With **2.23 Ping Wei San**, **1.38 Chien Chin Chih Tai Wan** or **1.36 Bi Xie Sheng Shi Wan** for Damp or recurrent Damp Heat accumulation in the lower body affecting the feet.
- With **14.1 Huang Lian Jie Du Wan** for Damp Heat pouring downwards.
- With **2.9 Xiang Sha Liu Jun Wan** for patients with Spleen Damp.

Dosage and method of administration
Wash the affected area with warm water and apply twice daily. In areas where the skin is thickened, soak in warm water to soften it first. Useful applied at night on a cotton ball wedged between the toes. Do not use soap, alcohol, hydrogen peroxide, iodine or sulphur compounds on the skin while using this product.

Cautions and Contraindications
For external use only. Avoid contact with the eyes.

SKIN

13.17 XIAO YAN TANG SHANG CREAM

消炎清毒烫伤膏

(Xiao Yan Qing Re Tang Shang Gao)

 Jing Xian Pharmaceutical Co. (Guangzhou)

'Anti-inflammatory, Detoxifying, Burns Ointment'

 Xiao Yan Tang Shang Cream is packaged in tubes of 20 grams ointment.

TCM actions

Clears Toxic Heat and Damp Heat from the skin, quickens and cools the Blood, reduces swelling and stops itch.

Biomedical actions

Anti-inflammatory, antibiotic, detoxicant.

INDICATIONS

- Inflammed and itchy skin diseases. Good for acute and chronic dermatitis, eczema, psoriasis, rosacea, urticaria and allergic eruptions, as well as superficial suppurative swellings, boils and sores. May also be useful for painful, inflammed or itchy hemorrhoids and anal fissure. Can be used for fungal skin infections such as tinea and ringworm.
- Used to alleviate the pain and swelling of burns and scalds, and to accelerate the healing process. Can be used on all types of burns including those from therapeutic radiation, electricity and sunburn.

Composition (each 1 gram contains extracts equivalent to dry)

Phellodendron amurense (huang bai, phellodendron) 924mg, *Scutellaria baicalensis* (huang qin, scute) 924mg, *Rheum palmatum* (da huang, rhubarb root) 924mg, *Sanguisorba officinalis* (di yu, sanguisorba) 924mg, *Paeonia suffruticosa* (mu dan pi, moutan) 924mg, *Arnebia euchroma* (zi cao, arnebia) 924mg, *Paeonia veitchii* (chi shao, red peony) 154mg, *Sophora angustifolia* (ku shen, sophora) 154mg, *Stemona sessifolia* (bai bu, stemona) 154mg

Dosage and method of administration

Apply locally to affected area 3-4 times daily.

Cautions and Contraindications

For external use only. Avoid contact with the eyes.

E

13.18 JI YAN GAO

鸡眼膏

(Corn Plaster)
Shanghai Hygienic Supply Factory (Shanghai)
'Chicken Eye Plaster'
Ji Yan Gao is packaged in boxes of six plasters.

TCM actions
Softens hardness, stops pain and removes warts and corns.

INDICATIONS

- Corns, calluses and warts (including plantar warts) on the feet.

Composition
Salicylic Acid 70%, ointment 2g.

Combinations
- With **14.5 Chuan Xin Lian Antiphlogistic Tablets** for chronic or recurrent warts.

Dosage and method of administration
Bathe the feet in warm water for ten minutes and dry thoroughly. Gently tear off the thin plastic strip covering the plaster and apply to the corn, callus or wart, making sure the red ointment is firmly in position against the lesion. After three days, the skin beneath the plaster should become soft and white and may be gently removed before applying another plaster. If the skin is not soft and white, keep the plaster in place for another couple of days. After the plaster has been changed three times, wait a week before applying another. The treatment may be repeated as often as necessary to remove the lesion.

Cautions and contraindications
For external use only.

SKIN

13.19 PEARL POWDER

珍珠末

(Zhen Zhu Mo)
Guangzhou Qixing Pharmaceutical Co.
(Guangzhou)
Pearl Powder is packaged in vials of 0.3 grams, twelve vials per box.

TCM actions
Promotes healing, soothes inflamed tissues, brightens the eyes, calms the *shen*, extinguishes Wind.

Biomedical actions
Anti-inflammatory, detoxicant, anodyne.

INDICATIONS

- Applied topically to ease inflammation and promote healing. Used for redness and irritation of the skin in conditions such as nappy (diaper) rash, moist eczema, and other wet skin conditions. Can be mixed with an emollient for dry or flaky skin conditions.
- Applied to minor open wounds to accelerate healing. Used topically for chronic non-healing ulcers and sores.
- Used internally for *shen* disturbances and tremors or spasms from internal Wind. Especially good for easy fright, fearfulness, anxiety, palpitations and insomnia in children.
- For visual weakness, inflammation of the eyes or growths over the eye, such as cataracts or pterygia.

Composition (each vial contains)
Pteria martensii (zhen zhu fen, pearl powder) 0.3g

Combinations
- With **13.2 Xiao Feng Wan** for moist eczema or dermatitis.
- With **8.1 Tian Wang Bu Xin Dan**, **8.2 Bai Zi Yang Xin Wan** or **1.9 Gui Pi Wan** for severe insomnia, anxiety, panic attacks or palpitations.
- With **9.21 Ming Mu Shang Ching Pien** for sore eyes or visual disturbances from Liver Heat.
- With **9.22 Ming Mu Di Huang Wan** or **7.2.2 Qi Ju Di Huang Wan** for visual weakness and cataracts from Liver and Kidney *yin* deficiency.
- With **7.16.1 Shi Quan Da Bu Wan** for chronic non-healing ulcers and sores.

Pattern identifying features

- inflammation of the skin
- minor wounds
- moist eczema

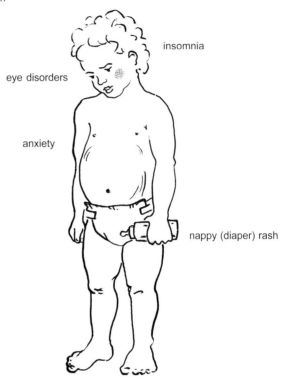

insomnia

eye disorders

anxiety

nappy (diaper) rash

SKIN

Dosage and method of administration

Apply the powder directly to red, itchy, moist eczema, 2-3 times daily. For dry flaking eczema or dermatitis, combine one vial of Pearl Powder with a half teaspoon of sorbolene and apply to the affected area. For nappy (diaper) rash, sprinkle the powder directly onto the childs' bottom after bathing.

When used internally the adult dose is 1-2 vials, twice daily, washed down with warm water. For children the dose is ½-1 vial twice daily. May be used alone, or more commonly, in combination with any other appropriate constitutional formula. Pearl Powder can also be made into eye-drops with saline for topical application.

Cautions and contraindications

Avoid soap while using Pearl Powder.

13.20 MOPIKO

E 无比膏

(Wu Bi Gao)
Ikeda Mohando Co. (Japan)
'Incomparable Ointment'
MOPIKO is packaged in 20 gram tubes of ointment.

TCM actions
Stops pain and itching.

Biomedical actions
Analgesic, antipruritic.

INDICATIONS

- Localised itching from eczema and other skin conditions.
- Itch and inflammation from insect bites and stings.

Composition (w/v)
Menthol crystals 3.92%, Camphor 5.83%, Methyl salicylate 3.75%

Dosage and method of administration
Apply locally to affected area 3-4 times daily.

Cautions and Contraindications
For external use only. Avoid contact with the eyes and broken skin.

14

Patent Medicines for Infection and Inflammation

14.1 Huang Lian Jie Du Wan
14.2 Huang Lian Su Tablets
14.3 Tabellae Berberini
14.4 Chuan Xin Lian
14.5 Chuan Xin Lian Antiphlogistic Tablets
14.6 Fu Fang Nan Ban Lan Gen
14.7 Niu Huang Qing Huo Wan
14.8 Wu Wei Xiao Du Wan
14.9 Bai Hu Tang Wan
14.10 Liang Ge Wan

See Also

3.16 Ching Fei Yi Huo Pien
4.9 DBD Capsule
6.6 Long Dan Xie Gan Wan
9.3 Peking Niu Huang Jie Du Pian
9.4 Huang Lien Shang Ching Pien
9.5 Pu Ji Xiao Du Wan
9.6 Ban Lan Gen Chong Ji
9.21 Ming Mu Shang Ching Pien
13.1 Lien Chiao Pai Tu Pien

14.1 HUANG LIAN JIE DU WAN

黄连解毒丸

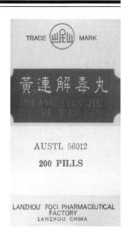

Lanzhou Foci Pharmaceutical Factory (Gansu)
'Coptis Pill to Eliminate Toxin'
Huang Lian Jie Du Wan is packaged in bottles of 200 pills.
Also available as: Huang Lian Jie Du Teapills (PF)

TCM actions

Clears Toxic Heat and Damp Heat from all three *jiao*,
purges Fire, cools the Blood.

Biomedical actions

Antipyretic, antibiotic, anti-inflammatory.

INDICATIONS

* Damp Heat, Toxic Heat or Fire affecting all three *jiao*. This important antibiotic
  formula has wide application in both systemic and localised patterns of Damp
  Heat, Toxic Heat or Fire characterised by fever, redness, suppuration, swelling
  and other signs of excess Heat. In severe cases, there may be febrile rashes,
  bleeding and disturbances of consciousness. Especially good for Damp or Toxic
  Heat affecting the gastro-intestinal system (in particular Dysenteric disorder),
  lungs and skin.
* Bleeding disorders from the reckless movement of Hot Blood.
* This formula may assist in the treatment of many biomedical conditions, if the
  appropriate identifying features are present. In the following selection, those
  considered most amenable to treatment are in bold type.
  – Systemic: **acute bacterial infections**, septicaemia, encephalitis, Beçhet's
    syndrome, fever of unknown origin, lymphangitis, hypertension
  – Skin: **pyogenic skin infections**, carbuncles, acne, boils, mastitis, erysipelas
  – Upper *jiao*: **acute bronchitis**, pneumonia, gingivitis, stomatitis, acute
    conjunctivitis, acute sinusitis, acute otitis
  – Middle *jiao*: acute hepatitis, cholecystitis, jaundice, *Helicobacter pylori*, gastritis
  – Lower *jiao*: acute colitis, **bacterial dysentery**, amebic dysentery, acute intestinal
    infections including those associated with *Giardia* and **Shigella**, **urinary tract
    infection**, acute pelvic inflammatory disease, acute appendicitis, acute gout

Composition (each pill contains powdered)

Coptis chinensis (huang lian, coptis) 30mg, *Gardenia jasminoides* (shan zhi zi, gardenia)
30mg, *Scutellaria baicalensis* (huang qin, scute) 20mg, *Phellodendron chinensis* (huang bai,
phellodendron) 20mg

Pattern identifying features

- **Damp Heat, Toxic Heat, Fire**
- **fever**
- insomnia, restlessness & irritability
- thirst, dry mouth, voracious appetite
- bleeding, especially from the upper body (nose, sclera, mouth)

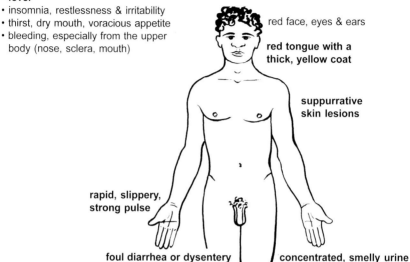

red face, eyes & ears

red tongue with a thick, yellow coat

suppurrative skin lesions

rapid, slippery, strong pulse

foul diarrhea or dysentery

concentrated, smelly urine

Combinations
- With **1.2 Si Wu Wan** for chronic menstrual bleeding from Blood deficiency and Hot Blood. This combination is also effective for stubborn skin diseases from the same etiology, such as psoriasis and dermatitis.
- With **2.26 Xiang Lian Wan** for epigastric pain and reflux from Stomach Heat and infection by *Helicobacter pylori*.
- With **14.5 Chuan Xin Lian Antiphlogistic Tablets** for acute bacterial dysentery or appendicitis (Intestinal abscess).
- With **14.6 Fu Fang Nan Ban Lan Gen** for encephalitis.

Dosage and method of administration
10 pills every two or three hours for acute disorders. When used long term (for constitutional Damp Heat or Fire), 6-8 pills three times daily is usually sufficient.

Cautions and contraindications
Contraindicated in patients (usually infants) with G6PD (Glucose-6-Phospate dehydrogenase) deficiency. This formula is very bitter and cold and can easily damage the Spleen and Stomach, and deplete *yin*. It should only be used for the duration of the acute excess Heat pattern, usually no longer than a few weeks. In those few circumstances where prolonged use is indicated (for example, when treating hypertension from a constitutional tendency to Fire), pay close attention to the patient's digestive function. Overdose can cause dizziness and vomiting.

INF

14.2 HUANG LIAN SU TABLETS

黄连素片

(Huang Lian Su Pian)
Jing Xian Pharmaceutical Co. (Guangzhou)
'Coptis Extract Tablets'
Huang Lian Su Tablets are packaged in bottles of 60 tablets.
Also available as: Coptis Teapills (PF)

TCM actions
Clears Damp Heat and Toxic Heat.

Biomedical actions
Antipyretic, antibiotic, anti-inflammatory.

INDICATIONS

- Damp Heat and Toxic Heat disorders, especially those affecting the gastro-intestinal system, lungs and skin. Especially effective against bacterial dysentery (*Shigella sp.*). Berberine, the main alkaloid, has been shown to possess growth inhibitory activity against other common parasites, including *Giardia lamblia*, *Trichomonas vaginalis* and *Entamoeba histolytica*. Also effective against *Helicobacter pylori*. May be useful for fungal infections and as an adjunct treatment for pulmonary tuberculosis. Effective for all types of suppurative sores and localised infections.
- May be useful in small doses (¼-½ normal dose) over a longer period of time for *gu* syndrome.
- **14.2 Huang Lian Su Tablets** can be combined with other formulae when a powerful Toxic Heat clearing action is desired.
- With the appropriate identifying features, this single herb formula can assist in the treatment of a wide variety of infectious conditions, including bacterial and amebic dysentery, acute colitis, appendicitis, acute infectious diarrhea, food poisoning, pyogenic skin infections, gout, cholecystitis, stomatitis, gingivitis, urinary tract infection, septicaemia and lymphangitis.

Composition (each tablet contains extract equivalent to dry)
Coptis japonica (huang lian, coptis) 1250mg

Combinations
- With **6.6 Long Dan Xie Gan Wan** for Damp Heat in the genito-urinary system— acute cystitis, urethritis, orchitis, prostatitis, pelvic inflammatory disease, etc.

Pattern identifying features

- **Toxic Heat & Damp Heat, especially of the gastro-intestinal system, Lung & skin**
- **suppurative infections**
- fever
- malaise

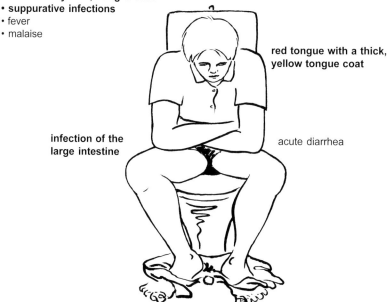

red tongue with a thick, yellow tongue coat

infection of the large intestine

acute diarrhea

- With **6.1 Xiao Chai Hu Tang Wan** for acute mastitis or otitis (of a *shao yang* type).
- With **2.3 So Hup Yuen Medical Pills** for *gu* syndrome.
- With **8.8 Wen Dan Wan** for severe Phlegm Heat patterns.
- With **4.6 Ba Zheng San Wan** for relatively severe urinary tract infection or pyelonephritis.

Dosage and method of administration

2-4 tablets three times daily on an empty stomach. For children the dose is ½-1 tablet three times daily.

Cautions and contraindications

Coptis is very bitter and cold and can easily damage the Spleen and Stomach, and deplete *yin*. It should only be used for the duration of the acute excess Heat pattern, usually no longer than a few weeks. Contraindicated in patients (usually infants) with G6PD (Glucose-6-Phospate dehydrogenase) deficiency.

INF

14.3 TABELLAE BERBERINI

黄连素片

(Huang Lian Su Pian)
Sing-Kyn Drug House (Guangzhou)
'Coptis Extract Tablets'
Tabellae Berberini is packaged in bottles of 100 small pills.

TCM actions
Clears Damp Heat and Toxic Heat.

Biomedical actions
Antipyretic, antibiotic, anti-inflammatory.

INDICATIONS

• As for **14.2 Huang Lian Su Tablets**.

Composition (each pill contains)
Berberine hydrochloride 50mg (extracted from *Coptis japonica* [huang lian and *Phellodendron chinensis* [huang bai])

Dosage and method of administration
1-3 tablets three times daily on an empty stomach. For children the dose is ½-1 tablet three times daily.

Cautions and contraindications
As for **14.2 Huang Lian Su Tablets**.

14.4 CHUAN XIN LIAN

穿心莲

Guanghua Pharmaceutical Co. (Guangzhou)
'*Andrographis panicuata*'
Chuan Xin Lian is packaged in bottles of 60 sugar coated tablets.

TCM actions

Clears Toxic Heat, cools the Blood, alleviates swelling.

Biomedical actions

General antibiotic action–antiviral and antibacterial; hypoglycemic, antithrombotic, antipyretic.

INDICATIONS

• As for **14.5 Chuan Xin Lian Antiphogistic Tablets**.

Composition (each tablet contains extract equivalent to dry)

Andrographis paniculata (chuan xin lian, andrographis) 1050mg

Dosage and method of administration

3-5 tablets, three times daily on an empty stomach.

Cautions and contraindications

Contraindicated during pregnancy. **14.4 Chuan Xin Lian** is an exceptionally bitter herb, and quite cold–it can easily damage Spleen *qi* so should only be used for a short time (i.e. the acute phase of an infection), except when used in small doses with an appropriate constitutional formula. Because it is so bitter it is best to avoid chewing the tablets.

INF

14.5 CHUAN XIN LIAN ANTIPHLOGISTIC TABLETS

穿心莲抗炎片

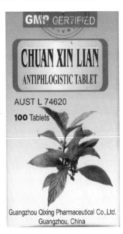

(Chuan Xin Lian Kang Yan Pian)
Guangzhou Qixing Pharmaceutical Factory (Guangzhou)
'Andrographis Anti-inflammatory Pills'
Chuan Xin Lian Antiphlogistic Tablets are packaged in
bottles of 100 pills.

TCM actions
Clears Toxic Heat, cools the Blood.

Biomedical actions
General antibiotic action–antiviral and antibacterial;
hypoglycemic, antithrombotic, antipyretic.

INDICATIONS

- Toxic Heat disorders and the early stage of Warm diseases (*see* glossary). Usually combined with a 'targeting' formula (such as **6.6 Long Dan Xie Gan Wan** to target the Liver, or **3.15 Qing Qi Hua Tan Wan** to target the Lungs) when a powerful Toxic Heat clearing action is desired. Useful against both bacterial and viral pathogens, but especially good against viruses. The broad action and current popularity of andrographis products lies in the ability of andrographis to stimulate the immune response. It operates by stimulating both the antigen-specific (where antibodies are made to counteract an invading microorganism), and nonspecific immune responses (where the body's macrophage cells scavenge and destroy intruders).
- With the appropriate identifying features, this formula can assist in the treatment of biomedical conditions such as acute tonsillitis, pharyngitis, bronchitis and pneumonia, acute pyelonephritis, cystitis, urethritis and prostatitis, shingles, herpes, hepatitis, cholecystitis, genital infections, ear infections, bacterial and amebic dysentery, suppurative sores, mastitis, erysipelas, pityriasis, mumps, systemic infections and encephalitis.

Composition (each tablet contains)
Andrographis paniculata (chuan xin lian, andrographis) 120mg, *Taraxacum mongolicum* (pu gong ying, dandelion) 60mg, *Isatis tinctora* (ban lan gen, isatis root) 60mg

Combinations
- With **6.6 Long Dan Xie Gan Wan** for Damp Heat or Toxic Heat in the genito-urinary system–acute cystitis, urethritis, prostatitis, pelvic inflammatory disease,

Pattern identifying features

- **Toxic Heat**
- **acute viral or bacterial infection**
- Warm diseases

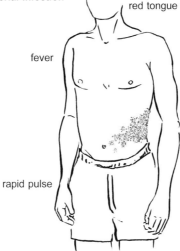

red tongue

fever

rapid pulse

- **tonsillitis**
- **dysentery, diarrhea**
- **urinary tract infection**
- mastitis
- bronchitis
- shingles
- suppurative sores

hepatitis and shingles.
- With **9.3 Peking Niu Huang Jie Du Pian** for respiratory or skin infection–tonsillitis, erysipelas, boils and sores.
- With **6.1 Xiao Chai Hu Tang Wan** for acute mastitis and otitis (of a *shao yang* type). This combination (with ¼-½ dose of **14.5 Chuan Xin Lian Antiphlogistic Tablets**) is also used for chronic low grade tonsillitis or salivary gland infection.
- With **14.1 Huang Lian Jie Du Wan** for a variety of infections with fever including bacterial and amebic dysentery and acute cholecystitis, Damp Heat acne and suppurative sores.
- With **6.5 Jia Wei Xiao Yao Wan** for severe premenstrual acne or boils.

Dosage and method of administration

3 pills three times daily on an empty stomach. In severe cases, 5 pills every 2 hours can be used.

Cautions and contraindications

Contraindicated during pregnancy. **14.5 Chuan Xin Lian Antiphlogistic Tablets** are very bitter and cold–they can easily damage Spleen *qi* so should only be used for a short time (i.e. the acute phase of an infection), except when used in small doses with an appropriate constitutional formula. Because they are so bitter it is best to avoid chewing the tablets.

INF

14.6 FU FANG NAN BAN LAN GEN

复方南板蓝根丸

(Fu Fang Nan Ban Lan Gen Wan)
Guangzhou Qixing Pharmaceutical Co. (Guangzhou)
'Southern Isatis Pills'
Fu Fang Nan Ban Lan Gen is packaged in bottles of 100 tablets.

TCM actions
Clears Toxic Heat, cools the Blood.

Biomedical actions
General antibiotic action—antiviral and antibacterial.

INDICATIONS

* Toxic Heat disorders. This formula is similar in general scope and action to **14.5 Chuan Xin Lian Antiphlogistic Tablets**, and may be combined in the same way with an appropriate targeting formula.
* Inflammatory skin disorders, such as acute eczema, psoriasis, dermatitis and pityriasis. Also used for various types of purpura (such as allergic and Henoch Schönlein) when associated with heat.

Composition (each pill contains)
Isatis tinctora (ban lan gen, isatis) 814.4mg, *Viola yedoensis* (zi hua di ding, viola) 814.4mg, *Taraxacum mongolicum* (pu gong ying, dandelion) 814.4mg

Combinations
* With **1.23 Zhi Bai Ba Wei Wan** for purpura associated with *yin* deficiency.

Dosage and method of administration
4 tablets three times daily. In severe cases 5 pills every 2 hours can be used.

Cautions and contraindications
This formula is bitter and cold and can damage Spleen *qi*. It should only be used for a short time (i.e. the acute phase of an infection), except when used in small doses with an appropriate constitutional formula.

14.7 NIU HUANG QING HUO WAN

GMP

牛黄清火丸

Tong Ren Tang (Beijing)
'Bovine Gallstone Fire Clearing Pills'
Niu Huang Qing Huo Wan is packaged
as three gram honey pills sealed in small
wax balls.

TCM actions
Clears Toxic Heat, purges Heat through *yang ming*.

Biomedical actions
Anti-inflammatory, antibiotic, purgative.

INDICATIONS

- Excess Heat patterns of the Liver, Lungs and Stomach, including toothache from Wind Fire, gingivitis, dental abscess, abscessed gum, acute otitis media and externa, mouth ulcers, acute boils and sores, tonsillitis and mumps.
- Used in *yang ming fu* excess Heat patterns, with high fever, thirst, sweating, big flooding pulse and constipation. May also be useful for Intestinal abscess (e.g. appendicitis), with focal abdominal pain and difficult bowel movements.
- To quickly clear Heat through the 'big exit' (i.e. the bowel) in cases of Liver Fire, Liver Wind or Phlegm Heat rushing up to the head. This occurs in Wind-stroke or pre-stroke conditions.

Composition
Synthetic Bovine Gallstone (ren gong niu huang), *Rheum palmatum* (da huang, rhubarb root), *Platycodon grandiflorum* (jie geng, platycodon), *Dryobalanops aromatica* (bing pian, borneol)

Dosage and method of administration
2 pills twice daily. The patient should expect loose stools or diarrhea.

Cautions and contraindications
Contraindicated during pregnancy.

INF

14.8 WU WEI XIAO DU WAN

五味消毒丸

Lanzhou Foci Pharmaceutical Factory (Gansu)
'Five Ingredient Detoxifying Pills'
Wu Wei Xiao Du Wan is packaged in bottles of 200 pills.

TCM actions
Clears Toxic Heat, reduces Toxic swellings.

Biomedical actions
Broad spectrum antibacterial agent, anti-inflammatory,
antipyretic, disinfectant.

INDICATIONS

- Toxic Heat lesions and sores, both internal and external. Used for a wide variety of pyogenic skin sores such as abscesses, boils, carbuncles and furuncles. Particularly good for hard, painful, deep rooted lesions. Generally considered best for bacterial infections.
- With the appropriate identifying features, this formula can also be used as a general antitoxic agent (or as an addition to a targeting formula) for localised Toxic Heat disorders such as erysipelas, cellulitis, paronychia, mastitis, otitis, tonsillitis and lymphangitis, acute urinary tract infections, acute pelvic inflammatory disease, orchitis and appendicitis.

Composition (each tablet contains powdered)
Lonicera japonica (jin yin hua, lonicera) 36.4mg, *Taraxacum mongolicum* (pu gong ying, dandelion) 36.7mg, *Chrysanthemum indicum* (ye ju hua, wild chrysanthemum) 36.7mg, *Viola yedoensis* (zi hua di ding, viola) 36.7mg, *Begonia fimbristipulata* (zi bei tian kui, begonia) 14.5mg

Combinations
- With **14.1 Huang Lian Jie Du Wan** for severe infections with high fever.
- With **6.1 Xiao Chai Hu Tang Wan** for acute mastitis, cystitis, or other acute infection characterised by distinct episodes of fever and chills.
- With **14.5 Chuan Xin Lian Antiphlogistic Tablets** for lymphangitis, bacteremia and impetigo.

Pattern identifying features

- **Toxic Heat focal lesions**
- localised suppurative infections
- redness, swelling, inflammation, pain, pus
- may be fever & chills

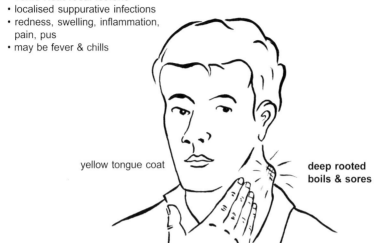

yellow tongue coat

deep rooted boils & sores

full, slippery, rapid pulse

- With **1.37 Yu Dai Wan** or **1.35 Fu Yan Qing Tablet** for Toxic Heat in the lower *jiao* causing leukorrhea or pelvic inflammatory disease.
- With **11.1 Qian Lie Xian Capsule** for acute prostatitis.

Dosage and method of administration

The recommended dose is 8-12 pills three times daily, however, in acute or severe disorders a higher dose is required to be effective, in general, 16-24 pills three times daily (or about 12 pills every two hours), on an empty stomach.

Cautions and contraindications

Contraindicated for *yin* type boils and swellings. Caution in patients with Spleen deficiency.

INF

GMP **14.9 BAI HU TANG WAN**

白虎汤丸

Available in the US,
UK and Europe
See Note 1, p.xxi

Lanzhou Foci Pharmaceutical Factory (Gansu)
'White Tiger Decoction Pills'
Bai Hu Tang Wan is packaged in bottles of 200 pills.
Available as: White Tiger Teapills (PF)

TCM actions
Clears Heat from the Lungs and Stomach (*yang ming* or *qi* level).

Biomedical actions
Antipyretic.

INDICATIONS

- Acute high fever associated with Heat accumulation in the *yang ming* channels. This pattern is classically attributed to the progress of a Cold pathogen through the superficial layers (*tai yang* and *shao yang*) into the interior of the body, where, confronted by strong resistance from *zheng qi*, it transforms from Cold to Heat. The *yang ming* level (corresponding to the gastro-intestinal system and Lungs) is the first point of contact between an invading pathogen and the internal organ systems, and as such represents a serious disorder. *Yang ming* channel syndrome is so called because at this stage of the invasion, the Heat is 'formless', and the *yang ming* organ (here the Large Intestine) is not yet obstructed by constipation. The main features of *yang ming* channel syndrome are quite specific and characterised by the 'four bigs'–fever, thirst, sweating and pulse. The intensity of the symptoms is the result of the clash between a strong pathogen and the *zheng qi* of an otherwise robust patient.
- With the appropriate identifying features, this formula can assist in the treatment of biomedical conditions such as the high fever of pneumonia, epidemic hemorrhagic fever, encephalitis, meningitis, heat stroke and childhood fevers such as measles.

Composition
Gypsum fibrosum (shi gao, gypsum) 51%, *Dioscorea opposita* (shan yao, dioscorea) 26%, *Anemarrhena aspheloides* (zhi mu, anemarrhena) 15%, *Glycyrrhiza uralensis* (gan cao, licorice) 5.5%

Pattern identifying features

- **Yang ming** channel syndrome (Heat accumulation in the Lungs & Intestines <u>without</u> constipation)
- irritability
- frontal headache
- bleeding gums, mouth ulcers

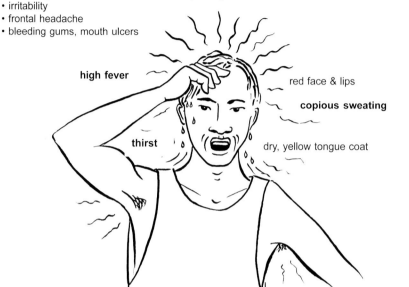

high fever

red face & lips

copious sweating

thirst

dry, yellow tongue coat

concentrated urine

rapid, big, bounding, slippery pulse

Dosage and method of administration

The recommended dose for adults is 8-12 pills three times daily, however, in acute or severe disorders a higher dose is required to be effective, in general, 16-24 pills three times daily (or about 12 pills every two hours), on an empty stomach. For infants and small children, the pills should be ground up and decocted, and 5-10ml of the resulting lukewarm liquid delivered with an eye-dropper or teaspoon (3-5 squirts or 2 teaspoons), every 2-3 hours.

Cautions and contraindications

Contraindicated in any other fever type other than the *yang ming* channel pattern described. Be careful with diagnosis because inappropriate usage can be dangerous. Watch for signs of over cooling, such as cold extremities and subjective feelings of cold, and stop the formula immediately if these symptoms occur.

14.9 Bai Hu Tang Wan is designed to be used for a maximum of a few days. If the fever has not subsided within 2-3 days, the patient must be reassessed. Excessive use of gypsum, which is very cold, easily damages Spleen *yang* and may lead to iatrogenic complications. Not suitable for the same presentation with constipation (*see* **3.16 Ching Fei Yi Huo Pien, 14.10 Liang Ge Wan** or **14.7 Niu Huang Qing Huo Wan**).

INF

GMP 14.10 LIANG GE WAN

凉膈丸

Available in the US, UK and Europe
See Note 1, p.xxi

Lanzhou Foci Pharmaceutical Factory (Gansu)
'Pills for Cooling the Diaphragm'
Liang Ge Wan is packaged in bottles of 200 pills.
Available as: Cool Valley Teapills

TCM actions

Clears and purges Toxic Heat and Fire from the *qi* (*yang ming*) level, benefits the throat, opens the bowels.

Biomedical actions

Antipyretic, antibiotic, purgative.

INDICATIONS

• Heat and Fire in the upper and middle *jiao*, (Lungs, Stomach and Intestines) with constipation. This pattern is a variation of the *yang ming* Heat pattern treated by **14.9 Bai Hu Tang Wan**, in which Heat has dried fluids and caused the complication of constipation. This formula simultaneously cools Heat and provides an outlet for Heat through the Large Intestine.

• Heat type skin rashes on the upper body. Rashes such as these are often associated with Heat in the Stomach and have a dietary component, being initiated or aggravated by heating food and alcohol.

• With the appropriate identifying features, this formula can assist in the treatment of biomedical conditions such as acute tonsillitis and laryngitis, stomatitis, gingivitis, conjunctivitis, suppurative and inflammatory skin lesions, pneumonia, cholecystitis, acute appendicitis, meningitis, encephalitis, acute infectious hepatitis, erysipelas and measles.

Composition

Lophatherum gracile dan zhu ye, bamboo leaves) 23.5%, *Forsythia suspensa* (lian qiao, forsythia) 23.5%, *Rheum palmatum* (da huang, rhubarb) 12%, Mirabilitum (mang xiao, sodium sulphate) 12%, *Glycyrrhiza uralensis* (gan cao, licorice) 9%, *Gardenia jasminoides* (shan zhi zi, gardenia) 6%, *Scutellaria baicalensis* (huang qin, scute) 6%, *Mentha haplocalycis* (bo he, mint) 5%

Combinations

• With **14.2 Huang Lian Su Tablets** or **14.5 Chuan Xin Lian Antiphlogistic Tablets** for severe infections with high fever.

Pattern identifying features

- **Heat & Fire accumulation in the middle & upper *jiao***
- **fever**
- irritability
- toothache, red, swollen gums
- mouth ulcers
- nosebleeds

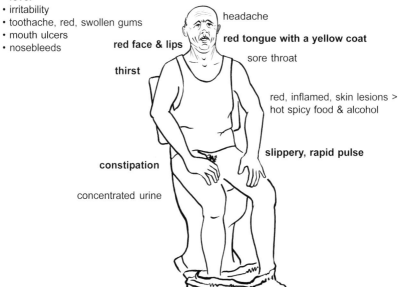

headache

red tongue with a yellow coat

sore throat

red face & lips

thirst

red, inflamed, skin lesions >
hot spicy food & alcohol

slippery, rapid pulse

constipation

concentrated urine

- With **14.6 Fu Fang Nan Ban Lan Gen** for infectious encephalitis.
- With **9.10 Sanjin Watermelon Frost** for mouth ulcers from Heart Fire.
- With **9.9 Superior Sore Throat Powder** for tonsillitis and Toxic Heat in the throat.

Dosage and method of administration

The recommended dose is 8-12 pills three times daily, however, in acute or severe disorders a higher dose is required to be effective, in general, 16-24 pills three times daily (or about 12 pills every two hours), on an empty stomach. The patient should be advised that diarrhea may occur.

Cautions and contraindications

Contraindicated during pregnancy and in the absence of excess Heat patterns with constipation.

INF

15

Patent Medicines for Wind and Exuberant Yang

GMP

15.1 PO LUNG YUEN MEDICAL PILLS

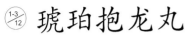

(1-3/12)

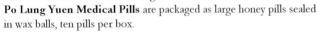

(Hu Po Bao Long Wan)
Chan Li Chai Medical Factory (Hong Kong)
'Amber Pills to Embrace the Dragon'
Po Lung Yuen Medical Pills are packaged as large honey pills sealed in wax balls, ten pills per box.

TCM actions

Extinguishes Liver Wind, clears and transforms Phlegm Heat, stops spasms and convulsions.

Biomedical actions

Calmative, sedative, antispasmodic.

INDICATIONS

- Liver Wind and Phlegm Heat patterns causing involuntary movements, tics, tremors or spasms.
- Acute or chronic seizure patterns, as in epilepsy (particularly the mild forms, such as Jacksonian, or absences), associated with Heat.
- Phlegm Heat patterns causing *shen* disturbance–frequent anxiety, easily startled, excess timidity, phobias, inappropriate emotional responses, sleep disturbances, nightmares.
- Fever, impaired consciousness, febrile convulsions, irritability and restlessness from Heat or Phlegm Heat affecting the Heart and Pericardium. This tends to occur in children. There may also be wheezing, cough and vomiting.

Composition

Gastrodia elata (tian ma, gastrodia) 16.5%, *Glycyrrhiza uralensis* (gan cao, licorice) 15%, *Arisaema cosnaguinium* (dan nan xing, bile treated arisaema) 11%, *Santalum album* (tan xiang, sandalwood) 11%, *Poria cocos* (fu ling, hoelen) 11%, *Mentha arvensis* (bo he, mint) 11%, *Atractylodes lancea* (cang zhu, red atractylodes) 11%, *Uncaria rhynchophylla* (gou teng, gambir) 5.5%, *Typhonium giganteum* (bai fu zi, typhonium) 5.5%, *Dryobalanops camphora* (bing pian, borneol) 1.5%, Amber (hu po) 1%

Pattern identifying features

- **Liver Wind & Phlegm Heat**
- spasms, convulsions, seizures
- febrile convulsions
- disturbances of consciousness, extreme emotional fragility
- tics, tremors

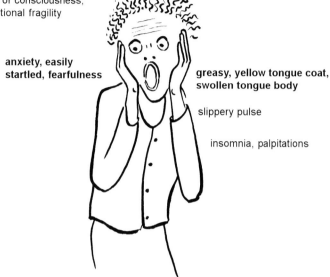

anxiety, easily startled, fearfulness

greasy, yellow tongue coat, swollen tongue body

slippery pulse

insomnia, palpitations

Combinations
- With **8.8 Wen Dan Wan** for severe Phlegm Heat and *shen* disturbances.
- With **6.6 Long Dan Xie Gan Wan** for Liver Fire with Phlegm Heat.

Dosage and method of administration
The recommended dose is one to two pills per day, with warm water or ginger tea. One third to half dose for children. These pills are often very hard and need to be softened in boiling water for 10 minutes before ingestion.

Cautions and contraindications
Contraindicated during pregnancy. Not suitable for timidity, anxiety states or emotional fragility due to Blood or *yin* deficiency.

WIND

15.2 NIU HUANG QING XIN WAN

同仁牛黄清心丸

(Tong Ren Niu Huang Qing Xin Wan)
Tong Ren Tang Pharmaceutical Factory
(Beijing)
'Bovine Gallstone Heart Cooling Pills from
Tong Ren Tang'
Niu Huang Qing Xin Wan is packaged as 3 gram honey pills sealed inside a wax ball, ten
balls per box.

TCM actions
Clears Heat from the Heart and Pericardium, transforms Phlegm Heat, extinguishes
Wind, supplements and regulates *qi* and quickens Blood, nourishes *yin*, opens the
sensory orifices, calms the *shen*.

Biomedical actions
Sedative, tranquilizer, tonic, expectorant.

INDICATIONS

- Internal Wind type movement disorders, seizures, tremors or loss of motor
  control in patients with underlying deficiency.
- In its original composition, this formula contained various endangered animal
  species to calm the Liver, clear Heat and extinguish Wind. Some elements of
  this still remain, however, this is a toned down version of the original prescription.
  This large and complex version is not as cooling, and is more focused on the
  underlying deficiency that has allowed generation of the Wind. It addresses
  multiple aspects of what are usually complicated mixtures of pathology–excess
  Heat, Phlegm, stagnation of *qi* and Blood, various deficiencies and Cold.
  Traditionally used in the treatment of tremor, spastic or flaccid paralysis,
  disturbances of consciousness, syncope, dizziness, muscular weakness, facial
  paralysis, aphasia, slurred speech and *wei* syndrome (*see* glossary).
- With the appropriate identifying features, this formula could be used to treat
  biomedical conditions such as Parkinson's disease, benign familial tremor, post
  Wind-stroke hemiplegia, paralysis or numbness, multiple sclerosis and peripheral
  neuropathy.

Composition (each pill contains extracts equivalent to)
Dioscorea officinalis (shan yao, dioscorea) 111mg, *Equus asinus* (e jiao, gelatin) 79.5mg,
Glycyrrhiza uralensis (gan cao, licorice) 73.5mg, *Siler divaricum* (fang feng siler) 46.5mg,

Pattern identifying features

- **Phlegm Heat, Wind, *qi* & Blood deficiency with mild stagnation**
- *wei* syndromes
- seizure disorders
- sequelae of Windstroke
- flaccid or spastic paralysis

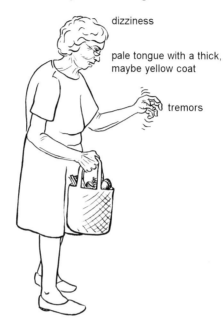

dizziness

pale tongue with a thick, maybe yellow coat

tremors

Atractylodes macrocephala (bai zhu, atractylodes) 45mg, *Panax ginseng* (ren shen, ginseng) 37.5mg, *Paeonia lactiflora* (bai shao, white peony) 37.5mg, *Poria cocos* (fu ling, hoelen) 37.5mg, *Cinnamomun cassia* (rou gui, cinnamon bark) 27mg, Massa Fermentata (shen qu) 27mg, *Angelica polymorpha* (dang gui, chinese angelica) 22.5mg, *Platycodon grandiflorum* (jie geng, platycodon) 22.5mg, *Astragalus membranaceous* (huang qi, astragalus) 22.5mg, *Zingiber officinale* (gan jiang, dry ginger) 22.5mg, *Ligusticum wallichi* (chuan xiong, cnidium) 19.5mg, *Bupleurum falcatum* (chai hu, bupleurum) 19.5mg, Bovine gallstone (niu huang) 12mg, *Prunus armenica* (xing ren, apricot seed) 9.5mg, *Typhae angustifolia* (pu huang, bulrush pollen) 7.5mg, *Ophiopogon japonicus* (mai dong, ophiopogon) 7.5mg, *Ampelopsis japonica* (bai lian, ampelopsis) 3mg, honey

WIND

Dosage and method of administration
One pill chewed twice daily on an empty stomach.

Cautions and contraindications
Contraindicated during pregnancy. Not suitable for children.

GMP ## 15.3 BAN XIA BAI ZHU TIAN MA WAN

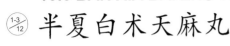
半夏白术天麻丸

Available in the US,
See Note 1, p.xxi

picture
unavailable at
time of printing

'Pinellia, Atractylodes and Gastrodia Pills'
Also available as: Head Clear Pill (BE)

TCM actions
Strengthens the Spleen, dries Dampness, transforms Phlegm
and extinguishes Wind.

Biomedical actions
Sedative, calmative.

INDICATIONS

- Wind Phlegm giving rise to sudden episodes of dizziness, vertigo accompanied
  by nausea, vomiting and tinnitus. There may also be frontal headaches, generalised
  heaviness and somnolence. The genesis of this pattern is twofold–Spleen
  deficiency allowing accumulation of Phlegm Damp, and Liver *qi* stagnation that
  weakens the Spleen and creates the conditions for the generation of internal
  Wind that carries the Phlegm to the Head. The vertigo of this pattern is distinctive.
  It is usually quite severe, even to the point of falling over and may occur when
  the patient is prone in bed. The sensation is sometimes likened to being on a
  ship or having the world spin around. Some people are even woken with vertigo,
  and it may be triggered by stress or exposure to strong penetrating smells such
  as perfume and petrol.
- With the appropriate identifying features, this formula may assist in the treatment
  of biomedical disorders such as Ménière's disease, aural vertigo, benign positional
  vertigo and hypertension.

Composition
Pinellia ternata (ban xia, pinellia) 15%, *Atractylodes macrocephala* (bai zhu, atractylodes)
15%, *Gastrodia elata* (tian ma, gastrodia) 15%, *Poria cocos* (fu ling, hoelen) 15%, *Citrus
reticulata* (chen pi, citrus) 10%, *Zingiber officinale* (sheng jiang, ginger) 10%, *Zizyphus
jujuba* (da zao, chinese dates) 8%, *Glycyrrhiza uralensis* (gan cao, licorice) 8%

Combinations
- With **7.22 Shen Qi Da Bu Wan** or **2.8 Liu Jun Zi Wan** for significant *qi*
  deficiency.

Pattern identifying features

- **Wind Phlegm**
- increased desire to sleep
- heavy sensations in the body
- poor appetite
- foggy head

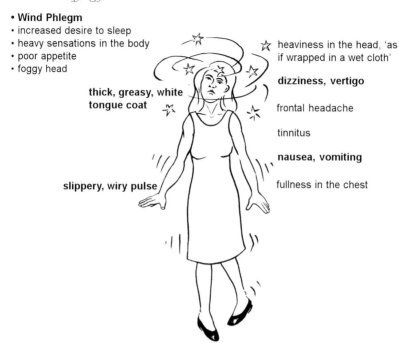

thick, greasy, white tongue coat

slippery, wiry pulse

heaviness in the head, 'as if wrapped in a wet cloth'

dizziness, vertigo

frontal headache

tinnitus

nausea, vomiting

fullness in the chest

- With **4.2 Wu Ling San Wan** for severe Dampness and fluid metabolism dysfunction.
- With **8.8 Wen Dan Wan** if there is Phlegm Heat.

Dosage and method of administration

8-12 pills three times daily, before meals. The dose may be spread out, or two lots of 12-18 pills may be taken, morning and evening. In severe cases or during the early stages of treatment (the first two weeks), a 50% increase in dose may be used, then reduced as the treatment takes effect.

Cautions and contraindications

Contraindicated in dizziness and vertigo patterns associated with Liver Fire or Blood deficiency.

WIND

15.4 TIAN MA GOU TENG WAN

天麻钩藤丸

Lanzhou Foci Pharmaceutical Factory (Gansu)
'Gastrodia and Uncaria Pills'
Tian Ma Gou Teng Wan is packaged in bottles of 200 pills.
Also available as: Tian Ma Gou Teng Teapills (PF)

TCM actions
Calms the Liver, extinguishes Wind, clears Heat and restrains rising Liver *yang*.

Biomedical actions
Antihypertensive, sedative to the nervous system, calmative.

INDICATIONS

- Liver *yang* rising and Liver Wind patterns. This important formula is frequently used for people with an acquired or constitutional tendency to too much *yang* in the upper body, characterised by a red plethoric complexion, temporal and vertical headaches, stiffness and pain in the neck and shoulders, dizziness, vertigo, facial flushing, irritability, insomnia and visual disturbances.
- Liver Wind patterns with numbness and paresthesia of the extremities, tics, tremors and spasms.
- With the appropriate identifying features, this formula may assist in the treatment of biomedical disorders such as migraine headaches, essential hypertension, renal hypertension, focal disorders of the central nervous system, preeclampsia and epilepsy.

Composition (each pill contains powdered)
Viscum coloratum (sang ji sheng, vaecium) 22mg, calcium sulphate (substitute for conch shell, shi jue ming) 22mg, *Uncaria rhynchophylla* (gou teng, gambir) 14mg, *Polygonatum multiflorum* (ye jiao teng, polygonatum stem) 14mg, *Poria cocos* (fu ling, hoelen) 14mg, *Achyranthes bidentata* (niu xi, achyranthes) 11mg, *Leonurus sibirica* (yi mu cao, motherwort) 11mg, *Gastrodia elata* (tian ma, gastrodia) 8mg, *Gardenia florida* (shan zhi zi, gardenia) 8mg, *Eucommia ulmoides* (du zhong, eucommia) 8mg

Combinations
- With **7.1.1 Liu Wei Di Huang Wan** for patients with significant underlying Liver and Kidney *yin* deficiency.

Pattern identifying features

- **Liver *yang* rising & Liver Wind**
- **hypertension**
- sleep disturbances
- irritability, irascibility

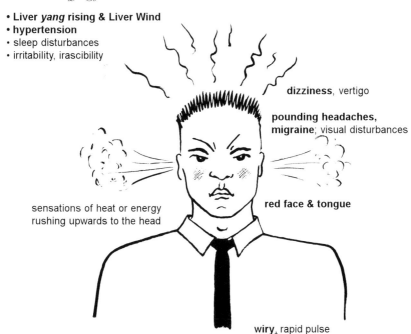

dizziness, vertigo

pounding headaches, migraine; visual disturbances

sensations of heat or energy rushing upwards to the head

red face & tongue

wiry, rapid pulse

- With **6.6 Long Dan Xie Gan Wan** for Liver Fire.
- With **8.8 Wen Dan Wan** for Phlegm Heat in the head.

Dosage and method of administration

8-12 pills three times daily on an empty stomach. The dose may be spread out, or two lots of 12-18 pills may be taken, morning and evening. In severe cases or during the early stages of treatment (the first few weeks), a 50% increase in dose may be used, then reduced to a maintenance dose as the treatment takes effect.

Cautions and contraindications

Contraindicated for patients without rising Liver *yang*, and for patients with dizziness and headaches arising from Blood deficiency.

WIND

15.5 TIAN MA WAN

天麻丸

Lanzhou Foci Pharmaceutical Factory (Gansu)
'Gastrodia Pills'
Tian Ma Wan is packaged in bottles of 200 pills.

TCM actions
Nourishes Liver and Kidney *yin*, nourishes Blood, restrains and anchors *yang*, extinguishes Wind.

Biomedical actions
Antihypertensive, sedative, calmative.

INDICATIONS

• Liver and Kidney *yin* deficiency with Liver *yang* rising. Similar in action and scope to **15.4 Tian Ma Gou Teng Wan**, the main differences are that this formula is slightly less cooling and better for neck stiffness and pain. The focus of this formula is fairly equally balanced between replenishing *yin* and restraining *yang* and this makes it ideal for mild cases of high blood pressure.

• May be used to treat a variety of other symptoms relating to *yin* deficiency and *yang* rising with or without hypertension, such as vascular and tension headaches, migraine headache, stiffness in the neck and shoulders, muscle spasms, dizziness, vertigo, tinnitus, tremors and numbness in the extremities.

• With the appropriate identifying features, this formula may be used to treat biomedical disorders such as migraine headaches, essential hypertension, renal hypertension, preeclampsia, focal disorders of the central nervous system and mild epilepsy.

Composition
Rehmannia glutinosa (sheng di, raw rehmannia) 14%, *Angelica polymorpha* (dang gui, chinese angelica) 14%%, *Notopterygium incisum* (qiang huo, notopterygium) 14%, *Eucommia ulmoides* (du zhong, eucommia) 10%, *Gastrodia elata* (tian ma, gastrodia) 8%, *Achyranthes bidentata* (niu xi, achyranthes) 8%, *Scrophularia ningpoensis* (xuan shen, scrophularia) 8%, *Dioscorea hypoglauca* (bei xie, fish poison yam) 8%, *Angelica pubescens* (du huo, Tu-huo) 7%, *Cyperus rotundus* (xiang fu, cyperus) 1.4%

Combinations
• With **7.2 Qi Ju Di Huang Wan** for significant *yin* deficiency.
• With **1.2 Si Wu Wan** for patients tending to Blood deficiency with *yang* rising.

Pattern identifying features

- **Liver *yang* rising & Liver Wind**
- **hypertension**
- sleep disturbances
- irritability, irascibility

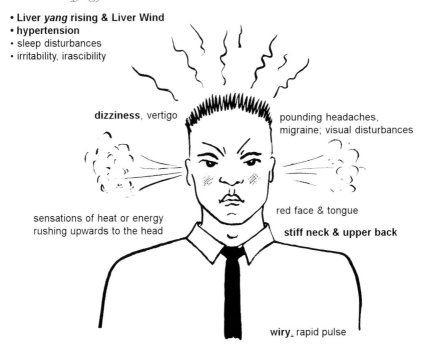

dizziness, vertigo

pounding headaches, migraine; visual disturbances

sensations of heat or energy rushing upwards to the head

red face & tongue

stiff neck & upper back

wiry, rapid pulse

Dosage and method of administration

8-12 pills three times daily, before meals. The dose may be spread out, or two lots of 12-18 pills may be taken, morning and evening. In severe cases or during the early stages of treatment (the first two weeks), a 50% increase in dose may be used, then reduced as the treatment takes effect.

Cautions and contraindications

Contraindicated for patients without rising Liver *yang*, and for patients with dizziness and headaches arising from Blood deficiency.

WIND

GMP

15.6 ZHEN GAN XI FENG WAN

镇肝熄风丸

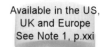
Available in the US, UK and Europe
See Note 1, p.xxi

Lanzhou Foci Pharmaceutical Factory (Gansu)
'Pills to Sedate the Liver and Extinguish Wind'
Zhen Gan Xi Feng Wan is packaged in bottles of 200 pills.
Available as: Zhen Gan Xi Feng Teapills (PF)

TCM actions
Sedates rising Liver *yang*, regulates Liver *qi*, extinguishes Wind, nourishes Liver and Kidney *yin* and anchors *yang*.

Biomedical actions
Antihypertensive, sedative to the nervous system, calmative.

INDICATIONS

* Liver *yang* rising and Liver Wind patterns with symptoms of dizziness and vertigo, temporal or vertical headaches, visual disturbances, tinnitus, facial flushing, tremors, disturbances of consciousness and hypertension. In contrast to the previous two formulae, **15.4 Tian Ma Gou Teng Wan** and **15.5 Tian Ma Wan**, this formula is much more focused on actively subduing *yang*, extinguishing the Wind and directing the excess out of the upper body, utilising several heavy mineral substances to weigh down the exuberant *yang*.
* With the appropriate identifying features, this formula can be used to treat biomedical conditions such as transient ischemic attacks, cerebral arteriosclerosis, cerebrovascular accident, essential hypertension, renal hypertension, arteriosclerosis, prevention of stroke in patients at risk and post stroke recovery when the patient continues to exhibit signs of Liver *yang* excess (but *see also* **5.8 Bu Yang Huan Wu Wan** for those with a *qi* deficiency sequelae).

Composition
Achyranthes bidentata (niu xi, achyranthes) 18%, *Hematitum* (dai zhe shi, hematite) 18%, *Chinemys reevesii* (gui ban, turtle shell) 8%, *Scrophularia ningpoensis* (xuan shen, scrophularia) 8%, *Paeonia lactiflora* (bai shao, white peony) 8%, *Asparagus lucidius* (tian dong, asparagus) 8%, *Os draconis* (long gu, dragon bone) 8%, *Ostrea gigas* (mu li, oyster shell) 8%, *Melia toosendan* (chuan lian zi, melia fruit) 3.5%, *Hordeum vulgare* (mai ya, sprouted barley) 3.5%, *Artemesia capillaris* (yin chen, capillaris) 3.5%, *Glycyrrhiza uralensis* (gan cao, licorice) 2.5%

Pattern identifying features

- **Liver *yang* rising, Liver Wind**
- pre-Windstroke conditions
- hypertension
- transient ischemic attacks (TIAs)
- confusion, disturbances of consciousness
- in severe cases, sudden collapse

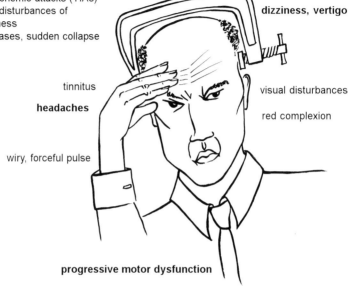

dizziness, vertigo

tinnitus

headaches

visual disturbances

red complexion

wiry, forceful pulse

progressive motor dysfunction

Combinations

- With **15.9 Headache & Dizziness Reliever** to enhance to antihypertensive aspects of the formula.
- With **2.18 Bao He Wan** or **2.17 Jian Pi Wan** to protect the Spleen and Stomach in patients with a tendency to digestive weakness.

Dosage and method of administration

8-12 pills three times daily on an empty stomach. The dose may be spread out, or two lots of 12-18 pills may be taken, morning and evening. In severe cases or during the early stages of treatment (the first few weeks), a 50% increase in dose may be used, then reduced to a maintenance dose as the treatment takes effect.

Cautions and contraindications

Contraindicated during pregnancy and in patients without rising *yang*. The mineral substances can be hard on the Spleen and Stomach, so caution in patients with Spleen *qi* deficiency.

WIND

15.7 YANG YIN JIANG YA WAN

养阴降压丸

Lanzhou Foci Pharmaceutical Factory (Gansu)
'Nourish *Yin* Antihypertensive Pills'
Yang Yin Jiang Ya Wan is packaged in bottles of 200 pills.

TCM actions

Nourishes *yin*, calms the Liver, restrains and anchors the *yang*, promotes urination.

Biomedical actions

Antihypertensive, sedative, calmative.

INDICATIONS

- Hypertension associated with Liver *yang* rising. This formula is designed specifically for hypertension and contains numerous herbs with well documented antihypertensive action.
- May be used for a variety of symptoms attributed to *yang* rising patterns, including headaches, dizziness, tinnitus, transient ischemic attacks, anger outbursts and sore eyes.

Composition (each pill contains powdered)

Polygonatum multiflorum (he shou wu, ho shou wu) 21.6mg, *Cassia tora* (jue ming zi, cassia seed) 20.7mg, *Paeonia lactiflora* (bai shao, white peony) 18mg, *Poria cocos* (fu ling, hoelen) 16.2mg, *Eucommia ulmoides* (du zhong, eucommia) 14.4mg, *Alisma orientale* (ze xie, alisma) 14.4mg, *Achyranthes bidentata* (niu xi, achyranthes) 12.6mg, *Dendrobium nobile* (shi hu, dendrobium) 12.6mg, *Uncaria rhyncophylla* (gou teng, gambir) 9mg; and extracts equivalent to dry: *Zea mays* (yu mi xu, corn silk) 109mg, *Polygonatum sibirica* (yuan zhi, polygala) 76.4mg, *Chysanthemum sinensis* (ju hua, chrysanthemum flower) 54.6mg

Combinations

- With **6.6 Long Dan Xie Gan Wan** for Heat in the Liver.
- With **7.2 Qi Ju Di Huang Wan** for significant *yin* deficiency.

Pattern identifying features

• **Liver *yang* rising**
• **hypertension**

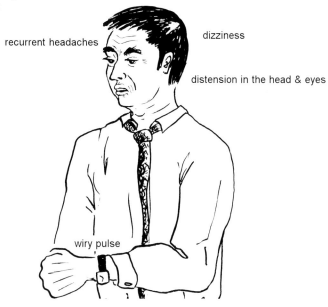

recurrent headaches

dizziness

distension in the head & eyes

wiry pulse

Dosage and method of administration

8-12 pills three times daily, before meals. The dose may be spread out, or two lots of 12-18 pills may be taken, morning and evening. In severe cases or during the early stages of treatment (the first two weeks), a 50% increase in dose may be used, then reduced as the treatment takes effect.

Cautions and contraindications

Contraindicated in patients without rising *yang* and with dizziness and headaches from Blood deficiency.

WIND

15.8 FU FANG JIANG YA CAPSULE

复方降压丸

(Fu Fang Jiang Ya Wan)
Jing Xian Pharmaceutical Co. (Guangzhou)
'Compound Antihypertensive Pills'
Fu Fang Jiang Ya Capsules are packaged in bottles of 36 capsules.

TCM actions

Calms the Liver and *shen*, extinguishes Wind, restrains *yang*, promotes urination.

Biomedical actions

Antihypertensive, diuretic, sedative.

INDICATIONS

• Hypertension associated with Liver *yang* rising or Liver Wind patterns. Similar to **15.7 Yang Yin Jiang Ya Wan**, with a focus on herbs with a known antihypertensive effect. Although this formula is best for hypertension associated with Liver *yang* or Liver Wind, it is broad enough to be useful in any type of hypertension when combined with an appropriate constitutional formula.

Composition (each capsule contains extracts equivalent to dry)

Alisma orientale (ze xie, alisma) 378mg, *Crategus pinnatifida* (shan zha, crategus) 378mg, *Prunella vulgaris* (xia ku cao, prunella) 378mg, *Chysanthemum sinensis* (ju hua, chrysanthemum flower) 315mg, *Uncaria rhyncophylla* (gou teng, gambir) 315mg, *Eucommia ulmoides* (du zhong, eucommia) 252mg, *Achyranthes bidentata* (niu xi, achyranthes) 252mg, *Ostrea gigas* (mu li, oyster shell) 54mg

Dosage and method of administration

3-4 capsules, three times daily on an empty stomach.

Cautions and contraindications

Contraindicated in patients without rising *yang* and with dizziness and headaches from Blood deficiency. Caution during pregnancy.

15.9 HEADACHE & DIZZINESS RELIEVER

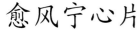

(Yu Feng Ning Xin Pian)
Tong Ren Tang (Beijing)
'Cure Wind and Calm the Heart Pills'
Headache and Dizziness Reliever is
packaged in boxes of 30 blister packed tablets.

TCM actions
Dispels Wind Heat, generates fluids, stops thirst, alleviates diarrhea, eases the muscles.

Biomedical actions
Antihypertensive, diaphoretic, antispasmodic.

INDICATIONS

- For the temporary relief of stiff neck and shoulders, headaches, dizziness and paresthesia associated with external pathogenic invasion, hypertension or Liver *yang* rising.
- Diarrhea. Can be used for a variety of types of diarrhea and Dysenteric disorder, depending on the formula with which it is combined.
- Recently researched for effects on reducing craving for alcohol. May be useful as an adjunct treatment for patients recovering from alcohol addiction.

Composition (each tablet contains)
Pueraria lobata (ge gen, pueraria) 810mg

Combinations
- With **14.1 Huang Lian Jie Du Wan** or **14.2 Huang Lian Su Tablets** for acute Damp Heat diarrhea.

Dosage and method of administration
5 tablets three times daily, on an empty stomach. In severe cases or during the early stages of treatment (the first two weeks), a 50% increase in dose may be used, then reduced as the treatment takes effect.

Cautions and contraindications
None noted.

WIND

CONCISE HERB FUNCTIONS

A brief summary of the main functions of all the herbs listed in the text. For more detailed information, consult Bensky D and Gamble A (1993) *Chinese Herbal Medicine: Materia Medica*, Eastland Press, Seattle, Washington.

Botanical name	Pin Yin	Common name	Function
Abrus cantoniensis	ji gu cao 鸡骨草	abrus	clears Damp Heat from the Liver and Gallbladder
Acacia catechu	hai er cha 孩儿茶	catechu	clears Damp Heat from the skin and Liver
Acanthopanax gracilistylus	wu jia pi 五加皮	acanthopanax	dispels Wind Damp, strengthens tendons and bones
Achyranthes bidentata	niu xi 牛膝	achyranthes	invigorates Blood, promotes menstruation, alleviates *bi* syndrome
Aconite carmichaeli	fu zi 附子	aconite	warms *yang*, rescues *yang* from collapse, moves fluids, dispels Wind Cold Damp
Aconitum carmichaeli	chuan wu 川乌	aconite	very powerful Cold Damp dispersing, analgesic, toxic
Aconitum kusnezoffii	cao wu 草乌	wild aconite	very powerful Cold Damp dispersing, analgesic, toxic
Acorus gramineus	shi chang pu 石菖蒲	acorus	opens the orifices, disperses Phlegm Damp, clears the mind
Adenophora tetraphylla	nan sha shen 南沙参	adenophora	nourishes and supplements Lung and Stomach *yin*
Agastache rugosa (*Pogostemon cablin*)	huo xiang 藿香	agastache	dispels Summerdamp, stops vomiting
Agkistrodon acutus	qi she 蕲蛇	tiger snake	powerfully unblocks the channels, extinguishes Wind, dispels Wind from the skin
Agrimonia pilosa	xian he cao 仙鹤草	agrimony	stops bleeding, alleviates diarrhea and Dysenteric disorder, kills parasites
Ailanthus altissima	chun gen pi 椿根皮	ailanthus	clears Damp Heat, kills parasites, astringes the Intestines, stops diarrhoea and bleeding
Akebia trifoliata (*Clematis armandii*)	mu tong 木通	akebia	diuretic, leaches out Dampness

Latin name	Pinyin / Chinese	Common name	Functions
Albizzia julibrissin	he huan pi 合欢皮	albizzia	calms the *shen*, alleviates stagnant Liver *qi*, quickens Blood, stops pain
Alisma orientalis	ze xie 泽泻	alisma	diuretic, drains Dampness
Allium macrostemon	xie bai 薤白	allium bulb	opens up *yang* circulation, moves *qi*, dissipates clumping in the chest
Allium odorum (tuberosum)	jiu zi 韭子	chinese chive seed	warms the Kidneys, astringes urine
Alpinia katsumadai	cao dou kou 草豆蔻	katsumadai cardamon	aromatically disperses Damp from the Spleen and Stomach
Alpinia officinarum	gao liang jiang 高良姜	galangal	warms the middle *jiao* and alleviates pain
Alpinia oxyphylla	yi zhi ren 益智仁	alpinia	warms the Kidneys, astringes urine
Amber	hu po 琥珀	amber	calms the *shen*, quickens Blood
Amomum cardamomum (Elettaria cardamomum)	bai dou kou 白豆蔻	amomum	aromatically disperses Damp from the Spleen and Stomach, regulates *qi*
Amomum tsao-ko	cao guo 草果	tsaoko fruit	aromatically disperses Cold Damp from the Spleen and Stomach, alleviates Malarial disorder
Amomum villosum	sha ren 砂仁	cardamon	aromatically disperses Damp from the Spleen and Stomach, regulates *qi*
Ampelopsis japonica	bai lian 白蔹	ampelopsis	clears Toxic Heat, promotes healing
Andrographis paniculata	chuan xin lian 穿心莲	andrographis	clears Toxic Heat, immunomodulating
Anemarrhena asphaloides	zhi mu 知母	anemarrhena	clear deficient Heat, clears *qi* level Heat from the Lungs and gastro-intestinal tract
Angelica dahurica	bai zhi 白芷	angelica	opens the nose, dispels Wind Cold, stops pain, aids in discharge of pus
Angelica pubescens	du huo 独活	Tu-huo	dispels Wind Damp (especially from the *tai yang* channels)
Angelica sinensis (polymorpha)	dang gui 当归	chinese angelica	nourishes Blood, regulates menstruation
Aquilaria agallocha	chen xiang 沉香	aquilaria	regulates *qi*, stops pain, calms wheezing and stops vomiting

Herb functions

Botanical name	Pin Yin	Common name	Function
Arctium lappa	niu bang zi 牛蒡子	burdock seeds	dispels Wind Heat and Toxic Heat, benefits the throat
Area catechu	bing lang 槟榔	betel nut	kills parasites, alleviates fullness, laxative, diuretic
Area catechu	da fu pi 大腹皮	betel husk	directs *qi* downward and alleviates fullness, diuretic
Arisaema cosanguinium	dan nan xing 胆南星	bile treated arisaema	disperses Phlegm and Phlegm Heat, sedative, expectorant
Arisaema cosanguinium	tian nan xing 天南星	arisaema	disperses Phlegm, dispels Wind Phlegm, stops spasms and pain
Ajuga reptans	jin gu cao 筋骨草	common bugle	astringent, quickens Blood, stops bleeding
Arnebia euchroma	zi cao 紫草	arnebia	cools the Blood, dissipates rashes
Artemesia anomala (Solidago viridaurea)	liu ji nu 刘寄奴	solidago	invigorates Blood, disperses stagnant Blood
Artemesia apiacea (annua)	qing hao 青蒿	artemesia	clears latent pathogens, dispels Summerheat, alleviates Malarial disorder
Artemesia argyi (vulgaris)	ai ye 艾叶	mugwort	dispels Cold Damp, warms the uterus, stops bleeding
Artemesia capillaris	yin chen 茵陈	capillaris	clears Damp Heat from the Liver and Gallbladder, alleviates jaundice
Asarum seiboldii	xi xin 细辛	asarum	dispels Wind Cold, warms the channels, analgesic
Asparagus lucidius	tian dong 天冬	asparagus	nourishes Lung and Kidney *yin*
Aster tataricus	zi wan 紫菀	aster	stops cough
Astragalus complanatus	sha yuan ji li 沙苑蒺藜	astragalus seed	astringent, supplements the Liver and Kidneys, benefits the eyes
Astragalus membranaceous	huang qi 黄芪	astragalus	supplements *qi*, strengthens *wei qi*, promotes urination
Atractylodes lancea	cang zhu 苍术	red atractylodes	powerfully dries Dampness
Atractylodes macrocephala	bai zhu 白术	atractylodes	strengthens the Spleen and supplements *qi*, dries Dampness

Latin name	Pinyin / Chinese	Common name	Functions
Bambusa textillis	tian zhu huang 天竺黄	bamboo sap	clears Phlegm Heat
Belamcanda chinensis	she gan 射干	belamcanda	clears Toxic Heat, benefits the throat
Biota orientalis	bai zi ren 柏子仁	biota seed	calms the *shen*, nourishes the Heart, lubricates the intestines
Bombyx mori	jiang can 僵蚕	silkworm	dispels Wind, Phlegm and Heat, stops spasm and itch
Borax	peng sha 硼砂	borax	clears Toxic Heat
Boswellia carteri	ru xiang 乳香	frankincense	invigorates Blood, disperses stagnant Blood, promotes healing, stops pain
Broussonetia papyrifera	chu shi zi 楮实子	broussonetia	supplements the Kidneys, brightens the eyes, promotes urination
Bufo bufo	chan su 蟾酥	cane toad venom	clears Toxic Heat
Bungarus parvus	bai hua she 白花蛇	golden coin snake	unblocks the channels, extinguishes Wind, dispels Wind from the skin
Bupleurum falcatum (chinensis)	chai hu 柴胡	bupleurum	dispels Wind Heat, elevates *yang*, harmonises *shao yang*
Buthus martensi	quan xie 全蝎	scorpion	extinguishes internal Wind, stops spasms, opens up the channels, stops pain
Callicarpa pedunculata	zi zhu 紫珠	callicarpa	stops bleeding
Cannabis sativa	huo ma ren 火麻仁	cannabis seeds	moistens the Intestines, nourishes *yin*
Camellia sinensis	cha ye 茶叶	tea	clears Heat, dispels Summerheat, alleviates Dysenteric disorder
Carpesium abrotanoides	he shi 鹤虱	carpesium	kills parasites, stops pain
Carthamus tinctorius	honghua 红花	carthamus	quickens Blood, disperses stagnant Blood
Cassia tora	jue ming zi 决明子	cassia seed	cools the Liver, benefits the eyes, laxative
Centipeda minima (Epates australis)	e bu shi cao 鹅不食草	centipeda	opens the nose
Cephaelis ipecacuanha		ipecac	emetic, expectorant
Cervus japonicus (nippon)	lu jiao jiao 鹿角胶	deer horn resin	benefits *jing*, warms and strengthens Kidney *yang*
Cervus japonicus (nippon)	lu rong 鹿茸	deer velvet	benefits *jing*, warms and strengthens Kidney *yang*

Herb functions

Botanical name	Pin Yin	Common name	Function
Chaenomeles lagenaria (speciosa)	mu gua 木瓜	chinese quince	dispels Wind Damp, stops spasms
Changium smyrnioides	ming dang shen 明党参	changium	moistens the Lungs, transforms Phlegm, harmonises the Stomach
Chinemys reevesii	gui ban 龟板	turtle shell	deeply enriches *yin* and anchors *yang*, benefits the Kidneys and strengthens the bones, cools the Blood
Chrysanthemum indicum	ye ju hua 野菊花	wild chrysanthemum	clears Toxic Heat
Chrysanthemum morifolium	ju hua 菊花	chrysanthemum flower	dispels Wind Heat, benefits the eyes and vision
Cibotium barometz	gou ji 狗脊	cibotium fern	supplements *yang*, strengthens the spine
Cimicifuga foetida	sheng ma 升麻	cimicifuga	dispels Wind Heat, elevates *yang*, clear Stomach Heat
Cinnamomum camphora	zhang nao 樟脑	camphor	dispels Wind, dries Dampness, kills parasites, invigorates Blood, stops pain
Cinnamomum cassia	rou gui 肉桂	cinnamon bark	warms *yang*, aids transformation of *qi*, dispels Cold, stops pain
Cinnamomum cassia	gui zhi 桂枝	cinnamon twigs	warms the channels, dispels Wind Cold
Cistanche deserticola	rou cong rong 肉苁蓉	cistanches	warms Kidney *yang*, laxative
Citrus aurantium	zhi ke (shi) 枳壳 (实)	aurantium	regulates *qi*, directs *qi* downwards
Citrus reticulata (nobilis)	chen pi 陈皮	citrus	transforms Phlegm Damp, regulates Spleen and Stomach *qi*
Citrus reticulata (nobilis)	ju he 橘核	citrus seed	regulates *qi*, dissipates nodules, stops pain
Citrus reticulata (nobilis)	qing pi 青皮	immature citrus	breaks up stagnant *qi*, alleviates fullness and swelling, stops pain
Clematis armandii (Akebia trifoliata)	mu tong 木通	akebia	diuretic, leaches out Dampness
Clematis sinensis	wei ling xian 威灵仙	chinese clematis	dispels Wind Damp, disperses Phlegm
Codonopsis pilosula	dang shen 党参	codonopsis	supplements Lung and Spleen *qi*

Latin name	Pinyin / Chinese	Common name	Functions
Coix lachryma-jobi	yi yi ren 薏苡仁	coix	strengthens the Spleen, clears Damp Heat
Commiphora myrrha	mo yao 没药	myrrh	invigorates Blood, promotes healing, analgesic
Coptis chinensis (japonica)	huang lian 黄连	coptis	clears Damp Heat and Fire from the Heart and Liver
Cordyceps sinensis	dong chong xia cao 冬虫夏草	cordyceps stroma	supplements the Lungs and Kidneys
Cornus officinalis	shan zhu yu 山茱萸	cornus	astringent, strengthens the Liver and Kidneys
Corydalis turtschaninovii (bulbosa)	yan hu suo 延胡索	corydalis	quickens *qi* and Blood, disperses stagnant Blood, stops pain
Cnidium monneri	she chuang zi 蛇床子	cnidium seed	dries Dampness, dispels Wind, kills parasites, stops itch, warms Kidney *yang*
Crategus pinnatifida	shan zha 山楂	crategus	improves digestion, alleviates food stagnation
Cryptotympana atrata	chan tui 蝉蜕	cicada shell	extinguishes internal Wind, dispels external Wind, stops spasms and itch
Curculigo orchioides	xian mao 仙茅	curculigo	supplements and warms Kidney *yang*, dispels Cold Damp, strengthens tendons and bones
Curcuma ezhu (zedoaria)	e zhu 莪术	curcuma	disperses Blood stagnation masses, alleviates food stagnation
Curcuma longa	jiang huang 姜黄	tumeric rhizome	invigorates *qi* and quickens Blood, dispels Wind Damp
Curcuma longa	yu jin 郁金	curcuma	invigorates *qi* and quickens Blood, disperses stagnant Blood, cools the Heart and Liver
Cuscuta chinensis (hygrophila)	tu su zi 菟丝子	cuscuta	supplements Kidney *yang* and *yin*, benefits *jing*
Cyathula officinalis	chuan niu xi 川牛膝	cyathula	dispels Wind Damp, opens the channels, moves Blood
Cynanchum atratum	bai wei 白薇	swallowwort root	clears Heat, cools the Blood, diuretic
Cynanchum stauntonii	bai qian 白前	cynanchum	directs *qi* downward and expels Phlegm
Cynomorium songariorum	suo yang 锁阳	cynomorium	supplements Kidney *yang*, laxative
Cyperus rotundus	xiang fu 香附	cyperus	regulates *qi*, regulates menstruation, stops pain
Daemonorops draco	xue jie 血竭	dragons blood	invigorates Blood, stops pain, promotes healing
Dalbergia odorifera	jiang xiang 降香	dalbergia wood	invigorates *qi* and Blood, disperses stagnant Blood, stops bleeding, stops pain

Herb functions

Botanical name	Pin Yin	Common name	Function
Dendrobium nobile	shi hu 石斛	dendrobium	nourishes Stomach *yin*, generates fluids, clears deficient Heat
Desmodium styracifolium	guang jin qian cao 广金钱草	desmodium	promotes urination, clears Damp Heat, dissolves urinary stones
Dictamnus dasycarpus	bai xian pi 白鲜皮	dictamnus	clears Damp Heat from the skin
Dioscorea hypoglauca	bei xie 萆解	fish poison yam	alleviates milky or turbid *lin* syndrome, dispels Wind Damp, clears Damp Heat
Dioscorea nipponica (japonica)	chuan shan long 穿山龙	japanese dioscorea	dispels Wind Damp, quickens Blood, opens the channels, stops pain
Dioscorea officinalis (opposita)	shan yao 山药	dioscorea	strengthens the Spleen, stops diarrhoea
Diospyros kaki	shi shu gen 柿树根	persimmon root	stops bleeding
Dipsacus asper	xu duan 续断	dipsacus	supplements the Liver and Kidneys, stops uterine bleeding, strengthens tendons and bones, promotes healing
Dolichos lablab	bian dou 扁豆	hyacinth bean	dispels Summerheat, strengthens the Spleen
Drynaria fortunei	gu sui bu 骨碎补	drynaria	supplements Kidney *yang*, promotes healing
Dryobalanops camphora	bing pian 冰片	borneol	aromatically opens the orifices, clears Heat, promotes healing
Eclipta prostrata	han lian cao 旱莲草	eclipta	nourishes the Liver and Kidneys, cools the Blood, stops bleeding
Ecklonia kurome	kun bu 昆布	kelp	softens hardness, dissipates nodules, transforms Phlegm
Elettaria cardamomum (Amomum cardamomum)	bai dou kou 白豆蔻	amomum	aromatically disperses Dampness, warms the Spleen and Stomach, moves *qi*
Epates australis (Centipeda minima)	e bu shi cao 鹅不食草	centipeda	opens the nose and clears the sinuses

Latin name	Pinyin / 中文	Common name	Functions
Ephedra sinica	ma huang 麻黄	ephedra	redirects *qi* downwards, aids dispersal of Lung *qi*, stops wheezing, dispels Wind Cold
Epimedium brevicornu	xian ling pi 仙灵脾	epimedium	warms Kidney *yang*, dispels Wind Damp
Erodium stephanianum	lao guan cao 老鹳草	cranebill	dispels Wind Damp, quickens Blood, stops diarrhea
Equus asinus	e jiao 阿胶	donkey skin gelatin	supplements Blood and *yin*, stops bleeding
Eriobotrya japonica	pi pa ye 枇杷叶	loquat leaf	clears Phlegm Heat, stops cough and vomiting
Erythrina variegata	hai tong pi 海桐皮	erythrina bark	dispels Wind Damp, unblocks the channels, promotes urination, stops itch
Eucommia ulmoides	du zhong 杜仲	eucommia	supplements Kidney *yang*, strengthens the low back
Eugenia caryophyllata (Syzygium aromaticum)	ding xiang 丁香	cloves	dispels Cold, redirects *qi* downwards, stops vomiting, hiccough and pain
Euphorbiae longana	long yan rou 龙眼肉	longan	nourishes Blood, calms the *shen*
Eupolyphaga sinensis	di bie chong 地鳖虫	field cockroach	breaks up stagnant Blood and softens hardness
Euryale ferox	qian shi 芡实	euryale seed	astringent, strengthens the Spleen
Evodia lepta	san jiao bie 三角别		clears Heat, stops itch
Evodia rutacarpae	wu zhu yu 吴茱萸	evodia	dispels Cold, stops pain and vomiting
Foeniculum vulgare	xiao hui xiang 小茴香	fennel seed	dispels Cold, stops pain, regulates *qi*, harmonises the Stomach
Forsythia suspensa	lian qiao 连翘	forsythia	clears Toxic Heat
Fritillaria cirrhosa	chuan bei mu 川贝母	fritillaria (Sichuan)	dissipates nodules, clears Phlegm Heat
Fritillaria thunbergii	zhe bei mu 浙贝母	fritillaria (Zhejiang)	clears Phlegm Heat from the Lungs, dissipates nodules
Ganoderma lucidum	ling zhi 灵芝	reishi mushroom	supplements *qi* and Blood, calms the *shen*, stops cough and wheezing
Gardenia jasminoides (florida)	shan zhi zi 山栀子	gardenia	clears Damp Heat, alleviates jaundice
Gastrodia elata	tian ma 天麻	gastrodia	extinguishes internal Wind, restrains *yang*
Gaultheria procumbens	dong qing you 冬青油	wintergreen	regulates *qi*, stops pain
Gecko gecko	ge jie 蛤蚧	gecko	strengthens the Lungs and Kidneys, benefits *yang* and augments *jing* and Blood

Herb functions

Botanical name	Pin Yin	Common name	Function
Gentiana macrophylla	qin jiao 秦艽	chin chiu	dispels Wind Damp, clears deficient Heat and Damp Heat, alleviates jaundice, laxative
Gentiana scabra	long dan cao 龙胆草	gentiana	clears Damp Heat and Fire from the Liver
Geranium wilfordii	lao guan cao 老鹳草	geranium	dispels Wind Damp, stops diarrhea
Ginko biloba	yin xing 银杏	ginko seed	astringent, stops cough and diarrhea
Gleditsia australis	zao jiao ci 皂角刺	gleditsia thorn	invigorates Blood, disperses Phlegm, dissipates nodules
Glehnia littoralis	bei sha shen 北沙参	glehnia	nourishes Lung and Stomach *yin*, nourishes the skin
Glycine max	dou chi 豆豉	prepared soybean	clears the exterior of Wind, alleviates irritability
Glycyrrhiza uralensis	gan cao 甘草	licorice	supplements the Spleen and *qi*, benefits the throat, stops cough, moderates harsh qualities of other herbs
Halloysitum rubrum	chi shi zhi 赤石脂	kaolin	stops diarrhoea and chronic Dysenteric disorder
Hedera nepalensis	chang chun teng 常春藤	hedera	dispels Wind Damp, stops pain
Hedyotis diffusa (*Oldenlandia diffusa*)	bai hua she she cao 白花蛇舌草	oldenlandia	clears Toxic Heat
Hematitum	dai zhe shi 代赭石	hematite	calms the Liver, anchors *yang*, directs *qi* downwards, cools the Blood
Hibiscus syricus	mu jin pi 木槿皮	hibiscus bark	clears Dampness from the skin
Hordeum vulgare	mai ya 麦芽	sprouted barley	alleviates food stagnation, improves digestion
Hypericum japonicum	di er cao 地耳草	hypericum	clears Toxic and Damp Heat, alleviates jaundice, invigorates Blood
Ilex aquifolium		english holly	dispels Wind
Ilex pubescens	mao dong qing 毛冬青	ilex	invigorates Blood, promotes circulation through the channels, clears toxic Heat
Ilex rotunda	jiu bi ying 救必应	iron holly bark	clears Damp Heat, astringes the Intestines, stops diarrhea

Latin name	Pinyin / Chinese / Common name	Functions
Illicium verum	di feng pi 地枫皮 illicium bark	dispels Wind Damp, regulates *qi*, stops pain
Imperata cylindrica	bai mao gen 白茅根 imperata	stops bleeding, diuretic, cools the Stomach and Lungs
Indigo Pulverata Levis	qing dai 青黛 indigo	clears Toxic Heat, cools the Liver and Blood
Inula britannica	xuan fu hua 旋复花 inula flower	directs *qi* downward, expels Phlegm, stops cough and vomiting
Inula cappa	bai niu dan 白牛胆 inula	clears Heat, quickens Blood, reduces swelling, stops pain
Isatis tinctoria (*Baphicacanthus cusia*)	ban lan gen 板蓝根 isatis root	clears Toxic Heat, cools the Blood, benefits the throat
Isatis tinctoria (*Baphicacanthus cusia*)	da qing ye 大青叶 isatis leaf	clears Toxic Heat, cools the Blood, benefits the throat
Juglans regia	hu tao ren 胡桃仁 walnut	supplements Kidney *yang*
Juncus effusus	deng xin cao 灯心草 juncus	clears Heat, promotes urination, cools the Heart, alleviates irritability
Kochia scoparia	di fu zi 地肤子 kochia	clears Wind from the skin, stops itch
Laminaria japonica	hai dai 海带 laminaria	softens hardness, dissipates nodules, transforms Phlegm
Lasiosphaera fenslii	ma bo 马勃 puffball	cools the Lungs, benefits the throat
Ledebouriella divaricata (*Siler divaricum*)	fang feng 防风 siler	dispels Wind Cold and Damp, stops spasms and pain
Leonurus sibirica (*heterophylla*)	yi mu cao 益母草 motherwort	regulates menstruation, quickens Blood
Lepidium apetalum	ting li zi 葶苈子 lepidium seed	promotes urination, drains the Lungs, transforms Phlegm, stops wheezing
Ligusticum sinense	gao ben 藁本 ligusticum	dispels Wind and stops pain
Ligusticum wallichii	chuan xiong 川芎 cnidium	regulates *qi* and Blood, analgesic
Ligustrum lucidum	nu zhen zi 女贞子 privet fruit	supplements the Liver and Kidneys, nourishes *yin*, clears deficient Heat, benefits the eyes
Lilium lancifolium (*brownii*)	bai he 百合 lily	nourishes Lung *yin*

Herb functions

Botanical name	Pin Yin	Common name	Function
Lindera strychnifolia	wu yao 乌药	lindera	regulates qi, stops pain, warms the Kidneys
Liquidamber orientalis	su he xiang 苏合香	liquidamber resin	aromatically opens the orifices, revives consciousness
Liquidamber taiwaniana	lu lu tong 路路通	sweetgum fruit	invigorates qi and Blood, unblocks the channels, promotes urination
Lobelia chinensis	ban bian lian 半边莲	lobelia	clears Toxic Heat
Lonicera japonica	jin yin hua 金银花	honeysuckle	clears Toxic Heat, dispels Wind Heat
Lophatherum gracile	dan zhu ye 淡竹叶	bamboo leaves	clears Heat from the Heart
Lycium chinense (barbarum)	di gu pi 地骨皮	lycium root bark	cools the Blood, clear deficient Heat, cools the Lungs, stops cough
Lycium chinense (barbarum)	gou qi zi 枸杞子	lycium fruit	supplements the Liver and Kidney, nourishes Blood, improves visual acuity
Lycopus lucidus	ze lan 泽兰	bugleweed	invigorates Blood and disperses stagnant Blood, promotes urination
Lygodium japonicum	hai jin sha 海金砂	lygodium spore	clears Heat, promotes urination, eases lin syndrome, dissolves stones and calculi
Lysimachia christina	jin qian cao 金钱草	lysimachia	clears Damp Heat, dissolves stones and calculi
Lysimachiae foeni-graeci	ling ling xiang 零陵香		dispels Wind Cold, moves qi, stops pain, kills parasites
Magnolia liliflora	xin yi hua 辛夷花	magnolia flower	opens the nose and clears the sinuses
Magnolia officinalis	hou po 厚朴	magnolia bark	regulates qi, disperses Phlegm Damp, warms the Spleen, alleviates wheezing
Malva verticilata	dong kui zi 冬葵子	malva	promotes urination and eases lin syndrome, promotes lactation, moistens the Intestines
Massa Fermentata	shen qu 神曲	medicated leaven	alleviates food stagnation, improves digestion
Melaleuca cajuputi		cajuput teatree oil	antiseptic, stops pain
Melia toosendan	chuan lian zi 川楝子	melia fruit	regulates qi and stops pain, clears Damp Heat, kills parasites

Botanical name	Pinyin 中文	Common name	Function
Mentha haplocalyxis (arvensis)	bo he 薄荷	mint	dispels Wind Heat, regulates *qi*
Momordica grosvenori (Siraitia grosvenori)	luo han guo 罗汉果	momordica fruit	nourishes Lung *yin*, transforms Phlegm
Morinda officinalis	ba ji tian 巴戟天	morinda	supplements Kidney *yang*
Morus alba	sang ye 桑叶	mulberry leaf	dispels Wind Heat, cools the Lungs and Liver
Morus alba	sang bai pi 桑白皮	mulberry root bark	cools the Lungs, stop cough and wheezing, promotes urination
Morus alba	sang zhi 桑枝	mulberry twig	dispels Wind Damp, unblocks the channels
Morus alba	sang zi 桑子	mulberry fruit	supplements Blood and *yin*
Mosla chinensis (Elsboltzia splendens)	xiang ru 香薷	madder	dispels Summerdamp, diuretic
Myristica fragrans	rou dou kou 肉豆蔻	nutmeg	astringent, stops diarrhoea, warms the Spleen and Stomach
Myroxylon balsamum		tolu	expectorant
Nelumbus nucifera (speciosum)	he ye 荷叶	lotus leaf	dispels Summerheat, raises *yang*, stops bleeding
Nelumbus nucifera (speciosum)	lian zi 莲子	lotus seed	supplements the Spleen, stops diarrhoea, calms the *shen*
Notopterygium incisum	qiang huo 羌活	notopterygium	dispels Wind Damp from *tai yang* channels
Oldenlandia diffusa (Hedyotis diffusa)	bai hua she she cao 白花蛇舌草	oldenlandia	clears Toxic Heat
Omphalia lapidescens	lei wan 雷丸	omphalis puffball	kills parasites
Ootheca Mantidis	sang piao xiao 桑螵蛸	mantis egg case	secures *jing*, restrains urine and astringes leakage of fluids
Ophiopogon japonicus	mai dong 麦冬	ophiopogon	nourishes and supplements Lung and Stomach *yin*
Oryza sativa (Setaria italica)	gu ya 谷芽	sprouted rice	alleviates food stagnation
Oryza sativa	nuo dao gen 糯稻根	glutinous rice root	stops sweating due to deficiency
Os draconis	long gu 龙骨	dragon bone	calms the *shen*, restrains *yang*, astringes leakage of fluids
Osmunda japonica	guan zhong 贯众	shield fern	kills parasites, cools the Blood

Herb functions

Botanical name	Pin Yin	Common name	Function
Ostrea gigas	mu li 牡蛎	oyster shell	calms the *shen*, restrains *yang*, astringes leakage of fluids, softens hardness
Paeonia lactiflora (alba)	bai shao 白芍	white peony	softens the Liver, nourishes *yin* and Blood
Paeonia suffruticosa	mu dan pi 牡丹皮	moutan	quickens Blood, disperses stagnant Blood, cools the Blood
Paeonia veitchii (rubra)	chi shao 赤芍	red peony	quickens Blood, disperses stagnant Blood, cools the Blood and Liver
Panax ginseng	ren shen 人参	ginseng	powerfully supplements yuan *qi*, strengthens the Spleen, generates fluids
Panax notoginseng (pseudoginseng)	tian qi 田七	tian qi ginseng	quickens Blood, stops bleeding
Panax quinquefolium	xi yang shen 西洋参	american ginseng	nourishes Lung *qi* and *yin*, clear deficient Heat
Paris polyphylla	cao he che 草河车	paris	clears Toxic Heat, reduces swelling, stops pain, extinguishes Wind, alleviates spasms
Patrinia villosa	bai jiang cao 败酱草	patrinia	clears Toxic Heat, dissipates inflammatory nodules
Perilla frutescens	su zi 苏子	perilla seed	stops cough and wheezing, transforms Phlegm, directs *qi* downwards
Perilla frutescens	zi su ye 紫苏叶	perilla leaf	dispels Wind Cold, harmonises the Stomach, stops vomiting
Periploca sepium	xiang jia pi 香加皮	periploca	dispels Wind Damp, strengthens the heart, diuretic
Peucedanum praeruptorum	qian hu 前胡	peucedanum	stops cough, dispels Wind Heat, resolves Phlegm
Pharbitis nil	qian niu zi 牵牛子	morning glory seed	cathartic diuretic, laxative
Phaseolus angularis	chi xiao dou 赤小豆	adzuki bean	diuretic, drains Dampness
Phellodendron amurense	huang bai 黄柏	phellodendron	clears Damp Heat from the lower jiao
Pheretima asiatica	di long 地龙	earthworm	clears Heat, extinguishes Wind, drills through obstruction in the channels, cools the Lungs

Latin name	Pinyin	Common name	Functions
Phragmites communis	lu gen 芦根	reed rhizome	clears Heat from the *qi* level, Lungs and Stomach, stops vomiting
Pinellia ternata	ban xia 半夏	pinellia	resolves Phlegm Damp, stops vomiting
Pinus massoniana		turpentine oil	dries Damp, kills parasites, promotes healing
Piper futokadsura	hai feng teng 海风藤	kadsura stem	dispels Wind Damp, unblocks the channels, disperses Cold, stops pain
Piper longum	bi ba 荜拨	long pepper	warms the Spleen and Stomach, disperses Cold, stops pain
Piper nigrum	hu jiao 胡椒	black pepper	warms the Spleen and Stomach, disperses Cold, stops pain
Plantago asiatica	che qian zi 车前子	plantago	diuretic, drains Dampness
Platycodon grandiflorum	jie geng 桔梗	platycodon	directs *qi* upwards, resolves Phlegm, stops cough, benefits the throat
Polygala sibiricum	yuan zhi 远志	polygala	disperses Phlegm, calms the *shen*
Polygonatum odoratum	yu zhu 玉竹	polygonatum	nourishes Lung and Stomach *yin*
Polygonatum sibiricum	huang jing 黄精	solomon seal rhizome	supplements Spleen *qi* and *yin*, moistens the Lungs, supplements the Kidneys and *jing*
Polygonum aviculare	bian xu 扁蓄	knotweed	clears Damp Heat from the Urinary Bladder, promotes urination, eases *lin* syndrome, stops itch
Polygonum chinense	huo tan mu 火炭母	chinese polygonum	clears Damp Heat and Toxic Heat, promotes urination, drains Dampness, brightens the eyes
Polygonum cuspidatum	hu zhang 虎杖	bushy knotweed	invigorates Blood, clears Damp Heat
Polygonum multiflorum	he shou wu 何首乌	ho shou wu	nourishes Blood, supplements the Liver and Kidneys
Polygonum multiflorum	ye jiao teng 夜交藤	ho shou wu stem	nourishes Heart Blood, calms the *shen*
Polyporus umbellatus	zhu ling 猪苓	polyporus	promotes urination, leaches out Dampness
Poria cocos	fu ling 茯苓	hoelen	strengthens the Spleen, promotes urination, calms the *shen*
Prunella vulgaris	xia ku ca 夏枯草	prunella	clears Heat, softens hardness

Herb functions

Botanical name	Pin Yin	Common name	Function
Prunus armenica	xing ren 杏仁	apricot seed	redirects Lung *qi* downwards, stops cough, lubricates the intestines
Prunus japonica	yu li ren 郁李仁	bush cherry seed	lubricates the intestines, promotes urination
Prunus mume	wu mei 乌梅	black plum	astringes leakage of fluids, generates fluids, stops cough, diarrhea and bleeding
Prunus persica	tao ren 桃仁	peach seed	quickens Blood, disperses stagnant Blood, lubricates the intestines
Pseudostellaria heterophylla	tai zi shen 太子参	pseudostellaria	Strengthens the Spleen, supplements *qi*, generated fluids
Psoralea corylifolia	bu gu zhi 朴骨脂	psoralea	warms *yang*, astringent
Pteria martensii	zhen zhu mu 珍珠母	mother of pearl	calms the *shen*, cools the Liver, promotes healing
Pueraria lobata	ge gen 葛根	kudzu	dispels Wind Heat, eases the muscles, stops diarrhoea
Punica granatum	shi liu pi 石榴皮	pomegranate skin	astringent, stops diarrhoea, kills parasites
Pyrola rotundifolia	lu xian cao 鹿衔草	pyrola	dispels Wind Damp, strengthens tendons and bones, supplements the Liver and Kidneys, stops bleeding
Quisqualis indica	shi jun zi 使君子	rangoon creeper fruit	kills parasites, strengthens the Spleen
Rabdosia lophanthoides	xi huang cao 溪黄草	rabdosia	clears Damp Heat from the Liver
Ranunculus ternatus	mao zhua cao 猫爪草	ranunculus	clears Toxic Heat, dissipates nodules
Raphanus sativus	lai fu zi 莱服子	radish seed	alleviates food stagnation, directs *qi* downwards and dries thin Phlegm
Rehmannia glutinosa	sheng di 生地	raw rehmannia	cools the Blood, nourishes *yin*
Rehmannia glutinosa	shu di 熟地	processed rehmannia	supplements Blood and Kidney *yin*
Rheum palmatum (officinale)	da huang 大黄	rhubarb root	purgative, clears Heat through the bowel, disperses stagnant Blood
Rosa laevingata	jin ying zi 金樱子	chinese rose	astringent for diarrhoea and frequent urination
Rubia cordifolia	qian cao gen 茜草根	rubia	cools the Blood, stops bleeding, quickens Blood

Latin name	Pinyin	Common name	Functions
Rubus chingii (coreanus)	fu pen zi 覆盆子	rubus	astringent, stops frequent urination, strengthens Kidneys, benefits the eyes
Saccharum Granorum	yi tang 飴糖	malt sugar	supplements Spleen *qi*, alleviates spasmodic pain, stops cough
Salvia miltiorrhiza	dan shen 丹参	salvia	quickens Blood, disperses stagnant Blood, calms the *shen*
Sanguisorba officinalis	di yu 地榆	sanguisorba	clears Damp Heat, stops bleeding
Santalum album	tan xiang 檀香	sandalwood	moves *qi*, stops pain, warms the Stomach, stops vomiting
Sargassum pallidum	hai zao 海藻	sargassum seaweed	softens hardness, dissipates nodules
Saussurea lappa (Auklandia lappa)	mu xiang 木香	saussurea	regulates *qi*, stops pain and diarrhoea
Schizandra chinensis	wu wei zi 五味子	schizandra	astringent, strengthens *wei qi*, stops cough and sweating
Schizonepeta tenuifolia	jing jie 荆芥	schizonepeta	dispels Wind, stops itch
Scolopendra subspinipes	wu gong 蜈蚣	centipede	extinguishes internal Wind, stops spasms, invigorates Blood
Scrophularia ningpoensis	xuan shen 玄参	scrophularia	cools the Blood, nourishes *yin*, softens hardness
Scutellaria baicalensis	huang qin 黄芩	scute	clears Damp Heat from the upper body
Selaginella tamariscana	juan bai 卷白	selaginella	astringent, stops bleeding, moves stagnant Blood, promotes urination
Senecio scandens	qian li guang 千里光	senecio	clears Toxic Heat, cools the Liver, brightens the eyes
Sepia esculenta	wu zei gu 乌贼骨	cuttlefish backbone	alleviates hyperacidity, promotes healing
Sesamum indicum	hei zhi ma 黑芝麻	sesame seed	nourishes *yin* and Blood, laxative, nourishes the skin
Setaria italica (Oryza sativa)	gu ya 谷芽	sprouted rice	alleviates food stagnation
Siegesbeckia orientalis	xixian cao 稀莶草	siegesbeckia	dispels Wind Damp, clears Damp Heat from the skin, stops itch, alleviates Malarial disorder
Siler divaricatum (Ledebouriella divaricata)	fang feng 防风	siler	dispels Wind Cold and Damp, stops spasms and pain

Herb functions

Botanical name	Pin Yin	Common name	Function
Smilax glabra	tu fu ling 土茯苓	smilax	clears Toxic Heat from the skin
Solidago virdaurea (*Artemesia anomala*)	liu ji nu 刘寄奴	solidago	invigorates Blood, disperses stagnant Blood
Sophora flavescentis	ku shen 苦参	sophora root	clears Damp Heat from the skin and Liver
Sophora japonica	huai hua 槐花	sophora flower bud	clears Damp Heat and cools the Liver, stops bleeding
Sophora japonica	huai jiao 槐角	sophora fruit	clears Damp Heat and cools the Liver
Sophora tonkinensis	shan dou gen 山豆根	sophora	clears Toxic Heat, cools the Lungs and throat
Sparganium stoloniferum	san leng 三棱	sparganium	disperses Blood stagnation masses, alleviates food stagnation
Spatholobus suberectus (*Milletia reticulata*)	ji xue teng 鸡血藤	spatholobus	moves *qi* and quickens Blood, opens the channels, promotes circulation to the extremities
Spirodela polyrrhiza	fu ping 浮萍	duckweed	dispels Wind Heat, diuretic
Stellaria dichotoma	yin chai hu 银柴胡	stellaria root	clears deficient Heat, cools the Blood
Stemona sessifolia	bai bu 百部	stemona	stops cough, kills parasites
Stephania tetrandra	fang ji 防己	stephania	dispels Wind Damp, diuretic
Styrax tonkinensis	an xi xiang 安息香	benzoinum	opens the orifices
Taraxicum mongolicum	pu gong ying 蒲公英	dandelion	clears Toxic Heat, cools the Liver, benefits the breasts
Terminalia chebula	he zi 诃子	terminalia	astringent, stops diarrhoea and cough
Tribulus terrestris	bai ji li 白蒺藜	tribulus	dispels Wind from the skin, calms the Liver, moves *qi*
Trichosanthes kirilowi	gua lou 栝楼	trichosanthes	clears Phlegm Heat, opens up circulation in the chest
Trichosanthes kirilowi	tian hua fen 天花粉	trichosanthes root	cools the Lungs, transforms Phlegm, generates fluids, clears Toxic Heat
Trigonella foenum-graecum	hu lu ba 葫芦巴	fenugreek seed	warms *yang*
Triticum aestivum	fu xiao mai 浮小麦	wheat	stops sweating from deficiency, nourishes the Heart and calms the *shen*

Latin	Pinyin	Common name	Functions
Trogopterus xanthipes	wu ling zhi 五灵脂	flying squirrel feces	invigorates Blood, disperses Blood stasis, stops pain
Tussilago farfare	kuan dong hua 款冬花	coltsfoot	stops cough
Typhae angustifolia	pu huang 蒲黄	bulrush pollen	invigorates Blood, stops bleeding
Typhonium giganteum	bai fu zi 白附子	typhonium	transforms Phlegm Damp, extinguishes Wind, stops pain
Uncaria rhyncophylla	gou teng 钩藤	gambir	extinguishes internal Wind, stops spasms, cools the Liver
Urginea scilla		squill	expectorant
Vaccaria segetalis	wang bu liu xing 王不留行	mustard seed	invigorates Blood, opens the channels, promotes menstruation and lactation
Viola yedoensis	zi hua di ding 紫花地丁	viola	clears Toxic Heat
Viscum coloratum	sang ji sheng 桑寄生	mistletoe	supplements the Liver and Kidneys, dispels Wind Damp, nourishes Blood, benfits the skin
Vitex negrundo	mu jing ye 牡荆叶	chinese vitex	dispels Wind, expels Phlegm, stops cough
Vitex trifolia	man jing zi 蔓荆子	vitex fruit	dispels Wind and clears Heat from the Liver channel, head and eyes
Xanthium sibiricum	cang er zi 苍耳子	xanthium	opens the nose, dispels Wind Damp
Zanthoxylum avicennae	ying bu bo 鹰不泊		dispels Wind Damp, moves *qi* and Blood, calms the Liver
Zanthoxylum nitidum	liang mian zhen 两面针	zanthoxylum root	invigorates *qi* and Blood, disperses stagnant Blood, stops pain
Zaocys dhummades	wu shao she 乌梢蛇	black striped snake	unblocks the channels, extinguishes Wind
Zingiber officinale	gan jiang 干姜	dry ginger	warms Spleen *jang*, warms the Lungs and transforms thin Phlegm
Zingiber officinale	sheng jiang 生姜	ginger	dispels Wind Cold, regulates Stomach *qi*, stops vomiting
Zizyphus jujuba	da zao 大枣	chinese dates	supplements the Stomach *qi*, harmonises the Stomach
Zizyphus spinoza	suan zao ren 酸枣仁	zizyphus	calms the *shen*, stops sweating

Possible Herb Drug Interactions

Many, if not most, of the patients presenting in Chinese medicine practices are taking (one or more) therapeutic substances of some description. These substances may include pharmaceuticals, herbal remedies, vitamins and minerals, either professionally prescribed or purchased over the counter. When wishing to prescribe a Chinese herbal formula, it is essential to have some idea of the potential for herb-drug or herb-herb interactions. In some cases, the patients existing medications will preclude the use of certain formulae, or warrant special monitoring of the patient when additional medications are prescribed.

Interaction refers to the possibility that one substance may alter the effectiveness or availability of another substance. The information following is based on both known interactions, and theoretical interactions based on an understanding of the pharmacology of the substances involved.

Drug	Herb	Mechanism	Interaction	Advice
Antiplatelet and anticoagulant drugs (warfarin, aspirin, NSAIDs, heparin)	Salvia miltiorrhizae (dan shen[1])	components may inhibit platelet aggregation	increased prothrombin time and INR[3], increased tendency to bleed	avoid concurrent use or monitor bruising and bleeding and stop herb if increased; have INR values monitored during initial therapy until stabilised, then routinely thereafter
	Angelica sinensis (dang gui[2])	unknown	increased prothrombin time and INR, increased tendency to bleed	
	Panax ginseng (ren shen[2])	unknown	may decrease the effectiveness of warfarin, decreased INR	have INR values monitored during initial therapy until stabilised, then routinely thereafter
	Ginko biloba (yin xing)	ginkgolide B may inhibit platelet activating factor	increases inhibition of platelet aggregation	monitor bruising and bleeding and stop herb if increased; have INR values monitored during initial therapy until stabilised, then routinely thereafter

1. Common and well documented.
2. Uncommon.
3. International Normalisation Ratio: A corrected measure of prothrombin time (the time it takes blood to clot) established against a premedication baseline. Usual values are in the range of 2-4.5 over baseline.

Drug	Herb	Mechanism	Interaction	Advice
Potassium retaining diuretics (aldactone, spironolactone)	*Glycyrrhiza uralensis* (gan cao)	glycyrrhizic acid prevents conversion of deoxycorticosterone into active glucocorticoids, cortisol and corticosterone	Na+ retention, K+ loss, edema, hypertension	avoid concurrent use
Potassium losing diuretics, loop diuretics (lasix)	*Glycyrrhiza uralensis* (gan cao) *Desmodium styracifolium* (jin qian cao)	aggravate K+ loss	hypokalaemia, numbness, muscle weakness, cramps, palpitations	monitor the patient carefully, or avoid concurrent use
Niacin (Vitamin B6)	yang supplementing and heating herbs	compounds heat elements	can cause the patient to overheat	avoid concurrent use
Theophylline	*Ephedra sinica* (ma huang)	ephedrine can cause stimulation	increases sympathetic and stimulatory effects	monitor changes in BP, heart rate, insomnia, tremors and headaches
Decongestants (Actifed, Sudafed)	*Ephedra sinica* (ma huang)	aggregate action with pseudoephedrine	increases sympathetic and stimulatory effects; insomnia, tachycardia, tremors	avoid concurrent use

Possible Herb Drug Interactions

Drug	Herb	Mechanism	Interaction	Advice
Hypoglycaemic agents (insulin, glyburide, tolbutamide, metformin)	*Glycyrrhiza uralensis* (gan cao)	glycyrrhizic acid prevents conversion of deoxyocorticosterone	reduced hypoglycaemic action	avoid concurrent use
	Panax ginseng (ren shen)	unknown	decreased blood glucose levels	monitor blood glucose, watch for signs of hypoglycaemia
Antihypertensive agents (beta blockers)	*Ephedra sinica* (ma huang)	ephedrine may oppose the effects of beta blockers	hypertension	monitor changes in BP, heart rate, or avoid concurrent use
	Glycyrrhiza uralensis (gan cao)	increase Na+ and water retention	counter the effects of medication and increase BP	monitor changes in BP, heart rate, or avoid concurrent use
Chloramphenicol	*Artemesia capillaris* (yin chen hao)	antagonise each other	reduced efficacy	allow some time between administration
Codeine	*Prunus persica* (xing ren) *Ginko biloba* (yin xing)	amygdaline suppresses the respiratory centre	respiratory centre depression	avoid concurrent use

Drug	Herb	Mechanism	Interaction	Advice
Corticosteroids	*Glycyrrhiza uralensis* (gan cao)	glycyrrhizic acid prevents conversion of deoxycorticosterone into active glucocorticoids, cortisol and corticosterone	potentiation of both oral and topical steroids	monitor use carefully
Cardiac glycosides (digoxin, lanoxin)	*Panax ginseng* (ren shen)	unknown	may falsely elevate digoxin levels; difficulty in monitoring drug response	avoid concurrent use
	Aconite spp. (fu zi, wu tou)	additive effect of aconitine	increased risk of digitalis toxicity	avoid concurrent use
	Glycyrrhiza uralensis (gan cao)	deoxycorticosterone like action causes retention of Na+, loss of K+ and increases cardiac muscle sensitivity to digoxin		avoid long term concurrent use
	Bufo bufo (gan chan, cane toad venom)	contains glycoside like action	additive effect can increase the risk of toxicity	avoid concurrent use

Possible Herb Drug Interactions

Drug	Herb	Mechanism	Interaction	Advice
MAO inhibitors (phenelzine, nardil)	*Ephedra sinica* (ma huang)	ephedrine can cause stimulation	increases sympathetic and stimulatory effects	monitor changes in BP, insomnia, nervousness, headaches and tremors
	Panax ginseng (ren shen)	inhibits cAMP phosphodiesterase activity	increases psychoactive stimulation and may induce mania in depressed patients	avoid concurrent use
Immunosuppressants (cyclosporin, azathioprine)	*Astragalus membranaceous* (huang qi)	stimulates T cell activity	decreases immunosuppressant effect	avoid concurrent use
Interferon	6.1 Xiao Chai Hu Tang Wan (formula)	unknown	may induce interstitial pneumonitis in susceptible patients	avoid concurrent use
Osmotic laxatives, bulking agents (psyllium)	all herbs	binding of herbs in insoluble matrix, increase transit time	actives carried out through the bowel	allow some time between administration

Medicines for acute exterior disorders

3.1 Yin Chiao Chieh Tu Pien	The formula of choice for typical Wind Heat *gan mao* patterns, especially when characterised by sore throat or acute itchy skin rashes.
3.2 Gan Mao Zhi Ke Chong Ji	For cough or Wind Heat *gan mao* that has been dragging on for a few days, or has begun to creep into the *shao yang* level.
3.3 Sang Ju Wan	Mild Wind Heat *gan mao* with cough.
3.4 Gan Mao Ling	A general medicine for non specific *gan mao* from Wind invasion. Although it leans towards Wind Heat, it can be used for non specific colds and flu, or those that are vague and without any clear Heat or Cold tendency.
3.5 Ma Huang Wan	Wind Cold *gan mao* with wheezing and dyspnoea, absence of sweating and cough. The classical formula for 'exterior excess', that is, tightly locked pores keeping the Cold pathogen from being ejected.
3. 6 Gui Zhi Wan	Wind invasion *gan mao* with exterior deficiency, that is, weak *wei qi* that allows the lingering presence of an invading pathogen.
3.8 Xiao Qing Long Wan	Wind Cold *gan mao* with watery sputum causing productive cough, wheezing and dyspnoea or runny nose and sinuses. Also used for acute hayfever.
3.9 Chuan Xiong Cha Tiao Wan	Wind Cold *gan mao*, especially when headache is a major features. Also used for headaches and facial pain triggered by exposure to cold or sudden temperature change.
3.10 Jing Fang Bai Du Wan	Wind Cold Damp *gan mao*, or Wind Cold *gan mao* that is beginning to transform into Heat.
3.11 Ge Gen Wan	Wind Cold *gan mao* with neck and upper back stiffness and pain.
3.12 Gan Mao Qing Re Chong Ji	Wind Cold *gan mao* with muscle aches as a prominent feature. Good for those who find pills hard to take.

Medicines for acute exterior disorders (cont.)

2.1 Xing Jun San	A powerful and fragrant powder for acute Summerdamp invasion and gastric upsets with nausea and vomiting. Strong tasting and fast acting.
2.2 Huo Hsiang Cheng Chi Pien	Similar to 2.1 Xing Jun San but not as strong. Also for Wind Cold *gan mao* with internal Dampness and for lingering or hidden Dampness patterns of the Spleen and Stomach.
2.4 Fu Ke An 2.5 Bao Ji Pills 2.6 Po Chai Pills	Acute Damp Heat invasion of the Intestines causing diarrhea. These medicines, while different in composition, are quite similar in effect.
2.13 Li Zhong Wan	While not usually considered for acute exterior disorders, this medicine can be used in severe acute patterns of vomiting and diarrhea with the threat of collapsing *yang*.
9.3 Peking Niu Huang Jie Du Pian	Acute Wind and Toxic Heat patterns of the upper body, including superficial infections, sore throat, conjunctivitis, abscess and otitis.
9.5 Pu Ji Xiao Du Wan	Toxic Heat in the head and throat; tonsillitis, strep throat, erysipelas.
9.6 Ban Lan Gen Chong Ji	Popular both as treatment and preventative for acute Wind Heat and Toxic Heat patterns, especially sore throat.
14.5 Chuan Xin Lian Antiphlogistic Tablets	A good all round antibiotic and antiviral agent for a range of acute exterior disorders and infectious processes. Especially good for infection of the throat and intestines.
14.9 Bai Hu Tang Wan	Acute Heat in *yang ming* channels. This pattern is often quite severe and may equate to biomedical conditions such as encephalitis, meningitis and pneumonia.
14.10 Liang Ge Wan	Acute Heat in *tai yang* and *yang ming* organs. This pattern is similar to that in 14.9 Bai Hu Tang Wan, with the added complication of constipation.

Qi stagnation

6.2 Si Ni San Wan	The base formula for Liver *qi* stagnation and the fundamental unit from which all other Liver *qi* regulating formulae are built. Good added to another constitutional medicine when a degree of *qi* regulating activity is required.
6.3 Chai Hu Shu Gan Wan	Similar to 6.2 Si Ni San Wan with additional *qi* regulating herbs. Especially good for Liver Spleen disharmony, this formula has no supplementing activity and is best for *qi* stagnation patterns with no deficiency. Most commonly used in young, robust, stressed individuals.
2.24 Shu Gan Wan	Strong *qi* moving formula with a focus on pain, especially hypochondriac, epigastric and abdominal.
6.3 Xiao Yao Wan	Liver *qi* stagnation with Spleen weakness and Blood deficiency. A good allround and gentle *qi* moving formula suitable for long term use. Particularly good for Liver *qi* stagnation patterns in women causing menstrual disorders and premenstrual syndrome.
6.4 Jia Wei Xiao Yao Wan	Similar to 6.3 Xiao Yao Wan with the addition of cooling herbs to clear Heat generated by chronic *qi* stagnation.
6.8 Yi Guan Jian Wan	Liver *qi* stagnation with Liver *yin* deficiency.
2.25 Tong Xie Yao Fang Wan	Liver *qi* invading the Spleen causing diarrhea preceded by spasmodic abdominal pain. An important formula for irritable bowel syndrome.
8.7 An Shen Jie Yu Capsule	Liver *qi* stagnation causing *shen* disturbances and sleep disorders.
2.10 Xiang Sha Yang Wei Wan	Middle *jiao qi* and Damp stagnation. Excellent for upper abdominal *qi* stagnation causing distension, epigastric discomfort, heartburn, reflux and belching.
2.29 Mu Xiang Shun Qi Wan	Middle *jiao qi* stagnation, disruption the *qi* mechanism causing abdominal distension and constipation.

Blood stagnation

5.1 Xue Fu Zhu Yu Wan	*Qi* and Blood stagnation. The most general and all purpose Blood stagnation eliminator. Particularly good for Blood stagnation complicated by, or resulting from Liver *qi* stagnation. Best for Blood stasis patterns of the upper body, chest and head.
1.18 Shao Fu Zhu Yu Wan	Blood stagnation and Cold in the lower *jiao*. Used for gynecological and urogenital pain, and masses in the pelvic basin.
6.12 Ge Xia Zhu Yu Wan	Blood stagnation masses. The strongest of the Zhu Yu formulae, designed for abdominal masses, especially those below the diaphragm, i.e. swelling and pathology of the liver and spleen.
10.12 Shen Tong Zhu Yu Wan	Blood stagnation type pain disorders. A powerful Blood moving formula designed for chronic pain and stiffness patterns in the joints and muscles. Used for chronic arthritis and fibromyalgia.
9.2 Tong Qiao Huo Xue Wan	Blood stagnation in the head, affecting the sense organs; post traumatic memory problems; post concussion syndrome.
5.2 Dan Shen Pill	Blood stagnation affecting the Heart. For angina and chest pain.
5.3 Dan Shen Wan	Blood stagnation affecting the Heart, chest or Stomach.
5.7 Sunho Multi Ginseng Tablets	Mild general Blood stagnation in the chest, stomach and periphery. Lowers cholesterol.
5.4 Xin Mai Ling	Blood stagnation affecting the Heart and periphery. For angina and peripheral vascular disease.
1.16 Tao Hong Si Wu Wan	Blood stagnation with Blood deficiency. Especially good for gynecological disorders. Good for prolonged use.
1.15 Tong Jing Wan	Relatively severe Blood stagnation in the uterus causing dysmenorrhea.

Blood stagnation

1.17 Gui Zhi Fu Ling Wan	Mild Blood stagnation patterns or the uterus, genito-urinary system and pelvic basin with small benign masses. Suitable for prolonged use.
1.13 Woo Garm Yuen Medical Pills	Relatively severe Cold accumulation and Blood stagnation in the uterus and pelvic basin with a degree of *qi* and Blood deficiency.
1.14 Wen Jing Tang Wan	Mild Blood stagnation and Cold in the uterus with deficiency of *qi*, Blood and *yang*.
10.21 Yan Hu Suo Wan	General analgesic formula for all types of Blood and *qi* stagnation pain.
1.12 Shi Xiao Wan	Simple formula for Blood stagnation pain, especially from the stomach and uterus. Usually added to another formula for added analgesia.
5.8 Bu Yang Huan Wu Wan	Blood stagnation and *qi* deficiency type hemiplegia and paralysis. Used in peripheral neuropathy and following Wind-stroke.
5.9 Dang Gui Si Ni Wan	Blood stagnation and Cold accumulation the channels and extremities.
10.1 Yunnan Paiyao	Blood stagnation with bleeding.
10.2 Raw Tienchi Tablets	Blood stagnation bleeding patterns and generalised Blood stagnation in the cardiovascular and hepatic systems. Lower blood cholesterol.
10.3 Die Da Zhi Tong Capsule	Acute traumatic Blood stagnation with bruising and pain.
10.4 Chin Gu Tie Shang Wan	Acute traumatic Blood stagnation with bruising and pain. Assists in slow healing of bone fractures.
10.5 Huo Luo Xiao Ling Wan	Traumatic Blood stagnation, Blood stagnation type pain, skin disease and inflammatory masses.
10.11 Shu Jin Huo Xue Wan	Chronic bi syndrome with Blood stasis causing joint and muscle pain and stiffness.

Blood stagnation (cont.)

10.23 Zheng Gu Shui	Topical application for acute traumatic Blood stagnation with bruising and pain. Assists in healing of bone fractures.
10.38 Plaster for Bruise and Analgesic	Similar to 10.23 Zheng Gu Shui on a sticky plaster. Good for overnight use.
11.1 Qian Lie Xian Capsule 11.2 Prostate Gland Pills	Blood stagnation and Damp Heat accumulation in the prostate gland. For chronic prostatitis.
11.3 Ji Sheng Ju He Wan	Mild Blood stagnation and Phlegm masses in the testicles.
11.8 Kang Wei Ling Wan	A combination of a powerful Blood moving substance with *qi*, Blood and *yang* supplementing herbs to assist in moving Blood in the penis. For *qi* and Blood stagnation vascular impotence.
12.11 Dan Shen Huo Xue Wan	Blood stagnation with Heat in the Blood type chronic skin disorders.

Dampness and Phlegm

2.1 Xing Jun San	A powerful and fragrant powder for acute gastro-intestinal Summerdamp with nausea and vomiting.
2.2 Huo Hsiang Cheng Chi Pien	Similar to 2.1 Xing Jun San but not as strong. Also for Wind Cold *gan mao* with internal Dampness and for lingering or hidden Dampness patterns of the Spleen and Stomach.
2.22 Er Chen Wan	The base formula for Phlegm Dampness and the fundamental unit from which all Phlegm formulae are built. Good added to an appropriate constitutional formula when a degree of Phlegm transformation is desired. Used for Phlegm anywhere in the body, but especially good for Phlegm in the Lung system and nausea.
2.23 Ping Wei San	Cold Damp accumulation in the Spleen and Stomach.
3.7 Su Zi Jiang Qi Wan	Wheezing, cough and asthma from thin Phlegm accumulation in the Lungs.
3.8 Xiao Qing Long Wan	Wheezing, cough and hayfever from Wind Cold *gan mao* with accumulation of thin Phlegm in the Lungs.
3.21 She Dan Chuan Bei Ye	Phlegm accumulation in the Lungs. Excellent for resolving residual and persistent Phlegm in the aftermath of an upper respiratory tract infection.
3.22 Orange Peel Powder	Phlegm accumulation in the Lungs.
4.5 Bi Xie Fen Qing Wan	Dampness accumulation in the reproductive system causing discharge and vesicular eruptions.
1.32 Ru Jie Xiao Tablets	Phlegm and *qi* stagnation type breast lumps.
1.33 Hai Zao Jing Wan	Phlegm type swellings, masses and nodules.
1.34 Nei Xiao Luo Li Wan	Hard Phlegm type masses, lumps and nodules.
11.3 Ji Sheng Ju He Wan	Cold Damp, Phlegm and mild Blood stagnation masses in the testicles.

Dampness and Phlegm (cont.)

6.10 Qing Gan Li Dan Tablets	Damp and mild Heat in the Liver and Gallbladder causing sludge accumulation and gall stones.
8.10 Cerebral Tonic Pills	Phlegm in the Head, misting the senses and mind.
8.11 Jian Nao Yi Zhi Capsule	Phlegm in the head causing poor memory and concentration.
9.12 Ban Xia Hou Po Wan	Phlegm and *qi* stagnation in the throat. 'Plum stone *qi*'.
9.18 Xin Yi San	Dampness accumulating in the sinuses.
10.8 Xiao Huo Luo Dan	Severe Cold Damp accumulation in the joints.
12.1 Bo Ying Compound	Phlegm accumulation in infants, accumulation disorder.
13.2 Xiao Feng Wan	Dampness and Wind accumulation in the skin.
13.5 Shi Du Qing Capsule	Dampness accumulation in the skin causing intense itching and weeping rashes.
13.15 Tujin Liniment	Dampness accumulation between the toes.
15.3 Ban Xia Bai Zhu Tian Ma Wan	Wind Phlegm in the head causing vertigo, nausea and tinnitus.
2.8 Liu Jun Zi Wan	Spleen *qi* deficiency with Phlegm Damp.
2.9 Xiang Sha Liu Jun Wan	Spleen *qi* deficiency with Phlegm Damp and *qi* stagnation disrupting the *qi* mechanism.
2.12 Shen Ling Bai Zhu Wan	Spleen *qi* deficiency with Dampness pouring downwards as diarrhea.

Damp Heat, Phlegm Heat, Toxic Heat, Fire

2.4 Fu Ke An 2.5 Bao Ji Pills 2.6 Po Chai Pills	Acute Damp Heat invasion of the Intestines causing diarrhea. These medicines, while different in composition, are quite similar in effect.
14.1 Huang Lian Jie Du Wan	General formula for systemic or focal Damp or Toxic Heat patterns. Also for Heat in the Blood.
14.5 Chuan Xin Lian Antiphlogistic Tablets	A good all round antibiotic and antiviral agent for a range of acute exterior disorders and infectious processes. Especially good for infection of the throat and intestines
14.6 Fu Fang Nan Ban Lan Gen	Toxic Heat and Hot Blood patterns with sores and boils, skin disorders, purpura and acute infections.
14.8 Wu Wei Xiao Du Wan	Toxic Heat in the skin causing deep rooted boils and sores, as well as infections such as mastitis, appendicitis and tonsillitis.
13.1 Lien Chiao Pai Tu Pien	Wind and Toxic Heat type skin disorders
9.6 Ban Lan Gen Chong Ji	Popular both as treatment and preventative for acute Wind Heat and Toxic Heat patterns, especially sore throat.
9.5 Pu Ji Xiao Du Wan	Toxic Heat in the head and throat; tonsillitis, strep throat, erysipelas.
9.3 Peking Niu Huang Jie Du Pian	Acute Toxic Heat patterns of the upper body, mouth and throat, including superficial infections, sore throat, conjunctivitis, abscess and otitis.
9.4 Huang Lian Shang Qing Pien	Toxic Heat patterns of the upper body, mouth skin and throat, including superficial infections, sore throat, conjunctivitis, abscess and otitis.
6.6 Long Dan Xie Gan Wan	Damp Heat or Fire in the Liver system.
6.7 Da Chai Hu Wan	Damp Heat in the Liver and Gallbladder systems; *shao yang/yang ming* syndrome.

Damp Heat, Phlegm Heat, Toxic Heat, Fire (cont.)

6.11 Lidan Tablets	Acute or chronic Damp Heat in the Liver and Gallbladder systems. Used for acute and chronic cholecystitis and hepatitis.
1.35 Fu Yan Qing Tablets	Damp Heat in the reproductive system and genitals.
1.36 Bi Xie Sheng Shi Wan	Damp Heat in the reproductive system, genitals and skin.
1.37 Yu Dai Wan	Damp Heat in the reproductive system with underlying Blood deficiency.
1.38 Chien Chin Chih Tai Wan	Chronic Damp Heat in the reproductive system with Kidney deficiency.
2.29 Mu Xiang Shun Qi Wan	Chronic Damp Heat Dysenteric Disorder.
3.15 Qing Qi Hua Tan Wan	Acute and chronic Phlegm Heat in the Lungs.
3.16 Ching Fei Yi Huo Pien	Acute Lung Fire.
3.19 Ding Chuan Wan	Phlegm Heat in the Lungs causing wheezing.
4.6 Ba Zheng San Wan	Acute Damp Heat in the Urinary Bladder causing dysuria and urinary tract infection.
4.8 Tao Chih Pien	Heart Fire invading the Small Intestine type dysuria.
8.8 Wen Dan Wan	Phlegm Heat affecting the Heart and *shen*, systemic Phlegm Heat, post febrile Phlegm Heat.
8.9 Chai Hu Long Gu Mu Li Wan	Phlegm Heat and Liver Fire type *shen* disturbances; withdrawal from drugs of addiction; mania; palpitations
9.8 Qing Wei San Wan	Heat in the Stomach causing oral and gingival inflammation.

Damp Heat, Phlegm Heat, Toxic Heat, Fire (cont.)

9.14 Bi Ye Ning Capsule	Phlegm Heat in the sinuses.
9.19 Cang Er Zi Wan	Wind Heat and Phlegm Heat in the sinuses.
9.21 Ming Mu Shang Ching Pien	Fire type eye disorders; also used for Damp Heat in the Urinary Bladder causing dysuria or hematuria.
10.9 Xuan Bi Tang Wan 10.10 Guan Jie Yan Wan	Damp Heat in the joints.
11.1 Qian Lie Xian Capsule 11.2 Prostate Gland Pills	Damp Heat and Blood stagnation in the prostate gland. For chronic prostatitis.
12.2 King Fung Powder	Phlegm Heat infantile fever and convulsions.
13.4 Ke Yin Wan	Stubborn Damp Heat in the skin.
13.10 Zhen Zhu An Chuang Tablets	Toxic Heat and Damp Heat type acne.
13.12 Chuan Xin Lian Cream	Topical ointment for Toxic Heat and Damp Heat type skin lesions.
15.1 Po Lung Yuen Medical Pills	Phlegm Heat and Wind type tics, tremors and seizures; febrile convulsions.
15.2 Niu Huang Qing Xin Wan	Phlegm Heat and Wind type movement disorders and post stroke syndrome.

Qi deficiency

2.7 Si Jun Zi Wan	The base formula for Spleen and systemic *qi* deficiency, and the fundamental unit from which all other *qi* supplementing formulae are built. Good added to any other constitutional formula when a degree of *qi* supplementation is desired.
2.8 Liu Jun Zi Wan	Spleen *qi* deficiency with Phlegm Damp.
2.9 Xiang Sha Liu Jun Wan	Spleen *qi* deficiency with Phlegm Damp and *qi* stagnation disrupting the *qi* mechanism.
2.11 Bu Zhong Yi Qi Wan	Spleen *qi* deficiency with sinking *qi*. An important formula for prolapse, *wei qi* deficiency, sweating disorders and immune weakness.
2.12 Shen Ling Bai Zhu Wan	Spleen *qi* deficiency with Dampness pouring downwards as diarrhea.
2.16 Zi Sheng Wan	Spleen *qi* deficiency with food stagnation, and chronic Dysenteric Disorder with diarrhea and food sensitivities.
2.17 Jian Pi Wan	Spleen *qi* deficiency with food stagnation.
3.38 Sheng Mai San Wan	Lung and Spleen *qi* and *yin* deficiency chronic respiratory problems and post febrile weakness.
3.40 Bu Fei Wan	Lung *qi* and *wei qi* deficiency chronic respiratory problems.
3.41 Xu Han Ting	*Wei qi* deficiency sweating.
4.12 San Yuen Medical Pills	Kidney *qi* deficiency urinary dysfunction.
7.22 Shen Qi Da Bu Wan	Simple formula for Spleen and *wei qi* deficiency. Good added to any other constitutional formula when a degree of *qi* supplementation is desired.
7.23 Yu Ping Feng Wan	*Wei qi* deficiency sweating and weakness; immune weakness, frequent colds; allergies.
7.24 Panax Ginseng Extractum	General Lung and Spleen *qi* deficiency.

Qi and Blood deficiency

1.1 Ba Zhen Wan	The fundamental *qi* and Blood supplementing formula; for all *qi* and Blood deficient patterns.
1.3 Ba Zhen Yi Mu Wan	Similar to 1.1 Ba Zhen Wan with the addition of the mild Blood regulating action of motherwort. Good for *qi* and Blood deficiency with mild Blood stagnation.
7.16 Shi Quan Da Bu Wan	Similar to 1.1 Ba Zhen Wan with the addition of the warming herbs. Good for *qi* and Blood deficiency with Cold.
1.30 Tangkwei Essence of Chicken	An excellent and powerful woman's *qi* and Blood supplement with black boned chicken for extra richness. Wonderful for insufficient lactation, anemia, fatigue and postpartum recovery.
1.6 Bai Feng Wan	A general and popular woman's *qi* and Blood supplement with black boned chicken for extra richness. Excellent for anemia and fatigue during pregnancy.
1.7 Wu Ji Bai Feng Wan	Similar to 1.6 Bai Feng Wan with the addition of the *yang* and Blood enriching deer horn for extra warmth and *yang* supplementation.
1.8 Tong Ren Wu Ji Bai Feng Wan	Similar to 1.6 Bai Feng Wan with the addition herbs to clear deficiency Heat. Good for Heat symptoms such as flushing and sweats following childbirth.
1.9 Gui Pi Wan	Spleen *qi* and Heart Blood deficiency type bleeding disorders, weakness and fatigue, *shen* disturbances and menstrual disorders.
1.10 Dang Gui Jing	Similar to 1.1 Ba Zhen Wan in liquid extract.
1.19 Yang Rong Wan	Qi and Blood deficiency with Kidney *yang* deficiency type menstrual disorders and infertility.
1.31 Shih San Tai Pao Wan	Qi and Blood deficiency during pregnancy and for Wind Cold gan mao in patients with *qi* and Blood deficiency.

Qi and Blood deficiency (cont.)

5.5 Zhi Gan Cao Wan	Heart *qi* and Blood deficiency arrhythmias.
7.6 Yang Xue Sheng Fa Capsule 7.7 Qi Bao Mei Ran Dan	*Qi* and Blood deficiency and Liver and Kidney deficiency type alopecia and hair disorders.
7.18 Yang Ying Wan	Similar to 7.16 Shi Quan Da Bu Wan with the addition of herbs to clam the Heart and *shen*.
7.26 Reishi Mushroom	Powerful immune enhancing and regulating herb for allergic, auto-immune or neoplastic disorders.
8.3 An Shen Ding Zhi Wan	*Qi* and Blood deficiency *shen* disturbances.
8.6 Suan Zao Ren Tang Pian	Liver Blood and *yin* deficiency *shen* disturbances. Also useful for night sweats from the same etiology.
1.2 Si Wu Wan	The fundamental Blood supplementing formula, and the base unit from which all Blood supplements are built. Good for combining with a constitutional formula when an enhanced degree of Blood supplementation is desired.
13.3 Dang Gui Yin Zi Wan	Blood deficiency with Wind in the skin.

Yin deficiency

7.1 Liu Wei Di Huang Wan	Kidney *yin* deficiency. The base formula for all Kidney deficiency patterns. Most Kidney *yin* and *yang* formulae are derivations or modifications of this formula. Wide application in general Kidney *yin* deficiency patterns and as a preventative for those at risk of *yin* depletion.
1.23 Zhi Bai Ba Wei Wan	Kidney *yin* deficiency with deficient Heat causing flushing, sweats and low grade fever. Also for Kidney *yin* deficiency with chronic Damp Heat in the lower *jiao*. A variation of 7.1 Liu Wei Di Huang Wan.
7.2 Qi Ju Du Huang Wan	Kidney and Liver *yin* deficiency. A variation of 7.1 Liu Wei Di Huang Wan.
9.22 Ming Mu Di Huang Wan	Lung and Kidney *yin* deficiency chronic visual and eye disorders. A variation of 7.1 Liu Wei Di Huang. Wan.
3.35 Mai Wei Di Huang Wan	Lung and Kidney *yin* deficiency chronic respiratory disorders. A variation of 7.1 Liu Wei Di Huang Wan.
9.1 Er Long Zuo Ci Wan	Liver and Kidney *yin* deficiency ear and hearing problems. A variation of 7.1 Liu Wei Di Huang Wan.
7. 3 Zuo Gui Wan	Similar to 7.1 Liu Wei Di Huang Wan, without the draining components and with extra supplementing herbs. More supplementing to *yin* generally.
1.24 Er Xian Wan	Kidney *yin* and *yang* deficiency with deficient Heat, flushing and sweats. An important formula for the symptoms of menopause.
2.35 Yu Quan Wan	Spleen, Stomach and Kidney *yin* and *qi* deficiency. Used to assist in the treatment of diabetes.
3.33 Yang Yin Qing Fei Wan	Lung and Kidney *yin* deficiency and dryness chronic throat and respiratory disorders.
3.34 Bai He Gu Jin Wan	Lung and Kidney *yin* deficiency chronic respiratory disorders; hemoptysis.
3.38 Sheng Mai San Wan	Lung *qi* and *yin* deficiency chronic respiratory disorders; wheezing.

Yin deficiency (cont.)

5.5 Zhi Gan Cao Wan	Heart *yin*, *qi* and Blood deficiency arrhythmias.
6.8 Yin Guan Jian Wan	Liver *yin* deficiency with *qi* stagnation. Excellent for chronic reflux and upper abdominal pain patterns.
7.4 Da Bu Yin Wan	Kidney *yin* deficiency with bone steaming fever and chronic consumptive disorders.
7.5 Gu Ben Wan	Lung, Stomach and Kidney *yin* deficiency with dryness and insufficient fluids.
8.1 Tian Wang Bu Xin Dan	Heart and Kidney *yin* deficiency; also known as Heart and Kidney not communicating; chronic *shen* disturbances, insomnia, palpitations, anxiety.
8.2 Bai Zi Yang Xin Wan	*Yin* and Blood deficiency *shen* disturbances.
8.4 An Shen Bu Xin Wan	Heart *yin* and Blood deficiency with rising *yang* type *shen* and *hun* disturbances.
8.6 Suan Zao Ren Tang Pian	Liver *yin* and Blood deficiency *shen* disturbances. Also useful for night sweats from the same etiology.
15.5 Tian Ma Wan	Liver *yin* deficiency with Liver *yang* rising type headaches, hypertension, dizziness and tinnitus.
15.6 Zhen Gan Xi Feng Wan	Liver *yang* rising with mild *yin* deficiency type headaches, hypertension, transient ischemic attacks, dizziness and tinnitus.

Yang deficiency

7.9 Fu Gui Ba Wei Wan	The base formula for warming and supplementing Kidney *yang*. Widely applicable for all Kidney *yang* deficiency patterns.
7.10 You Gui Wan	Supplements and warms Kidney *yang* and *jing*.
1.20 Cu Yun Yu Tai Wan 1.21 Tiao Jing Cu Yun Wan	Warms Kidney *yang* for infertility and menstrual disorders; weak progesterone phase and anovulation disorders.
2.13 Li Zhong Wan	Spleen *yang* deficiency.
2.14 Li Chung Yuen Medical Pills	Spleen *yang* deficiency. Very warming formula for relatively severe Cold and very weak digestion.
2.15 Xiao Jian Zhong Wan	Spleen *yang* deficiency with abdominal pain and *yang* deficiency type low grade fever.
3.39 Yulin Bu Shen Wan	Lung and Kidney *yang* deficiency respiratory problems; Kidney not grasping Lung *qi*; chronic wheezing.
4.1 Zhen Wu Tang Wan	Heart and Kidney *yang* deficiency fluid metabolism disorders, urinary disfunction and edema.
4.11 Ba Ji Yin Yang Wan 4.13 Zi Shen Da Bu Capsule	Kidney *yang* deficiency urinary disfunction; nocturia, frequency, incontinence.
7.11 Deer Velvet 7.12 Lu Rong Jiao	Kidney *yang* and *jing* deficiency. Usually combined with an appropriate constitutional formula for developmental problems or infertility.
2.34 Cong Rong Bu Shen Wan	*Yang* deficiency chronic atonic constipation and impotence.
7.13 Huan Shao Dan	Heart and Kidney *qi* and *yang* deficiency type memory disorders and disorders of aging.
7.20 Cordyceps Essence of Chicken	An excellent general *yang* and *yin* supplement for Kidney and Lung deficiency patterns.

Glossary of Chinese Medicine Terminology

Abdominal masses (*ji ju* 积聚)

Abdominal masses (*ji ju*) are masses and lumps that can be palpated in the abdomen. They are classified into two types, *ji* and *ju* masses.

Ji masses are obvious and firm, clearly defined, fixed in location and often painful. *Ji* masses (commonly known as Blood masses) are a deeper level of disharmony than *ju* masses, and are usually associated with chronic disease states involving the Blood and elements of Blood stagnation. In general, they are associated with disorders of the *zang* organs. *Ji* masses are associated with structural change in tissues, for example, the proliferative growth of benign and malignant tumours, enlargement or swelling of organs, or inflammatory masses such as chronic appendicitis and diverticulitis.

Ju masses (commonly known as *qi* masses) are soft, ill defined on palpation, may or may not be painful, and tend to be intermittent. When present they move around, or come and go depending on the emotional state of the patient. They are associated with the *qi* and disorders associated with *qi* stagnation. *Ju* masses are generally mild functional disorders, that is, they are the result of functional changes in the tissues involved. They affect the *fu* organs, primarily the Stomach and Intestines.

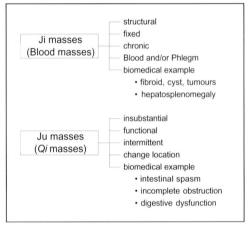

Accumulation disorder (*gan ji* 疳积)

Accumulation disorder is a feeding disorder that underlies a large number of infant illnesses, and at its most basic is simply the inability of the delicate digestive system of the child to cope with the amount of food it is called on to process. When very small, infants are essentially feeding tubes dedicated to converting food into baby at an astonishing rate. Infants digestive systems are working at full capacity and are easily overtaxed. Feeding too much food too quickly, or giving hard to digest foods (as in weaning to solids too early) can cause a backlog of partially digested materials that accumulate and ferment in the gut. As a by-product of this accumulation, Phlegm is produced. Once Phlegm is present, a host of other pathologies may result. Phlegm can gum up the digestive process further causing gastro-intestinal complaints. It can cause obstruction, pressure build up and the generation of heat and fever. It can accumulate in the lungs, ear or sinuses.

Many common, and some not so common, symptoms and disorders of infants such as fevers, convulsions, epilepsy, sleep and feeding problems, colic, reflux, vomiting, diarrhea and mucus congestion and its various complications (for example glue ear, asthma and allergies), may have their beginnings in accumulation disorder.

Basal Body Temperature (BBT)

The Basal Body Temperature is a method of graphically representing a woman's hormonal cycle, and serves as a relatively accurate diagnostic tool for detecting problems in either the follicular (*yin*) or luteal (*yang*) phase. During the *yin* phase (day 4-14) the channels most closely associated with reproduction, the *chong* and *ren* channels, fill with Blood (analogous to the thickening endometrium), and fertile mucus develops, a physical manifestation of the growing *yin*. The BBT remains steady around 36.1°C-36.6°C. At midcycle the resting body temperature of a normally ovulating woman rises by about 0.4°C, signalling the beginning of the *yang* phase, and this elevation in temperature is maintained for 10-12 days, falling again with the onset of menstruation. Fertility relies upon sufficient *yin* and adequately maintained *yang*, and variations in the balance of these physiological elements may contribute to infertility and other menstrual disorders. Charting variations from the normal pattern enables a very focused diagnosis and clear response, and is particularly useful when no clear pattern emerges from the standard diagnostic methods.

Bi syndrome (*bi zheng* 痹症)

Bi syndrome is a class of disorders characterized by pain, stiffness, numbness and paresthesia of muscles and joints. It is usually due to an invasion of the channel system by pathogenic Wind, Cold, Damp and/or Heat. *Bi* syndrome is usually a chronic disorder, but may be acute or have occasional acute flare-ups. *Bi* literally means to obstruct or block, and the term refers to the statement 'where there is obstruction there is pain'. It may correspond to biomedical conditions characterized primarily by pain, such as osteo-arthritis and rheumatoid arthritis, sciatica, infectious arthritis, lumbago, cervical and lumbar spondylosis, ankylosing spondylitis, rheumatic fever, systemic lupus erythematosus and polymyositis.

Blood (*xue* 血)

Blood in Chinese medicine is a technical term describing the function and structure of the fluid that circulates with *qi* through the channel and vessel network. While Blood shares many features in common with the biomedical understanding of blood, it has some unique characteristics. In addition to its general nutritive, lubricating and distributive function, Blood has a special relationship with certain parts of the body, in particular the eyes, the tendons, skin and hair. A variety of visual, neurological and dermatological diseases are associated with Blood problems. Blood also anchors *qi*, preventing it from 'floating' away. This is particularly important in relationship to the *shen*, the most rarefied form of *qi*, which relies on Blood for its foundation. Blood deficiency often causes *shen* disturbances such as insomnia, anxiety states and palpitations.

GLOSSARY

Blood stagnation (*xue yu* 血瘀)

Blood stagnation refers to a continuum of states in which the movement of Blood is in some way impeded or slowed. Blood stagnation syndrome can range from poor or obstructed blood circulation, in which drainage or supply of blood to a particular area is poor and the flow sluggish, to actual stasis, in which the blood circulation at some locus has ceased and a physical obstruction has formed further impeding circulation.

Blood stagnation may be localised or systemic, with a multitude of presentations depending on the site and the severity, and may be the result of a large variety of pathological processes. Trauma is a common cause of localised Blood stagnation, however stagnant *qi*, obstruction to circulation by external pathogens especially Cold, insufficient motive force behind the circulation, emotional factors and surgery may all contribute.

Herbs for treating stagnant Blood are of varying strengths, designated by different terms in Chinese. The mildest are those that quicken Blood (*huo xue* 活血), suitable for mild Blood stasis patterns characterized primarily by sluggish Blood flow. Herbs that quicken the Blood are gentle in action, well tolerated, have a low incidence of side effects and are generally suitable for prolonged use. Quickening implies not only restoring correct flow, but also promoting the normal physiological ability of the Blood to nourish and moisten. Stronger are the herbs that invigorate Blood (*xing xue* 行血) and disperse stagnant Blood (*qu yu* 祛瘀). These herbs are more dynamic in activating Blood flow and clearing obstructions from stopped Blood. Blood invigorating and stasis dispersing herbs have the potential for side effects in some cases. The strongest are herbs that break up stagnant Blood (*po xue* 破血). These are powerful and very dispersing to *zheng qi* as well as pathological accumulation of Blood, and are usually reserved for severe stasis patterns and masses. They have a high potential for side effects in inexperienced hands.

In biomedical terms, Blood stagnation syndrome may be associated with a wide variety of disorders, in particular those associated with diseases of the hepatic and cardiovascular systems, connective tissue diseases, sclerotic disorders and tumors.

Cold (*han* 寒)

Cold in Chinese medicine is a technical term describing the physical response of the body to environmental cold or insufficient generation of body heat due to *yang* deficiency. Cold has a tendency to 'freeze and constrict'–narrowing vessels and channel pathways, impeding the smooth circulation of *qi* and Blood. The typical features of a Cold pattern are generalized chilliness, coldness in the body either perceived by the patient or felt by the examining hand, fairly severe localised pain that is significantly improved with heat and thin clear watery discharges.

Cyclical treatment

Cyclical treatment refers to various methods aimed at restoring the menstrual cycle to normality, based on promoting the correct physiological event at the right time. For example, based on an average 28 day menstrual cycle, the main principle of treatment in the pre-ovulation phase (day 4-14) is to supplement *qi*, Blood and *yin*, as they are relatively deficient following menstruation and need to be replaced. At ovulation around day 14, the aim of treatment is to assist the transformation of *yin* into *yang*. The normal post ovulation phase (day 15-28) is characterized by an abundance of *yang*, *qi* and Blood until menstruation begins around day 28, therefore the general principle of treatment is to support *yang*, regulate *qi* and facilitate blood flow.

Dampness (*shi* 湿)

Dampness in Chinese medicine is a technical term describing a pathological entity that results in a variety of gastro-intestinal disorders, various swellings and discharges and a host of chronic and often difficult disease patterns. Dampness has two origins; it can seep into the body from the environment or it can be manufactured internally by internal organ dysfunction. In either case, Dampness seeps into muscles and cavities obstructing the circulation of *qi* and Blood and clogging the channels with its wet, heavy, cloying nature.

External Damp is usually an acute disorder, similar to Summerdamp and is associated with exposure to humid or wet environments, including damp housing. External Damp can also seep into the joints causing pain and swelling. Internally generated Damp is the product of poor digestive function, being the residue remaining from inefficient digestion and distribution of ingested material. Internal and external Damp causes symptoms such as abdominal distension, indigestion, flatulence, loss of appetite, nausea, heaviness, lethargy, poor concentration, slippery pulses and a thick, greasy tongue coat. Dampness is rather heavy and so tends to sink downwards, preferentially affecting the gastro-intestinal system and the lower body. Discharges such as heavy leukorrhea and diarrhea are physical manifestations of Damp.

There are several methods of dealing with Dampness, depending on its nature and location. Each method has a specific designation in Chinese. Dampness in the lower body may be eliminated through the urine (*li shui shen shi* 利水渗湿). Dampness affecting the Spleen and Stomach is either dried (*zao shi* 燥湿) with bitter parching herbs, or transformed (*hua shi* 化湿). Dampness is generally dried when it is introduced into the body by Damp natured food or by invasion of a Damp pathogen. Transformation of Dampness involves strengthening the function of the Spleen in processing food and fluids so Dampness is not created. Dampness in the upper body can be dispelled (*qu shi* 祛湿). Dispelling Dampness involves the use of fragrant or pungent herbs that stimulate Lung function and the Lungs regulatory control of the 'water passages'. By stimulating the Lungs, fluids and Dampness are sent down to the Kidneys for reprocessing and to the exterior to be eliminated with sweat.

Damp Heat (*shi re* 湿热)

Damp Heat is a pathogenic entity that combines the cloying nature of Dampness intermingled with the inflammatory stimulus of Heat. Damp Heat patterns are characterized by having symptoms of both Dampness (discharge, swellings, thick tongue coat) and Heat (redness, fever, inflammation). Damp Heat disorders are often associated with problems that cause offensive, coloured discharges.

Damp Heat can invade from the environment, in which case the associated disorder is typically acute and seasonal, or it can be generated internally by internal organ dysfunction or by ingestion of an excess of Damp Heat generating substances, such as alcohol and rich fatty foods. Uncomplicated Damp Heat is usually cleared (*qing shi re* 清湿热) with bitter cold herbs

Biomedical conditions that are frequently diagnosed as Damp Heat include acute hepatitis and cholecystitis, pelvic inflammatory disease, acute inflammatory arthritis, dysentery, cystitis and suppurative skin diseases.

Dysenteric disorder (*li ji* 痢疾)

Dysenteric disorder refers to a variety of patterns characterized by acute or chronic diarrhea with pus and/or blood in the stool. Dysenteric disorder overlaps with biomedical conditions such as amebic and bacterial dysentery, as well as chronic disorders such as ulcerative colitis and Crohn's disease.

Deficient patterns (*xu zheng* 虚证)

Deficient patterns in Chinese medicine are those characterized by insufficiency of a normal physiological substrate (*qi*, Blood, *yin* or *yang*, *jing*, body fluids), or hypofunction of an organ or metabolic system. Deficient patterns are usually chronic. In practice, deficient patterns are often complicated by excess patterns. For example, deficiency of Lung and *wei qi* (defensive *qi*) enables the penetration and lodgement of external pathogenic Wind into the body; deficiency of Liver Blood leads to a tendency to Liver *qi* stagnation; Spleen *qi* deficiency often leads to the accumulation of Dampness.

Excess patterns (*shi zheng* 实证)

Excess patterns are characterized by the presence of a pathogen of some type in the body (Wind, Heat, Cold, Damp, Phlegm or Fire), or by a pathological accumulation of normal physiological substrates, i.e. *qi* and/or Blood, either systemically or at some locus. Excess patterns are often acute but may be chronic. Excess patterns often have a degree of deficiency at their root, for example, Spleen *qi* deficiency easily gives rise to an accumulation of Dampness or Phlegm.

Food stagnation (*shi ji* 食积)

Food stagnation is an important and often overlooked etiological component in a host of gastro-intestinal and other disorders. Food stagnation patterns have traditionally been underrated in TCM textbooks, disregarded as a mechanical event related to a single episode of overeating. In reality, food stagnation is usually more insidious and patients can become conditioned to ignoring, or may not even be conscious of, the traditional symptoms—abdominal and epigastric distension and discomfort, nausea and vomiting, belching, bad breath and flatulence. The eating patterns that give rise to food stagnation may be so ingrained that patients cease to be aware of the symptoms, or the symptoms experienced are considered to be normal.

By habitually overloading the Spleen and Stomach and exceeding their capacities to process the food ingested, a cycle is begun that can have profound ramifications. Firstly, instead of being sent through the intestine, the food lingers longer than it should, clogging the digestive system. The stagnant food may produce Heat. The Spleen and Stomach are weakened, further inhibiting their abilities to perform their digestive tasks efficiently. The weakened Spleen produces Dampness which in turn may be congealed into Phlegm by the Heat. The Phlegm or Phlegm Heat so produced can then affect other systems. For example, Phlegm accumulation (with or without the frequently complicating Blood stagnation) in the chest and cardiovascular system is a major cause of angina and heart disease; Phlegm in the respiratory system can contribute to asthma, allergies and sinus problems. In addition, some neurological conditions such as tremors, anxiety states, insomnia, vertigo and paralysis, and dermatological disorders such as cysts, ulcerations, and chronic sores and swellings may be linked to Phlegm, Phlegm Heat and other complicating pathogens produced by food stagnation.

Gan mao 感冒

Gan mao is the Chinese expression for the common cold. In TCM terms it can refer to any external invasion that causes acute symptoms consistent with colds or flu–fever and chills, sneezing, cough, sore throat, myalgia and so on.

Gu syndrome (*gu zheng* 蛊证)

Gu syndrome is a complex type of systemic infection involving a host with a weakened constitution in a pathological equilibrium with a lingering pathogen, either viral, amebic, vermiform, bacterial or fungal. *Gu* pathogens have been likened to 'oil seeping into flour–they are everywhere and cannot be separated out' (Fruehauf 1998). Treatment of *gu* syndrome is frequently lengthy, requiring months or even years. Clinically, patients with this type of problem often appear to be clearly *qi* deficient, or *qi* deficient with accumulated Dampness, but they typically get worse with standard *qi* supplementing therapies. The symptoms are typical of Spleen disorder–chronic diarrhea or alternating bowel habits, abdominal distension and pain, nausea, loss of appetite or ravenous hunger or odd food cravings, muscle aches, weakness and physical and mental exhaustion.

Heart (*xin* 心)

The organ system referred to as the Heart incorporates the cardiovascular system and certain aspects of the neurological system and higher consciousness. Functional weakness of the Heart (*qi* or *yang* deficiency) causes circulatory problems and various types of arrhythmia. In addition, the Heart is closely associated with maintenance of the *shen*, and disturbances of Heart function may give rise to various disturbances of consciousness, including manic behaviour, anxiety, panic attacks, palpitations, depression and insomnia.

Hun 魂

The *hun* is a subgroup of the *shen* closely associated with the Liver organ system. Functionally, the *hun* is closely associated with certain aspects of the sleep wake cycle, resoluteness, determination, and sensitivity to subtle elements of the human experience. Patients with *hun* disturbances may experience insomnia, prophetic dreams, sleepwalking, timidity or anxiety. Those with *hun* predominance may experience a kind of sensitive insight that may be described as 'extra sensory'.

Indeterminate gnawing hunger (*cao za* 嘈杂)

Indeterminate gnawing hunger is an uncomfortable sensation in the epigastric region that mimics hunger without the patient wanting to eat. Patients will often wake in the middle of the night with a nagging discomfort in the pit of the stomach, feeling the need to eat something but not knowing what. Often associated with peptic ulcer disease or chronic gastritis.

Jiao 焦

The trunk of the body is divided into three functional units or *jiao*, each with its own specific contents and physiological activity. The translation of the character is usually rendered as 'burning space' or 'heater', as in the *san jiao*–the triple heater. What this implies is that dynamic physiological activity, including the generation and maintenance of body heat, occurs within these distinct units. The Heart and Lungs are located in the upper *jiao* above the diaphragm, and as a unit are responsible for the motive force behind the circulation of *qi* and Blood. The Spleen and Stomach are located in the middle *jiao*, and the functional activity of digestion and acquisition of *qi*, and thus the Spleen and Stomach, is often referred to as middle *jiao qi*. The Liver and Kidneys are situated, in a functional sense, in the lower *jiao* and are the foundation of the constitutional strength of the individual.

Jing 精

Jing is the fundamental substance inherited from the parents that confers the ability to grow, develop and reproduce. The quality and quantity of *jing* inherited determines the constitutional strength, and to a certain extent, the duration of life of an individual. *Jing* also provides the ground substance from which the bones and 'marrow' (here the brain and spinal cord) are formed. *Jing* is stored in the Kidney system and is closely associated with Kidney function. Deficiency of *jing* leads to disorders characterized by bony deformity, learning difficulties, failure to thrive, growth problems, infertility and disorders of ageing.

Kidneys (*shen* 肾)

The organ system referred to as the Kidneys incorporates the genito-urinary system, fluid metabolism, the ability to reproduce, and the development and maintenance of the bones, central nervous system and ears. The Kidneys are the foundation of constitutional health, the source of the body's *yin* and *yang* and the storehouse of inherited *jing*. The *yang* aspect of Kidney function underwrites all dynamic *yang* physiology, including fluid metabolism, digestion and circulation. The complement of *yang*, Kidney *yin*, maintains the integrity of the structural components upon which the *yang* acts and is the basis of the body's lubricating and moistening fluids, including fertile mucus, vaginal lubrication, prostatic and synovial fluids. Kidney deficiency problems include those associated with the ageing process, disorders of fluid metabolism and reproduction, energy weakness, some skeletal, neurological and aural disorders, loss of structural integrity as occurs in some atrophic disorders, and congenital abnormalities.

Lin syndrome (*lin zheng* 淋证)

Lin syndrome, generally translated as painful urination syndrome, describes a variety of disorders characterized by pain associated with urination. The key feature in *lin* syndrome is pain, and it is the presence of pain that differentiates this group of disorders from other urinary disorders. Biomedically, painful urination syndrome includes such diseases as urinary tract infections, urinary calculi, pyelonephritis, tumours of the urogenital system, prostatic diseases, chyluria and albuminuria. There are six classifications of *lin* syndrome.

- Heat or Damp Heat *lin* syndrome is clinically the most common variety, and is characterized by being acute and by rather intense burning pain upon urination.
- Stone (or sand) *lin* syndrome is characterized by the presence of urinary calculi, and, depending on their location, intense radiating pain and/or obstructed urination.
- *Qi lin* syndrome is traditionally divided into two types, deficiency (of *qi*) and excess (*qi* stagnation). The deficiency type is associated with Spleen *qi* deficiency and often follows recurrent Heat types that have not been treated, or have been treated with antibiotics or excessively cold natured herbs. It is characterized by a dragging discomfort which is relieved by pressure, or a feeling of burning that improves with warmth and pressure. The excess type is characterized by discomfort during or following urination aggravated or initiated by stress and emotional upset.
- Blood *lin* syndrome is painful urination with bleeding.
- Cloudy or turbid *lin* syndrome is painful urination with cloudy or milky urine.
- Exhaustion *lin* syndrome is chronic and recurrent, initiated or aggravated by sex, overexertion and fatigue. It is characterized by incomplete or dribbling urination, lumbar pain and weakness and mild dysuria that is often worse following urination.

Liver (*gan* 肝)

The organ system referred to as the Liver incorporates the functional activity of the Liver, as well as the tissues and structures traversed by the channel pathways of the Liver and it's partner, the Gallbladder. These structures include the reproductive system, external genitals, flanks, breasts, throat and eyes. Functionally, the Liver is responsible for the regular and uninterrupted distribution of *qi* and Blood. It is the coordinator of the other organ systems, ensuring a steady supply of *qi* where and when it is needed. Failure of *qi* distribution leads to localised accumulations and obstructions. In pathological terms this results in hypertonicity of the affected tissues with consequent decrease in perfusion and nutrition. The Liver is very susceptible to emotional turmoil and stress, and conversely, malfunction of the Liver can give rise to various emotional or psychological problems, most notably depression and mood swings.

Lungs (*fei* 肺)

The organ system referred to as the Lungs incorporates the respiratory system, the skin and large intestine. The Lungs perform the function of respiration and as such are part of the energy generating system of the body, in concert with the Spleen. The Lungs are a fundamental component of the immune system via the media of defensive *qi* or *wei qi*, and play an important role in the distribution and metabolism of fluids. Healthy Lung function facilitates elimination of waste products. Weakness of the Lungs leads to various respiratory and energy problems, immune weakness, poor elimination, sweating disorders, some skin disorders and problems of the large intestine.

Malarial Disorder (*nue ji* 疟疾)

Malarial disorders are a collection of conditions characterized by alternating fever and chills or a cyclical fever pattern. The diseases that fall into this category include true *Plasmodium* malaria, but also Dengue fever, Ross River fever and numerous fevers of the subtropic and tropical regions.

Masses and nodules

There are three main types of mass defined by Chinese medicine, *qi*, Phlegm and Blood stagnation. They may occur anywhere in the body.

Qi masses are intermittent, can vary in location, are quite soft upon palpation and will generally dissipate with prolonged pressure. They are usually associated with a functional disorder of an organ or tissue.

Phlegm masses do not move location, feel smooth, rubbery and round on palpation, and are usually not painful. Phlegm masses often occur in the neck, extremities and gynecological system.

Blood masses are hard, fixed in location and feel very firm or irregular on palpation. They are often painful, especially when palpated. Blood masses can be associated with relatively benign lesions such as benign gynecological tumours, chronic inflammatory masses like diverticulosis, chronic salpingitis, ulcerative colitis, chronic appendicitis and more sinister problems including malignant tumors.

Paradoxical pulse

The paradoxical pulse is so called because it is the opposite of the pulse expected for the pattern it reflects. The paradoxical pulse is a very clear indicator of Liver invading Spleen and Stomach patterns, where the expected pulse is an excess pulse–wiry, strong etc., at the left middle position (Liver) and a deficient pulse–weak, thready etc., at the right middle position (Spleen/Stomach). The paradoxical pulse presents as a large bulge at the right middle position and a clear dip at the left middle position.

Primary Pathological Triad (PPT)

The Primary Pathological Triad represents three patterns of pathology which are frequently found to occur simultaneously, are tightly interlinked and mutually engendering. The triad comprises Spleen deficiency, Liver *qi* stagnation and Heat, usually Damp Heat or stagnant Heat. In addition to the basic triad of pathology, there may be further complication by Blood and/or *yin* deficiency, Blood stagnation, disruption to communication between the Heart and Kidney, and Phlegm.

The three main patterns of the PPT reinforce each other in the following way. Liver *qi* stagnation impacts on the Spleen and Stomach, weakening their functions and encouraging the generation of Dampness. Dampness is heavy in nature and tends to sink downwards to the lower body and the depths of the gastro-intestinal system. *Qi* stagnation, and the increase in *qi* pressure behind an obstruction, tend to generate Heat. Stagnant Heat, once present and applied to pre-existing Dampness, creates Damp Heat. Dampness on its own, as a consummate stagnator, can also generate Heat and become Damp Heat.

The Western lifestyle seems to be particularly adept at producing the PPT. A combination of stress, inappropriate diet and eating habits, alcohol, sedentary occupations, and overuse of pharmaceuticals, in particular antibiotics and analgesics, may all contribute.

The frequency of this combination of pathologies and the complex interactions

GLOSSARY

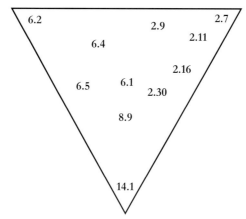

Figure 1. Mapping of selected formulae according to their relative action on the PPT.

Liver *qi* stagnation

Spleen and Stomach *qi* deficiency

6.2
2.9
2.7
6.4
2.11
6.5 6.1
2.16
2.30
8.9
14.1

6.1 Xiao Chai Hu Tang Wan
8.9 Chai Hu Long Gu Mu Li Wan
6.4 Xiao Yao Wan
6.5 Jia Wei Xiao Yao Wan
2.11 Bu Zhong Yi Qi Wan
2.9 Xiang Sha Liu Jun Wan

14.1 Huang Lian Jie Du Wan
6.2 Si Ni San Wan
2.7 Si Jun Zi Wan
2.16 Zi Sheng Wan
2.30 Chen Xiang Hua Qi Wan

between them is the reason the 'harmonising' category of prescriptions is the most widely used group of formulations worldwide. Harmonising prescriptions combine herbs with several different, often opposing, actions. They are typically complex, utilising pungent hot, bitter cold and sweet warm substances to disperse stagnation, clear Heat and supplement *qi*. As a group, the harmonizing formulae work on various aspects of the PPT, with varying degrees of emphasis.

Successful treatment of the triad of pathological patterns requires that each pattern be addressed at the same time, otherwise the condition will either not improve or will quickly relapse. For example, if only the Spleen is treated, the repeated insult by invasive Liver *qi* will continue to weaken it and the Spleen will be damaged again. If only Damp Heat is treated, the weakened Spleen will continue to produce Dampness and will likely be damaged by the bitter cold herbs or substances used to clear the Damp Heat.

The major prescriptions for treating the various elements of the PPT can be mapped according to the hierarchy of therapeutic features they display. Figure 1 charts a selection of prescriptions commonly used for this purpose. Their position inside the triangle indicates the relative balance of the formula's activity on Spleen *qi* deficiency, Liver *qi* stagnation and the Heat component. For example, **6.1 Xiao Chai Hu Tang Wan** can be mapped in the centre of the triangle, as it is equally balanced between the three major principles of treatment. It strengthens the Spleen and supplements *qi*, regulates Liver *qi* and clears Damp Heat, in about equal proportions.

Phlegm (*tan* 痰)

Phlegm in Chinese medicine is a technical term describing a pathological product resulting from the stagnation and congealing of body fluids or Dampness. There are two broad types of Phlegm, material (or substantial) and latent (or insubstantial). Material Phlegm has physical form and can be observed in the thin or thick sputum of acute and chronic respiratory problems, the congesting mucus of sinus disease, and the rounded rubbery masses of various benign nodules, such as lipomas and thyroid nodules. Latent Phlegm has no physical form, instead it is detected through the symptoms and constitutional patterns it produces. The symptoms of latent Phlegm are mostly associated with its inhibiting effect on the clear expression of the *shen*– disturbances of consciousness, anxiety states, insomnia, foggy headedness and palpitations–and its cloying effects on the circulation and distribution of *yang*, *qi* and Blood.

There are several methods of dealing with Phlegm, depending on it's nature and location. Phlegm in the Lungs is usually expelled by promoting expectoration (*qu tan* 祛痰). Phlegm can be transformed (*hua tan* 化痰) by strengthening fluid metabolism and the organ systems responsible for production of the Phlegm in the first place. Phlegm that accumulates in masses and lumps can be dispersed (*xiao tan* 消痰) with pungent herbs, or, if particularly hard, softened first (*ruan jian* 软坚) with salty substances.

Qi 气

Qi is the functional component of Chinese physiology. *Qi* is required and necessary to enable people to perform the various tasks associated with life; gathering and harvesting food, transforming the *qi* of the raw materials into a form the human body can use, performing the daily maintenance tasks of respiration, protection from pathogens and generation of body heat. All the organ systems rely on a steady supply of *qi* in order to be able to perform their various functions. An inadequate supply of *qi* usually means that one or more systems is in a state of hypofunction.

Qi can be supplemented (*bu qi* 补气) by strengthening the source of *qi*, the Spleen and Lungs. The distribution of *qi* can be facilitated by using pungent herbs to regulate *qi* (*li qi* 理气), spread Liver *qi* (*shu gan jie yu* 疏肝解郁), invigorate *qi* (*xing qi* 行气) or break up stagnant *qi* (*po qi* 破气). Regulating *qi* is the mildest method and generally applies to stagnant *qi* in the Spleen, Stomach and Intestines. Spreading Liver *qi* and invigorating *qi* are stronger, and are utilized when Liver dysfunction leads to uneven distribution of *qi*, especially in the structures of the Liver and Gallbladder organ systems. Breaking up stagnant *qi* is the strongest, utilizing intensely pungent herbs to powerfully disperse pathological accumulation of *qi*, often in the form of masses of lumps.

Qi mechanism (*qi ji* 气机)

The *qi* mechanism is one of the fundamental axes of normal physiological function in the body. Essentially, it is the dynamic created by the natural tendency of Spleen *qi* to rise ('the raising of the pure'), and Stomach *qi* to descend ('descent of the turbid'). Spleen and Stomach *qi* acts as the dynamo, or pivot, of ascending and descending throughout the body, thus the *qi* mechanism, in association with the Liver, facilitates the general movement and distribution of *qi* throughout the body.

Disruption to the *qi* mechanism features prominently in many gastro-intestinal problems. Nausea and vomiting are associated with blockage to, and consequent rising of, Stomach *qi*; abdominal distension occurs when *qi* fails to descend and accumulates in the middle *jiao*. Constipation often reflects a failure of the descent of Stomach *qi*.

There are two main types of disruption to the *qi* mechanism, excess and deficient. The excess type of *qi* blockage is usually related to Liver *qi* stagnation and its retarding action on the movement of Spleen and Stomach *qi*. Pathogenic accumulations, such as Dampness, Phlegm or stagnant food can also obstruct *qi* and disrupt the *qi* mechanism. Less commonly, excess *qi* blockage may be associated with obstruction of Lung *qi*. Lung *qi* is spread to the surface and should descend. When this process is blocked by a pathogen, the subsequent accumulation of *qi* in the Lungs has a disruptive effect on the ascent of Spleen *qi*. The result is disruption of the *qi* mechanism, the natural movement of *qi*, and consequent accumulation of *qi* in the middle *jiao*.

The deficient type of *qi* mechanism dysfunction is due to a weakness of middle *jiao qi*. Put simply, there is insufficient motive force behind the rising of Spleen *qi*, or the descent of Stomach *qi*. Deficient type *qi* blockage will often be further complicated by excess accumulation. The obstruction in this case occurs because the *qi* is too feeble to move adequately, or the weakened Spleen/Stomach invite the attention and overcontrol of Liver *qi*, or because they are too weak to process food adequately so that food or Dampness and Phlegm accumulate.

Shan disorders (*shan qi* 疝气)

Shan disorders are conditions associated with pain and/or swelling of the lower abdomen and external genitals, in particular the testicles and scrotum. A number of biomedical conditions may be diagnosed as *shan qi*, including some types of inguinal or scrotal herniae, varicocele and hydrocele, tumours of the testicles, testicular torsion, orchitis, eczema and chronic inflammatory conditions with pain, such as chronic prostatitis. There are different classifications of *shan qi*.

• Cold *shan qi* (*han shan qi*) is characterized by coldness, shrinkage and firmness of the testicles.

• Watery *shan qi* (*shui shan qi*) is an accumulation of fluid in the scrotum (hydrocele), or swollen veins in the scrotum (varicocele), or eczema.

• *Qi shan qi* is distension and pain in the testicles, perineum and lower abdomen, with an obvious emotional component.

• Foxy *shan qi* (*hu shan qi*) occurs when a portion of the intestine is intermittently squeezed through an aperture or weakness in the abdominal wall, usually through the inguinal canal into the testicles. A type of hernia.

• Hard *shan qi* (*tui shan qi*) is a hard, solid mass with loss of testicular sensation.

Shao Yang syndrome (*shao yang bing* 少阳病)

Shao yang syndrome is a pattern of disharmony characterized by the residence of a pathogen in the second of the six levels (*see* Six level disease differentiation, p.639), the *shao yang* level. The *shao yang* is considered to be neither external, that is, on the surface of the body, the *tai yang* level, nor internal, affecting the internal organs, *yang ming* and the three *yin* levels. It represents a transitional zone where pathogens can hide and get locked away, sometimes for prolonged periods. From a clinical perspective, numerous common post acute and chronic infections, as well as a host of hepatic and gastro-intestinal disorders may manifest as variations of *shao yang* syndrome.

Shen 神

Usually translated as 'spirit' or 'mind', the *shen* is at the most rarefied end of the spectrum of *qi*. The most condensed is *jing*; in between are the various functional types of *qi* (*zong qi*, *wei qi*, *zang fu qi* etc.). These three aspects of *qi* (*jing*, *qi*, *shen*) are termed the 'three treasures' and are the foundation of Chinese physiology and at the root of Daoist meditation techniques. Indeed, it is the transformation of *jing* into *shen* that preoccupies some of the daoist and other esoteric schools of Chinese philosophical thought and practice.

The *shen* plays a key role in higher mental functions, including many of the intellectual and spiritual aspects of consciousness. In practical terms, the *shen* is most closely associated with our conscious awareness, and is essentially our ability to perceive, interact and communicate with our world clearly. In addition, the *shen* and the Heart share an intimate and interdependent relationship. TCM describes the Heart as the residence of the *shen*. *Shen* pathology is associated with disturbances of consciousness and perception, sleep, higher mental function and some aspects of Heart function.

Six level disease differentiation (*liu jing bian zheng* 六经辨证)

Six level theory, elucidated in the magnificent *Shang Han Lun* (Treatise on Diseases with Fever, Han dynasty, circa 200AD) by Zhang Zhong Jing, describes the events that occur as a pathogen, usually Wind Cold, drives into the body, interacting with the body's *zheng qi*. The *Shang Han Lun* systematised the prevailing concepts of feverish diseases, the most significant cause of mortality of the time, into a series of levels through which a pathogen can penetrate, each successive level deeper in the body than the one preceding it. In the three *yang* levels, the body's *qi* is generally intact and able to put up a defence against the pathogen, hence the key manifestation of this stage of the conflict, the fever. By the time a pathogen reaches the internal organs, the *zheng qi* has been significantly weakened, and the remaining levels represent various aspects of internal organ deficiency. The symptoms characteristic of each level are due to the interaction and relative strengths of the pathogen and the body's *zheng qi*. Zhang clearly laid out the clinical features of the interaction between the pathogen and the body at each level, with common variations, and designed diagnostic strategies and treatments which are still in use today.

The six levels are the *tai yang, shao yang, yang ming, tai yin, shao yin* and *jue yin*. The *tai yang* level is the most superficial, generally the first point of contact between a pathogen and the body, and corresponds anatomically to the channel system, skin and muscles. The *shao yang* level represents a transitional zone between the interior of the body and the exterior (*see* above). The *yang ming* is the most superficial part of the interior, corresponding to the *yang fu* organ systems of the Stomach and Large Intestine. The *tai yin* level is the first true internal level as it represents the *yin* organ systems of the Spleen and Lungs. The *shao yin* level is the most dangerous of the *yin* levels, representing as it does a significant deficiency of Heart and Kidney *yang* or *yin*. The final level, the *jue yin* represents a complex of heat and cold signs and symptoms, and primarily involves the Liver.

Zhang's achievement was far reaching—of the 100 or so formulae he describes, a significant number are still being used today, including many in this book, and are among the most popular and effective.

Spleen (*pi* 脾)

In Chinese medicine the organ system referred to as the Spleen incorporates the functions attributed to the Spleen organ, as well as the tissues and structures along the pathway of the Spleen channel, the muscles and oral cavity. The Spleen performs several fundamental processes that are critical to daily functional maintenance and metabolism. The Spleen is the basis of digestion, the harvesting of nutrients and the transformation of the raw materials of food into usable physiological *qi*. The Spleen plays a crucial role in maintaining vascular integrity and preventing leakage of Blood from the circulatory system. Healthy Spleen function maintains muscular tone and bulk and provides the complimentary force to counter the relentless pull of gravity. Spleen weakness can lead to a variety of digestive, metabolic and energy problems, bleeding disorders, muscular weakness and wasting and prolapse of various structures.

Sudden Turmoil Disorder (*huo luan* 霍乱)

Sudden Turmoil Disorder is a group of conditions characterised by acute and usually violent simultaneous vomiting and diarrhea. There may or may not be abdominal pain. The most common cause is an acute invasion of a strong, epidemic or pestilential pathogen that disrupts the *qi* mechanism. As the pressure builds up due to the obstruction in the middle *jiao*, the conglomerate of turbid untransformed materials and pathogen is forcefully ejected upwards and downwards.

Even though the pathogenic influence is usually quite strong, patients with Sudden Turmoil Disorder can present with varying degrees of disharmony, from mild to severe. The common types in the Western clinic are generally relatively mild and self limiting, but should always be treated to fully clear the offending pathogen, and thereby preventing recurrence. Patients with Sudden Turmoil Disorder may be diagnosed with biomedical conditions such as acute gastroenteritis associated with infection by numerous bacterial, viral or parasitic agents, including *Campylobacter*, *Salmonella*, *Shigella*, *Giardia* and *Cryptosporidium*, gastric 'flu', food poisoning or cholera.

Summerdamp (*shu bing* 暑病)

Summerdamp is an acute disorder primarily affecting the gastro-intestinal system. It tends to be seasonal, most frequently occurring during the humid months of late summer or during periods of hot humid weather. Summerdamp is always an external environmental pathogen and is often epidemic, sweeping through offices and schools. It has a tendency to linger or recur if not promptly or correctly resolved. The typical features are nausea and vomiting, urgent diarrhea, muscle aches, foggy headedness and malaise.

Surgery, using patent medicines in association with

Certain patent medicines can be used to enhance recovery from, and decrease the risk of complications of, surgical procedures. Surgery of any type disrupts the circulation of *qi* and Blood and leaves a residue of stagnant Blood. Certain surgical procedures appear to damage *yang qi*. There are two main groups of patent medicines that are frequently used, depending on the constitution and medical condition of the patient, and the nature of the surgery. These are the supplementing and the Blood invigorating medicines. For patients who are weakened from illness or in some way deficient in the lead up to a surgical procedure, building *qi*, Blood or *yang* can be useful to help them to better weather the trauma of the procedure and to hasten recovery during convalescence. This is especially the case in the elderly and debilitated, and those who tend to heal slowly. A gentle *yang qi* supplementing approach, used both before and after a procedure is also useful for those undergoing abdominal surgery, which can in some cases damage Spleen *yang qi*. Common preparatory formulae include **1.1 Ba Zhen Wan, 7.16 Shi Quan Da Bu Wan, 1.6 Bai Feng Wan, 2.11 Bu**

Zhong Yi Qi Wan, **2.12 Shen Ling Bai Zhu Wan** and **2.13 Li Zhong Wan**.

For more robust patients, those having surgery following a traumatic injury or broken bones, and for those prone to keloid scarring, quickening and invigorating the Blood clearly accelerates healing, promotes osteogenesis and decreases the likelihood of excessive fibrosis. The famous hemostatic medicine **10.1 Yunnan Paiyao** has been used and studied extensively in China in this regard, and has been found to significantly decrease post-surgical blood loss, while improving circulation to encourage and accelerating healing. Other suitable medicines, drawn mostly from the Cardiovascular and Pain and Trauma sections of the text, can be found under the relevant headings in the index.

Even though supplementing and Blood invigorating formulae are the most commonly used medicines to enhance healing and recovery around surgery, practitioners are not restricted to these groups. Other medicines can be used as appropriate. For example, patent medicines that clear Damp Heat from the Gallbladder are often useful in the run up to a cholecystectomy or keyhole gallstone removal.

In all cases however, patent medicines should be discontinued at least one week prior to the surgical procedure. This is especially important for medicines which influence blood viscosity and clotting time. This includes not only Blood regulating medicines, but also those with high doses of ginseng. The appropriate medicine can be resumed once the patient is able to ingest the medicine in the convalescent stage.

Toxic Heat (*re du* 热毒)

Toxic Heat refers to two types of disorder. The first is a severe localised accumulation of Heat or Damp Heat that reaches a level of intensity sufficient to destroy tissue and create pus. Abscesses and carbuncles, acute appendicitis or diverticulitis and suppurative tonsillitis are all examples of localised Toxic Heat disorders. Toxic Heat patterns may also be systemic, in which case they are observed in the generalized malaise, sickness, nausea and vomiting that accompanies serious infections like lymphangitis, lymphadenitis, bacteremia and septicemia.

Warm disease (*wen bing* 温病)

Warm diseases are acute disorders caused by invasion of powerful external pathogens, usually occurring in epidemics and affecting the weak and strong alike. They superficially resemble simple Wind Heat patterns in the early stages. Unlike simple Wind Heat disorders however, quick intervention does not always bring a quick cure, and the pathogen often swiftly penetrates deep into the body through the theoretical four levels into the deepest reaches of the body. The four levels are the *wei* level, corresponding to the surface, an external disorder, the *qi* level involving the Lungs, chest, Stomach and Intestines, the *ying* or nutritive level, and the Blood level. By the time a pathogen has entered the *ying* and Blood levels, the disorder is serious, and is characterized by febrile rashes, disordered consciousness and convulsions. Warm diseases include biomedical conditions such as meningitis and encephalitis, febrile rashes, scarlet fever, measles, chicken pox and numerous tropical fevers.

Wei syndrome (*wei zheng* 痿证)

Wei syndrome is a class of disorders characterized by wasting and weakness of the muscles of the extremities. There is usually no pain associated with the wasting. Disorders like multiple sclerosis, muscular dystrophy and polio may be diagnosed as *wei* syndrome.

Wind (*feng* 风)

Wind in Chinese medicine is a pathological entity that gives rise to disorders characterized by sudden onset, rapid development, mobile symptoms and involuntary movements and spasms. There are two types of Wind defined by Chinese medicine, external and internal. External Wind invades the body from the environment, usually in combination with Cold, Heat or Dampness, and is implicated in acute colds, influenza, gastric flu and some skin disorders. External Wind is usually dispelled from the body with diaphoretic herbs (*qu feng* 祛风). Internal Wind is a more complex phenomena, being generated by pathological processes within the body. There are three common mechanisms that can create internal Wind, *yin* deficiency, Blood deficiency and extreme Heat. Internal Wind is extinguished (*xi feng* 熄风) by supplementing *yin* and Blood, clearing Heat, or applying heavy mineral substances or herbs that sedate.

• **Yin deficiency**: The body's *yin* is the anchor that secures *yang* and provides a counterweight to *yang's* active and rising nature. At some critical point of deficiency, *yin* is unable to restrain Liver *yang* which, at a certain point of volatility and movement, becomes Wind. This type of Wind can be sudden and catastrophic–it is the type of Wind that can cause severe dizziness, to the point of Wind stroke, leading to hemiplegia or death. It typically follows years of *yin* depletion.

• **Blood deficiency**: This type of Wind is similar in etiology to the *yin* deficiency in that the Wind is generated by failure of the Blood to anchor *qi*–when *qi* moves without the grounding control of Blood, a mild form of Wind is generated. Blood deficient Wind is more likely to cause mild rhythmic tics, tremors, fasiculations and spasms.

• **Extreme Heat**: Because Heat and movement are closely related physiologically, at a certain level of intensity, internal Heat can generate sufficient movement to become Wind. This most frequently manifests as the convulsions of a high fever.

Wind edema (*feng shui* 风水)

Wind edema is due to Wind disrupting the Lungs' normal fluid descending and dispersing function. The fluids that should be directed to the skin and the Kidneys though the 'water passages', back up and accumulate, primarily in the face and upper *jiao*. The main feature is sudden onset of orbital and facial edema. In the early stages the eyes, then the face, become swollen and puffy. Swelling of the limbs and rest of the body may follow. The edema generally develops quickly. This is a *yang* type of edema. The Wind can combine with either Cold, Heat or Dampness producing a variable secondary symptom picture. With Cold, there are generalized muscle and joint aches, cold and wind intolerance, no sweating, chills, mild fever, scanty urination, dyspnea or wheezing, cough, a thin, white tongue coat and a floating, tight pulse. With Heat, there is fever, aversion to wind, sore throat, cough, scanty concentrated urine, a red tipped tongue with a thin, yellow coat and a floating, rapid pulse. With Damp, there is heaviness and lethargy, swelling in the lower body and a floating, soggy pulse.

Edema of this type may follow an acute upper respiratory tract infection, or disorders such as acute boils and sores, acute (post streptococcal) glomerulonephritis, or tooth extraction. It tends predominantly to affect young people, although older people may also be affected.

Wind stroke (*zhong feng* 中风)

The TCM classification of Wind stroke is closely analogous to the biomedically defined cerebrovascular accident (CVA), although it also incorporates some non central nervous system conditions such as Bell's Palsy. There are two main classifications of Wind Stroke:

- **Channel stroke** is a mild type of Wind stroke that only affects the channels and does not cause loss of consciousness. The main manifestations are facial paralysis, dysphasia and hemiplegia. The general prognosis for recovery is good, or at least better than when consciousness is lost.
- **Organ** (*zang fu*) **stroke** is a serious disorder thought to involve severe damage to the internal organs. This type causes loss of consciousness as well as hemiplegia, facial paralysis and dysphasia. This type frequently leads to permanent disability or death.

Xiao Ke 消渴

The term *xiao ke* is usually translated literally as 'wasting and thirsting', a description that refers to the main features that were observed in patients before insulin treatment became widespread–intense thirst, copious urination, frequent hunger and weight loss. In biomedical terms *xiao ke* is broadly analogous to diabetes mellitus or, occasionally, diabetes insipidus.

Yang 阳

Yang is a technical term describing all the functional activity of body's tissues and organ systems, and the energetic principle responsible for generation of body heat. Insufficient *yang* leads to problems associated with severe hypofunction of tissues and organ systems and insufficient thermogenesis. Patients tend to be weak, sluggish and cold. Many disorders may be associated with insufficient *yang*, in particular reproductive problems, fluid and urinary disorders, circulatory and some endocrine disorders.

Yang Ming syndrome (*yang ming bing* 阳明病)

Yang ming syndrome refers to a variety of disorders characterized by an accumulation of excess Heat in the Stomach and Intestines. The main symptoms are fever, thirst, sweating and a large rapid pulse. If the *yang ming* organ is involved there will be constipation. *Yang ming* syndrome may begin as an acute invasion of Wind Cold or Heat that penetrates through the surface into the interior (*see* Six level disease differentiation, p.639), or may occur due to Heat generated by some pathological process internally. In biomedical terms, *yang ming* syndrome may correspond to disorders as diverse as meningitis, pneumonia, acute appendicitis, heat stroke and dysentery.

Yin 阴

Yin is a technical term describing the structural components of the body upon which the *yang* acts, and the cool moistening fluid components that contain, balance and cool the heat and activity of the *yang* elements. Many problems associated with weakness of *yin* involve a loss of structural integrity, actual atrophy or deterioration of tissues (such as chronic atrophic gastritis and glossitis), decrease in fluids or an increase in fluid viscosity. *Yin* deficiency also leads to overheating in much the same way as a car engine with insufficient water in the radiator tends to overheat. *Yin* deficient patients tend to be hot, dry and agitated. Disorders that may have a component of *yin* deficiency include menopausal syndrome, sleep disturbances, chronic inflammatory states such as interstitial cystitis, pelvic inflammatory disease and prostatitis, hearing or visual weakness, some endocrine problems such as diabetes and hyperthyroidism, and chronic respiratory disorders.

General index

This index does not list every patent medicine that can be used for a particular symptom or pathology. In the interests of brevity and clarity the list includes the most commonly used medicines, with the ones considered the most effective toward the top.

Huang Lian Jie Du Wan 552 (*Toxic Heat, Damp Heat*)

• **pharyngeal**

Lien Chiao Pai Tu Pien 522 (*Wind Heat, Toxic Heat*)

Huang Lian Shang Ching Pien 386 (*Wind Heat, Toxic Heat, Damp Heat*)

Peking Niu Huang Jie Du Pian 384 (*Toxic Heat*)

DBD Capsule 238 (*severe Toxic Heat*)

Wu Wei Xiao Du Wan 562 (*Toxic Heat*)

Chuan Xin Lian Antiphlogistic Tablets 558 (*Toxic Heat*)

Jie Geng Wan 391

Superior Sore Throat Powder 394 (*topical*)

Accumulation disorder

Bo Ying Compound 506

Qi Xing Tea 518

Acid reflux

Xiang Lian Wan 120 (*Stomach Heat*)

Wei Te Ling 122 (*hyperacidity*)

Xiang Sha Yang Wei Wan 90 (*qi stag.*)

Chai Hu Shu Gan Wan 280 (*Liver qi stag.*)

Shu Gan Wan 116 (*Liver qi stag.*)

Yi Guan Jian Wan 290 (*yin def., qi stag*)

Wei Tong Ding 124 (*Cold, yang def.*)

Bao He Wan 106 (*food stag.*)

Ping Wei San 114 (*Phlegm Damp*)

Jian Pi Wan 104 (*pregnancy*)

Bo Ying Compound 506 (*infants*)

Qi Xing Tea 518 (*infants*)

Acne

Qing Re An Chuang Pian 536 (*Toxic Heat & Hot Bld.*)

Zhen Zhu An Chuang Tablet 537 (*Toxic & Damp Heat*)

Huang Lian Jie Du Wan 552 (*Damp Heat*)

Wu Wei Xiao Du Wan 562 (*Toxic Heat*)

Lien Chiao Pai Tu Pien 522 (*Wind Heat, Toxic Heat*)

Chuan Xin Lian Cream 540 (*topical*)

Acne–premenstrual

Jia Wei Xiao Yao Wan 284 (*Liver qi stag. with stagnant Heat*)

Xiao Yan Tang Shang Cream 546 (*topical*)

Acne Rosacea

Peking Niu Huang Jie Du Pian 384 (*Toxic Heat*)

Ban Lan Gen Chong Ji 390 (*Toxic Heat*)

Fu Fang Nan Ban Lan Gen 560 (*Toxic Heat*)

Chin Gu Tie Shang Wan 426 (*Bld stag.*)

Huo Luo Xiao Ling Wan 428 (*Bld stag.*)

Xiao Yan Tang Shang Cream 546 (*topical*)

Adaptogen

Reishi Mushroom 354 (*immune regulator*)

Panax Ginseng Extractum 350

Deer Velvet 328

Deer Antler and Ginseng 332

Adenoma

Hai Zao Jing Wan 60 (*Phlegm*)

Nei Xiao Luo Li Wan 62 (*Phlegm & Bld stag.*)

Adhesions–intestinal

Dang Gui Si Ni Wan 268 (*Cold & Bld stag.*)

Adnexitis (see pelvic inflammatory disease)

Adrenal cortex–to regulate

Liu Wei Di Huang Wan 304 (*kid. yin def.*)

Fu Gui Ba Wei Wan 324 (*Kid. yang def.*)

Panax Ginseng Extractum 350 (*qi def.*)

Agitation–in drug withdrawal

Chai Hu Long Gu Mu Li Wan 372 (*qi stag., Phlegm Heat, rising ying*)

AIDS–low grade fever in

Da Bu Yin Wan 314 (*yin def.*)

American Ginseng Essence of Chicken 344 (*qi & yin def.*)

Albuminuria

Chien Chin Chih Tai Wan 70 (*Damp Heat & Kid. def.*)

Bi Xie Fen Qing Wan 230 (*Kid. qi def.*)

Alcohol abuse

Headache and Dizziness Reliever 585

Po Chai Pills 84 (*Damp Heat*)

Bao Ji Pills 83 (*Damp Heat*)

Allergic purpura (see purpura)

Allergies

Yu Ping Feng Wan 348 (*wei qi def.*)

Reishi Mushroom 354 (*immune regulator*)

Antisperm antibodies
Gui Zhi Fu Ling Wan 30 (*Bld stag.*)
Wu Zi Yan Zong Wan 496 (*jing def.*)

Anuria (*see* Urination–scanty)

Anus–burning of
Huang Lian Jie Du Wan 552 (*Damp Heat*)
Hua Zhi Ling Tablet 140 (*Damp Heat*)
Chuan Xin Lian Antiphlogistic Tablets 558
(*Toxic Heat*)

Anus–itching of (*see* Pruritus–anal)

Anxiety
Tian Wang Bu Xin Dan 358 (*Heart & Kid. yin def.*)
Gui Pi Wan 16 (*Heart & Spleen qi def.*)
Bai Zi Yang Xin Wan 360 (*Bld & yin def.*)
An Shen Ding Zhi Wan 362 (*Bld & yin def. with Phlegm*)
An Shen Bu Xin Wan 364 (*yin def., yang rising*)
Wen Dan Wan 370 (*Phlegm Heat*)
Chai Hu Long Gu Mu Li Wan 372 (*qi stag., Phlegm Heat, yang rising*)
Ban Xia Hou Po Wan 400 (*qi & Phlegm stag.*)
Po Lung Yuen Medical Pills 570 (*Phlegm Heat*)

Aphasia
Hua Tuo Zai Zao Wan 272 (*qi & yin def.*)
Da Huo Luo Dan 444 (*Kid. def.*)
Niu Huang Qing Xin Wan 572 (*Phlegm Heat*)

Aphonia (*see* Voice, loss of)

Appendicitis
• **acute, uncomplicated**
Huang Lian Jie Du Wan 552 (*Damp & Toxic Heat*)
Wu Wei Xiao Du Wan 562 (*Toxic Heat*)
Ching Fei Yi Huo Pien 176 (*yang ming organ syndrome*)
Niu Huang Qing Huo Wan 561 (*yang ming organ syndrome*)
Liang Ge Wan 566 (*yang ming organ syndrome*)
• **chronic**
Nei Xiao Luo Li Wan 62 (*Phlegm & Bld stag.*)
Huo Luo Xiao Ling Wan 428 (*Bld stag.*)

Appetite
• **excessive**
Huang Lian Jie Du Wan 552 (*Stomach Heat*)
Qing Wei San Wan 392 (*Stomach Heat*)
Gu Ben Wan 316 (*Stomach yin def.*)
• **poor**
Si Jun Zi Wan 86 (*Spleen qi def.*)
Xiang Sha Liu Jun Wan 88 (*Spleen qi def. with Phlegm Damp*)
Li Zhong Wan 96 (*yang def.*)
Ping Wei San 114 (*Phlegm Damp*)
Bao He Wan 106 (*food stag.*)
Bu Zhong Yi Qi Wan 92 (*Spleen qi def.*)
Huan Shao Dan 331 (*yang def.*)
Bo Ying Compound 506 (*infants*)
Healthy Child Tea 514 (*Spleen def., infants*)
Qi Xing Tea 518 (*food intolerance, infants*)

Apthous ulcers (*see* Ulcers, apthous)

Arrhythmia
Zhi Gan Cao Wan 260 (*Heart qi, Bld & yin def.*)
Chai Hu Long Gu Mu Li Wan 372 (*qi stag. Phlegm Heat*)
Wen Dan Wan 370 (*Phlegm Heat*)
Tian Wang Bu Xin Dan 358 (*Heart yin def.*)
Sheng Mai San Wan 212 (*qi & yin def.*)
Gui Pi Wan 16 (*Heart qi def.*)
Xue Fu Zhu Yu Wan 252 (*Bld stag.*)
Dan Shen Pill 254 (*Bld & Phlegm stag.*)

Arteriosclerosis
Dan Shen Pill 254 (*Bld & Phlegm stag.*)
Dan Shen Yin Wan 256 (*qi & Bld stag.*)
Raw Tienqi Tablets 424 (*Bld stag.*)
Guan Xin An Kou Fu Ye 262 (*Bld stag.*)
Sunho Multi Ginseng Tablets 264 (*Bld stag.*)
Xue Fu Zhu Yu Wan 252 (*Bld stag.*)
Liu Wei Di Huang Wan 304 (*yin def.*)
Zhen Gan Xi Feng Wan 580 (*yang rising*)

Arthritis (*see also Bi* syndrome)
Juan Bi Wan 430 (*Wind Cold Damp*)
Qu Feng Zhen Tong Capsule 432 (*Wind Cold Damp*)
Xuan Bi Tang Wan 436 (*Damp Heat*)

Niu Huang Qing Huo Wan 561 (*Lung & Stomach excess Heat*)
Liang Ge Wan 566 (*yang ming syndrome*)
Pu Ji Xiao Du Wan 389 (*Toxic Heat*)

• **skin**

Huang Lian Jie Du Wan 552 (*Toxic & Damp Heat*)
Wu Wei Xiao Du Wan 562 (*Toxic Heat*)
Peking Niu Huang Jie Du Pian 384 (*Toxic Heat*)
Fu Fang Nan Ban Lan Gen 560 (*Toxic Heat*)
Chuan Xin Lian Antiphlogistic Tablets 558 (*Toxic Heat*)
Lien Chiao Pai Tu Pien 522 (*Wind Heat, Toxic Heat*)
Niu Huang Qing Huo Wan 561 (*Toxic Heat, yang ming Heat*)
Fang Feng Tong Sheng Wan 534 (*recurrent*)
Yunnan Paiyao 422
Chuan Xin Lian Cream 540 (*topical*)

• **systemic**

Huang Lian Jie Du Wan 552 (*Damp & Toxic Heat*)
Wu Wei Xiao Du Wan 562 (*Toxic Heat*)
Chuan Xin Lian 557 (*Toxic Heat*)
Chuan Xin Lian Antiphlogistic Tablets 558 (*Toxic Heat*)
Bai Hu Tang Wan 564 (*yang ming channel syndrome*)
Liang Ge Wan 566 (*yang ming organ syndrome*)

Bad breath (*see* Halitosis)

Bartholin's cyst

Qing Re Qu Shi Tea 234 (*Damp & Toxic Heat*)
Long Dan Xie Gan Wan 286 (*Liver Fire, Damp Heat*)
Huang Lian Jie Du Wan 552 (*Damp & Toxic Heat*)
Fu Fang Nan Ban Lan Gen 560 (*Toxic Heat*)
Chuan Xin Lian Antiphlogistic Tablets 558 (*Toxic Heat*)
Xue Fu Zhu Yu Wan 252 (*recurrent*)
Chuan Xin Lian Cream 540 (*topically*)

Bedwetting (*see* Enuresis)

Bed sores (*see* Ulcers, chronic non-healing)

Beçhets syndrome

Tian Wang Bu Xin Dan 358 (*Heart & Kid yin def.*)
Huang Lian Jie Du Wan 552 (*Heart Fire*)
Qing Wei San Wan 392 (*Stomach Heat*)
Reishi Mushroom 354 (*immune regulator*)

Belching

Xiang Lian Wan 120 (*stomach Heat*)
Bao He Wan 106 (*food stag.*)
Ping Wei San 114 (*Phlegm Damp*)
Xiang Sha Yang Wei Wan 90 (*qi & Damp stag.*)
Chai Hu Shu Gan Wan 280 (*Liver qi stag.*)
Mu Xiang Shun Qi Wan 126 (*qi & Damp stag.*)
Chen Xiang Hua Qi Wan 128 (*qi def. with qi blockage*)

Bell's palsy

Chuan Xiong Cha Tiao Wan 164 (*Wind Cold, acute*)
Hua Tuo Zai Zao Wan 272 (*qi & yin def.*)
Bu Yang Huan Wu Wan 266 (*qi def. with Bld stag.*)
Xiao Shuan Zai Zao Wan 270
Da Huo Luo Dan 444
Kang Wei Ling Wan 502 (*Bld stag., Wind*)
Tong Luo Zhi Tong Tablet 453 (*Bld def.*)
Niu Huang Qing Xin Wan 572 (*Phlegm Heat*)

Benign Familial Tremor

San Bi Wan 446 (*Wind Damp with Kid. & Bld def.*)
Niu Huang Qing Xin Wan 572 (*Phlegm Heat*)

Benign prostatic hypertrophy (*see* Prostatic hypertrophy)

Bi Syndrome

• **Wind Cold**

Ma Huang Tang Wan 156

• **Wind Cold Damp**

Juan Bi Wan 430
Qu Feng Zhen Tong Capsule 432

Bu Zhong Yi Qi Wan 92 (*qi def.*)
Bai Feng Wan 10 (*Bld def.*)
Shi Quan Da Bu Wan 336 (*qi & Bld def. with Cold*)
Woo Garm Yuen Medical Pills 22 (*Cold & Blood stag.*)
Shao Fu Zhu Yu Wan 32 (*Cold & Blood stag.*)
Tao Hong Si Wu Wan 28 (*Bld stag. with Bld def.*)
Huang Lian Jie Du Wan 552 (*Heat in the Bld*)
Jia Wei Xiao Yao Wan 284 (*Liver qi stag. with stag. Heat*)
Li Zhong Wan 96 (*yang def.*)
• vomiting blood (*see* Hematemesis)
• yin deficiency
Da Bu Yin Wan 314

Blepharitis
Ming Mu Shang Ching Pien 416 (*Wind Heat, Liver Heat*)
Peking Niu Huang Jie Du Pian 384 (*Toxic Heat*)
Huang Lien Shang Ching Pien 386 (*Wind Heat, Toxic Heat*)
Ming Mu Di Huang Wan 418 (*Liver yin def.*)

Blood sugar–regulation of
Yu Quan Wan 136 (*qi & yin def.*)
Liu Wei Di Huang Wan 304 (*yin def.*)
Shen Ling Bai Zhu Wan 94 (*Spleen qi def.*)
Sugarid 138
Panax Ginseng Extractum 350

Boils (*see* Abscess)
Bone marrow, to protect (*see* Chemotherapy)
Bones–breaks and fractures
Chin Gu Tie Shang Wan 426 (*Bld stag.*)
Die Da Zhi Tong Capsule 425 (*Bld stag.*)
Zheng Gu Shui 460 (*topical*)
Plaster for Bruise and Analgesic 478 (*topical*)

Bones and tendons–weakness of
Deer Velvet 328 (*jing def.*)
Lu Rong Jiao 330 (*jing def.*)
You Gui Wan 326 (*yang def.*)

Blood Pathology

deficiency
Si Wu Wan 4 (*Heart & Liver*)
Ba Zhen Wan 2 (*qi & Bld*)
Ba Zhen Yi Mu Wan 6 (*with mild Bld stag.*)
Bai Feng Wan 10 (*qi & Bld*)
Gui Pi Wan 16 (*Heart Bld & Spleen qi def.*)
Dang Gui Jing 18 (*qi & Bld*)
Shi Quan Da Bu Wan 336 (*qi & Bld with Cold*)
Tangkwei Essence of Chicken 54 (*qi & Bld*)
Dang Gui Su 20
Tao Hong Si Wu Wan 28 (*with Bld stag.*)
Zhi Gan Cao Wan 260 (*with qi & yin def.*)
Yang Xue Sheng Fa Capsule 318 (*with Liver & Kid. def.*)
Qi Bao Mei Ran Dan 320 (*with kid. yin def.*)
Shou Wu Chih 322
Shou Wu Pian 341
Yang Ying Wan 340
Bai Zi Yang Xin Wan 360
An Shen Bu Xin Wan 364 (*with yang excess*)
Suan Zao Ren Tang Pian 367
Dang Gui Yin Zi Wan 526 (*with Wind in the skin*)

Heat in
Huang Lian Jie Du Wan 552
Stagnation
see Box, p.652

Bu Gai Zhuang Gu Capule 53 (*yang def.*)
Bones–slow healing of
Chin Gu Tie Shang Wan 426 (*Bld stag.*)
Zheng Gu Shui 460 (*topical*)
Bu Gai Zhuang Gu Capule 53 (*yang def.*)
Xue Fu Zhu Yu Wan 252 (*Bld stag.*)
Sunho Multi Ginseng Tablets 264 (*Bld stag. & qi def.*)
Shi Quan Da Bu Wan 336 (*qi & Bld def.*)

GENERAL INDEX

Su Zi Jiang Qi Wan 160 (*Cold Phlegm*)
Da Bu Yin Wan 314 (*yin def.*)

Bronchitis
• acute
Ching Fei Yi Huo Pien 176 (*Lung Fire*)
Qing Qi Hua Tan Wan 174 (*Phlegm Heat*)
Niu Huang Qing Huo Wan 561 (*Toxic Heat*)
Huang Lian Jie Du Wan 552 (*Toxic & Damp Heat*)
Xiao Chai Hu Tang Wan 276 (*post acute*)
• asthmatic
Ma Huang Tang Wan 156 (*Wind Cold*)
Xiao Qing Long Wan 162 (*Wind Cold with congested fluids*)
Ding Chuan Wan 182 (*Phlegm Heat*)
• chronic
Su Zi Jiang Qi Wan 160 (*Cold Phlegm*)
Qi Guan Yan Ke Sou Tan Chuan Wan 184 (*Phlegm Damp*)
Ding Chuan Wan 182 (*Phlegm Heat*)
Wen Dan Wan 370 (*Phlegm Heat*)
Qing Qi Hua Tan Wan 174 (*Phlegm Heat*)
Xiang Sha Liu Jun Wan 88 (*with Spleen qi def.*)
Li Chung Yuen Medical Pills 98 (*yang def.*)
Li Zhong Wan 96 (*yang def.*)
She Dan Chuan Bei Ye 186 (*Phlegm*)
Orange Peel Powder 188 (*Phlegm*)
Sheng Mai San Wan 212 (*qi & yin def.*)
Bu Fei Wan 216 (*Lung qi def.*)

Bruising–to resolve
Die Da Zhi Tong Capsule 425
Chin Gu Tie Shang Wan 426
Huo Luo Xiao Ling Wan 428
Yunnan Paiyao 422
Raw Tienchi Tablets 424
Zheng Gu Shui 460
Die Da Tian Qi Yao Jiu 463

Bruising–easy
Gui Pi Wan 16 (*Heart Bld & Spleen qi def.*)
Ge Xia Zhu Yu Wan 298 (*Bld stag.*)

Bruxism
Xiao Yao Wan 282 (*Liver qi stag.*)
Jia Wei Xiao Yao Wan 284 (*Liver qi stag.*)

Chai Hu Shu Gan Wan 280 (*Liver qi stag.*)
An Shen Jie Yu Capsule 368 (*qi stag. with shen disturbance*)

Buerger's disease
Xue Fu Zhu Yu Wan 252 (*Bld stag.*)
Dan Shen Pill 254 (*Bld stag.*)
Xin Mai Ling 258 (*Bld stag. with Heat*)
Bu Yang Huan Wu Wan 266 (*Bld stag. with qi def.*)
Shi Quan Da Bu Wan 336 (*qi & Bld def.*)
Dang Gui Si Ni Wan 268 (*Cold & Bld stag.*)

Burning feet syndrome (see also Peripheral neuropathy)
Zhi Bai Ba Wei Wan 42 (*yin def.*)
Hua Tuo Zai Zao Wan 272 (*qi & yin def.*)

Burns and scalds
Ching Wan Hung 542 (*topical*)
Xiao Yan Tang Shang Cream 546 (*topical*)
Sanjin Watermelon Frost 396 (*topical*)

Bursitis
Juan Bi Wan 430 (*Wind Cold Damp*)
Jian Bu Qiang Shen Wan 454 (*with Kid. def.*)
Zheng Gu Shui 460 (*topical*)
Trans Wood Lock Liniment 470 (*topical*)

C

Calculi, urinary
Shi Lin Tong 239

Cancer–lung, to alleviate dry cough of
Yang Yin Qing Fei Wan 204 (*Lung yin def.*)
Bai He Gu Jin Wan 206 (*Lung yin def.*)
Mai Wei Di Huang Wan 208 (*Lung yin def.*)

Cancer–general immune support for
Reishi Mushroom 354 (*immune regulator*)
American Ginseng Essence of Chicken 344
Cordyceps Essence of Chicken 342
Bu Zhong Yi Qi Wan 92

Candidiasis–gastro-intestinal
So Hup Yuen Medical Pills 80 (*gu syndrome*)

Xiang Sha Liu Jun Wan 88 (*Spleen qi def. with Phlegm Damp*)
Huo Hsiang Cheng Chi Pien 76 (*Damp*)
Ping Wei San 114 (*Phlegm Damp*)
Da Huang Jiang Zhi Wan 133

Candidiasis–vaginal (thrush)

Bi Xie Sheng Shi Wan 66 (*Damp Heat*)
Yu Dai Wan 68 (*Damp Heat, Bld def.*)
Chien Chin Chih Tai Wan 70 (*Damp Heat, def.*)
Bi Xie Fen Qing Wan 230 (*Damp*)
Ping Wei San 114 (*Phlegm Damp*)

Carbuncle (*see* Abscess)

Cardiomyopathy

Zhi Gan Cao Wan 260 (*Heart qi & Blood def.*)

Cardiovascular disease

Dan Shen Pill 254 (*Bld & Phlegm stag.*)
Keep Fit Capsule 111 (*Bld & Phlegm stag.*)
Dan Shen Yin Wan 256 (*Bld stag.*)
Xue Fu Zhu Yu Wan 252 (*qi & Bld stag.*)
Guan Xin An Kou Fu Ye 262 (*Bld stag.*)
Sunho Multi Ginseng Tablets 264 (*Bld stag.*)

Cardiovascular system, preventitive treatment for

Sunho Multi Ginseng Tablets 264 (*Bld stag.*)
Raw Tienchi Tablets 424 (*Bld stag.*)

Carotid stenosis

Dan Shen Pill 254 (*Bld & Phlegm stag.*)
Xin Mai Ling 258 (*Bld stag. with Heat*)

Cataracts

Ming Mu Di Huang Wan 418 (*Liver yin def.*)
Ming Mu Shang Ching Pien 416 (*Liver Heat, Fire*)
Fu Gui Ba Wei Wan 324 (*Kid. yang def.*)
Pearl Powder 548

Cellulitis

Huang Lien Shang Ching Pien 386 (*Wind Heat, Toxic Heat*)
Ming Mu Shang Ching Pien 416 (*Liver Heat, Fire*)
Lien Chiao Pai Tu Pien 522 (*Wind Heat, Toxic Heat*)

Wu Wei Xiao Du Wan 562 (*Toxic Heat*)
Chuan Xin Lian Cream 540 (*topical*)

Cerebrovascular hemorrhage, sequelae of

Raw Tienchi Tablets 424 (*Bld stag.*)
Bu Yang Huan Wu Wan 266 (*Bld stag., qi def.*)

Cerebrovascular insufficiency

Xue Fu Zhu Yu Wan 252 (*qi & Bld stag.*)
Dan Shen Pill 254 (*Bld & Phlegm stag.*)
Xin Mai Ling 258 (*Bld stag. with Heat*)
Guan Xin An Kou Fu Ye 262 (*Bld stag.*)

Cervix

- erosion of
  Gui Zhi Fu Ling Wan 30 (*Bld stag.*)
- incompetent
  Shih San Tai Pao Wan 56 (*Bld def.*)
  Bu Zhong Yi Qi Wan 92 (*qi def.*)
- inflammation of
  Fu Yan Qing Tablet 64 (*Damp & Toxic Heat*)
  Yu Dai Wan 68 (*Damp Heat*)

Chemotherapy

- fever following
  Da Bu Yin Wan 314 (*yin def.*)
- hair loss following
  Yang Xue Sheng Fa Capsule 318 (*Bld def.*)
  Qi Bao Mei Ran Dan 320 (*Liver, Kid. & Bld def.*)
  Tangkwei Essence of Chicken 54 (*qi & Bld def.*)
- nausea, vomiting from
  Wen Dan Wan 370 (*Phlegm Heat*)
  Er Chen Wan 112 (*Phlegm Damp*)
  Xiang Sha Liu Jun Wan 88 (*Spleen def. with Phlegm Damp*)
- oral dryness following
  American Ginseng Essence of Chicken 344
  Yang Yin Qing Fei Wan 204
- to protect bone marrow during
  Wu Ji Bai Feng Wan 12
  Cordyceps Essence of Chicken 342
  Reishi Mushroom 354 (*immune regulator*)

- **weakness following**
  Cordyceps Essence of Chicken 342
  Shi Quan Da Bu Wan 336

Chest, fullness and discomfort in
Ping Wei San 114 (*Phlegm Damp*)
Chai Hu Shu Gan Wan 280 (*qi stag.*)
Wen Dan Wan 370 (*Phlegm Heat*)
Chai Hu Long Gu Mu Li Wan 372 (*qi stag,
Phlegm Heat, Liver yang*)
Dan Shen Pill 254 (*Bld stag.*)

Chest pain (*see* Pain–chest)

Chicken Pox
Yin Chiao Chieh Tu Pien 146 (*Wind Heat*)
Lien Chiao Pai Tu Pien 522 (*Wind Heat,
Toxic Heat*)
Peking Niu Huang Jie Du Pian 384 (*Toxic
Heat*)

Childhood eczema (*see* Eczema)

Chillblains
Hua Tuo Zai Zao Wan 272 (*qi & yin def.*)
Xue Fu Zhu Yu Wan 252 (*qi & Bld stag.*)

Chlamydia
Fu Yan Qing Tablet 64 (*Toxic Heat*)
Bi Xie Sheng Shi Wan 66 (*Damp Heat*)
Chuan Xin Lian Antiphlogistic Tablets 558
(*Toxic Heat*)

Chloasma
Yang Yan Qu Ban Tablet 72 (*qi & Bld
stag., Bld def.*)

Cholangitis
Li Dan Tablets 296 (*Damp Heat*)

Cholecystitis
- **acute**
  Da Chai Hu Wan 288 (*shao yang/yang
  ming syndrome*)
  Long Dan Xie Gan Wan 286 (*Liver Fire*)
  Li Dan Tablets 296 (*Damp Heat*)
  Ching Fei Yi Huo Pien 176 (*Fire*)
  Huang Lian Jie Du Wan 552 (*Damp &
  Toxic Heat*)
  Niu Huang Qing Huo Wan 561 (*yang
  ming syndrome*)
- **chronic**
  Chai Hu Shu Gan Wan 280 (*Liver qi
  stag.*)
  Shu Gan Wan 116 (*Liver qi stag.*)

Da Chai Hu Wan 288 (*shao yang/yang
ming syndrome*)
Qing Gan Li Dan Tablets 294 (*Damp
Heat*)
Li Dan Tablets 296 (*Damp Heat*)
Jigucao Wan 292 (*Damp Heat*)

Cholera
Li Zhong Wan 96 (*Spleen yang def.*)
Xing Jun San 74 (*Summerdamp*)

Cholesterol–high
Keep Fit Capsule 111 (*Phlegm & Bld
stag.*)
Bojenmi Chinese Tea 110
Dan Shen Pill 254 (*Bld stag.*)
Raw Tienchi Tablets 424 (*Bld stag.*)
Sunho Multi Ginseng Tablets 264 (*Bld
stag.*)
Reishi Mushroom 354 (*immune regulator*)

Chronic fatigue syndrome
Xiao Chai Hu Tang Wan 276 (*shao yang*)
Bu Zhong Yi Qi Wan 92 (*Spleen qi def.*)
Gui Pi Wan 16 (*Heart & Spleen def.*)
Xiang Sha Liu Jun Wan 88 (*Spleen qi def.
with Phlegm Damp*)

Chyluria
Chien Chin Chih Tai Wan 70 (*Damp Heat
with qi def.*)
Bi Xie Fen Qing Wan 230 (*Damp*)
Chin So Ku Ching Wan 246 (*Kid. def.*)

Circulation–poor
Si Ni San Wan 278 (*Liver qi stag.*)
Sunho Multi Ginseng Tablets 264 (*qi def.,
Bld stag.*)
Xin Mai Ling 258 (*Bld stag.*)
Dang Gui Si Ni Wan 268 (*Cold stag. in
the channels*)
Xiao Huo Luo Dan 434 (*severe Cold stag.
in the channels*)
Bu Yang Huan Wu Wan 266 (*qi def., Bld
stag.*)
Li Chung Yuen Medical Pills 98 (*Spleen
yang def.*)
Fu Gui Ba Wei Wan 324 (*Kid. yang def.*)

Cirrhosis of the liver
Shu Gan Wan 116 (*qi stag.*)
Xiao Yao Wan 282 (*qi stag., Bld def.,
early*)

Concentration–poor

Jian Nao Yi Zhi Capsule 376 (*qi def. with Bld. stag*)

Xiang Sha Liu Jun Wan 88 (*Spleen def. with Phlegm Damp*)

Gui Pi Wan 16 (*Heart Bld & Spleen qi def.*)

Ping Wei San 114 (*Phlegm Damp*)

Wen Dan Wan 370 (*Phlegm Heat*)

Tian Wang Bu Xin Dan 358 (*Heart & Kid yin def.*)

Cerebral Tonic Pills 374 (*Phlegm & Kid. def.*)

Concussion–sequelae of

Tong Qiao Huo Xue Wan 382 (*Bld stag.*)

Xue Fu Zhu Yu Wan 252 (*Bld stag.*)

Raw Tienchi Tablets 424 (*Bld stag.*)

Congenital abnormalities

Deer Velvet 328 (*jing def.*)

Lu Rong Jiao 330 (*jing def.*)

Liu Wei Di Huang Wan 304 (*general Kid. def.*)

You Gui Wan 326 (*yang def.*)

Zuo Gui Wan 312 (*yin def.*)

Congestive cardiac failure

Zhen Wu Tang Wan 222 (*Heart yang def.*)

Conjunctivitis

Yin Chiao Chieh Tu Pien 146 (*Wind Heat*)

Ming Mu Shang Ching Pien 416 (*Liver Fire*)

Peking Niu Huang Jie Du Pian 384 (*Toxic Heat*)

Huang Lien Shang Ching Pien 386 (*Wind Heat, Toxic Heat*)

Xiao Er Gan Mao Chong Ji 516 (*infants*)

Gan Mao Tea 513 (*infants*)

Connective tissue disorders

Reishi Mushroom 354 (*immune regulator*)

Xue Fu Zhu Yu Wan 252 (*Bld stag.*)

Guan Jie Yan Wan 438 (*Damp Heat*)

Xuan Bi Tang Wan 436 (*Damp Heat*)

Constipation

Run Chang Wan 130 (*Bld & fluid def.*)

Wu Ren Wan 132 (*Bld & fluid def.*)

Cong Rong Bu Shen Wan 134 (*yang def., atonic*)

Mu Xiang Shun Qi Wan 126 (*qi stag., habitual*)

Chen Xiang Hua Qi Wan 128 (*qi stag, qi def.*)

Da Huang Jiang Zhi Wan 133 (*excess*)

Ching Fei Yi Huo Pien 176 (*yangming syndrome, Lung Fire*)

Da Chai Hu Wan 288 (*shao yang/yang ming syndrome*)

Yang Yin Qing Fei Wan 204 (*yin def., dry post febrile*)

Consumptive lung disease

Bai He Gu Jin Wan 206 (*yin def.*)

Zhi Gan Cao Wan 260 (*qi & Bld def.*)

Shi Quan Da Bu Wan 336 (*qi & Bld def.*)

Da Bu Yin Wan 314 (*yin def.*)

Contact dermatitis (*see Dermatitis*)

Convulsions

Po Lung Yuen Medical Pills 570 (*Phlegm Heat*)

Wen Dan Wan 370 (*Phlegm Heat*)

King Fung Powder 508 (*Phlegm, Wind*)

Li Zhong Wan 96 (*yang def, chronic childhood*)

Cor pulmonale

Zhen Wu Tang Wan 222 (*Heart yang def.*)

Coronary artery bypass, convalescence from

Sheng Mai San Wan 212 (*qi & yin def.*)

Coronary artery disease

Dan Shen Pill 254 (*Bld & Phlegm stag.*)

Xue Fu Zhu Yu Wan 252 (*qi & Bld stag.*)

Dan Shen Yin Wan 256 (*Bld stag.*)

Xin Mai Ling 258 (*Bld stag.*)

Raw Tienchi Tablets 424 (*Bld stag.*)

Guan Xin An Kou Fu Ye 262 (*Bld stag.*)

Zhi Gan Cao Wan 260 (*qi & Bld def.*)

Sheng Mai San Wan 212 (*qi & yin def.*)

Corpus luteum failure

Tiao Jing Cu Yun Wan 38 (*yang def.*)

Corticosteroids, to alleviate side effects of

Liu Wei Di Huang Wan 304 (*Kid yin def.*)

Costochondritis

Shu Gan Wan 116 (*qi stag.*)

Xue Fu Zhu Yu Wan 252 (*qi & Bld stag.*)

Bi Xie Fen Qing Wan 230 (*Damp*)
Ba Ji Yin Yang Wan 240 (*Kid. yang def.*)
Bu Zhong Yi Qi Wan 92 (*qi def.*)
• **interstitial**
Zhi Bai Ba Wei Wan 42 (*Kid yin def.*)
Da Bu Yin Wan 314 (*yin def.*)
Xue Fu Zhu Yu Wan 252 (*Bld stag.*)

Cysts (*see* Breast, Bartholin's, Ovarian, Sebaceous)

D

Dacryocystitis
Ming Mu Shang Ching Pien 416 (*Wind Heat, Liver Fire*)
Peking Niu Huang Jie Du Pian 384 (*Toxic Heat*)
Huang Lien Shang Ching Pien 386 (*Wind Heat, Toxic Heat*)
Ming Mu Di Huang Wan 418 (*Liver yin def.*)

Deafness (*see* Hearing, loss of)

Deep venous thrombosis
Xue Fu Zhu Yu Wan 252 (*Bld stag.*)
Raw Tienchi Tablets 424 (*Bld stag.*)
Bu Yang Huan Wu Wan 266 (*qi def, Bld stag.*)
Sunho Multi Ginseng Tablets 264 (*qi def, Bld stag.*)

Delirium
Niu Huang Qing Xin Wan 572 (*Phlegm Heat*)
Niu Huang Qing Huo Wan 561 (*yang ming Heat*)
Huang Lian Jie Du Wan 552 (*Toxic Heat*)

Dental abscess (*see* Abscess, dental)

Dental caries
Qing Wei San Wan 392 (*Stomach Heat*)

Depression
Chai Hu Shu Gan Wan 280 (*Liver qi stag.*)
Xiao Yao Wan 282 (*qi stag. & Bld def.*)
Tao Hong Si Wu Wan 28 (*Bld stag., Bld def.*)
Xue Fu Zhu Yu Wan 252 (*chronic, Bld stag.*)

Damp pathology
joints
Juan Bi Wan 430
Qu Feng Zhen Tong Capsule 432
knees
Fang Ji Huang Qi Wan 228
lungs
Su Zi Jiang Qi Wan 160
Xiao Qing Long Wan 162
prostate
Bi Xie Fen Qing Wan 230
skin
Xiao Feng Wan 524
Fu Yin Tai Liniment 541
Tujin Liniment 544
Hua Tuo Gao 545
Pearl Powder 548
Bo Ying Compound 506
stomach, intestines
Ping Wei San 114
Liu Jun Zi Wan 87
Shen Ling Bai Zhu Wan 94
Xing Jun San 74
Huo Hsiang Cheng Chi Pien 76
systemic
Wu Ling San Wan 224
urinary bladder
Wu Ling San Wan 224
Bi Xie Fen Qing Wan 230

Wen Dan Wan 370 (*Phlegm Heat*)
Xiang Sha Yang Wei Wan 90 (*qi & Damp stag.*)

Depression–postnatal
Gui Pi Wan 16 (*Heart Bld def.*)
Tangkwei Essence of Chicken 54 (*qi & Bld def.*)
Xiao Yao Wan 282 (*qi stag.*)
Tao Hong Si Wu Wan 28 (*Bld stag., Bld def.*)
Gan Mai Da Zao Wan 378

Dermatitis
acute
Lien Chiao Pai Tu Pien 522 (*Wind Heat, Toxic Heat*)

Damp Heat pathology

joints
Xuan Bi Tang Wan 436
Guan Jie Yan Wan 438

large intestine
Bao Ji Pills 83
Po Chai Pills 84
Fu Ke An 82
Huang Lian Jie Du Wan 552
Hua Zhi Ling Tablet 140
Huai Jiao Wan 139
Fargelin for Piles 142
Xiang Lian Wan 120

liver& gall bladder
Da Chai Hu Wan 288
Long Dan Xie Gan Wan 286
Qing Gan Li Dan Tablets 294
Jigucao Wan 292
Li Dan Tablets 296

prostate
Qian Lie Xian Capsule 488
Prostate Gland Pills 490

uterus
Bi Xie Sheng Shi Wan 66
Yu Dai Wan 68
Fu Yan Qing Tablet 64

skin
Ming Mu Shang Ching Pien 416
Bi Xie Sheng Shi Wan 66
Ke Yin Wan 528

systemic
Huang Lian Jie Du Wan 552
Huang Lian Su Tablets 554

urinary bladder
Ba Zheng San Wan 232
Qing Re Qu Shi Tea 234

with *yin* deficiency
Zhi Bai Ba Wei Wan 42

with Blood deficiency
Yu Dai Wan 68

with Dampness greater than Heat
Bi Xie Sheng Shi Wan 66

with *qi* stagnation
Mu Xiang Shun Qi Wan 126

with Spleen qi deficiency
Zi Sheng Wan 102

with *qi* deficiency and *qi* stagnation
Chen Xiang Hua Qi Wan 128

with Spleen and Kidney deficiency
Chien Chin Chih Tai Wan 70

Huang Lien Shang Ching Pien 386 (*Wind Heat, Toxic Heat*)
Ming Mu Shang Ching Pien 416 (*Liver Fire*)
Xiao Feng Wan 524 (*Wind Damp*)
Xiao Yan Tang Shang Cream 546 (*topical*)

chronic
Bi Xie Sheng Shi Wan 66 (*Damp Heat*)
Dang Gui Yin Zi Wan 526 (*Bld def. with Wind in the skin*)
Jia Wei Xiao Yao Wan 284 (*qi stag. with Heat*)
Fang Feng Tong Sheng Wan 534 (*internal & external Heat*)
Huo Luo Xiao Ling Wan 428 (*Bld stag.*)
Pearl Powder 548 (*topical*)
Fu Yin Tai Liniment 541 (*topical*)
Xiao Yan Tang Shang Cream 546 (*topical*)

Developmental delay in children
Liu Wei Di Huang Wan 304 + Deer Velvet 328 or Lu Rong Jiao 330 (*jing def.*)
Zuo Gui Wan 312 (*yin def.*)
You Gui Wan 326 (*yang def.*)
Yulin Bu Shen Wan 214 (*Kid. yang def.*)

Diabetes insipidus
Sang Piao Xiao Wan 248 (*Heart & Kid. yang qi def.*)

Diabetes mellitus
Yu Quan Wan 136 (*qi & yin def.*)
Sugarid 138
Liu Wei Di Huang Wan 304 (*Kid yin def.*)
Shen Ling Bai Zhu Wan 94 (*Spleen qi def.*)
Gu Ben Wan 316 (*Stomach & Kid yin def.*)
Fu Gui Ba Wei Wan 324 (*Kid. yang def.*)

Diabetic neuropathy (see Neuropathy, diabetic)

Diabetic vascular disease

Xin Mai Ling 258 (*Bld stag. with Heat*)
Xue Fu Zhu Yu Wan 252 (*Bld stag.*)
Bu Yang Huan Wu Wan 266 (*qi def., Bld stag.*)
Sunho Multi Ginseng Tablets 264 (*Bld stag.*)
Huo Luo Xiao Ling Wan 428 (*Bld stag.*)
Raw Tienchi Tablets 424 (*Bld stag.*)

Diaper rash (see Nappy rash)

Diarrhea

• **acute**

Po Chai Pills 84 (*Damp Heat*)
Xing Jun San 74 (*Summerdamp*)
Huo Hsiang Cheng Chi Pien 76 (*Wind Cold with Damp*)
Ge Gen Wan 168 (*Wind Cold*)
Huang Lian Jie Du Wan 552 (*Damp or Toxic Heat*)
Bo Ying Compound 506 (*infantile*)

• **chronic**

Shen Ling Bai Zhu Wan 94 (*Spleen qi def.*)
Tong Xie Yao Fang Wan 118 (*Liver invading Spleen*)
Li Zhong Wan 96 (*Spleen yang def.*)
Zi Sheng Wan 102 (*Spleen def. with food stag.*)
Ba Ji Yin Yang Wan 240 (*Spleen & Kid yang def., cockcrow*)
Yulin Da Bu Wan 334 (*yang def., cockcrow*)
Healthy Child Tea 514 (*infantile*)

Digestion–weak

Si Jun Zi Wan 86 (*Spleen qi def.*)
Xiang Sha Liu Jun Wan 88 (*Spleen qi def.*)
Li Zhong Wan 96 (*Spleen yang def.*)
Li Chung Yuen Medical Pills 98 (*Spleen yang def.*)
Shen Ling Bai Zhu Wan 94 (*Spleen qi def.*)
Jian Pi Wan 104 (*Spleen def. with food stag.*)
Zi Sheng Wan 102 (*Spleen def. with food stag.*)

Diptheria

Yang Yin Qing Fei Wan 204 (*Lung yin def.*)

Discharge–vaginal (see Leukorrhea)

Diverticulitis

Huang Lian Jie Du Wan 552 (*Damp & Toxic Heat*)
Huang Lian Su Tablets 554 (*Damp Heat*)
Niu Huang Qing Huo Wan 561 (*yang ming organ syndrome*)
Ching Fei Yi Huo Pien 176 (*yang ming organ syndrome*)
Wu Wei Xiao Du Wan 562 (*Toxic Heat*)
Liang Ge Wan 566 (*yang ming organ syndrome*)
Chuan Xin Lian Antiphlogistic Tablets 558 (*Toxic Heat*)

Diverticulosis

Nei Xiao Luo Li Wan 62 (*Phlegm & Bld stag.*)
Huo Luo Xiao Ling Wan 428 (*Bld stag.*)

Dizziness

• **postural, lightheadedness**

Ba Zhen Wan 2 (*qi & Bld def.*)
Gui Pi Wan 16 (*qi & Bld def.*)
Tangkwei Essence of Chicken 54 (*qi & Bld def., postpartum*)
Qi Ju Di Huang Wan 309 (*Liver & Kid. yin def.*)
Ming Mu Di Huang Wan 418 (*Liver & Kid. yin def.*)
Xiao Chai Hu Tang Wan 276 (*shao yang syndrome*)
Er Xian Wan 46 (*Kid. yin & yang def.*)

• **premenstrual**

Xiao Yao Wan 282 (*Liver qi stag.*)
Jia Wei Xiao Yao Wan 284 (*Liver qi stag. with Heat*)

• **severe, vertigo**

Ban Xia Bai Zhu Tian Ma Wan 574 (*Wind Phlegm*)
Zhen Gan Xi Feng Wan 580 (*Liver yang rising*)
Tian Ma Gou Teng Wan 576 (*Liver yang rising*)
Tong Qiao Huo Xue Wan 382 (*Bld stag., post concussion*)

Dysmenorrhea

Gui Zhi Fu Ling Wan 30 (*mild Bld stag., masses*)

Tao Hong Si Wu Wan 28 (*mild Bld stag with Bld def.*)

Tong Jing Wan 26 (*severe Bld stag.*)

Shao Fu Zhu Yu Wan 32 (*Cold & Bld stag., severe*)

Woo Garm Yuen Medical Pills 22 (*Bld stag. with Cold*)

Dang Gui Si Ni Wan 268 (*Cold*)

Tong Luo Zhi Tong Tablet 453 (*Bld stag., Cold*)

Xiao Yao Wan 282 (*Liver qi stag.*)

Tian Tai Wu Yao Wan 494 (*Cold in Liver channel*)

Ba Zhen Yi Mu Wan 6 (*mild Bld def.*)

Yi Mu Tiao Jing Tablet 8 (*Bld def. with Bld stag.*)

Shi Xiao Wan 21 (*Bld stag.*)

Shi Quan Da Bu Wan 336 (*qi & Bld def. with Cold*)

Ba Zhen Wan 2 (*qi & Bld def.*)

Dyspepsia

Xiang Lian Wan 120 (*Stomach Heat*)

Xiang Sha Yang Wei Wan 90 (*qi & Damp stag.*)

Bao He Wan 106 (*food stag.*)

Chai Hu Shu Gan Wan 280 (*Liver qi stag.*)

Wei Te Ling 122 (*hyperacidity*)

Dysphagia

Hua Tuo Zai Zao Wan 272 (*qi & yin def.*)

Da Huo Luo Dan 444

Gu Ben Wan 316 (*Stomach & Lung dryness*)

Ban Xia Hou Po Wan 400 (*qi & Phlegm stag.*)

Dysuria (*see also* Urinary tract infection)

Tong Jing Wan 26 (*Bld stag.*)

Yunnan Paiyao 422 (*Bld stag.*)

Qian Lie Xian Capsules 488 (*Damp Heat*)

Tian Tai Wu Yao Wan 494 (*Cold in Liver channel*)

E

Ear–ringing (*see* Tinnitus)

Ear–infection of (*see* Otitis media)

Eczema

Lien Chiao Pai Tu Pien 522 (*Wind, Toxic Heat*)

Xiao Feng Wan 524 (*Wind Damp*)

Bi Xie Sheng Shi Wan 66 (*Damp Heat*)

Gui Zhi Tang Wan 158 (*Wind, worse in cold*)

Dang Gui Yin Zi Wan 526 (*Bld def. with Wind in the skin*)

Jia Wei Xiao Yao Wan 284 (*qi stag. with Heat*)

Fang Feng Tong Sheng Wan 534 (*internal & external Heat*)

Dan Shen Huo Xue Wan 538 (*Bld stag. with Hot Bld*)

Huo Luo Xiao Ling Wan 428 (*Bld stag.*)

Eczema Herbal Formula 532

Chuan Xin Lian Cream 540 (*topical*)

Xiao Yan Tang Shang Cream 546 (*topical*)

Fu Yin Tai Liniment 541 (*topical*)

Pearl Powder 548 (*topical*)

Si Wu Wan 4 (*Bld def.*)

• **genital**

Long Dan Xie Gan Wan 286 (*Liver Damp Heat*)

Bi Xie Sheng Shi Wan 66 (*Damp Heat*)

Qing Re Qu Shi Tea 234 (*Damp Heat*)

Ke Yin Wan 528 (*Damp Heat*)

Fu Yin Tai Liniment 541 (*topical*)

Xiao Yan Tang Shang Cream 546 (*topical*)

• **infants**

Bo Ying Compound 506 (*accumulation disorder*)

Qi Xing Tea 518 (*accumulation disorder*)

King Fung Powder 508

Pearl Powder 548 (*topical*)

Edema

Ma Huang Tang Wan 156 (*Wind Cold, acute facial*)

Wu Ling San Wan 224 (*Spleen def. with congested fluids*)

Wu Pi Yin 226 (*generalised, pregnancy, menopause*)

Fang Ji Huang Qi Wan 228 (*Wind*)

Epigastric pain (see Pain–epigastric)

Epilepsy

Po Lung Yuen Medical Pills 570 (*Phlegm Heat*)

Wen Dan Wan 370 (*Phlegm Heat*)

Chai Hu Long Gu Mu Li Wan 372 (*qi stag., Phlegm Heat, Liver Fire*)

Tian Ma Gou Teng Wan 576 (*Liver yang*)

Tong Qiao Huo Xue Wan 382 (*Bld stag.*)

Epistaxis

Yunnan Paiyao 422

Raw Tienchi Tablets 424

Liang Ge Wan 566 (*Heat in the Lungs & Stomach*)

Huang Lian Jie Du Wan 552 (*Hot Bld*)

Epstein Barr virus

Xiao Chai Hu Tang Wan 276 (*shao yang syndrome*)

Chuan Xin Lian Antiphlogistic Tablets 558 (*Toxic Heat*)

So Hup Yuen Medical Pills 80 (*Cold Damp*)

Erectile dysfunction (see Impotence)

Esophageal spasm

Ban Xia Hou Po Wan 400 (*qi & Phlegm stag.*)

Shu Gan Wan 116 (*Liver qi stag.*)

Xue Fu Zhu Yu Wan 252 (*qi & Bld stag.*)

Extremities–cold

Dang Gui Si Ni Wan 268 (*Cold stag. in the channels*

Xiao Huo Luo Dan 434 (*severe Cold stag. in the channels*)

Si Ni San Wan 278 (*Liver qi stag.*)

Li Chung Yuen Medical Pills 98 (*Spleen yang def.*)

Fu Gui Ba Wei Wan 324 (*Kid. yang def.*)

Yulin Da Bu Wan 334 (*Kid yang def.*)

Xin Mai Ling 258 (*Bld stag.*)

Hua Tuo Zai Zao Wan 272 (*qi & yin def.*)

Extremities–numbness & paresthesia in (see *also* Neuropathy)

Shi Quan Da Bu Wan 336 (*qi & Bld def.*)

Hua Tuo Zai Zao Wan 272 (*qi & yin def.*)

Bu Yang Huan Wu Wan 266 (*qi def., Bld stag.*)

Jian Bu Qiang Shen Wan 454 (*Kid. def.*)

Sunho Multi Ginseng Tablets 264 (*Bld stag.*)

Xue Fu Zhu Yu Wan 252 (*qi & Bld stag.*)

Xiao Huo Luo Dan 434 (*severe Cold in the channels*)

Erysipelas

Pu Ji Xiao Du Wan 389 (*Toxic Heat*)

Lien Chiao Pai Tu Pien 522 (*Wind Heat, Toxic Heat*)

Huang Lien Shang Ching Pien 386 (*Wind Heat, Toxic Heat*)

Ming Mu Shang Ching Pien 416 (*Liver Heat, Fire*)

Huang Lian Jie Du Wan 552 (*Toxic Heat*)

Wu Wei Xiao Du Wan 562 (*Toxic Heat*)

Liang Ge Wan 566 (*yang ming organ syndrome*)

Chuan Xin Lian Cream 540 (*topical*)

Exopthalamos

Tian Wang Bu Xin Dan 358 (*Heart & Kid. yin def.*)

Eyelids–edema of

Si Jun Zi Wan 86 (*Spleen qi def.*)

Wu Ling San Wan 224 (*Spleen def.*)

Fang Ji Huang Qi Wan 228 (*Wind*)

Ma Huang Tang Wan 156 (*Wind Cold*)

Eyes

• dry, itchy, photophobic

Ming Mu Di Huang Wan 418 (*Liver yin def.*)

Qi Ju Di Huang Wan 309 (*Liver yin def.*)

Si Wu Wan 4 (*Bld def.*)

• floaters & spots before

Ba Zhen Wan 2 (*qi & Bld def.*)

Shi Quan Da Bu Wan 336 (*qi & Bld def.*)

Ming Mu Di Huang Wan 418 (*Liver yin def.*)

Ming Mu Capsule 420 (*yin & Blood def.*)

• red and sore (see *also* Conjunctivitis)

Huang Lien Shang Ching Pien 386 (*Wind Heat, Toxic Heat*)

Ming Mu Shang Ching Pien 416 (*Damp Heat*)

Long Dan Xie Gan Wan 286 (*Liver Fire*)

Jia Wei Xiao Yao Wan 284 (*qi stag. with Heat*)

- **postpartum**

  Gui Zhi Tang Wan 158 (*ying wei disharmony*)

  Xiao Chai Hu Tang Wan 276 (*shao yang syndrome*)

- **premenstrual**

  Jia Wei Xiao Yao Wan 284 (*qi stag. with Heat*)

Fever of unknown origin

Da Bu Yin Wan 314 (*yin def.*)

Zhi Bai Ba Wei Wan 42 (*yin def.*)

Xue Fu Zhu Yu Wan 252 (*qi& Bld stag.*)

Bu Zhong Yi Qi Wan 92 (*qi def.*)

Xiao Jian Zhong Wan 100 (*yang def.*)

Huang Lian Jie Du Wan 552 (*Damp Heat*)

Fibrocystic breast disease

Ru Jie Xiao Tablet 58 (*qi & Bld stag. with Phlegm*)

Chai Hu Shu Gan Wan 280 (*qi stag.*)

Xiao Yao Wan 282 (*qi stag.*)

Jia Wei Xiao Yao Wan 284 (*qi stag. with Heat*)

Nei Xiao Luo Li Wan 62 (*hard Phlegm*)

Hai Zao Jing Wan 60 (*Phlegm*)

Fibroids

Woo Garm Yuen Medical Pills 22 (*Bld & Cold stag.*)

Gui Zhi Fu Ling Wan 30 (*mild Bld stag.*)

Tao Hong Si Wu Wan 28 (*Bld stag. & Bld def.*)

Tong Jing Wan 26 (*Bld stag.*)

Shao Fu Zhu Yu Wan 32 (*Cold & Bld stag.*)

Xue Fu Zhu Yu Wan 252 (*qi & Bld stag.*)

Nei Xiao Luo Li Wan 62 (*hard Phlegm stag.*)

Hai Zao Jing Wan 60 (*Phlegm stag.*)

Ru Jie Xiao Tablet 58 (*qi, Phlegm & Bld stag.*)

Ji Sheng Ju He Wan 492 (*qi & Phlegm stag.*)

Shi Quan Da Bu Wan 336 (*Qi & Bld def. with Cold*)

Fibromyalgia (*see also* Pain, muscular)

Shu Gan Wan 116 (*qi stag.*)

Chai Hu Shu Gan Wan 280 (*qi stag.*)

Xiao Yao Wan 282 (*qi stag.*)

Shen Tong Zhu Yu Wan 442 (*Bld stag.*)

Xue Fu Zhu Yu Wan 252 (*qi & Bld stag.*)

Hua Tuo Zai Zao Wan 272 (*qi & yin def.*)

Juan Bi Wan 430 (*Wind Damp*)

Qu Feng Zhen Tong Capsule 432 (*Wind Cold Damp*)

Fingers and toes–cold

Si Ni San Wan 278 (*Liver qi stag.*)

Chai Hu Shu Gan Wan 280 (*Liver qi stag.*)

Fifty year shoulder

Huo Luo Xiao Ling Wan 428 (*Bld stag.*)

Flatulence

Bao He Wan 106 (*food stag.*)

Xiang Sha Yang Wei Wan 90 (*qi & Damp stag. with Spleen def.*)

Mu Xiang Shun Qi Wan 126 (*qi & Damp stag.*)

Flu (**see Influenza**)

Fluid retention (**see Edema**)

Folliculitis

Peking Niu Huang Jie Du Pian 384 (*Toxic Heat*)

Lien Chiao Pai Tu Pien 522 (*Wind Heat, Toxic Heat*)

Qing Re An Chuang Pian 536 (*Toxic Heat*)

Zhen Zhu An Chuang Tablet 537 (*Toxic Heat*)

Wu Wei Xiao Du Wan 562

Fontanel–failure to close (**see *also* Failure to thrive**)

Deer Velvet 328 (*jing def.*)

Deer Antler and Ginseng 332 (*qi & jing def.*)

Food allergies/intolerance

Xiang Sha Liu Jun Wan 88 (*Spleen def. with Phlegm Damp*)

Bao He Wan 106 (*food stag.*)

Xiang Sha Yang Wei Wan 90 (*qi & Damp stag. with Spleen def.*)

Shen Ling Bai Zhu Wan 94 (*Spleen def.*)

Li Zhong Wan 96 (*Spleen yang def.*)

Jian Pi Wan 104 (*food stag. with Spleen def.*)

Qi Xing Tea 518 (*infants*)

Food poisoning

Xing Jun San 74 (*Summerdamp*)
Huo Hsiang Cheng Chi Pien 76 (*Damp*)
Po Chai Pills 84 (*Damp Heat*)
Shen Chu Cha 108 (*Damp*)

Food stagnation

Bao He Wan 106
Jian Pi Wan 104
Shen Qu Cha 108

Forgetfulness

Gui Pi Wan 16 (*Bld def.*)
Jian Nao Yi Zhi Capsule 376 (*qi def., Bld & Phlegm stag.*)
Bai Zi Yang Xin Wan 360 (*Bld & yin def.*)
Cerebral Tonic Pills 374 (*Phlegm & Kid. def.*)
Tian Wang Bu Xin Dan 358 (*Heart & Kid. yin def.*)
Liu Wei Di Huang Wan 304 (*Kid yin def.*)

Fractures–acute

Die Da Zhi Tong Capsule 425 (*Bld stag.*)
Huo Luo Xiao Ling Wan 428 (*Bld stag.*)
Zheng Gu Shui 460 (*topical*)
Plaster for Bruise and Analgesic 478 (*topical*)

Fractures–slow healing of

Chin Gu Tie Shang Wan 426 (*Bld stag.*)
Shu Jin Huo Xue Wan 440 (*Bld & Phlegm stag.*)
Huo Luo Xiao Ling Wan 428 (*Bld stag.*)
Bu Gai Zuang Gu Capsule 53 (*Kid. def.*)
Zheng Gu Shui 460 (*topical*)

Frostbite

Dang Gui Si Ni Wan 268 (*Cold in the channels*)
Gui Zhi Tang Wan 158 (*ying wei disharmony*)
Hua Tuo Zai Zao Wan 272 (*qi & yin def.*)

Fungal infection

• intestines

Da Huang Jiang Zhi Wan 133 (*Damp Heat*)
Huang Lian Jie Du Wan 552 (*Damp Heat*)

• skin

Bi Xie Sheng Shi Wan 66 (*Damp Heat*)
Xiao Feng Wan 524 (*Wind, Damp*)
Xiao Yan Tang Shang Cream 546 (*topical*)

Gallbladder Pathology

Damp Heat

Da Chai Hu Wan 288
Li Dan Tablets 296
Jigucao Wan 292
Qing Gan Li Dan Tablets 294

Gallbladder deficiency

Wen Dan Wan 370

Fu Yin Tai Liniment 541 (*topical*)
Hua Tuo Gao 545 (*topical*)
Tujin Liniment 544 (*topical*)

• toes

Hua Tuo Gao 545 (*topical*)
Tujin Liniment 544 (*topical*)
Xiao Yan Tang Shang Cream 546 (*topical*)

Furuncle (*see* Abscess)

G

Galactorrhea

Jia Wei Xiao Yao Wan 284 (*qi stag. with Heat*)
Wen Dan Wan 370 (*Phlegm Heat*)

Gall bladder inflammation (*see* cholecystitis)

Gallstones

Da Chai Hu Wan 288 (*Damp Heat*)
Qing Gan Li Dan Tablets 294 (*Damp Heat*)
Li Dan Tablets 296 (*Damp Heat*)
Mu Xiang Shu Qi Wan 126 (*qi & Damp stag.*)
Chai Hu Shu Gan Wan 280 (*Liver qi stag.*)

Gastric hyperacidity

Wei Te Ling 122 (*antacid*)
Xiang Lian Wan 120 (*Damp Heat*)

Gastric neurosis

Yi Guan Jian Wan 290 (*Liver yin def. with qi stag.*)

Gastric ulcers (*see* Ulcers, gastric)

Gastritis

• **acute**

Huang Lian Jie Du Wan 552 (*Damp Heat*)
Qing Wei San Wan 392 (*Stomach Heat*)
Xiang Lian Wan 120 (*Stomach Heat*)
Wen Dan Wan 370 (*Phlegm Heat*)
Xiang Sha Yang Wei Wan 90 (*qi & Damp stag.*)
Bao He Wan 106 (*food stagnation*)

• **atrophic**

Xiao Jian Zhong Wan 100 (*Spleen yang def.*)
Yi Guan Jian Wan 290 (*Liver yin def., qi stag.*)

• **chronic**

Xiang Sha Liu Jun Wan 88 (*Spleen def. with Damp & qi stag.*)
Chai Hu Shu Gan Wan 280 (*Liver Stomach disharmony*)
Yi Guan Jian Wan 290 (*Liver yin def., qi stag.*)
Gu Ben Wan 316 (*stomach yin def.*)
Ping Wei San 114 (*Phlegm Damp*)
Mu Xiang Shun Qi Wan 126 (*qi & Damp stag.*)
Dan Shen Yin Wan 256 (*qi & Bld stag.*)
Xiao Yao Wan 282 (*Liver qi stag., Bld def.*)
Wen Dan Wan 370 (*Phlegm Heat*)
Bao He Wan 106 (*food stagnation*)
Wei Te Ling 122 (*antacid*)

Gastroenteritis

• **acute**

Xing Jun San 74 (*Summerdamp*)
Huo Hsiang Cheng Chi Pien 76 (*Wind Cold with Damp*)
Fu Ke An 82 (*Damp Heat*)
Po Chai Pills 84 (*Damp Heat*)
Ping Wei San 114 (*Phlegm Damp*)
Wu Ling San Wan 224 (*Spleen Damp*)
Qi Xing Tea 518 (*infants*)

• **chronic**

Shen Ling Bai Zhu Wan 94 (*Spleen Damp*)
Li Zhong Wan 96 (*Spleen yang def.*)

Gastro-esophageal reflux (GERD)

Xiang Lian Wan 120 (*Stomach Heat*)
Wei Te Ling 122 (*hyperacidity*)

Xiang Sha Yang Wei Wan 90 (*qi stag.*)
Chai Hu Shu Gan Wan 280 (*Liver qi stag.*)
Shu Gan Wan 116 (*Liver qi stag.*)
Yi Guan Jian Wan 290 (*yin def., qi stag*)
Wei Tong Ding 124 (*Cold, yang def.*)
Bao He Wan 106 (*food stag.*)
Ping Wei San 114 (*Phlegm Damp*)
Bo Ying Compound 506 (*infants*)
Qi Xing Tea 518 (*infants*)

Genital pain (see Pain–genital)

Genital inflammation and infection

Long Dan Xie Gan Wan 286 (*Liver Damp Heat*)
Bi Xie Sheng Shi Wan 66 (*Damp Heat*)
Fu Yan Qing Tablet 64 (*Toxic & Damp Heat*)
Qing Re Qu Shi Tea 234 (*Toxic & Damp Heat*)
Fu Yin Tai Liniment 541 (*topical*)
Xiao Yan Tang Shang Cream 546 (*topical*)

German measles

Yin Chiao Chieh Tu Pien 146 (*Wind Heat*)
Lien Chiao Pai Tu Pien 522 (*Wind Heat, Toxic Heat*)

Giardia lamblia

Huang Lian Jie Du Wan 552 (*Damp & Toxic Heat*)
Xiang Lian Wan 120 (*Stomach Heat*)
Huang Lian Su Tablets 554 (*Damp Heat*)

Gingivitis

Qing Wei San Wan 392 (*Stomach Heat*)
Peking Niu Huang Jie Du Pian 384 (*Toxic Heat*)
Huang Lian Jie Du Wan 552 (*Stomach Fire*)
Niu Huang Qing Huo Wan 561 (*yang ming syndrome*)
Liang Ge Wan 566 (*Lung & Stomach Fire*)
Superior Sore Throat Powder 394 (*topical*)
Sanjin Watermelon Frost 396 (*topical*)

Glands–swollen

Hai Zao Jing Wan 60 (*chronic Phlegm*)
Peking Niu Huang Jie Du Pian 384 (*Toxic Heat*)
Long Dan Xie Gan Wan 286 (*Liver Fire*)

Zuo Gui Wan 312 (*yin def.*)
You Gui Wan 326 (*yang def.*)

Halitosis (*see also* Sinusitis, Gingivitis, Tonsillitis)
Qing Wei San Wan 392 (*Stomach Heat*)
Bao He Wan 106 (*food stag.*)
Qi Xing Tea 518 (*infants*)

Hand, foot and mouth disease
Lien Chiao Pai Tu Pien 522 (*Wind Heat, Toxic Heat*)
Xiao Er Gan Mao Chong Ji 516 (*Heat, infants*)

Hangover
Bao Ji Pills 83 (*Damp Heat*)
Po Chai Pills 84 (*Damp Heat*)
Headache and Dizziness Reliever 585
Shen Chu Cha 108
Huang Lian Jie Du Wan 552 (*Damp Heat*)

Hay fever (*see Rhinitis*)

Head trauma–sequelae of
Tong Qiao Huo Xue Wan 382 (*Bld stag.*)
Xue Fu Zhu Yu Wan 252 (*qi & Bld stag.*)

Headache
• **acute**
Tian Ma Tou Tong Capsule 457 (*Cold, Wind, yang rising*)
Chuan Xiong Cha Tiao Wan 164 (*Wind Cold*)
Zhen Gan Xi Feng Wan 580 (*Liver yang rising, Liver Wind*)
Tian Ma Gou Teng Wan 576 (*Liver yang rising*)
Qu Feng Zhen Tong Capsule 432 (*Wind Cold Damp*)
Tong Luo Zhi Tong Tablet 453 (*Bld def., Bld stag.*)
Long Dan Xie Gan Wan 286 (*Liver Fire*)
Jia Wei Xiao Yao Wan 284 (*Liver qi stag. with Heat*)
Yan Hu Suo Zhi Tong Wan 458 (*analgesic*)

• **dull, worse with extertion**
Ba Zhen Wan 2 (*qi & Bld def.*)
Qi Ju Di Huang Wan 309 (*Kid & Liver yin def.*)

Heat

Heat in the Intestines
Huang Lian Jie Du Wan 552
Hua Zhi Ling Tablet 140
Run Chang Wan 130

Toxic Heat
Chuan Xin Lian Antiphlogistic Tablets 558
Fu Fang Nan Ban Lan Gen 560
Chuan Xin Lian 557
Ban Lan Gen Chong Ji 390
Peking Niu Huang Jie Du Pian 384

Heat in the Stomach
Qing Wei San Wan 392

Heat in the Uterus
Fu Yan Qing Tablet 64
Bi Xie Sheng Shi Wan 66

Heat in the Urinary Bladder
Ba Zheng San Wan 232

Heat in the Liver
Long Dan Xie Gan Wan 286
Ming Mu Shang Ching Pien 416

Heat in the Lungs
Ching Fei Yi Huo Pien 176
Qing Qi Hua Tan Wan 174
Pi Pa Cough Tea 178
Pu Ji Xiao Du Wan 389

Heat in the skin
Lien Chiao Pai Tu Pien 522
Fang Feng Tong Sheng Wan 534
Chuan Xin Lian Cream 540

Heat in the joints
Xuan Bi Tang Wan 436
Guan Jie Yan Wan 438

• **frontal, sinus**
Qian Bai Bi Yan Pian 408 (*Heat*)
Ban Xia Bai Zhu Tian Ma Wan 574 (*Wind Phlegm*)

• **migraine, cluster**
Tian Ma Gou Teng Wan 576 (*Liver yang rising*)
Tian Ma Wan 578 (*yin def., yang rising*)
Chai Hu Shu Gan Wan 280 (*Liver qi stag.*)

Heel spur
Kang Gu Zeng Sheng Pian 456

Helicobacter pylori, infection by
Huang Lian Jie Du Wan 552 (*Damp & Toxic Heat*)
Huang Lian Su Tablets 554 (*Damp & Toxic Heat*)

Hemaspermia
Yunnan Paiyao 422 (*hemostatic*)
Raw Tienchi Tablets 424 (*hemostatic*)
Gui Zhi Fu Ling Wan 30 (*Bld stag.*)

Hematemesis
Yunnan Paiyao 422 (*hemostatic*)
Raw Tienchi Tablets 424 (*hemostatic*)
Huang Lian Jie Du Wan 552 (*Stomach Heat*)
Xue Fu Zhu Yu Wan 252 (*Bld stag.*)
Shi Xiao Wan 21 (*Bld stag.*)

Hematuria
Yunnan Paiyao 422 (*hemostatic*)
Raw Tienchi Tablets 424 (*hemostatic*)
Tao Chih Pien 236 (*Heart Fire*)
Ba Zheng San Wan 232 (*Damp Heat*)
Qian Lie Xian Capsules 488 (*Damp Heat*)
DBD Capsule 238 (*Toxic Heat*)
Zhi Bai Ba Wei Wan 42 (*yin def.*)
Tong Jing Wan 26 (*Bld stag.*)

Hemiplegia
Bu Yang Huan Wu Wan 266 (*qi def. Bld stag.*)
Xiao Shuan Zai Zao Wan 270
Raw Tienchi Tablets 424 (*Bld stag.*)
Sunho Multi Ginseng Tablets 264 (*Bld stag.*)
Hua Tuo Zai Zao Wan 272 (*qi & yin def.*)
Xiao Huo Luo Dan 434 (*Cold, Phlegm & Bld stag. in the channels*)
Da Huo Luo Dan 444 (*Kid. def.*)

Hemochromatosis
Xue Fu Zhu Yu Wan 252 (*qi & Bld stag.*)

Hemoptysis
Yunnan Paiyao 422 (*hemostatic*)
Raw Tienchi Tablets 424 (*hemostatic*)
Ching Fei Yi Huo Pien 176 (*Lung Fire*)
Bai He Gu Jin Wan 206 (*Lung yin def.*)
Da Bu Yin Wan 314 (*yin def. with Heat*)

Cordyceps Essence of Chicken 342 (*consumptive disease*)

Hemorrhoids
Hua Zhi Ling Tablet 140 (*Damp Heat, Bld stag.*)
Fargelin for Piles 142 (*Damp Heat*)
Huai Jiao Wan 139 (*Intestinal Wind*)
Bu Zhong Yi Qi Wan 92 (*sinking Spleen qi*)
Gui Pi Wan 16 (*Spleen qi def.*)
Hemorrhoids Ointment 143 (*topical*)
Ching Wan Hung 542 (*topical*)
Xiao Yan Tang Shang Cream 546 (*topical*)

Henoch Schönlein purpura
Gui Pi Wan 16 (*Spleen qi def.*)
Fu Fang Nan Ban Lan Gen 560 (*Heat in the Bld*)

Hepatitis
• acute
Long Dan Xie Gan Wan 286 (*Liver Damp Heat*)
Li Dan Tablets 296 (*Damp, Damp Heat*)
Ban Lan Gen Chong Ji 390 (*Toxic Heat*)
Chuan Xin Lian Antiphogistic Tablets 558 (*Toxic Heat*)
Herba Abri Fruticulosi Beverage 300 (*Damp Heat*)
Xi Huang Cao 301 (*Damp Heat*)

• chronic
Xiao Chai Hu Tang Wan 276 plus Jigucao Wan 292
Da Chai Hu Wan 288 (*Damp Heat*)
Chai Hu Shu Gan Wan 280 (*Liver qi stag.*)
Shu Gan Wan 116 (*Liver qi stag.*)
Yi Guan Jian Wan 290 (*Liver yin def. with qi stag.*)
Qing Gan Li Dan Tablets 294 (*Damp Heat*)
Xue Fu Zhu Yu Wan 252 (*Bld stag.*)
Sunho Multi Ginseng Tablets 264 (*Bld stag.*)
Herba Abri Fruticulosi Beverage 300
Xi Huang Cao 301
Reishi Mushroom 354 (*immune regulator*)

Hepatitis C–chronic
Xiao Chai Hu Tang Wan 276 plus Jigucao Wan 292

Bu Zhong Yi Qi Wan 92 (*Spleen qi def.*)
Yang Ying Wan 340 (*qi & Bld def.*)
Yi Guan Jian Wan 290 (*Liver yin def. with qi stag.*)
Qi Ju Di Huang Wan 309 (*Liver yin def.*)
Reishi Mushroom 354 (*immune regulator*)

Hepatosplenomegaly

Nei Xiao Luo Li Wan 62 (*hard Phlegm*)
Ge Xia Zhu Yu Wan 298 (*Bld stag.*)
Huo Luo Xiao Ling Wan 428 (*Bld stag.*)

Hernia

- **hiatus**

  Bu Zhong Yi Qi Wan 92 (*Spleen qi def.*)
  Li Zhong Wan 96 (*Spleen yang def.*)

- **inguinal**

  Bu Zhong Yi Qi Wan 92 (*Spleen qi def.*)
  Tian Tai Wu Yao Wan 494 (*Cold in Liver channel*)

Herpes–aural and ocular

Long Dan Xie Gan Wan 286 (*Liver Fire*)
Ming Mu Shang Ching Pien 416 (*Liver Fire*)
Chuan Xin Lian Antiphlogistic Tablets 558 (*Toxic Heat*)
Chuan Xin Lian 557 (*Toxic Heat*)

Herpes genitalis

- **acute**

  Bi Xie Sheng Shi Wan 66 (*Damp Heat*)
  Long Dan Xie Gan Wan 286 (*Liver Damp Heat*)
  Chuan Xin Lian Antiphlogistic Tablets 558 (*Toxic Heat*)
  Chuan Xin Lian 557 (*Toxic Heat*)
  Fu Yan Qing Tablet 64 (*Toxic & Damp Heat*)
  Qing Re Qu Shi Tea 234 (*Damp & Toxic Heat*)

- **recurrent**

  Bi Xie Sheng Shi Wan 66 (*Damp Heat*)
  Bi Xie Fen Qing Wan 230 (*Damp*)
  Chuan Xin Lian Antiphlogistic Tablets 558 (*Toxic Heat*)
  Chuan Xin Lian 557 (*Toxic Heat*)

Herpes simplex

Lien Chiao Pai Tu Pien 522 (*Wind Heat, Toxic Heat*)

Peking Niu Huang Jie Du Pian 384 (*Toxic Heat*)
Huang Lien Shang Ching Pien 386 (*Wind Heat, Toxic Heat*)
Ban Lan Gen Chong Ji 390 (*Toxic Heat*)
Chuan Xin Lian Antiphlogistic Tablets 558 (*Toxic Heat*)
Chuan Xin Lian 557 (*Toxic Heat*)

Herpes zoster

Lien Chiao Pai Tu Pien 522 (*Wind Heat, Toxic Heat*)
Long Dan Xie Gan Wan 286 (*Damp Heat, Liver Fire*)
Chuan Xin Lian Antiphlogistic Tablets 558 (*Toxic Heat*)
Chuan Xin Lian 557 (*Toxic Heat*)
Bi Xie Sheng Shi Wan 66 (*Damp Heat*)
Ban Lan Gen Chong Ji 390 (*Toxic Heat*)
Superior Sore Throat Powder 394 (*topical*)

Hiccough

Wei Tong Ding 124 (*Cold, yang def.*)
Bao He Wan 106 (*food stagnation*)
Xiang Sha Yang Wei Wan 90 (*qi & Damp stag.*)

HIV–to assist immunity in

Cordyceps Essence of Chicken 342 (*Lung & Kid. yang qi & yin def.*)
Reishi Mushroom 354

Hong Kong foot

Hua Tuo Gao 545 (*topical*)

Hives (*see* Urticaria)

Hoarse voice (*see* Voice–hoarse)

Hordeolum (stye)

Huang Lien Shang Ching Pien 386 (*Wind Heat, Toxic Heat*)
Ming Mu Shang Ching Pien 416 (*Liver Fire*)
Peking Niu Huang Jie Du Pian 384 (*Toxic Heat*)
Huang Lien Shang Ching Pien 386 (*Wind Heat, Toxic Heat*)

Hot flushing

Er Xian Wan 46 (*Kid. yin & yang def.*)
Da Bu Yin Wan 314 (*Kid. yin def.*)
Zhi Bai Ba Wei Wan 42 (*Kid yin def.*)
Geng Nian Ling 52 (*yin & yang def.*)

Jia Wei Xiao Yao Wan 284 (*qi stag. with Heat*)

Kun Bao Wan 48 (*yin def. with yang rising*)

Tong Ren Wu Ji Bai Feng Wan 14 (*Bld def. postpartum*)

Hydrocele

Ji Sheng Ju He Wan 492 (*qi & Phlegm stag.*)

Hai Zao Jing Wan 60 (*Phlegm*)

Hypercholesterolemia

Dan Shen Pill 254 (*Bld & Phlegm stag.*)

Xin Mai Ling 258 (*Bld stag.*)

Sunho Multi Ginseng Tablets 264 (*Bld stag.*)

Raw Tienchi Tablets 424 (*Bld stag.*)

Keep Fit Capsule 111 (*qi, Phlegm & Bld stag.*)

Hyperglycemia

Sugarid 138

Yu Quan Wan 136 (*qi & yin def.*)

Liu Wei Di Huang Wan 304 (*Kid. yin def.*)

Panax Ginseng Extractum 350 (*qi def.*)

American Ginseng Essence of Chicken 344 (*qi & yin def.*)

Hyperpigmentation–hormonal

Yang Yan Qu Ban Tablet 72 (*qi & Bld stag., Bld def*)

Hypersalivation (see Salivation–excessive)

Hypertension

Zhen Gan Xi Feng Wan 580 (*Liver yang rising, Liver Wind*)

Tian Ma Gou Teng Wan 576 (*Liver yang rising*)

Tian Ma Wan 578 (*yin def., yang rising*)

Yang Yin Jiang Ya Wan 582 (*yang rising*)

Fu Fang Jiang Ya Capsule 584 (*yang rising*)

Qi Ju Di Huang Wan 309 (*Liver yin def.*)

Chai Hu Long Gu Mu Li Wan 372 (*Liver Fire, Phlegm Heat*)

Ban Xia Bai Zhu Tian Ma Wan 574 (*Wind Phlegm*)

Huang Lian Jie Du Wan 552 (*Damp Heat*)

Xue Fu Zhu Yu Wan 252 (*qi & Bld stag.*)

Da Chai Hu Wan 288 (*shao yang/yang ming syndrome*)

• **menopausal**

Er Xian Wan 46 (*yin & yang def., menopausal*)

• **portal**

Ge Xia Zhu Yu Wan 298 (*Bld stag.*)

Hyperthyroidism

Tian Wang Bu Xin Dan 358 (*Heart yin def.*)

Zhi Bai Ba Wei Wan 42 (*Kid yin def.*)

Er Xian Wan 46 (*yin & Yang def.*)

Da Bu Yin Wan 314 (*yin def. with Heat*)

Zhi Gan Cao Wan 260 (*Heart qi & yin def.*)

Chai Hu Long Gu Mu Li Wan 372 (*Liver Fire, Phlegm Heat*)

Long Dan Xie Gan Wan 286 (*Liver Fire*)

Nei Xiao Luo Li Wan 62 (*Phlegm Heat*)

Hypochondriac pain (see Pain, hypochondriac)

Hypoglycemia

Si Jun Zi Wan 86 (*Spleen qi def.*)

Xiang Sha Liu Jun Wan 88 (*Spleen qi def. with Damp*)

Shen Ling Bai Zhu Wan 94 (*Spleen qi def.*)

Bu Zhong Yi Qi Wan 92 (*Spleen qi def.*)

Hypoproteinemia

Gui Pi Wan 16 (*Heart & Spleen def.*)

Hypotension

Bu Zhong Yi Qi Wan 92 (*Spleen qi def.*)

Hypothyroidism

Fu Gui Ba Wei Wan 324 (*Kid. yang def.*)

You Gui Wan 326 (*Kid. yang def.*)

Zhen Wu Tang Wan 222 (*Heart & Kid. yang def.*)

Hysteria

Chai Hu Long Gu Mu Li Wan 372 (*Liver Fire, Phlegm Heat*)

Gan Mai Da Zao Wan 378

I

Immunity–weak or insufficient

Bu Zhong Yi Qi Wan 92 (*Spleen & Lung qi def.*)

Reishi Mushroom 354 (*immune regulator*)

Tong Luo Zhi Tong Tablets 453 (*Bld def.*)

Deer Antler and Ginseng 332 (*qi & jing def.*)

Yu Ping Feng Wan 348 (*wei qi def.*)

Sheng Mai San Wan 212 (*qi & yin def.*)

Cordyceps Essence of Chicken 342 (*qi & yang def.*)

American Ginseng Essence of Chicken 344 (*qi & yin def.*)

Panax Ginseng Extractum 350 (*qi def.*)

Immunisation–side effects of

Xiao Chai Hu Tang Wan 276

Bo Ying Compound 506 (*Heat, fever following*)

Impetigo

Lien Chiao Pai Tu Pien 522 (*Wind Heat, Toxic Heat*)

Peking Niu Huang Jie Du Pian 384 (*Toxic Heat*)

Huang Lian Su Tablets 554 (*Damp & Toxic Heat*)

Chuan Xin Lian Antiphlogistic Tablets 558 (*Toxic Heat*)

Huang Lian Jie Du Wan 552 (*acute, Damp Heat*)

Qing Re An Chuang Pian 536 (*Toxic Heat*)

Xiao Er Gan Mao Chong Ji 516 (*infants*)

Chuan Xin Lian Cream 540 (*topical*)

Impotence

Gu Ben Fu Zheng Capsule 498 (*Kid. yang def.*)

Kang Wei Ling Wan 502 (*Bld stag.*)

Zi Shen Da Bu Capsules 244 (*Kid. yang def.*)

Nan Bao Capsules 500 (*yang def.*)

Fu Gui Ba Wei Wan 324 (*Kid. yang def.*)

Gui Pi Wan 16 (*Heart & Spleen def.*)

Chai Hu Shu Gan Wan 280 (*Liver qi stag.*)

Wu Zi Yan Zong Wan 496 (*jing def.*)

Deer Velvet 328 (*jing def.*)

Deer Antler and Ginseng 332 (*qi & jing def.*)

Incontinence of urine (*see* Urination–incontinence of)

Indeterminate gnawing hunger

Shen Ling Bai Zhu Wan 94 (*Spleen qi def.*)

Shu Gan Wan 116 (*Liver Spleen disharmony*)

Yi Guan Jian Wan 290 (*Liver yin def., qi stag.*)

Tung Hsuan Li Fei Pien 180 (*dryness, Heat*)

Gu Ben Wan 316 (*Stomach qi & yin def.*)

Wen Dan Wan 370 (*Phlegm Heat*)

Indigestion

Bao He Wan 106 (*food stag.*)

Jian Pi Wan 104 (*food stag., during pregnancy*)

Ping Wei San 114 (*Cold Damp*)

Zi Sheng Wan 102 (*food stag. with Spleen def.*)

Mu Xiang Shun Qi Wan 126 (*qi & Damp stag.*)

Li Zhong Wan 96 (*Spleen yang def.*)

Wei Tong Ding 124 (*Cold*)

Xiang Lian Wan 120 (*Stomach Heat*)

Xiang Sha Yang Wei Wan 90 (*qi & Damp stag.*)

Shu Gan Wan 116 (*Liver Spleen disharmony*)

Wei Te Ling 122 (*antacid*)

Infantile colic

Bo Ying Compound 506 (*accumulation disorder*)

Infection (*see* Bacterial infection, Viral infection)

Infertility (*see also* Endometriosis, Fibroids, Ovarian cysts)

• **female**

Tiao Jing Cu Yun Wan 38 (*yang def., weak progesterone phase*)

Cu Yun Yu Tai Capsule 36 (*yang def., weak progesterone phase*)

Wu Ji Bai Feng Wan 12 (*Bld & yang def.*)

Ba Zhen Wan 2 (*qi & Bld def.*)

Shi Quan Da Bu Wan 336 (*qi & Bld def. with Cold*)

Gui Pi Wan 16 (*Heart & Spleen def.*)

Wen Jing Tang Wan 24 (*Cold & def., Bld stag.*)

You Gui Wan 326 (*Kid. yang def.*)

Zuo Gui Wan 312 (*Kid. yin def.*)

Deer Velvet 328 (*jing def.*)

Lu Rong Jiao 330 (*jing def.*)

Gui Zhi Fu Ling Wan 30 (*Bld stag., masses*)

Tao Hong Si Wu Wan 28 (*Bld def., Bld stag., masses*)

Hai Zao Jing Wan 60 (*polycystic ovaries*)

Shao Yao Gan Cao Wan 459 (*polycystic ovaries*)

• **male**

Wu Zi Yan Zong Wan 496 (*jing def.*)

Gu Ben Fu Zheng Capsule 498 (*yang def.*)

Zi Shen Da Bu Capsule 244 (*yang def.*)

Gui Zhi Fu Ling Wan 30 (*Bld stag.*)

Inflammation of the bile duct

Li Dan Tablets 296 (*Damp Heat*)

Inflammatory joint disorders

Xuan Bi Tang Wan 436 (*Damp Heat*)

Guan Jie Yan Wan 438 (*Damp Heat*)

Inflammatory bowel disorders (see Ulcerative colitis, Crohn's disease)

Influenza

Gan Mao Ling 155 (*Wind*)

Yin Chiao Chieh Tu Pien 146 (*Wind Heat*)

Ma Huang Tang Wan 156 (*Wind Cold*)

Jing Fang Bai Du Wan 166 (*Wind Cold Damp*)

Chuan Xiong Cha Tiao Wan 164 (*Wind Cold*)

Gan Mao Qing Re Chong Ji 170 (*Wind Cold*)

Gan Mao Zhi Ke Chong Ji 152 (*tai yang / shao yang syndrome*)

Gui Zhi Tang Wan 158 (*persistent, postpartum*)

Shih San Tai Pao Wan 56 (*during pregnancy*)

Insect bites (see Bites & stings)

Insomnia

Gui Pi Wan 16 (*Heart & Spleen def.*)

Tian Wang Bu Xin Dan 358 (*Heart yin def.*)

Wen Dan Wan 370 (*Phlegm Heat*)

An Shen Bu Xin Wan 364 (*yang rising*)

Tao Chih Pien 236 (*Heart Fire*)

Xue Fu Zhu Yu Wan 252 (*qi & Bld stag., chronic refractory*)

An Shen Jie Yu Capsule 368 (*qi stag., premenstrual*)

Bao He Wan 106 (*food stag.*)

Qi Xing Tea 518 (*children*)

Intercostal neuralgia (see Neuralgia–intercostal)

Interstitial cystitis (see Cystitis)

Intestinal abscess (see Appendicitis, Diverticulitis)

Intestinal flu (see Gastroenteritis)

Intestinal parasites

Baby Fat Powder 510

Intestinal Wind

Huai Jiao Wan 139

Irritability

Chai Hu Shu Gan Wan 280 (*qi stag.*)

Chai Hu Long Gu Mu Li Wan 372 (*Liver Fire, Phlegm Heat*)

Jia Wei Xiao Yao Wan 284 (*qi stag. with Heat*)

Long Dan Xie Gan Wan 286 (*Liver Fire*)

Fu Gui Ba Wei Wan 324 (*Kid yang def.*)

Kun Bao Wan 48 (*Kid yin def.*)

Irritable Bowel Syndrome

• **diarrhea predominant**

Tong Xie Yao Fang Wan 118 (*Liver invading Spleen*)

Chai Hu Shu Gan Wan 280 (*Liver invading Spleen*)

Xiao Yao Wan 282 (*Liver qi stag.*)

Zi Sheng Wan 102 (*qi def. & food stag.*)

• **constipation predominant**

Mu Xiang Shun Qi Wan 126 (*qi & food stag.*)

Ischemia

Raw Tienchi Tablets 424 (*Bld stag.*)

Knee pain (see Pain, knee)

Knees–weakness of
Zhuang Yao Jian Shen 450 (*Wind Damp with Kid def.*)
Zhuang Yao Jian Shen Tablet 452 (*Wind Damp with Kid def.*)
Jian Bu Qiang Shen Wan 454 (*Kid. def.*)
Bu Gai Zhuang Gu Capsule 53 (*Wind Cold Damp with kid. def.*)
San Bi Wan 446 (*Kid. def. with Cold Damp*)
Du Huo Ji Sheng Wan 448 (*Wind Damp with Kid def.*)

L

Labour–difficult
Bu Zhong Yi Qi Wan 92 (*qi def.*)
Ba Zhen Yi Mu Wan 6 (*qi & Bld def.*)
Tao Hong Si Wu Wan 28 (*Bld def., Bld stag.*)

Labour–to induce at term
Ping Wei San 114 (*dispersing*)

Labyrinthitis–chronic
Er Long Zuo Ci Wan 380 (*Kid. yin def.*)

Lacrimation–excessive
Ming Mu Di Huang Wan 418 (*Kid. yin. def.*)
Ming Mu Capsule 420 (*yin & Bld def.*)

Lactation–insufficient
Tangkwei Essence of Chicken 54 (*qi & Bld def.*)
Bai Feng Wan 10 (*qi & Bld def.*)
Shi Quan Da Bu Wan 336 (*qi & Bld def. with Cold*)

Laryngitis
• acute
Gan Mao Qing Re Ke Li 171 (*Wind Heat*)
Huang Lien Shang Ching Pien 386 (*Wind Heat, Toxic Heat*)
Peking Niu Huang Jie Du Pian 384 (*Wind & Toxic Heat*)
Yin Chiao Chieh Tu Pien 146 (*Wind Heat*)
Superior Sore Throat Powder 394 (*topical*)
Sanjin Watermelon Frost 396 (*topical*)

Large Intestine Pathology

Excess Heat
Ching Fei Yi Huo Pien 176
Niu Huang Qing Huo Wan 561
Liang Ge Wan 566

Toxic Heat (intestinal abscess)
Huang Lian Jie Du Wan 552
Chuan Xin Lian Antiphlogistic Tablets 558
Niu Huang Qing Huo Wan 561

Damp Heat
Huang Lian Jie Du Wan 552
Da Chai Hu Wan 288
Hua Zhi Ling Tablet 140
Po Chai Pills 84
Bao Ji Pills 83
Fu Ke An 82

Chronic residual Damp Heat
Mu Xiang Shun Qi Wan 126

Deficiency with Damp and food accumulation
Zi Sheng Wan 102

Qi stagnation
Mu Xiang Shun Qi Wan 126
Chen Xiang Hua Qi Wan 128
Shu Gan Wan 116

Blood stagnation
Shao Fu Zhu Yu Wan 32
Gui Zhi Fu Ling Wan 30

Large Intestine dryness
Run Chang Wan 130
Wu Ren Wan 132

Invasion by Liver qi
Tong Xie Yao Fang Wan 118
Chai Hu Shu Gan Wan 280
Shu Gan Wan 116

• chronic
Qing Yin Wan 398 (*Lung dryness & Heat*)
Ban Xia Hou Po Wan 400 (*qi & Phlegm stag.*)
Mai Wei Di Huang Wan 208 (*Lung yin def.*)
Yang Yin Qing Fei Wan 204 (*yin def., dryness*)

Yu Ping Feng Wan 348 (*wei qi def.*)
Sheng Mai San Wan 212 (*qi & yin def.*)
Cordyceps Essence of Chicken 342 (*qi & yang def.*)
American Ginseng Essence of Chicken 344 (*qi & yin def.*)
Panax Ginseng Extractum 350 (*qi def.*)

Leukorrhea

• **white mucoid watery**
Shen Ling Bai Zhu Wan 94 (*Spleen Damp*)
Xiang Sha Liu Jun Wan 88 (*Spleen def. with Phlegm Damp*)
Cu Yun Yu Tai Capsule 36 (*yang def., Cold*)
Bi Xie Fen Qing Wan 230 (*Kid. def., Damp*)
Ba Ji Yin Yang Wan 240 (*Kid. yang def.*)
Bai Feng Wan 10 (*qi & Bld def.*)

• **yellow malodorous**
Yu Dai Wan 68 (*Damp Heat*)
Bi Xie Sheng Shi Wan 66 (*Damp Heat*)
Long Dan Xie Gan Wan 286 (*Liver Damp Heat*)
Fu Yan Qing Tablet 64 (*Toxic Heat*)
Chien Chin Chih Tai Wan 70 (*Damp Heat with def.*)

Libido–loss of
Cu Yun Yu Tai Capsule 36 (*yang def., Cold*)
Tiao Jing Cu Yun Wan 38 (*yang def., Cold*)
You Gui Wan 326 (*Kid. yang def.*)
Gu Ben Fu Zheng Capsule 498 (*yang def.*)
Qian Lie Xian Capsule 488 (*Damp Heat*)

Lichen simplex
Xiao Feng Wan 524 (*Wind, Damp*)

Lichen sclerosis
Lien Chiao Pai Tu Pien 522 (*Wing & Toxic Heat*)

Ligament–damage to
Chin Gu Tie Shang Wan 426 (*Bld. stag.*)
Die Da Zhi Tong Capsule 425 (*Bld stag.*)
Zheng Gu Shui 460 (*topical*)

Limbs–cold (*see* Extremities–cold)

Lipoma
Hai Zao Jing Wan 60 (*Phlegm*)
Ru Jie Xiao Tablet 58 (*qi, Phlegm, Bld stag.*)
Nei Xiao Luo Li Wan 62 (*hard Phlegm*)
Ji Sheng Ju He Wan 492 (*qi, Phlegm, Bld stag.*)

Liver spots
Yang Yan Qu Ban Tablet 72 (*qi & Bld stag., Bld def.*)

Lower back ache–chronic (*see* Pain–lower back)

Lower back–weakness of
Zhuang Yao Jian Shen Tablet 452 (*Kid. yang def.*)
You Gui Wan 326 (*Kid. Yang def.*)
Zuo Gui Wan 312 (*Kid. yin def.*)
Jian Bu Qiang Shen Wan 454 (*Kid. def.*)
Ba Ji Yin Yang Wan 240 (*Kid. yang def.*)

Lung cancer–chronic dry cough of
Yang Yin Qing Fei Wan 204 (*Lung dryness*)
Bai He Gu Jin Wan 206 (*Lung & Kid yin def.*)
Cordyceps Essence of Chicken 342 (*yin & yang def.*)
Tung Hsuan Li Fei Pien 180 (*dryness*)

Lungs–weakness of
Bu Fei Wan 216 (*qi def.*)
Sheng Mai San Wan 212 (*qi & yin def.*)
Yulin Bu Shen Wan 214 (*Lung & Kid. yang def.*)
Mai Wei Di Huang Wan 208 (*Lung yin def.*)
Yu Ping Feng Wan 348

Lupus (*see* Systemic Lupus Erythematosus)

Lymphadenitis
• **acute**
Pu Ji Xiao Du Wan 389 (*Lung & Stomach Heat*)
Peking Niu Huang Jie Du Pian 384 (*Toxic Heat*)
Lien Chiao Pai Tu Pien 522 (*Wind Heat, Toxic Heat*)

GENERAL INDEX

Xiang Sha Yang Wei Wan 90 (*Spleen qi def. with qi stag.*)

Ping Wei San 114 (*Phlegm Damp*)

Malarial disorder

Xiao Chai Hu Tang Wan 276 (*shao yang*)

Da Chai Hu Wan 288 (*shao yang/yang ming*)

Ping Wei San 114 (*Phlegm Damp*)

Ge Xia Zhu Yu Wan 298 (*Bld stag.*)

Mania

Chai Hu Long Gu Mu Li Wan 372 (*Liver Fire, Phlegm Heat*)

Manic depressive psychosis

Chai Hu Long Gu Mu Li Wan 372 (*Liver Fire, Phlegm Heat, qi stag.*)

Masses

• **abdominal**

Xue Fu Zhu Yu Wan 252 (*qi & Bld stag.*)

Ge Xia Zhu Yu Wan 298 (*Liver Bld stag.*)

Huo Luo Xiao Ling Wan 428 (*Bld stag.*)

Woo Garm Yuen Medical Pills 22 (*Cold & Bld stag.*)

Nei Xiao Luo Li Wan 62 (*Phlegm & Bld stag.*)

Shu Gan Wan 116 (*Liver qi stag.*)

Bao He Wan 106 (*food stag.*)

Gui Zhi Fu Ling Wan 30 (*Bld stag. in the uterus*)

• **gynecological (*See* Breast; Endometriosis; Fibroids; Ovarian cysts**

• **prostatic, testicular**

Ji Sheng Ju He Wan 492 (*qi, Bld, Phlegm stag.*)

Shao Fu Zhu Yu Wan 32 (*Bld stag., Cold*)

Qian Lie Xian Capsule 488 (*Damp Heat*)

Gui Zhi Fu Ling Wan 30 (*Bld stag. in the uterus*)

Fu Gui Ba Wei Wan 324 (*Kid. yang def.*)

• **thyroid**

Hai Zao Jing Wan 60 (*Phlegm*)

Nei Xiao Luo Li Wan 62 (*Phlegm & Heat.*)

Ru Jie Xiao Tablet 58 (*qi, Bld, Phlegm*)

Mastalgia (*see* Breast–swelling and tenderness)

Mastitis

• **acute**

Xiao Chai Hu Tang Wan 276 + Chuan Xin Lian Antiphlogistic Tablets 558

Xiao Chai Hu Tang Wan 276 + Wu Wei Xiao Du Wan 562

Lien Chiao Pai Tu Pien 522 (*Toxic Heat*)

• **chronic or recurrent after antibiotics**

Xiang Sha Liu Jun Wan 88 (*Spleen def. with Phlegm*)

Li Zhong Wan 96 (*Spleen yang def.*)

Measles

Ge Gen Wan 168 (*Wind Cold, early stage of*)

Yin Chiao Chieh Tu Pien 146 (*Wind Heat*)

Lien Chiao Pai Tu Pien 522 (*Wind Heat, Toxic Heat*)

Ban Lan Gen Chong Ji 390 (*Toxic Heat*)

Bai Hu Tang Wan 564 (*yang ming syndrome, high fever*)

Liang Ge Wan 566 (*Lung & Stomach Heat*)

Xiao Er Gan Mao Chong Ji 516

Melasma

Yang Yan Qu Ban Tablet 72 (*qi & Bld def., Bld stag.*)

Memory–poor, loss of

Jian Nao Yi Zhi Capsule 376 (*qi def., Bld stag.*)

Cerebral Tonic Pills 374 (*Bld def. & Phlegm Heat*)

Gui Pi Wan 16 (*qi & Bld def.*)

Tian Wang Bu Xin Dan 358 (*Heart & Kid. yin def.*)

Huan Shao Dan 331 (*Heart & Kidney def.*)

Zhi Gan Cao Wan 260 (*Heart qi & Bld def.*)

Bai Zi Yang Xin Wan 360 (*general*)

Wen Dan Wan 370 (*Phlegm Heat*)

Tong Qiao Huo Xue Wan 382 (*Bld stag., post traumatic*)

Ménière's disease

Ban Xia Bai Zhu Tian Ma Wan 574 (*Wind Phlegm*)

Zhen Wu Tang Wan 222 (*yang def.*)

Er Long Zuo Ci Wan 380 (*Liver & Kid. yin def.*)

Wen Dan Wan 370 (*Phlegm Heat*)

Meningitis
Ge Gen Wan 168 (*Wind Cold, early stage of*)
Pu Ji Xiao Du Wan 389 (*Toxic Heat*)
Ban Lan Gen Chong Ji 390 (*Toxic Heat*)
Bai Hu Tang Wan 564 (*yang ming syndrome, high fever*)
Liang Ge Wan 566 (*Lung & Stomach Heat*)

Menopausal syndrome
Kun Bao Wan 48 (*Kid yin def.*)
Er Xian Wan 46 (*yin & yang def.*)
Geng Nian Ling 52 (*yin & yang def.*)
Zhi Bai Ba Wei Wan 42 (*Kid yin def.*)
Tian Wang Bu Xin Dan 358 (*Heart & Kid yin def.*)
Da Bu Yin Wan 314 (*yin def., severe Heat*)
Gan Mai Da Zao Wan 378

Menopausal hypertension
Er Xian Wan 46 (*yin & yang def.*)

Menorrhagia
Yunnan Paiyao 422 (*hemostatic*)
Raw Tienchi Tablets 424 (*hemostatic*)
Gui Pi Wan 16 (*Spleen qi def.*)
Tao Hong Si Wu Wan 28 (*Bld stag., Bld def.*)
Si Wu Wan 4 + Huang Lian Jie Du Wan 552 (*Hot Bld with Bld def.*)
Jia Wei Xiao Yao Wan 284 (*Liver qi stag. with Heat*)
Li Zhong Wan 96 (*Spleen yang def.*)

Menstruation
• **irregular**
Si Wu Wan 4 (*Bld def.*)
Xiao Yao Wan 282 (*Liver qi stag.*)
Jia Wei Xiao Yao Wan 284 (*Liver qi stag. with Heat*)
Ba Zhen Wan 2 (*qi & Bld def.*)
Bai Feng Wan 10 (*qi & Bld def.*)
Wu Ji Bai Feng Wan 12 (*qi, Bld & yang def.*)
• **low or short progesterone phase of**
Cu Yun Yu Tai Capsules 36 (*yang def.*)
Tiao Jing Cu Yun Wan 38 (*yang def.*)

• **prolonged**
Cu Yun Yu Tai Capsule 36 (*yang def.*)
Tiao Jing Cu Yun Wan 38 (*yang def.*)
Woo Garm Yuen Medical Pills 22 (*Bld stag. with Cold & def.*)
Tao Hong Si Wu Wan 28 (*Bld stag with Bld def.*)
Ba Zhen Wan 2 (*qi & Bld def.*)
Shi Quan Da Bu Wan 336 (*qi & Bld def., with Cold*)
• **scant**
Ba Zhen Wan 2 (*qi & Bld def.*)
Shi Quan Da Bu Wan 336 (*qi & Bld def.*)
Bai Feng Wan 10 (*qi & Bld def.*)
Tao Hong Si Wu Wan 28 (*Bld stag with Bld def.*)
Shao Fu Zhu Yu Wan 32 (*Bld stag. Cold*)
• **Wind Cold during**
Shih San Tai Pao Wan 56 (*Bld def., Wind*)
Gui Zhi Tang Wan 158 (*ying wei disharmony*)

Mental
• **agitation**
Chai Hu Long Gu Mu Li Wan 372 (*Phlegm Heat, Liver yang*)
An Shen Bu Xin Wan 364 (*yang excess*)
Gui Pi Wan 16 (*Bld def.*)
Cerebral Tonic Pills 374 (*Phlegm Heat*)
Wen Dan Wan 370 (*Phlegm Heat*)
Tian Wang Bu Xin Dan 358 (*Heart yin def.*)
Xue Fu Zhu Yu Wan 252 (*Bld stag.*)
• **cloudiness**
Xiang Sha Yang Wei Wan 90 (*qi & Damp stag.*)
Jian Nao Yi Zhi Capsule 376 (*qi def.*)
• **fatigue**
Xiang Sha Liu Jun Wan 88 (*Spleen def. with Damp*)
Jian Nao Yi Zhi Capsule 376 (*qi def.*)

Migraine headache (*see* Headache–migraine)

Miscarriage
• **habitual**
You Gui Wan 326 (*Kid. yang def.*)
Zuo Gui Wan 312 (*Kid. yin def.*)
Cu Yun Yu Tai Capsule 36 (*yang def.*)

Tiao Jing Cu Yun Wan 38 (*yang def.*)
Ba Zhen Wan 2 (*qi & Bld def.*)
Bu Zhong Yi Qi Wan 92 (*sinking Spleen qi*)
• **persistent bleeding following (see Bleeding)**
• **threatened**
Shih San Tai Pao Wan 56

Mittlesmertz
Woo Garm Yuen Medical Pills 22 (*Cold, Bld stag.*)
Gui Zhi Fu Ling Wan 30 (*Bld stag.*)
Tao Hong Si Wu Wan 28 (*Bld stag., Bld def.*)
Tong Jing Wan 26 (*Bld stag., severe*)
Tiao Jing Cu Yun Wan 38 (*yang def.*)

Mixed connective tissue disease
Xue Fu Zhu Yu Wan 252 (*qi & Bld stag.*)

Mood swings
Gan Mai Da Zao Wan 378
Chai Hu Shu Gan Wan 280 (*qi stag.*)
Xiao Yao Wan 282 (*qi stag., Bld def.*)
Xue Fu Zhu Yu Wan 252 (*qi & Bld stag.*)
Kun Bao Wan 48 (*yang def.*)

Morning sickness
Zi Sheng Wan 102 (*Spleen def., food & Damp stag.*)
Liu Jun Zi Wan 87 (*Spleen def. with Phlegm Damp*)
Xiang Sha Liu Jun Wan 88 (*Spleen def. with Phlegm Damp & qi stag.*)
Er Chen Wan 112 (*Phlegm Damp*)
Wen Dan Wan 370 (*Phlegm Heat*)
Shih San Tai Pao Wan 56

Motion sickness
Xing Jun San 74 (*Damp*)
Huo Hsiang Cheng Chi Pien 76 (*Damp*)
Er Chen Wan 112 (*Phlegm*)
White Flower Embrocation 467

Mucus congestion–chronic
Er Chen Wan 112 (*Phlegm Damp*)
Wen Dan Wan 370 (*Phlegm Heat*)
Liu Jun Zi Wan 87 (*Spleen def. with Phlegm Damp*)
Xiang Sha Liu Jun Wan 88 (*Spleen def. with Phlegm Damp & qi stag.*)
Orange Peel Powder 188 (*Phlegm*)

Multiple sclerosis
Bu Zhong Yi Qi Wan 92 (*Spleen qi def.*)
Hua Tuo Zai Zao Wan 272 (*qi & yin def.*)
Bu Yang Huan Wu Wan 266 (*qi def., Bld stag.*)
You Gui Wan 326 (*Kid. yang def.*)
Niu Huang Qing Xin Wan 572 (*Phlegm Heat*)

Mumps
Jing Fang Bai Du Wan 166 (*Wind Cold, early stage of*)
Peking Niu Huang Jie Du Pian 384 (*Toxic Heat*)
Pu Ji Xiao Du Wan 389 (*Lung & Stomach Heat*)
Chuan Xin Lian Antiphlogistic Tablets 558 (*Toxic Heat*)

Muscle aches (see Pain–muscular)

Muscle spasm and tension (see Cramps and spasms)

Muscle strain
Die Da Zhi Tong Capsule 425 (*Bld stag. acute*)
Zheng Gu Shui 460 (*topical*)
Trans Wood Lock Liniment 470 (*topical*)

Muscle weakness
Bu Zhong Yi Qi Wan 92 (*Spleen qi def.*)
American Ginseng Essence of Chicken 344 (*qi & yin def.*)

Muscular dystrophy
Bu Zhong Yi Qi Wan 92 (*Spleen qi def.*)
Hua Tuo Zai Zao Wan 272 (*qi & yin def.*)
Bu Yang Huan Wu Wan 266 *qi def., Bld stag.*)
Xiao Huo Luo Dan 434 (*severe Cold in the channels*)
You Gui Wan 326 (*Kid. yang def.*)

Myasthenia gravis
Bu Zhong Yi Qi Wan 92 (*Spleen qi def.*)
Hua Tuo Zai Zao Wan 272 (*qi & yin def.*)
Bu Yang Huan Wu Wan 266 *qi def., Bld stag.*)
Xiao Huo Luo Dan 434 (*severe Cold in the channels*)
You Gui Wan 326 (*Kid. yang def.*)

Hua Tuo Zai Zao Wan 272 (*qi & yin def., Wind Damp*)
Qing Wei San Wan 392 (*Stomach Heat*)
Xiao Huo Luo Dan 434 (*severe Cold*)
Tong Luo Zhi Tong Tablet 453 (*Bld stag., def*)
Yan Hu Suo Zhi Tong Wan 458 (*Bld stag.*)
Shao Yao Gan Cao Wan 459 (*antispasmodic*)

• **intercostal**
Shu Gan Wan 116 (*Liver qi stag.*)
Xiao Chai Hu Tang Wan 276 (*shao yang syndrome*)
Xue Fu Zhu Yu Wan 252 (*qi & Bld stag.*)
Long Dan Xie Gan Wan 286 (*Damp Heat, Liver Fire*)
Yi Guan Jian Wan 290 (*Liver yin def., qi stag.*)
Tong Luo Zhi Tong Tablet 453 (*Bld stag., def*)
Yan Hu Suo Zhi Tong Wan 458 (*Bld stag.*)
Shao Yao Gan Cao Wan 459 (*antispasmodic*)

• **postherpetic**
Shu Gan Wan 116 (*Liver qi stag.*)
Xue Fu Zhu Yu Wan 252 (*qi & Bld stag.*)
Huo Luo Xiao Ling Wan 428 (*Bld stag.*)
Shen Tong Zhu Yu Wan 442 (*Bld stag.*)
Yan Hu Suo Zhi Tong Wan 458 (*Bld stag.*)

Neurodermatitis (see *also* Dermatitis)
Dang Gui Yin Zi Wan 526 (*Bld def. with Wind in the skin*)
Xiao Feng Wan 524 (*Wind, Damp*)
Lien Chiao Pai Tu Pien 522 (*Wind Heat, Toxic Heat*)
Eczema Herbal Formula 532

Neurogenic bladder dysfunction
Sang Piao Xiao Wan 248 (*Heart & Kid. qi def.*)

Neuropathy–diabetic, peripheral
Hua Tuo Zai Zao Wan 272 (*qi & yin def.*)
Bu Yang Huan Wu Wan 266 (*qi def., Bld stag.*)
Sunho Multi Ginseng Tablets 264 (*Bld stag.*)
Xue Fu Zhu Yu Wan 252 (*Bld stag.*)

Dang Gui Si Ni Wan 268 (*Cold in the channels*)
Xiao Huo Luo Dan 434 (*severe Cold in the channels*)
Xin Mai Ling 258 (*Bld stag. with Heat*)
Shi Quan Da Bu Wan 336 (*qi & Bld stag., with Cold*)

Neurosis
Gui Pi Wan 16 (*Heart & Spleen def.*)
Tian Wang Bu Xin Dan 358 (*Heart & Kid. yin def.*)
Bai Zi Yang Xin Wan 360 (*Bld & yin def.*)
Gan Mai Da Zao Wan 378
Wen Dan Wan 370 (*Phlegm Heat*)
Chai Hu Long Gu Mu Li Wan 372 (*Liver Fire, Phlegm Heat*)
Ban Xia Hou Po Wan 400 (*qi & Phlegm stag.*)

Nightmares
An Shen Bu Xin Wan 364 (*yang excess*)
Po Lung Yuen Medical Pills 570 (*Phlegm Heat*)
Tian Wang Bu Xin Dan 358 (*Heart & Kid. yin def.*)
Bai Zi Yang Xin Wan 360 (*Bld & yin def.*)
Gui Pi Wan 16 (*Heart & Spleen def.*)

Night blindness
Ming Mu Di Huang Wan 418 (*Liver & Kid. yin def.*)
Qi Ju Di Huang Wan 309 (*Liver & Kid. yin def.*)
Ming Mu Capsules 420 (*yin & Blood def.*)

Night sweats (see Sweating)

Night terrors (infants)
King Fung Powder 508

Nocturia
Fu Gui Ba Wei Wan 324 (*Kid yang def.*)
Ba Ji Yin Yang Wan 240 (*Kid yang def.*)
Zhuang Yao Jian Shen 450 (*yang def.*)
Sang Piao Xiao Wan 248 (*Heart & Kid. qi def.*)
San Yuen Medical Pills 242 (*astringent*)
Chin So Ku Ching Wan 246 (*astringent*)

Nodules (see Masses)

Nosebleed
Yunnan Paiyao 422 (*hemostatic*)

Osteophytosis
Kang Gu Zeng Sheng Pian 456
Qu Feng Zhen Tong Capsule 432 (*Wind Cold Damp*)

Osteoporosis
Bu Gai Zhuang Gu Capsule 53 (*yang def.*)

Otitis externa
Long Dan Xie Gan Wan 286 (*Liver Fire*)
Superior Sore Throat Powder 394 (*topical*)
Chuan Xin Lian Cream 540 (*topical*)
Tujin Liniment 544 (*topical for fungal infection*)

Otitis media
Xiao Chai Hu Tang Wan 276 (*shao yang*)
Long Dan Xie Gan Wan 286 (*Liver Fire*)
Peking Niu Huang Jie Du Pian 384 (*Toxic Heat*)
Huang Lien Shang Ching Pien 386 (*Wind Heat & Toxic Heat*)
Chuan Xin Lian Antiphlogistic Tablets 558 (*Toxic Heat*)
Huang Lian Jie Du Wan 552 (*Damp & Toxic Heat*)
Wu Wei Xiao Du Wan 562 (*Toxic Heat*)
Fang Feng Tong Sheng Wan 534 (*internal & external excess pattern*)
Xiao Er Gan Mao Chong Ji 516 (*infants*)

Ovarian cysts (see also Polycystic ovarian disease)
Hai Zao Jing Wan 60 (*Phlegm*)
Nei Xiao Luo Li Wan 62 (*hard Phlegm*)
Ji Sheng Ju He Wan 492 (*Phlegm & qi stag.*)
Ru Jie Xiao Tablet 58 (*qi & Bld stag. with Phlegm*)
Woo Garm Yuen Medical Pills 22 (*Cold & Bld stag.*)
Gui Zhi Fu Ling Wan 30 (*Bld stag.*)
Tao Hong Si Wu Wan 28 (*Bld def. with Bld stag.*)
Shao Fu Zhu Yu Wan 32 (*Bld stag. severe*)
Tong Jing Wan 26 (*Bld stag.*)
Chai Hu Shu Gan Wan 280 (*Liver qi stag.*)
Shi Quan Da Bu Wan 336 (*qi & Bld def.*)

P

Pain
• **abdominal**
Si Ni San Wan 278 (*Liver qi stag.*)
Shu Gan Wan 116 (*Liver invading Spleen*)
Chai Hu Shu Gan Wan 280 (*Liver invading Spleen*)
Tong Xie Yao Fang Wan 118 (*Liver invading Spleen*)
Huo Hsiang Cheng Chi Pien 76 (*Summerdamp*)
Xiao Jian Zhong Wan 100 (*Spleen yang def.*)
Bao He Wan 106 (*food stag.*)
Xue Fu Zhu Yu Wan 252 (*Bld stag.*)
Wei Tong Ding 124 (Cold, *yang* def.)
Dang Gui Si Ni Wan 268 (*Cold, Bld stag.*)

• **chest**
Dan Shen Pill 254 (*Bld stag.*)
Xin Mai Ling 258 (*Bld stag.*)
Guan Xin An Kou Fu Ye 262 (*Bld stag.*)
Xue Fu Zhu Yu Wan 252 (*Bld & qi stag.*)
Sunho Multi Ginseng Tablets 264 (*mild Bld stag.*)

• **epigastric**
Shu Gan Wan 116 (*qi stag.*)
Wei Tong Ding 124 (*Cold, yang* def.)
Chai Hu Shu Gan Wan 280 (*qi stag.*)
Dan Shen Yin Wan 256 (*Bld stag.*)
Shi Xiao Wan 21 (*Bld stag.*)
Qing Wei San Wan 392 (*Stomach Heat*)
Xiang Sha Yang Wei Wan 90 (*qi & Damp stag.*)
Li Zhong Wan 96 (*yang def.*)
Wei Te Ling 122 (*hyperacidity*)
Bao He Wan 106 (*food stag.*)

• **ear**
Qing Gan Li Dan Tablets 294 (*Damp Heat*)
Long Dan Xie Gan Wan 286 (*Liver Damp Heat*)
Xiao Chai Hu Tang Wan 276 (*shao yang*)
Tong Qiao Huo Xue Wan 382 (*Bld stag.*)

• **facial**
Chuan Xiong Cha Tiao Wan 164 (*Wind Cold*)

Xiao Huo Luo Dan 434 (*severe Cold stag. in channels*)
Hua Tuo Zai Zao Wan 272 (*qi & yin def., Wind Damp*)
Kang Wei Ling Wan 502 (*Bld stag., neuralgic*)
Tong Luo Zhi Tong Tablet 453 (*Bld def.*)
Qing Wei San Wan 392 (*Stomach Heat*)
• **generalised**
Yan Hu Suo Zhi Tong Wan 458 (*analgesic*)
Shao Yao Gan Cao Wan 459 (*antispasmodic*)
Du Huo Ji Sheng Wan 448 (*Wind Damp with Kid def.*)
Xiao Huo Luo Dan 434 (*severe Cold*)
Xing Jun San 74 (*Summerdamp, acute*)
Huo Hsiang Cheng Chi Pien 76 (*Wind Cold with Damp, acute*)
Xiao Yao Wan 282 (*Liver qi stag.*)
Po Sum On Medicated Oil 468 (*muscle tension, qi stag.*)
Shu Jin Huo Xue Wan 440 (*chronic, Bld stag.*)
Zhuang Yao Jian Shen 450 (*Kid def.*)
• **genital**
Tian Tai Wu Yao Wan 494 (*Cold in the Liver channel*)
Hua Tuo Zai Zao Wan 272 (*qi & yin def., Wind Damp*)
Long Dan Xie Gan Wan 286 (*Damp Heat*)
Chai Hu Shu Gan Wan 280 (*Liver qi stag.*)
Ji Sheng Ju He Wan 492 (*qi, Bld, Phlegm stag.*)
Gui Zhi Fu Ling Wan 30 (*Bld stag., postsurgical*)
• **hip**
Qing Gan Li Dan Tablets 294 (*Gallbladder channel dysfunction*)
Zhuang Yao Jian Shen 450 (*yang def*)
Juan Bi Wan 430 (*Wind Cold Damp*)
Shen Tong Zhu Yu Wan 442 (*Bld stag.*)
Xuan Bi Tang Wan 436 (*Damp Heat*)
• **hypochondriac**
Shu Gan Wan 116 (*qi & Bld stag.*)
Xiao Chai Hu Tang Wan 276 (*shao yang*)
Chai Hu Shu Gan Wan 280 (*Liver qi stag.*)

Xue Fu Zhu Yu Wan 252 (*Bld stag.*)
Long Dan Xie Gan Wan 286 (*Damp Heat*)
Li Dan Tablets 296 (*Damp Heat*)
Jigucao Wan 292 (*chronic hepatitis*)
• **inguinal**
Tian Tai Wu Yao Wan 494 (*Cold in the Liver channel*)
Qian Lie Xian Capsule 488 (*Damp Heat*)
• **jaw**
Qing Gan Li Dan Tablets 294 (*Gallbladder channel dysfunction*)
• **joint (*see Bi* syndrome)**
• **knee**
Fang Ji Huang Qi Wan 228 (*Wind Damp., qi def.*)
Jian Bu Qiang Shen Wan 454 (*Kid def.*)
Zhuang Yao Jian Shen 450 Tablets 452 (*Kid. yang def.*)
Du Huo Ji Sheng Wan 448 (*Wind Damp with Kid def.*)
Xiao Huo Luo Dan 434 (*severe Cold*)
Fu Gui Ba Wei Wan 324 (*Kid yang def.*)
Zuo Gui Wan 312 (*Kid yin def.*)
Xuan Bi Tang Wan 436 (*Damp Heat*)
Tiger Balm 476 (*topical*)
Plaster for Bruise and Analgesic 478 (*topical*)
Porous Capsicum Plaster 482 (*topical*)
Gou Pi Gao 484 (*topical*)
• **lower back**
Zhuang Yao Jian Shen 450 (*Kid def.*)
Liu Wei Di Huang Wan 304 (*yin def.*)
Zuo Gui Wan 312 (*yin def.*)
Fu Gui Ba Wei Wan 324 (*Kid yang def.*)
You Gui Wan 326 (*yang def.*)
Jian Bu Qiang Shen Wan 454 (*Kid def.*)
San Bi Wan 446 (*Wind Damp with Kid. def.*)
Kang Gu Zeng Sheng Pian 456 (*spondylosis*)
Shu Jin Huo Xue Wan 440 (*Wind Damp with Bld stag.*)
Shi Lin Tong 239 (*renal calculi*)
Bi Xie Sheng Shi Wan 66 (*Damp Heat*)
Die Da Zhi Tong Capsule 425 (*acute Bld stag.*)
Plaster for Bruise and Analgesic 478 (*topical*)

Porous Capsicum Plaster 482 (*topical*)
Gou Pi Gao 484 (*topical*)

- **menstrual (*see* Dysmenorrhea)**
- **muscular (*see also Bi* syndrome)**
  Shao Yao Gan Cao Wan 459
    (*antispasmodic*)
  Jing Fang Bai Du Wan 166 (*Wind Cold*)
  Xiao Yao Wan 282 (*Liver qi stag., Bld def.*)
  Shu Gan Wan 116 (*Liver qi stag.*)
  Xing Jun San 74 (*Summerdamp, acute*)
  Huo Hsiang Cheng Chi Pien 76 (*Wind Cold with Damp, acute*)
  Trans Wood Lock Liniment 470 (*topical*)
  Po Sum On Medicated Oil 468 (*topical*)
- **neck & upper back**
  Ge Gen Wan 168 (*Wind Cold*)
  Headache and Dizziness Reliever 585
  Chuan Xiong Cha Tiao Wan 164 (*Wind Cold*)
  Xiao Yao Wan 282 (*Liver qi stag.*)
  Ba Zhen Wan 2 (*qi & Bld def.*)
  Hua Tuo Zai Zao Wan 272 (*qi & yin def., Wind Damp*)
- **phantom limb**
  Shen Tong Zhu Yu Wan 442 (*Bld stag.*)
  Dang Gui Si Ni Wan 268 (*Cold, Bld stag.*)
- **postoperative**
  Shen Tong Zhu Yu Wan 442 (*Bld stag.*)
  Raw Tienchi Tablets 424 (*Bld stag.*)
  Xue Fu Zhu Yu Wan 252 (*qi & Bld stag.*)
- **sinus (*see* Headache)**
- **temporomandibular**
  Qing Gan Li Dan Tablets 294 (*Gallbladder channel dysfunction*)
  Xiao Yao Wan 282 (*Liver qi stag., Bld def.*)
- **testicular (*see* Pain–genital)**
- **traumatic acute**
  Die Da Zhi Tong Capsule 425 (*Bld stag.*)
  Chin Gu Tie Shang Wan 426 (*Bld stag.*)
  Huo Luo Xiao Ling Wan 428 (*Bld stag.*)
  Xue Fu Zhu Yu Wan 252 (*qi & Bld stag.*)
  Zheng Gu Shui 460 (*topical*)
  Die Da Tian Qi Yao Jiu 463 (*topical*)
  Plaster for Bruise and Analgesic 478
    (*topical*)

Pallor
Ba Zhen Wan 2 (*qi & Bld def.*)
Tangkwei Essence of Chicken 54 (*qi & Bld def.*)
Shi Quan Da Bu Wan 336 (*qi & Bld def.*)
Fu Gui Ba Wei Wan 324 (*Kid yang def.*)
Bu Zhong Yi Qi Wan 92 (*qi def.*)
Bu Fei Wan 216 (*Lung qi def.*)

Palms, hot and dry
Liu Wei Di Huang Wan 304 (*Kid. yin def.*)
Zhi Bai Ba Wei Wan 42 (*Kid. yin def.*)
Tian Wang Bu Xin Dan 358 (*Heart yin def.*)
Da Bu Yin Wan 314 (*Kid. yin def.*)

Palms, sweating of
Gui Pi Wan 16 (*Heart & Spleen def.*)
Xu Han Ting 218 (*wei qi def.*)

Palpitations
Tian Wang Bu Xin Dan 358 (*Heart yin def.*)
Gui Pi Wan 16 (*Heart Bld def.*)
Zhi Gan Cao Wan 260 (*Heart qi, yin, Bld def.*)
Chai Hu Long Gu Mu Li Wan 372 (*Liver Fire, Phlegm Heat*)
Wen Dan Wan 370 (*Phlegm Heat*)
Dan Shen Pill 254 (*Bld & Phlegm stag.*)
Sheng Mai San Wan 212 (*qi & yin def.*)
Zhen Wu Tang Wan 222 (*Heart yang def.*)

Pancreatitis
Ching Fei Yi Huo Pien 176 (*yang ming Heat*)
Da Chai Hu Wan 288 (*Damp Heat*)
Niu Huang Qing Huo Wan 561 (*yang ming organ syndrome*)
Shu Gan Wan 116 (*qi stag., chronic*)

Panic attacks
Tian Wang Bu Xin Dan 358 (*Heart yin def.*)
Gui Pi Wan 16 (*Heart Bld def.*)
Chai Hu Long Gu Mu Li Wan 372 (*qi stag., Phlegm Heat, yang rising*)
Wen Dan Wan 370 (*Phlegm Heat*)
An Shen Ding Zhi Wan 362 (*Bld & yin def. with Phlegm*)
An Shen Bu Xin Wan 364 (*yin def., yang rising*)

Phlegm pathology

Phlegm Damp

Er Chen Wan 112 (*Lungs, GIT, general*)
Ping Wei San 114 (*GIT*)
Jie Geng Wan 391 (*throat, Lungs*)
Su Zi Jiang Qi Wan 160 (*Lungs*)
Tong Xuan Li Fei Kou Fu Ye 198 (*Lungs*)
Tendrilleaf Fritillary Powder 189 (*Lungs*)
Hai Zao Jing Wan 60 (*nodules, thyroid*)
Ji Sheng Ju He Wan 492 (*nodules, testicles*)
Liu Jun Zi Wan 87 (*with Spleen def.*)
Xiang Sha Liu Jun Wan 88 (*with Spleen def. & qi stag.*)

Phlegm Heat

Wen Dan Wan 370 (*Heart & Lungs*)
Po Lung Yuen Medical Pills 570 (*Heart*)
Chai Hu Long Gu Mu Li Wan 372 (*Heart*)
Qing Qi Hua Tan Wan 174 (*Lungs*)
Ding Chuan Wan 182 (*Lungs*)
She Dan Chuan Bei Ye 186 (*Lungs*)
Orange Peel Powder 188 (*Lungs*)
Tendrilleaf Fritillary Powder 189 (*Lungs*)
Qian Bai Bi Yan Pian 408 (*sinuses*)
Cang Er Zi Wan 412 (*sinuses*)
Nei Xiao Luo Li Wan 62 (*nodules, thyroid*)

Wind Phlegm

Ban Xia Bai Zhu Tian Ma Wan 574

Phlegm misting the Heart

Cerebral Tonic Pills 374
An Shen Ding Zhi Wan 362

Phlegm and qi stagnation

Ban Xia Hou Po Wan 400 (*Lungs, throat*)
Ru Jie Xiao Tablet 58 (*breast, nodules*)

Phlegm and Blood stagnation

Xiao Huo Luo Dan 434 (*pain & numbness*)
Nei Xiao Luo Li Wan 62 (*nodules, thyroid*)
Dan Shen Pill 254 (*Heart, vessels*)
Keep Fit Capsule 111 (*Heart, vessels*)

Phlegm and yin deficiency

Tian Wang Bu Xin Dan 358

Photophobia

Ming Mu Di Huang Wan 418 (*Liver yin def.*)
Ming Mu Capsule 420 (*yin & Bld def.*)
Ming Mu Shang Ching Pien 416 (*Liver Heat*)

Pityriasis rosea

Huang Lien Shang Ching Pien 386 (*Wind Heat, Toxic Heat*)
Lien Chiao Pai Tu Pien 522 (*Wind Heat, Toxic Heat*)
Chuan Xin Lian Antiphlogistic Tablets 558 (*Toxic Heat*)
Fu Fang Nan Ban Lan Gen 560 (*Toxic Heat*)
Ban Lan Gen Chong Ji 390 (*Toxic Heat*)
Dan Shen Huo Xue Wan 538 (*Bld stag. with Heat*)

Placenta–retention of (*see Birth products–incomplete expulsion of*)

Plantar warts

Ji Yan Gao 547 (*topical*)

Pleurisy

Ching Fei Yi Huo Pien 176 (*Lung Fire*)
Qing Qi Hua Tan Wan 174 (*Phlegm Heat*)
Pi Pa Cough Tea 178 (*Phlegm Heat*)
Xiao Chai Hu Tang Wan 276 (*shao yang*)

Plum stone throat

Ban Xia Hou Po Wan 400 (*qi & Phlegm stag.*)
Xiao Yao Wan 282 (*Liver qi stag., Bld def.*)
Chai Hu Shu Gan Wan 280 (*Liver qi stag.*)

Pneumonia

Ching Fei Yi Huo Pien 176 (*Lung Fire*)
Qing Qi Hua Tan Wan 174 (*Phlegm Heat*)
Niu Huang Qing Huo Wan 561 (*Toxic Heat*)
Huang Lian Jie Du Wan 552 (*Toxic & Damp Heat*)
Chuan Xin Lian Antiphlogistic Tablets 558 (*Toxic Heat*)
Chuan Xin Lian 557 (*Toxic Heat*)
Liang Ge Wan 566 (*Lung & Stomach Heat*)
Xiao Chai Hu Tang Wan 276 (*post acute*)

- **heartburn, indigestion**
  Jian Pi Wan 104 (*Spleen def. with food stag.*)
  Bao He Wan 106 (*food stag.*)
- **high blood pressure (see Preeclampsia)**
- **hyperpigmentation following**
  Yang Yan Qu Ban Tablet 72 (*Bld def., Bld stag.*)
- **nausea**
  Zi Sheng Wan 102 (*Spleen def., food & Damp stag.*)
  Liu Jun Zi Wan 87 (*Spleen def. with Phlegm Damp*)
  Xiang Sha Liu Jun Wan 88 (*Spleen def. with Phlegm Damp & qi stag.*)
  Er Chen Wan 112 (*Phlegm Damp*)
  Wen Dan Wan 370 (*Phlegm Heat*)
  Shih San Tai Pao Wan 56 (*Bld def.*)
- **weakness during**
  Tangkwei Essence of Chicken 54 (*qi & Bld def.*)
  Ba Zhen Wan 2 (*qi & Bld def.*)
  Bai Feng Wan 10 (*qi & Bld def.*)
  Shi Quan Da Bu Wan 336 (*qi & Bld def.*)
  Shih San Tai Pao Wan 56 (*Bld def.*)

Premature ectopic systole
Zhi Gan Cao Wan 260 (*Heart qi, Bld, yin def.*)

Premenstrual
- **dizziness**
  Xiao Yao Wan 282 (*Liver qi stag., Bld def.*)
  Jia Wei Xiao Yao Wan 284 (*Liver qi stag. with Heat*)
- **edema**
  Ba Zhen Yi Mu Wan 6 (*qi & Bld def., Bld stag*)
  Si Wu Wan 4 + Xiao Yao Wan 282
- **fever**
  Jia Wei Xiao Yao Wan 284 (*Liver qi stag. with Heat*)
- **lower back ache**
  Wen Jing Tang Wan 24 (*Cold, def. Bld stag.*)
  Shao Fu Zhu Yu Wan 32 (*Cold, Bld def.*)
  Yang Rong Wan 34 (*Bld and Kid. def.*)

You Gui Wan 326 (*yang def.*)
- **syndrome, general**
  Xiao Yao Wan 282 (*Liver qi stag., Bld def.*)
  Gui Pi Wan 16 (*Heart & Spleen def.*)
  Chai Hu Shu Gan Wan 280 (*Liver qi stag.*)
  Tong Luo Zhi Tong Tablet 453 (*Bld def.*)

Prickly heat
Fu Yin Tai Liniment 541 (*topical*)

Prolapse–uterus, rectum, bladder
Bu Zhong Yi Qi Wan 92 (*sinking Spleen qi*)
Zi Shen Da Bu Capsule 244 (*Kid. yang def.*)

Proliferative bone disorders
Kang Gu Zeng Sheng Pian 456

Prostatitis
- **acute**
  Ba Zheng San Wan 232 (*Damp Heat*)
  Long Dan Xie Gan Wan 286 (*Liver Damp Heat*)
  Ming Mu Shang Ching Pien 416 (*Liver Fire*)
  Fu Yan Qing Tablet 64 (*Damp & Toxic Heat*)
  Bi Xie Sheng Shi Wan 66 (*Damp Heat*)
  Chuan Xin Lian Antiphlogistic Tablets 558 (*Toxic Heat*)
  Fu Fang Nan Ban Lan Gen 560 (*Toxic Heat*)
- **chronic**
  Qian Lie Xian Capsule 488 (*Damp Heat, Bld stag.*)
  Prostate Gland Pills 490 (*Damp Heat, Bld stag.*)
  Chien Chin Chih Tai Wan 70 (*smouldering Damp Heat with qi, Bld & Kid. yang def.*)
  Bi Xie Fen Qing Wan 230 (*Kid. def, Damp*)
  Tian Tai Wu Yao Wan 494 (*Cold in Liver channel*)
  Gui Zhi Fu Ling Wan 30 (*Bld stag.*)
  Chai Hu Shu Gan Wan 280 (*Liver qi stag.*)

GENERAL INDEX

Long Dan Xie Gan Wan 286 (*Liver Damp Heat*)

Ming Mu Shang Ching Pien 416 (*Liver Fire*)

Huang Lian Jie Du Wan 552 (*Toxic & Damp Heat*)

Chuan Xin Lian Antiphlogistic Tablets 558 (*Toxic Heat*)

Xiao Chai Hu Tang Wan 276 (*shao yang syndrome*)

Pyogenic skin diseases (see Abscess)

Q

Qi level–Heat affecting

Ching Fei Yi Huo Pien 176 (*Lung Fire*)

Qing Qi Hua Tan Wan 174 (*Phlegm Heat*)

Niu Huang Qing Huo Wan 561 (*Toxic Heat*)

Qi lin syndrome

Tian Tai Wu Yao Wan 494 (*Cold*)

Chai Hu Shu Gan Wan 280 (*qi stag.*)

Shu Gan Wan 116 (*qi stag.*)

Quinsy

Niu Huang Qing Huo Wan 561 (*Toxic Heat*)

DBD Capsule 238 (*Toxic Heat*)

Huang Lian Jie Du Wan 552 (*Toxic Heat*)

Huang Lian Su Tablets 554 (*Toxic Heat*)

Peking Niu Huang Jie Du Pian 384 (*Toxic Heat*)

Jie Geng Wan 391 (*Phlegm*)

Lien Chiao Pai Tu Pien 522 (*Wind Heat, Toxic Heat*)

Huang Lien Shang Ching Pien 386 (*Wind Heat, Toxic Heat, Damp Heat*)

Superior Sore Throat Powder 394 (*topical*)

R

Radiation therapy

• fever following

Da Bu Yin Wan 314 (*yin def.*)

Qi Pathology

Qi deficiency

Si Jun Zi Wan 86 (*Spleen qi*)

Liu Jun Zi Wan 87 (*Spleen qi with Damp*)

Xiang Sha Liu Jun Wan 88 (*Spleen qi with Damp & qi stag.*)

Bu Fei Wan 216 (*Lung qi def.*)

Bu Zhong Yi Qi Wan 92 (*Spleen & Lung qi*)

Shen Ling Bai Zhu Wan 94 (*Spleen qi with Damp*)

Yu Ping Feng Wan 348 (*wei qi def.*)

Xu Han Ting 218 (*wei qi def.*)

Qi and yin deficiency

Sheng Mai San Wan 212

Zhi Gan Cao Wan 260

Qi stagnation

Si Ni San Wan 278 (*Liver qi*)

Xiao Yao Wan 282 (*Liver qi, Bld def*)

Chai Hu Shu Gan Wan 280 (*Liver qi*)

Xiang Sha Yang Wei Wan 90 (*Spleen qi & Damp*)

Mu Xiang Shun Qi Wan 126 (*qi & Damp*)

Qi and Phlegm stagnation

Ban Xia Hou Po Wan 400 (*Lungs, throat*)

Ru Jie Xiao Tablet 58 (*breast, nodules*)

Qi and Blood stagnation

Xue Fu Zhu Yu Wan 252

Sinking Spleen qi

Bu Zhong Yi Qi Wan 92

Rebellious qi

Xiang Lian Wan 120 (*Stomach Heat*)

• hair loss following

Yang Xue Sheng Fa Capsule 318 (*Bld def.*)

Qi Bao Mei Ran Dan 320 (*Liver, Kid. & Bld def.*)

Tangkwei Essence of Chicken 54 (*qi & Bld def.*)

• nausea, vomiting from

Wen Dan Wan 370 (*Phlegm Heat*)

Xin Mai Ling 258 (*Bld stag., sequelae of*)
Zhi Gan Cao Wan 260 (*Heart qi, Bld, yin def., sequelae of*)

Rheumatoid arthritis (*see also* Arthritis)

Reishi Mushroom 354 (*immune regulator*)
Xue Fu Zhu Yu Wan 252 (*qi & Bld stag.*)

Rhinitis

• allergic
Xin Yi San 410 (*Wind Cold*)
Cang Er Zi Wan 412 (*Wind Heat*)
Xiao Qing Long Wan 162 (*Wind Cold with congested fluids*)
Hayfever Relieving Tea 414 (*Phlegm Heat*)
Qian Bai Bi Yan Pian 408 (*Heat & pain*)
Gui Zhi Tang Wan 158 (*ying wei disharmony*)

• perennial, chronic
Qian Bai Bi Yan Pian 408 (*Heat & pain*)
Bi Yen Ning Capsule 404 (*Phlegm Heat*)
Pe Min Kan Wan (Nasal Clear) 406
Cang Er Zi Wan 412 (*Wind & Phlegm Heat*)
Yu Ping Feng Wan 348 (*wei qi def.*)
Xu Han Ting 218 (*wei qi def.*)
Ba Ji Yin Yang Wan 240 (*Kid. yang def.*)

Ringworm

Hua Tuo Gao 545 (*topical*)
Xiao Yan Tang Shang Cream 546 (*topical*)
Tujin Liniment 544 (*topical*)

Rosacea

Dan Shen Huo Xue Wan 538 (*Bld stag. with Heat*)
Huo Luo Xiao Ling Wan 428 (*Bld stag.*)

Ross River fever–post acute stage of

Xiao Chai Hu Tang Wan 276 (*shao yang syndrome*)

Roundworm

Baby Fat Powder 510

S

Salivary gland infection

Chuan Xin Lian Antiphlogistic Tablets 558 (*Toxic Heat*)

Peking Niu Huang Jie Du Pian 384 (*Toxic Heat*)
Huang Lian Jie Du Wan 552 (*Toxic Heat*)

Salivation

• excessive
Wei Tong Ding 124 (*Stomach Cold*)
Li Zhong Wan 96 (*Spleen yang def.*)
Bo Ying Compound 506 (*accumulation disorder*)
Healthy Child Tea 514 (*Spleen qi def., infants*)

Salpingitis (*see* Pelvic inflammatory disease)

Sarcoidosis

Cordyceps Essence of Chicken 342 (*yin & yang def.*)

Scabies

Tujin Liniment 544 (*topical*)
Hua Tuo Gao 545 (*topical*)

Scarlet fever

Peking Niu Huang Jie Du Pian 384 (*Toxic Heat*)
Pu Ji Xiao Du Wan 389 (*Lung & Stomach Heat*)
Ban Lan Gen Chong Ji 390 (*Toxic Heat*)

Schizophrenia

Xue Fu Zhu Yu Wan 252 (*qi & Bld stag.*)
Chai Hu Long Gu Mu Li Wan 372 (*Liver Fire, Phlegm Heat*)
Wen Dan Wan 370 (*Phlegm Heat*)

Sciatica

Dang Gui Si Ni Wan 268 (*Cold in the channels*)
Xiao Huo Luo Dan 434 (*severe Cold in the channels*)
Huo Luo Xiao Ling Wan 428 (*Bld stag.*)
Juan Bi Wan 430 (*Wind Cold Damp*)
Qu Feng Zhen Tong Capsule 432 (*Wind Cold Damp*)
Shu Jin Huo Xue Wan 440 (*Bld stag., Wind Damp*)
Du Huo Ji Sheng Wan 448 (*Kid. def. with Wind Damp*)
Tong Luo Zhi Tong Tablet 453 (*Bld def. Bld stag.*)
Kang Wei Ling Wan 502 (*neuralgic pain*)

Sinusitis

• acute

Ching Fei Yi Huo Pien 176 (*Lung Heat*)

Chuan Xin Lian Antiphlogistic Tablets 558 (*Toxic Heat*)

Peking Niu Huang Jie Du Pian 384 (*Toxic Heat*)

Qian Bai Bi Yan Pian 408 (*Heat*)

Cang Er Zi Wan 412 (*Wind Heat*)

Xin Yi San 410 (*Wind Cold*)

• chronic

Bi Yen Ning Capsule 404 (*Heat*)

Qing Qi Hua Tan Wan 174 (*Phlegm Heat*)

Jia Wei Xiao Yao Wan 284 (*Liver qi stagnation with Heat*)

Sjögren's syndrome

Qing Yin Wan 398 (*dryness & Heat*)

Yang Yin Qing Fei Wan 204 (*yin def. & dryness*)

Bai He Gu Jin Wan 206 (*Lung yin def.*)

Gu Ben Wan 316 (*Stomach yin def.*)

Ming Mu Di Huang Wan 418 (*Liver yin def.*)

Qi Ju Di Huang Wan 309 (*Liver yin def.*)

Skin (*see also* Eczema; Psoriasis etc.)

• dry

Jing An Oral Liquid 50 (*Bld & yin def.*)

Lady Oral Liquid 51(*Bld & yin def.*)

Ba Zhen Wan 2 (*Bld def.*)

Si Wu Wan 4 (*Bld def.*)

Shou Wu Chih 322 (*yin & Bld def.*)

Yang Yin Qing Fei Wan 204 (*Lung yin def.*)

• hyperpigmentation of

Yang Yan Qu Ban Tablet 72 (*qi & Bld def., Bld stag.*)

• itch in cold weather

Xiao Feng Wan 524 + Si Wu Wan 4

Gui Zhi Tang Wan 158 (*Wind Cold*)

• suppurative lesions (*see* Abscess)

Sleep apnea

Bu Zhong Yi Qi Wan 92 (*Spleen def.*)

Reishi Mushroom 354

Spleen Pathology

Spleen qi deficiency

Si Jun Zi Wan 86

Liu Jun Zi Wan 87 (*with Phlegm Damp*)

Xiang Sha Liu Jun Wan 88 (*with Phlegm Damp & qi stag.*)

Bu Zhong Yi Qi Wan 92

Shen Ling Bai Zhu Wan 94

Shen Qi Da Bu Wan 346

Healthy Child Tea 514 (*infants*)

Zi Sheng Wan 102 (*with Damp Heat*)

Wu Ling San Wan 224 (*with fluid accumulation*)

Spleen not controlling Blood

Gui Pi Wan 16

Sinking Spleen qi

Bu Zhong Yi Qi Wan 92

Spleen yang deficiency

Li Zhong Wan 96

Li Chung Yuen Medical Pills 98

Xiao Jian Zhong Wan 100

Spleen yin deficiency

Sheng Mai San Wan 212

Gu Ben Wan 316

Spleen Damp

Ping Wei San 114

Er Chen Wan 112

Xiang Sha Liu Jun Wan 88

Damp Heat in the Spleen

Huang Lian Jie Du Wan 552

Spleen and Liver disharmony

Tong Xie Yao Fang Wan 118

Si Ni San Wan 278

Shu Gan Wan 116

Chai Hu Shu Gan Wan 280

Sleep disturbance (*see* Insomnia)

Sleepwalking

An Shen Bu Xin Wan 364 (*yin def., yang excess*)

Sleepiness after eating

Xiang Sha Liu Jun Wan 88 (*Spleen qi def. with Phlegm Damp*)

• motility disorder
Fu Gui Ba Wei Wan 324 (*kid yang def.*)
You Gui Wan 326 (*Kid. yang def.*)
Wu Zi Yan Zong Wan 496 (*jing def.*)
Deer Velvet 328 (*jing def.*)
San Yuen Medical Pills 242 (*Kid. yang qi def.*)

Splenomegaly
Ge Xia Zhu Yu Wan 298 (*Bld stag.*)

Spondylitis–ankylosing
Kang Gu Zeng Sheng Pian 456

Spondylosis–cervial, lumbar
Kang Gu Zeng Sheng Pian 456
Ge Gen Wan 168 (*Wind Cold, neck*)
Qu Feng Zhen TongCapsule 432 (*Wind Cold Damp*)
Xiao Huo Luo Dan 434 (*severe Cold*)
Juan Bi Wan 430 (*Wind Cold Damp*)
Shu Jin Huo Xue Wan 440 (*Wind Damp with Bld stag.*)

Sprains
Die Da Zhi Tong Capsule 425 (*Bld stag.*)
Zheng Gu Shui 460 (*topical*)
Die Da Tian Qi Yao Jiu 463 (*topical*)

Spurs
Kang Gu Zeng Sheng Pian 456
Qu Feng Zhen Tong Capsule 432 (*Wind Cold Damp*)

Stomach ache (*see* Epigastric pain)

Stomach flu (*see* Gastoenteritis)

Stomatitis
Qing Wei San Wan 392 (*Stomach Heat*)
Peking Niu Huang Jie Du Pian 384 (*Toxic Heat*)
Tao Chih Pien 236 (*Heart Fire*)
Huang Lian Jie Du Wan 552 (*Stomach Fire*)
Liang Ge Wan 566 (*Lung & Stomach Fire*)
Tian Wang Bu Xin Dan 358 (*Heart yin def.*)
Superior Sore Throat Powder 394 (*topical*)
Sanjin Watermelon Frost 396 (*topical*)

Stools
• alternating constipation and diarrhea
Tong Xie Yao Fang Wan 118 (*Liver Spleen disharmony*)
Mu Xiang Shun Qi Wan 126 (*qi & Damp stag.*)
Chai Hu Shu Gan Wan 280 (*Liver qi stag.*)
Xiao Yao Wan 282 (*Liver qi stag.*)
Bao He Wan 106 (*food stag.*)

• dry
Run Chang Wan 130 (*Bld def.*)
Ching Fei Yi Huo Pien 176 (*yang ming syndrome, Lung Fire*)
Niu Huang Qing Huo Wan 561 (*Toxic Heat*)
Yang Yin Qing Fei Wan 204 (*yin def.*)

• loose (*see also* Diarrhea)
Shen Ling Bai Zhu Wan 94 (*Spleen qi def.*)
Zi Sheng Wan 102 (*Spleen qi def. with food stag.*)
Po Chai Pills 84 (*Damp Heat*)
Huo Hsiang Cheng Chi Pien 76 (*acute Damp invasion*)

Strep throat
Peking Niu Huang Jie Du Pian 384 (*Toxic Heat*)
Pu Ji Xiao Du Wan 389 (*Toxic Heat*)
Huang Lian Su Tablets 554 (*Toxic Heat*)
Chuan Xin Lian Antiphlogistic Tablets 558 (*Toxic Heat*)
Superior Sore Throat Powder 394

Stress
Chai Hu Shu Gan Wan 280 (*qi stag.*)
Xiao Yao Wan 282 (*qi stag.*)
American Ginseng Essence of Chicken 344 (*general*)
Panax Ginseng Extractum 350 (*general*)

Stroke
• prevention of
Raw Tienchi Tablets 424 (*Bld stag.*)
Zhen Gan Xi Feng Wan 580 (*yin def. yang rising & Wind*)

• recovery from
Bu Yang Huan Wu Wan 266 (*qi def., Bld stag.*)

Temporomandibular pain (see Pain–temporomandibular)

Tendonitis
Qu Feng Zhen Tong Wan 432 (*Wind Cold Damp*)
Shen Tong Zhu Yu Wan 442 (*Bld stag.*)

Tenesmus (see Dystenteric disorder)

Testicular pain and swelling
Ji Sheng Ju He Wan 492 (*qi & Phlegm stag.*)
Tian Tai Wu Yao Wan 494 (*Cold in Liver channel*)
Xue Fu Zhu Yu Wan 252 (*qi & Bld stag., trauma, post operative*)
Gui Zhi Fu Ling Wan 30 (*Bld stag., postoperative*)
Nei Xiao Luo Li Wan 62 (*hard Phlegm*)
Long Dan Xie Gan Wan 286 (*Damp Heat*)
Bi Xie Sheng Shi Wan 66 (*Damp Heat*)

Thermoregulation–poor
Er Xian Wan 46 (*yin & yang def.*)

Thirst
Huang Lian Jie Du Wan 552 (*Stomach Fire*)
Luo Han Kuo Beverage 210 (*Lung yin def.*)
Liu Wei Di Huang Wan 304 (*Kid yin def.*)
Qing Yin Wan 398 (*yin & fluid def.*)
Yang Yin Qing Fei Wan 204 (*yin & fluid def. after febrile illness*)

Threadworms
Baby Fat Powder 510
Hua Ji Xiao Zhi Oral Liquid 512 (*infants*)

Throat abscess (see Abscess–pharyngeal)

Throat–sore
• acute
Yin Chiao Chieh Tu Pien 146 (*Wind Heat*)
Peking Niu Huang Jie Du Pian 384 (*Toxic Heat*)
Chuan Xin Lian Antiphlogistic Tablets 558 (*Toxic Heat*)
Ban Lan Gen Chong Ji 390 (*Toxic Heat*)
Ching Fei Yi Huo Pien 176 (*Lung Fire*)
Superior Sore Throat Powder 394 (*topical*)

Gan Mao Tea 513 (*children*)
• chronic, recurrent
Tung Hsuan Li Fei Pien 180 (*Heat & dryness*)
Yang Yin Qing Fei Wan 204 (*Lung yin def.*)
Zhi Bai Ba Wei Wan 42 (*yin def.*)
Mai Wei Di Huang Wan 208 (*yin def.*)
Qing Yin Wan 398 (*Lung dryness*)

Thrombocytemia
Xue Fu Zhu Yu Wan 252 (*qi & Bld stag.*)

Thrombocytopenia
Cordyceps Essence of Chicken 342 (*yin, yang, Bld def.*)
Tangkwei Essence of Chicken 54 (*qi & Bld def.*)
Wu Ji Bai Feng Wan 12 (*Bld & jing def.*)
Shi Quan Da Bu Wan 336 (*qi & Bld def. with Cold*)

Thrombophlebitis
Xin Mai Ling 258 (*Bld stag.*)
Sunho Multi Ginseng Tablets 264 (*Bld def.*)
Xue Fu Zhu Yu Wan 252 (*qi & Bld def.*)
Raw Tienchi Tablets 424 (*Bld stag.*)
Tao Hong Si Wu Wan 28 (*Bld stag. Bld def.*)
Dang Gui Si Ni Wan 268 (*Cold in the channels*)

Thrush
• gastro-intestinal
So Hup Yuen Medical Pills 80 (*gu syndrome*)
Xiang Sha Liu Jun Wan 88 (*Spleen qi def. with Phlegm Damp*)
Huo Hsiang Cheng Chi Pien 76 (*Damp*)
Ping Wei San 114 (*Phlegm Damp*)
Da Huang Jiang Zhi Wan 133 (*antifungal*)
• infantile
Bo Ying Compound 506
• vaginal
Bi Xie Sheng Shi Wan 66 (*Damp Heat*)
Yu Dai Wan 68 (*Damp Heat, Bld def.*)
Chien Chin Chih Tai Wan 70 (*Damp Heat, def.*)
Bi Xie Fen Qing Wan 230 (*Damp*)
Ping Wei San 114 (*Phlegm Damp*)

GENERAL INDEX

Peking Niu Huang Jie Du Pian 384 (*Toxic Heat*)

Chuan Xiong Cha Tiao Wan 164 (*Wind Cold*)

Sanjin Watermelon Frost 396 (*topical*)

Torticollis

Ge Gen Wan 168 (*Wind Cold*)

Chuan Xiong Cha Tiao Wan 164 (*Wind Cold*)

Headache and Dizziness Reliever 585

Tracheitis (*see* Laryngitis)

Transient ischemic attacks (TIAs)

Zhen Gan Xi Feng Wan 580 (*yin def., yang rising & Wind*)

Xue Fu Zhu Yu Wan 252 (*qi & Bld stag.*)

Dan Shen Pill 254 (*Bld stag.*)

Xin Mai Ling 258 (*Bld stag.*)

Sunho Multi Ginseng Tablets 264 (*Bld stag.*)

Raw Tienchi Tablets 424 (*Bld stag.*)

Yang Yin Jiang Ya Wan 582 (*yang rising*)

Traumatic injury (*see* Pain–traumatic)

Travellers diarrhea

Po Chai Pills 84 (*Damp Heat*)

Bao Ji Pills 83 (*Damp Heat*)

Fu Ke An 82 (*Damp Heat*)

Huang Lian Su Tablets 554 (*Toxic Heat*)

Xing Jun San 74 (*Summerdamp*)

Huo Hsiang Cheng Chi Pien 76 (*Wind Cold with Damp*)

Trichomonas vaginitis

Fu Yan Qing Tablet 64 (*Damp & Toxic Heat*)

Bi Xie Sheng Shi Wan 66 (*Damp Heat*)

Long Dan Xie Gan Wan 286 (*Liver Damp Heat*)

Huang Lian Jie Du Wan 552 (*Damp Heat*)

Huang Lian Su Tablets 554 (*Damp Heat*)

Fu Yin Tai Liniment 541 (*topical*)

Triglycerides–high

Keep Fit Capsule 111 (*Bld & Phlegm stag.*)

Dan Shen Pill 254 (*Bld stag.*)

Raw Tienchi Tablets 424 (*Bld stag.*)

Trigeminal neuralgia (*see* Neuralgia–trigeminal)

Tuberculosis–adjunct therapy for

• **debility in**

Zhi Gan Cao Wan 260 (*Heart qi, yin, Bld def.*)

• **dry cough of**

Bai He Gu Jin Wan 206 (*Lung yin def.*)

Mai Wei Di Huang Wan 208 (*Lung & Kid yin def.*)

Yang Yin Qing Fei Wan 204 (*Lung yin def.*)

• **sweating, fevers**

Cordyceps Essence of Chicken 342 (*yin & yang def.*)

Da Bu Yin Wan 314 (*Kid. yin def.*)

Zhi Bai Ba Wei Wan 42 (*yin def.*)

Turbid (cloudy) *lin* syndrome

Bi Xie Fen Qing Wan 230 (*Kid def., Damp*)

U

Ulcers–apthous

• **acute**

Peking Niu Huang Jie Du Pian 384 (*Heart or Stomach Fire*)

Huang Lien Shang Ching Pien 386 (*Wind Heat, Toxic Heat*)

Qing Wei San Wan 392 (*Stomach Heat*)

Tao Chih Pien 236 (*Heart Fire*)

Niu Huang Qing Huo Wan 561 (*yang ming organ syndrome*)

Liang Ge Wan 566 (*yang ming organ syndrome*)

Qi Xing Tea 518 (*infants*)

Sanjin Watermelon Frost 396 (*topical*)

Superior Sore Throat Powder 394 (*topical*)

• **chronic, recurrent**

Tian Wang Bu Xin Dan 358 (*Heart yin def., with Phlegm*)

Li Zhong Wan 96 (*chronic, Spleen yang def.*)

Jia Wei Xiao Yao Wan 284 (*Liver qi stag. with Heat*)

Sanjin Watermelon Frost 396 (*topical*)

Zhuang Yao Jian Shen 450 (*yiang def.*)

Chin So Ku Ching Wan 246 (*astringent*)

San Yuen Medical Pills 242 (*Kid def. & astringent*)

Bu Zhong Yi Qi Wan 92 (*sinking qi, bladder prolape, postpartum*)

Bu Yang Huan Wu Wan 266 (*qi def., Bld stag., post stroke*)

• scanty (anuria)

Wu Ling San Wan 224 (*tai yang fu syndrome*)

Fu Gui Ba Wei Wan 324 (*Kid. yang def.*)

Zhen Wu Tang Wan 222 (*Heart & Kid. yang def.*)

Urticaria

Gui Zhi Tang Wan 158 (*with exposure to cold*)

Xiao Feng Wan 524 (*Wind, Damp*)

Yin Chiao Chieh Tu Pien 146 (*Wind Heat*)

Lien Chiao Pai Tu Pien 522 (*Wind, Toxic Heat*)

Ming Mu Shang Ching Pien 416 (*Damp Heat*)

Shi Du Qing 531 (*pruritus*)

Tian Wang Bu Xin Dan 358 (*Heart yin def.m chronic*)

Xiao Yan Tang Shang Cream 546 (*topical*)

Uterine bleeding (*see Bleeding–uterine*)

Uterine fibroids (*see Fibroids*)

Uterine prolapse (*see Prolapse*)

Uterus–Damp or Toxic Heat in

Fu Yan Qing Tablets 64 (*Damp Heat*)

Bi Xie Sheng Shi Wan 66 (*Damp Heat*)

Long Dan Xie Gan Wan 286 (*Liver Damp Heat*)

Wu Wei Xiao Du Wan 562 (*Toxic Heat*)

Huang Lian Jie Du Wan 552 (*Damp & Toxic Heat*)

Huang Lian Su Tablets 554 (*Damp & Toxic Heat*)

Uveitis

Ming Mu Shang Ching Pien 416 (*Liver Fire*)

Long Dan Xie Gan Wan 286 (*Liver Fire*)

V

Vaccination (*see Immunisation*)

Vaginal discharge (*see Leukorrhea*)

Vaginal itch (*see Pruritis–genital*)

Vaginal inflammation and infection

Fu Yan Qing Tablet 64 (*Damp Heat*)

Bi Xie Sheng Shi Wan 66 (*Damp Heat*)

Long Dan Xie Gan Wan 286 (*Liver Damp Heat*)

Wu Wei Xiao Du Wan 562 (*Toxic Heat*)

Huang Lian Jie Du Wan 552 (*Damp & Toxic Heat*)

Huang Lian Su Tablets 554 (*Damp & Toxic Heat*)

Fu Yin Tai Liniment 541 (*topical*)

Vaginal thrush (*see Thrush–vaginal*)

Vaginitis–non specific

Zhi Bai Ba Wei Wan 42 (*Kid yin def.*)

Bi Xie Sheng Shi Wan 66 (*Damp Heat*)

Yu Dai Wan 68 (*Damp Heat, Bld def.*)

Long Dan Xie Gan Wan 286 (*Damp Heat*)

Jia Wei Xiao Yao Wan 284 (*Liver qi stag. with stag. Heat*)

Chien Chin Chih Tai Wan 70 (*Damp Heat with def.*)

Fu Yin Tai Liniment 541 (*topical*)

Varicocoele

Ji Sheng Ju He Wan 492 (*qi, Bld, Phlegm stag.*)

Hai Zao Jing Wan 60 (*Phlegm*)

Nei Xiao Luo Li Wan 62 (*Phlegm & Bld stag.*)

Gui Zhi Fu Ling Wan 30 (*mild Bld stag.*)

Varicose veins

Tao Hong Si Wu Wan 28 (*mild Bld stag.*)

Xue Fu Zhu Yu Wan 252 (*qi & Bld stag.*)

Sunho Multi Ginseng Tablets 264 (*Bld stag.*)

Bu Zhong Yi Qi Wan 92 (*qi def.*)

Varicosity–testicular

Gui Zhi Fu Ling Wan 30 (*mild Bld stag.*)

Vasculitis

Xue Fu Zhu Yu Wan 252 (*qi & Bld stag.*)

W

Warm disease

Pu Ji Xiao Du Wan 389 (*Lung & Stomach Heat*)
Yin Chiao Chieh Tu Pien 146 (*Wind Heat*)
Lien Chiao Pai Tu Pien 522 (*Wind Heat, Toxic Heat*)
Chuan Xin Lian Antiphlogistic Tablets 558 (*Toxic Heat*)

Warts

• **general**
Chuan Xin Lian Antiphlogistic Tablets 558
Ban Lan Gen Chong Ji 390
• **plantar**
Ji Yan Gao 547 (*topical*)

Weakness

• **following surgery or illness**
Tangkwei Essence of Chicken 54 (*qi & Bld def.*)
American Ginseng Essence of Chicken 344 (*qi & yin def.*)
Cordyceps Essence of Chicken 342 (*yin & yang def.*)
Shi Quan Da Bu Wan 336 (*qi & Bld def.*)
Wu Ji Bai Feng Wan 12 (*qi & Bld def.*)
• **generalised**
Bu Zhong Yi Qi Wan 92 (*Spleen qi def.*)
Shi Quan Da Bu Wan 336 (*qi & Bld def.*)
Tangkwei Essence of Chicken 54 (*qi & Bld def.*)
American Ginseng Essence of Chicken 344 (*qi & yin def.*)
Cordyceps Essence of Chicken 342 (*yin & yang def.*)
• **immune**
Bu Zhong Yi Qi Wan 92 (*Spleen & Lung qi def.*)
Reishi Mushroom 354 (*immune regulator*)
Tong Luo Zhi Tong Tablet 453 (*Bld def.*)
Deer Antler and Ginseng 332 (*qi & jing def.*)
Yu Ping Feng Wan 348 (*wei qi def.*)
Sheng Mai San Wan 212 (*qi & yin def.*)
Cordyceps Essence of Chicken 342 (*qi & yang def.*)
American Ginseng Essence of Chicken 344 (*qi & yin def.*)

Panax Ginseng Extractum 350 (*qi def.*)
• **legs, lower back**
Jian Bu Qiang Shen Wan 454 (*Kid. def.*)
Hua Tuo Zai Zao Wan 272 (*qi & yin def., Wind Damp*)
Ba Ji Yin Yang Wan 240 (*Kid. yang def.*)
Zhuang Yao Jian Shen Tablet 452 (*Kid. yang def.*)
Si Jun Zi Wan 86 (*Spleen qi def.*)
• **pregnancy (see Pregnancy)**

Wei syndrome

Hua Tuo Zai Zao Wan 272 (*qi & yin def.*)
Da Huo Luo Dan 444 (*Kid. def.*)
Xiao Shuan Zai Zao Wan 270
Niu Huang Qing Xin Wan 572 (*Phlegm Heat*)
Du Huo Ji Sheng Wan 448 (*Wind Damp, Kid. def.*)
Xiao Huo Luo Dan 434 (*Cold, Phlegm, Bld stag.*)
Bu Yang Huan Wu Wan 266 (*qi def., Bld stag.*)

Wheezing

Ma Huang Tang Wan 156 (*Wind Cold*)
Xiao Qing Long Wan 162 (*Wind Cold with congested fluids*)
Su Zi Jiang Qi Wan 160 (*Cold Phlegm*)
Ding Chuan Wan 182 (*Phlegm Heat*)
Yulin Bu Shen Wan 214 (*Lung & Kid. def.*)
Mai Wei Di Huang Wan 208 (*chronic Lung & Kid yin def.*)
Sheng Mai San Wan 212 (*qi & yin def.*)
Bu Fei Wan 216 (*Lung qi def.*)

Whooping cough

Ching Fei Yi Huo Pien 176 (*Lung Fire*)
Qing Qi Hua Tan Wan 174 (*Phlegm Heat*)
She Dan Chuan Bei Ye 186 (*Phlegm Heat*)
Orange Peel Powder 188 (*Phlegm Heat*)
Chuan Xin Lian Antiphlogistic Tablets 558 (*Toxic Heat*)
Chuan Xin Lian 557 (*Toxic Heat*)

Wind Damp bi syndrome (see *Bi* syndrome)

Worms

Baby Fat Powder 510
Hua Ji Xiao Zhi Oral Liquid 512 (*infants*)

GENERAL INDEX

Patent Medicine Index

PATENT INDEX

PATENT INDEX

Bibliography and references

Bensky D and Gamble A (1993) *Chinese Herbal Medicine: Materia Medica*, Eastland Press, Seattle, Washington

Bensky D and Barolet R (1990) *Chinese Herbal Medicine: Formulas and Strategies*, Eastland Press, Seattle, Washington

Beers M and Berkow R, et al. (1999) *The Merck Manual* (17th Ed). Merck Research Laboratories, Whitehouse Station, New Jersey

Chen J (1999) Recognition and Prevention of Herb-Drug Interaction. Medical Acupuncture Journal 10(2).

Chu Han Zhu (1989) *Clinical Handbook of Chinese Prepared Medicines*, Paradigm Publications, Brookline, Mass.

Clavey S (1995) *Fluid Physiology and Pathology in Traditional Chinese Medicine*, Churchill Livingstone, Melbourne

Edwards CRW et al. (1995) *Davidson's Principles and Practice of Medicine* (17th Ed), Churchill Livingstone, Edinburgh

Fratkin J (2001) *Chinese Herbal Patent Formulas*, *The Clinical Desk Reference*, Shya Publications, Boulder, Colorado.

Fruehauf H (1998) *Gu* syndrome. The Journal of Chinese Medicine, 57:10-17

Fugh-Bergman A (2000) Herb-Drug Interactions. Lancet 355:134-138.

Ko RJ (1998) Adulterants in Asian Patent Medicines. N Engl J Med 339:847.

Maclean W and Lyttleton J (1998) *Clinical Handbook of Internal Medicine Volume 1 Disorders of the Lungs, Kidney, Liver and Heart*. University of Western Sydney.

Maclean W and Lyttleton J (2002) *Clinical Handbook of Internal Medicine Volume 2 Disorders of the Spleen and Stomach*. University of Western Sydney.

Miller LG (1998) Herbal Medicinals: Selected Clinical Considerations Focusing on Known or Potential Drug-Herb Interactions. Arch Intern Med 158(20):2200-2211

Naeser M (1992) *Outline to Chinese Herbal Patent Medicines in Pill Form* (2nd ed.), Boston Chinese Medicine.

Shi Yong Fang Ji Xue 实用方剂学 (Practical Chinese Herbal Formulas) 1989 Zhou Feng-Wu (ed.), Shandong Science and Technology Press, Shandong

Shi Yong Zhong Cao Yao Yuan Se Tu Pu 实用中草药原色图谱 (Color Atlas of Chinese Herbs) 1993 Gao Shi-Xian (ed.), Guangxi Science and Technology Press, Guangxi

Townsend P (1997) Chinese Herb and Modern Drug Interactions. (Unpublished).

Zhong Yao Xue 中药学 (Chinese Herbal Medicine) 1991 Yan Zheng-Hua (ed.), Peoples Medical Publishing Company, Beijing

Zui Xin Fang Ji Shou Ce 最新方剂手册 (Handbook of the Latest Prescriptions) 1998 Fan Wei-Hong (ed.), Central Plains Publishing Company, Henan

1.1 Ba Zhen Wan	1.1 Ba Zhen Wan (US)	1.2 Si Wu Wan	1.3 Ba Zhen Yi Mu Wan
1.4 Yi Mu Tiao Jing Wan	1.5 Bu Xue Tiao Jing Wan	1.6 Bai Feng Wan	1.7 Wu Ji Bai Feng Wan
1.8 Tong Ren Wu Ji Bai Feng Wan	1.9 Gui Pi Wan	1.9 Gui Pi Wan (US)	1.10 Dang Gui Jing
1.11 Dang Gui Su	1.11 Dang Gui Su (US)	1.12 Shi Xiao Wan	1.13 Woo Garm Yuen Medical Pills
1.15 Tong Jing Wan	1.16 Tao Hong Si Wu Wan	1.17 Gui Zhi Fu Ling Wan	1.19 Yang Rong Wan

		1.22 Rehmannia Glutinosa Compound Pills	1.22 Rehmannia Glutinosa Compond Pills (US)
1.20 Cu Yun Yu Tai Capsule	1.21 Tiao Jing Cu Yun Wan		

1.23.1 Zhi Bai Ba Wei Wan	1.23.2 Zhi Bai Di Huang Wan	1.23.3 Zhi Bai Ba Wei Wan	1.23 Zhi Bai Ba Wei Wan (US)
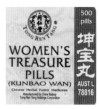			
1.25 Kun Bao Wan	1.26 Jing An Oral Liquid	1.27 Lady Oral Liquid	1.28 Geng Nian Ling

1.29 Bu Gai Zhuang Gu Capsule	1.30 Tangkwei Essence of Chicken	1.31 Shih San Tai Pao Wan	1.32 Ru Jie Xiao Tablet

1.33 Hai Zao Jing Wan	1.34 Nei Xiao Luo Li Wan	1.35 Fu Yan Qing Tablet	1.36 Bi Xie Sheng Shi Wan

1.37 Yu Dai Wan

1.37 Yu Dai Wan (US)

1.38 Chien Chin Chih
Tai Wan

1.38 Chien Chin Chih
Tai Wan (US)

1.39 Yang Yan Qu Ban Tablet

2.1 Xing Jun San

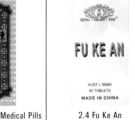

2.2.1 Huo Hsiang
Cheng Chi Pien

2.2.2 Huo Xiang Zheng Qi Wan

2.2.3 Cold and Abdpminal
Discomfort Reliever

2.2.3 Huo Xiang
Zheng Qi Wan (US)

2.3 So Hup Yuen Medical Pills

2.4 Fu Ke An

2.5 Bao Ji Pills

2.6 Po Chai Pills

2.9 Xiang Sha Liu Jun Wan

2.9 Xiang Sha Liu Jun Wan (US)

2.10 Xiang Sha Yang Wei Wan

2.10 Xiang Sha Yang Wei Wan (US)

2.11 Bu Zhong Yi Qi Wan

2.11 Bu Zhong Yi Qi Wan (US)

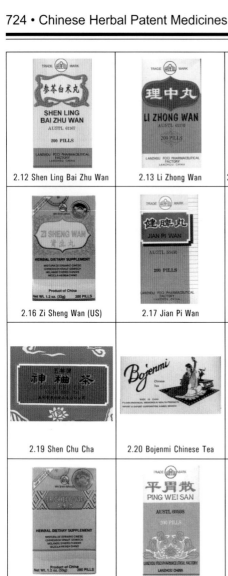

2.12 Shen Ling Bai Zhu Wan	2.13 Li Zhong Wan	2.14 Li Chung Yuen Medical Pills	2.16 Zi Sheng Wan
2.16 Zi Sheng Wan (US)	2.17 Jian Pi Wan	2.17 Jian Pi Wan (US)	2.18 Bao He Wan
2.19 Shen Chu Cha	2.20 Bojenmi Chinese Tea	2.21 Keep Fit Capsule	2.22 Er Chen Wan
2.22 Er Chen Wan (US)	2.23 Ping Wei San	2.24 Shu Gan Wan	2.24 Shu Gan Wan (US)
2.26 Xiang Lian Wan	2.27 Wei Te Ling	2.28 Wei Tong Ding	2.29 Mu Xiang Shun Qi Wan

2.29 Mu Xiang Shun Qi Wan (US)	2.30 Chen Xiang Hua Qi Wan	2.30 Chen Xiang Hua Qi Wan (US)	2.31 Run Chang Wan
2.31 Run Chang Wan (US)	2.34 Cong Rong Bu Shen Wan	2.36 Sugarid	2.38 Hua Zhi Ling Tablet
2.39 Fargelin for Piles	3.1.1 Yin Chiao Chieh Tu Pien	3.1.2 Yin Chiao Jie Du Pian	3.1.3 Yin Chiao Jie Du Wan
3.1.4 Peking Yin Chiao Jie Du Pian	3.1.5 Influenza and Cold Reliever	3.2 Gan Mao Zhi Ke Chong Ji	3.3 Sang Ju Wan
3.4 Gan Mao Ling	3.7 Su Zi Jiang Qi Wan	3.8 Xiao Qing Long Wan	3.9 Chuan Xiong Cha Tiao Wan

3.9 Chuan Xiong Cha Tiao Wan (US)	3.12 Gan Mao Qing Re Chong Ji	3.12 Gan Mao Qing Re Chong Ji	3.13 Gan Mao Qing Re Ke Li
3.15 Qing Qi Hua Tan Wan	3.15 Qing Qi Hua Tan Wan (US)	3.16 Ching Fei Yi Huo Pien	3.17 Pi Pa Cough Tea
3.18 Tung Hsuan Li Fei Pien	3.19 Ding Chuan Wan	3.20 Qi Guan Yan Ke Sou Tan Chuan Wan	3.21 She Dan Chuan Bei Ye
3.22 Orange Peel Powder	3.23 Tendrilleaf Fritillary Powder	3.24 She Dan Chuan Bei Pi Pa Gao	3.25 Nin Jiom Pei Pa Kao
3.26 Mi Lian Chuan Bei Pi Pa Gao	3.27 Fritillary & Loquat Leaf Mixture	3.28 Loquat Leaf Cough Syrup	3.29 African Sea Coconut Cough Syrup

3.30 Tong Xuan Li Fei Kou Fu Ye	3.31.1 Zhi Sou Wan	3.31.2 Zhi Sou San	3.33 Yang Yin Qing Fei Wan
3.34 Bai He Gu Jin Wan	3.34 Bai He Gu Jin Wan (US)	3.35 Mai Wei Di Huang Wan	3.35 Mai Wei Di Huang Wan (US)
3.36 Lo Han Kuo Beverage	3.38 Sheng Mai San Wan	3.39 Yulin Bu Shen Wan	3.41 Xu Han Ting
4.5 Bi Xie Fen Qing Wan	4.6 Ba Zheng San Wan	4.7 Qing Re Qu Shi Tea	4.8 Tao Chih Pien
4.9 DBD Capsule	4.10 Shi Lin Tong	4.11 Ba Ji Yin Yang Wan	4.12 San Yuen Medical Pills

4.13 Zi Shen Da Bu Capsule	4.14 Chin So Ku Ching Wan	5.1 Xue Fu Zhu Yu Wan	5.2 Dan Shen Pill
5.4 Xin Mai Ling	5.6 Guan Xin An Kou Fu Ye	5.7 Sunho Multi Ginseng Tablets	5.8 Bu Yang Huan Wu Wan
5.10 Xiao Shuan Zai Zao Wan	5.11 Hua Tuo Zai Zao Wan	6.1 Xiao Chai Hu Tang Wan	6.1 Xiao Chai Hu Tang Wan (US)
6.3 Chai Hu Shu Gan Wan	6.4 Xiao Yao Wan	6.4 Xiao Yao Wan (US)	6.5 Jia Wei Xiao Yao Wan
6.6 Long Dan Xie Gan Wan	6.6 Long Dan Xie Gan Wan (US)	6.9 Jigucao Wan	6.10 Qing Gan Li Dan Tablet

6.11 Lidan Tablets	6.13 Herba Abri Fruticulosi Beverage	6.14 Xi Huang Cao	7.1.1 Liu Wei Di Huang Wan
7.1.2 Liu Wei Di Huang Wan	7.1.3 Tinnitus Herbal Treatment	7.1.4 Liu Wei Di Huang Pills	7.2.1 Qi Ju Di Huang Wan
7.2.2 Qi Ju Di Huang Wan	7.2 Qi Ju Di Huang Wan (US)	7.3 Zuo Gui Wan	7.4 Da Bu Yin Wan
7.5 Gu Ben Wan	7.5 Gu Ben Wan (US)	7.6 Yang Xue Sheng Fa Capsule	7.8 Shou Wu Chih
7.9 Fu Gui Ba Wei Wan	7.9 Fu Gui Ba Wei Wan (US)	7.10 Yuo Gui Wan	7.11 Deer Velvet

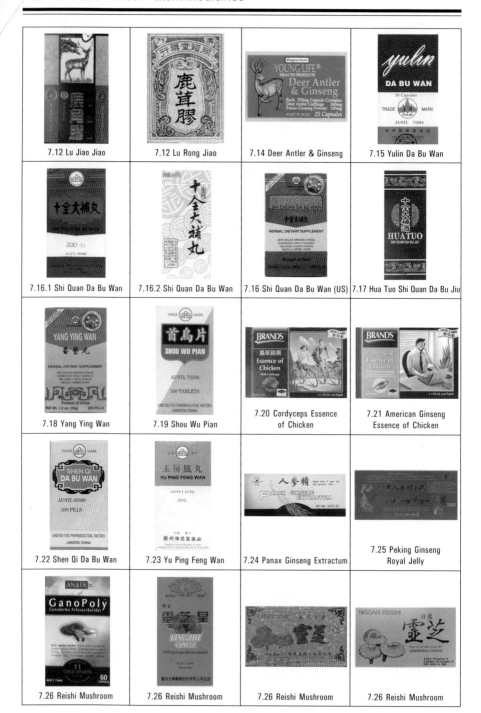

7.12 Lu Jiao Jiao	7.12 Lu Rong Jiao	7.14 Deer Antler & Ginseng	7.15 Yulin Da Bu Wan
7.16.1 Shi Quan Da Bu Wan	7.16.2 Shi Quan Da Bu Wan	7.16 Shi Quan Da Bu Wan (US)	7.17 Hua Tuo Shi Quan Da Bu Jiu
7.18 Yang Ying Wan	7.19 Shou Wu Pian	7.20 Cordyceps Essence of Chicken	7.21 American Ginseng Essence of Chicken
7.22 Shen Qi Da Bu Wan	7.23 Yu Ping Feng Wan	7.24 Panax Ginseng Extractum	7.25 Peking Ginseng Royal Jelly
7.26 Reishi Mushroom	7.26 Reishi Mushroom	7.26 Reishi Mushroom	7.26 Reishi Mushroom

8.1 Tian Wang Bu Xin Dan	8.2 Bai Zi Yang Xin Wan	8.2 Bai Zi Yang Xin Wan (US)	8.3 An Shen Ding Zhi Wan
8.4 An Shen Bu Xin Wan	8.5 Shuian Capsule	8.7 An Shen Jie Yu Capsule	8.8 Wen Dan Wan
8.10 Cerebral Tonic Pills	8.11 Jian Nao Yi Zhi Capsule	8.12 Zao Ren An Shen Ye	9.1 Er Long Zuo Ci Wan
9.1 Er Long Zuo Ci Wan (US)	9.3 Peking Niu Huang Jie Du Pian	9.3 Peking Niu Huang Jie Du Pian	9.4.1 Huang Lien Shang Ching Pien
9.4.2 Huang Lian Shang Qing Tablet	9.6 Ban Lan Gen Chong Ji	9.7 Jie Geng Wan	9.7 Jie Geng Wan (US)

 9.9 Superior Sore Throat Powder	 9.10 Sanjin Watermelon Frost	 9.11 Qing Yin Wan	 9.13 Pe Min Kan Wan
9.15 Pe Min Kan Wan	 9.16 Hay Fever Tablet	 9.17 Qian Bai Bi Yan Pian	 9.18 Xin Yi San
9.20 Hay Fever Relieving Tea	 9.21 Ming Mu Shang Ching Pien	 9.22 Ming Mu Di Huang Wan	 9.22 Ming Mu Di Huang Wan (US)
 9.23 Ming Mu Capsule	 10.1 Yunnan Paiyao	 10.1 Yunnan Paiyao	 10.2 Raw Tienchi Tablets
 10.3 Die Da Zhi Tong Capsule	 10.4 Chin Gu Tie Shang Wan	 10.7 Qu Feng Zhen Tong Capsule	 10.8 Xiao Huo Luo Dan

| 10.9 Xuan Bi Tang Wan | 10.11 Shu Jin Huo Xue Wan | 10.13 Da Huo Luo Dan | 10.15 Du Huo Ji Sheng Wan |

| 10.16.1 Zhuang Yao Jian Shen | 10.16.2 Zhuang Yao Jian Shen Tablet | 10.17 Tong Luo Zhi Tong Tablet | 10.18 Jian Bu Qiang Shen Wan |

| 10.20 Tian Ma Tou Tong Capsule | 10.23 Zheng Gu Shui | 10.24 Zheng Gu Ging | 10.25 Die Da Tian Qi Yao Jiu |

| 10.26 Minjak Gosok | 10.27 Zhi Tong You | 10.28 Wong Lop Kong Medicated Oil | 10.29 White Flower Embrocation |

| 10.30 Po Sum On Medicated Oil | 10.31 Trans Wood Lock Liniment | 10.32 Die Da Jiu | 10.33 Wood Lock Medicated Balm |

10.34 Imada Red Flower Oil

10.35 Eagle Brand Medicated Oil

10.36 Kung Fu Oil

10.37 Tiger Balm

10.38 Plaster for Bruise and Analgesic

10.39 Die Da Feng Shi Plaster

10.40 Porous Capsicum Plaster

10.41 Gou Pi Gao

11.1 Qian Lie Xian Capsule

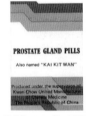

11.2 Prostate Gland Pills

11.3 Ji Sheng Ju He Wan

11.5 Wu Zi Yan Zong Wan

11.6 Gu Ben Fu Zheng Capsule

11.7 Nan Bao Capsules

11.8 Kang Wei Ling Wan

12.1 Bo Ying Compound

12.2 King Fung Powder

12.3 Baby Fat Powder

12.4 Hua Ji Xiao Zhi Oral Liquid

12.5 Gan Mao Tea

12.6 Healthy Child Tea	12.7 Xiao Er Gan Mao Chong Ji	12.8 Qi Xing Tea	12.9 Xiaoér Qi Xing Cha Chong Ji
13.1 Lien Chiao Pai Tu Pien	13.2 Xiao Feng Wan	13.4 Ke Yin Wan	13.5 Shi Du Qing Capsule
13.6 Shi Du Qing	13.7 Eczema Herbal Formula	13.8 Fang Feng Tong Sheng Wan	13.9 Qing Re An Chuang Pian
13.10 Zhen Zhu An Chuang Tablet	13.12 Chuan Xin Lian Cream	13.13 Fu Yin Tai Liniment	13.14 Ching Wan Hung
13.15 Tujin Liniment	13.16 Hua Tuo Gao	13.17 Xiao Yan Tang Shang Cream	13.18 Ji Yan Gao

13.19 Pearl Powder	13.20 Mopiko	14.1 Huang Lian Jie Du Wan	14.2 Huang Lian Su Tablets
14.3 Tabellae Berberini	14.4 Chuan Xin Lian	14.5 Chuan Xin Lian Antiphlogistic Tablet	14.6 Fu Fang Nan Ban Lan Gen
14.7 Niu Huang Qing Huo Wan	14.8 Wu Wei Xiao Du Wan	15.1 Po Lung Yuen Medical Pills	15.2 Niu Hung Qing Xin Wan
15.4 Tian Ma Gou Teng Wan	15.5 Tian Ma Wan	15.7 Yang Yin Jiang Ya Wan	15.8 Fu Fang Jiang Ya Capsule
15.9 Headache & Dizziness Reliever			